The Ancient Maya

New Perspectives

The Ancient Maya

New Perspectives

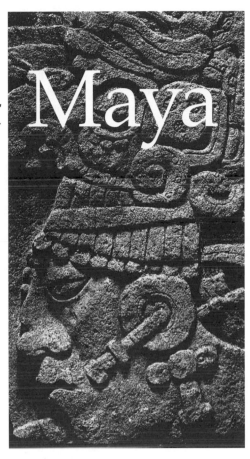

HEATHER McKILLOP

W.W. Norton & Company

New York   London

All maps by Mary Lee Eggart.

Library of Congress Cataloging-in-Publication Data
McKillop, Heather Irene
  The ancient Maya : new perspectives / Heather McKillop.
     p. cm. — (Understanding ancient civilizations)
Includes bibliographical references and index.
  ISBN 1-57607-696-2 (alk. paper) — ISBN 1-57607-697-0 (e-book)
  1. Mayas—History. 2. Mayas—Antiquities. 3. Mayas—Social life and
customs. 4. Mexico—Antiquities. 5. Central America—Antiquities.
I. Title. II. Series.
F1435.M485 2003
972.81'016—dc22
2003016239

ISBN-13: 978-0-393-32890-5 pbk.
ISBN-10: 0-393-32890-2 pbk.

W. W. Norton & Company, Inc.
500 Fifth Avenue, New York, N.Y. 10110
www.wwnorton.com

W. W. Norton & Company Ltd.
Castle House, 75/76 Wells Street, London W1T 3QT

1 2 3 4 5 6 7 8 9 0

To GORDON, BOB, ELEANOR, and TIGER

Contents

List of Maps

Series Editor's Preface

In recent years, there has been a significant and steady increase of academic and popular interest in the study of past civilizations. This is due in part to the dramatic coverage—real or imagined—of the archaeological profession in popular film and television, and to the extensive journalistic reporting of spectacular new finds from all parts of the world. Yet, because archaeologists and other scholars have tended to approach their study of ancient peoples and civilizations exclusively from their own disciplinary perspectives and for their professional colleagues, there has long been a lack of general factual and other research resources available for the nonspecialist. The Understanding Ancient Civilizations series is intended to fill that need.

Volumes in the series are principally designed to introduce the general reader, student, and nonspecialist to the study of specific ancient civilizations. Each volume is devoted to a particular archaeological culture (for example, the ancient Maya of southern Mexico and adjacent Guatemala) or cultural region (for example, Israel and Canaan) and seeks to achieve, with careful selectivity and astute critical assessment of the literature, an expression of a particular civilization and an appreciation of its achievements.

The keynote of the Understanding Ancient Civilizations series is to provide, in a uniform format, an interpretation of each civilization that will express its culture and place in the world as well as the qualities and background that make it unique. Series titles include volumes on the archaeology and prehistory of the ancient civilizations of Egypt, Greece, Rome, and Mesopotamia, as well as the achievements of the Celts, Aztecs, and Inca, among others. Still more books are in the planning stage.

I was particularly fortunate in having Kevin Downing from ABC-CLIO contact me in search of an editor for a series about archaeology. It is a simple statement of the truth that there would be no series without him. I am also lucky to have Simon Mason, Kevin's successor from ABC-CLIO, continue to push the production of the series. Given the scale of the project and the schedule for production, he deserves more than a sincere thank you.

John Weeks

Preface

It is indeed a pleasure and a wonderful opportunity to present an overview of the ancient Maya civilization and to include my interpretations and perspectives as well as those of my colleagues. Readers might notice my interest in ancient economy and may notice the variability within ancient Maya culture, including both the dynastic rulers and the common folk, the large cities as well as the smaller communities.

I hope that this book helps address the insatiable interest among the public and students about the ancient Maya. In writing the book, I was targeting it to the educated public (or, as my senior editor put it, "the educated reader of the *New York Times*"!), as well as students. I hope the book will be useful both as a reference and as a text for classes. I have used the text to teach both a graduate class on the Maya and an advanced undergraduate class.

There are many variant spellings for ancient Maya words, and a new lexicon was recently introduced that more carefully reflects the indigenous Mayan languages developed by Maya linguists and indigenous Maya in Guatemala (Coe and Stone 2001, 19; Freidel, Schele, and Parker 1993). The new orthography better represents words phonetically than the orthography imposed by the Spaniards in colonial times, replacing, for example, *Uaxactun* with *Waxaktun,* and *Yukatek* with *Yucatec.* Acceptance of the new orthography will standardize the varied spellings used by researchers, missionaries, and others that have previously resulted in a disturbing array of spellings of Maya words and place names. For example, Freidel et al. (1993, 16) point out that the Maya word for *lord* is variously written *ahaw, ahau, ajau, ajaw,* or *axaw.* In order to communicate most easily to a broad audience, including specialists, students, and the educated public, I have chosen to use traditional spellings that are more familiar and commonly used in the published literature. In addition, I have omitted accents and other diacritics to facilitate communication and reading.

Here are some basic guidelines for pronouncing the names of Maya sites and other Maya words. Generally, all letters are pronounced. The "au" in the word *ahau* is pronounced like "ow" in the English word *how.* For the site of Uaxactun, the letter "u" is pronounced "w," the letter "x" is pronounced "sh," and "c" is pronounced "k." *Tun* is a common word, meaning day, and is pronounced like the English word *tune.* Phonetically, Uaxactun is pronounced "Wash-ak-tune," with the emphasis on the last syllable, as is the rule. For other words, generally "a" is short as in the English word *father,* so that the site name Altun Ha is pronounced "All tune ha," with the emphasis on the last syllable. Knowing that the letter "i" is pronounced like the "ea" in *eat*, the site name Tikal can be pronounced "Tea-kal." The above guidelines can be applied to other sites, such as Copan, Lubaantun (with the "aa" a short "a" as in *father*), Dzibilchaltun, Cozumel (with the "e" sound short as in *elephant*), and Kaminaljuyu (with the "j" pronounced like "h").

Although this book is about the ancient Maya, especially the civilization that developed in the rainforest of Central America between A.D. 300 and 900, I remind readers that the Maya people continue to live in Belize, Guatemala, Mexico, Honduras, and El Salvador, as well as having emigrated and continuing to emigrate to other countries.

REFERENCES

Coe, Michael D., and Mark Van Stone. 2001. *Reading the Maya Glyphs*. New York: Thames & Hudson.

Friedel, David A., Linda Schele, and Joy Parker. 1993. *Maya Cosmos: Three Thousand Years on the Shaman's Path*. New York: Morrow.

Acknowledgments

I appreciate this wonderful opportunity and hope that this book brings some of my work and that of my colleagues to a broader audience. I would like to thank those who encouraged, instructed, and talked with me about Maya archaeology, who listened to me in classes, and who participated with me in fieldwork in Belize, including students, Earthwatch workers, and other volunteers. In particular, I would like to thank Paul Healy, my M.A. advisor at Trent University, and Barbara Voorhies, my Ph.D. advisor at University of California, Santa Barbara. I thank the government of Belize, and particularly the present and past archaeological commissioners, for granting me permits to carry out fieldwork for many years along the coast of Belize.

I thank John Weeks for providing me the opportunity to write this book and thereby express my views on the ancient Maya. I thank my senior editor at ABC-CLIO, Simon Mason, for patiently encouraging me in this endeavor, as well as the many other people at ABC-CLIO who helped in various ways. I appreciate the thoughtful discussions of the graduate students in my Meso-american Archaeology class in the Spring of 2003 at Louisiana State University (LSU), who accepted e-mailed chapters from this book for class discussion: Samantha Euraque, Marsha Hernandez, Jamie Hughes, Erin Lund, Lara Lundy, Hampton Peele, Kevin Pemberton, Erika Roberts, Bretton Somers, Fiona Vasbinder, and Olga Yermakonov.

Several individuals provided me with slides for this book, including Jaime Awe, Pat Colquette, Ed Kurjack, Virginia Ochoa, Bretton Somers, and Terance Winemiller, for which I am grateful. I thank Mary Lee Eggart of LSU for drawing the maps. I appreciate the assistance of Bretton Somers and Saraphine Latchie, who helped with the bibliography. Bill Davidson, as chair of the Department of Geography and Anthropology at LSU, provided me with a semester course release, which gave me time to begin writing this book, for which I am grateful.

I appreciate the encouragement and insights of my husband, Robert Tague, and the enthusiastic interest of our daughter, Eleanor, in the ancient and modern Maya.

PART I
Introduction

CHAPTER 1

Introduction

The ancient Maya evoke images of temples shrouded by rainforest vegetation, of partially deciphered hieroglyphs, and of carved and painted pictures of ritual bloodletting. Widespread public attention was drawn to Maya cities following John Lloyd Stephens's 1841 publication of *Incidents of Travel in Central America, Chiapas, and Yucatan* (Stephens 1969). Misconceptions about the rise and fall of the Maya civilization developed in part from the difficulty of carrying out archaeological fieldwork in the rainforest landscape of Guatemala, Belize, and parts of Mexico, Honduras, and El Salvador, where the ancient Maya civilization developed.

Unlike with the Aztec and Inca civilizations encountered by the sixteenth-century Spanish explorers, the earlier collapse of the Maya civilization and

View from Tikal's Temple 4 overlooking the rainforest to Temples 5, 1, and 2
(Courtesy B. Somers)

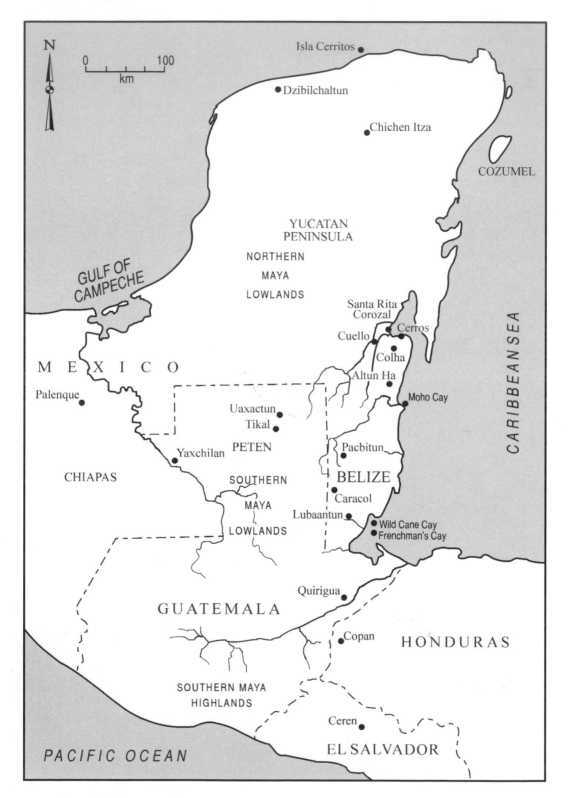

Map of the Maya area showing subareas and sites mentioned in the text

abandonment of its cities in the ninth century only added to the mystery. By the turn of the twenty-first century, however, significant strides had been made in understanding the development and demise of the Maya civilization. Insights were due to an exponential growth in the amount of fieldwork, to the deciphering of many of the hieroglyphs, and to the study of the painted and carved iconography on pottery, stone, and other media.

The tropical rainforest setting has seemed to scholars and the public alike as an unlikely location for the rise of a great civilization. Most other ancient civilizations developed in arid landscapes and arguably were based on elite management of water resources through irrigation. Not only was this the case for Teotihuacan, the highland Mexican state contemporaneous with the Classic Maya, but also for the river valley kingdoms that developed along the coast of Peru, along the Nile, along the Tigris-Euphrates, and in China. If the "slash and burn" farming technique of the modern Maya was used by the ancient Maya, urban populations must have been quite small (Morley 1946). In fact, population estimates based on early twentieth-century excavations at Uaxactun, Chichen Itza, Copan, and other sites supported the idea that Maya capitals were "empty ceremonial centers" where the priests and other leaders lived, but that the bulk of the Maya were rural farmers who lived in the surrounding countryside (Thompson 1970). Subsequent surveys beyond the central part of the region where most of the cities were concentrated indicated, however, that there were populations in the tens of thousands or perhaps more at big cities such as Tikal (Harrison 1999). The discovery that the ancient Maya also used more intensive farming techniques than slash and burn led to much research on ancient Maya food production. The discovery of the use of terraced hillslopes, raised fields created by canals through swamps, orchards, household kitchen gardens, hunting, and fishing meant both that more food was produced and that larger population densities were supported than had been previously imagined (Harrison and Turner 1978; McKillop 1994; White 1999).

Decipherment of many of the Mayan hieroglyphs by the beginning of the twenty-first century transformed our modern understanding of the ancient Maya. The discovery by the Russian scholar Yuri Knorozov (1958) that Mayan hieroglyphs were phonetic contrasted with the popular view that the Mayan hieroglyphs were based on picture writing (logographs). As a result, tremendous strides were made in decipherment and the tracing of modern Mayan languages to ancestral Classic Chol Mayan (Houston, Mazariegos, and Stuart 2001; Matthews 2003). Tatiana Proskouriakoff (1960) made the other critical discovery in Maya epigraphy that was a catalyst for further research. She pointed out that the hieroglyphs on the carved stone monuments (stelae) recorded historical information and the military exploits of Classic Maya royalty. This discovery contrasted to popular views of Maya priests being focused on astronomy and fixated on mathematics. Although the Classic Maya were very knowledgeable in these areas, the main use for hieroglyphs was historical. The hieroglyphs and accompanying images also enmeshed the lives of Maya kings and queens into rituals, myths, and stories of creation as told in the *Popol Vuh,* a historic text (Freidel, Schele, and Parker 1993; Milbrath 1999; Tedlock 1985).

Main Plaza at Tikal, Guatemala (Courtesy B. Somers)

Only by the late twentieth century did Maya researchers recognize that the Maya lowlands were environmentally diverse and that this diversity was important in the course of Maya prehistory. This diversity includes food resources as well as materials such as chert and granite used to make stone tools; stingray spines and seashells used in rituals; and even the basic building blocks of Maya buildings: Limestone, sandstone, and coral rock were variously locally available and used in construction. This diversity of resources indicated that there was more trade within the Maya lowlands than had been previously thought. Local exchange played an important role in the development of the Maya political economy—even though it may not seem to us as glamorous as long-distance trade by canoe in the sea or by trade along rivers or by human porters on overland trails. Maya trade studies were dominated in the late twentieth century by studies of obsidian, which does not naturally occur in the limestone platform of the Maya lowlands but which was ubiquitous at Maya sites throughout prehistory. Obsidian was commonly used for ritual bloodletting but also as a sharp-edged cutting implement for other tasks. Moreover, the facility to chemically "fingerprint" obsidian artifacts to their origins in the volcanic highlands of Guatemala, Mexico, and Honduras allowed archaeologists to present skeletal structures of long-distance Maya trade (Hammond 1972; Healy, McKillop, and Walsh 1984; McKillop et al. 1988; Nelson 1985). By the turn of the twenty-first century, it was clear that the ancient Maya economy included goods and resources of fine manufacture that sometimes had value added by their exotic origin and that were part of the "political economy" of Maya royalty, as well as goods and resources that formed the backbone of the subsistence economy, obtained from a variety of locations both close to home and farther away (Graham 1987; Masson and Freidel 2002; McKillop 2002).

The collapse of the Maya civilization in the ninth century continues to arouse the interest of the public and to entertain heated debates among Mayanists. Three competing theories remain popular among a plethora of other hypotheses. In the first model, overpopulation and overuse of the land from extensive clearing of the rainforest precipitated ecological disaster and abandonment of the cities. This model was popular in the late twentieth century and provided a cautionary analog for modern Western society (Culbert 1973). In a second model, endemic warfare among competing city-states led to military, marriage, and trading alliances among lowland city-states that aggressively attacked, plundered, and overpowered their neighbors. Some archaeologists believe this caused the breakdown of dynastic power and caused the urban centers to collapse like a house of cards (Demarest 1997), but others attribute endemic warfare to ecological collapse (Webster 2002). A third view holds that catastrophic environmental change was instrumental in an ecological disaster that caused the Classic Maya civilization to collapse (Gill 2000; Hodell, Curtis, and Brenner 1995). In this scenario, a drought occurred that was both more dramatic and more devastating than the regular fluctuations in rainfall, and this catastrophic environmental change meant insufficient rainfall for agriculture, ultimately resulting in famine and loss of life (Gill 2000). The relationship between environmental and cultural agents, and these agents' part in social change, has a long and tempestuous history among Maya researchers (Meggers 1954). There was likely a complex interplay between the two that was often coincidental rather than causal (McKillop 2002; McKillop 2003).

OVERVIEW OF MAYA CIVILIZATION

Paleoindian and Archaic Periods

Although the earliest evidence of people in Central America dates to the time of the retreat of the Pleistocene glacier, the first traces of ancient Maya culture (as indicated by the first appearance of pottery) are from much later. The earliest inhabitants of the Maya area used stone tools to hunt ice age animals during the Paleoindian period, which began about 9500 B.C. Following the extinction of ice age animals, smaller animals such as deer and rabbits were hunted by people during the Archaic period, which ends with the first pottery in the Maya area. Both the Paleoindian and Archaic periods are poorly known in the Maya area, but comparisons with other areas in Mexico and North America provide important clues about the ancient adaptation of the earliest inhabitants of the Maya area.

Preclassic Period

The earliest Maya date to about 1800 B.C. along the Pacific coast of Guatemala and to 1000 B.C. in the southern Maya lowlands, marking the beginning of the

Early and Middle Preclassic periods in each area, respectively. These early Maya were farmers living in small villages, with pole and thatch houses on low, earthen platforms, such as found at Cuello in northern Belize. The early pottery of Cuello, Santa Rita, Colha, and other sites is quite sophisticated, arguing for as yet undiscovered precursors to the Maya (Hammond 1991). The Middle Preclassic, as well as other time periods, includes smaller divisions of times called phases, each characterized by a specific ceramic complex—all the pottery styles used in that phase.

The Late Preclassic period (300 B.C.–A.D. 300) marked the rise of cultural complexity, as seen in temples with stuccoed and painted façades, built by the common folk at the instructions of the emerging elite rulers. The site of Cerros, Belize, was an important Late Preclassic community, with a core area consisting of temples and other elite buildings and a larger area of dispersed small households beyond. The Late Preclassic is also noted for the development of long-distance trade for elite items, such as jade and obsidian. These goods were commissioned by the ruling elite, used during their lifetimes, and often ritually buried as grave offerings, building dedications, or building terminations (rituals involving smashing pots or other offerings before a building was abandoned). Stucco masks on temple façades at Cerros, Tikal, Uaxactun, and Dzibilchaltun point to long-distance communication among emerging elites, communication that may actually have fostered the development of the Classic Maya civilization.

Classic Period

The Classic period (A.D. 300–900) is defined as the time when the Maya erected stelae, carved monuments with dates in the Maya long count (a counting system dating events to the beginning of the Maya calendar, equivalent to the year 3114 B.C. in our calendar). The earliest dated stela is from A.D. 292 at Tikal. The last dated monument is from A.D. 909 at Tonina, Mexico. The stelae are stone slabs, each with a depiction of an important Maya person on one face, hieroglyphic writing and dates on the other face, and sometimes writing on the sides as well. The stelae were erected in front of temples and palaces in the central areas of Classic period cities for public viewing. The monuments recounted significant events in a ruler's life, notably birth, marriage, accession to the throne, battles won, and death (Martin and Grube 2000).

The kings and queens of royal Maya dynasties ruled the Classic Maya. The ruler and the royal court of each city-state were supported in part by subsistence farmers who provided labor and food to the Maya royalty. The royal Maya courts were located in the cities, including craft specialists producing finely made goods for the elite; artisans working on a variety of building, plastering, and craft projects; and bureaucrats.

Royal Maya women had power, sometimes by virtue of a marriage alliance with another city-state, as the mother of a young king, or as a ruling queen. They are often depicted in high art involved in rituals and ceremonies. Grave offerings were associated with women of all ranks, reflecting their royal dynasty or membership in a lower-class lineage. Artistic depictions show women of various ranks involved in a variety of tasks, including weaving and grinding corn on metates (flat grinding stones). Royal Maya women were more politically visible than their modern or historic counterparts (Ardren 2002).

Although the basic features of Maya civilization crystalized during the Early Classic period (A.D. 300–600), the height of the Maya civilization was during the Late Classic period (A.D. 600–900), when building efforts, population, and artistic endeavors reached their peaks. The high population densities in cities increasingly taxed the Maya farmers: They provided labor to construct the Maya temples and palaces and to produce food for the city folk. By the Late Classic period, warfare was endemic among the lowland Maya city-states. Maya kings and queens competed for control of neighboring cities, their territory, tribute and tax base, trade routes, and political power. The last hundred years of unrest in the Late Classic period are referred to as the Terminal Classic period (A.D. 800–900).

Maya settlement patterns reveal a hierarchical social structure. Each city-state had a capital with towns and villages located around it, owing political and economic allegiance to that city. The basic unit of Maya architecture was the plazuela (plaza group), consisting of several buildings around a central plaza. The plazuela was the basis for household architecture as well as for the architecture of the temples and palaces in the city cores. Consequently, the urban area of Maya cities was dispersed. The main plaza of a city consisted of a temple along one or two sides, with palaces or elite administrative buildings along the other two sides, with a ball court (see explanation following) nearby. The temple consisted of a large, rubble-filled platform with a small room on top and often a decorative architectural extension termed a "roof comb" that further elevated the temple.

Ball courts were a feature of Maya cities but not of smaller communities (Whittington 2001). The court was located at the city center, and the ball game was an important political event, with the cost of losing sometimes being death. The game was played with a rubber ball (made from the latex of indigenous rubber trees, *Castilla elastica*), and the players had elaborate gear. Depictions of the ball game in progress can be seen in carvings at the ball court at Chichen Itza and on a ball court marker from Lubaantun in southern Belize, for example. The ritual significance of the ball game is tied to the origin myth of the Maya Hero Twins recorded in the *Popol Vuh,* a historic text (Tedlock 1985).

The Maya had no separate cemeteries but instead buried people under the floors and in the foundations of residences and temples. The royal Maya were interred in stone tombs in the temples that had been the foci of their rituals and political lives. This tradition reflects the importance the Maya placed on ancestry, lineage membership, and, during the Classic period, in the dynastic records of Maya kings and queens. Pottery vessels, obsidian and chert artifacts, shell, carved bone, and various perishable items were placed as grave offerings, with the number of items and their level of craftsmanship reflecting the deceased's social standing.

The Maya developed systems of agriculture to suit their varied living environments and the increasing population. Although slash-and-burn agriculture

Ball court at Chichen Itza (Courtesy T. Winemiller)

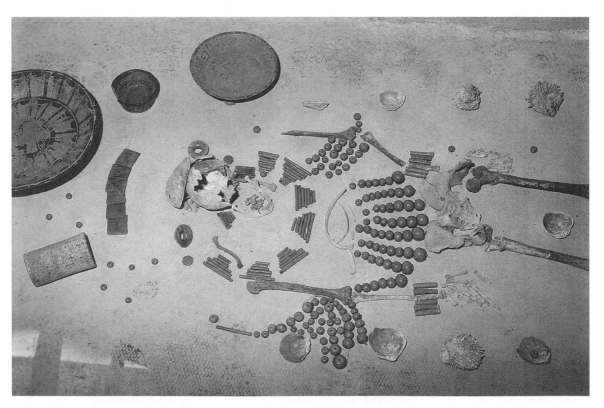

A reconstruction of a burial at Tikal containing jade, obsidian, and finely made pottery
(Corbis/Wolfgang Kaehler)

was carried out, hillslopes were terraced, canals were dug in swamps to create drained or raised-field agriculture, and people had kitchen gardens and orchards. Traces of agricultural activity—notably at Ceren where fields and orchards were preserved by a volcanic eruption—together with preserved plant remains from Cerros, Colha, Copan, Wild Cane Cay, Frenchman's Cay, and Ceren, reveal that the Maya ate corn, beans, and tree crops such as native palms and forest fruits. With few domesticated animals—dogs, Muscovy ducks, and stingless bees—the Maya relied on wild animals for meat, including fish at coastal sites and deer and peccary inland. Human skeletal studies indicate that the Maya were relatively healthy. Some studies indicate that the common Maya were shorter than the elite Maya (Haviland 1967), although this estimate may be unreliable as the sample size is small (Danforth 1999).

Although most of the everyday goods and resources were obtained from nearby locations, obsidian, jade, exotic pottery, marine resources, and mercury were obtained from distant areas by the elite and were displayed as status symbols. Some exotics, such as obsidian, a volcanic rock used to make sharp-edged blades, were traded to even the common Maya. Trade, as well as fairs and religious events, was focused in the city. Trading ports along the Caribbean included sites at Wild Cane Cay, Cozumel, and Isla Cerritos. Boat models recovered from Altun Ha, Moho Cay, and Orlando's Jewfish, as well as drawings of canoes incised on bone objects from a burial in Temple 1 at Tikal, indicate that the Classic Maya had boats and paddles, but there is no evidence of sails (McKillop 2002). Their settlement of offshore islands also indicates the use of boats. Overland transportation was by trails and sacbes (limestone roadways). Human porters, sometimes slaves, were used to carry goods and resources. Technologically, the Maya had no domesticated draft animals and did not use the wheel, either for transportation or in the production of pottery vessels, which were produced by hand using the coil technique, in which long coils of clays were used to make pots whose surfaces were then smoothed by hand or tools.

The Maya were sophisticated artists and craftspeople whose skill was reflected in their pottery and chert stone tools and also in their organization and construction of temples and palaces. They displayed art publicly, from stone or stuccoed masks on temple façades and the brightly colored temples and other public architecture, to murals at Bonampak and cave paintings. Multicolored painted pots were typical of the Classic period, with ritual and historic themes of figures depicted on Late Classic vases, many of which also had hieroglyphic writing. Fancy pots were used in public feasting and in the ritual ceremonies of the royal Maya, with vessels for chocolate, tamales, and other foods depicted in scenes of court life on painted pots. Figures were also depicted on stone monument buildings and stelae, which, along with the hieroglyphs, were historical documents and public statements by the elite Maya. Stone carvings figured in architecture at some Classic cities, such as Yaxchilan, Mexico. There are artistic depictions of dancers and musicians on pottery vessels and actual musical instruments from Pacbitun and Lubaantun, Belize, and from other Maya sites (Miller 1986; Reents-Budet 1994).

The Classic Maya had a hieroglyphic writing system that is preserved on stelae and other carved monuments, on pottery vessels, and on stone carvings. The writing was used to record historical information about the royal Maya and to describe important rituals, but it was not about commerce and only incidentally about astronomy and mathematics as they were used in the calendars. The ability to read and write was evidently limited to the upper class, as hieroglyphs at some smaller communities were decorative but not real glyphs, indicating that the medium was the message (Coe and Van Stone 2001; Matthews 2003a; Montgomery 2002a; Montgomery 2002b).

The Maya had a complex mathematical system involving the advanced concept of zero, and they had a complicated calendrical system. They had two time cycles based on multiples of twenty that intersected every fifty-two years to form the calendar round. The beginning of the Maya calendar corresponds to the year 3114 B.C. in the Christian calendar. Archaeologists develop chronologies of the Maya by reference to the dated stelae and also from study of the changing styles of pottery vessels from excavations. Generally, red-painted pots are characteristic of the Preclassic period, polychrome pottery is typical of the Classic period, and carved or incised decoration is typical of the Postclassic period.

The Maya had a pantheon of gods, but the Maya king or queen was the paramount ritual figure. Fasting, bloodletting, tobacco smoking, and taking ritual enemas were part of vision quests carried out by the royal Maya at important state events—notably accession to the throne, marriage, the birth of a child, and death. Bloodletting was done with a stingray spine or obsidian blade piercing the tongue, penis, or other soft body part. The public display of royal Maya bloodletting and other rituals is shown on stelae, other stone carvings, and on painted pots.

Postclassic Period

One by one, the Late Classic cities in the southern Maya lowlands were abandoned. The collapse may have been precipitated by overpopulation and by ecological disasters brought on by extensive clearing of the rainforest and overuse of the land for agriculture. Climatic or other environmental changes made have also contributed to the ecological problems. Certainly, warfare was endemic among the lowland city-states, and some archaeologists contend that it was what caused the collapse. The downfall of cities was recorded on stelae at the conquering city. By A.D. 900, most of the important Classic period cities in the southern Maya lowlands were abandoned. Rural farmers and small communities continued, but there was also significant depopulation in the rural area of the southern Maya. However, there is no skeletal evidence of disease decimating the population or of bodies strewn in the streets or in hastily made graves, as would have resulted from disease or large-scale warfare. What happened to the Classic Maya people when the political-economic fabric of the dynastic Maya disintegrated? Was there a mass exodus out of the southern lowlands? Certainly there was continued settlement, even an increase in population, to the east in parts of Belize and in the northern Maya lowlands. A

Stela P at Copan, front view showing royal figure
(Courtesy B. Somers)

Stela P at Copan, side view showing hieroglyphic text
(Courtesy B. Somers)

few cities in the southern Maya lowlands, such as Lamanai in Belize, continued during the subsequent Postclassic period (A.D. 900–1500). Chichen Itza and later Mayapan rose to prominence in the Postclassic in the northern Maya lowlands. Population dynamics at the end of the Classic period in the Maya lowlands remain a pressing unresolved issue.

Still, important strides have been made since John Lloyd Stephens explored ancient Maya cities in the mid-nineteenth century. Old views of the empty ceremonial center supported by rural slash-and-burn farmers have been replaced by new views of densely populated cities supported, in part, by more intensive agriculture. Reasons for the collapse of the civilization still focus on ecological and demographic problems, but the roles of warfare and climatic change are now considered as viable alternatives. Once considered a peaceful people, the Classic Maya as revealed through the decipherment of the hieroglyphs were shown to be quite bellicose. Current examinations of the nature of craft production and the trade of salt, obsidian, chert, and other materials will enhance our knowledge of the Classic Maya economic and political structure.

SOURCES OF INFORMATION ON THE MAYA

Journals

Ancient Mesoamerica and *Latin American Antiquity* are the premier journals that have a significant focus on Maya archaeology, but many other leading archaeology journals carry articles on the ancient Maya. *Journal of Field Archaeology* publishes reports of fieldwork and analysis and has a Web page providing an alphabetical listing of articles on the Maya by author under the category "Mesoamerica," at http://jfa-www.bu.edu/Indices/MesoAm.htm/. *Mexicon* is a good source of recent research. It also lists recent journal articles and books that focus on Mesoamerica, including the Maya. Their Web page (http://www.mexicon.de) has an index of articles arranged by author, including some articles with abstracts.

Other major journals that often include articles on Maya archaeology include *Journal of Archaeological Science, World Archaeology, Archaeology, Science, Nature, Journal of World Prehistory, American Anthropologist, Current Anthropology, Antiquity, Journal of Anthropological Research,* and *Cambridge Archaeological Journal. Antiquity* has an index by subject and author of articles in their journal (http://antiquity.ac.uk/Listing/listingindex.html), as well as the table of contents of recent journal issues. *Archaeology* magazine (http://www.archaeology.org) has an index of articles by author, with abstracts from 1991 to the present, as well as an archive of articles from 1996 to 2001 (http://www.archaeology.org/index/msubject.html). The *PARI Journal* provides important recent articles on hieroglyphs, as well as articles on the Maya city of Palenque and other Maya research, with information also being provided on their Web page (http://www.mesoweb.com/pari).

Increasingly, entire journal articles are available on the Internet, either by a per-article fee, or gratis to students and faculty at universities, for example. Ingenta, an electronic source, provides overnight delivery of articles from thousands of journals (http://www.Ingenta.com). JStor, another electronic source, provides electronic access to the full text of articles from *American Antiquity, Latin American Antiquity, World Archaeology, Current Anthropology,* and *Annual Review of Anthropology,* although not the most recent issues. Importantly, both JStor and Ingenta can be used without charge as online search engines by topic or by viewing the table of contents of each issue. Members of the Society of American Archaeology, which publishes *American Antiquity* and *Latin American Antiquity,* can subscribe to JStor for a modest annual fee (http://www.jstor.org).

Books

The University of Texas Press, University Press of Florida, University of Oklahoma Press, Thames & Hudson, and University of Utah Press publish general texts on the Maya, edited volumes, and other books on the ancient Maya. For more suggested reading on the Maya, see the Resources for Further Study section at the end of this book.

Andrews, E. Wyllys, IV, and E. Wyllys Andrews V. 1980. *Excavations at Dzibilchaltun, Yucatan, Mexico.* Middle American Research Institute Publication 48. New Orleans: Tulane University.

Ashmore, Wendy, ed. 1981. *Lowland Maya Settlement Patterns.* Albuquerque: University of New Mexico Press.

Chase, Arlen F., and Prudence M. Rice, eds. 1985. *The Lowland Maya Postclassic.* Austin: University of Texas Press.

Clancy, Flora F., and Peter D. Harrison, eds. 1990. *Vision and Revision in Maya Studies.* Albuquerque: University of New Mexico Press.

Culbert, T. Patrick, ed. 1973. *The Classic Maya Collapse.* Albuquerque: University of New Mexico Press.

———. 1991. *Classic Maya Political History.* New York: Cambridge University Press.

Culbert, T. Patrick, and Don S. Rice, eds. 1990. *Precolumbian Population History in the Maya Lowlands.* Albuquerque: University of New Mexico Press.

Ford, Anabel. 1986. *Population Growth and Social Complexity: An Examination of Settlement and Environment in the Central Maya Lowlands.* Anthropological Research Paper 35. Tempe: Arizona State University.

Freidel, David A., and Jeremy A. Sabloff. 1984. *Cozumel: Late Maya Settlement Patterns.* New York: Academic Press.

Hammond, Norman. 1975. *Lubaantun: A Classic Maya Realm.* Peabody Museum of Archaeology and Ethnology Monograph, vol. 2. Cambridge, MA: Harvard University.

Houston, Stephen D. 1993. *Hieroglyphs and History at Dos Pilas: Dynastic Politics of the Classic Maya.* Austin: University of Texas Press.

Kurjack, Edward. 1974. *Prehistoric Lowland Maya Community and Social Organization: A Case Study at Dzibilchaltun, Yucatan, Mexico.* Middle American Research Institute Publication 38. New Orleans: Tulane University.

Lowe, John W. G. 1985. *The Dynamics of Apocalypse: A Systems Simulation of the Classic Maya Collapse.* Albuquerque: University of New Mexico Press.

Marcus, Joyce. 1976. *Emblem and State in the Classic Maya Lowlands.* Washington, DC: Dumbarton Oaks.

Martin, Simon, and Nickolai Grube. 2000. *Chronicle of the Maya Kings and Queens.* New York: Thames & Hudson.

Masson, Marilyn, and David Freidel, eds. 2002. *Ancient Maya Political Economies.* New York: Altamira.

McAnany, Patricia A., and Barry Isaac, eds. 1989. *Prehistoric Maya Economies of Belize.* Research in Economic Anthropology Supplement 4. Greenwich, CT: JAI Press.

McKillop, Heather. 2002. *Salt: White Gold of the Ancient Maya.* Gainesville: University Press of Florida.

Miller, Mary Ellen. 1986. *The Murals of Bonampak.* Princeton, NJ: Princeton University Press.

Morley, Sylvanus G. 1946. *The Ancient Maya*. Palo Alto, CA: Stanford University Press.

Sabloff, Jeremy A., and E. Wyllys Andrews V, eds. 1986. *Late Lowland Maya Civilization: Classic to Postclassic*. Albuquerque: University of New Mexico Press.

Sabloff, Jeremy A., and John S. Henderson, eds. 1993. *Lowland Maya Civilization in the Eighth Century A.D.* Washington, DC: Dumbarton Oaks Research Library and Collection.

Schlesinger, Victoria. 2001. *Animals and Plants of the Ancient Maya: A Guide*. Austin: University of Texas Press.

Sheets, Payson, ed. 2002. *Before the Volcano Erupted: The Ancient Ceren Village in Central America*. Austin: University of Texas Press.

White, Christine D., ed. 1999. *Reconstructing Ancient Maya Diet*. Salt Lake City: University of Utah Press.

Monographs

Monograph series that focus on the ancient Maya include *Papers (and Memoirs) of the Peabody Museum of Archaeology and Ethnology* published by Harvard University, *Middle American Research Institute Papers* of Tulane University, the Tikal reports and other Maya monographs published by the University of Pennsylvania Museum, Vanderbilt University's series on the Petexbatun project, and the Royal Ontario Museum on Altun Ha and other sites. The University of Texas Press, the University Press of Florida in their Maya Studies series, the Pre-Columbian Art Research Institute (PARI), and Thames & Hudson have a focus on publishing Maya monographs. Monographs also are published by other universities, museums, and private publishers.

CDs and Videos

UCSB Maya Forest GIS 2000 by Anabel Ford and Keith Clarke includes maps and satellite imagery for the Peten, Guatemala, and upper Belize River area corresponding to Ford's research. Ford's (2003) *Welcome to El Pilar* CD describes the El Pilar Archaeological Reserve for Maya Flora and Fauna. *Mesolore: Exploring Mesoamerican Culture* (Bakewell and Hammann 2001) includes discussion of the ancient Maya. The *Living Maya* CD explores the modern Mopan and Kekchi Maya of southern Belize (Marsden and Leupold 2001). Payson Sheets's CD on the Ceren site, *An Interactive Guide to Ancient Cerén: Before the Volcano Erupted,* contains field reports, illustrations, and data that are summarized in the text *Before the Volcano Erupted* (Sheets 2002). The CD is available on the Internet at http://ceren.colorado.edu. Merle Green Robertson's rubbings of Palenque stelae and other carved monuments can be downloaded for free from the Pre-Columbian Art Research Institute (PARI) at http://www.mesoweb.com/pari. Increasingly, electronic access to Maya archaeology is being provided on the Internet without charge.

Educational videos are available on the ancient Maya. *Lost Kingdoms of the Ancient Maya* (Weber 1993) includes interviews of Maya archaeologists at Copan, Caracol, Dos Pilas, and other Classic Maya sites in the 1990s. *Lost King of the Maya* (Glassman 2001) explores the life of Yax K'uk Mo, the first king of the Copan dynasty, a Classic Maya polity in western Honduras. An earlier video, *Maya: Lords of the Jungle,* provides an informative discussion of population increase and methods of intensifying agricultural production during the Late Classic, with interviews of Maya archaeologists (Ambrosino 1993).

Research Programs

Research programs focusing on Maya archaeology and involving fieldwork are offered at many universities with Maya archaeologists, as well as through government agencies in several Central American countries. Maya research has been carried out for many years through several institutions, notably Harvard University, the University of Pennsylvania, and the Royal Ontario Museum. Beginning in the 1980s, there was a tremendous increase in the number of Maya archaeologists with field programs through their universities. Institutions developing programs at that time included Vanderbilt University, Southern Methodist University, the University of Arizona, Trent University, the University of Texas at Austin, the University of Texas at San Antonio, the University of Central Florida, and Southern Illinois University at Carbondale. By 2000, there were many more universities with active field programs in Maya archaeology.

Many of the currect and ongoing projects involve opportunities for university students to participate, and some projects allow volunteers to participate. Many projects permit visitors, so public knowledge of "who is digging where" is useful to those interested in participating in or visiting Maya sites so that the project director may be contacted in advance. The Guatemalan government initiated excavation and restoration at Tikal, under the direction of Juan Valdez LaPorte, following the long-term University of Pennsylvania Museum project at the site. After a multiyear project in the Petexbatun region of the Peten, Guatemala, Arthur Demarest of Vanderbilt University initiated work at Cancuen, Guatemala. Several of Demarest's former students who worked on the Petexbatun project have initiated their own fieldwork, including Antonia Foias at Motul de San Jose and Takeshi Inomata at Aguateca. Francisco Estrada-Belli began excavations at Holmul, where distinctive Protoclassic pottery had been reported decades earlier (Merwin and Vaillant 1932). Don and Prudence Rice have carried out fieldwork in the central Peten, Guatemala, through the University of Southern Illinois at Carbondale. Stephen Houston of Brigham Young University directs research at Piedras Negras, Guatemala, along with David Webster of Penn State University. Other projects include William Saturno's research on the murals of San Bartolo and Richard Hansen's research at the Preclassic cities of El Mirador and Nakbe through UCLA.

The Institute of Archaeology of the Belize government is occupied both with overseeing the many field projects by foreign archaeologists and in carrying out government-sponsored fieldwork. The Institute is part of the National Institute of Culture and History (http.//www.nichbelize.org.) Belizean archaeologists Jaime Awe and Allan Moore initiated an excavation and restoration project at Caracol and other public sites in Belize funded by the Inter-American Development Bank to develop ancient sites for tourism, which is a major focus of the Belize government for archaeological research in their country. This follows Awe's earlier work in Belizean caves through the University of New Hampshire and Trent University, and at Cahal Pech through Trent University and the University of London. Allan Moore's previous research was at Baking Pot through the University of London. Both Awe and Moore studied at Trent University under Paul Healy, who had projects on terraces in the Maya Mountains and at Pacbitun. Elizabeth Graham has ongoing research at Lamanai through the Institute of Archaeology at the University of London, England, continuing research done by David Pendergast, retired from the Royal Ontario Museum. Boston University has a Maya research program, with Norman Hammond doing research at La Milpa (following earlier work at Cuello, Nohmul, and Lubaantun) and Patricia McAnany doing a project along the Sibun River (following earlier work at K'axob near Pulltrouser Swamp).

Others working in Belize include Diane and Arlen Chase of the University of Central Florida, who have carried out a long-term project at Caracol, following earlier work at Santa Rita Corozal, Belize. The author of this book has a long-term research program on

Archaeological research programs in the Maya area

the coast and cays of southern Belize (Port Honduras Marine Reserve and Paynes Creek National Park) through Louisiana State University, following earlier work at Moho Cay, Wild Cane Cay, and Frenchman's Cay. The Program for Belize, directed by Fred Valdez of the University of Texas, Austin, includes a variety of research efforts by many archaeologists in northwestern Belize. Other major research programs in Belize include K. Anne Pyburn's excavations at Chau Hiix through Indiana University (following her earlier work at Nohmul and on Albion Island); Anabel Ford's project at El Pilar, following her earlier work along the Belize River (both through the University of California at Santa Barbara); Joe Ball's project at Cahal Pech and nearby sites through San Diego State University; Marilyn Masson's project in northern Belize through SUNY, Albany; Shirley Mock's study of northern coastal Belize through the University of Texas at San Antonio; Jon Lohse's project at Blue Creek (following Thomas Guderjan's research); Geoffrey Braswell's project at Pusilha through SUNY, Buffalo; and Peter Dunham's Maya Mountain research through Cleveland State University.

Other multiyear projects ended in the late twentieth century, including Thomas Hester and Harry Shafer's projects at Colha through the University of Texas at Austin and Texas A & M University, respectively; Richard Leventhal and Wendy Ashmore's project at Xunantunich through UCLA and UC, Riverside (following Leventhal's previous work at Nim li punit, Pusilha, and elsewhere in southern Belize).

The Institute of Anthropology and History (INAH) in Mexico carries out excavation and restoration projects and also oversees research programs directed by foreign archaeologists; these must have a Mexican co-director. A research program directed by George Bey of Millsap's College and Bill Ringle of Davidson College focused on Ek Balam and other sites in the Yucatan. Rani Alexander has directed a rare historical archaeology project in the Yucatan, with continuing work at Isla Cilvituk through New Mexico State University. Other recent projects include Marilyn Masson's project at Mayapan, Bruce Dahlin and Traci Ardren's project at Chunchucmil, Michael Smyth's excavations at Chac, Anthony Andrews's research on the Yucatan coast, and Terance Winemiller's study of water resources at ancient Maya sites in the northern Maya lowlands. The Mexican government itself continues excavation and restoration of architecture at a number of sites, notably Peter Schmidt's project at Chichen Itza.

Several universities have been involved in research at Copan, Honduras. Bill Fash of Harvard University, David Webster and William T. Sanders of Penn State, Robert Sharer of the University of Pennsylvania, and E. Wyllys Andrews V of Tulane University have directed recent projects. Elsewhere in Honduras, Rosemary Joyce of the University of California at Berkeley, John Henderson, and others are carrying out ongoing fieldwork.

In El Salvador, Payson Sheets of the University of Colorado at Boulder has carried out research since the 1970s at the Ceren site. Elsewhere in El Salvador, Jane Kelly, Bill Fowler, and E. Wyllys Andrews V also have carried out fieldwork in recent years.

Several institutions host regular events focusing on Maya archaeology that are open to the public. The Maya Weekend, held each spring at the University of Pennsylvania Museum, hosts a series of speakers. A similar Maya weekend has been offered at UCLA in the fall. Beginning in 2002, Tulane University's Middle American Research Institute initiated a Maya weekend during the fall. The Maya Hieroglyph Workshop at the University of Texas, Austin, initiated by the late Linda Schele, is offered annually in March for a week and focuses on learning and interpreting Maya glyphs. Louisiana State University has offered LSU Maya Archaeology Night in early November, highlighting student research in Maya archaeology for a public audience (http://www.ga.lsu.edu/

Maya_Night.htm). Dumbarton Oaks in Washington, D.C. (http://www.doaks.org), and the School for American Research in Santa Fe, New Mexico (http://www.sarweb. org) periodically host seminars on Maya archaeology, with the Dumbarton Oaks event open to the public.

A number of exhibitions of Maya pottery and other objects in recent years have produced publications. E. Michael Whittington (2001) organized the exhibit The Sport of Life and Death: The Mesoamerican Ball Game in 2002 at the Mint Museum of Art in Charlotte, North Carolina, the New Orleans Museum of Art, the Joslyn Art Museum in Omaha, Nebraska, and the Newark Museum, in New Jersey, in 2001–2002. The exhibit entitled Maya, with a lavishly illustrated book edited by Peter Schmidt, Mercedes de la Garza, and Enrique Nalda (1998), was held in Venice, Italy. *Painting the Maya Universe: Royal Ceramics of the Classic Period* by Dorie Reents-Budet (1994) accompanied an exhibit at the Duke Museum of Art, the Museum of Fine Arts in Boston, the Denver Art Museum, the Los Angeles County Museum, and Yale University Art Gallery in 1994 and 1995. *The Blood of Kings: Dynasty and Ritual in Maya Art* by Linda Schele and Mary Miller (1986) accompanied an exhibit at the Kimbell Art Museum in Fort Worth, Texas, and the Cleveland Museum of Art in 1986. The book *Cenote of Sacrifice: Maya Treasures from the Sacred Well at Chichen Itza* (Coggins and Shane 1984) was a joint venture by the Science Museum of Minnesota and Harvard's Peabody Museum. Other recent exhibits include Maya: Treasures of an Ancient Civilization (with a book by the same name written by Clancy et al. 1985), which toured the American Museum of Natural History, the Los Angeles County Museum, the Dallas Museum of Art, the Royal Ontario Museum, Nelson-Atkins Museum of Art in Kansas City, and the Albuquerque Museum from 1985 to 1987. Diane and Arlen Chase had exhibits on Caracol (with a book by Chase and Chase 1987) and Santa Rita Corozal (with a book by Chase and Chase 1986) at the Orlando Museum of Art. Michael Coe has organized several important exhibitions of Maya art with well-illustrated catalogs (Coe 1973; Coe 1978; Coe 1982).

Internet

Perhaps the best Maya archaeology Web pages are those created by the archaeologists (or in consultation with them) about their fieldwork. There are other informative websites that provide more general information on the ancient Maya, including useful information on how modern people can travel to see Maya sites. Some websites are valuable resources for research, as they include reports and illustrations. For example, Diane and Arlen Chase created the website http://www.caracol.org about their project at Caracol. The site includes background on Caracol, field season summaries, photos, and information on publications. The site also has journals from the archaeologists and their children, plus fun Maya games for kids to play. Anabel Ford's website on El Pilar (http://www.marc.ucsb.edu/elpilar//) provides sophisticated computer illustrations, other informative illustrations, and text on her successful efforts to create a binational park at El Pilar, which straddles the border between Belize and Guatemala.

Payson Sheets's excavations at El Ceren, an ancient Maya community in El Salvador buried by a volcanic eruption, are highlighted in his Web page at http://ceren. colorado.edu. The site provides stunning graphics. Rani Alexander's excavations at Isla Cilvituk, an island off the west coast of the Yucatan peninsula, Mexico, are well documented in her website at http://www.nmsu.edu/~anthro/islacilvituk/ICmast. html. The LSU Maya Archaeology website (http://www.ga.lsu.edu/Maya_Night.html) includes descriptions, photos, and newsletters about this author's own fieldwork at Wild Cane Cay, Frenchman's Cay, Punta Ycacos Lagoon, and elsewhere in the Port

Honduras Marine Reserve and Paynes Creek National Park in southern Belize. Research at Lamanai, Altun Ha, and Marco Gonzalez in northern Belize by David Pendergast and Elizabeth Graham is detailed at http://www.rom.on.ca./digs/belize.html/. Much of the site highlights Lamanai (http://www.rom.on.ca./digs/belize/what-we-know.html), with a section on the history of excavations and a wonderful summary of the research. Patricia McAnany's fieldwork at the Maya community of K'axob by Pull-trouser Swamp in northern Belize and at Xibun along the Sibun River in central Belize is presented in her Web page, http://www.bu.edu/tricia/. The Programme for Belize Archaeological Project in northwestern Belize directed by Fred Valdez includes description of the fieldwork (http://uts.cc.utexas.edu/~marl/), as well as a new digital journal on Maya and Texas prehistory, *Mono y Conejo: Journal of the Mesoamerican Archaeological Research Laboratory,* with volume 1 published in 2003 on the Internet and downloadable for free (http://uts.cc.utexas.edu/~marl/Publications/mono_y_conejo.htm). Sophisticated computer mapping using geographic information system (GIS) software maps by Francisco Estrada-Belli, as well as informative reports, are on the La Milpa website at http://www.bu.edu/lamilpa). A status report on Tom Hester and Harry Shafer's Colha Preceramic Project is available at http://www.utexas.edu/cola/llilas/centers/publications/papers/latinamerica/9503.html. Bill and Barbara Fash present some of their research findings at Copan, Honduras, in their Web page, http://www.peabody.harvard.edu/profiles/fash.html. Marilyn Masson's website at http://www.albany.edu/anthro/fac/masson.htm is mainly about the field school in northern Belize. Jaime Awe's Western Belize Cave Project includes video tours and other information (http://www.indiana.edu/~belize/; see also http://www.bvar.org).

The governments of Belize, Guatemala, Mexico, Honduras, and El Salvador provide information on Maya archaeology in their countries. In Mexico, the Instituto Nacional de Antropologia e Historia (INAH) is in charge of Maya archaeology, and you can find information at http://www.inah.gob.mx. The Tikal website (http://www.tikalpark.com) includes the site map, general information about the ruins, history of research, flora, fauna, and photographs.

In the late twentieth century, the Belize government initiated a program to develop museums, launched with the Belize Museum in Belize City, the Museum in Belmopan, and overall management of cultural and archaeological development through the National Institute of Culture and History (NICH). The Belize government's Institute of Archaeology in Belmopan provides tours of their collections and houses an outstanding research library.

The Foundation for Mesoamerican Research, Inc. (FAMSI) is the main source for Justin Kerr's (2003a, 2003b) fabulous "rollouts" of Maya vases and other pottery that provide a full photo of the painted decoration on a pottery vessel using a special photographic technique he developed. The FAMSI website also includes research reports from FAMSI grants at http://www.famsi.org. Their online "research facility" is an important source of primary information for students and researchers, who can search by word or phrase through the combined Kerr portfolio (2003a); John Montgomery heiroglyph dictionary, including Maya speakers pronouncing the words (Matthews 2003a); and Linda Schele drawing archive (Matthews 2003b; http://www.famsi.org/search.htm). The FAMSI website makes it possible to carry out original research utilizing the Web data, thereby marking an important turning point in the use of the Internet. Additionally, FAMSI hosts the ongoing Mesoamerican bibliography project, which is a joint project with John Weeks (2003) of the University of Pennsylvania and is founded on the thousands of sources compiled by Ignacio Bernal. The FAMSI website also hosts the

University of Pennsylvania Museum's Tikal Digital Access Project (Mesdia 2003) providing data on the project. FAMSI also maintains an up-to-date listing of Maya-related events (http://www.famsi.org/events/htm) and continues to add new information, such as a photographic database of Stephen Houston's 1997–2000 fieldwork at Piedras Negras (http://www.famsi.org/research/piedras_negras.htm).

Pre-Columbian Studies at Dumbarton Oaks also has useful online material and information for Maya archaeology, including an online tour of their Maya gallery (http://www.doaks.org/Pre-Columbian.html/). Maya pots, including rollouts, are shown on their "slide sets" listing. The Dumbarton Oaks website also lists conferences and other activities on Maya archaeology, as well as an important online library catalog of Maya books and articles in their collections. Tulane University's Middle American Research Institute provides a listing of their collections http://www.tulane.edu/~mari/collect.html), as well as of their publication series http://www.tulane.edu/~mari/pubmenu.html).

There are several excellent websites on Mayan hieroglyphs, calendars, astronomy, and related topics in addition to John Montgomery's (Matthews 2003a) digital dictionary, which includes sound. The Maya astronomy page (http://www.michielb.nl/maya/) provides very useful information on Maya mathematics, calendars, hieroglyphic writing, and astronomy. The Mayan Epigraphic Database Project (http://www.iath.virginia.edu/med/) provides a stellar glyph catalog for the serious researcher, as well as other information for researchers and for novice Maya hieroglyph aficionados. David Stuart of Harvard's Peabody Museum provides an outstanding introduction to the hieroglyphs and history at Copan http://www.peabody.harvard.edu/Copan/text.html).

The Mesoamerican ball game website is a sophisticated companion to the exhibit of the same name (http://www.ballgame.org/main.asp). The companion website to the National Geographic Society video *Lost Kingdoms of the Maya* (Weber 1993; http://www.pbs.org/wgbh/nova/maya) includes detailed information on the ancient Maya under "Tour Copan with David Stuart," "Incidents of Travel," "Map of Maya World" (which has a clickable map with information on fifteen Maya sites), and "Reading Maya Hieroglyphs." They are available in video format or as a transcript online. National Geographic provides information on the ancient Maya (http://www.nationalgeographic.com), including, for example, field reports such as the one from Jaime Awe's cave research in Belize (http://www.nationalgeographic.com/chiquibul/intro.html). Information on many Maya sites in Belize is available at http://www.ambergriscaye.com/pages/mayan/mayasites.html. Links to Maya archaeology websites in Belize are available through the website http://archaeology.about.com/blbelize.htm. A valuable website for researchers and travelers interested in Spanish colonial sites in the Yucatan is http://www.colonial-mexico.com, published by Richard Perry. The website has selected Yucatecan monasteries, churches, and other Spanish colonial monuments, with a focus on the art and architecture as well as links to related websites. Information about Maya sites and Maya archaeology is widely available from many other websites, but the viewer must exercise judgment about the scientific quality of secondary sources not prepared by Maya archaeologists.

Field Schools

There are opportunities for students and volunteers to participate in excavations at Maya sites as part of archaeological field schools offered through universities with Maya archaeologists, through various volunteer organizations, or as part of a research team (although this last is normally for students registered in academic programs). Maya archaeologists have offered field schools through university departments of anthropology (University of Texas, Austin, Trent University, Southwest Texas State University, UC Riverside, Louisiana State University) and departments of archaeology (Boston University). Earthwatch (http://www.earthwatch.org), University of California Research Expeditions or UREP (http://extension.ucdavis.edu/urep/), and the Maya Research Program (http://www.mayaresearchprogram.org) provide opportunities for volunteers to participate in fieldwork at Maya sites.

REFERENCES

Ambrosino, Michael, prod. [1981] 1993. *Maya: Lords of the Jungle.* VHS video, PBS Home Video. Los Angeles: The Pacific Arts Corporation.

Ardren, Traci, ed. 2002. *Ancient Maya Women.* Walnut Creek, CA: Altamira.

Bakewell, Liza, and Byron Hammann. 2001. *Mesolore: Exploring Mesoamerican Culture.* Version 2.0. CD. Providence, RI: Brown University.

Chase, Arlen F., and Diane Z. Chase. 1987. *Glimmers of a Forgotten Realm: Maya Archaeology at Caracol, Belize.* Orlando: Orlando Museum of Art and Loch Haven.

Chase, Diane Z., and Arlen F. Chase. 1986. *Offerings to the Gods: Maya Archaeology at Santa Rita Corozal.* Orlando: University of Central Florida.

Clancy, Flora S., Clemency C. Coggins, T. Patrick Culbert, Charles Gallenkamp, Peter D. Harrison, and Jeremy A. Sabloff. 1985. *Maya: Treasures of an Ancient Civilization.* New York: Harry N. Abrams.

Coe, Michael D. 1973. *The Maya Scribe and His World.* New York: Grolier Club.

———. 1978. *Lords of the Underworld: Masterpieces of Classic Maya Ceramics.* Princeton, NJ: Art Museum, Princeton University, and Princeton University Press.

———. 1982. *Old Gods and Young Heroes: The Pearlman Collection of Maya Ceramics.* Jerusalem: Israel Museum.

Coe, Michael D., and Mark Van Stone. 2001. *Reading the Maya Glyphs.* New York: Thames & Hudson.

Coggins, Clemency, and Orrin C. Shane III, eds. 1984. *Cenote of Sacrifice: Maya Treasures from the Sacred Well at Chichen Itza.* Austin: University of Texas Press.

Culbert, T. Patrick, ed. 1973. *The Classic Maya Collapse.* Albuquerque: University of New Mexico Press.

Danforth, Marie. 1999. "Coming up Short: Stature and Nutrition among the Ancient Maya of the Southern Lowlands." In *Reconstructing Ancient Maya Diet,* edited by Christine White, 103–117. Salt Lake City: University of Utah Press.

Demarest, Arthur. 1997. "The Vanderbilt Petexbatun Regional Archaeological Project 1989–1994: Overview, History, and Major Results of a Multidisciplinary Study of the Classic Maya Collapse." *Ancient Mesoamerica* 8: 209–227.

Ford, Anabel. 2003. *Welcome to El Pilar: Come Explore the Trails of the El Pilar Archaeological Reserve for Maya Flora and Fauna.* CD. Santa Barbara: University of California at Santa Barbara.

Ford, Anabel, and Keith Clark. 2000. *UCSB Maya Forest GIS 2000.* Santa Barbara: University of California at Santa Barbara.

Freidel, David, Linda Schele, and Joy Parker. 1993. *Maya Cosmos.* New York: Morrow.

Gill, Richardson. 2000. *The Great Maya Droughts: Water, Life, and Death.* Albuquerque: University of New Mexico Press.

Graham, Elizabeth. 1987. "Resource Diversity in Belize and Its Implications for Models of Lowland Trade." *American Antiquity* 52 (4): 753–767.

Hammond, Norman. 1972. "Obsidian Trade Routes in the Mayan Area." *Science* 178: 1092–1093.

———, ed. 1991. *Cuello.* New York: Cambridge University Press.

Harrison, Peter D. 1999. *The Lords of Tikal.* New York: Thames & Hudson.

Harrison, Peter D., and B. L. Turner, eds. 1978. *Pre-Hispanic Maya Agriculture.* Albuquerque: University of New Mexico Press.

Haviland, William A. 1967. "Stature at Tikal, Guatemala: Implications for Ancient Maya Demography and Social Organization." *American Antiquity* 32: 117–125.

Healy, Paul F., Heather I. McKillop, and Bernetta Walsh. 1984. "Analysis of Obsidian from Moho Cay, Belize: New Evidence on Classic Maya Trade Routes." *Science* 225: 414–417.

Hodell, David A., Jason H. Curtis, and Mark Brenner. 1995. "Possible Role of Climate in the Collapse of Classic Maya Civilization." *Nature* 375: 391–394.

Houston, Stephen, Oswaldo Chinchilla Mazariegos, and David Stuart, eds. 2001. *The Decipherment of Ancient Maya Writing.* Norman: University of Oklahoma Press.

Kerr, Justin. 2003a. *Maya Vase Data Base: An Archive of Rollout Photographs Created by Justin Kerr.* http://www.mayavase.com.

———. 2003b. *The Grolier Codex.* http://www.mayavase.com/grol/grolier.html.

Knorozov, Yuri V. 1958. "The Problem of the Study of Maya Hieroglyphic Writing" (translated by Sophie Coe). *American Antiquity* 23: 284–291.

Marsden, Anne-Michelle, and Eric Leupold. 2001. *The Living Maya.* Punta Gorda, Belize: Maya Viewkeeper.

Martin, Simon, and Nikolai Grube. 2000. *Chronicle of the Maya Kings and Queens.* New York: Thames & Hudson.

Masson, Marilyn, and David Freidel, eds. 2002. *Ancient Maya Political Economies.* New York: Altamira.

Matthews, Peter. 2003a. John Montgomery's *Dictionary of Maya Hieroglyphs.* http://www.famsi.org/mayawriting/dictionary/montgomery/index.html.

———. 2003b. *The Linda Schele Drawings.* http://www.famsi.org/research/schele/bypmathews.htm.

McKillop, Heather. 1994. "Ancient Maya Tree Cropping: A Viable Subsistence Adaptation for the Island Maya." *Ancient Mesoamerica* 5: 129–140.

———. 2002. *Salt: White Gold of the Ancient Maya.* Gainesville: University Press of Florida.

———. 2003. "Catastrophic and Other Environmental Factors in the Classic Maya Collapse." Paper presented at the annual meeting of the American Association of Geographers, New Orleans, March.

McKillop, Heather, L. J. Jackson, Helen Michel, Fred Stross, and Frank Asaro. 1988. "Chemical Sources Analysis of Maya Obsidian Artifacts: New Perspectives from Wild Cane Cay, Belize." In *Archaeometry 88,* edited by R. M. Farqhuar, R. G. V. Hancock, and Larry A. Pavlish, 239–244. Toronto: Department of Physics, University of Toronto.

Meggers, Betty. 1954. "Environmental Limitation on the Development of Culture." *American Anthropologist* 56: 801–824.

Merwin, Raymond E., and George C. Vaillant. 1932. "The Ruins of Holmul, Guatemala." In *Memoirs of the Peabody Museum of Archaeology and Ethnology.* Cambridge, MA: Harvard University.

Mesdia, Sharon. 2003. The Tikal Digital Access Project. http://www.museum.upenn. edu/tdap/. For part of the digital project data, see also http://www.famsi.org/ research/tikal/index.html.

Milbrath, Susan. 1999. *Star Gods of the Maya: Astronomy in Art, Folklore, and Calendars.* Austin: University of Texas Press.

Miller, Mary. 1986. *The Murals of Bonampak.* Princeton, NJ: Princeton University Press.

Montgomery, John. 2002a. *How to Read Maya Hieroglyphs.* New York: Hippocrene.

————. 2002b. *Dictionary of Maya Hieroglyphs.* New York: Hippocrene.

Morley, Sylvanus. 1946. *The Ancient Maya.* Palo Alto, CA: Stanford University Press.

Nelson, Fred W. 1985. "Summary of the Results of Analysis of Obsidian Artifacts from the Maya Lowlands." *Scanning Electron Microscopy* 2: 631–649.

Proskouriakoff, Tatiana. 1960. "Historical Implications of a Pattern of Dates at Piedras Negras, Guatemala." *American Antiquity* 25: 454–475.

Reents-Budet, Dorie. 1994. *Painting the Maya Universe.* Durham, NC: Duke University Press.

Schele, Linda, and Mary Miller. 1986. *The Blood of Kings: Dynasty and Ritual in Maya Art.* New York: George Braziller.

Schmidt, Peter, Mercedes de la Garza, and Enrique Nalda, eds. 1998. *Maya.* Venice: Bompiani.

Stephens, John L. [1841] 1969. *Incidents of Travel in Central America, Chiapas, and Yucatan.* New York: Dover.

Tedlock, Dennis, trans. 1985. *Popol Vuh: The Definitive Edition of the Mayan Book of the Dawn of Life and the Glories of Gods and Kings.* New York: Simon and Schuster.

Thompson, J. Eric S. 1970. *Maya History and Religion.* Norman: University of Oklahoma Press.

Weber, Christie. 1993. *Lost Kingdoms of the Maya.* VHS. Washington, DC: National Geographic Society.

Webster, David. 2002. *The Fall of the Ancient Maya.* New York: Thames & Hudson.

Weeks, John. 2003. *Bibliografia Mesoamericana.* http://www.famsi.org/research/ bibliography.htm.

White, Christine D., ed. 1999. *Reconstructing Ancient Maya Diet.* Salt Lake City: University of Utah Press.

Whittington, E. Michael, ed. 2001. *The Sport of Life and Death: The Mesoamerican Ballgame.* New York: Thames & Hudson.

PART 2
Maya Civilization

CHAPTER 2

Location of Maya Area and Environmental Setting

By definition, the Maya area includes the region where the ancient Maya civilization developed. This area consists of what is now Guatemala, Belize, El Salvador, the Yucatan peninsula and parts of adjacent Chiapas in Mexico, and western Honduras. According to historical linguist Lyle Campbell (1984), the Mayan language had developed in this area before 2100 B.C. The Maya of the Classic period civilization evidently spoke Cholan Mayan, which is close to modern Chorti, spoken by the Maya west of the ruins of Copan. Indigenous Maya people still live throughout much of the area, and many still speak one of the some thirty-one Mayan languages.

GENERAL NATURAL AND CULTURAL SUBDIVISIONS

Cultural Subareas

Archaeologists divide the Maya area into three subareas that reflect both environmental and cultural differences. The northern Maya lowlands are on the Yucatan peninsula. The southern Maya lowlands include Belize, the Peten district of Guatemala, and parts of adjacent Chiapas, Mexico, as well as the lowland area of Guatemala along the Motagua River and adjoining lowland Honduras. The southern Maya highlands are the mountainous region of southern Guatemala. The Classic period civilization developed in the southern Maya lowlands. Although there was early settlement in the northern Maya lowlands, it was not until the collapse of the southern lowland Maya cities after A.D. 900 that the northern lowlands flourished. Similarly, there was precocious early cultural development in the southern Maya highlands and also on the adjacent Pacific littoral, but the area remained in the cultural shadows of the southern lowland civilization.

Topography

Although evident on a gross scale, the topographic differences between the Maya highlands and lowlands often have been exaggerated. The Maya lowlands of the Yucatan peninsula of Mexico, of Belize, and of the Peten district of Guatemala are a limestone platform that is relatively flat. It looks particularly so being covered with the tropical rainforest vegetation of much of the southern Maya lowlands or the scrub vegetation of the northern Maya lowlands. From the top of a Maya temple, the panoramic view over the rainforest would

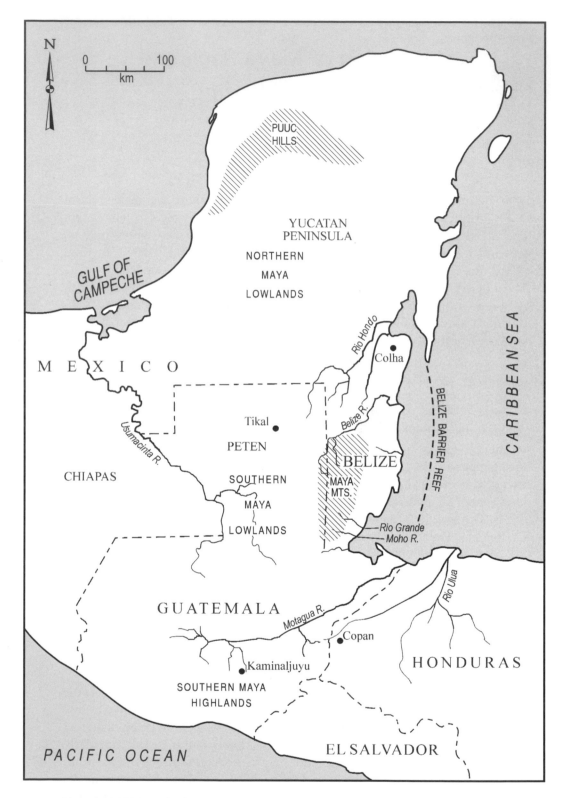

Rivers, mountains, and subareas in the Maya area

Cenote are deep water filled sinkholes formed by water percolating through the soft limestone above. Maya and Toltec city of Chichen Itza, Yucatan, Mexico (Art Directors/Martin Barlow)

mask much of what topographic variation there is on the ground in this region. The limestone platform itself was formed during the Cretaceous period and is of marine origin. Much like in the topography of Florida, sinkholes in this karstic landscape provide natural wells that tap the water table.

To the east is the Belize barrier reef—the longest reef system in the western hemisphere and surpassed in length only by the Great Barrier Reef off the coast of Australia. The reef parallels the coastline at a distance of 10 to 25 miles offshore. Cozumel, Cancun, and Isla Mujeres form the northern extension of the reef off the eastern coast of the Yucatan in Quintana Roo, Mexico. The reef system includes the barrier reef as well as hundreds of cays (islands) located between the reef and the mainland in what is the barrier lagoon. The reef system is a limestone extension of the Yucatan peninsula that was submerged by rising seas at the end of the Pleistocene, when sea level rose worldwide resulting from melting of the ice age glaciers (McKillop 2002). As sea level rose, beginning about 9500 B.C., red mangroves (*Rhizophora mangle*) and coral (*Acropora palmata*) took root on areas of high elevation within the barrier lagoon. Both mangroves and coral grow in salt water and at specific depths below sea level.

As sea levels continued to rise, the mangroves and coral continued to grow, depositing mangrove peat and coral, respectively, and forming land. The ancient Maya settled on some of the dry land cays (McKillop 2002).

The limestone bedrock on the mainland provided the building material for construction of buildings, sacbes (roadways), and carved stone monuments, as well as the plaster for facing the buildings. Limestone was quaried at Maya cities using stone tools to cut pits into the limestone and to shape limestone blocks for construction. The soft limestone hardens when exposed to air. Plaster—used for the exterior of buildings, plaza floors, and room interiors—was produced by burning crushed limestone. Natural depressions, cenotes (sinkholes), and underground cave systems found throughout the limestone platform were used by the ancient Maya for water storage and, in the case of caves, for various rituals. The ancient Maya used chert (a durable stone that can be chipped into a variety of stone tools, often referred to erroneously as flint) that occurs naturally in the limestone to make tools for clearing the forest, farming, various cutting and chopping tasks, and ritual or nonutilitarian tasks. Chert of varying qualities is widely available in limestone deposits in the lowlands. However, exceptionally high-quality chert—large outcrops of fine-grained stone—occurs in northern Belize around the ancient settlement of Colha. This site emerged as an important quarrying and manufacturing center.

Although much of the Maya lowlands are indeed a relatively flat limestone platform, the Puuc Hills in the northern lowlands and the Maya Mountains in southern Belize provide significant topographic relief, as well as a variety of natural resources that were of use for the ancient Maya (Graham 1987; West 1964; Wright et al. 1959). The Puuc Hills form an upland region that was used for defensive settlements. The Maya Mountains consist of three granite batholiths that rise up to 1,000 meters above the limestone platform. They provided granite for the ubiquitous corn grinding stones (metates) of the ancient Maya. Pine forests and granite outcrops in this area are a stark reminder of the variability in the lowland landscape.

The volcanic backbone of the Americas passes through the southern Maya highlands of Guatemala, Honduras, and El Salvador. The volcanic Maya highlands provided the people with important resources, such as obsidian—the volcanic glass so popular as a sharp cutting tool in ancient times. The major outcrops of obsidian used by the ancient Maya include El Chayal near Guatemala City, Ixtepeque (about 85 kilometers to the southeast), and San Martin Jilotepeque (also known as Rio Pixcaya) west of modern Guatemala City. Obsidian from these outcrops is gray in color. The Maya also obtained obsidian from outside the Maya area, including a "bottle-glass" green obsidian from the Pachuca outcrop north of Mexico City, as well as gray obsidian from a variety of other outcrops in that area. The chemical fingerprinting of obsidian artifacts to their outcrops of origin has formed the foundations of many models of ancient Maya trade and communication.

Large, heavy blocks of volcanic basalt were imported to the Maya lowlands for corn grinding stones—certainly more durable than those made from locally available limestone.Although periodic volcanic eruptions shrouded ancient

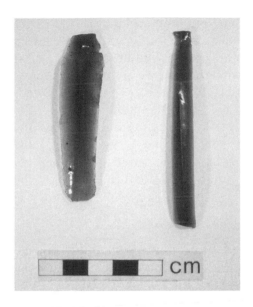

Obsidian blade fragments from Wild Cane Cay. The edges of a freshly made blade are at least twice as sharp as surgical steel. Depictions on painted pots and sculpture indicate they were used in ritual bloodletting by the ancient Maya but were also used for other purposes (Courtesy H. McKillop)

communities under volcanic material, the volcanic soils provided tremendously rich farmland once the land was again habitable. These eruptions have been beneficial to modern researchers, as they preserved ancient communities "Pompeii style," notably Ceren in El Salvador (Sheets 2002).

Lagoons formed along the coastlines, providing shelter for canoe traders and aquatic resources for fisher folk (West 1964). Rivers certainly provided important avenues of trade and transportation, both between the southern Maya highlands and the lowlands, and within the lowlands. The Motagua River was a major transportation route between the Maya highlands and the Caribbean coast of Guatemala. Originating near the ancient city of Kaminaljuyu in the outskirts of modern Guatemala City, the Motagua provided a water route for transporting obsidian from the Maya highlands, jade and other green stones from along the Motagua River, and other goods and resources to the Caribbean coast. From there, canoe traders transported goods north along the coast of Belize, inland by rivers to cities in the southern Maya lowlands, and farther north along the coast and around the Yucatan peninsula. The Pasion and Chixoy Rivers provided an alternate inland route between the southern Maya highlands and the lowlands.

The southern and northern Maya lowlands stand in sharp contrast in terms of river transportation. There are no rivers for waterborne transportation in the northern Maya lowlands. By way of contrast, Belize has many navigable rivers that provided significant avenues of communication and trade in antiquity. On the west, the Usumacinta River forms the modern boundary between Mexico's Yucatan peninsula and Chiapas and provided the ancient Maya with access between the Gulf of Mexico and the heart of the southern Maya lowlands in the Peten. Belize abounds in navigable rivers that connect the Caribbean with the interior. The Rio Hondo forms the boundary between Mexico's Yucatan peninsula and Belize, and it also provided a riverine link for the Maya between the Caribbean and the Peten region. Continuing south, the New River widens to form an inland lagoon where the city of Lamanai persisted—perhaps in part due to its access to fresh water—from the Middle Preclassic period through the Postclassic. The Belize River certainly was an important transportation avenue in antiquity as it was even into the twentieth century, extending to the Guatemalan border and into the Maya Mountains. Many of the rivers in central Belize drain from the Maya Mountains. In southern Belize, the Rio Grande, Deep River, and Moho River provided access between the Caribbean and nearby inland cities during the Classic period. The Ulua River in western Honduras surely provided a transportation route between the Caribbean and inland cities.

Climate

Rainfall and temperature in the Maya area are affected by topography, as well as external air masses (West and Augelli 1989, 43). Climatologists describe the northern Maya lowlands as a tropical wet and dry climate (West 1964; West and Augelli 1989). This pattern is characterized by a well-defined dry season of four to six months duration between January and June, with most of the deciduous trees losing their leaves in the dry season. Mean annual rainfall is 1,000 to 2,000 millimeters, except in the northwestern quarter of the Yucatan in the modern state of Campeche, where rainfall is 500 to 1,000 millimeters and less than 500 millimeters in the extreme northwestern Yucatan. Average annual temperatures are between 25° and 30° C.

Most of the southern Maya lowlands fall into the tropical monsoon climate pattern (West 1964; West and Augelli 1989). The February to May dry season can have substantial rainfall. Mean annual rainfall is 2,000 to 3,000 millimeters and is more evenly distributed throughout the year than in the northern Maya lowlands. Consequently, the rainforest of the southern Maya lowlands is described as evergreen, since few of the trees lose their leaves in the dry season (Wright et al. 1959). Average annual temperatures are between 25 and 30° C, with temperatures rising to 38°C in the dry season (West and Augelli 1989, figure 2.21). Cold fronts called "northers" periodically drop the rainy season temperature as low as 10°C for up to several days.

There is more rain along the Caribbean side of the southern Maya lowlands than in the rest of the subarea. Climatologists describe the Caribbean side as true tropical rainforest, with no distinct dry season. The Caribbean side is affected by northeast trade winds that develop in the mid-Atlantic, move southeast over warm Caribbean waters, and bring unstable hot moist air to the southern Maya lowlands (West and Augelli 1989, 43–46). Although there is generally more rainfall in the rainy season, the dry season, usually abbreviated to between February and May, can have substantial rain, so that there is no clear seasonality of rainfall. The weather is particularly unstable from July through November, with five to a dozen hurricanes, as well as thunderstorms, and tropical waves. The overall impact is more rainfall, with 3,000 to 4,000 millimeters annual rainfall (or more), compared to the rest of the southern Maya lowlands. The periodic affect of major hurricanes in the Maya lowlands, such as Iris (October 8, 2001) and Hattie (1961), is devastation of the natural and cultural landscape from high wind and torrential rain. Hurricane Iris made landfall in southern Belize at 140 mph and continued at this speed across Belize, resulting in widespread clear cutting of the rainforest. Entire villages were blown away and some 8,000 Belizeans, mainly Maya, were homeless within a couple of hours. In addition to strong winds, Hurricane Hattie was associated with heavy rain and tides, which resulted in deaths of hundreds of people in Belize City.

The southern Maya highlands have a Mesothermal highland climatic pattern (West and Augelli 1989). Annual rainfall is between 1,000 and 2,000 millimeters, with 500 to 1,000 millimeters rainfall at higher elevations in the mountains. Precipitation is seasonal, usually associated with thunderstorms. However, on the Caribbean side of the hillslopes, rainfall resembles the pattern of the southern Maya lowlands, since the hillslopes are exposed to the Caribbean trade winds that affect the southern Maya lowlands. Consequently, on the Caribbean hillslopes of the southern Maya highlands, rainfall is 2,000 to 3,000 millimeters, and there is no seasonality of rainfall. Annual temperatures average 20° to 25° C at lower elevations, 15° to 20° C at moderate elevations, and below 15°C at the highest elevations. There is little seasonal variation in temperature, less than 5°C.

Flora

The diverse vegetation of the Maya area reflects different patterns of climate and underlying geology (West 1964; Wright et al. 1959). Much of the southern Maya lowlands can be characterized as tropical rainforest. The substantial, year-round rainfall results in evergreen rainforest (West and Augelli 1989, figure 2.21; Wright et al. 1959). The rainforest consists of a dense canopy of overlapping tree crowns of trees that rise 40 to 70 meters above the ground surface. Trees include broad-leaved evergreens, such as mahogany, Ceiba (*Ceiba pendandra*, West and Augelli 1989, figure 2.2), and rosewood. A lower canopy at 25 to 50 meters above the ground surface includes chicle (*Achras zapote*), tropical cedar, rubber, sapodilla, and native palms such as cohune (*Orbignya cohune*). The ground surface below the tree canopies is relatively free of vegetation since little sunlight penetrates the canopies. The underbrush and vines are impenetrable in areas such as near clearings or at the edge of rivers, where sunlight penetrates the forest canopies. The northern area of the northern Maya lowlands is drier and has scrub forest. The northern Maya lowlands has less rainfall resulting in a low deciduous forest whose trees shed their leaves in the dry season. There is no high rainforest canopy of tall mahogany or sapodilla trees such as grow in the southern Maya lowlands. However, there are isolated trees that rise above the low forest, including Ceiba and Guanacaste (*Enterolobium* sp.). The southern Maya highlands and Maya Mountains include vegetation suited to more temperate areas. The dominant vegetation is oak and coniferous forest, with pine forests above 2,000 meters elevation. However, much of the area is cleared for settlement, farming, and plantations, and even within the southern Maya lowlands, there are diverse vegetation associations (Sanders and Michels 1977; West 1964; Wright et al. 1959). Mangrove trees dominate *because* there is little or no dry land in the offshore islands and coastlines up to 15 miles inland. Savannahs, sometimes dotted with palmettos and pine trees, occur in southern Belize and parts of Honduras but are absent in the northern Maya lowlands. Pine forests on the granite soils of the Maya Mountains and the adjacent coastal lowlands provide a dramatic contrast to the tropical rainforest vegetation dominated by mahogany, rosewood, native palms, and other tropical trees.

Fauna

A variety of animals populated the Americas, including the Maya area, during the Pleistocene. Bones of giant ground sloths, extinct elephants (mammoths and mastodons), horses, and camels are among the remnants of a host of large animals that would have coexisted with the earliest inhabitants of the Maya area at the end of the Pleistocene, around 9500 B.C. More than thirty-one genera of animals, including the horse, became extinct in the area over the following millenium, so that the assortment of wild animals available to the ancient Maya for food, transportation, or farming was greatly reduced.

A variety of different animals, however, inhabit the Maya area today and would have been available to the ancient Maya also (Olsen 1982; Schlesinger 2001). The Caribbean and Pacific waters provide marine fishes, mollusks, and other animals that are depicted on painted Maya pots and murals and whose bones and shells are found, sometimes carved into objects, in ancient garbage, offerings, and burials (Emery 2004). The Belize barrier reef system, in particular, provides a rich array of marine animals, including manatee; conch; lobster; hawksbill and green sea turtles; reef fishes such as parrotfish, triggerfish, and yellow-tail snappers; and estuarine fishes such as groupers, barracudas, permit, bonefish, and tarpon (McKillop 1985; Randall 1983). The rivers host turtles, fishes, and shellfish, notably the popular "jute" (*Pachychilus* sp.) shell, as well as shrimp, iguana, and crocodiles. Rainforest animals include the tapir, jaguar, jaguarundi, margay, white-lipped and collared peccaries, paca, and white-tailed and brocket deer, all of which were exploited in ancient times by the Maya. Deer and peccary, in particular, were favored for food by the inland Maya. Domesticated fauna included the dog, stingless bee, Muscovy duck, and perhaps the turkey.

Absent in this inventory are animals suitable as draft animals for transporting people or goods or for farming. The horse was not reintroduced until the sixteenth century (when the Spanish conquerors brought it with them), after the extinction of the giant horse at the end of the Pleistocene. The cows, sheep, and goats of the Near East; water buffalo of China; camels of Egypt; and llamas and related vicuna of Peru that provided significant transportation (and, in some cases, draft animals for farming) were not available to the ancient Maya. Hence, the Maya did not use the wheel.

MODERN ENVIRONMENTAL CHANGES

Maya archaeologists agree that the landscape and environment of the ancient Maya, and in particular of the Classic period, were different than they are today. However, there is considerable controversy about the ancient environ-

The mayans
dident care for
the rain
fores

pectives: "Women in Combat: U.S.
e Monitor; "In a New Elite Army Unit,
Make the Cut" from *The Washington Post*;
Corps Gazette; and "G.I. Janes" from *The*

some of the challenges female service

2.

Iraq and Afghanistan, over 283,000
ded and over 130 have died. According to
er 20,000 female members have or are
s of Dec. 2011.) On numerous occasions
ver Star medals. This outcome has
nd beyond in reviewing and possibly

nalysis and Statisti

Milpa farmer using a digging stick to plant corn, Belize (Courtesy Jaime Awe)

mental changes and in particular their impact on the course of ancient Maya civilization.

Popular views of the ancient Maya as conserving and protecting the rainforest simply do not fit with the evidence. Clearly, the rainforest vegetation that covers much of the southern Maya lowlands developed after A.D. 900 when the Classic Maya cities were abandoned. Before that time, much of the area would have been cleared for agriculture to feed the Maya in the densely populated cities and surrounding countryside. In particular, as the population density increased in the Late Classic period, between A.D. 600 and 900, increasingly more rainforest was cleared for farming. When well-drained uplands were occupied, swamps were drained to create fields, and hillslopes were cleared and terraced. The slash and burn or milpa farming that characterized at least a part of Classic Maya agriculture uses extensive tracts of rainforest in the cycle of clearing, use, and fallowing of fields. The abandonment of southern lowland cities at the end of the Classic period meant that many agricultural fields also were abandoned. The natural vegetation succession ultimately resulted in the modern rainforest.

The forest that shrouds ancient Maya cities and smaller settlements today more likely consisted back then of carefully planned useful trees and other plants, resembling a "garden city" (Chase and Chase 2001). Kitchen gardens around houses, and trees throughout the communities, included economically valuable trees with edible fruits, shade trees, and useful palms with fronds for thatching roofs. These trees were deliberately planted.

In some cases, the modern vegetation patterns of ancient Maya sites are an adaptation to the soil that developed on Maya ruins instead of an indication of the vegetation that existed during ancient times. For example, the modern association of ramón trees (*Brosimum alicastrum*), which are prolific producers of an edible nut, derives from the lime-rich soil from deteriorating ancient limestone buildings rather than from the ancient Maya's selection of these nuts for food. Dennis Puleston (1982) had suggested that the large population of the city of Tikal during the Classic period could have been supported, in part, by ramón nuts, which he observed were common at the site. Evidently, however, the ramón trees populated already-abandoned cities but were not likely as popular when the cities were occupied (Lambert and Arnason 1978). Ramón nuts certainly did not form a major component of the Classic Maya diet, as they are virtually absent in the assemblages of plant food remains from Classic Maya sites (McKillop 1994; McKillop 1996).

A dramatic rise in worldwide sea level at the end of the Pleistocene also raised sea level along Maya coastlines, and rising sea level continued over the course of Maya prehistory to submerge low-lying coastal areas (McKillop 2002). As a result, some ancient Maya sites were inundated with water and still lie under coastal waters or shrouded under mangroves in low-lying coastal areas. The sea level rise also changed the vegetation patterns where the land was inundated. Along the coastlines, red mangroves (*Rhizophora mangle*) thrived in the salt water. Black mangroves (*Avicennia germinans*), white mangroves (*Laguncularia racemosa*), and buttonwood (*Conocarpus erectus*) took over in seasonally inundated and salty soil. Low-lying inland areas turned to marshes or swamps. The sea level rise has removed many coastal sites from modern view, either placing them underwater or submerged in mangrove vegetation, and it also has dramatically altered the coastal landscape from the time of ancient Maya settlement (McKillop 2002). This is indeed a sobering reminder of the fate of low-lying areas worldwide, which are subject to sea level rise.

Accepting that the ancient Maya landscape and vegetation were different from today's, were there environmental changes in antiquity that impacted the course of Maya prehistory? According to Richardson Gill (2000), drought caused the Classic Maya collapse and indeed was responsible for many of the major cultural changes in Maya prehistory. Is there any foundation for Gill's hypothesis? In fact, soil scientists have found changes in pollen, sediments, and geochemistry of soils from coring sediments in lake beds. Scientists attribute these differences to climatic change, and drought in particular, between A.D. 800 and 1000—the time of the Classic Maya collapse. Hodell et al. (1995) suggest that a drought coincides with the end of the Classic period collapse and that it may have precipitated an ecological disaster and the collapse. Furthermore, soil scientists think that droughts occurred at the end of the Preclassic period, about A.D. 300, and during a time in the fifth century that Mayanists refer to as the "Classic Maya hiatus," when there was an unexplained cultural disruption.

The impact of climatic change on the Classic Maya has been minimized by Arthur Demarest (2001), who argues that these interpretations are tantamount to "environmental determinism" (an extremist view that environmental change causes major cultural change) and did not cause the Classic Maya's collapse (see also McKillop 2003). Certainly, old views of environmental determinism for the ancient Maya expressed by Betty Meggers (1954) have been set aside for more demographic, political, and warfare-related models of the collapse. Still, environmental changes and their possible impact on the ancient Maya are poorly articulated and need further research to elucidate both their nature and their role in the course of Maya prehistory, especially the Classic period collapse.

Adding to the differences in the environment between the Classic period and today, many plants and animals characteristic of the Maya area in modern times are not indigenous but were introduced by European explorers and settlers. Perhaps the most dramatic change was the replacement of native palms with the more productive coconut palm, now ubiquitous along the coastline and offshore islands in the Maya area and beyond. Sugarcane was introduced with the rise of the plantation economy of the Caribbean. Other plants, notably citrus and banana, also became plantation staples. The British introduced breadfruit, tamarind, and mangos, which are vegetation markers of the historic presence of the British in the area. The Europeans also introduced horses, cattle, sheep, chickens, and goats. Rice, not indigenous to the Americas (apart from the wild rice of North America), replaced corn as the carbohydrate staple in many areas. Asian settlers in the late twentieth century introduced water buffalo to the area. These and other changes have altered the environmental and cultural landscape of the Maya area from its ancient appearance. These changes must be considered when making analogies between prehistoric and modern Maya lifeways.

REFERENCES

Campbell, Lyle R. 1984. "The Implications of Mayan Historical Linguistics for Glyphic Research." In *Phoneticism in Mayan Hieroglyphic Writing,* edited by John Justeson and Lyle Campbell, 1–16. Institute for Mesoamerican Studies, Publication 9. Albany: State University of New York.

Chase, Arlen F., and Diane Z. Chase. 2001. "Ancient Maya Causeways and Site Organization at Caracol, Belize." *Ancient Mesoamerica* 12: 273–281.

Demarest, Arthur A. 2001. "Climatic Change and the Classic Maya Collapse: The Return of Catastrophism." *Latin American Antiquity* 12: 105–123.

Emery, Kitty, ed. 2004. *Maya Zooarchaeology.* Los Angeles: Costen Institute of Archaeology, UCLA.

Gill, Richardson. 2000. *The Great Maya Droughts: Water, Life, and Death.* Albuquerque: University of New Mexico Press.

Graham, Elizabeth. 1987. "Resource Diversity in Belize and Its Implications for Models of Lowland Trade." *American Antiquity* 54: 753–767.

Hodell, David A., Jason H. Curtis, and Mark Brenner. 1995. "Possible Role of Climate in the Collapse of Classic Maya Civilization." *Nature* 375: 391–394.

Lambert, John D. H., and Thor Arnason. 1978. "Distribution of Vegetation on Maya Ruins and Its Relation to Ancient Land-Use at Lamanai, Belize." *Turrialba* 28 (1): 33–41.

McKillop, Heather. 1985. "Exploitation of the Manatee in the Maya and Circum-Caribbean Areas." *World Archaeology* 16: 337–353.

———. 1994. "Ancient Maya Tree Cropping: A Viable Subsistence Adaptation for the Island Maya." *Ancient Mesoamerica* 5: 129–140.

———. 1996. "Prehistoric Maya Use of Native Palms." In *The Managed Mosaic: Ancient Maya Agriculture and Resource Use,* edited by Scott L. Fedick, 278–294. Salt Lake City: University of Utah Press.

———. 2002. *Salt: White Gold of the Ancient Maya.* Gainesville: University Press of Florida.

———. 2003. "Catastrophic and Other Environmental Factors in the Classic Maya Collapse." Paper presented at the annual meeting of the American Association of Geographers, New Orleans, March.

Meggers, Betty. 1954. "Environmental Limitation on the Development of Culture." *American Anthropologist* 56: 801–824.

Olsen, Stanley J. 1982. *An Osteology of Some Maya Mammals.* Papers of the Peabody Museum of Archaeology and Ethnology, vol. 73. Cambridge, MA: Harvard University.

Puleston, Dennis. 1982. "The Role of Ramón in Maya Subsistence." In *Maya Subsistence,* edited by Kent V. Flannery, 353–366. New York: Academic Press.

Randall, John E. 1983. *Caribbean Reef Fishes.* Neptune City, NJ: T. F. H.

Sanders, William T., and Joseph W. Michels, eds. 1977. *Teotihuacan and Kaminaljuyu: A Study in Prehistoric Culture Contact.* University Park: Pennsylvania State University Press.

Schlesinger, Victoria. 2001. *Animals and Plants of the Ancient Maya.* Austin: University of Texas Press.

Sheets, Payson, ed. 2002. *Before the Volcano Erupted.* Austin: University of Texas Press.

West, Robert C., ed. 1964. *Natural Environment and Early Cultures: Handbook of Middle American Indians,* vol. 1. Austin: University of Texas Press.

West, Robert C., and John P. Augelli. 1989. *Middle America: Its Land and Peoples.* 3d ed. Englewood Cliffs, NJ: Prentice Hall.

Wright, A. Charles S., D. H. Romney, R. H. Arbuckle, and V. E. Vial. 1959. *Land Use in British Honduras: Report of the British Land Use Survey Team.* Colonial Research Publication 24. London: Colonial Office.

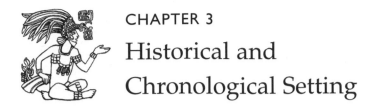

CHAPTER 3

Historical and Chronological Setting

HISTORY OF RESEARCH

The historical context of Maya archaeology lies in the discovery and excavation of stone temples and palaces in the rainforest and the study of associated carved stone monuments with hieroglyphic texts. The difficulty of working in the rainforest, the emphasis on major sites, and the dominance by a few institutions in the first part of the twentieth century led to criticism by scholars of the atheoretical and descriptive nature of Maya archaeology (Kluckhohn 1940).

Nineteenth-Century Explorers

Although there had been some enduring earlier interest in the ancient Maya ruins (Hammond 1983), it was the accounts of explorations of Maya cities in Mexico and Central America by John Lloyd Stephens (Stephens 1963; Stephens 1969) that brought the ancient Maya to the attention of the educated public in the United States and Europe in the mid-nineteenth century. The descriptions of Maya ruins were accompanied by accurate illustrations of the buildings and monuments made from camera lucida and daguerreotype by Frederick Catherwood, an artist and Stephens's traveling companion. The public's interest in lost cities in the "jungle" was sparked, and this further entrenched the already-popular characterization of the Maya as enigmatic and unique among ancient civilizations. Stephens's books were both more widely read and more accurate than other popular Maya accounts during the nineteenth century, notably the travels by Augustus and Alice Le Plongeon in the Yucatan (Desmond and Messenger 1988).

The late nineteenth and early twentieth centuries were characterized by a number of adventurers, explorers, and early archaeologists who explored, excavated, and recorded sites in the Maya area (Brunhouse 1975; Hammond 1983; Willey and Sabloff 1980). Some were independently wealthy or secured money from sponsors for their explorations, but others, such as Dr. Thomas E. F. Gann, the medical officer of health for British Honduras (Belize), visited and dug at Maya sites as a vocation.

The work was of variable quality, even destructive in some cases. There were no standards for excavating and recording. There were also no laws protecting archaeological sites or prohibiting the export of artifacts and monuments. The recovery of artifacts and monuments suitable for museum display

Underworld god on stone carving from Late Preclassic period at Izapa, Chiapas, Mexico (The Art Archive / National Anthropological Museum Mexico / Dagli Orti)

was a major goal of American and European museums at the time. In addition, there was limited institutional support of Maya research. Universities, museums, and other institutions, such as Harvard, the University of Pennsylvania, and the Carnegie Institution of Washington, would later sponsor major archaeological expeditions that had a profound impact on our modern understanding of Maya prehistory.

Still, significant and insightful research was directed to the study of Mayan hieroglyphs, to the calendar and counting system, and to indigenous literature. Ernst Förstemann (1906) was able to decipher much of the calendar and count-

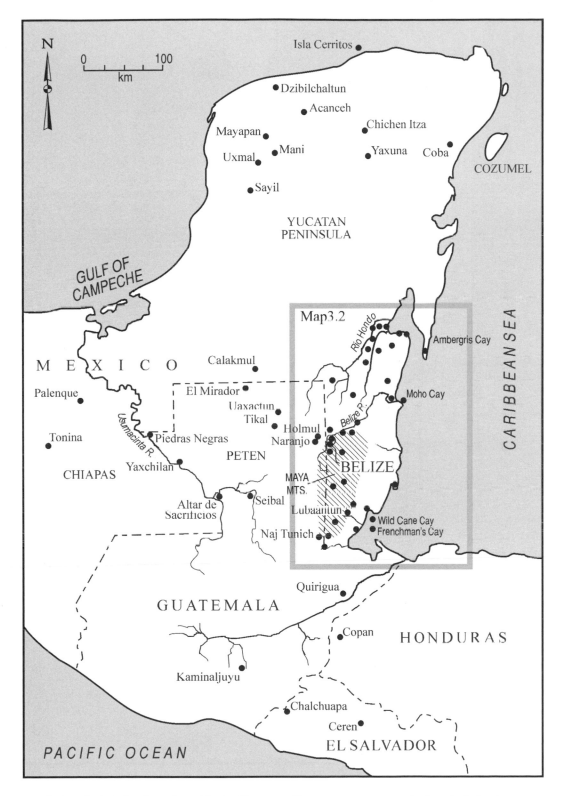

Archaeological sites investigated in the Maya area (See map on next page for insert of sites in Belize)

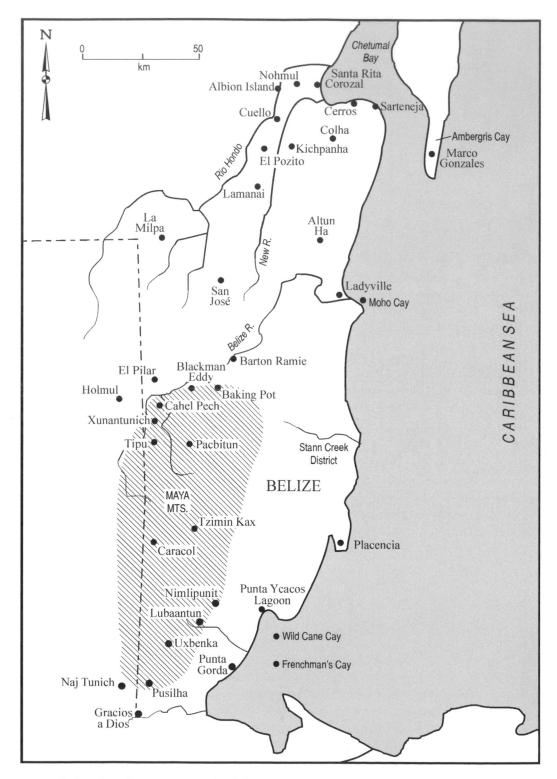

Archaeological sites investigated in Belize

Reconstructed temple at Lubaantun (Courtesy B. Somers)

ing system from study of the Dresden Codex, an ancient Maya book with images and heiroglyphs painted on bark paper. This allowed people to read the dates on Maya monuments. Brasseur de Bourbourg discovered and interpreted Bishop de Landa's *Relación de las Cosas de Yucatan* (*Relation of the Things of the Yucatan*), as well as other documents (see Tozzer 1941 for a later translation).

Thomas Gann, sometimes with his wife Mary, explored and excavated at more sites in Belize than any modern archaeologist, leaving "Gann holes" in the center of stone mounds, but he fortunately provided some written documentation of his work. He was frequently sent by the governor of the colony of British Honduras (now Belize) to explore new sites that were reported (Gann 1925).

British adventurer Frederick Mitchell-Hedges was along with Gann on an expedition to Lubaantun in 1927—an expedition often cited in popular literature due to the alleged discovery of a crystal skull. Mitchell-Hedges's adopted Canadian daughter Sammy found the crystal skull, which was likely brought from Europe and placed for her discovery. There are no other similar crystal skulls in the Maya area. Moreover, Mitchell-Hedges is more commonly known for his adventure stories than for scientific accuracy, such as his 1931 book *Land of Wonder and Fear,* principally a story of adventure and fishing in the Caribbean.

By way of contrast, some earlier researchers, notably Teobert Maler, Alfred P. Maudslay, Herbert Spinden, and Robert Merwin, stand out for their important contributions to the nascent field of Maya archaeology. Independently wealthy from an inheritance, Maler had a long and important career exploring, documenting, photographing, and excavating Maya sites beginning with a visit to the site of Palenque in 1877. His photographic record of sites made a lasting contribution to Maya archaeology, in part because many sites were subsequently destroyed by looters or weather. His last expeditions to the Peten and Usumacinta from 1895 to 1905 were sponsored by Harvard's Peabody Museum and subsequently published in the Peabody Museum Memoirs (Maler 1901; Maler 1908). Much of Maler's writing and photographs are unpublished in the Ibero-American Institute of Berlin and the Ethnographic Museum in Hamburg, with some published by Gerdt Kutscher (1971). As a young archaeologist, Sylvanus Morley met Maler in Merida, as did the wealthy battery manufacturer Theodore A. Willard, who pursued Maya archaeology as an avocation. Willard's (1926) *City of the Sacred Well* describes Maler's hostile attitude toward Edward Thompson, the American Consul in Yucatan, who dredged the sacred cenote at Chichen Itza (Coggins 1992; Coggins and Shane 1984).

Another independently wealthy early researcher, Alfred Maudslay, carefully photographed and described many important Maya sites between 1881 and 1894 (Graham 2002). His wife Anne accompanied him on his last expedition in 1894 to 1895. Maudslay supported his own work, except for one season at Copan sponsored by the Peabody Museum. His major publication, *Archaeology*, is published in the multivolume *Biologia Centrali-Americana* (Maudslay 1961).

Herbert J. Spinden, born in 1879 in what would become South Dakota, rose from modest beginnings (a sod house with windows made from oiled paper) to graduate from Harvard. His 1906 Ph.D. dissertation, "A Study of Maya Art," was published in 1913 and remains a pivotal work in Maya art and architecture. Spinden continued his studies of Maya art while a curator at the American Museum of Natural History (AMNH) and at the Brooklyn Museum. His lasting contributions were in interpretation of Maya art and in understanding the Maya calendar. Although it was subsequently overtaken in popularity by the GMT (Goodman-Martinez-Thompson) correlation, one of Spinden's important contributions was his correlation of the Maya and western (Gregorian) calendars. By Spinden's calculations, the zero date of the Maya calendar was 3373 B.C. The GMT correlation placed the dates about 260 years later. Spinden's artistic analysis of Maya art enabled him to date Maya art by its place in his evolutionary framework of stylistic change. He was an ardent opponent of diffusion—the view that cultural changes are due to borrowing or influence from other cultures rather than independent origins or development. Diffusion was popular at the time as an explanation for cultural change, and he argued instead for multiple origins of various cultural innovations. Among his many hypotheses, his idea that the Classic Maya collapse was due to a yellow fever epidemic is not considered as a possible explanation. His interpretation was not out of line with Ernest Hooton's (1940) view, after studying skeletons recovered from the Cenote of Sacrifice, that osteoporosis caused the collapse.

Robert Merwin's Holmul study was the first stratigraphic ceramic sequence (the description of the different decorative styles of pottery charactersitc of each time excavated from different soil layers) in the Maya area (Merwin and Vaillant 1932). Even though it was published before Robert E. Smith's (1955) Uaxactun ceramic chronology, the latter was circulated to researchers first in unpublished form so the Uaxactun report became the standard reference. In fact, the names of the ceramic complexes (the styles of pottery characterstic of each time) are still used by Maya researchers and became the foundation for other ceramic studies in the Maya area. Furthermore, the Uaxactun ceramic chronology was correlated with dated monuments and extended farther back in time to the Middle Preclassic period, providing a known age to the ceramic complexes.

The Twentieth-Century Institutional Period

The 1920s through 1970 featured several institutions sponsoring major excavations at Maya cities that both set the tradition of fieldwork and created an intellectual lineage of Maya archaeologists that continues to the present (Black 1990; Coe 1990; Hammond 1983). As Hammond (1983) appropriately mentions, much of the work was focused on the description of art and architecture at major Maya sites. For the researchers working during this time frame, the emphasis on careful excavation and description—for which later generations of Mayanists are very grateful—took precedence over theory. Many of their techniques of trenching and horizontal peeling of the construction layers of structures, correlating architectural and ceramic sequences, and using survey transects are still in vogue in Maya archaeology (Black 1990).

There were relatively few Maya archaeologists at the time, but they were a close-knit group. They communicated with one another with some regularity, in some cases facilitated by physical proximity of their institutions, as with the Carnegie and Peabody Museums at Harvard. Most had a Harvard education or affiliation and most were upper middle class men. The Carnegie Institution of Washington carried out long term projects at Uaxactun, Chichen Itza, Kaminaljuyu, and Mayapan between 1924 and the closing of the institution in 1958. The University of Pennsylvania Museum carried out long-term fieldwork at Piedras Negras and subsequently at Tikal. Tulane's Middle American Research Institute sponsored fieldwork in the northern Yucatan, specifically at Dzibilchaltun. The British Museum made expeditions to southern Belize in the late 1920s, but these did not result in lasting fieldwork by that institution in the Maya area. Finally, although less well known, the Royal Ontario Museum carried on fieldwork in Belize, first with William Bullard's work in northern Belize and at Baking Pot, and subsequently with David M. Pendergast's cave studies, his 1964 to 1970 Altun Ha project (Pendergast 1979), and his 1974 to 1980 Lamanai project, which began in 1974 and is ongoing (Pendergast 1981).

The institutional period began after the First World War, with a program of excavation and restoration at Chichen Itza by the Carnegie Institution and directed by Sylvanus Morley between 1924 and 1933, and one at Uaxactun from 1926 through 1938 under the direction of Oliver Ricketson and others (Black

1990; Hammond 1983). The Carnegie archaeologists were researchers who didn't have the teaching responsibilities of their Harvard or University of Pennsylvania contemporaries. However, Carnegie's impact on the discipline has been much greater, as archaeologists who worked on Carnegie projects subsequently formed the bulk of university faculty influencing the next generations of Maya archaeologists. Unlike other institutions in United States and Europe at the time, Carnegie's policy was not to accept artifacts but to support the restoration of ancient Maya buildings, which certainly facilitated research at Chichen Itza and promoted Mexican nationalism.

Sylvanus Morley, educated in archaeology at Harvard under the encouragement of Alfred M. Tozzer and Charles Bowditch, was hired by the Carnegie Institution of Washington in 1914 to excavate at Chichen Itza, but this work was delayed by the onset of war. Morley persuaded the Carnegie president to allow Morley to work on deciphering Mayan hieroglyphs and building a chronology, which he did for some ten years, traveling to Maya sites (see Morley 1920). In 1916, Morley discovered Uaxactun and named it "Eight Stone," after the eight-cycle date from a carved monument that placed the site as the earliest known at that time. He secured permits to excavate at Uaxactun and Chichen Itza, spending half of each year from 1924 to 1940 at Chichen Itza directing the work of Earl Morris, Karl Ruppert, Harry E. D. Pollock, J. Eric S. Thompson, Gustav Strömsvik, and Tatiana Proskouriakoff. The focus of the fieldwork at Chichen Itza on restoration for tourism meant that relatively little is understood today about the site's chronology or cultural history.

By way of contrast, the focus on research at Uaxactun has had long-lasting impacts on modern knowledge of Maya ceramic and architectural chronology, architecture, and city planning. Frans Blom recognized the astronomical significance of a cluster of Maya buildings named Group E at Uaxactun: From the steps of a temple, as one stood looking at a line of three low buildings, the sun rose over the building on the left on the longest day of the year, over the building on the right on the shortest day, and on the central building on the two equinoxes. The same arrangement of buildings has been found at other sites, and they are referred to as "E groups" after the first recognized one at Uaxactun. Ricketson discovered and excavated the first Late Preclassic temple to have stucco masks and central staircases. This temple—known as E-VII-sub—became known as a hallmark for the precocious beginnings of ancient Maya civilization (Ricketson and Ricketson 1937).

A. Ledyard Smith (1950) initiated a style of major architectural excavation at Uaxactun that he later continued through Harvard at Altar de Sacrificios (A. L. Smith 1972) and Seibal (A. L. Smith 1982), setting standards that were widely used by others who worked with him. For example, he trenched plaza floors to search for the exteriors of buildings, followed the exterior to establish the building's size and shape, located and excavated along the central staircase of a building, and then excavated the building's exterior, either partially by trenches or completely by horizontal exposure (Black 1990). Smith coordinated dated monuments with architectural trenching. His brother, Robert E. Smith, also a Harvard graduate, excavated test pits adjacent to structures and coordinated architectural and stratigraphic ceramic profiles. His landmark publication of the Uaxactun ceramics (R. E. Smith 1955) remains the starting point for Maya ceramicists and was followed by the important Mayapan ceramic report (A. L. Smith 1971). The first settlement density study also was carried out at Uaxactun under the direction of Oliver Ricketson (Ricketson and Ricketson 1937). He established a cruciform pattern of four transects radiating in cardinal directions from the site center, recorded house mounds (mounded remains of houses), and established the first field-based population studies. Ricketson assigned Robert Wauchope to excavate a 5 percent sample of the mounds, resulting in his seminal report on Maya house mounds (Wauchope 1934) along with his important work on modern Maya houses (Wauchope 1938).

Major changes at the Carnegie Institution took place when Alfred V. Kidder, also educated at Harvard, was appointed Director of Historical Research in the late 1920s. Maya archaeology now became of limited interest to the institution. Kidder instead initiated a program of interdisciplinary research, enlisting specialists in Maya culture, flora, fauna, and disease, among others. Ultimately, the eclectic nature of Maya research was resoundingly criticized by the eminent Clyde Kluckhohn (1940) in his often-cited article "The Conceptual Structure in Middle American Studies." Carnegie closed down its Chichen Itza project in 1940. With the dissolution of the Division of Historical Research at Carnegie in 1958, the records and remaining archaeologists—Proskouriakoff, Shook, and Pollock—moved next door to the Peabody Museum. In addition to the earlier research at Uaxactun, the published accounts of the last Carnegie projects at Kaminaljuyu (Kidder, Jennings, and Shook 1946) and Mayapan (Pollock et al. 1962; R. E. Smith 1971) remain landmark studies for Maya research.

Sir J. Eric S. Thompson, one of the leading Maya archaeologists of the twentieth century, began his fieldwork at Chichen Itza in 1926 under Earl Morris at the Temple of the Warriors. Thompson joined the second British Museum expedition to southern British Honduras in 1927 under the direction of Thomas Joyce, working at Lubaantun and exploring Pusilha at the end of the field season. Based on his 1929 fieldwork at Tzimin Kax in the Maya Mountains, Thompson defined the plazuela—a house mound cluster that subsequent researchers have confirmed as the basic unit of ancient Maya households and community patterning. In contrast to the large Maya ruins typically explored and excavated, Thompson (1939) elected to work at the smaller community of San Jose, which remains a lasting contribution to excavation reporting and artifact description. Thompson joined the Carnegie Institution in 1936, and they continued the sponsorship of his San Jose fieldwork. Thompson subsequently carried out fieldwork at Xunantunich (then called Benque Viejo) in 1938, and from 1954 to 1957 he worked on the Carnegie's Mayapan project.

The University of Pennsylvania Museum initiated fieldwork at Piedras Negras in 1929 under the direction of J. Alden Mason. The subsequent Tikal project, under the direction of Edwin Shook (from 1955 to 1961), Robert Dyson (in 1962), and William Coe (from 1963 to 1969), was arguably the largest archaeological project in the Americas (Harrison 1999). The training of many Maya archaeologists (with 113 professional participants on the project, according to

Harrison 1999) and the creation of graduate theses, dissertations, and preliminary Tikal reports preceded the publication of final reports on ceramics (Culbert 1993) and Central Acropolis architecture (Harrison 1999), for example.
The results of the Tikal project have had a lasting influence on interpretations
of Maya cities as urban centers instead of empty ceremonial centers. The results have also had a lasting impact on controversies about population densities and agricultural techniques, economy, and politics, as discussed by project
staff such as William Haviland, Peter Harrison, Dennis Puleston, Payson
Sheets, and T. Patrick Culbert (Sabloff 2003). The government of Guatemala
initiated long-term excavations at Tikal in 1969 under the direction of Juan Pedro Laporte, who focused on the "Lost World Complex" and, with the collaboration of the Spanish government, on the tunneling and restoration of a particular temple known as Temple V. Only two temples were excavated by the
University of Pennsylvania Museum project mentioned above, leaving three
major temples uninvestigated, despite the many years of research at the site.

Harvard's tradition of Maya fieldwork had begun with work at Copan,
Quirigua, Palenque, and Chichen Itza. The first major expedition sponsored by
Harvard was carried out at Copan under the direction of Marshall Saville,
John Owens, and George Gordon (see Gordon 1896 and Gordon 1902). This
and subsequent fieldwork by Alfred Tozzer, Raymond Merwin, and Sylvanus
Morley was published in the new Peabody Museum memoirs and provided
detailed and accurate descriptions of sites, architecture, and pottery (Merwin
and Vaillant 1932). With the appointment of Gordon R. Willey to the prestigious Bowditch Chair of Mexican and Central American Archaeology and Ethnology at Harvard, that institution's focus on Maya archaeology was ce-
mented. Also, the location of the Carnegie Institute of Washington building
beside the Peabody Museum at Harvard resulted in a long association of Maya
archaeologists from the two institutions. Willey's major projects include his
seminal work on settlement patterns at Barton Ramie and the Belize River
(Willey et al. 1965) between 1953 and 1956, followed by major excavation projects at Altar de Sacrificios (1958–1963) and at Seibal (1964–1968).

The Middle American Research Institute was formed at Tulane University in
1925 under the direction of William Gates, with Frans Blom (who worked at
Uaxactun in 1924) as his assistant. Gates had persuaded Samuel Zemurray, a
New Orleans area resident and the owner of the United Fruit Company, to buy
Gates's collections of Mesoamerican books and manuscripts, donate them to
Tulane, and also donate funds to start the institute. Blom, accompanied by his
assistant and former fellow Harvard student, Oliver La Farge, traveled
through Central America recording sites and their experiences and observations of the natural and cultural environment (Blom and La Farge 1926–1927).
In 1926, Frans Blom was appointed acting director, and later head, of the Department of Middle American Research, where he remained until 1941 (Brunhouse 1975, 205). As well as editing the quarterly publication *Maya Research,* he
initiated the Middle American Research series, Middle American Pamphlets
series, and *Middle American Papers.* He also directed the affairs of the museum,
did fundraising, and sent off research expeditions. Notable exhibitions in-

cluded a display featuring molds of the Nunnery from Uxmal at the 1933 Century of Progress Exposition in Chicago. He also organized a large display of Maya artifacts at the Greater Texas and Pan American Exposition in Dallas in 1937, among others. E. Wyllys Andrews IV initiated major field projects in the northern Yucatan, notably at Dzibilchaltun.

During the institutional period, there was an enduring interest and some important insights into decipherment of the Mayan hieroglyphs, calendar, and counting system. Although J. Eric S. Thompson wrote much, others made more important discoveries. As mentioned previously, Proskouriakoff (1960) made the pivotal discovery that the hieroglyphs recorded historical information about the Maya rulers, based on her work on Piedras Negras monuments. Heinrich Berlin (1958) interpreted "emblem glyphs" as the names of Maya cities. Yuri Knorozov's discovery that Mayan hieroglyphs were phonetic was a turning point in the decipherment of the glyphs. Volumes 2 and 3 of the *Handbook of Middle American Indians* includes summaries of various aspects of Maya prehistory by the leading Mayanists of the time and remains to this day an important research tool (Willey 1965).

Late Twentieth-Century Sites

Whereas most Maya projects of the early part of the twentieth century were long-term field projects funded by major institutions, smaller thematic field projects supported by government or private funding agencies dominated the late twentieth century. Graduate students pursued Maya archaeology at an increasing number of universities, often under the tutelage of researchers who had gained their training and field experiences from the Harvard, Carnegie, or University of Pennsylvania projects. Competition for limited grants for fieldwork contributed to the shorter duration and problem-oriented nature of many projects during this period. With civil war in El Salvador, political unrest in Guatemala, and a 15 percent surcharge levied on grants by the Mexican government, many Maya archaeologists initiated fieldwork in Belize.

By the late 1970s, there were several archaeological projects in Belize, notably at Lubaantun, Cuello, Colha, Cerros, Santa Rita Corozal, and Moho Cay, as well as regional surveys. There were also a number of projects focusing on ancient Maya agriculture and other topics, such as MacNeish's search for pre-Maya sites. David Pendergast continued his long-term fieldwork in Belize, with research at Lamanai from 1974 to 1980 and beyond in collaboration with Elizabeth Graham. Norman Hammond (1975) carried out Ph.D. research in southern Belize from 1970 to 1972, with excavations at Lubaantun and regional survey in what he termed the realm of Lubaantun. Subsequently, Hammond initiated a regional survey project in northern Belize, resulting in the discovery of the stone tool workshop site of Colha, the earliest ceramics at Cuello, and a host of other sites of various ages.

Hammond's fieldwork at Cuello, in the backyard of the Cuello Brothers rum distillery near Orange Walk, became a landmark in defining the earliest evidence of pottery, villages, and agriculture in the Maya lowlands (Hammond 1991). Instead of excavating the rather modest stone temple at the site, Ham-

Classic building at Santa Rita Corozal, northern Belize, after excavation and reconstruction by Diane and Arlen Chase (Courtesy H. McKillop)

mond opened a large 10-by-10-meter excavation area, searching for early evidence of settlement. The earliest pottery was quite well made, suggesting that there were antecedents, but they remain unknown. Shallow bowls and dishes with out-flaring walls, jars, and other vessels were often painted red (Kosakowsky 1987). The early houses at Cuello were evidently pole and thatch and oval in shape, as indicated by oval house floors with circular "post molds," where the rotted house posts had left stains in the ground (Hammond 1991). Corn, or *Zea mays,* was identified at Cuello, as were a variety of other domesticated and wild plant foods (Miksicek 1991). Hammond's very important research at Cuello sparked other archaeologists to "dig deeper" and search for early pottery, to use advanced recovery techniques (such as flotation with fine sieves) to recover plant food remains, and to go beyond the Classic period temple mound focus. The early Cuello pottery, referred to as the "Swasey" ceramic complex, was subsequently found at many sites in northern Belize, notably Santa Rita Corozal, Colha, and Lamanai.

Colha was the focus of intensive excavations directed by Tom Hester and Harry Shafer through the University of Texas at Austin and through Texas A & M University (Shafer and Hester 1983). The site consists of low house mounds where people quarried outcrops of high-quality chert and made a variety of stone tools for local use and for distribution to other Maya communities in northern Belize and beyond. The tools were produced in "cottage workshops" associated with the residences, in contrast to the physically separated independent workshops, for example the ones where salt was made at Punta Ycacos (McKillop 2002a). Hester and Shafer's excavations resulted in enormous quantities of debitage (flakes left over from making stone tools) and production errors from the process of manufacturing stone tools. The thematic focus on stone tool production marked a major shift from research in the institutional period, which focused on temples and other major architecture at big cities. The Colha project prompted other Maya archaeologists to look at the production and trade of chert and other stone tools, such as those made of obsidian, to help reconstruct the ancient Maya economy. Although the site of El Pozito was arguably the first known chert tool workshop in Belize, there remains little published about it (Neivens and Libbey 1976). Certainly the Colha research indicated that not all production and distribution was centered at lowland cities, so that even modest-looking communities like Colha played an important role in the economy.

Following his Ph.D. dissertation research on Cozumel, David Freidel carried out major excavations and surveys at Cerros in northern Belize. Excavations revealed that Cerros was a precocious Late Preclassic community that grew to importance due to communication and trade among various emerging elites in the Maya lowlands at that time (Freidel 1979; Robertson and Freidel 1986). Cerros was virtually abandoned at the end of the Late Preclassic period, so that the architecture in the central precinct is Late Preclassic, without the encumbrance of the Classic buildings so common at other sites. Freidel credits the coastal location of Cerros on Chetumal Bay, near the New River and Hondo River, with facilitating the community leaders' participation in what he termed an interregional interaction sphere of the Late Preclassic. Freidel and his team of students from Southern Methodist University, along with Maya workers from Belize, uncovered large stucco masks of the Maya sun god on either side of a central staircase at a rather modest temple (Freidel 1979). Traces of red and blue paint on the masks served as reminders that they were once vividly painted for public viewing. Visitors to the site, however (which is managed by the Belize government's Institute of Archaeology), will not see the masks, which Freidel protected from weathering and looting by building stone walls in front with sand between the masks and the walls. A dedication offering of small jade heads showed both the participation of the Cerros elite in long-distance trade (in this case from the Motagua Valley jade sources) as well as the Maya's sophisticated craftsmanship in working jade (Garber 1989). Freidel's work tied Cerros with a temple at Uaxactun called E-VII-sub, as well as with other masked temples elsewhere in the Maya lowlands such as at Dzibilchaltun in the northern Yucatan and Lamanai in northern Belize. The central precinct at Cerros, where several temples and other early monumental buildings were located, was bounded by the sea and, on the inland side, by a canal. Residences of the common folk, as well as a complex system of agricultural canals located beyond the main canal, showed an early interest by the Cerros Maya in intensifying their agriculture activities (Freidel and Scarborough 1982; Scarborough 1991).

The site of Santa Rita, now virtually engulfed by modern Corozal Town in northern Belize, was of some interest to archaeologists since Thomas Gann's discovery of painted murals there. Diane Chase's Ph.D. dissertation fieldwork at Santa Rita focused on comparing documentary evidence from sixteenth-century visits by the Spaniards with the Late Postclassic site. In addition to horizontal exposure of domestic architecture and other Late Postclassic remains, she identified a long prehistoric record of settlement. She restored an Early Classic building, now maintained by the Belize government's Institute of Archaeology, as a public site open to visitors. Santa Rita owed much of its success as a community to its coastal location and participation in waterborne trade and communication (Chase and Chase 1988).

Moho Cay was a Late Classic trading port located at the mouth of the Belize River that provided access to communities in the interior of Belize and the adjacent Peten of Guatemala—the heartland of Late Classic civilization (Healy, McKillop, and Walsh 1984; McKillop 1980; McKillop 2004). The author's 1979 excavations at Moho Cay were the fieldwork for my M.A. thesis and also initiated what has become a long tradition of Trent University archaeological field schools in Belize. Excavations revealed Late Classic settlement on the northern point of the island, with a large area having eroded into a shallow offshore zone beyond. The larger remaining part of the island was mangrove swamp and devoid of ancient settlement. Unfortunately the site was destroyed in 1980 in the process of dredging a harbor for a marina on the island, despite the protests of the government Archaeological Commissioner, the late Harriot Topsey. A subsequent attempt to develop another island trading port, Wild Cane Cay, as a tourism lodge was thwarted by environmental protection laws that, since the 1990s, have required archaeological impact assessments prior to development, even on private land, at the discretion of the Belize government (McKillop 1998).

Regional surveys established settlement patterns and laid the foundations for subsequent specialized and thematic projects. Hammond's British Museum (Cambridge) Corozal Project in northern Belize discovered both Cuello and Colha. Elizabeth Graham (1989, 1994) carried out Ph.D. dissertation fieldwork in the Stann Creek district, with a comprehensive survey and test excavation program in an area that was virtually unknown. Ernestine Green carried out a survey in northern Belize. Raymond V. Sidrys's (1983) survey in northern Belize included important work at the coastal site of Sarteneja. Richard "Scotty" MacNeish's 1982–1983 survey of the coastline and rivers of Belize was an ambitious search for early, preceramic settlement. The major success of his project was in prompting other researchers to look for pre-Maya settlement, as his claims for a chronological sequence from Paleoindian through Archaic have been disputed. In contrast, a Paleoindian stone spear point was fortuitously found at Ladyville by Tom Hester's survey team, led by Thomas Kelly (1993). Hester and Harry Shafer have discovered Archaic occupation stratigraphically below the Maya occupation layers at Colha.

Some projects during the later twentieth century were thematically focused on ancient Maya agriculture, often including botanists, agronomists, and other specialists on the projects. With the growing estimates of large populations at

Maya cities, particularly by the Late Classic period, archaeologists began to wonder what kind of farming systems would have provided enough food— clearly it would have to be more than is provided by the area's modern system of slash and burn agriculture. The untimely death of Dennis Puleston, who was struck by lightning at Chichen Itza, abruptly ended his project with Alfred Siemens investigating drained fields on Albion Island in northern Belize. However, Mary Pohl (1990) continued the work, finding evidence of intensification of farming in the form of drained fields by precocious Late Preclassic power-mongering elite. By way of contrast, Peter Harrison and Billie Lee Turner (Harrison and Turner 1978; Turner and Harrison 1983) related drained fields in Pulltrouser Swamp to the Late Classic population increase. Similarly, Paul F. Healy (Healy et al. 1983) found that terraced hillslopes in the Maya Mountains and around Caracol in western Belize were a response to a Late Classic period population increase. Controversy over whether or not the swamps were drained for agriculture still continues. Peter Harrison has found evidence of agriculture in the Bajo de Morocoy (a swamp that was drained for farming) in Quintana Roo, Mexico. Whether the Bajo de Santa Fe near Tikal was drained for farming remains unclear because of limited research in the swamp.

Anthony P. Andrews and this author have maintained long-term field projects on the coasts of Mexico and Belize, respectively, and other researchers have carried out coastal work before moving inland. The Harvard-Arizona project on Cozumel directed by Jeremy Sabloff and William Rathje (1975) from 1972 to 1973 established a theoretical interest in the nature of ancient Maya trading ports and economy. Andrews has carried out extensive survey and excavation on the east, north, and west coasts of the Yucatan, and also excavated Isla Cerritos, which he identified as the trading port for Chichen Itza (Andrews et al. 1989). My own excavations at Wild Cane Cay from 1982 to 1992, at Frenchman's Cay in 1994 and 1997, and elsewhere in the Port Honduras Marine Reserve and Paynes Creek National Park in southern Belize, including the salt works in Punta Ycacos Lagoon (McKillop 2002a; McKillop 2005) identified a complex economy from Late Preclassic through colonial days (McKillop 1989; McKillop 1996). Important coastal fieldwork also has been carried out by Diane and Arlen Chase at Santa Rita (1986, 1988), Matthew Boxt at Sarteneja, Tom Guderjan and James Garber on northern Ambergris Cay, Elizabeth Graham and David Pendergast at Marco Gonzalez on southern Ambergris Cay, J. Jefferson MacKinnon in the Placencia area, among others (McKillop and Healy 1989).

Since 1980, there has been a glut of Maya archaeologists carrying out fieldwork, particularly in northern Belize. Competition for National Science Foundation (NSF), Earthwatch, and other grants has meant that some projects were funded primarily through university archaeological field schools. In 1985, Diane and Arlen Chase initiated a multiyear project investigating major architecture and community settlement patterning at Caracol, a city of some interest since, according to some scholars, its leaders defeated Tikal in a war (Chase and Chase 1987a; Chase and Chase 1987b; Chase and Chase 1994). Norman Hammond directed a project at Nohmul, a city that is interesting in part due to its city planning, with two urban areas connected by a causeway (Hammond

El Castillo at Chichen Itza (Courtesy Ed Kurjack)

et al. 1985). Hammond subsequently began a multiyear investigation of La Milpa, collaborating with Gair Tourtellot for a settlement survey and Vernon Scarborough for investigation of water management (Hammond et al. 1998; Scarborough 1998). A number of archaeologists, notably Fred Valdez, have carried out fieldwork associated with the Programme for Belize, a nongovernmental organization charged with managing a vast tract of park in northwestern Belize. Tom Guderjan established the Maya Research Program to investigate the site of Blue Creek, following his dissertation work on Ambergris Cay.

A new interest developed in the northern Maya lowlands late in the twentieth century. Much of the research, at least initially, focused on understanding the rise of cities in the northern lowlands along with the Classic period collapse of most southern lowland cities. The last 100 years of the Late Classic period are also referred to as the Terminal Classic period (A.D. 800–900). In the northern Maya lowlands, the Terminal Classic (A.D. 800–1000) extended for a longer time. Sabloff and Tourtellot initiated research at Sayil, a Terminal Classic city in the Yucatan, where they were able to investigate the Terminal Classic unencumbered by later archaeological surface remains. David Freidel carried out excavations at Yaxuna, and George Bey and Bill Ringle directed a project at Ek Balam. Fieldwork at Chichen Itza by Charles Lincoln, Rafael "Rach" Cobos, Terance Winemiller, and others has begun to provide basic chronological and settlement information about this poorly understood city. The focus of the

Main Ball Court at Copan (Courtesy B. Somers)

Mexican government in the Yucatan continues to emphasize restoration and consolidation for tourism at a number of sites.

Maya archaeologists periodically attempt to better understand the Classic Maya collapse, with warfare being an important factor under consideration in the late twentieth century among Mayanists. Arthur Demarest's (1997) project in Petexbatun intertwined hieroglyphic data on the rise and fall of various Maya kings and queens with field investigations at Dos Pilas and other communities, along with regional studies of settlement, soils, human biology, and caves.

Despite early research by David Pendergast in a number of karstic caves in western Belize, it was not until the late twentieth century that Maya caves became a prime focus of fieldwork. Naj Tunich (Stone 1995), caves in the Petexbatun (Brady et al. 1997), and caves in western Belize investigated by Jaime Awe of Trent University indicate ancient Maya use of caves for a variety of rituals.

An interest in excavating large Maya sites continues. Following excavations at Pusilha, Nim li punit, and Uxbenka in southern Belize, Richard Leventhal directed major excavation and restoration with Wendy Ashmore at Xunantunich in western Belize. A number of teams have investigated Copan, sometimes simultaneously, notably E. Wyllys Andrews V of Tulane University, William T. Sanders and David Webster of Penn State University, Robert Sharer of the University of Pennsylvania, and Bill Fash of Harvard. Nearby Quirigua was the scene of major excavations by Robert Sharer and Wendy Ashmore.

Robert Sharer investigated Chalchuapa, El Salvador, with important dissertation research on obsidian done by Payson Sheets. There was also the Chases' research at Caracol, Norman Hammond and Gair Tourtellot's project at La Milpa, and Stephen Houston and David Webster's research at Piedras Negras.

Innumerable other projects have been carried out that provide significant insights into our understanding of the ancient Maya. Projects in the upper Belize River valley include Paul Healy's excavations at Pacbitun, Jaime Awe's investigations of Middle Preclassic pottery and architecture at Cahal Pech, Joseph Ball and Jennifer Taschek's excavation and restoration at Cahal Pech and other sites, James Garber's excavations at Blackman Eddy, Trent University research at Baking Pot and nearby Berdan site, Anabel Ford's excavations at El Pilar and her establishment of a binational park to preserve the natural and cultural resources, and Anabel Ford's Belize River survey. Elsewhere in Belize, Anne Pyburn investigated Chau Hiix with community input, research continued at Cerros and Colha, and Leslie Shaw investigated Kichpanha. One of the longer-running field programs has been Payson Sheets's investigations of Ceren, initially discovered and excavated in the 1970s, with excavations continuing after the conclusion of the civil war in El Salvador. Perhaps no other Maya site has provided so much in situ preserved evidence of everyday life than El Ceren, which was covered suddenly, and therefore well preserved, by a volcanic eruption (Sheets 2002).

In the Yucatan, Susan Kepecs carried out regional survey and excavations in the Chinkinel area, Michael Smyth at Chac, Smyth and Chris Dore carried out research at Sayil, and Richard Folan and colleagues excavated Coba. Bruce Dahlin and Traci Ardren carried out mapping and excavation at the enigmatic inland city of Chunchucmil, a large site without major monumental architecture whose importance they attribute to control of the salt trade and other mercantile affairs. In Campeche, Mexico, Joyce Marcus, Richard Folan, and others have investigated the major Classic city of Calakmul for a number of years. Richard Hansen excavated Nakbe and El Mirador. Antonia Foias at Motul de San Jose, Francisco Estrada-Belli at Holmul, and Juan Pedro Laporte and colleagues at Tikal and Uaxactun figure among other important ongoing field projects.

Archaeological research in the Maya area has occasionally turned to the time of the arrival of the Spanish explorers; the Franciscan and Dominican missionaries; and the British pirates, log workers, and settlers (Alexander 1998; Andrews 1991; Graham, Pendergast, and Jones 1989; Hanson 1995; McKillop 2002b; McKillop and Roberts 2003; Pendergast 1985). In some cases, as at Lamanai, this focus resulted from the continuity of settlement from prehistoric into historical times (Pendergast 1985). At Lamanai, David Pendergast investigated two Franciscan churches and an associated historic cemetery, as well as a nineteenth-century sugar mill, in the course of his excavations of the ancient Maya city. Elizabeth Graham investigated the Franciscan mission at Tipu, following its discovery in archives by Grant Jones and David Pendergast (Graham 1991; Graham, Pendergast, and Jones 1989). The Tipu church was excavated by Robert Kautz and Grant Jones in 1981, and the burials in and around the church were excavated under the direction of Mark Cohen (Jacobi 2000). Rani Alexander (1998) investigated colonial communities in the Yucatan (McKillop 2002b).

CHRONOLOGY OF THE MAYA

The Maya Calendar

The Maya Long Count was the system used to record the dates of events of historical or ritual significance associated with the Classic Maya kings and queens. Using a horizontal bar to designate the number five, a stylized shell to designate zero, and a dot for the number one, numbers were written based on multiples of twenty. A date recorded the number of days, months, and years from the beginning of the Maya calendar (3114 B.C. in our calendar) to the described event. The dates are associated with hieroglyphic texts that describe events such as birth, accession to the throne, and the conquering of city-states. Unfortunately, calendrical histories are recorded for relatively few of the Classic cities. Smaller communities lack written histories. Moreover, the written records pertain only to Maya royalty and are limited in duration—from the earliest date of A.D. 292 on a stela from Tikal to the last date of A.D. 909 on a stone carving from Tonina. No books have been preserved from the Classic period. The written history of the Maya is known principally from hieroglyphic texts and associated calendar dates on stelae and other carved monuments, as well as on a few painted pots. Although the Postclassic Maya continued to use the same calendar, they used an abbreviated "Maya Short Count" (comparable to our modern practice of shortening 1870 to '70), so that their calendar is difficult to interpret. Relatively few Postclassic sites, with the major exception of Chichen Itza, used the calendar to record dates.

Type-Variety System of Pottery Classification

Most Maya sites are dated by studying the changing decoration on pottery found in burials and caches associated with successive building renovations (and sometimes from the foundations themselves) and from different depths in household midden deposits. Using the principle of stylistic change over time commonly accepted by archaeologists, temporal frameworks have been established from excavated pottery from individual sites. The chronologies can generally only narrow time frames down to within several hundred years, based on the length of time a particular style of pottery was used. In addition, the dates are relative and need to be anchored in time, either by reference to Maya calendar dates (as at Uaxactun, for example) or by radiocarbon dating that provides an absolute date in years, albeit with a broad range. Most Maya ceramicists use a number of major pottery reports for comparison of their pottery in order to tie their sequences with other Maya sites and to investigate the amount of interaction among various communities. Perhaps the most widely referenced ceramic chronologies are for Uaxactun (R. Smith 1955), Seibal (Sabloff 1975), Mayapan (R. Smith 1971), Altar de Sacrificios (Adams 1971), Barton Ramie and the Belize Valley (Gifford 1976), Holmul (Merwin and Vaillant 1932), and Cuello (Kosakowsky 1987).

Radiocarbon Dating

Radiocarbon dating has been used to establish chronologies for relatively few Maya sites. This may be due to the misconception that carbon is poorly preserved at Maya sites; to the facility, interest, or past successes of dating sites by study of the pottery; or to the cost of radiocarbon dating, which at this writing in 2003 is about $260 in U.S. currency for a sample that will provide a single date. Radiocarbon dating has, however, been used as a means to tie in ceramic chronologies at a number of Maya sites.

Radiocarbon dating was used extensively at Cuello and Wild Cane Cay to provide site chronologies. Radiocarbon dating at Cuello allowed Andrews and Hammond (1990) to assign the earliest pottery at the site to about 1000 B.C., the beginning of the Middle Preclassic period. At Wild Cane Cay, a series of radiocarbon dates of wood charcoal from midden deposits in different excavations provided Classic through Postclassic dates for the site, corresponding to the ceramic chronologies. The problem with using radiocarbon dating for establishing chronologies is that it only provides a range of dates, and it also depends on the archaeologist selecting organic material for dating from a reliable, undisturbed context. The radiocarbon date of A.D. 770 ± 60 indicates that there is a 68 percent probability that the true age of the sample is somewhere within a 120-year span of A.D. 770. In order to increase the probability to 95 percent, one has to accept a 240-year time span.

Obsidian hydration is another dating method that has been successfully used in California and elsewhere, where, as with the ancient Maya, obsidian was widely used for making sharp cutting implements. The technique is based on the assumption that a freshly exposed (e.g., when the artifact is made) surface of obsidian begins to hydrate, and it hydrates at a known rate. The rate of hydration is constant but varies by the particular outcrop of obsidian, which can be identified by chemical analysis of trace elements. The amount of hydration is measured by visually examining the "hydration band," visible microscopically where the artifact was broken. An obsidian hydration sequence was established for Copan using 2,150 obsidian dates (Freter 1992), and sequences are available for several other Maya sites, including Wild Cane Cay (McKillop 1987). This technique holds promise for future research, as obsidian was so widely used and traded by the Maya throughout their prehistory.

Literary or Folkloric Evidence for Interpretation of Maya Civilization

In addition to the dated events and rituals recorded by the Classic Maya pertaining to Maya royalty, four texts of some antiquity written in the Mayan language have survived. In addition, a number of Europeans recorded folk tales told to them by the colonial period Maya. The Spanish explorers, missionaries, and other travelers and explorers also recorded their observations about Maya people. Modern ethnographic studies by cultural anthropologists and cultural geographers also provide analogies for interpreting the ancient Maya way of life.

Mayan Hieroglyphs

The Mayan hieroglyphs record events and rituals about Classic Maya royalty that were considered important by the kings and queens who wielded political power in the Maya lowlands. The hieroglyphs record the names, birth dates, marriages, accessions to the throne, battles won and cities conquered, and

Stelae and altars in front of temple at Tikal (Courtesy H. McKillop)

deaths of individuals in this rather limited group of Classic Maya royalty. Martin and Grube (2000, 22–23) list the known rulers of eleven Classic Maya cities, namely Tikal, Dos Pilas, Naranjo, Caracol, Calakmul, Yaxchilan, Piedras Negras, Palenque, Tonina, Copan, and Quirigua. Emblem glyphs, the symbols used to refer to the names of cities, are known for many more cities. There are estimates by some researchers that there were some eighty city-states in the Maya lowlands during the Classic period. Presumably, each city-state had an emblem glyph and a written dynastic history of its rulers, but for some, such as Altun Ha, there are no carved and dated stone stelae. Hieroglyphs and dates record the political histories of many important cities. A summary of the types of political, military, and ritual events can be seen in the following summary of the dynastic record of Tikal (see also Sabloff 2003).

Tikal had a dynastic record of at least 33 rulers over some 800 years (Martin and Grube 2000). The Tikal rulers traced their lineage to Yax Ehb' Xook, who probably lived and ruled during the Late Preclassic period. The first known depiction of a Tikal ruler is on Stela 29 dated A.D. 292, but the area with his name is missing. Various hieroglyphic texts reveal the arrival at Tikal of Siyaj K'ak' from the central Mexican state of Teotihuacan, who placed Yax Nuun Ayiin as the new ruler, replacing the Tikal lineage. The hieroglyphic texts clarify that there was a political takeover of Tikal, whereas the various interpretations of Teotihuacan-style artifacts and buildings had been interpreted as trade, marriage ties, or military takeovers. Siyaj Chan K'awiil II ascended to the throne in A.D. 411, claimed lineal descent to the Tikal lineage, and reduced Teotihuacan power at Tikal.

The city's twenty-first ruler, Wak Chan K'awiil, developed close ties with Caracol and sponsored the inauguration of one of Caracol's rulers Yajaw Te' K'inich II in A.D. 553, but he was defeated in A.D. 562, either by Calakmul (Martin and Grube 2000, 39) or by Caracol. Tikal's power dissipated, and the city sank into a dark age. This "hiatus" lasted from A.D. 562–692 and was marked by a lack of carved, dated monuments at Tikal. During this time B'alaj Chan K'awiil from Tikal established a royal lineage at Dos Pilas to the south, initiating a rivalry between the two cities. The new Dos Pilas ruler seems to have been supported in this and other efforts by Calakmul. Subsequently, another Tikal ruler, Nuun Ujol Chaak, was evidently rousted from Tikal by Calakmul and went to visit King Pacal of Palenque in A.D. 659. Nuun Ujol Chaak regained power at Tikal, ousted his rival from Dos Pilas in A.D. 672, was defeated again by Calakmul in A.D. 677, and was defeated by Dos Pilas in A.D. 679 in concert with Calakmul.

Nuun's son, Jasaw Chan K'awiil I, defeated Calakmul in A.D. 695 and returned Tikal to its former glory and power. This battle is recorded on one of the lintels over the doorway of the room at the top of Tikal's Temple 1 (one of the temples named and excavated by the University of Pennsylvania project). The actual event recorded on the lintel was a ritual in which the king let blood and participated in a vision quest, in which the successful battle is replayed. The other lintel shows the king in Teotihuacan military attire, replete with Teotihuacan spear thrower and darts, in a revitalization of the power associated with the former Tikal ally. The façade of a nearby structure shows the king holding a captive, who may be the defeated Calakmul king, by a rope during a ceremony before the captive was sacrificed. Jasaw Chan K'awiil I sponsored the construction of several important buildings that were noted in the hieroglyphs at katun (twenty-year) intervals during his reign. His burial in newly renovated Temple 1 in an elaborate tomb with many finely made and exotic grave offerings—including delicately incised images of figures in canoes on human bones—marks the king as an important and powerful leader. Still, hieroglyphs record skirmishes with neighboring cities, especially Naranjo and Dos Pilas.

Jasaw's son, Yik'in Chan K'awiil, led Tikal to even greater political and military prominence and directed the construction and renovation of many major buildings at the city, including the renovation of Temple 1 for his father's burial. His victory over nearby El Perú in A.D. 743 is recorded in a carved wooden lintel in Temple 4, the tallest temple at Tikal. There is also a depiction of the Naranjo king, bound prostrate on Stela 5 at Tikal. Although a series of rulers followed after Yik'in, Tikal's power began to diminish in the wake of endemic warfare in the southern lowlands, with the last dynastic reference to a Tikal king being that of Jasaw Chan K'awiil II in A.D. 869, after which Tikal was virtually abandoned.

CREATION MYTH

The ancient Maya creation myth was evidently passed down through generations and was discovered and translated by Brasseur de Bourbourg in 1861 as the *Popol Vuh* (see Tedlock 1985 for a modern translation). The same creation story is pictorially depicted on Classic Maya painted pots (Coe 1978; Reents-Budet 1994). An animated story of the *Popol Vuh* is available on video (Amlin 1989). In addition to discovering and translating the *Popol Vuh,* Brasseur de Bourbourg transcribed a series of Maya plays from the town of Rabinal, Guatemala (see Houston, Mazariegos, and Stuart 2001).

The *Popol Vuh* recounts the story of the creation of humans, their arrival in the world, and their relations with the gods of the underworld and heaven. In particular, the story underscores the importance of corn and the ball game for the ancient Maya: The myth recounts that after several unsuccessful attempts at creating humans from clay, which dissolved in the rain, and wood, which burned, humans were created from corn. The *Popol Vuh* introduces two young men called the Hero Twins and describes their travels to the Maya underworld, where they meet underworld gods. The adventures of the Hero Twins, as well as their participation in the ball game, become the foundation for the creation of the world and the relations between gods and humans. The imagery also is recorded in Classic Maya painted pots.

ETHNOHISTORIC ACCOUNTS

The ethnohistoric record of written accounts by European explorers, missionaries, pirates, and other travelers provides a rich description of the Maya during the sixteenth and later centuries. Perhaps the most cited and useful ethnohistoric account is Bishop de Landa's *Relación de las Cosas de Yucatan* (*Relation of the Things of the Yucatan*), translated by Alfred Tozzer (1941). As Bishop of Yucatan, de Landa had presided over a horrible auto-da-fé at the town of Mani in 1562 at which quantities of Maya books were burned. Recalled to Spain by the Spanish Inquisition, who felt he had overextended his zest for converting the Maya, de Landa wrote the *Relación* as a defense of his position. His careful and thorough description of the way of life of the Maya became an often-cited documentary source for modern researchers.

A variety of European explorers also described their encounters with the Maya. Certainly among the most commonly mentioned is Columbus's alleged encounter with a large Maya trading canoe off the north coast of Honduras near the Bay Islands, recently revealed to be local native traders from Honduras rather than Maya traders (Davidson 1991). Hernan Cortes's assistant, Bernal Diaz, reports on their travels through the Peten and near Gracios a Dios in southern Belize. Various other explorers, notably Davila, report encounters with the Maya (Chamberlain 1948). The archives in Seville, Spain—as well as others in various Central American countries, notably Belize, Guatemala, Honduras, and Mexico—house records of taxation, labor disputes, and other events that often provide useful information about the Maya's interactions with Europeans (Jones 1998). In searching original archival documents, Grant Jones, an ethnohistorian specializing in the Maya, discovered that there had been many skirmishes between the British log workers and indigenous Maya in northern Belize. His findings contradicted popular histories, perhaps presented as a historical justification of territorial expansion, that incorrectly described the Maya as having fled into the interior of the Yucatan before the

British arrived. Historical accounts for southern Belize also describe the Maya as having fled inland prior to the arrival of the British, but this also seems to be contradicted by ethnohistoric documents (McKillop 2005). Even historical accounts not pertaining to the Maya mention the presence, location, or condition of Maya archaeological sites.

Historical archaeology provides important insights on Spanish missions and colonial expansion in the Maya lowlands (Alexander 1998; Andrews 1991; Jacobi 2000; Graham Pendergast, and Jones 1989; Hanson 1995; McKillop 2002b). Archaeological excavations of Spanish churches at Tipu and Lamanai in northern Belize and at Ek Balam in the Yucatan document the religious conversion of indigenous Maya people. Interment of hundreds of Maya in the churches and churchyards at Tipu and Lamanai were in Christian fashion. Many other churches remain unexcavated (Andrews 1991). The later colonial period in Mexico also has received some attention, although much of the work at colonial sites has been on restoration for tourism purposes.

The modern Maya provide a valuable analogue for interpreting the ancient Maya. However, considerable changes have occurred among the people, particularly since the Classic period. The pole and thatch houses (Wauchope 1938); the dietary triad of corn, beans, and squash; and the modern way of life described in various ethnographies (Redfield and Villa Rojas 1962; Vogt 1970; Wilk 1991) all provide analogies for the ancient Maya. Population estimates of ancient cities are based, in part, on there being 5.6 people per modern household. However, the ancient diet seems to have been more variable and to have included more seafood than the diet of the modern Maya. There have been many changes to the Maya way of life since the Classic period that mean that comparisons between the modern and ancient Maya must be approached cautiosly: The sixteenth-century arrival of Europeans brought diseases that decimated the Maya, who were subsequently driven into marginal land. The Maya in southern Belize, for example, now live on Indian reservations, and the lack of sufficient farmland has driven many into nonnative lands. There have also been significant movements of people fleeing economic or political persecution, notably Mopan and Kekchi Maya fleeing Guatemala since the late nineteenth century into Belize, Yucatecan Maya fleeing Mexico into northern Belize after the mid-nineteenth century Caste War of the Yucatan, and modern Maya fleeing the civil war in El Salvador in the late twentieth century.

REFERENCES

Adams, Richard E. W. 1971. *The Ceramics of Altar de Sacrificios.* Papers of the Peabody Museum of Archaeology and Ethnology, vol. 63, no. 1. Cambridge, MA: Harvard University Press.

Alexander, Rani. 1998. "Community Organization in the Parroquia de Yaxcaba, Yucatan, Mexico, 1750–1847: Implications for Household Adaptation within a Changing Colonial Economy." *Ancient Mesoamerica* 9: 39–54.

Amlin, Patricia. 1989. *Popol Vuh: The Creation Myth of the Maya.* VHS video. Berkeley: Extension Center for Media and Independent Learning, University of California.

Andrews, Anthony P. 1991. "The Rural Chapels and Churches of Early Colonial Yucatan and Belize: An Archaeological Perspective." In *Columbian Consequences*, vol. 3, edited by David Hurst Thomas, 355–374. Washington, DC: Smithsonian Institution Press.

Andrews, Anthony P., Frank Asaro, Helen V. Michel, Fred H. Stross, and Pura Cervera Rivero. 1989. "The Obsidian Trade at Isla Cerritos, Yucatan, Mexico." *Journal of Field Archaeology* 16: 355–363.

Andrews, E. Wyllys, V, and Norman Hammond. 1990. "Redefinition of the Swasey Phase at Cuello, Belize." *American Antiquity* 54: 570–584.

Berlin, Heinrich. 1958. "El gifto 'emblema' en las inscripciones Mayas." *Journal de la Société des Américanistes* 47: 111–119.

Black, Stephen L. 1990. "The Carnegie Uaxactun Project and the Development of Maya Archaeology." *Ancient Mesoamerica* 1: 257–276.

Blom, Frans, and Oliver La Farge. 1926–1927. *Tribes and Temples.* Publications 1 and 2. New Orleans: Middle American Research Institute, Tulane University.

Brady, James E., Ann Scott, Allan Cobb, Irma Rodas, John Fogarty, and Monica Urquizu Sanchez. 1997. "Glimpses of the Dark Side of the Petexbatun Project: The Petexbatun Regional Cave Study." *Ancient Mesoamerica* 8 (2): 353–364.

Brunhouse, Robert L. 1975. *Pursuit of the Ancient Maya.* Albuquerque: University of New Mexico Press.

Chamberlain, Robert S. 1948. *The Conquest and Colonization of Yucatan, 1517–1550.* Washington, DC: Carnegie Institution of Washington.

Chase, Arlen F., and Diane Z. Chase. 1987a. *Glimmers of a Forgotten Realm: Maya Archaeology at Caracol, Belize.* Orlando, FL: Orlando Museum of Art and Loch Haven.

———. 1987b. *Investigations at the Classic Maya City of Caracol, Belize: 1985–1987.* Monograph 3. San Francisco: Pre-Columbian Art Research Institute

Chase, Diane Z., and Arlen F. Chase. 1986. *Offerings to the Gods: Maya Archaeology at Santa Rita Corozal.* Orlando: University of Central Florida.

———. 1988. *A Postclassic Perspective: Excavations at the Maya Site of Santa Rita Corozal, Belize.* Monograph 4. San Francisco: Pre-Columbian Art Research Institute.

———, eds. 1994. *Studies in the Archaeology of Caracol, Belize.* Monograph 7. San Francisco: Pre-Columbian Art Research Institute.

Coe, Michael D. 1978. *Lords of the Underworld: Masterpieces of Classic Maya Ceramics.* Princeton, NJ: Art Museum, Princeton University, and Princeton University Press.

———. 1990. "Next Door to Olympus: Reminiscences of a Harvard Student." *Ancient Mesoamerica* 1: 253–255.

Coggins, Clemency, ed. 1992. *Artifacts from the Cenote of Sacrifice, Chichen Itza, Yucatan.* Memoirs of the Peabody Museum of Archaeology and Ethnology, vol. 10, no. 3. Cambridge, MA: Peabody Museum, Harvard University.

Coggins, Clemency, and Orrin C. Shane III. 1984. *Cenote of Sacrifice: Maya Treasures from the Sacred Well at Chichen Itza.* Austin: University of Texas Press.

Culbert, T. Patrick. 1993. *The Ceramics of Tikal.* Philadelphia: University of Pennsylvania Museum.

Davidson, William V. 1991. "Geographical Perspectives on Spanish-Pech (Paya) Indian Relationships, Northeast Honduras, Sixteenth Century." In *Columbian Consequences*, vol. 3, edited by David Hurst Thomas, 205–226. Washington, DC: Smithsonian Institution Press.

Demarest, Arthur. 1997. "The Vanderbilt Petexbatun Regional Archaeological Project 1989–1994: Overview, History, and Major Results of a Multidisciplinary Study of the Classic Maya Collapse." *Ancient Mesoamerica* 8: 209–227.

Desmond, Lawrence, and Phyllis Messenger. 1988. *A Dream of Maya: Augustus and Alice Le Plongeon in Nineteenth-Century Yucatan.* Albuquerque: University of New Mexico Press.

Förstemann, Ernst W. 1906. *Commentary on the Maya Manuscript in the Royal Public Library of Dresden.* Papers of the Peabody Museum, vol. 4, no. 2, 49–266. Cambridge, MA: Harvard University.

Freidel, David A. 1979. "Culture Areas and Interaction Spheres: Contrasting Approaches to the Emergence of Civilization in the Maya Lowlands." *American Antiquity* 44: 36–54.

Freidel, David A., and Vernon Scarborough. 1982. "Subsistence, Trade, and Development of the Coastal Maya." In *Maya Subsistence,* edited by Kent V. Flannery, 131–155. New York: Academic Press.

Freter, AnnCorinne. 1992. "Chronological Research at Copan: Methods and Implications." *Ancient Mesoamerica* 3: 117–133.

Gann, Thomas H. F. 1925. *Mystery Cities: Exploration and Adventure in Lubaantun.* London: Duckworth.

Garber, James F. 1989. *Archaeology at Cerros, Belize, Central America,* vol. 2: *The Artifacts.* Dallas: Southern Methodist University Press.

Gifford, James C. 1976. *Prehistoric Pottery Analysis and the Ceramics of Barton Ramie in the Belize Valley.* Papers of the Peabody Museum of Archaeology and Ethnology, vol. 18. Cambridge, MA: Harvard University Press.

Gordon, George Byron. 1896. *Prehistoric Ruins of Copan, Honduras.* Memoirs of the Peabody Museum of Archaeology and Ethnology, vol. 1, no. 1. Cambridge, MA: Peabody Museum, Harvard University.

———. 1902. *The Hieroglyphic Stairway: Ruins of Copan.* Memoirs of the Peabody Museum of Archeaology and Ethnology, vol. 1, no. 6. Cambridge, MA: Harvard University.

Graham, Elizabeth. 1989. "Brief Synthesis of Coastal Site Data from Colson Point, Placencia, and Marco Gonzalez, Belize." In *Coastal Maya Trade,* edited by Heather McKillop and Paul F. Healy, 135–154. Occasional Papers in Anthropology 8. Peterborough, Ontario: Trent University.

———. 1991. "Archaeological Insights into Colonial Period Maya Life at Tipu, Belize," In *Columbian Consequences,* vol. 3, edited by David Hurst Thomas, 319–335. Washington, DC: Smithsonian Institution Press.

———. 1994. *The Highlands of the Lowlands: Environment and Archaeology in the Stann Creek District, Belize, Central America.* Monographs in World Archaeology 19. Madison, WI: Prehistory Press.

Graham, Elizabeth A., David M. Pendergast, and Grant D. Jones. 1989. "On the Fringes of Conquest: Maya-Spanish Contact in Colonial Belize." *Science* 246: 1254–1259.

Graham, Ian. 2002. *Alfred Maudslay and the Maya.* Norman: University of Oklahoma Press.

Hammond, Norman. 1975. *Lubaantun: A Classic Maya Realm.* Peabody Museum of Archaeology and Ethnology Monograph, vol. 2. Cambridge, MA: Harvard University.

———. 1983. "Lords of the Jungle: A Prosopography of Maya Archaeology." In *Civilization in the Ancient Americas,* edited by Richard M. Leventhal and Alan L. Kolata, 3–32. Albuquerque: University of New Mexico Press.

———, ed. 1991. *Cuello.* New York: Cambridge University Press.

Hammond, Norman, Amanda Clarke, M. Horton, M. Hodges, Logan McNatt, Laura Kosakowsky, and K. Anne Pyburn. 1985. "Excavation and Survey at Nohmul, Belize, 1983." *Journal of Field Archaeology* 12: 177–200.

Hammond, Norman, Gair Tourtellot, Sara Donaghey, and Amanda Clarke. 1998. "No Slow Dusk: Maya Urban Development and Decline in La Milpa, Belize." *Antiquity* 278: 831–837.

Hanson, Craig A. 1995. "The Hispanic Horizon in Yucatan: A Model of Franciscan Missionization." *Ancient Mesoamerica* 6: 15–28.

Harrison, Peter D. 1999. *The Lords of Tikal.* New York: Thames & Hudson.

Harrison, Peter D., and B. L. Turner, eds. 1978. *Pre-Hispanic Maya Agriculture.* Albuquerque: University of New Mexico Press.

Healy, Paul F., John D. H. Lambert, J. T. Arnason, and Richard J. Hebda. 1983. "Caracol, Belize: Evidence of Ancient Maya Agricultural Terraces." *Journal of Field Archaeology* 10: 397–410.

Healy, Paul F., Heather I. McKillop, and Bernetta Walsh. 1984. "Analysis of Obsidian from Moho Cay, Belize: New Evidence on Classic Maya Trade Routes." *Science* 225: 414–417.

Hooten, Earnest A. 1940. "Skeletons from the Cenotes of Sacrifice at Chichen Itza." In *The Maya and Their Neighbors,* edited by Clarence L. Hay, Ralph L. Linton, Samuel K. Lothrop, Harry L. Shapiro, and George C. Vaillant, 272–280. New York: D. Appleton-Century.

Houston, Stephen, Oswaldo Chinchilla Mazariegos, and David Stuart, eds. 2001. *The Decipherment of Ancient Maya Writing.* Norman: University of Oklahoma Press.

Jacobi, Keith. 2000. *Last Rites for the Tipu Maya: Genetic Structuring in a Colonial Cemetery.* Tuscaloosa: University of Alabama Press.

Jones, Grant D. 1998. *The Conquest of the Last Maya Kingdom.* Stanford: Stanford University Press.

Kelly, Thomas C. 1993. "Preceramic Projectile-Point Typology in Belize." *Ancient Mesoamerica* 4: 205–227.

Kidder, Alfred V., Jessie D. Jennings, and Edwin M. Shook. 1946. *Excavations at Kaminaljuyu, Guatemala.* Publication 561. Washington, DC: Carnegie Institution of Washington.

Kluckhohn, Clyde. 1940. "The Conceptual Structure in Middle American Studies." In *The Maya and Their Neighbors,* edited by Clarence L. Hay, Ralph L. Linton, Samuel K. Lothrop, Harry L. Shapiro, and George C. Vaillant, 41–51. New York: D. Appleton-Century

Kosakowsky, Laura J. 1987. *Preclassic Maya Pottery at Cuello, Belize.* Anthropological Papers of the University of Arizona 47. Tucson: University of Arizona Press.

Kutscher, Gerdt, ed. 1971. *Teobert Maler: Bauten der Maya.* Berlin.

Maler, Teobert. 1901. *Researches in the Central Portion of the Usumatsintla Valley.* Memoirs of the Peabody Museum of Archaeology and Ethnology, vol. 2, no. 2. Cambridge, MA: Harvard University.

———. 1908. *Explorations of the Upper Usumatsintla and Adjacent Region: Altar de Sacrificios, Seibal, Itsimte-Sacluk, Cankuen.* Memoirs of the Peabody Museum of Archaeology and Ethnology, vol. 4, no. 1. Cambridge, MA: Harvard University.

Martin, Simon, and Nicholai Grube. 2000. *Chronicle of the Maya Kings and Queens: Deciphering the Dynasties of the Ancient Maya.* New York: Thames & Hudson.

Maudslay, Alfred P. [1889–1902] 1961. *Archaeology.* Vols. 55–59 of Biologica Centrali-Americana. 59 vols., edited by Frederic DuCane Goodman and Osbert Salvin. London: R. H. Porter and Dulau.

McKillop, Heather. 1980. "Moho Cay, Belize: Preliminary Investigations of Trade, Settlement, and Marine Resource Exploitation." Master's thesis, Department of Anthropology, Trent University, Peterborough; University Microfilms, Ann Arbor, MI.

———. 1987. "Wild Cane Cay: An Insular Classic Period to Postclassic Period Maya Trading Station." Unpublished Ph.D. dissertation, Department of Anthropology, University of California, Santa Barbara; University Microfilms, Ann Arbor, MI.

———. 1989. "Coastal Maya Trade: Obsidian Densities from Wild Cane Cay, Belize." In *Prehistoric Maya Economies of Belize,* edited by Patricia McAnany and Barry Isaac, 17–56. Research in Economic Anthropology, Supplement 4. Greenwich, CT: JAI Press.

———. 1996. "Ancient Maya Trading Ports and the Integration of Long-Distance and Regional Economies: Wild Cane Cay in South-Coastal Belize." *Ancient Mesoamerica* 7: 49–62.

———. 1998. *Archaeological Survey of Wild Cane Cay, Port Honduras, Toledo, Belize: Archaeological Impact Assessment.* Report on file, Institute of Archaeology, National Institute of Culure and History, Belmopan, Belize, Central America.

———. 2002a. *Salt: White Gold of the Ancient Maya.* Gainesville: University Press of Florida.

———. 2002b. "Central America." *Encyclopedia of Historical Archaeology,* edited by Charles Orser, 355–358. London: Routledge.

———. 2003. "Catastrophic and Other Environmental Factors in the Classic Maya Collapse." Paper presented at the annual meeting of the American Association of Geographers, New Orleans, March.

———. 2004. "The Ancient Maya Trading Port on Moho Cay, Belize." In *The Ancient Maya of the Belize Valley: Half a Century of Archaeological Research,* edited by James F. Garber. Gainesville: University Press of Florida.

———. 2005. *In Search of Maya Sea Traders.* College Station: University of Texas Press.

McKillop, Heather, and Paul F. Healy, eds. 1989. *Coastal Maya Trade.* Occasional Papers in Anthropology 8. Peterborough, Ontario: Trent University.

McKillop, Heather, and Erika Roberts. 2003. *Nineteenth-Century Settlement of the Port Honduras Coast, Southern Belize.* Unpublished manuscript.

Merwin, Raymond E., and George C. Vaillant. 1932. *The Ruins of Holmul, Guatemala.* Memoirs of the Peabody Museum of Archaeology and Ethnology, vol. 3, no. 2. Cambridge, MA: Harvard University.

Miksicek, Charles H. 1991. "The Ecology and Economy of Cuello." In *Cuello: An Early Maya Community in Belize,* edited by Norman Hammond, 70–97. New York: Cambridge University Press.

Mitchell-Hedges, Frederick. 1931. *Land of Wonder and Fear.* New York: Century.

Morley, Sylvanus G. 1920. *The Inscriptions of Copan.* Washington, DC: Carnegie Institution of Washington.

Neivens, Mary, and David Libbey. 1976. "An Obsidian Workshop at El Pozito, Northern Belize." In *Maya Lithic Studies: Papers from the 1976 Belize Field Symposium,* edited by Thomas R. Hester and Norman Hammond, 137–149. Special Report No. 4. San Antonio: Center for Archaeological Research, University of Texas.

Pendergast, David M. 1979. *Excavations at Altun Ha,* vol. 1. Toronto: Royal Ontario Museum.

———. 1981. "Lamanai, Belize: Summary of Excavation Results 1974–1980." *Journal of Field Archaeology* 8: 29–53.

———. 1985. "Stability through Change: Lamanai, Belize, from the Ninth to the Seventeenth Century." In *Late Lowland Maya Civilization,* edited by Jeremy Sabloff and E. Wyllys Andrews V, 223–249. Albuquerque: University of New Mexico Press.

Pohl, Mary D., ed. 1990. *Ancient Maya Wetland Agriculture: Excavations on Albion Island, Northern Belize.* Boulder, CO: Westview.

Pollock, Harry E. D., Ralph L. Roys, Tatiana Proskouriakoff, and A. Ledyard Smith. 1962. *Mayapan, Yucatan, Mexico.* Carnegie Institution of Washington Publication 619. Washington, DC: Carnegie Institution of Washington.

Proskouriakoff, Tatiana. 1960. "Historical Implications of a Pattern of Dates at Piedras Negras, Guatemala." *American Antiquity* 25: 454–475.

Redfield, Robert, and Alfonso Villa Rojas. 1962. *Chan Kom: A Maya Village.* Chicago: University of Chicago Press.

Reents-Budet, Dorie. 1994. *Painting the Maya Universe.* Durham, NC: Duke University Press.

Ricketson, Oliver G., Jr., and Edith B. Ricketson. 1937. *Uaxactun, Guatemala, Group E: 1926–1937.* Carnegie Institution of Washington Publication 477. Washington, DC: Carnegie Institution of Washington.

Robertson, Robin A., and David A. Freidel, eds. 1986. *Archaeology at Cerros, Belize, Central America,* vol. 1: *An Interim Report.* Dallas: Southern Methodist University Press.

Sabloff, Jeremy A. 1975. *Excavations at Seibal, Guatemala, Department of the Peten, Guatemala: The Ceramics.* Memoirs of the Peabody Museum of Archaeology and Ethnology, vol. 13, no. 2. Cambridge, MA: Harvard University.

———, ed. 2003 *Tikal: Dynasties, Foreigners, and Attairs of State.* Santa Fe, NM: School of American Research Press.

Sabloff, Jeremy A., and William L. Rathje, eds. 1975. *A Study of Changing Pre-Columbian Commercial Systems: The 1972–73 Seasons at Cozumel, Mexico.* Monographs of the Peabody Museum of Archaeology and Ethnology, vol. 3. Cambridge, MA: Harvard University.

Scarborough, Vernon L. 1991. *Archaeology at Cerros, Belize, Central America,* vol. 3: *The Settlement System in a Late Preclassic Maya Community.* Dallas: Southern Methodist University Press.

———. 1998. "Ecology and Ritual: Water Management and the Maya." *Latin American Antiquity* 9: 135–159.

Shafer, Harry J., and Thomas R. Hester. 1983. "Ancient Maya Chert Workshops in Northern Belize, Central America." *American Antiquity* 48: 519–543.

Sheets, Payson, ed. 2002 *Before the Volcano Erupted: The Ancient Ceren Village in Central America.* Austin: University of Texas Press.

Sidrys, Raymond V. 1983. *Archaeological Excavations in Northern Belize, Central America.* Monograph XVII. Los Angeles: Institute of Archaeology, University of California.

Smith, A. Ledyard. 1950. *Uaxactun, Guatemala: Excavations of 1931–1937.* Carnegie Institution of Washington Publication 588. Washington, DC: Carnegie Institution of Washington.

———. 1972. *Excavations at Altar de Sacrificios: Architecture, Settlement, Burials, and Caches.* Papers of the Peabody Museum of Archaeology and Ethnology, vol. 62, no. 2. Cambridge, MA: Harvard University.

———. 1982. *Major Architecture and Caches: Excavations at Seibal, Department of Peten, Guatemala.* Papers of the Peabody Museum of Archaeology and Ethnology, vol. 15, no. 1. Cambridge, MA: Harvard University.

Smith, Robert E. 1955. *Ceramic Sequence at Uaxactun, Guatemala.* 2 vols. Publication 20. New Orleans: Middle American Research Institute, Tulane University.

———. 1971. *The Pottery of Mayapan.* 2 vols. Papers of the Peabody Museum of Archaeology and Ethnology, vol. 66. Cambridge, MA: Harvard University.

Spinden, Herbert J. 1913. *A Study of Maya Art.* Memoirs of the Peabody Museum of Archaeology and Ethnology, vol. 6. Cambridge, MA: Harvard University.

Stephens, John Lloyd. [1843] 1963. *Incidents of Travel in Yucatan.* 2 vols. New York: Dover.
———. [1841] 1969. *Incidents of Travel in Central America, Chiapas, and Yucatan.* New York: Dover.
Stone, Andrea. 1995. *Images from the Underworld: Naj Tunich and the Tradition of Maya Cave Painting.* Austin: University of Texas Press.
Tedlock, Dennis, trans. 1985. *Popol Vuh: The Definitive Edition of the Mayan Book of the Dawn of Life and the Glories of Gods and Kings.* New York: Simon and Schuster.
Thompson, J. Eric S. 1939. *Excavations at San Jose, British Honduras.* Carnegie Institution of Washington Publication 506. Washington, DC: Carnegie Institution of Washington.
Tozzer, Alfred M., trans. 1941. *Relación de las Cosas de Yucatan.* Papers of the Peabody Museum of Archaeology and Ethnology, vol. 18. Cambridge, MA: Harvard University.
Turner, B. L., and Peter D. Harrison, eds. 1983. *Pulltrouser Swamp: Ancient Maya Habitat, Agriculture, and Settlement in Northern Belize.* Austin: University of Texas Press.
Vogt, Evon Z. 1970. *The Zinacantecos of Mexico: A Modern Maya Way of Life.* New York: Holt, Rinehart, and Winston.
Wauchope, Robert. 1934. *House Mounds of Uaxactun, Guatemala.* Carnegie Institution of Washington Publication 436, Contributions to American Archaeology 7. Washington, DC: Carnegie Institution of Washington.
———. 1938. *Modern Maya Houses.* Carnegie Institution of Washington Publication 502. Washington, DC: Carnegie Institution of Washington.
Wilk, Richard R. 1991. *Household Ecology: Economic Change and Domestic Life among the Kekchi Maya in Belize.* Tucson: University of Arizona Press.
Willard, Theodore A. 1926. *City of the Sacred Well.* New York: Century.
Willey, Gordon R., ed. 1965. *Handbook of Middle American Indians.* Vols. 2 and 3. Austin: University of Texas Press.
Willey, Gordon R., William R. Bullard, John B. Glass, and James C. Gifford. 1965. *Prehistoric Maya Settlement Patterns in the Belize Valley.* Papers of the Peabody Museum of Archaeology and Ethnology, vol. 54. Cambridge, MA: Harvard University.
Willey, Gordon R., and Jeremy A. Sabloff. 1980. *A History of American Archaeology,* 2d ed. New York: Thames & Hudson.

CHAPTER 4

Origins, Growth, and Decline of the Maya Civilization

Beneath the temples and other stone buildings of the Classic Maya lie the clues to the modest origins and development of this rainforest civilization. A handful of stone tools provide the only evidence that people occupied what would later become the Maya area as early as 9500 B.C. There they left stone spear points characteristic of the Paleoindians who hunted large animals at the end of the Pleistocene, the most recent ice age. Following the extinction of the ice age animals, Archaic people hunted the remaining animals, which were smaller, and gathered wild plant foods. They followed the seasonal abundance of various wild plant and animal foods in what archaeologists term a seasonal round. Domesticated plant and animal foods played an increasing part of their diet over time, however.

Whether or not the Paleoindians and the Archaic occupants of the Maya area were ancestors of the ancient Maya is undetermined. The earliest ethnically Maya people are identified by the introduction of pottery vessels in their society. This occurred about 1800 B.C. along the Pacific coast of Guatemala and Chiapas, Mexico, but not until about 1000 B.C. in the Maya lowlands of Guatemala, Mexico, and Belize. The Middle (1000–300 B.C.) and Late (300 B.C.–A.D. 300) Preclassic periods mark the rise of social and political complexity, culminating in the Classic period civilization.

The Classic period is defined as the time between approximately A.D. 300 and 900 when Maya kings and queens had stone monuments erected with historical information and dates in the Maya long count. During this time, the civilization reached its peak in population, in size and complexity of architecture, and in the arts. Monumental pieces of architecture built during the Late Classic (A.D. 600–900) height of the civilization in the rainforests of Guatemala, Belize, and Mexico still stand for public viewing today, covering much of the Early Classic period (A.D. 300–600) construction. Smaller temporal divisions within the Early and Late Classic periods are often described by their constituent ceramic complexes—the array of pottery styles characteristic of a particular time. The ceramic complexes from Uaxactun are commonly used throughout the southern Maya lowlands: The Early Classic period includes Tzakol 1 and Tzakol 2, whereas the Late Classic period includes Tepeu 1, 2, and 3, with Tepeu 3 also known as Terminal Classic.

After endemic warfare and the collapse of the Classic civilization, the seats of power moved to the northern Maya lowlands. There were various Postclassic period city-states in the northern lowlands, dominated by Chichen Itza in the Early Postclassic (A.D. 900–1200) and Mayapan and others in the Late Post-classic (A.D. 1200–1519). When the Spaniards arrived in the sixteenth century, they encountered Maya people living in cities and smaller communities, but the culture had changed dramatically since the time of the Classic period civilization. The Europeans brought disease and superior weaponry, both of which helped them to decimate the Maya. This colonial period after the Europeans' arrival was marked by Maya rebellions, Spaniards' attempts to convert the Maya to Christianity, and, eventually, large-scale farming using the Maya as laborers. Today, many of the modern Maya are unaware of their rich ancient history.

PRE-MAYA PEOPLE: THE PALEOINDIANS

The lush tropical rainforest as well as millennia of ancient stone buildings now cover much of the Maya area, obscuring the earliest evidence of human occupation. However, clues have been discovered both in the highlands and in the lowlands that the first people there belonged to the group known elsewhere in the Americas as the Paleoindians. They evidently traveled from Asia during the Pleistocene, when the two continents were joined by a land bridge called Beringea. This land bridge formed when the advancing glaciers trapped much of the Earth's water, and sea level was lowered as much as 30 meters. Beringea formed a bridge between Siberia and Alaska that was up to 1,000 kilometers wide several times during the late Pleistocene, coinciding with periodic advances of the glaciers across Europe, Asia, and North America. When the continents were joined, large ice age herbivores, called megafauna—including mammoth and mastodon—as well as giant horses, armadillos, camels, bears, and other large animals, wandered across Beringea into the open grasslands of the Americas. People followed these game animals and both populated North, Central, and South America.

Genetic studies of mitochondrial DNA (mtDNA) reveal that most Native Amerindians can be traced to one of four founding maternal lineages, A to D. Mitochondrial DNA studies of modern Yucatecan Maya and ancient human skeletal remains from Xcaret on the east coast of the Yucatan indicate that these areas' high frequency of lineage group A corresponds to similar results from elsewhere in Mesoamerica and North America (Gonzalez-Oliver et al. 2001). By way of contrast, groups C and D are more common farther south in the Americas.

The Paleoindians had reached the southern tip of South America at Tierra del Fuego within 1,000 years of arriving in Alaska. Archaeologist Paul S. Martin (1973) developed a compelling explanation for the rapid settlement of the Americas by the Paleoindians and for the close similarity of their stone tools throughout the Americas. Martin suggested that, given a lack of competitors in the open grasslands along with a high birth rate characteristic of human habitation of a new territory, an initial group of 100 people who moved south 10 kilometers per year would have doubled their population every 20 years. Following this model, researchers have determined that humans settled the

Americas within 1,000 years (Fagan 1987 provides a popular account of the scientific data).

Evidence that the Paleoindians lived in the Maya area is based on the discovery of a handful of diagnostic stone points made of obsidian and chert. These fluted points are long and narrow blades with a characteristic flute or channel coming from the base on each side, where the point would have been hafted onto a spear. An obsidian fluted point was recovered in the southern Maya highlands near Guatemala City at Los Tapiales and another on the ground surface near Huehuetenango. But were the Maya lowlands unoccupied until pottery-making people arrived there? The absence of evidence for Paleoindian or Archaic sites in the Maya lowlands led Richard "Scotty" Mac-Neish to search for such evidence. Unfortunately, his 1980–1984 Belize Archaic Archaeological Reconnaissance Project did not yield a single Paleoindian point or any solid evidence of other pre-Maya use of the lowlands. However, Mac-Neish's project did prompt other researchers to focus attention on pre-Maya use of the Maya lowlands. As sometimes happens with the serendipity of discovery, at the same time MacNeish was searching for pre-Maya settlement, other researchers found a chert Paleoindian point at Ladyville, near the Belize International Airport. This discovery marks the first evidence of Paleoindian use of the Maya lowlands, and it was followed by the discovery of later-period Archaic stone points elsewhere in northern Belize (Kelly 1993, figure 5a).

What can we say about the way of life of the Paleoindians in what would later become the Maya area? Based on the known distribution of ice age megafauna in Central America and on comparison to Paleoindians elsewhere in the Americas, the few fluted points suggest a similar lifestyle throughout the Americas. Reports of bones from extinct megafauna found in Loltun Cave in the Yucatan, for example, as well as a giant sloth bone found near San Ignacio, Belize, and now in the Belize government's Institute of Archaeology provide clues about Pleistocene animals in the region that may have been available to Paleoindians. Although the popular view of Paleoindians is of great hunters of ice age megafauna, the Paleoindian diet certainly also included a variety of wild plant foods and smaller animals that were more readily captured. Excavations by MacNeish in the Tehuacan Valley south of Mexico City, for example, yielded relatively few bones from megafauna but many bones from rabbits and other small animals.

There are tantalizing clues, however, that people may have occupied the Americas much earlier than the Paleoindians' arrival. These "pre-projectile point" people did not use the distinctive fluted points of the Paleoindians. Instead, bone and stone objects found at Monte Verde in Chile, Pedra Furada in Brazil, Meadowcroft Rockshelter in Pennsylvania, and Bluefish Cave in the Yukon, among other localities, point to the possibility of sites predating the Paleoindians. Their dates, origins, culture, and very existence as pre-Paleoindian sites remain controversial, however. Many previously accepted localities for pre-Paleoindian sites have been discounted. Still, one must remember the discovery of a fluted point embedded in the rib cage of an extinct bison at Folsom, New Mexico, in 1927. This discovery marked a turning point in our knowl-

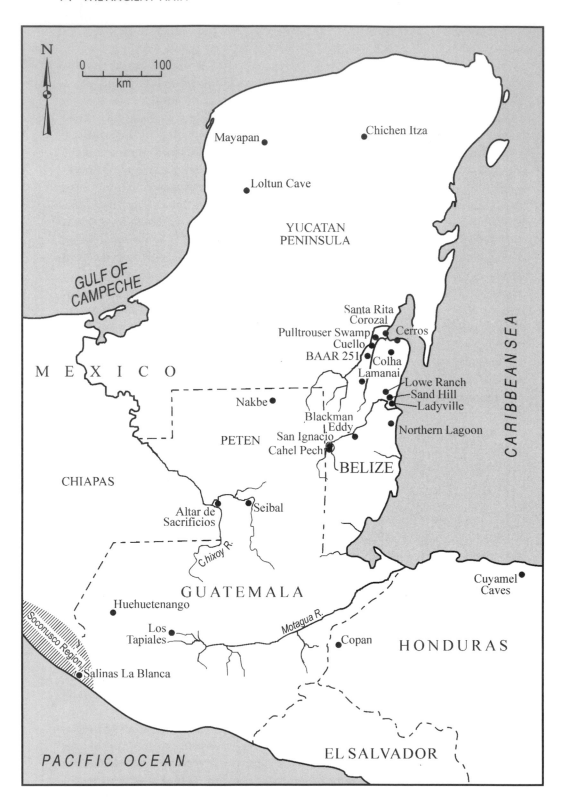

Preceramic and early ceramic sites

edge of prehistory when scientists accepted the contemporaneity of extinct ice age animals and humans in the New World.

SMALL GAME HUNTERS OF THE ARCHAIC

Massive extinction of the large Pleistocene animals, including more than thirty genera in Mexico, required a change in diet by humans, if they were to survive. What caused the extinction of the giant horse, giant ground sloth, mammoth, and mastodon, among others? Was it a changing postglacial landscape, reducing the vast grasslands in a natural succession to forest? Was it excessive hunting by Paleoindians? There are supporters of each hypothesis, and others who believe the explanation can be found in a combination of hunting overkill and environmental change. Regardless of the reason, humans survived and changed their diets to focus on small animals and wild plant foods. The period of this new adaptation, called the Archaic period, describes the way of life that persisted until the introduction of agriculture and permanent settlements.

The Archaic hunting and gathering way of life in the Maya area is poorly understood. Fortunately, the Archaic is better known elsewhere in Mesoamerica from a variety of archaeological sites in Mexico, notably from the Tehuacan Valley (south of Mexico City), the Valley of Mexico, and the Pacific coast of Chiapas, Mexico. In those areas, archaeologists have documented a gradual transition from reliance on wild plants and animals to a dependence on domesticated plants and animals. This transition eventually resulted in a change from temporary to permanent settlements by farming groups.

It was Richard MacNeish's persistent search for early corn that ultimately led to our best understanding of the origins and development of agriculture in highland Mesoamerica. Why corn? MacNeish focused his search on corn because it became the main carbohydrate of farmers and underwrote the subsistence regime of the early Mesoamerican civilizations. He spent several field seasons searching dry caves where corn would be preserved before he found the evidence he was searching for at Tehuacan. The outstanding preservation of organic remains in dry conditions of caves in the Tehuacan Valley allowed MacNeish and his colleagues to document the Archaic way of life and the origins of agriculture. The Tehuacan Valley provides evidence of a gradual change in the diet from the reliance on wild plants and animals to the incorporation of domesticated plants and animals into the diet. Even when people became increasingly more reliant on domesticated foods, they continued to follow the seasonal round in search of wild foods. At some point, a threshold was reached in the amount of domesticated foods used, allowing or even requiring people to remain near their crops to tend them.

The Archaic period transition to farming undoubtedly occurred elsewhere in Mesoamerica besides the Tehuacan Valley, including the Maya area, as ongoing fieldwork by Mary Pohl and colleagues (1996) indicates. However, the tropical rainforest setting and the expansive Maya buildings of later times make the evidence difficult to find. The earliest ethnically identifiable Maya were farmers living in permanent villages, with sophisticated pottery. Neither the presumed gradual transition from an Archaic way of life nor the first attempts at pottery making are well documented in the Maya area. Barbara Voorhies (1976) excavated shell middens along the Pacific coast of Chiapas, Mexico, that date to 3000 to 2000 B.C. Voorhies describes the Chantuto people as exploiting shrimp and mollusks in coastal mangrove lagoons and moving inland seasonally to exploit other wild resources. Perhaps in the Chantuto setting, the local abundance of wild resources allowed people to live a settled way of life most of the year, even without agriculture.

The best evidence for the Archaic lifestyle in the Maya lowlands comes from Harry Shafer and Thomas Hester's work at Colha in northern Belize (Hester et al. 1996; Iceland 1997). The Colha site is best known as a major stone tool manufacturing community utilized by the later Maya, who quarried the high-quality chert at the site (Shafer and Hester 1983). Hester and Shafer returned to Colha in 1993 to search for pre-Maya evidence of humans, based on clues from their earlier work at the site. In particular, excavations in Operation 4046 in the late 1980s by graduate student Greg Wood pointed to evidence for pre-Maya occupation of the area. Excavations yielded a different style of stone tool not previously found. These distinctive "constricted unifaces" were located in rock strata that were below the earliest pottery. The constricted unifaces were oval-shaped blades chipped on one side only and tapered at one end. At the time of Wood's fieldwork, the layer containing the constricted unifaces was undated, and the notion of a pre-Maya occupation was left as a conjecture.

The Colha Project Regional Survey directed by Thomas Kelly (1993) found constricted unifaces at two of MacNeish's sites, Sand Hill and Lowe Ranch. Their great antiquity was not clear, as they were from the ground surface. Interestingly, this style of stone tool was not found associated with later Maya occupation at Colha or other Maya sites. In their 1993 excavations, Hester and Shafer found two upper soil layers, called A and B, that contained Maya pottery, and two lower soil layers, which they referred to as C and D, that contained stone tools but not Maya pottery, suggesting that these lower layers were pre-Maya. Layer C, from 80 to 100 centimeters (cm) in depth, contained constricted unifaces.

Hester and Shafer's lowest soil layer at Colha—layer D, from 100 to 160 centimeters depth—did not contain constricted unifaces, but it did contain chert blades, cores, flakes, and debitage (waste material from the cutting of stone into implements). The dates for horizons C and D are 1400 to 2500 B.C., which predate the earliest evidence of Maya occupation. This is the first stratigraphic, dated evidence for the Archaic lifestyle in the Maya lowlands and is an exciting avenue for future researchers.

Mounting evidence for a pre-Maya occupation of the southern Maya lowlands comes from other sites as well. In 1996, Mary Pohl and colleagues reported a constricted uniface and an Archaic dart point (see Pohl 1996, Figure 4.1) at Pulltrouser Swamp, located near Colha. Soil cores in Cobweb Swamp near Colha by John Jones (1994) of Texas A & M University revealed that the swamp edge had been cleared by 2500 B.C. and that corn was being grown in the area. Jones reported similar results from soil cores at Pulltrouser Swamp. This predates the earliest known Maya use of the area, which is about 1000 to

800 B.C. Mary Pohl led a team to investigate the origins of corn farming in the Mesoamerican lowlands, including the Maya area, and reported corn predating the Maya in several locations (Pohl et al. 1996).

THE EARLY PRECLASSIC PERIOD

Ethnically, who were the Archaic people living in what would later become known as the Maya area? It is not until the first pottery in the Maya area that we see the origins of a ceramic tradition that can be identified as ethnically "Maya." The stone tools produced by the earlier Archaic people were similar in style and manufacture to those produced throughout much of North America. Perhaps the pottery-making tradition of the Maya grew out of the Archaic tradition in the area. Perhaps, on the other hand, a new group of Maya people moved into the area. Linguist Lyle Campbell (1984) tells us that the Mayan languages could be distinguished from the parent proto-Mayan languages by 2100 B.C. Hopefully, future fieldwork will elucidate the transition and clarify the ethnic identity and origins of the Archaic and earliest Maya people in the area.

The introduction of pottery in the Maya area marks the transition from the Archaic to the Preclassic period. This transition coincides with a change from a hunting and gathering way of life to a life based in permanent villages, usually dependent on farming. In some instances, the local abundance of wild food resources allowed early settlers to live permanently in one location with little or no dependence on farming, as discovered by Christine Niederberger for lakeside settlers in central Mexico. Archaic hunting and gathering people evidently used baskets and gourds for containers, with more friable pottery containers only being commonly used by more sedentary groups. For reasons that remain unclear, the transition to pottery use and village farming in the Maya area occurred first along the Pacific coast by 1800 B.C. and not in the southern Maya lowlands where the later Classic Maya civilization developed. The earliest villages, pottery, and agriculture do not appear in the Maya lowlands until 1000 B.C. This lag is perplexing, owing to the subsequent elaboration of Classic Maya civilization in that area. Similarly, the cultural or ecological conditions for the precocious development of early Maya society along the Pacific coast are unexplained.

THE EARLIEST MAYA ON THE PACIFIC COAST

The earliest appearance of pottery in the Maya area is during the Barra Phase (ceramic complex) of the Early Preclassic, beginning in 1800 B.C. along the Pacific coast. This includes the Soconusco region of Pacific coastal Guatemala and adjacent Chiapas, Mexico, as well as western El Salvador. Coastal mangrove lagoons, rivers, and a hot, humid climate dominate this region. According to linguists, Mayan language was spoken in the area before 2100 B.C., but the earliest archaeological evidence is 1800 B.C. (Justeson and Campbell 1984).

The pottery vessels from this complex are surprisingly well made and decorated for the earliest attempts at pottery making. Most of the vessels are round, neckless jars with markedly incurved walls, called tecomates, which resemble gourds in shape. In addition, there are some deep bowls from this complex. The lack of the usual inventory of plates, dishes, and large, necked water jars used by subsequent Maya groups begs explanation. John Clark, Michael Blake, and Barbara Voohries (Blake et al. 1992a; Blake et al. 1992b; Clark 1994), who have investigated the Preclassic in the Soconusco, provide an explanation for the peculiar vessel inventory of the earliest Maya. As most of these vessels were nicely painted or decorated with incising, grooving, or modeling, they suggest that the early pots were used in rituals. The introduction of pottery figurines at this time corroborates a ritual interpretation. Fire-cracked rocks found in the area suggest that cooking was done using heated rocks, with the food being placed in waterproof baskets and not in the finely decorated pottery vessels. This sort of "stone boiling" is a common technique used in antiquity elsewhere in the Americas, so the explanation seems reasonable.

The Early Preclassic Barra complex marks a significant change in lifestyle for the people of the area. People now lived in permanent villages away from the coast of their Archaic predecessors (such as the Chantuto people described above) and relied on a variety of wild and domestic plants and animals. Barra villages in the Soconusco were located beside seasonally inundated bajos (swamps) that may have allowed these early farmers to cultivate up to three crops per year. To the east in Guatemala, Francisco Estrada-Belli, Laura Kosakowsky, and colleagues (Estrada-Belli 1999) report early pottery-making groups as well.

Social and economic inequality—ranked societies—emerge along the Pacific coast between 1700 and 1500 B.C., during the Locona complex. This inequality is marked by two tiers of settlements, with one larger community surrounded by many small settlements. One building that is significantly larger than regular houses was evidently a chief's house, where community rituals took place. The Locona complex also witnesses an expansion of ceramic technology, with the introduction of two new decorative techniques. In rocker stamping, the edge of a shell is moved across wet clay in zigzags, perhaps improving the grip on a vessel. The use of an iridescent pink paint to make stripes on pottery vessels seems more decorative than functional.

Much of our knowledge of the Early Preclassic Maya on the Pacific coast derives from Michael Coe and Kent Flannery's (1967) research in coastal Guatemala focusing on the Salinas La Blanca site. This Ocos complex (1500–1400 B.C.) marks a time of elaboration of pottery figurines and the introduction of cord marking on pottery. In that technique, string is wrapped around a stick or paddle, which is then pressed against the walls of the wet clay before the vessel is fired. Perhaps intended as decoration, cord marking also provides a good gripping surface for lifting or carrying storage and cooking jars.

MIDDLE PRECLASSIC EXPANSION OF VILLAGE FARMING

During the succeeding Middle Preclassic period, the village farming way of life by pottery-making Maya people spread throughout the Maya highlands and lowlands. Elsewhere in Mesoamerica, the Middle Preclassic saw the rise and fall of the Olmec civilization, which certainly influenced the later development of Maya and other Mesoamerican civilizations.

The Earliest Maya in the Lowlands: The Middle Preclassic (1000–300 B.C.)

As mentioned previously, the course of Maya prehistory in the Maya lowlands begins with the earliest evidence of pottery. But the sophistication of this early pottery begs the questions of its origins. Was the pottery introduced from somewhere else, or are there local antecedents yet to be discovered?

Much of our understanding of the earliest lowland Maya derives from excavations from the 1970s to the 1990s under the direction of Norman Hammond (1991). Excavations at Cuello revealed oval platforms with circular stains interpreted by Hammond as post holes, providing the earliest modest glimpse of Maya architecture. As with later Classic and then with modern Maya houses, palm thatch was probably used for the roofs, and the walls were likely made of poles lightly held together with vines. Plant food remains identified by Charles Miksicek (1991) provide a rare glimpse of the early diet, which included corn (*Zea mays*), yams (*Dioscorea*), and another root crop, cocoyan (*Xanthosoma*). The project ceramicist, Laura Kosakowsky (1987), describes open, flaring-sided dishes, spouted jars, and bowls, painted in red and well fired. The earliest pottery, called the Swasey ceramic complex, was well made, suggesting that earlier attempts at pottery making might be found elsewhere that pre-date Swasey. Whether the Swasey Maya developed from local preceramic groups such as the Archaic remains reported from Colha is unknown. The prior development of pottery along the Pacific littoral and the widespread distribution of red-painted pottery in the lowlands suggest that interregional communication or migration were important factors in the transition and development of early lowland Maya culture.

Following Hammond's discovery of Swasey pottery at Cuello, other researchers have found this early pottery elsewhere in northern Belize, including Colha, Santa Rita, and Lamanai. The earliest Maya were corn farmers who lived in permanent villages, with little social or economic differentiation within a community, as indicated by modest houses and grave offerings. The people were relatively egalitarian, without differential access to basic food, shelter, or other resources. They obtained chert and other materials from nearby for making stone tools and other basic daily goods (Hammond 1991; Awe et al. 1990; Garber 2004).

The Swasey Maya in northern Belize are contemporary with the Xe Maya at Seibal and Altar de Sacrificios on the Chixoy River in the Peten district of Guatemala. Both Altar de Sacrificios (Willey 1973) and Seibal (Willey 1990) were excavated by Harvard University researchers under the direction of Gordon Willey. Both sites gained preeminence during the Classic period but are among the few documented sites with early settlement in the Peten. Jeremy Sabloff (1975) and Richard E. W. Adams (1971) identified the earliest Xe complex pottery at Seibal and Altar de Sacrificios, respectively. Xe artifacts point to connections beyond the Maya lowlands at this early time period. Some of the pottery resembles white-slipped pottery vessels at contemporary sites in Chiapas. Willey reported a cache of Olmec-style jade celts (ceremonial axes) from

Xe deposits at Seibal, demonstrating that there was communication or trade with the Olmec civilization of the Gulf of Mexico coast.

Later Middle Preclassic Period in the Maya Lowlands (700–300 B.C.)

Discoveries of early monumental architecture at Nakbe have pushed back in time the origins of social complexity that led to the rise of Maya civilization in the southern Maya lowlands. The large size of the buildings at Nakbe indicates a growing economic and social differentiation in society in which the elite were able to manipulate the masses to build significant public works and to otherwise support and sustain the elite. Richard Hansen (1991) of UCLA discovered and excavated impressive temples measuring up to 18 meters in height, as well as other monumental public architecture dating to 750 B.C., all of which marks an important transition in lowland Maya culture. The precocious developments at Nakbe are important because they are contemporary with the Olmec civilization, which was previously considered to predate the Maya in terms of significant monumental architecture and cultural complexity (Clark and Hansen 2001). It is not yet known what other early monumental architecture lies buried under large Classic period buildings elsewhere in the Maya lowlands.

Excavations at Cahal Pech and Blackman Eddy in the upper Belize River Valley by Jaime Awe and James Garber, respectively (Garber 2004; Garber et al. 2004), revealed public architecture and village ritual that were previously considered to have been later developments. One can expect that Maya archaeologists will continue to search for similar precocious developments at other sites.

In other lowlands areas, the latter part of the Middle Preclassic appears to be a continuation of the village farming way of life of earlier times, only marked by a new pottery complex, Mamon. The ceramics of this complex are painted red or orange-red and include a variety of vessel forms. Mamon pottery has been found from all over the Maya lowlands and dates to between 700 and 300 B.C. The emergence of social complexity is also seen in western Belize, albeit in less dramatic form than at Nakbe.

ANTECEDENTS TO THE CLASSIC MAYA CIVILIZATION: OLMEC AND IZAPA

The degree to which the Classic Maya civilization developed over time in isolation or through communication and sharing of knowledge and resources with neighboring cultures is a matter of continued debate. At least some features that are characteristic of the later Classic Maya have their origins in cultures elsewhere in Mesoamerica. Both in the highlands of Mexico and along the Gulf of Mexico lowlands, there were socially and economically more complex cultures that impacted the course of early Maya cultural complexity. This was at a time when the Early Preclassic Maya on the Pacific littoral lived a relatively simple way of life as village farmers. The beginning of inequality and ranking was just emerging by 1700 B.C. In the Maya lowlands, people continued to

Late Preclassic sites

La Venta, Olmec head (Corbis/Danny Lehman)

follow a hunting and gathering Archaic way of life, as evidenced by the remains of preceramic Archaic people at Colha.

Two of the hallmarks of Maya civilization, writing and the calendar, had their origins in Middle Preclassic cultures outside the Maya area. The Maya derived their number system and calendar from the Olmec of the Gulf Coast of Mexico in the modern Mexican states of Veracruz and Tabasco. The writing system was evidently derived from the Olmec or from the Zapotec of Oaxaca in highland Mexico. Although there is no date on the stela, the earliest known hieroglyph on a monument in Mesoamerica predates the Olmec stelae. Monument 3 from a building at San Jose Mogote in the State of Oaxaca, Mexico, depicts a naked human body with the heart removed, along with a hieroglyph of the name of the person, interpreted as a war captive (Flannery and Marcus 2003, figure 3b). The building within which the stela was placed is radiocarbon dated to 590 B.C., plus or minus 90 years. The earliest dates in Mesoamerica are at Chiapa de Corzo, with a date of 36 B.C., and on a stela from the Olmec site of Tres Zapotes, Tabasco, with a date of 31 B.C. It is interesting to note that when Matthew Sterling found and deciphered the date on a fragment of the Tres Zapotes stela, the scientific community of the 1940s did not believe him because the early date gave the Olmec greater antiquity than the Maya and the scientific community believed the Maya predated the Olmec. He was later vindicated when the remaining part of the stela was found.

Two early monuments from Veracruz were apparently written in Mixe-Zoque, which was likely the language of the Olmec and an ancestral language of the Maya. One stela from La Mojarra has dates of A.D. 143 and A.D. 156 and a text of some 400 signs. Another monument, the Tuxtla statuette, dates to A.D. 162. This evidence indicates that writing spread from the Olmec area to the Pacific coast of Guatemala, to the Maya highlands, and subsequently into the Maya lowlands, and mirrors the adoption of Olmec artistic conventions along the Pacific coast. In turn, artistic styles of the Pacific coast were copied by the Maya in the southern lowlands.

The Olmec were arguably Mesoamerica's first civilization. The Middle Preclassic Olmec capital of San Lorenzo (1200–900 B.C.), with its colossal basalt heads of Olmec rulers, was the first capital of the earliest civilization in Mesoamerica. La Venta (900–400 B.C.) became the second Olmec capital, with its finely carved objects from imported jade and other greenstone. The Olmec developed extensive trade networks throughout much of Mesoamerica. The construction of large earthen mound temples, placement of stone-lined drainage systems at San Lorenzo, and deliberate burial of tons of imported serpentine blocks at La Venta point to significant organization of labor. Carved basalt altars, sculptures, and colossal heads representing the Olmec rulers were transported from the Tuxtla Mountains, some 60 kilometers north of the island site of La Venta. The Olmec rulers likely dominated the common folk through ritually acquired powers. The Olmec art style, focusing on a shamanistic combination of human and jaguar forms known as the were-jaguar motif, was widely copied in portable art and in monumental carved stone altars and sculptures. Olmec style was copied throughout Mesoamerica, providing evidence of the pervasive spiritual influence of the Olmec as well as the development of early trade networks (Grove 1997).

There is clear evidence of Olmec influence along the Pacific coast as far as El Salvador dating back to the Early Preclassic and continuing in the Middle Preclassic. Olmec-style ceramics and carved monuments are common, even at some distance from the Olmec area, for example in the Copan valley of Honduras. The flame eyebrow and the paw-wing motifs of the Olmec, like the were-jaguar, were widely copied. In an outlying community of Copan, Bill Fash excavated a Middle Preclassic burial with Olmec-style artifacts including pottery vessels, stone celts, and some 300 drilled jade objects. Elsewhere in Honduras, Paul Healy has found Olmec-style artifacts from Cuyamel Cave. An Olmec-style jade spoon is reported from Uxbenka in southern Belize (Healy and Awe 2001). Certainly the Olmec desired and acquired quantities of jade, serpentine, and other greenstones from outcrops along the Motagua River drainage in Guatemala. Copying of the artistic motifs may represent incorporation of the shamanistic were-jaguar ritual into local beliefs or perhaps simply emulation of the more affluent Olmec culture.

Early evidence of the Olmec artistic style, as well as the use of dated stone monuments, places the Izapan culture of the Pacific coast midway stylistically and temporally between the Olmec and the Maya. At Abaj Takalik in the western highlands of Guatemala, there is a boulder carved in relief of a bearded were-jaguar in pure Olmec style. Of particular interest is the fact that other stone monuments at the site are in the style of the nearby Izapa site, and one includes traces of a Maya long count date. Otherwise unimpressive, Abaj Takalik consists of earthen mounds. Izapa, by way of contrast, is a large site located about 20 miles inland from the Pacific coast in Chiapas. It lacks writing and the calendar but shows clear stylistic and iconographic similarities to later lowland Maya art. The site consists of more than eighty earthen mounds faced with river cobbles. Izapa dates from the Early Preclassic through the Early Classic, but most of the mounds and the stone monuments evidently date to the site's time of prominence during the Late Preclassic. The Izapan art style consists of low-relief carvings of scenes combining historical and mythical themes, including elaborately costumed and plumed individuals, in a somewhat cluttered appearance. The style shows a focus on two-dimensional renditions characteristic of later Classic Maya art.

What is most exciting for tracing the origins of the Maya civilization is that precursors of Maya gods appear on stone monuments in Izapan style at the site. They include a "long-lipped god," part human and part fish, that is a prototype of the Maya rain god, Chac. Also depicted is the earliest known rendition of God K (a name given to the god by archaeologists), a supernatural being with one leg ending in a serpent's body and head, who was in Classic times an important deity for Maya ruling houses. A clear link between Izapa and the lowland Maya is seen in representations of Vucub Caquix, depicted as the anthropomorphic vulture shown in the *Popol Vuh* as the sun in the previous creation. This same deity is depicted on giant stucco masks at Late Preclassic sites in the Maya lowlands.

The earliest dated monument in the Maya area is the Herrera Stela from El Baul, located in the Maya highlands southeast of Abaj Takalik and not far from Kaminaljuyu. The stela depicts a profile figure holding a spear, with two vertical columns of glyphs to the right. The glyphs on the left column provide a Maya long count date of A.D. 36, later than dates in Chiapas and the Olmec area but earlier than lowland Maya dates. Perhaps also antecedent to the lowland Maya are large, potbellied figures and a puffy-faced colossal stone head at nearby Monte Alto, also dating to the Late Preclassic.

The Pacific coast of Guatemala, Chalchuapa, and other sites in western El Salvador and the highlands of Guatemala centered on Kaminaljuyu experienced a cultural florescence during the Middle and Late Preclassic periods. The dominance of Chalchuapa is evident in monumental sculpture and architecture (Sharer 1978). The community may have controlled the distribution of Ixtepeque obsidian from the nearby outcrop.

The Maya highland city of Kaminaljuyu is culturally and temporally intermediate between the Izapan culture of the Pacific coast and the lowland Maya. Although Kaminaljuyu is now virtually engulfed by urban sprawl in the outskirts of modern Guatemala City, excavations have provided provocative clues about its ancient importance. Several archaeological projects have worked at the site, but most of the information derives from the Carnegie Institute projects in the 1930s and 1940s (Kidder, Jennings, and Shook 1946) and the Pennsylvania State University project in the 1960s and 1970s (Sanders and Michels 1977).

Kaminaljuyu had its origins in the Las Charcas culture of the Middle Pre-classic period or earlier, but it is better known for its Late Preclassic cultural florescence of the Miraflores complex, beginning about 200 B.C. Two carved monuments from the site indicate that the Kaminaljuyu Maya had writing and a system of recording and depicting ritual leaders on stone monuments for public display. One of the monuments is a granite stela of a human figure wearing a mask of the bird-monster Vucub Caquix in Izapan style.

Although the size of the site is unknown, there were at least two hundred mounds, including one that was well known to archaeologists for its elaborate tombs. The mound contained several superimposed temples, each with a central staircase and flat top that once supported a building of pole and thatch that has been preserved. The topmost temple measured 18 meters in height. Elaborate tombs were associated with each construction episode, evidently marking the temples as funerary monuments, a feature that was to become characteristic of the Maya area. Tomb II contained dozens of pottery vessels, sacrificial victims—both adults and children—jade, mica, obsidian, and bone objects, among others.

During the Late Preclassic Miraflores complex, Kaminaljuyu shares the same ceramic tradition as communities from El Salvador, the Pacific lowlands, and Maya highlands, but it stands apart in the sophistication and elaboration of its pottery. Among other ceramics found there is the distinctive Usulutan pottery, a type of pottery called resist ware, made by applying wavy lines of wax to the exterior of the vessel. Removing the wax after firing revealed a pattern of yellow wavy lines on an orange or brown background.

The Late Preclassic florescence at Kaminaljuyu was followed by a decline until the Early Classic influence of Teotihuacan. Kaminaljuyu probably derived its Early Classic power from control of the nearby obsidian outcrop of El Chayal, which was at that time just becoming a major source for the lowland Maya. Certainly the monumental architecture, high quality of grave goods, and size of the city show extraordinary wealth and power compared to earlier times. Although most of Kaminaljuyu is buried by urban sprawl from modern Guatemala City as mentioned previously, ground-penetrating radar has helped discover remains of ancient buildings (Valdes and Kaplan 2000).

The Rise of Lowland Maya Civilization in the Late Preclassic (300 B.C.–A.D. 300)

The rise of the great Maya civilization is a story of growing social and economic inequality that was wonderful for the emerging elite but placed increasing burdens of tribute and labor on the bulk of the population. The magnificent stone temples and finely made painted pots, carved jade, and stone monuments with the history of the rulers laid out in only partially deciphered hieroglyphs are a measure of the power of the Classic Maya elite. The material evidence for growing social and economic inequality dates to the Late Preclassic period between 300 B.C. and A.D. 300 and, at sites such as Nakbe, even earlier. Painted stucco masks adorn the façades of a number of important Late Preclassic communities, notably Cerros, Uaxactun, Tikal, El Mirador, Nakbe, Dzibilchaltun, and Lamanai. Many Late Preclassic settlements subsequently grew in size and population density during the Classic period, with the early architecture buried under later construction efforts. Fortunately for archaeologists, this is not the case at Cerros in northern Belize and in El Mirador in the Peten district of Guatemala, both of which witnessed major Late Preclassic settlement without major rebuilding in later times.

Major architectural excavations at Cerros, directed by David Freidel of Southern Methodist University, provide a good picture of early public architecture (Freidel 1979; Robertson and Freidel 1986). Perched on the edge of Chetumal Bay, Cerros derived its wealth and emerging power from coastal trade. A core precinct of monumental buildings at the site contains several temples and palace structures, with a residential zone beyond. The sheer size of the nondomestic buildings indicates an organized labor force focused on construction efforts beyond family needs. Public ritual with a ruler-priest is represented on a temple with an outset central staircase flanked on each side by large painted stucco masks of the sun god. Freidel and epigrapher Linda Schele (1988) describe the iconography of the four masks and an offering of jade heads at the temple's summit as evidence of the origins of kingship in the Late Preclassic.

A person standing four steps from the base and nine steps from the top of the temple would be centered on a stage of the four masks, representing the four corners of the Maya universe. Four post molds on the flat top of the temple evidently are the remains of posts that held up a structure representing the four corners of the world. Carved greenstone heads placed on the temple summit include one with the tripartite pointed hat of the Jester God, who accompanies Classic Maya kings in rituals. Freidel and Schele (1988) suggest that the Classic Maya concept of kingship focused on a charismatic leader who, through shamanistic transformation during rituals depicted in Maya art, drew power from and transformed into the creators of the Maya world. This power was sanctified by dynastic links to the creators. Dynastic power of charismatic shaman-leaders was displayed on stone monuments for public viewing during the Classic period. Freidel and Schele suggest that the Late Preclassic public knew how to interpret the symbolism in public architecture.

Early masked temples at other Late Preclassic sites include E-VII-sub at Uaxactun with staircases on four sides leading to a flat summit. The entire temple was once painted red. The staircases are flanked on each side by monumental stucco masks of the jaguar god. As at Cerros, four post molds at the temple summit suggest the corners of a perishable superstructure of pole and thatch that once stood on the limestone temple. Oliver and Edith Ricketson (Ricketson and Ricketson 1937) of the Carnegie Institution excavated this temple in the 1930s. The temple is regarded as prototypical of the Late Preclassic public architecture in the Maya lowlands. More recent fieldwork at Uaxactun by the Guatemalan Institute of Anthropology and History under the direction of Juan Valdes (1986) revealed another area of Late Preclassic monumental architecture at Uaxactun, called Group H. This group includes several buildings on a large stone platform, including H-sub-3, a tall temple with a central staircase flanked on each side by two massive stucco masks with polychrome paint. The complex also supports buildings that once had corbelled and vaulted rooms—a defining characteristic of later Classic period construction.

Above: Corbelled vault room construction in uppermost building of the Castillo at Xunantunich, Belize (Courtesy H. McKillop)

Interior of room on top of Tikal's Temple I showing corbelled vault construction, with plastered walls and original roof supports (Courtesy H. McKillop)

Both Nakbe and El Mirador, connected through swampy terrain by an 8-kilometer causeway, have major architectural construction, replete with stucco-masked temples, from the Late Preclassic. Research at El Mirador, by Richard Hansen (1984), indicates that the site was a huge Late Preclassic city with temples measuring up to 70 meters in height. Raised causeways radiated from the city center. One temple has enormous stucco masks of Vucub Caquix, like the ones that are so common at other Late Preclassic sites. Nakbe, following its precocious Middle Preclassic origins, reached its apogee of monumental construction early in the Late Preclassic (Hansen 1991). Among nine masks and panels, Richard Hansen has excavated an expansive painted stucco mask of Vucub Caquix on the façade of Temple 1 at Nakbe. Fragments of a stone stela were reconstructed to reveal two human figures whose apparel resembles that shown on the Miraflores granite stela from Kaminaljuyu, underscoring highland-lowland interaction at this time. Painted murals discovered at San Bartolo in the Peten district of Guatemala also include a depiction of Vucub Caquix (Saturno 2003).

The Late Preclassic witnessed a widespread development in cultural complexity as a prelude to the subsequent Classic civilization. The unequal access to both basic resources and luxury goods that is typical of the growth of civilization is seen in Late Preclassic burials, houses, and public architecture. Elite burials contained jade, obsidian, and finely made pottery. The common Maya, though, had qualitatively and quantitatively less. For example, elite Maya lived in palaces in the city center, but the common Maya lived on houses built of perishable pole and thatch built on modest stone platforms or even directly on the ground surface.

Public architecture became increasingly associated with elite rituals and ceremonies, in temples that the common Maya were invited to witness in the plazas below. Elite people's power and authority were publicly reinforced by shamanistic transformations through pain and blood loss from ritual bloodletting, for example. Obsidian blades obtained via long-distance trading partners, and stingray spines—associated with the elaborate imagery of the sea and the watery underworld—were common bloodletting instruments. Both are shown in pictorial scenes in Classic Maya art. Obsidian blades made a clean cut. Stingray spines, the barbed and venomous weapons of the stingray, were perhaps more painful.

THE ORIGINS OF MAYA CIVILIZATION

What factors led to the precocious development of some settlements and the rise of the Classic Maya civilization? In the previous section, the changes in Maya architecture and artifacts are discussed, but what caused the rise of the social complexity? Although there is no consensus among Maya archaeologists, several innovative hypotheses have been advanced. The similar style and iconography of Late Preclassic masked temples at several sites in the lowlands led David Freidel (1979) to suggest that the origins of Maya civilization were related to communication and trade among emerging elite at various lowland Maya polities: In what he referred to as the "interaction sphere model" of the rise of Maya civilization, the communication was indicated in the archaeological record by the shared ceremonial and elite ritual paraphernalia, including the temple masks, the imported jade beads carved into heads, and the existence of monumental architecture.

By way of contrast, William Rathje (1971) suggested a basic resource deficiency model to explain the origins of Maya civilization in what he referred to as the resource-deficient central Maya lowlands around Tikal. He believed that the lack of salt, obsidian for cutting stone, and basalt for grinding stones led to the development of sophisticated trade networks and social complexity in order to import critical resources in bulk from the northern Maya lowlands and southern Maya highlands. Although not a popular model for the origins of Maya civilization, Rathje's model has prompted considerable discussion and research. The lack of volcanic rock, including obsidian and basalt, in the southern Maya lowlands was not really a problem, as locally available chert was used for cutting implements. Granite and limestone were commonly used as grinding stones. Even some salt was available from animal meat and from burning palm fronds in the central Maya lowlands. Fieldwork has revealed extensive salt production along the coast of Belize that was much closer to the southern lowland cities than the north coast of the Yucatan (McKillop 2002).

William T. Sanders (1977) argued against Rathje's characterization of the central Maya lowlands as resource-poor, suggesting instead that it was the rich agricultural soil of the well-drained uplands that first attracted settlers to the region and acted as a catalyst for continued settlement and population increase. From Sanders's perspective, it was competition for limited water and good agricultural land that led to growing inequality and the development of Classic Maya civilization. Access to water and management of water resources are viewed by archaeologist Vernon Scarborough (1998, 2003), as critical in the development of Maya civilization.

The sudden appearance of a new pottery style similar to ceramics from El Salvador has led to another interpretation of the origins of complex Maya culture as being "intrusive" from outside the Maya lowlands. The intrusive pottery includes vessels with wavy lines called Usulutan as well as polychrome bowls with four mammiform vessel supports (Merwin and Vaillant 1932; Gifford 1976). Contemporaneous with the eruption of the Ilopango volcano in El Salvador, there was a migration of people to new areas, perhaps including the southern Maya lowlands of Belize and Guatemala. Recent dating places the Ilopango volcanic eruption in A.D. 425, with a range between 410 and 532 (Dull, Southon, and Sheets 2001), much later than was previously thought. Certainly some of the settlements in El Salvador were buried along with their occupants. People most affected lived within 100 kilometers west of Ilopango where no one survived the airborne volcanic ejecta of 1000° C (Dull, Southon, and Sheets 2001). The indirect effect was wider, with heavy rainstorms and daytime darkness. There was a demographic collapse with immediate evacuation, continued emigration due to starvation and disease, and a regional economic collapse. The cultural florescence ended. In 1,000-square-kilometer area, everyone was killed. Some 25 kilometers from the vent, pyroclastic flows carbonized biota, including trees, and people. In western El Salvador, the landscape was denuded and sterile for decades, precluding agriculture. It took 100 to 125 years for the area to be suitable for farming and thus human settlement. Central El Salvador and southeastern Guatemala were abandoned. The regional economy focused on Chalchuapa collapsed, that city was abandoned, and Kaminaljuyu was weakened. People moved north to Copan, which was unaffected by the volcanic eruption. There was a cultural hiatus in the areas affected by the volcanic eruption of about 100 to 150 years. Chalchuapa was resettled at the end of the sixth century A.D. The Ceren site (Sheets 2002) was buried under meters of volcanic deposits after the Loma Caldera eruption at about A.D. 600. That eruption devastated the landscape nearby. Discovery and excavation of the Ceren village, with fields and houses preserved by the Loma Caldera volcanic eruption, provide a Pompeii-like glimpse of ancient Maya village life (Sheets 2002).

Was this new pottery style in the Maya lowlands a result of intrusive or "in situ" development? Although it has been designated as being from the Protoclassic period, this implies that it was a separate ceramic complex between the Late Preclassic and the Early Classic, a conclusion for which there is no clear evidence. The elaborate polychrome pottery vessels, including the distinctive mammiform tetrapod shape, are sometimes viewed as a funeral subcomplex popular at some Late Preclassic or Early Classic settlements. From her studies of pottery in the Stann Creek District of southern Belize, Elizabeth Graham (1994) raised the possibility that this introduction of polychrome painting was simply part of the experimentation in pigments that preceded the elaborate Classic period pottery.

Originally defined by the burial pottery from the site of Holmul, Guatemala, by Robert Merwin and George Vaillant (1932), the Protoclassic pottery consists of tetrapod vessels with characteristic mammiform vessel supports, as well as the first polychrome painted decorations on the exterior of bowls and dishes. In a seminal volume on Maya pottery, *Prehistoric Pottery Analysis and the Ceramics of Barton Ramie in the Belize Valley,* James Gifford (1976) described the Floral Park complex as the Protoclassic style in the upper Belize River valley. The pottery is stylistically similar to pottery from El Salvador, notably from Chalchuapa. The widespread occurrence of Protoclassic ceramics in the southern Maya lowlands, together with significant fieldwork pointing to a long trajectory of local development of Maya culture, points to the Protoclassic pottery as a component of the Late Preclassic and Early Classic, encompassing a time between around 75 B.C. to A.D. 400 (Brady et al. 1998). Graham (1994) suggests that Maya in central Belize were experimenting with paint during the Late Preclassic and that this experimentation was widespread. Was polychrome painted pottery introduced from outside the Maya lowlands? Perhaps the distinctive Protoclassic tetrapod mammiform style was intrusive, but the origins of polychrome were also within the southern Maya lowlands.

CLASSIC MAYA CIVILIZATION

The Classic period is defined as the time in which carved monuments called stelae were erected at lowland Maya cities with hieroglyphic inscriptions and dates carved in the Maya long count, roughly between A.D. 300 and 900. The

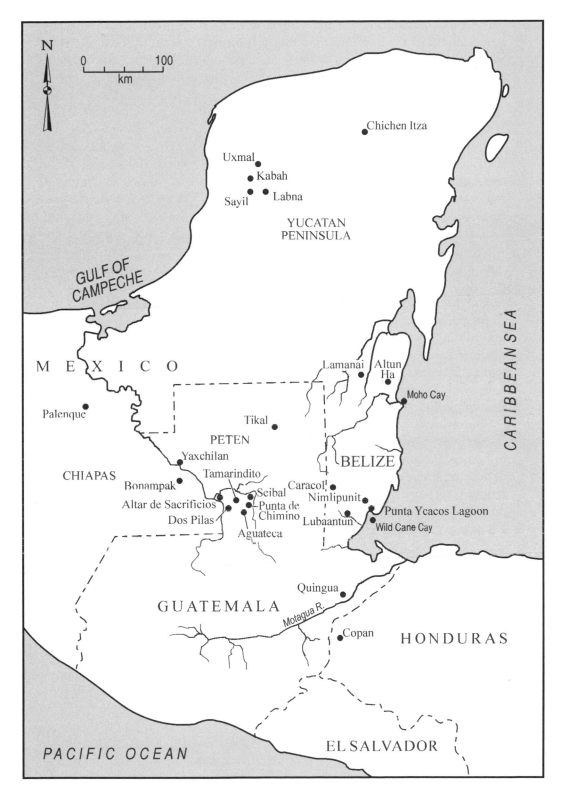

Classic and Postclassic sites

earliest dated monument is Stela 29, dated to A.D. 292 from Tikal. The last dated monument is from A.D. 909 from Tonina, near Palenque, Chiapas, Mexico. Although this definition of the Classic period might appear arbitrary, in fact it refers to the time period of dynastic rule of lowland city-states as recorded on stelae.

Features of Classic Maya Civilization

The expression of the culture has left clear evidence of distinctive features of the Classic Maya civilization in the archaeological record. The Classic Maya civilization is characterized by monumental temples and palaces, built around plazas that represent the marshaling and organizing of a tremendous labor force of common Maya by the ruling elite. Based on the basic Maya architectural feature of buildings around a plaza typical of Maya households throughout the lowlands, the royal Maya of the Classic period organized the construction of temples and palaces in the centers of cities. Temples consisted of stone rubble fill with a cut stone façade that served as a platform for a temple structure on top. Reached by a steep, central staircase with narrow treads and high risers, the temple structure was difficult to reach. The temples were renovated periodically by covering the platform and temple with a layer of rubble and then constructing a new stone façade. The result was both a higher and larger temple platform. Height was further increased by the addition of a roof comb, a decorative stone or stone and stucco architectural element constructed above the temple structure.

The periodic renovation of temples followed a tradition of rebuilding even the simplest Maya houses, as well as the practice of burying dead relatives in buildings. Patricia McAnany (1995) has argued convincingly that the practice of burying relatives below house floors or in the construction fill prior to house renovation focused on ancestor veneration, in which the Maya traced their importance and their standing in society according to their lineage history. What better way to record and venerate ancestors than by keeping them at home and maintaining a tie of family and place over generations? The interment of Maya royalty in the foundations of temples in central plazas at Maya cities was simply the public display of the ancestor veneration practice that had become entrenched in dynastic kingship by the Classic period. Deaths of Maya kings and queens were recorded in heiroglyphs for public notice on carved monuments in front of the temples. Although the renovation of temples often coincided with the death of an important royal Maya, the periodicity of burial and house renovation for the common Maya is unknown.

The small temple room at the top of Maya temples was the center of important royal rituals that are depicted on stelae and on painted pots (Reents-Budet 1994). These rituals helped to codify and reinforce the power, authority, and royal lineage rights of the royal Maya. Rituals were performed on the occasion of accession to the throne and to mark other important personal and public events. The rituals often featured blood offerings using stingray spines or lancets made of obsidian. Blood loss helped induce a state of trance in which, the Maya believed, the royal person attained supernatural powers by contact with the gods following age-old shamanistic practices. Blood offerings are de-

Tikal stucco mask on temple façade (Courtesy B. Somers)

picted on carved monuments at Palenque, Yaxchilan, Nim li punit, and elsewhere, with droplets of blood falling onto bark paper in a brazier where they were burned, allowing smoke to rise to invoke the vision serpent.

The temple room at the summit of temples was small because of the construction technique known as the corbelled vault, used for building stone walls and roofs. The Maya did not use the true arch in buildings. Their corbelled vault resulted in narrow rooms, which could be of considerable length but not width. In making a corbelled vault, successive cut stone blocks were placed on opposite walls progressively closer to the center line, with a capstone placed over the center. The corbelled vault roof required thick stone walls to transfer the weight of the roof and just a narrow distance between the supporting walls. The original corbelled vault rooms, complete with plastered walls and ceilings, and wooden beam supports, still remain at Tikal's Temple 1 and 2.

Stone and stucco masks flank the central staircases of temples at various Classic period cities, notably Tikal, Lamanai, and Altun Ha. The masks, like the entire stone temples, were plastered and painted, but only traces of plaster and paint remain to give visitors to these sites a vision of the multicolored splendor of the monumental architecture during its use by the Classic Maya. The Classic period masks are materialistic depictions of dynastic rulers, displaying and reinforcing the importance of kingship. By way of contrast, the Late Preclassic masks are abstract depictions of deities from which Maya leaders obtained power through rituals.

Palaces flanking the sides of central plazas were for residential and administrative uses by the Classic Maya royalty and their royal courts. Palaces consisted of large stone-faced platforms, with stone buildings on top, as at Tikal. There would also have been pole and thatch structures that have not been preserved, as at Nim li punit, Lubaantun, Altun Ha, and others. The palaces at Tikal include multiroom buildings with corbelled vaults and interior chambers, some of which have stone benches, for thrones or for sleeping (Christie 2003).

The ball game, an important feature of the Maya origin myth and likely commonly played in Maya communities, was a central part of life in Maya city-states, as stone ball courts are found in the central area of the cities (Whittington 2001, http://www.ballgame.org/main.asp). At Tikal, for example, there is a stone ball court behind Temple 1 in the central plaza. The ball courts are formed by the space created between two parallel buildings, often with circular ball court markers placed along the center line of the playing field, which was plastered.

Stelae were placed in front of temples and palaces in the central plazas of major cities. The stelae provided historical information about Maya royalty who were the leaders of Maya city-states. Hence, stelae with hieroglyphs and dates are found principally at lowland cities and only at smaller communities that were key players in the political maneuverings of Classic Maya geopolitics. The information on stelae focused on Maya kings and queens, including personal information as well as their military conquests and their marriages and other alliances. These events were accompanied by dates in the Maya long count, a system used exclusively during the Classic period and now used by researchers to define that time period.

The purpose of the stelae was surely to provide the public with information on the importance of the ruler and the ruler's exploits, with propaganda certainly being a feature of the public monumental display of information. Usually there was a depiction of a royal person, with hieroglyphic text and dates on each face of the stela and often on the sides as well. The stelae were carved in low relief. Limestone mined from the immediate environs of the city was used in most cases, as with the construction of buildings. In some areas, locally available sandstone or volcanic tuff was used instead. The sandstone stelae at Nim li punit in southern Belize and Quirigua, along the Motagua River in southeastern Guatemala, include the tallest stelae in the Maya lowlands.

Archaeologists once thought that the stelae recorded astronomical information, until an important discovery was made by Tatiana Proskouriakoff, published in 1960 in *American Antiquity*. She proposed that the hieroglyphs recorded historical information about the Maya rulers, an interpretation that has been underscored by further work by a corps of epigraphers, including Linda Schele, David Stuart, Joyce Marcus, Stephen Houston, Simon Martin, Nicholai Grube, and Barbara MacLeod, among others (Houston, Mazariegos, and Stuart 2001). As a result of the hieroglyphic research, we now know that the Maya had dynasties whose kings ruled lowland city-states for generations and formed military and marriage alliances with royalty in neighboring city-states. Over the course of about 150 years beginning in the eighth century A.D., the city-states fell to the greater military force of neighboring city-states. By A.D. 900, the hieroglyphic record on stelae was silent and the southern lowland Maya cities virtually abandoned.

Unlike in the Near Eastern cities in Mesopotamia, the Mayan hieroglyphs do not record economic transactions or the lives of the more common or rural Maya, which must instead be understood from archaeological excavations. However, the rich historical and political information, with accompanying dates, has provided a detailed culture history of the urban and royal Maya to enhance information from excavations of buildings, tombs, and middens.

Decipherment of the Maya calendar system and its correlation with the Gregorian calendar used by modern Western cultures moved the ancient Maya into a specific place in history and anchored archaeological research into chronometric dates in years. Maya archaeologists use the GMT correlation of the Maya and Gregorian calendars (so named because it was advanced by Goodman, Martinez, and Thompson [Houston, Mazariegos, and Stuart 2001]), which placed the beginning of the Maya calendar at 3114 B.C. in the Gregorian calendar. Importantly, the Classic Maya had the concept of zero, unknown by other ancient civilizations at the time, and mathematically a sophisticated concept. Reading a date on a Classic period stela, altar, or painted pot requires an understanding of the Maya counting system. Based on multiples of twenty, a date is read in five sections, from top to bottom. There are four basic symbols, including a dot to represent the number 1, a bar to represent the number 5, a stylized shell to represent the number 0, and a stylized shell with a dot above it to represent 20. Using those symbols to read a number, the top section records multiples of 400 years (baktuns) from the inception of the Maya calendar. The next section records multiples of 20 years (katuns), followed by multiples of 1 year (tuns), multiples of 20 days (uinals), and finally, at the bottom, the number of days (kins) from 1 to 19. The date, then, records the number of years, months, and days that have elapsed from the beginning of the Maya calendar to the recorded event. Epigraphers transcribe the date in its sections, from top to bottom, as 8.12.14.8.15, for example (Coe and Van Stone 2001, 37–58).

Classic Maya pottery is quite distinctive, with decorations painted on the vessels in multiple colors. Prior to the Classic period, most of the pottery was simply painted red or was unpainted. Following the collapse of the Classic period culture, there were few polychrome painted pots. Instead, Postclassic potters decorated their vessels by incising, molding, or carving. If pots were painted, it was usually red or orange. Classic Maya polychrome pottery was characteristically decorated in red and black on an orange background, although sometimes the background was cream or off-white, and orange also was used in the decoration. Rarely, other colors, such as brown and blue, were used. Early Classic pottery features an open bowl or dish with an interior painted design and, in the case of bowls, decoration on the vessel's exterior as well. The interior of the vessel often depicts a single figure, human or animal, with bands or other decoration below the vessel rim. A flange (or skirt) around the lower part of bowls is diagnostic of the early part of the Early Classic, both in polychrome and monochrome bowls.

Polychrome vases with elaborate scenes painted on the vessel exterior are diagnostic of the Late Classic period. Specialists attached to the royal Maya court painted the finest pots and inscribed hieroglyphs on them. Takeshi Inomata's (1997) excavations of suddenly abandoned elite residences at Aguateca show the tools of elite specialists on the floors. The Classic elite polychrome vessels these specialists painted show carefully rendered scenes of royal Maya engaged in ritual and political activities. Vertical bands of hieroglyphs often separate panels on the vase exterior. A band of hieroglyphs below the vessel rim often holds a standard set of information that archaeologists term the primary standard sequence (PSS), which indicates the date and other essential information about the activity depicted (see Reents-Budet 1994).

Polychrome pots served as a medium for the royal Maya to express and publicize important ritualized behavior (often mythological events from the *Popol Vuh*, for example) that was a recognized part of society, and even though the common Maya were illiterate, they could recognize symbols and the structure and icons of ceramic communication (bands of hieroglyphs, royal Maya in elaborate costume, ritual bloodletting), and they repeated it in their more modest painted pots, which were widely distributed at all levels of Classic Maya society.

Maya population levels reached their maximum during the Classic period, in terms of both overall population and density. Population increased in both the cities and in the rural areas. Public buildings were renovated many times, with each successive temple or palace being larger because it was constructed over the ruins of its predecessor. Although population estimates for the Classic period vary considerably, researchers agree that the Maya civilization reached its peak in population during the Late Classic period. Residential population estimates are based on 5.6 people per household multiplied by the number of contemporary mounded remains considered to have been houses, but these vary quite a bit. Peter Harrison (1999) estimates that the Late Classic population of Tikal reached 100,000 people.

By the Late Classic period, the Maya lowlands consisted of regional city-states, each with a hierarchy of smaller settlements in their hinterland. Joyce Marcus (1976, 1993) explained the regular spacing of major cities, identified by their emblem glyphs on carved monuments, by Central Place Theory. This model was created to explain the distribution of modern cities to minimize travel and transportation costs and to maximize profit (Haggett 1965). Takeshi Inomata and Kazuo Aoyama (1996) found that even without a modern market economy, the hierarchical distribution of Late Classic Maya settlements and the regular spacing of large cities fit Central Place Theory. In their study of settlement distribution in northwestern Honduras, Inomata and Aoyama found that the administrative principle of the model explains the relations among Maya leaders who extracted tribute and labor from the common folk.

Development and Maximum Expansion of Maya Civilization

The Classic Maya civilization, as well as the size of its buildings, reached its apogee during the Late Classic period, at a time when competing city-states were both making alliances with friendly neighbors and carrying out military campaigns, often coordinated with allies, against less friendly neighbors. The maximum growth of the civilization is marked across the southern Maya lowlands by Late Classic monumental architecture. It is these latest renovations that are seen by modern visitors to the southern lowland Maya sites. Maya royalty who publicly displayed their lives, alliances, and military conquests ruled city-states that extended from the Peten district of Guatemala to southern Belize and adjacent Mexico and western Honduras, as well as into Chiapas, Mexico. Northern Belize and the northern Maya lowlands, although beyond the areas that had concentrations of dated stelae, also were densely occupied. The story of the Classic Maya continues to unfold as the hieroglyphic record of Maya kings and queens is deciphered and as field archaeologists uncover new settlements of both the royal and common Maya.

Classic Maya Collapse

Perhaps the most frequently asked question about the ancient Maya is why the civilization collapsed. Many insightful theories have been advanced to explain the Classic Maya collapse, as noted, for example, in an edited volume resulting from a symposium, *The Classic Maya Collapse* (Culbert 1973). Invasion, earthquake, drought, hurricane, and civil war are featured among the various interpretations of the collapse. Three interpretations are popular among early twenty-first-century Maya archaeologists: a systemic ecological collapse model, a political/warfare model, and a drought model. The first model stresses ecological factors. The second model places more weight on cultural factors in the collapse of the Classic Maya civilization. The third model attributes the collapse to environmental change.

In order to evaluate the various competing theories about the collapse of the Classic Maya civilization, it is important to determine what collapsed. The descendants of the Classic Maya people still live in many parts of the Yucatan of Mexico, Guatemala, Belize, and Honduras where the Classic period civilization developed. The result of the Classic period collapse was a virtual abandonment of cities in the southern Maya lowlands. However, the rural population in the southern lowlands persisted, at least for several generations. It was the political and economic power of the urban royal Maya that fell apart. This did not happen as a single event but rather was associated with the defeat and abandonment of lowland city-states, one by one, at the hand of more powerful lowland city-states over the course of some 150 years. There was, in fact, a population increase along the coasts of the Yucatan and in the northern Maya lowlands. Perhaps some or much of this increase was due to migration of people from the southern Maya lowlands.

In the systemic/ecological collapse model, the tremendous population increase in some areas during the Late Classic placed burdensome taxation in labor and food on the common Maya farming families in those areas. At the same time, the rainforest was being more extensively cleared than before, and the fallow cycle for fields was diminished. There was more pressure on some areas of the land to produce more food to feed the growing populations. The overuse of the land led to ecological disaster, coupled with a revolt of the common Maya, who felt overworked.

In the warfare/political model, by way of contrast, self-aggrandizing royal Maya precipitated the collapse. In a search for power and glory, they formed alliances and fought wars that got out of hand and led to their ultimate demise. Arthur Demarest is a leading proponent of the warfare/political explanation for the Classic Maya collapse, supported by fieldwork at Dos Pilas, Aguateca, and Tamarindito, among other sites, in the Petexbatun region of Guatemala. Demarest (1997) explains his warfare/political downfall model in these words: "increasing political rivalry, competition, and warfare spiraled out of control by the middle of the eighth century, disrupting cultural, economic, and ecological systems and leading to rapid depopulation and sociopolitical devolution." He focuses on the expanding and escalating competition among rival elites that was manifested in showy displays of exotic and high-crafted paraphernalia, more elaborate architecture, and elaborate ritual, as well as interregional alliances that further exacerbated tensions among elites. David Freidel (1992) also discusses the importance of warfare, specifically the capture of war victims for sacrifice, to Classic Maya kingship. He also finds that the fragmentation of the lowlands into many polities is related to this ritual aspect of warfare.

According to Demarest (1997), the effect of elite competition was a debilitating stress on the economic system, the local populations, and the area's resources. A cycle of endemic, destructive warfare began in the mid-eighth century, with fortifications, sieges, and devastation of the cities in the Petexbatun. One by one, the cities fell, monumental construction ended, and population levels dropped to 10 percent of their former sizes. As warfare progressed, settlements were fortified with walls and palisades. Finally, the rural population moved to defensible hilltops and the artificial fortified island of Punta de Chimino. The collapse in the Petexbatun was early (compared to the other areas in the southern lowland), between A.D. 760 and 830, is well dated on stelae, and was associated with extensive defensive systems and dramatic depopulation of settlements. This seventy-year period also is marked by a decrease in imported Peten pottery and an increase in the variety of ceramic pastes—indicating more local manufacture of pottery vessels—and a general decline in the quality of artifacts.

The Petexbatun researchers (Demarest 1997; Dunning, Beach, and Rue 1997; Wright 1997) found that the agricultural and other subsistence systems were well adapted to the various environmental niches. Furthermore, according to osteological findings by Lori Wright (1997), the people were well nourished, so that ecological disaster (including overuse of the land, overpopulation, and nutritional stress) were not found to be factors in the collapse in the area. Soil cores studied by Nick Dunning and colleagues (Dunning, Beach, and Rue 1997) found that there were no climatological changes, so climate change was also not found to be a causal factor in the Petexbatun collapse. The production and distribution of pottery in the Petexbatun region indicates that the changes in the economy followed from the political turmoil and warfare of the late eighth century (Foias and Bishop 1997).

By the mid-eighth century, defensive position was the main criterion for the location of settlements, with settlements being situated along the edge of the Petexbatun escarpment, which was defensible but still near good arable land. As time went on, defensibility became of paramount concern, as reflected in the hilltop locations of sites, which were then located at some distance from arable land but in optimally defensive locations.

In the drought model of the Classic Maya collapse, it was a lack of rainfall that was said to have caused crop failure, famine, and massive loss of life. Geographers base the model of climatic change on analysis of sediment from soil cores in several lakes in the Maya area. Pollen identified from the cores documents a change to drier-climate vegetation. Of course, the change in climate could have followed an ecological disaster instead of precipitating cultural changes. The leading proponents of the drought model are David Hodell, Jason Curtis, and Mark Brenner (1995) and Richardson Gill (2000). Demarest (2001) alleges that the political disintegration was complete in the Petexbatun before the proposed desiccation occurred and cautions that the emphasis on climate in Gill's book appears to be environmental determinism.

There are various other interpretations of the Classic Maya collapse (see Culbert 1973). An old view of the collapse that remains popular is the intrusion by Mexicanized Maya, perhaps the Putun Maya traders, from the Xicalango region of the western base of the Yucatan. Both Seibal and Altar de Sacrificios had non-Maya, perhaps Mexican, stylistic influences during the ninth century A.D. This is also the time of the spread of Fine Orange and Fine Gray pottery from the Gulf coast to the southern Maya lowlands. Perhaps the effects of foreign intrusion into the Maya lowlands can be better understood with reference to the fall of the great city of Teotihuacan by A.D. 700 and the subsequent scrambling for political and economic power throughout Mesoamerica.

Importantly, the Terminal Classic period saw the rise to prominence of two great powers in Mesoamerica, Tula north of Mexico City and Chichen Itza in the northern Maya lowlands (Chase and Rice 1985; see http://www.le.ac.uk/cgi-bin/lab_int/server/docs/ar/image_collection/images.tab?operation=retrieve&record=240).

Lessons from the Classic Maya Collapse

The collapse of the Classic period Maya civilization in the southern lowlands is a sobering reminder of the eventual fate of many civilizations and begs the question as to whether there are any parallels with modern Western civilization. Certainly, overpopulation and overuse of the land for agriculture are pressing issues in today's world that many believe were also instrumental in the fall of the Classic Maya civilization. The ancient Maya cut the rainforest for farming, leading to soil erosion, depletion of the soil nutrients, and subsequent use of less desirable swamp land for farming. These internal forces seem difficult to manage and control, and clearly the ancient Maya were not able to do so.

According to Arthur Demarest (1997), this ecological model does not explain the Classic Maya collapse. As previously outlined, his research in the Petexbatun region of Guatemala indicates that internecine warfare founded on escalating elite competition was spiraling out of control and led to the reallocation of resources and redirection of all activities toward defense. Certainly there are historic and modern parallels for the deleterious effects of warfare from ethnic, national, or international conflicts and competition. Whatever the factors precipitating Maya warfare, it did lead to their ultimate demise.

Perhaps more problematic in any culture's decline are external factors, such as invasion or climate change, that are unexpected and for which a culture is not prepared to deal. Changing vegetation patterns identified from soil cores in the Maya area point to sudden climatic changes at the end of the Classic period that may have precipitated the collapse or may have contributed in some way to the spiraling downfall (Gill 2000; Hodell, Curtis, and Brenner 1995). Whether there was a drought as some have argued, fluctuations in rainfall would have negatively impacted farming and the Late Classic Maya's ability to feed their society. Did the Classic Maya take steps to avert the effects of climate change? In coastal areas subject to sea level rise, buildings were raised onto stone platforms, and some low-lying locations were abandoned (McKillop 2002). Modern worldwide rise of sea level threatens to inundate low-lying coastal areas, including many heavily populated places. New Orleans is already below sea level and keeps its streets dry by pumping out water.

The collapse of the Classic Maya provides an opportunity for modern society to evaluate the consequences of increasing social, economic, and political complexity and the precarious relationship people have with the Earth's natural resources. In so doing, we may learn how to avert calamity in modern times.

THE TERMINAL CLASSIC FLORESCENCE IN THE NORTHERN MAYA LOWLANDS (A.D. 800–1000)

As the polities in the southern Maya lowlands collapsed and fell into obscurity, cities in the northern Maya lowlands rose to prominence. The impetus for the northern advances is unclear. Even some communities in the southern lowlands continued uninterrupted into the Postclassic. Among these, Lamanai, Santa Rita, and Wild Cane Cay are on waterways—an inland lagoon in the case of Lamanai, and the Caribbean for the others. Although some parts of the southern lowlands, such as Tikal and the northeastern Peten, were virtually abandoned, other nearby areas, such as the lakes district, experienced a continuity of settlement into the Postclassic. As work by Don and Prudence Rice (1990) has documented, there was a sharp population decline in the Terminal Classic period, but the population increased in the Early Postclassic period.

The diminution of the hinterland population after the collapse of Copan evidently was more gradual, occurring over several generations. According to David Webster (2002), one of the project directors of the Penn State Copan Project in the 1970s and 1980s, lesser nobility were vying for political control during the last reigns of the Copan dynasty. The lesser lords may have grasped power after the death of Yax Pac, the last king to leave hieroglyphic records on carved monuments at Copan. And people continued to live for several generations in the Copan hinterland, with migration and a gradually declining population ultimately contributing to the near abandonment of the area.

The ruins of Uxmal (Corel)

The Terminal Classic in the northern lowlands witnessed the development of distinctive Cehpech ceramics, a continuity of earlier architectural traditions and external influences in ceramics, architecture, and by inference, culture. Warfare must have become a common aspect of life, as many communities are fortified, and some, such as Chichen Itza, display battle scenes on buildings and stone carvings showing skull racks (presumably artistic renditions of decapitated war victims or sacrificial victims). Sacbes continued to be common roadways between northern communities. The use of sacbes as ritual pathways, avenues of opportunity for merchants, or even roads for moving armies is a matter of some discussion among Mayanists (Chase and Chase 2001; Cobos and Winemiller 2001).

The Puuc Hills region of the northern lowlands has rich agricultural soil and has settlement dating from Preclassic times, including a number of competing small cities. The area grew to prominence during the Terminal Classic, with important cities at Sayil (Sabloff and Tourtellot 1992), Edzna, Labna, Kabah, Chichen Itza, and Uxmal (Kowalski 2003). A wall surrounds Uxmal's major temples, the Great Pyramid and the House of the Magician, as well the Nunnery and other buildings. The wall and moat system built during the Late Preclassic around Edzna may still have been in use during the Terminal Classic at the site. Most of the Puuc cities fell into obscurity, though, perhaps due to warfare, with the exception of Chichen Itza, which became the principal power in the Maya lowlands.

The distinctive Puuc architectural style is evident in a number of well-preserved buildings. The Nunnery at Uxmal consists of four palaces enclosing a central square. According to Jeff Kowalski (2003), the building's iconography depicts the Maya world: The north building is elevated and has thirteen doors, representing the thirteen layers of heaven and celestial serpents. The south building is lower and has nine doors, representing the nine layers of Xibalba, the Maya underworld. The seven entrances on the west building represent the middle world, where the sun descends into Xibalba. It has depictions of the Earth god, Pauahtun, as a turtle. The Puuc architectural style is unmistakable in the ornateness of the building façades. Buildings there were constructed with thin stone façades made of small cut limestones over a rubble core. The façades include ornate patterns of frets, latticework, and mosaics with masks. Buildings include rows of columns, as well as round columns in doorways. Elsewhere in the Puuc area, there is a five-storied building at Edzna, a three-storied building replete with an elaborate façade and round columns at Sayil, and a magnificent arch set in an elaborate wall at Labna, drawn by Frederick Catherwood during his travels to Maya ruins with John Lloyd Stevens (1963, 1969).

CHICHEN ITZA

Significant and ongoing research at Chichen Itza leaves most questions about the ancient city unexplained. The central area of the city has been mapped, and many of the principal buildings were restored for tourism, largely due to work by the Carnegie Institution of Washington. In the focusing of their research interests on Uaxactun and their restoration interests on Chichen Itza, we are left with a preponderance of data on Uaxactun's Preclassic and Classic prehistory but relatively little on the cultural history of Chichen Itza, which dates mainly to the Postclassic. Several of the site's buildings are in the Puuc style, notably the Caracol, Nunnery, Temple of the Three Lintels, and Temple of the Four Lintels. Other buildings, such as the Temple of the Warriors, the great ball court, and El Castillo, are in the style of the Toltec capital of Tula in central Mexico. Mapping by Rafael Cobos and Terance Winemiller (2001) indicates that some fifty-five causeways connected various parts of the city. The causeways were constructed during two time periods, the Late Classic and the Terminal Classic, linking important buildings in each time period.

Despite much work at Chichen Itza, the age of the site and the degree of Toltec control or influence over the city are still in question. Much debate centers on whether or not the Toltec style of architecture at Chichen results from invaders from Tula. What was the impact, if any, of Mexicanized Maya traders or Putun Maya traders from the Gulf of Mexico coast? Frescoes in the Temple of the Warriors and low-relief carvings elsewhere at the site depict Toltec warriors and the capture of the city. The layout, the use of rows of columns, and the chacmool sacrificial stone (showing a reclining human figure with a flat area in his stomach to receive offerings) of the Temple of the Warriors closely resemble a building at Tula. The Tzompantli, with its rows of profile heads on skewers, is reminiscent of the Toltec emphasis on sacrifice (Ferguson and Adams 2001, 223). Stone carvings around the site are in Toltec style, and the use of large stone rings on the sides of the ball court is a Toltec and not Maya tradition.

Caracol at Chichen Itza (Courtesy T. Winemiller)

The glyph dates at Chichen Itza are in the Maya short count, which is restricted to a fifty-two-year cycle. Moreover, the hieroglyphs record ritual and
not history, and they record only a short time during the latter part of the tenth
century A.D. Hieroglyphs on lintels in the Nunnery and elsewhere at Chichen
Itza, as deciphered by Ruth Krochok (1988) and others, refer to dedication rituals and not to royal dynastic histories. They are restricted temporally to the latter part of the ninth century.

Controversy about the age of Chichen Itza centers on the dates of two major
ceramic complexes, the Cehpech and Sotuta, and on whether they are coeval,
partially overlap, or are sequential. Traditional ceramic analyses in the Yucatan
place Cehpech earlier than Sotuta, but stratigraphic excavations in which pottery from both ceramic complexes are found have challenged this sequence.
Unfortunately, only limited ceramic analysis at Chichen Itza has been carried
out (Lincoln 1985), so the answer to the age of Chichen Itza awaits further
excavations.

According to Fernando Robles and Anthony Andrews (1985), Chichen Itza
was established after A.D. 900 by foreigners who introduced a new ceramic
style, the Sotuta. By way of contrast, Arlen Chase (1985) contends that Cehpech

Tulum, Maya ceremonial center on Caribbean Sea, Yucatan, Mexico (Corel)

and Sotuta overlap substantially, perhaps entirely. George Bey's (Bey et al. 1998) analysis of ceramics from Ek Balam and other sites in the northern Maya lowlands indicates that Cehpech and Sotuta overlap. Most Maya ceramicists tend to follow this interpretation. Unfortunately, the overlap of Cehpech and Sotuta ceramics does not help address the age and duration of Puuc Maya and Toltec Maya architecture at Chichen Itza (see Sabloff and Andrews 1985).

MAYAPAN AND THE LATE POSTCLASSIC MAYA

The Late Postclassic period (A.D. 1250–1550) witnessed an expansion of settlement along the eastern coast of the Yucatan, for example at Tulum and Cozumel, as well as the rise to dominance of Mayapan in the interior of the northern Maya lowlands. Mayapan was a densely nucleated, walled city that dominated a multiplicity of independent polities in a loosely integrated federation. The city was mapped and excavated by Carnegie Institution of Washington archaeologists during the 1920s and 1930s as part of the Chichen Itza project (Pollock et al. 1962). According to historic texts (Kowalski 2003), provincial nobles were required to have residences in the capital at Mayapan. The elite residence compounds at Mayapan probably served this function (Kowalski 2003). Tatiana Proskouriakoff (Pollack et al. 1962) noted that the number of colonnaded buildings at Mayapan corresponds to the city's subject provinces, suggesting a cooperative government rather than a centralized authority. The Spaniards witnessed a decentralized political and economic organization in the northern Maya lowlands in the sixteenth century (Tozzer 1941). David

Freidel (1981) contrasts the decentralized organization of Mayapan with the centralized organization of earlier Chichen Itza, where elite residence and administration was centrally focused on three plaza groups around the major temple, the Castillo. By way of contrast, Mayapan's Castillo functioned as the location of an elite cult. By the time the Spaniards arrived in the sixteenth century, Mayapan had long been abandoned (likely around A.D. 1441) and the rest of the northern Maya lowlands was fragmented into small polities. At the time of Spanish contact, Maya communities were concentrated in the northwestern part of the Yucatan and along the northern and eastern coasts of the Yucatan.

Settlement continued and even expanded on Cozumel Island from the Terminal Classic through the Late Postclassic. The basic house plan at Mayapan and Tulum during the Late Postclassic included two rooms, with the front room being open. This pattern marked a change from the single rooms of earlier Chichen Itza and elsewhere. In addition to uniformity in house type, Mayapan is very nucleated compared to earlier communities. Bishop de Landa noticed the Mayapan two-room plan when he arrived in the Yucatan in the sixteenth century. According to Ed Kurjack (2003), an oval form was more common in buildings at Dzibilchaltun in the Late Preclassic, Late Classic, and Late Postclassic periods. Cozumel houses tended to be single rooms. The two-room-plan houses at Dzibilchaltun tended to be elite residences showing alliances with Mayapan, as at Cozumel and Isla Cilvituk (Freidel 1981).

The Late Postclassic was a time of outside contacts, trade, and, arguably, invasions in the Maya area. Coastal canoe trade around the Yucatan was extensive, with trading ports at Nito, Wild Cane Cay, Cozumel, and Tulum. The Maya at Santa Rita Corozal in northern Belize traded for turquoise, gold, and other exotics from beyond the Maya area. There is a widely discussed account of an alleged Maya trading canoe encountered by Columbus during his fourth voyage to the New World in 1502. However, this canoe was apparently not Maya but belonged to some local people from the north coast of Honduras, according to geographer Bill Davidson (1991).

THE SPANISH CONQUEST

Beginning with the arrival of Hernan Cortez in Mexico in 1519 and subsequent travels by other Spanish explorers, the Maya area was affected by religious, economic, and political changes imposed by the Spaniards that had devastating effects on indigenous populations. The earliest Spanish presence in the Yucatan was 1525. Native people were relocated to towns where Spanish churches were built, often on demolished indigenous temples. Natives were required to pay tribute to the conquerors in labor and goods. Historians (Jones 1989) have documented the decimation of the native populations by European diseases including smallpox, measles, and influenza, and the impact of relocation and tribute that resulted in the virtual elimination of some native groups and the dramatic diminution of their numbers elsewhere. The mission programs of the Franciscans and Dominicans in Mexico and Belize and of the Mercedarians in Honduras have been investigated by archaeological studies, aided by historic documents, at Tipu and Lamanai in Belize and in Honduras. These studies reveal the impact of colonialism and missionization on natives, not well documented by the Spaniards. Mexican churches have been mapped and investigated at Ek Balam by Craig Hanson (1995), and other locations in the Yucatan (Andrews 1991), including Dzibilchaltun and Xcaret.

The historic mission at Tipu in western Belize, established on the Maya community of Negroman in 1544, was the political center of the Dzuluinicob Province and grew cacao for trade and tribute (Graham, Pendergast, and Jones 1989). Robert Kautz (Graham, Jones, and Kautz 1985) found and partially excavated the church and mapped the surrounding area between 1980 and 1982. Elizabeth Graham's (1991) excavations from 1984 to 1987 included mapping and excavation of the historic area, with a team led by Mark Cohen excavating almost 600 burials associated with the church (see Jacobi 2000 for a summary of the church burials).

Tipu was a Maya community that was visited by Franciscan missionaries, who established a church and used the community as a point of embarkation to subdue the nearby Itza Maya in the Peten of Guatemala. Hundreds of Tipu Maya were interred in the church and its adjacent churchyard, lying on their backs facing east toward the altar of the church, as in Christian tradition. The presence of shroud pins further indicates that the bodies were prepared and wrapped with cloth in Christian tradition. The significant impact of the Spaniards is further indicated by Elizabeth Graham's excavations (Graham, Pendergast, and Jones 1989), which show a basic change in community patterns from the traditional Maya focus on the household patio group to the Spanish pattern of central square and streets.

The Tipu Maya accepted Christianity and maintained good relations with the visiting Franciscan friars until the Maya rebelled for unknown reasons during one of the friars' rare visits in 1638. The continuation of Christian burials in the church indicates that Christianity made an impact on the indigenous religious practices. The historic architecture from this period marked a dramatic change from the earlier styles. The old Maya style of erecting buildings of stone or of pole and thatch on earth or rubble platforms faced with stone around a plaza was replaced by buildings placed directly on the ground. Some structures from this period were built on the demolished foundations of prehistoric platforms. Other departures were the use of cobblestone pavement for plazas and walkways, and the building of different type of houses, perhaps with roofed patios. The church was a rectangular structure with a thatch roof and open sides typical of the earliest Yucatecan churches.

Few European goods were brought to Tipu, probably due to its remote, frontier location. Majolica and olive jar sherds found around the church and plaza suggest that these pieces were used on a limited basis by visiting friars or Christianized Maya of high status. There was also a continuity of the prehistoric Maya ceramic tradition into historic times. Since there are no historic records describing the pottery styles, the cutoff between prehistoric Maya and the historic times when the Spaniards arrived is poorly understood. Among the European goods found have been rosary beads, silver earrings, metal needles, and coffin nails. Silver earrings and beads recovered from children's graves in the church suggested that Maya children had been a focus of proselytizing by the Franciscans, who had given them gifts.

During the 1970s and 1980s, David Pendergast excavated a Franciscan mission established after 1544 at the Maya community of Lamanai (Graham, Pendergast, and Jones 1989; Pendergast 1981; Pendergast 1985). In historic times, Maya were resettled at Lamanai from outlying areas in order to more easily convert and control the Maya. A small early church measuring 6 by 9 meters, with a thatched roof, earth floor, and partial masonry walls, was a blend of Spanish style and local building techniques. A later, larger church with a masonry chancel built in Spanish style reflects the growing role of Lamanai in the Spanish reduction system. The few European ceramics from excavations of a midden and historic building include Spanish olive jars and several Majolica sherds, but most of the pottery was a continuity of local Maya unpainted pots. The Spanish colonial mission at Lamanai was successful in converting the Maya to Catholicism, but it had little impact on the economy and politics of the community, which remained unchanged in settlement patterns beyond the church and associated warehouse or convent. After the 1638 uprising, visiting friars Fuensaldia and Orbita found the church and associated buildings burned and abandoned during their visit in 1641, marking the end of Spanish influence at Lamanai. Some Maya fled Chichen Itza before the city fell and they established a new town in the Peten of Guatemala where the modern community of Flores is located. After several unsuccessful attempts by the Spaniards to conquer and convert these "Itza" Maya, they were subdued in 1697.

Limited attention has been directed to archaeology studying later periods in Central America. David Pendergast (1985) reported a nineteenth-century sugar mill and settlement at Lamanai. A regional survey and mapping project in the Yaxcaba region of the Yucatan, Mexico, by Rani Alexander (1998) examined the surface evidence for the Spanish impact on native populations from 1750 until 1847, beginning with the population increase associated with the introduction of large haciendas, until the Caste War of the Yucatan. She mapped a pueblo, hacienda, and independent ranch to examine acculturation of Yucatec Maya.

Charles Cheek (1997) reported on ceramics found at Campamento and another site near Trujillo, Honduras. The descendants of Garifuna, or Black Caribs (descendents of African slaves and native Carib Inidans from the Caribbean and South America), who had been deported by the British from St. Vincent's Island in the Caribbean in 1799, dominated the area. A relatively high proportion of English tea wares in the artifact inventories was attributed to the Garifunas's intent to identify ethnically with the British.

Fieldwork in Port Honduras Marine Reserve and Paynes Creek National Park region of southern Belize revealed historic camps attributed to the nineteenth- and early twentieth-century mahogany industry in the Deep River area at Muschamp Creek and Pineapple Grove. In addition, a nineteenth- to twentieth-century fishing community was identified on the Maya site of Wild Cane Cay (McKillop 2005; McKillop and Roberts 2003).

The burgeoning field of historical archaeology in Central America has focused since its inception in the 1970s on the colonial period, particularly the impact of missions on the native populations, which is not well articulated in

Spanish documents. The historical archaeology of Central America will ultimately be better understood within a broader context of Spanish and British colonialism in the Americas. Despite the collapse of the Classic Maya civilization of the southern Maya lowlands by A.D. 900 and the later rise and fall of cities in the northern Maya lowlands, the Maya people continued to live throughout the Maya area. The Maya still practice their traditional way of village farming today.

REFERENCES

Adams, Richard E. W. 1971. *The Ceramics of Altar de Sacrificios.* Papers of the Peabody Museum of Archaeology and Ethnology, vol. 63, no. 1. Cambridge, MA: Harvard University.

Alexander, Rani. 1998. "Community Organization in the Parroquia de Yaxcaba, Yucatan, Mexico, 1750–1847: Implications for Household Adaptation within a Changing Colonial Economy." *Ancient Mesoamerica* 9: 39–54.

Andrews, Anthony P. 1991. "The Rural Chapels and Churches of Early Colonial Yucatan and Belize: An Archaeological Perspective." In *Columbian Consequences,* vol. 3, edited by David Hurst Thomas, 355–374. Washington, DC: Smithsonian Institution Press.

Ashmore, Wendy, ed. 1981. *Lowland Maya Settlement Patterns.* Albuquerque: University of New Mexico Press.

Awe, Jaime, Cassandra Bill, Mark Campbell, and David Cheetham. 1990. "Early Middle Formative Occupation in the Central Maya Lowlands: Recent Evidence from Cahal Pech, Belize." Papers from the Institute of Archaeology 1: 1–5, London: University College London.

Bey, George J., III, Tara M. Bond, William M. Ringle, Craig A. Hanson, Charles W. Houck, and Carlos Peraza Lope. 1998. "The Ceramic Chronology of Ek Balam, Yucatan, Mexico." *Ancient Mesoamerica* 9: 101–120.

Blake, Michael, B. Chisholm, John Clark, Barbara Voorhies, and Michael Love. 1992a. "Prehistoric Subsistence in the Soconusco Region." *Current Anthropology* 33: 83–94.

Blake, Michael, John Clark, B. Chisholm, and K. Mudar. 1992b. "Non-Agricultural Staples and Agricultural Supplements: Early Formative Subsistence in the Soconusco Region, Mexico." In *Transitions to Agriculture in Prehistory,* edited by A. B. Gebauer and T. Douglas Price, 133–152. Madison, WI: Prehistory Press.

Brady, James E., Joseph W. Ball, Ronald L. Bishop, Duncan C. Pring, Norman Hammond, and Rupert A. Housley. 1998. "The Lowland Maya 'Protoclassic:' A Reconsideration of its Nature and Significance." *Ancient Mesoamerica* 9: 17–38.

Braswell, Geoffrey E., ed. 2003. *The Maya and Teotihuacan: Reinterpreting Early Classic Interaction.* Austin: University of Texas Press.

Campbell, Lyle R. 1984. "The Implications of Mayan Historical Linguistics for Glyphic Research." In *Phoneticism in Mayan Hieroglyphic Writing,* edited by John Justeson and Lyle Campbell, 1–16. Institute for Mesoamerican Studies Publication 9. Albany: State University of New York.

Chase, Arlen F., and Diane Z. Chase. 2001. "Ancient Maya Causeways and Site Organization at Caracol, Belize." *Ancient Mesoamerica* 12: 273–281.

Chase, Arlen F., and Prudence M. Rice, eds. 1985. *The Lowland Maya Postclassic.* Austin: University of Texas Press.

Cheek, Charles. 1997. "Setting an English Table: Black Carib Archaeology on the Caribbean Coast of Honduras." In *Approaches to the Historical Archaeology of Mexico, Central, and South America,* edited by Jan Gasco, Greg C. Smith, and Patricia Fournier-

Garcia, 101–109. Los Angeles: Costen Institute of Archaeology, University of California.

Christie, Jessica J., ed. 2003. *Maya Palaces and Elite Residences*. Austin: University of Texas Press.

Clancy, Flora, and Peter D. Harrison, eds. 1990. *Vision and Revision in Maya Studies*. Albuquerque: University of New Mexico Press.

Clark, John E. 1994. "The Development of Early Formative Ranked Societies in the Soconusco, Chiapas, Mexico." Ph.D. dissertation, Department of Anthropology, University of Michigan, Ann Arbor.

Clark, John E., and Richard Hansen. 2001. "The Architecture of Early Kingship: Comparative Perspectives on the Origin of the Maya Royal Court." In *Royal Courts of the Ancient Maya*, Vol. 2, edited by Takeshi Inomata and Stephen Houston, 1–45. Boulder, CO: Westview.

Cobos, Raphael, and Terance L. Winemiller. 2001. "The Late and Terminal Classic-Period Causeway Systems of Chichen Itza, Yucatan, Mexico." *Ancient Mesoamerica* 12: 283–291.

Coe, Michael D., and Kent V. Flannery. 1967. *Early Cultures and Human Ecology in South Coastal Guatemala*. Washington, DC: Smithsonian Institution Press.

Coe, Michael D., and Mark Van Stone. 2001. *Reading the Maya Glyphs*. New York: Thames & Hudson.

Culbert, T. Patrick, ed. 1973. *The Classic Maya Collapse*. Albuquerque: University of New Mexico Press.

———. 1991. *Classic Maya Political History: Hieroglyphic and Archaeological Evidence*. Albuquerque: University of New Mexico Press.

Culbert, T. Patrick, and Don S. Rice, eds. 1990. *Precolumbian Population History in the Maya Lowlands*. Albuquerque: University of New Mexico Press.

Davidson, William V. 1991. "Geographical Perspectives on Spanish-Pech (Paya) Indian Relationships, Northeast Honduras, Sixteenth Century." In *Columbian Consequences*, vol. 3, edited by David Hurst Thomas, 205–226. Washington, DC: Smithsonian Institution Press.

Demarest, Arthur. 1997. "The Vanderbilt Petexbatun Regional Archaeological Project 1989–1994: Overview, History, and Major Results of a Multidisciplinary Study of the Classic Maya Collapse." *Ancient Mesoamerica* 8: 209–227.

———. 2001. "Climatic Change and the Classic Maya Collapse: The Return of Catastrophism." *Latin American Antiquity* 12: 105–123.

Dull, Robert A., John R. Southon, and Payson Sheets. 2001. "Volcanism, Ecology, and Culture: A Reassessment of the Volcán Ilopango TBJ Eruption in the Southern Maya Realm." *Latin American Antiquity* 12: 25–44.

Dunning, Nicholas, Timothy Beach, and David Rue. 1997. "The Paleoecology and Ancient Settlement of the Petexbatun Region, Guatemala." *Ancient Mesoamerica* 8: 255–266.

Estrada-Belli, Francisco. 1999. *The Archaeology of Complex Societies in Southeastern Pacific Coastal Guatemala: A Regional GIS Approach*. Oxford: British Archaeology Reports, International Series 820.

Fagan, Brian. 1987. *The Great Journey: The Peopling of Ancient America*. New York: Thames & Hudson.

Fash, William. 2001. *Scribes, Warriors, and Kings*, 2d ed. New York: Thames & Hudson.

Ferguson, William M., and Richard E. W. Adams. 2001. *Mesoamerica's Ancient Cities*, rev. ed. Albuquerque: University of New Mexico Press.

Flannery, Kent V., and Joyce Marcus. 2003. "The Origin of War: New 14C Dates from Ancient Mexico." *Proceedings of the National Academy of Sciences* 100: 11801–11805.

Foias, Antonia E., and Ronald L. Bishop. 1997. "Changing Ceramic Production and Ex-change in the Petexbatun Region, Guatemala: Reconsidering the Classic Maya Collapse." *Ancient Mesoamerica* 8: 275–291.

Freidel, David A. 1979. "Culture Areas and Interaction Spheres: Contrasting Approaches to the Emergence of Civilization in the Maya Lowlands." *American Antiquity* 44: 36–54.

———. 1981. "The Political Economics of Residential Dispersion among the Lowland Maya." In *Lowland Maya Settlement Patterns,* edited by Wendy Ashmore, 371–382. Albuquerque: University of New Mexico Press.

———. 1992. "Children of the First Father's Skull: Terminal Classic Warfare in the Northern Maya Lowlands and the Transformation of Kingship and Elite Hierarchies." In *Mesoamerican Elites: An Archaeological Assessment,* edited by Diane Z. Chase and Arlen F. Chase, 99–117. Norman: University of Oklahoma Press.

Freidel, David A., and Linda Schele. 1988. "Kingship in the Late Preclassic Maya Lowlands: The Instruments and Places of Ritual Power." *American Anthropologist* 90: 547–567.

Garber, James F., ed. 2004. *The Ancient Maya of the Belize Valley.* Gainesville: University Press of Florida.

Garber, James F., Jaime J. Awe, M. Kathryn Brown, and Christopher J. Hartman. 2004. "Middle Formative Prehistory of the Central Belize Valley: An Examination of Architecture, Material Culture, and Sociopolitical Change at Blackman Eddy." In *The Ancient Maya of the Belize Valley,* edited by James F. Garber, 25–47. Gainesville: University Press of Florida.

Gifford, James C. 1976. *Prehistoric Pottery Analysis and the Ceramics of Barton Ramie in the Belize Valley.* Papers of the Peabody Museum of Archaeology and Ethnology, vol. 18. Cambridge, MA: Harvard University.

Gill, Richardson. 2000. *The Great Maya Droughts.* Albuquerque: University of New Mexico Press.

Gonzalez-Oliver, Angelica, Lourdes Marquez-Morfin, Jose C. Jimenez, and Alfonso Torre-Blanco. 2001. "Founding Amerindian Mitochondrial DNA Lineages in Ancient Maya from Xcaret, Quintana Roo." *American Journal of Physical Anthropology* 116: 230–235.

Graham, Elizabeth A. 1991. "Archaeological Insights into Colonial Period Maya Life at Tipu, Belize," In *Columbian Consequences,* vol. 3, edited by David H. Thomas, 319–335. Washington, DC: Smithsonian Institution Press.

———. 1994. *The Highlands of the Lowlands: Environment and Archaeology in the Stann Creek District, Belize, Central America.* Monographs in World Archaeology 19. Madison, WI: Prehistory Press.

Graham, Elizabeth, Grant D. Jones, and Robert R. Kautz. 1985. "Archaeology and Ethnohistory on a Spanish Colonial Frontier: An Interim Report on the Macal-Tipu Project in Western Belize." In *The Lowland Maya Postclassic,* edited by Arlen F. Chase and Prudence M. Rice, 206–214. Austin: University of Texas Press.

Graham, Elizabeth, David M. Pendergast, and Grant D. Jones. 1989. "On the Fringes of Conquest: Maya-Spanish Contact in Colonial Belize." *Science* 246: 1254–1259.

Grove, David. 1997. "Olmec Archaeology: A Half Century of Research and Its Accomplishments." *Journal of World Prehistory* 11: 51–101.

Haggett, Peter. 1965. *Locational Analysis in Human Geography.* London: Edward Arnold.

Hammond, Norman, ed. 1991. *Cuello.* New York: Cambridge University Press.

Hansen, Richard D. 1984. "Excavation on Structure 34 and the Tigre Area, El Mirador, Peten, Guatemala: A New Look at the Preclassic Lowland Maya." Master's thesis, Department of Anthropology, Brigham Young University, Provo, UT.

————. 1991. "The Maya Rediscovered: The Road to Nakbe." *Natural History* 91 (5): 8–14.

Hanson, Craig A. 1995. "The Hispanic Horizon in Yucatan: A Model of Franciscan Missionization." *Ancient Mesoamerica* 6: 15–28.

Harrison, Peter D. 1999. *The Lords of Tikal.* New York: Thames & Hudson.

Healy, Paul F., and Jaime J. Awe. 2001. "Middle Preclassic Jade Spoon from Belize." *Mexicon* 23: 61–64.

Hester, Thomas R., Harry B. Iceland, Dale B. Hudler, and Harry B. Shafer. 1996. "The Colha Preceramic Project: Preliminary Results from the 1993–1995 Field Seasons." *Mexicon* 18: 45–50.

Hodell, David A., Jason H. Curtis, and Mark Brenner. 1995. "Possible Role of Climate in the Collapse of Classic Maya Civilization." *Nature* 375: 391–394.

Houston, Stephen, Oswaldo Chinchilla Mazariegos, and David Stuart, eds. 2001. *The Decipherment of Ancient Maya Writing.* Norman: University of Oklahoma Press.

Iceland, Harry B. 1997. "The Preceramic Origins of the Maya: The Results of the Colha Preceramic Project in Northern Belize." Ph.D. dissertation, Department of Anthropology, University of Texas, Austin.

Inomata, Takeshi. 1997. "The Last Day of a Fortified Maya Center: Archaeological Investigations at Aguateca, Guatemala." *Ancient Mesoamerica* 8: 337–351.

Inomata, Takeshi, and Kazuo Aoyama. 1996. "Central-Place Analysis in the La Entrada Region, Honduras: Implications for Understanding the Classic Maya Political and Economic Systems." *Latin American Antiquity* 7: 291–312.

Jacobi, Keith P. 2000. *Last Rites for the Tipu Maya: Genetic Structuring in a Colonial Cemetery.* Tuscaloosa: University of Alabama Press.

Jones, Grant D. 1989. *Maya Resistance to Spanish Rule: Time and History on a Colonial Frontier.* Albuquerque: University of New Mexico Press.

Jones, John. 1994. "Pollen Evidence for Early Settlement and Agriculture in Northern Belize." *Palynology* 18: 205–211.

Justeson, John S., and Lyle Campbell, eds. 1984. *Phoneticism in Mayan Hieroglyphic Writing.* Institute for Mesoamerican Studies, Publication 9. Albany: State University of New York.

Kelly, Thomas C. 1993. "Preceramic Projectile-Point Typology in Belize." *Ancient Mesoamerica* 4: 205–227.

Kidder, Alfred V., Jessie D. Jennings, and Edwin M. Shook. 1946. *Excavations at Kaminaljuyu, Guatemala.* Carnegie Institution of Washington, Publication 561. Washington, DC: Carnegie Institution of Washington.

Kosakowsky, Laura J. 1987. *Preclassic Maya Pottery at Cuello, Belize.* Anthropological Papers of the University of Arizona 47. Tucson: University of Arizona Press.

Kosakowsky, Laura, Francisco Estrada-Belli, and Hector Neff. 1999. "Late Preclassic Ceramic Interaction Spheres: The Pacific Coast as Love, Not Periphery." *Journal of Field Archaeology* 26: 377–390.

Kowalski, Jeff. 2003. "Evidence for the Functions and Meanings of Some Northern Maya Palaces." In *Maya Palaces and Elite Residences,* edited by Jessica J. Christie, 204–252. Austin: University of Texas Press.

Kurjack, Edward B. 2003. "Palace and Society in the Northern Maya Lowlands." In *Maya Palaces and Elite Residences,* edited by Jessica J. Christie, 274–290. Austin: University of Texas Press

Lincoln, Charles. 1985. "The Chronology of Chichen Itza: A Review of the Literature." In *Late Lowland Maya Civilization,* edited by Jeremy A. Sabloff and E. Wyllys Andrews V, 141–196. Albuquerque: University of New Mexico Press.

Marcus, Joyce. 1976. *Emblem and State in the Classic Maya Lowlands.* Washington, DC: Dumbarton Oaks.

———. 1993. "Ancient Maya Political Organization." In *Lowland Maya Archaeology in the Eighth Century A.D.,* edited by Jeremy A. Sabloff and John S. Henderson, 111–183. Washington, DC: Dumbarton Oaks Research Library and Collections.

Martin, Paul S. 1973. "The Discovery of America." *Science* 179: 969–974.

Martin, Simon, and Nicholai Grube. 2000. *Chronicle of the Maya Kings and Queens: Deciphering the Dynasties of the Ancient Maya.* New York: Thames & Hudson.

McAnany, Patricia A. 1995. *Living with the Ancestors.* Austin: University of Texas Press.

McKillop, Heather. 2002. *Salt: White Gold of the Ancient Maya.* Gainesville: University Press of Florida.

———. 2005. *In Search of Maya Sea Traders.* College Station: University of Texas Press.

McKillop, Heather, and Erika Roberts. 2003. *Nineteenth-Century Settlement of the Port Honduras Coast, Southern Belize.* Unpublished manuscript.

Merwin, Raymond E., and George C. Vaillant. 1932. *The Ruins of Holmul, Guatemala.* Memoirs of the Peabody Museum of Archaeology and Ethnology, vol. 3, no. 2. Cambridge, MA: Harvard University.

Miksicek, Charles H. 1991. "The Ecology and Economy of Cuello." In *Cuello: An Early Maya Community in Belize,* edited by Norman Hammond, 70–97. New York: Cambridge University Press.

Pendergast, David M. 1981. "Lamanai, Belize: Summary of Excavation Results 1974–1980." *Journal of Field Archaeology* 8: 29–53.

———. 1985. "Stability Through Change: Lamanai, Belize, from the Ninth to the Seventeenth Century." In *Late Lowland Maya Civilization,* edited by Jeremy Sabloff and E. Wyllys Andrews V, 223–249. Albuquerque: University of New Mexico Press.

Pohl, Mary D., Kevin O. Pope, John G. Jones, John S. Jacob, Dolores R. Piperno, Susan D. deFrance, David L. Lentz, John A. Gifford, Marie E. Danforth, and J. Kathryn Josserand. 1996. "Early Agriculture in the Maya Lowlands." *Latin American Antiquity* 7: 355–372.

Pollock, Harry E. D., Ralph L. Roys, Tatiana Proskouriakoff, and A. Ledyard Smith. 1962. *Mayapan, Yucatan, Mexico.* Carnegie Institution of Washington Publication 619. Washington, DC: Carnegie Institution of Washington.

Proskouriakoff, Tatiana. 1960. "Historical Implications of a Pattern of Dates at Piedras Negras, Guatemala." *American Antiquity* 25: 454–475.

Rathje, William L. 1971. "The Origin and Development of Lowland Classic Maya Civilization." *American Antiquity* 36: 275–285.

Reents-Budet, Dorie. 1994. *Painting the Maya Universe.* Duke University Press, Durham.

Rice, Don S., and Prudence M. Rice. 1990. "Population Size and Population Change in the Central Peten Lakes Region, Guatemala." In *Precolumbian Population History in the Maya Lowlands,* edited by T. Patrick Culbert and Don S. Rice, 123–148. Albuquerque: University of New Mexico Press.

Ricketson, Oliver G., Jr., and Edith B. Ricketson. 1937. *Uaxactun, Guatemala, Group E, 1926–1937.* Carnegie Institution of Washington Publication 477. Washington, DC: Carnegie Institution of Washington.

Robertson, Robin A., and David A. Freidel, eds. 1986. *Archaeology at Cerros, Belize, Central America,* vol. 1:, *An Interim Report.* Dallas: Southern Methodist University Press.

Robles, Fernando, and Anthony P. Andrews. 1985. "A Review and Synthesis of Recent Postclassic Archaeology in Northern Yucatan." In *Late Lowland Maya Civilization,* edited by Jeremy A. Sabloff and E. Wyllys Andrews V., 53–98. Albuquerque: University of New Mexico Press.

Sabloff, Jeremy A. 1975. *Excavations at Seibal, Guatemala, Department of the Peten, Guatemala: The Ceramics.* Memoirs of the Peabody Museum of Archaeology and Ethnology, vol. 13, no. 2. Cambridge, MA: Harvard University.

————, ed. 2003. *Tikal: Dynasties, Foreigners, and Affairs of State*. Santa Fe, NM: School of American Research Press.

Sabloff, Jeremy A., and E. Wyllys Andrews V, eds. 1985. *Late Lowland Maya Civilization: Classic to Postclassic*. Albuquerque: University of New Mexico Press.

Sabloff, Jeremy, and Gair Tourtellot. 1992. "Beyond Temples and Palaces: Recent Settlement Pattern Research at the Ancient Maya City of Sayil (1983–1985)." In *New Theories on the Ancient Maya*, edited by Elin C. Danien and Robert J. Sharer, 155–160. Philadelphia: University Museum, University of Pennsylvania.

Sanders, William T. 1977. "Environmental Heterogeneity and the Evolution of Lowland Maya Civilization." In *The Origins of Maya Civilization*, edited by Richard E. W. Adams, 287–297. Albuquerque: University of New Mexico Press.

Sanders, William T., and Joseph W. Michels, eds. 1977. *Teotihuacan and Kaminaljuyu: A Study in Prehistoric Culture Contact*. University Park: Pennsylvania State University Press.

Saturno, William. 2003. *Proyecto San Bartolo*. http://www.sanbartolo.org/index.htm.

Scarborough, Vernon L. 1998. "Ecology and Ritual: Water Management and the Maya." *Latin American Antiquity* 9: 135–159.

————. 2003. *The Flow of Power: Ancient Water Systems and Landscapes*. Sante Fe, NM: School of American Research Press.

Shafer, Harry J., and Thomas R. Hester. 1983. "Ancient Maya Chert Workshops in Northern Belize, Central America." *American Antiquity* 48: 519–543.

Sharer, Robert J. 1978. "Summary of Architecture and Construction Activity." In *The Prehistory of Chalchuapa, El Salvador*, vol. 1, edited by Robert J. Sharer, 121–132. Philadelphia: University of Pennsylvania Press.

Sheets, Payson, ed. 2002. *Before the Volcano Erupted: The Ancient Ceren Village in Central America*. Austin: University of Texas Press.

Stephens, John Lloyd. [1843] 1963. *Incidents of Travel in Yucatan*. 2 vols. New York: Dover.

————. [1841] 1969. *Incidents of Travel in Central America, Chiapas, and Yucatan* New York: Dover.

Tozzer, Alfred M., trans. 1941. *Landa's "Relación de las Cosas de Yucatan."* Papers of the Peabody Museum of Archaeology and Ethnology, vol. 18. Cambridge, MA: Harvard University.

Valdes, Juan Antonio. 1986. "Uaxactun: Recientes Investigaciones." *Mexicon* 7 (6): 125–128.

Valdes, Juan Antonio, and Jonathan Kaplan. 2000. "Ground-Penetrating Radar at the Maya Site of Kaminaljuyu, Guatemala." *Journal of Field Archaeology* 27: 329–342.

Voorhies, Barbara. 1976. *The Chantuto People: An Archaic Period Society of the Chiapas Littoral, Mexico*. Papers of the New World Archaeological Foundation 41. Provo, UT: Brigham Young University.

Webster, David. 2002. *The Fall of the Ancient Maya*. New York: Thames & Hudson.

Whittington, E. Michael, ed. 2001. *The Sport of Life and Death: The Mesoamerican Ballgame*. New York: Thames & Hudson.

Willey, Gordon R. 1973. *The Altar de Sacrificios Excavations: General Summary and Conclusions*. Papers of the Peabody Museum of Archaeology and Ethnology, vol. 64, no. 3. Cambridge, MA: Harvard University.

————. 1990. *Excavations at Seibal: General Summary and Conclusions*. Memoirs of the Peabody Museum of Archaeology and Ethnology, vol. 14, no. 4. Cambridge, MA: Harvard University.

Wright, Lori E. 1997. "Biological Perspectives on the Collapse of the Pasion Maya." *Ancient Mesoamerica* 8: 267–273.

CHAPTER 5

Economics

Perhaps no other aspect of Maya archaeology has received so much attention and yielded so much controversy as the nature of the ancient Maya economy. In very general terms, the ancient Maya economy consisted of the prestige or ritual economy and the subsistence economy. These two spheres of the economy may have had different systems of production, distribution (including trade), and use. Although Maya scribes were prolific in their accounts of political and genealogical aspects of the Classic Maya royal dynasties, the hieroglyphs contain little information about the Maya economy. Even the painted pictorial scenes on Late Classic vases only indirectly point to the economy—they might, for example, depict a royal personage receiving a bundle of chocolate, perhaps as tribute from a subservient lord. Certainly, opinions about the dynamics of the prestige and subsistence economies vary dramatically among scholars.

Mayanists agree that the prestige economy included the production, distribution, and use of goods and resources for the royal Maya and other elites. Although royal Maya used prestige items during their lifetimes, archaeologists recover most prestige goods from burials, where they were placed as offerings. Prestige goods also come from caches associated with the dedication or termination of a building's use. These items were often highly crafted. They were sometimes made from imported materials such as jade or marine shells. Prestige items were used in elite rituals, as is known from pictorial depictions on painted pots and on carved monuments. In fact, these good's rarity—due to their exotic origin, high degree of craftsmanship, or both—helped to denote, reinforce, and effectively create the higher status of the Maya royalty and other elite Maya personages. The public display and burial of highly crafted and nonlocal items by Maya royalty reminded the general public of their own lower status and provided symbols of status enhancement to emulate. For example, the largest carved jade item in the Maya lowlands, weighing almost 4.4 kilograms, is a representation of the head of Kinich Ahau, the sun god, which was taken out of view and use by the living to be buried in a royal tomb in a temple at Altun Ha, Belize (Pendergast 1979).

The subsistence economy, on the other hand, refers to goods and resources for basic daily use by all classes of Maya society. Subsistence items, or their residual remains, are often found in garbage heaps where they were discarded from household use. Certainly everyone, from the dynastic leaders to the common Maya, needed subsistence goods and resources such as food and tools for basic daily needs. So, it is quite clear who used and benefited from both

Seated chief (Ah Cacau), from cylindrical vase, polychrome, Late Classic burial 116 from Temple 1 at Tikal, A.D. 600–900, Guatemala (detail) (The Art Archive / Archaeological Museum Tikal Guatemala/Dagli Orti)

Sites mentioned in the text about workshops and economic specialization

Structure of society in Maya civilization, pictorial chart (The Art Archive/National Anthropological Museum Mexico/Dagli Orti)

prestige and subsistence goods. However, less clear is who controlled the production and distribution of these items at any given time in Maya prehistory.

Systems of Maya production and distribution, including trade, became more complex over time, mirroring the growth and development of the ancient civilization. The earliest Maya farmers living in modest villages such as Cuello in northern Belize relied on the household as the basic unit of production for food, pottery, and other goods (Hammond 1991). Even at this early time during the Middle Preclassic (beginning about 1000 B.C.), long-distance trade networks had been established. Jaime Awe and Paul Healy (1994) of Trent University in Canada document obsidian from the Maya highlands of Guatemala being found at Cahal Pech, Belize. As with trade in egalitarian societies elsewhere, the obsidian was likely traded "down the line" by reciprocal exchanges between relatives in adjacent villages, ultimately resulting in the long-distance movement of obsidian from outcrops in the southern Maya highlands of Guatemala to communities in the Maya lowlands.

During the succeeding Late Preclassic period, between 300 B.C. and A.D. 300, production and distribution became more complex with the rise of cities such as Cerros, Calakmul, Dzibilchaltun, El Mirador, Uaxactun, Lamanai, and Tikal—and even earlier at Nakbe, Guatemala. At Cerros there is evidence for more intensive agriculture that may have required community organization

(Scarborough 1991). The construction of large-scale public buildings indicates a growing division within Maya society between the rulers who used the buildings and the common Maya. It was the common Maya's labor that built the temples and supplied the food for the rulers. In turn, the rulers organized public rituals and ceremonies related to the agricultural cycle, the origins of the world, and people's place in the world. On these and other occasions, the Maya elite displayed exotic and highly crafted goods not available to the common Maya that further reinforced the growing social and economic divisions within society. The imported obsidian and jade were concentrated in elite burials and offerings, suggesting a growing inequality of access to luxury goods. An offering of jade beads carved into the shape of human heads was recovered from a temple at Cerros by the site's investigator, David Freidel (1979).

The Classic period witnessed the development of a variety of intensive agricultural systems and other food procurement systems to meet the needs of a growing population (Harrison and Turner 1978; Turner and Harrison 1983). At the height of the civilization during the Late Classic, between A.D. 600 and 900, the elite may have had preferential access to imported foods from the sea as well as to local foods, as reflected in heights measured from skeletons and in differences in the bone chemistry of elites and commoners (White 1999; Whittington and Reed 1997).

The Classic period also saw the rise of royal scribes and other specialized craft workers attached to royal Maya households, making fancy painted pots, clothing, and other ritual goods (Coe and Kerr 1998; Inomata 2001; Masson and Freidel 2002; Reents-Budet 1994). In addition, there was production by others elsewhere of more mundane goods, such as stone tools and salt cakes, to meet the daily needs of the masses (Shafer and Hester 1983; McKillop 1995a; McKillop 2002).

Most Maya archaeologists see a correlation between political centralization and elite control over the economy. But how centralized was the ancient Maya economy in the hands of the urban elite—the Maya royalty—during the Classic period? The degree of elite control over the economy is an important question central to the debate on the nature of Maya political organization during the Classic period: Was the Maya state centralized, with the urban elite having control over the economy (Chase and Chase 1996; Fox and Cook 1996; Marcus 1993)? Alternatively, were Maya states only weakly integrated, with less central control and management of the economy by the urban elite within each polity and with little integration between polities (Ball and Taschek 1991; Demarest 1996; Freidel 1981; Houston 1993; Schele and Freidel 1990; Schele and Mathews 1991)? A third and more likely possibility is that there was geographic variation in the level of centralized elite urban Maya control of both politics and the economy—as suggested, for example, in Marcus's (1993) "dynamic" model of fluctuations over time. Certainly a higher level of centralized political control is evident in the central Maya lowlands, including Tikal, Naranjo, and eastward to Caracol, than is evident farther north in the Yucatan or east in Belize. Furthermore, trading ports such as Wild Cane Cay operated independently from the polity capitals of Nim li punit or Lubaantun during the Late Classic period. In some cases, such as for salt on the southern coast of

Belize or high-quality chert outcrops at Colha, the distribution of natural resources did not coincide with the location of polity capitals, so that one might also argue for decentralization of economic control of production in the subsistence economy (McKillop 2002).

Those who support a centralized view of the Maya economy argue that the elite controlled both the prestige and subsistence economies. Those who believe that the Maya economy was more decentralized believe that only the prestige economy was managed by the upper class. These contrasting views reflect the continuing debates over various parts of the Classic Maya economy: the degree of craft specialization; the scale of intraregional and interregional exchange; and the nature of exchange. Some have suggested the existence of a well-developed Maya middle class of craft specialists (Adams 1970; Shafer and Hester 1983; McKillop 2002). Others see a low degree of economic specialization, probably with crafts being done on a part-time basis (Abrams 1987; Ball 1993; Fry 1979; Fry 1980; McAnany 1989a; McAnany 1989b; McAnany and Isaac 1989; Rice 1987a). The amount of trade has been interpreted as low by some (Sanders and Price 1968), and as extensive by others (Shafer and Hester 1983; Shafer and Hester 1986; McAnany 1989a; McAnany 1989b; McKillop 1989). Furthermore, there is an ongoing argument about the nature of this exchange: was it market exchange (Fry 1979; Fry 1980), gift exchange and redistribution (Tourtellot and Sabloff 1972; Sabloff and Rathje 1975; Rice 1987), or both (Fry 1980)?

MAYA WORKSHOPS AND CRAFT PRODUCTION

Classic Maya workshops, where prestige and/or subsistence goods were manufactured, have rarely been identified (Adams 1970; Becker 1973; Foias and Bishop 1997; Fry 1980; McKillop 1995a; McKillop 2002; Rice 1987a; Rice 1987b; Shafer and Hester 1983). Occupational specialization certainly existed among the Classic Maya: skilled workers were needed for construction (Abrams 1994), quarrying (Winemiller 1997), production of the most finely made painted pots and stone tools, and for creating written records on paper, stelae, architecture, pottery, and other objects (Adams 1970; Becker 1973; Fash 2001; Inomata 2001; Joyce 2000; McKillop 2002; Reents-Budet 1994; Shafer and Hester 1983).

How specialized was the Classic Maya economy? Relatively few craft workers were needed to supply the limited number of highly crafted goods acquired by Maya royalty at lowland cities and left in their graves or depicted on pottery vessels and carved monuments. In contrast, the bulk of Maya craft production was geared to making utilitarian and ceremonial goods that were less highly crafted. These included polychrome pottery that had a wide distribution within elite Maya society as well as utilitarian stone tools, ceramics, salt, clothing, and other goods, including imports such as obsidian, for distribution to the Maya populace. But was this more mundane production carried out in separate workshops or just part of daily household activities? Relatively little research has focused on the production of utilitarian goods, the extraction of natural resources, and the integration of their production and distribution in the political economy of the Classic period dynastic rulers (Foias and Bishop

Maya Pots in Che Chem Ha Cave, Vaca Plateau, Maya Mountains, Belize, ca 1996
(Corbis/Kevin Schafer)

1997; Fry 1980; Rice 1987a; Shafer and Hester 1983). More is known about the production and distribution of the limited number of highly crafted goods for Maya royalty and the import of obsidian and other exotics from beyond the Maya lowlands where archaeologists have concentrated their efforts because of the ease of identifying them as trade goods.

Did the royal Maya control production and distribution of all craft goods, except those made within common households for their own residents' use? What if production was not state controlled? Did the Classic Maya have cottage industries, or were there separate workshops (Foias and Bishop 1997; McKillop 2002)? Was production associated with urban centers? If the production of craft goods was not in the cities, how did the royal Maya ensure a supply of the goods they wanted? Were there large-scale workshops where some goods were mass-produced, as Harry Shafer and Tom Hester (1983) suggest for stone tool manufacture at Colha? Or was workshop production of all goods—both prestige and subsistence—less intensive, even part-time, with relatively few goods being produced, as at Copan (Fash 2001)?

Elaborately painted pots and other highly crafted items were used in royal rituals and public feasts. These events are depicted on painted pottery and on carved monuments, sometimes accompanied by hieroglyphic inscriptions describing the ritual or feast (Coe 1978; Coe 1982; Reents-Budet 1994; Schele and

Carving of Ruler Eighteen Rabbit on stela at Copan, Honduras (Corel)

Miller 1986). Gifts often were given at such events. Dynastic leaders used feasts to establish, maintain, and solidify political and economic relationships (Leventhal 1990; Marcus 1995; Reents-Budet 1994; Schele and Miller 1986). Much of this gifting was with kings and queens who were the dynastic rulers of other city-states. The Quetzal Vase, found in a royal burial at Copan, was in the style of ceramics from Altun Ha, where it was likely made (Reents-Budet 1994, 338–339, plate 57). In addition to this horizontal movement of goods, there was vertical exchange to lesser lords who governed smaller towns, even villages, within a city-state. By the Late Classic, political relations among city-states were unstable and fragile. Diplomatic ties based on marriage and military alliances were celebrated by feasting. But alliances eventually succumbed to hostilities, border skirmishes, and ultimately endemic warfare throughout much of the southern Maya lowlands.

HOUSEHOLD PRODUCTION

Using the modern Maya as a model, researchers have concluded that the ancient Maya household was the basic unit of production for the subsistence economy. The houses are identified archaeologically by the distribution of low mounds over the landscape, the mounds shrouding the remains of stone or earth platforms that once supported pole and thatch structures. A house was periodically renovated, with the roof and walls being deliberately collapsed and a new foundation and building being constructed on the existing foundation, raising the building farther off the ground surface. The continuity of the dwelling locations over generations reflected, in part, the fact that family members were interred in the foundations and under the floors of houses, marking a material record of the family's ancestry and importance in relation to other households.

The household economy focused on the procurement of food and basic goods and resources related to the subsistence economy. Following the modern Maya model, each household had farmland that was planted in corn, beans, squash, and other foods. These slash and burn, or "milpa," fields were located at various distances from the household, as the system of milpa agriculture required periodic fallowing of the land due to depletion of the soil nutrients and increased growth of weeds. Depending on soil fertility, the fallow cycle might require the temporary abandonment of fields after as little as two years' planting and for a fallow period of ten or more years. This extensive system of agriculture was complemented by other food procurement systems, including kitchen gardens around the household, various other forms of intensive agriculture that may have required community cooperation, hunting wild animals, fishing, and gathering wild plant foods.

Although there is general agreement that the household was the unit for production of food resources, there is no consensus on organization of production of other subsistence goods and resources, such as pottery vessels, stone tools, salt, and clothing. In some cases, the subsistence economy may have focused on household production, but in other cases, production may have been in selected households, by community specialization (as is the case in the highlands of Guatemala today), or in seasonal workshops where craft workers produced goods either part-time or full-time. The production of everyday cooking pots may have been a household task, for example, whereas the production of pots for boiling brine to produce salt may have been carried out in nondomestic workshops (McKillop 2002). Traditional potters in highland Guatemala currently make cooking pots in household workshops for distribution throughout a community, so that not every household is engaged in pottery making (Reina and Hill 1978). Workshops for the production of stone tools made from locally occurring chert at the site of Colha in northern Belize were attached to households, but the large quantity of stone tools produced in each household far exceeded the needs of the family. The tools were distributed to other households at Colha and to other communities in northern Belize. In some instances, local chert was used in addition to the Colha chert tools, indicating that even the subsistence economy acted on several levels for the same resources. If the subsistence economy was not centrally controlled, how was it organized? Was production for daily subsistence needs part of household activities? Did the Maya have a "cottage industry" in which some households produced goods, such as water jars, beyond their own needs, for exchange within a community or beyond? Did independent craft workers work outside the home and outside of the geographic and political control of the urban elite?

Little attention has been paid to the gender division of labor within households. The modern Maya and those encountered by the Spaniards during the sixteenth century (Clark and Houston 1998) indicate a strict division of labor by gender, but this may not have been the case in antiquity, particularly during the Classic period civilization. Even though Wauchope (1938) has argued for continuity in the Maya household structure from ancient to modern times, it is hard to believe that the fundamental economic changes beyond the household did not impact the Maya household, especially after the Classic period collapse and European conquest, in particular. In any event, both the modern Maya and the ethnohistoric Maya encountered by the sixteenth-century Spaniards can be used only as a model to test against the archaeological record, not as an analogy to apply blindly. Archaeological evidence for the gender division of labor does exist, and some researchers have begun to draw the evidence together (Ardren 2002; Joyce 2000). Figurines from the Classic Maya island site of Jaina off the west coast of the Yucatan depict common Maya engaged in a variety of activities and, in particular, show women grinding corn on metates, weaving, and using pots. These activities are also depicted on figurine whistles that were common throughout the southern lowlands during the Late Classic period, particularly at Lubaantun, where both molds and figurines have been found. A promising avenue for future study of gender differences in activities would be examination of grave goods associated with men and with women.

CLASSIC MAYA WORKSHOPS

As mentioned previously, relatively few workshops have been identified in the Maya lowlands, and in fact, relatively few areas of production activity have been found. Workshop production of Maya objects is assumed from finished goods that, for example, required a high level of craftsmanship indicating that some kind of craft specialists existed (Adams 1970; Becker 1973). Much of the evidence for actual production, either within households or in workshops, is not from the production areas themselves. Instead, in many cases evidence for production comes from material that was moved in ancient times (Moholy-Nagy 1997); the finished goods may have been stored temporarily in or near a workshop but ultimately used elsewhere, for example. So what was left at a workshop? There might be production errors, debitage (flakes left over from the manufacturing process), and used cores in the case of stone tools, or other remains from the manufacture of stone tools, pottery vessels, or other goods. Even these by-products of manufacturing may have been moved from the workshops simply to continue to work without debris underfoot—or to have a safe working environment. Imagine an obsidian knapper chipping blades in the midst of a growing pile of sharp-edged waste flakes.

If both the finished goods and the waste from the manufacturing process were moved in antiquity, what might Maya archaeologists reasonably expect to find that would indicate that there once was a workshop in a particular location? Workshops themselves have been identified from residues from the production process, such as obsidian microdebitage (Moholy-Nagy 1990) or shell and obsidian debitage (Fash 2001) that have become embedded in floors. The brine-boiling hearths at the Stingray Lagoon site in Punta Ycacos Lagoon show evidence of equipment and activity areas where production took place (McKillop 2002).

Case Study: Punta Ycacos Salt Works

Salt was produced in Punta Ycacos Lagoon, a large salt water lagoon in Paynes Creek National Park in southern Belize, by the "sal cocida" method of boiling brine in pots over fires to make salt cakes (McKillop 1995a; McKillop 2002). By analogy with the modern Maya in the highlands of Guatemala and elsewhere, a dozen or more pots were placed together over fires and used to boil brine to produce the salt cakes (Reina and Monaghen 1981). This sal cocida method was a good strategy in the Paynes Creek National Park region, where the short, unpredictable dry season was not ideally suited to solar evaporation of salt. A slag heap at one of the Punta Ycacos sites, Killer Bee, indicated that seawater was preprocessed by pouring it through salt-saturated soil to produce a salt-enriched brine for boiling. Salt was produced in the form of hard cakes suitable for storage or transport without additional individual containers, although some loose salt for local use in the coastal region of Paynes Creek National Park and Port Honduras Marine Reserve to the south or for inland trade may also have been made. In addition to preprocessing the salt water and boiling the brine, other activities included the manufacture of the salt-boiling vessels and the vessel supports from local clays and sand temper, the material added to clay before pots were made to prevent them from cracking when fired.

The Punta Ycacos Lagoon sites were workshops for salt production by people who lived elsewhere. Similar artifact assemblages were recovered from each of the four salt workshops in the lagoon. Most of the artifacts were the same type of pottery jars and bowl sherds and their vessel supports, associated with abundant charcoal, corroborating the interpretation that a specific and limited activity was carried out at the workshops. The most striking feature of the artifact assemblages was the lack of diversity of ceramic types and the abundance of sherds from similar large utilitarian vessels. In addition to the sherds from brine-boiling vessels, sherds from two types of water jars suitable for storing brine were recovered. There is not the variety of vessel forms and vessel quality—everyday to ceremonial—that has been found at settlements in the area, such as Wild Cane Cay. The few stone tools from Punta Ycacos do not match standard stone tool assemblages found at other settlements in the area. The nature of the artifact assemblages at the salt workshops indicates low variability, arguing for a specific task.

Several lines of evidence from the Punta Ycacos salt works indicate that salt production was specialized beyond the household level into workshops focused on production for export to nearby inland Maya cities. For example, the production was geographically localized near the raw material source. Also, production was spatially segregated from households and settlements. In fact, production was spatially segregated from other activities as well, such as eating, sleeping, and burial. The pots themselves were standardized in shape and size, which would have facilitated mass production of salt: A dozen or more pots could be placed over a fire at one time, for example (McKillop 2002).

Salt production at the Punta Ycacos salt works was likely seasonal, coinciding with the dry season for maximum solar evaporation, ease of boiling the brine, and saving the off-season for agricultural work.

The inland Maya at large cities such as Lubaantun and Nim li punit were the consumers of the Punta Ycacos salt works. Water jars with stamped decoration and pottery whistles, both made at inland sites, are found at the salt workshops. Pottery whistles were traded from inland cities and used in rituals that reinforced vertical ties between the coastal and inland elite. Who supplied the inland Maya with salt and the salt workers with whistles and other inland trade goods? Arguably, it was the island Maya at Wild Cane Cay and Frenchman's Cay, who also supplied the inland Maya with long-distance coastal resources. Not only salt works, but other utilitarian goods such as chert, were desired by the urban Maya. Ritualized trading and marriage alliances may have tied independent craft specialists in outlying areas near raw material sources with the urban elite Maya. Craft specialists thereby obtained elite paraphernalia for rituals, as well as status. This facilitated the maintenance of the regular supply of utilitarian goods and resources from the peripheries to the cities.

Case Study: Stone Tool Workshops at Colha, Belize

Craft specialists produced stone tools at Colha, a small community with modest architecture in northern Belize located adjacent to outcrops of high-quality chert (Shafer and Hester 1983; Shafer and Hester 1986). The presence of production errors and debitage at Colha has been interpreted to indicate that more goods were produced than could have been used by the occupants of the local households. The production was interpreted as specialized production, even though it occurred within the context of households. The production and distribution of stone tools at Colha were spatially separated from the Maya elite at major lowland cities. Elite participation is evident as consumers of a limited number and array of objects, notably eccentrics (large chipped objects of no clear utilitarian use, sometimes in the shape of human figures or animals).

Tools were produced in household workshops at Colha, but domestic debris was not intermixed with the workshop items, indicating a separation of activities. The household location of the workshops suggests a cottage industry. The large quantity of chert debitage, occurrence of several workshops, and the array of tools argue for significant production of stone tools at Colha. Shafer and Hester (1986) point out that it was a mass-production area, based on their calculations of the large quantity of tools produced. Certainly the distribution of Colha chert tools to a variety of communities in northern Belize, where they form the core of the stone tool assemblages found, demonstrates an intensity of production beyond household or even community needs. Colha chert was distributed to a variety of communities in northern Belize, including Ambergris Cay, Cerros, Cuello, Moho Cay, Pulltrouser Swamp, and Santa Rita Corozal (Dockall and Shafer 1993; Hult and Hester 1995; McAnany 1989a; McKillop 1980; McKillop 2004; McKillop 2005; Mitchum 1991). Lower-quality local chert and other stone also were used to make some tools at these communities.

CRAFT PRODUCTION FOR MAYA ROYALTY

Artisans attached to royal courts in Maya cities made some of the most highly crafted pots, stone tools, and ritual clothing. Although not even traces of the elaborate clothing and headdresses made from perishable materials of Maya royalty have been preserved, their existence is well documented on painted pottery and carved monuments. The amount of time needed, high level of skill demanded, and inclusion of imported materials in these items indicates that specialists produced them.

Attached specialists were sponsored by Maya royalty and made many of the items found in elite burials. Dorie Reents-Budet and Ron Bishop identified separate schools of style among Late Classic painted pottery vessels by analysis of vessel style and of chemical composition of the vessel clay (Reents-Budet 1994). Some vessels were attributable to individual artists, with a few vessels even being signed by the painter (Reents-Budet 1994, figure 2.20). The high level of artistic skill indicates that there were specialized painters in royal court workshops, painting vessels made by other specialists. Some painters of elite painted pottery even depicted themselves in scenes with Maya royalty, attesting to the importance and high rank of these artisans in Late Classic Maya society. Takeshi Inomata (1997, 2001) found artisans' tools, including inkpots used by scribes, on the floors of elite residences that were abandoned at Aguateca, Guatemala, when the city was invaded.

SYSTEMS OF SUBSISTENCE

The Maya developed a diversity of subsistence systems reflecting the variability in the landscape and the demands of a growing population. Archaeologists once considered that the ancient Maya relied on slash and burn agriculture like the Maya encountered by the Spaniards in the sixteenth century and the modern Maya. Slash and burn agriculture is considered an extensive form of agriculture because it requires farmers to abandon their fields after a few years due to depletion of the nutrients in the soil and the growth of weeds. Only a relatively low population can be supported with this method, as is typical of many modern Maya villages today. The earliest Maya farmers during the Middle Preclassic, living at such communities as Cerros, Tikal, Colha, Seibal, and Altar de Sacrificios, may have relied on slash and burn agriculture. Population densities were quite low at that time.

With significantly higher populations during the Classic period—and particularly by the Late Classic period, when the population was at its greatest—most Maya archaeologists think that slash and burn agriculture would have not provided enough food. Traces of a variety of other relict agricultural systems have been uncovered that would have allowed the Classic Maya to more intensively exploit the environment and produce more food. Hillslopes were terraced for agriculture in the Maya Mountains of western Belize and the Rio Bec region of Campeche, Mexico (Harrison and Turner 1978; Healy et al. 1983). This extended arable land into new areas, allowing more food to be grown. Canals were dug through low-lying swamps, creating drained fields at Pulltrouser Swamp in northern Belize, in Quintana Roo, Mexico (Turner and Harrison 1983; Harrison 1978), the Candelaria region of Campeche (Siemens 1978), and arguably elsewhere (Adams, Brown, and Culbert 1981). This drained field agriculture allowed year-round farming in areas that were otherwise not arable. The drained field system of Cerros (Freidel and Scarborough 1982) and on Albion Island (Pohl 1990) show the Preclassic origins and development of drained field farming.

Most researchers see intensive agriculture as a Late Classic response to dramatic increases in human populations within the southern Maya lowlands. In contrast, Mary Pohl interprets the Preclassic drained fields on Albion Island as the precocious development of elite Maya who were able to coerce workers into draining fields for agriculture. The extent of intensive agriculture is hotly debated among Maya archaeologists, with a need for basic fieldwork, including exploration of the Bajo de Santa Fe beside Tikal and other swamps near cities within the lowlands. A stimulating article by Richard E. W. Adams and colleagues (1981) in *Science*, in which he suggested that the entire Maya lowlands were covered by canals (a theory taken from his interpretation of side-scan radar imagery, which cuts through the vegetation and provides an oblique view of the ground surface, including canals) has been called into question by other researchers.

The Classic Maya also cultivated and tended plants in a variety of settings, ultimately enhancing their diet and reflecting the diversity of environments

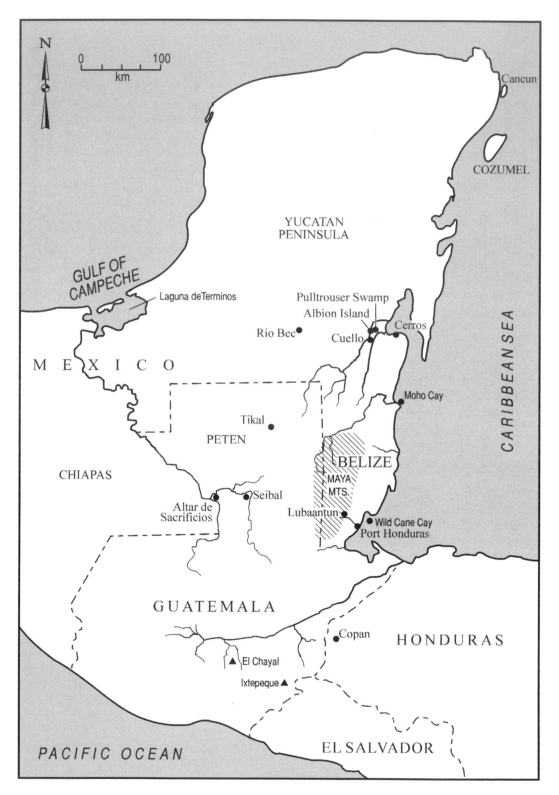

Sites mentioned in the text about subsistence

within the Maya lowlands. Orchards were a specialized adaptation on offshore islands, where several native palms, as well as other trees, were grown for their fruits (McKillop 1994; McKillop 1996a). The rainforest itself was managed by the selective culling of cacao (chocolate) trees and by weeding (see various articles in Fedick 1996). Along with kitchen gardens around households, the Maya had a sophisticated specialization in their agriculture to the various environments within the Maya area.

Actual plant food remains have been recovered only from a handful of sites, but they provide intriguing clues to the ancient diet. The Mesoamerican triad of corn, beans, and squash of the modern and sixteenth-century Maya have been identified in ancient Maya sites, but not in any great enough quantity to allow researchers to evaluate their contribution to the Late Classic Maya diet or to that of earlier times. Archaeologists assume that corn was the mainstay of the ancient diet, providing essential carbohydrates. John Jones (1994) identified corn pollen from Cobweb Swamp in northern Belize dating to 2500 B.C., indicating that the area was cleared by that time and at least some corn was planted. Other plant food remains include avocado, chocolate, native palm fruits, and wild forest fruits such as mammee apples from Cerros, Cuello, Copan, Colha, and the Port Honduras sites of Wild Cane Cay, Frenchman's Cay, Tiger Mound, Pelican Cay, and Orlando's Jewfish (McKillop 1994; McKillop 1996a; Turner and Miksicek 1984; also see various articles in Fedick 1996, McAnany and Isaac 1989, and White 1999). Clearly, the recovery of plant food remains by flotation or from dry or waterlogged settings that provide unusual conditions of preservation is urgently needed to better evaluate the ancient Maya diet.

The identification of a variety of animal bones show that wild game, freshwater and marine fishes, and mollusks added to the Maya diet. White-tailed deer and peccary were the main meats selected by the ancient Maya, except along the coast, where seafood comprised a significant part of the diet. Elizabeth Wing's (1978) research indicates that dogs were a part of the Maya diet as well. A provocative article by Frederick Lange (1971) suggesting that dried or salted seafood provided protein to feed the growing populations in the Late Classic has not been substantiated by the (admittedly limited) research identifying animal remains or by the chemical analysis of human bones. At offshore island sites on Cozumel, Cancun, Frenchman's Cay, and Moho Cay, seafood comprised the bulk of the Maya's animal foods (Andrews et al. 1975; Hamblin 1984; McKillop 1984; McKillop and Winemiller 2004). However, even at communities such as Cerros, located on the coast, mainland animals contributed a significant amount to the diet (Carr 1986). Seafood was a dietary supplement, perhaps for the elite, at inland cities. Still, pictorial depictions on painted pots and in carvings reveal that the sea figured prominently in Maya cosmology as a portal to the underworld (Reents-Budet 1994). A variety of resources from the sea, such as stingray spines and conch shells, were imported to inland cities for rituals.

Artistic depictions of food, artifacts used in food preparation and procurement, and studies of human bone and bone chemistry corroborate the rather meager evidence about Maya diet obtained from the plant and animal remains (White 1999; White et al. 2001a; Whittington and Reed 1997; Wright and White 1996). Classic Maya painted pots show feasts and regal meals with tamales piled on dishes and chocolate in vases, and they show deer being hunted. The corn grinding implements, mano (hand-held grinding cylinder) and metate (the flat stone on which corn was ground using the mano), fishhooks and fishing weights, and spear points found also provide clues to the Maya diet. Skeletal analyses indicate that anemia was widespread and that dental plaque was quite extensive from a diet rich in corn (Wright and White 1996; Whittington and Reed 1997). William Haviland's (1967) pioneering study indicating that human stature declined over the course of the Classic Period at Tikal—adding fuel to the model of ecological collapse ending the Classic Maya society—seems not to be supported by more extensive skeletal studies at a variety of other sites (Wright and White 1996). From Lynette Norr's initial carbon isotope analysis of Maya bones from Moho Cay, Belize (McKillop 1980), there have been tremendous insights from carbon, nitrogen, and oxygen isotopic studies, particularly by Christine White (1999; White et al. 2000; White, Longstaffer, and Law 2001; White et al. 2001) of the University of Western Ontario and by Lori Wright (1997) of Texas A & M University, among others (see Whittington and Reed 1997). These chemical and morphological studies of human bone, together with sophisticated analyses of plant food and animal remains (Emery 2004; Fedick 1996; White 1999), promise to provide significant insights into the ancient Maya diet.

MAYA TRADE

Although the presence of nonlocal goods and resources at Maya sites from the Middle Preclassic through the Postclassic indicates that the Maya participated in a variety of trading networks from both nearby and distant locations, there is much discussion about the mechanisms by which trade goods were obtained, the quantity of goods traded, and the importance of trade to the development of Maya civilization. By the Classic period, the urban Maya elite had developed sophisticated trade networks in prestige items, but their involvement in the exchange of subsistence goods and resources is polarized into contrasting views of the political economy. As outlined previously, some scholars regard the political economy as having been centralized under the control and management of the urban elite of regional polities (Chase and Chase 1996). By way of contrast, others believe that the political economy was more decentralized, with the Maya in various communities near resource and nonurban production areas having control and management of trade (Demarest 1996; Foias and Bishop 1997; McKillop 2002; Shafer and Hester 1983). There is no doubt, however, that quite a variety of prestige and subsistence goods and resources were traded in various networks of exchange involving nearby and more distant locations.

Although archaeologists often discuss long-distance versus local or regional trade, this dichotomy masks the fact that goods were traded from short, medium, and long distances, depending on the distance of the source location from any particular Maya site (Graham 1987). Although often underestimated, there was an active trade of goods and resources within the Maya lowlands. Even though many perishable trade goods have left no material remains, both organic materials, such as shell and bone, and inorganic materials, including rocks, minerals, and pottery, are commonly recovered from Maya sites of various sizes. Marine shells and bone were traded from the coasts to inland Maya settlements (E. W. Andrews 1969), but the distance these items were transported was often not very great (McKillop 1984; McKillop 1985). Although the chert outcrops in northern Belize centered on the stone tool manufacturing community of Colha were arguably of the highest quality, chert is distributed in limestone deposits throughout the Maya lowlands (Shafer and Hester 1983). The Maya Mountains of southern Belize were a source of granite for manos and metates used to make grinding stones (Shipley and Graham 1989), as well as a source for quartz and slate. Granite from the Maya Mountains was not a long-distance trade good for the Maya in southern Belize or in the upper Belize Valley. Chemical and petrographic studies of the composition of the clays and tempering materials added to clay indicate that pottery vessels were traded both within and between lowland Maya polities, including some cases of considerable distance, such as a vessel from Altun Ha in a burial at Copan. Salt was traded from the salt flats along the northern Yucatan coast as well as from workshops along the Belizean coast, where it was produced by boiling brine in pots over fires as detailed earlier in this chapter (McKillop 2002).

From Christopher Columbus's encounter with an alleged Maya trading canoe off the north coast of Honduras in 1502 (Davidson 1991), right through to modern times, long-distance Maya trade has fascinated Mayanists and the public alike. Goods and resources traded to lowland Maya settlements from outside the area have attracted considerable attention, both because of their exotic origin and often because they are finely crafted as well. The presence of these exotic items demonstrates that the Maya had far-flung trading systems. Marine shells from the Pacific coast were found at a variety of lowland Maya sites (Feldman 1974). Mercury from Honduras was placed under a ball court marker at Lamanai (Pendergast 1982). Turquoise from northern Mexico or lower Central America was found at Santa Rita Corozal. Gold from western Mexico was found at Chichen Itza, Santa Rita Corozal, and Wild Cane Cay. Copper bells, rings, and other items from Honduras were found at a variety of lowland Maya sites. Whether or not the central Mexican state of Teotihuacan had a military presence in the Maya area, there is clear evidence of many Teotihuacan trade goods there (Braswell 2003). Teotihuacan-style pottery vessels were excavated at Kaminaljuyu, Altun Ha, Tikal, and Rio Azul. Green obsidian from the Pachuca outcrop north of Mexico City was recovered from Tikal, Wild Cane Cay, Frenchman's Cay, Becan, and Altun Ha, among other settlements (McKillop et al. 1988; Moholy-Nagy 1999; Spence 1996). Some materials, such as jade and other greenstones from the Motagua River drainage in Guatemala, were elaborately carved at lowland Maya sites. They include a cache of jade head pendants at Cerros (Freidel 1979), jaguar and hunchback figures at

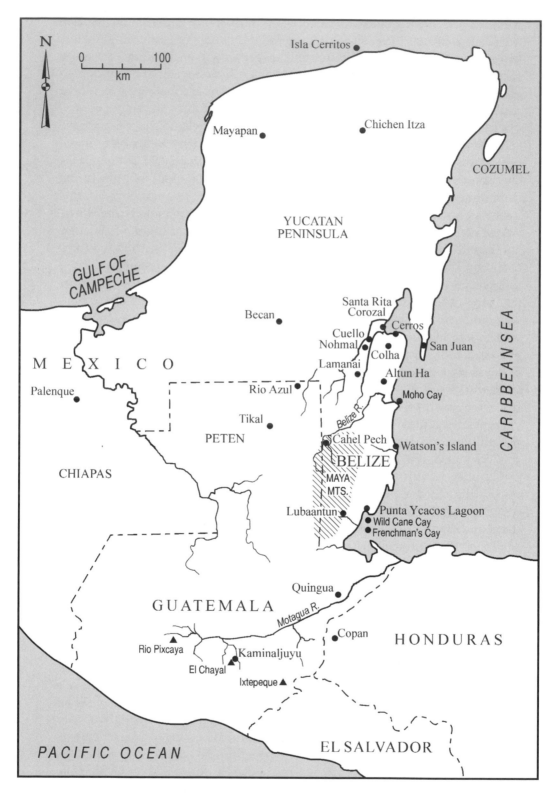

Sites mentioned in the text about trade

Lamanai (Pendergast 1981), and a jade head of Kinich Ahau, the sun god, from Altun Ha, which, at 4.4 kilograms, makes it the largest jade carving in the Maya lowlands (Pendergast 1979). Basalt for grinding stones and obsidian for ritual bloodletting and other cutting purposes were traded from volcanic regions of Mesoamerica, particularly from outcrops in the highlands of Guatemala.

Obsidian Trade

Obsidian, perhaps more than any other material, has been used to reconstruct models of ancient Maya trade. Because obsidian is not naturally available in the limestone platform of the Maya lowlands, all obsidian in that area was imported. And, obsidian is ubiquitous at lowland Maya sites throughout the course of Maya prehistory, from the largest cities to the small communities. The ability to chemically match obsidian from which artifacts were made to specific outcrops in the volcanic ranges of highland Mesoamerica has allowed archaeologists to reconstruct various trade routes (Hammond 1972; Healy, McKillop, and Walsh 1984; McKillop et al. 1988; Nelson 1985; P. Rice 1984). As obsidian is a volcanic mineral that is spewed in liquid form from volcanic eruptions and that subsequently solidifies into glass, it is quite uniform chemically, both within and among outcrops. However, chemists have found that obsidian from different outcrops varies in chemical trace elements such as zirconium and rubidium. This makes chemical fingerprinting of obsidian artifacts to their highland outcrops possible. Chemists use X-ray fluorescence (XRF) and neutron activation analysis (NAA) to identify the trace elements of obsidian artifacts and to assign them to particular obsidian outcrops. XRF is nondestructive, but NAA destroys the artifact. The main labs for obsidian research are the Lawrence Berkeley Lab and the Missouri Lab.

Experiments with visually assigning Maya artifacts to their sources have also met with success, but visual identification has only been used for a few Maya sites (Braswell et al. 2000; McKillop 1995b; McKillop et al. 1988). Some researchers question its accuracy in distinguishing among gray obsidians from different sources; some researchers are also skeptical because the method fits obsidians into visual groups of known sources but artifacts from unknown sources will not be recognized (Moholy-Nagy 1999; Moholy-Nagy 2003). The value of using visual identification is that virtually all obsidian artifacts can be assigned to their source locations, allowing more statistically valid trade models to be tested than is typical of the small samples that are usually chemically tested. This method, combined with chemical identifications, may prove to have wider use and validity as more and more samples are visually sourced.

The small number of obsidian artifacts typically subjected to chemical sourcing for Maya sites has struck serious flaws into reconstructions of Maya obsidian trade (McKillop and Jackson 1988). Small samples tend to show the dominant source but not the minor sources, and so do not include the diversity of sources used by the ancient Maya during a particular time. Some researchers propose the use of visual identification of each obsidian to its outcrop to overcome the small sample size problem (Braswell et al. 2000).

Several major and many minor outcrops of obsidian utilized by the ancient Maya have been located throughout the volcanic highland region of Meso-america. Apart from the green obsidian at Pachuca, north of modern Mexico City, and a less common darker green obsidian from Tulancingo, the other obsidian sources were various colors of gray or black. Pachuca is translucent and is a shade of "bottle-glass" green (Spence 1996). Three main outcrops of gray obsidian in the Maya highlands of Guatemala produced the bulk of the obsidian used by the lowland Maya throughout their prehistory: the El Chayal outcrop near modern Guatemala City, the Ixtepeque outcrop to the southeast near the modern community of that name, and the Rio Pixcaya (also called San Martin Jilotepeque) outcrop to the west. The La Esperanza obsidian outcrop near the modern community by that name in western Honduras was a minor source of obsidian used at Quirigua and Wild Cane Cay (McKillop et al. 1988; Sheets et al. 1990). At least a dozen outcrops in central Mexico produced gray obsidians used in the Maya area, as evidenced by the chemical identification of Mexican obsidian artifacts from Tikal (Moholy-Nagy 1999), Wild Cane Cay (McKillop et al. 1988), Isla Cerritos (Andrews et al. 1989), and Ambergris Cay (Guderjan and Garber 1995), among other places.

Did the royal Maya in lowland cities control the import of obsidian from volcanic regions of Mesoamerica and its distribution to smaller communities within their polities? This would represent quite a centralized model of the Maya economy. Or did Maya merchants, perhaps sponsored by royal Maya, ply their wares at cities, at coastal ports, and along transportation routes? This model describes the Maya economy as more decentralized, with less control by the urban elite. Or was obsidian traded down the line from one community to the next, from highland outcrop to lowland site, outside the control of the royal Maya? How did obsidian trade change over time? These questions about the nature of obsidian trade are related to the aforementioned hotly debated perspectives on how centralized the ancient Maya economy was. Perhaps obsidian will resolve the economy issue.

Tracing the production of obsidian artifacts at highland outcrops and lowland Maya sites has led archaeologists to suggest times when the pieces were transported as finished artifacts or were made at various cities and smaller communities. Obsidian was extracted from surface outcrops or mined from tunnels in the outcrops and was prepared at these source locations into cylindrical cores. The virtual lack of green obsidian cores at Maya sites suggests that green obsidian—and, in fact, other Mexican obsidian—was traded in the form of finished artifacts. However, gray obsidian from the highlands of Guatemala was undoubtedly traded as cores. This is known because, first, partly used or "exhausted" cores are a frequent recovery at lowland sites. More importantly, perhaps, is the fragile nature of a finished obsidian blade, prone to breakage or wearing down of its sharp edges. Unless carefully protected, obsidian would have needed to be transported as cores and then made into blades when it reached its destination. Whether or not blade production occurred at all communities is unknown. Perhaps, in some instances, finished blades were transported to small communities. Perhaps itinerant obsidian knappers traveled to various communities as "door-to-door craftsmen," producing blades on demand.

Early Maya trade—trade occurring during the Middle Preclassic—consisted of the import of obsidian flakes, perhaps made from nodules, as at Cahal Pech (Awe and Healy 1994) and Butterfly Wing (McKillop 1996b). Classic Maya lowland cities had the greatest abundance of obsidian (often found in burials or caches as special dumps of debris), and smaller communities within their realms had less obsidian. Wild Cane Cay, and perhaps other coastal trading ports, are exceptions. Owing to its role in coastal trade, the community evidently had access to regular supplies of obsidian cores from which a considerable number of blades and other artifacts were produced (McKillop 1989). By Postclassic times, following the collapse of the Classic Maya royal dynasties and their control of regional polities, obsidian seems to have been available to a wider sector of Maya society (Rice 1987a). Presumably, the mechanisms by which obsidian was traded from highland outcrops to lowland cities, towns, and villages changed as well.

Most of the green obsidian that came from Pachuca was traded to the Maya area in the Early Classic period during the heyday of Teotihuacan (Spence 1996), as well as during the Postclassic, associated with the rise of Chichen Itza and its central Mexican ties to the site of Tula, although it is reported from as early as the Middle Preclassic at Tikal and as late as the Postclassic at Mayapan. Gray-colored Mexican obsidians, such as Ucareo, were traded at these times as well, but their distribution at Maya sites is not as well known as green, which is visually distinctive. Gray-colored Mexican obsidian has been chemically identified in artifacts from a number of Maya sites including Tikal (Moholy-Nagy 1999), Becan, and Altun Ha, as well as at the coastal trading ports of Wild Cane Cay (McKillop et al. 1988), San Juan on Ambergris Cay in Belize (Guderjan and Garber 1995), and Isla Cerritos, the trading port for Chichen Itza located off the north coast of the Yucatan (Andrews et al. 1989).

Maya archaeologists disagree on the coastal or inland transportation routes for obsidian from the volcanic highlands to the Maya lowlands and on how these routes changed over time. Resolving this issue impacts researchers' understanding of obsidian trade and hence the broader Maya economy. Norman Hammond's (1972) pioneer model of Maya obsidian trade stands as the baseline for other studies. In his model, Hammond proposed that there were competing routes for obsidian during the Classic period. He suggested that El Chayal obsidian was transported along overland routes and that Ixtepeque obsidian traveled along the Yucatan coast, following its initial transport down the Motagua River to the Caribbean. Second, the accumulation of obsidian source results have indicated that time, and not space, was the important criterion in looking at the use of El Chayal versus Ixtepeque obsidian. Instead of competing coastal and inland transportation routes for Ixtepeque and El Chayal obsidian, respectively, these outcrops were actually dominant at different times. The lowland Maya utilized both El Chayal and Ixtepeque during the Classic period, but El Chayal was dominant. Ixtepeque rose to prominence in the Terminal Classic and became the main outcrop used during the Postclassic.

The ruins of one of the main buildings in the ancient Maya city of Chichen Itza, on the Yucatan Peninsula of Mexico, is surrounded by numerous columns known as the "Group of a Thousand Columns." (Corel)

Both Ixtepeque and El Chayal obsidian were likely traded along the Belize coast. Healy et al. (1984) found that El Chayal was more common at the Classic Maya coastal trading port of Moho Cay, indicating the transport of El Chayal obsidian along coastal routes during the Classic period. Although Ixtepeque was the main source used farther south along the Belizean coast at Wild Cane Cay, El Chayal was an important secondary source at that island trading port.

The selection of sources of gray obsidian changed over time, although the political and economic implications of these changes are not always well articulated (Andrews et al. 1989; Guderjan and Garber 1995; Healy, McKillop, and Walsh 1984; McKillop and Jackson 1988; McKillop et al. 1988; Moholy-Nagy 1999; Moholy-Nagy and Nelson 1990; Moholy-Nagy, Asaro, and Stross 1984; Nelson 1985; Rice 1984; Stross et al. 1978). The Maya traded for obsidian from as early as the Middle Preclassic at Cuello, the central Peten lakes region (Rice 1984), and Cahal Pech (Awe and Healy 1994), and continued to do so through the Classic and Postclassic and into historic times. The dominant source used by the Middle Preclassic Maya was Rio Pixcaya, also known as San Martin Jilotepeque (SMJ), located in the Maya highlands west of Guatemala City. El Chayal eclipsed SMJ in popularity during the Late Preclassic, perhaps associated with the rise of nearby Kaminaljuyu. El Chayal was the dominant source used by the Classic Maya, with a few exceptions such as at Nohmul in Belize, where another Maya highland outcrop, Ixtepeque, was more common. At Wild Cane Cay, Ixtepeque was more common than El Chayal in the Late and Terminal Classic deposits and into the Postclassic as well. It may be that the landscape and human settlement in the area around the Ixtepeque outcrop had by this time recovered from the Ilopango volcanic eruption that had blanketed much of western El Salvador and beyond with volcanic materials around A.D. 410 (Dull, Southon, and Sheets 2001).

The Terminal Classic period witnessed the rise in use of Ixtepeque, which became the dominant source used during the Postclassic at such sites as Tulum, San Juan, and Wild Cane Cay. The Postclassic also saw a rise in diversity of source use, as shown at Wild Cane Cay and Isla Cerritos in particular. Six sources were used in the Postclassic at Wild Cane Cay, including Pachuca and Ucareo in central Mexico; SMJ, El Chayal, and Ixtepeque in Guatemala; and La Esperanza in Honduras. La Esperanza was a common source used in antiquity in lower Central America, so its known restricted distribution in the Maya area at Wild Cane Cay and Quirigua indicates trade to the south. The decline in importance of Kaminaljuyu and recovery of the area around Ixtepeque from the Ilopango volcanic eruption of A.D. 410 may account for the rise in importance of Ixtepeque obsidian, although this conjecture begs further research. Future assignment of obsidian artifacts to their highland sources will clarify patterns of obsidian distribution within the lowlands, particularly within Maya polities.

Food Trade

Without much evidence of preserved food remains at Maya sites, the debate about whether or not food was traded remains undecided. Fred Lange (1971) has suggested that seafood was sun-dried or salted and was traded inland in large quantities to feed the expanding Classic Maya population. On the basis of statistical calculations, Andrew Sluyter (1993) proposed that corn and other foodstuffs were transported long distances in the Maya area and elsewhere in Mesoamerica. Anthony Andrews (1983) proposed that the basic daily salt needs of the large lowland Maya population of the Classic period were met by bulk transport of salt from the north coast of the Yucatan. T. Patrick Culbert (1974) makes a convincing argument for transport of agricultural produce over shorter distances, both within and between polities. Common to these perspectives is the belief that the inland Maya, particularly those at large cities in the southern lowlands, could not produce sufficient food, either by swidden or more-intensive agriculture, to feed their urban populations. The lack of nonlocal food remains at Maya cities is not surprising, considering the very few cases in which any plant food remains have been recovered from Maya sites. Carbon and nitrogen isotope studies of human bone indicate that for the most part the bulk of the diet, both from meat and plants, came from nearby the communities in which the people lived. Some elites at Lamanai have isotopic signatures in their bones suggesting that they had greater access to seafood than did commoners, but the sample is small and shows a need for more research. The few instances of nonlocal food remains are usually found in burials and caches, so it is not clear whether or not the items were imported for their dietary uses or for ritual uses of the animal bones or shells.

Trade within the Maya Lowlands

Studies of production and distribution of everyday goods within the Maya lowlands have been overshadowed by research on long-distance trade of prestige items. This research focus can be attributed to the facility to chemically or even visually match obsidian and other artifacts from lowland Maya sites to distant origins and thereby to facilitate the development of models of production and distribution. Notable exceptions are the study of chert tool production and distribution identified in northern Belize (Dockall and Shafer 1993; Hult and Hester 1995; McAnany 1989a; Mitchum 1991; Shafer and Hester 1983); the production and distribution of utilitarian vessels near Tikal, Palenque, and in the Petexbatun area (Foias and Bishop 1997; Fry 1980; Rice 1987a); the specialized production units for salt, shellfish processing, and other activities at Watson's Island (Graham 1994); and the production of salt cakes in Punta Ycacos Lagoon (McKillop 1995a). These studies indicate there was a variety of everyday goods and resources traded short distances within the Maya lowlands, suggesting more research should be focused here.

Trade and Civilization

Many Mayanists have argued for the importance of long-distance trade in prestige goods (Freidel 1979) or basic subsistence resources (Rathje 1971) in the rise of social complexity. However, other researchers suggest that it was instead the local exchange of less highly crafted, often bulky, utilitarian goods over short distances for the common folk that was critical to the rise of complex civilization (Marcus 1995; Sanders and Price 1968). The economics of salt production in Punta Ycacos Lagoon and of stone tool manufacture at Colha

Case study: THE TRADING PORT AT WILD CANE CAY

The sea was important to the ancient Maya as an avenue of transportation, the origin of ritual and subsistence items, and the source of watery imagery related to death, rebirth, and the underworld (McKillop 2002; McKillop 2004; McKillop 2005). The Spaniards who arrived in the sixteenth century encountered coastal inhabitants along the Yucatán peninsula of Mexico. Cerros and other Preclassic coastal settlements underscore the antiquity and importance of sea trade in Maya society. By the Classic period, coastal trading ports became an important link for the dynastic Maya in southern lowland cities in their quest for goods and resources from near and far. The trading port on Wild Cane Cay in the Port Honduras of southern Belize developed such a level of economic and political autonomy that it withstood the collapse of nearby inland cities with which its inhabitants had developed an extensive trade. The Wild Cane Cay inhabitants, as opportunistic traders, simply realigned their economy to link with emerging powers in the northern Maya lowlands, notably Chichen Itza and later Tulum (McKillop 1989; McKillop 1996b; McKillop 2005).

both underscore the importance of production and distribution of subsistence resources within the southern Maya lowlands.

The collapse of the Classic period civilization in the southern Maya lowlands was marked by an economic collapse of the production and distribution systems in that area. At the same time, cities such as Chichen Itza in the northern Maya lowlands, Lamanai in Belize, and coastal trading ports such as Wild Cane Cay in southern Belize, San Juan on Ambergris Cay, and Isla Cerritos off the northern Yucatan coast rose to prominence.

Wild Cane Cay is strategically located for trading both along the coast and inland. Although a relatively small village community of only about ten acres in size, Wild Cane Cay was densely settled in the Late Classic, as well as in the Early and Late Postclassic. It was the northernmost island of the Port Honduras, and the island's natural harbor provided protection from the rough seas to the north and from pirates or other boat travelers in the coastal waters. The island also was well situated for coastal-inland trade, being located near several navigable rivers that provided avenues of communication and trade to such Late Classic cities as Lubaantun, Nim li punit, and Uxbenka. During the Late Classic, Wild Cane Cay was integrated in a coastal-inland exchange economy providing subsistence resources, such as seafood and the Punta Ycacos salt, as well as ritual paraphernalia, such as stingray spines, to nearby inland cities. In return, the Wild Cane Cay Maya received Lubaantun-style pottery figurine whistles, and distinctive "unit-stamped" pottery with stamped impressions, among other objects.

These exchanges tied the ritual and subsistence economies of the coast to the dynastic Maya of nearby lowland cities. These ties were through alliances that likely included marriage and economic alliances, celebrated by feasting and gift exchange between the dynastic inland leaders and the lowly, yet economically and politically independent, coastal merchants on Wild Cane Cay. Perhaps the inland elite reluctantly accepted the independence of their coastal neighbors in order to maintain a steady supply of salt—without which they would not survive. The independence of the Wild Cane Cay Maya from their inland counterparts is underscored by the ability of the Wild Cane Cay Maya to weather the political and economic collapse at the end of the Late Classic, when the inland cities in southern Belize were abandoned. The Wild Cane Cay Maya simply adjusted their economy to focus more on long-distance sea trade with the emerging powers in the northern Maya lowlands.

What features identify Wild Cane Cay as a trading port, and what was traded during the Late Classic and Postclassic, respectively? During the Late Classic, the island participated in the coastal transport of gray obsidian from the El Chayal and Ixtepeque obsidian outcrops in the southern Maya highlands of Guatemala to southern lowland Maya cities. At that time, sea trade was well integrated with inland trade of salt and other subsistence resources from the sea, as well as ritual items like shells for carving and stingray spines for ritual bloodletting. The collapse of the Late Classic dynasties and the abandonment of nearby inland cities terminated inland trade for Wild Cane Cay. However, there was an exponential increase in obsidian trade and an increase in the places from which obsidian and other goods were traded to Wild Cane Cay. There was, for example, an 800 percent increase in the amount of obsidian traded to the island in the Early Postclassic as compared to the Late Classic (McKillop 1989; McKillop 2005). The presence of green obsidian from Pachuca and gray obsidian from Ucareo points to trading ties with central Mexico. Pottery was traded from the Pacific coast of Guatemala or Chiapas, Mexico, as indicated by the presence of distinctive Tohil Plumbate pottery at Wild Cane Cay. Trade and communication to points farther north along the Caribbean coast are indicated by pottery very similar to that from Tulum. Gold and copper also arrived at the island trading port.

A variety of quantitative measures support the view that the island was a port where traders stopped overnight to trade and rest. The manufacture of blades that are both wide and thick indicates a lack of conservation of such scarce, imported material. Evidently the Wild Cane Cay Maya had a steady and regular supply of obsidian from which they could make blades without much care to conservation (McKillop 2005). There were more cores (or core fragments) found than would be expected for the number of blades, indicating production of blades on the island for use there as well as for distribution elsewhere, evidently at other Port Honduras communities where cores are rare or absent (McKillop 1989; McKillop 2005). In general, Wild Cane Cay's access to exotic gold, copper, Mexican obsidian, and imported pots and stones (jade, volcanic basalt) was unexpected for a rather small community. Ordinarily one might expect the Maya at small communities to obtain exotics by trade or by gift exchange with the urban capital of their city-state. This exchange pattern would not result in much in the way of exotics, either in quantity, diversity, or quality (such as gold). A trading port, on the other hand, had access, albeit for a limited time, to abundant and diverse imports of high quality. Some of these evidently were acquired in exchange for services.

SUMMARY

Was the Maya political economy centralized in the hands of the dynastic leaders and their royal court in the major cities? Were specialists who crafted prestige goods part of royal courts where they had workshops? Alternatively, was economic control decentralized into the hands of leaders of smaller cities and even towns? Or was some production, especially that of elite items for the prestige economy, centrally controlled, with goods produced for the subsistence economy not controlled or controlled to a lesser degree? Given the lack of consensus on production, it is not surprising that there are varied opinions on the distribution of locally produced goods and resources, as well as the import and distribution of exotic items. They are compelling areas for research.

REFERENCES

Abrams, Elliot. 1987. "Economic Specialization and Construction Personnel in Classic Period Copan, Honduras." *American Antiquity* 52 (3): 485–499.

———. 1994. *How the Maya Built Their World.* Austin: University of Texas Press.

Adams, Richard E. W. 1970. "Suggested Classic Period Occupational Specialization in the Southern Maya Lowlands." In *Monographs and Papers in Maya Archaeology,* edited by William R. Bullard Jr., 487–502. Papers of the Peabody Museum of Archaeology and Ethnology, vol. 61. Cambridge, MA: Harvard University.

Adams, Richard E. W., Walter E. Brown Jr., and T. Patrick Culbert. 1981. "Radar Mapping, Archaeology, and Ancient Maya Land Use." *Science* 213: 1457–1463.

Andrews, Anthony P. 1983. *Maya Salt Production and Trade.* Tucson: University of Arizona Press.

———. 1991. "The Rural Chapels and Churches of Early Colonial Yucatan and Belize: An Archaeological Perspective." In *Columbian Consequences,* vol. 3, edited by David Hurst Thomas, 355–374. Washington, DC: Smithsonian Institution Press.

Andrews, Anthony P., Frank Asaro, Helen V. Michel, Fred H. Stross, and Pura Cervera Rivero. 1989. "The Obsidian Trade at Isla Cerritos, Yucatan, Mexico." *Journal of Field Archaeology* 16: 355–363.

Andrews, E. Wyllys, IV. 1969. *The Archaeological Use and Distribution of Mollusca in the Maya Lowlands.* Middle American Research Institute, Publication 34. New Orleans: Tulane University.

Andrews, E. Wyllys, IV, Michael P. Simmons, Elizabeth S. Wing, and E. Wyllys Andrews V. 1975. "Excavations of an Early Shell Midden on Isla Cancun, Quintana Roo, Mexico." *Middle American Research Institute, Publication* 31: 147–197. New Orleans: Tulane University.

Ardren, Traci, ed. 2002. *Ancient Maya Women.* New York: Altamira.

Awe, Jaime, Cassandra Bill, Mark Campbell, and David Cheetham. 1990. "Early Middle Formative Occupation in the Central Maya Lowlands: Recent Evidence from Cahal

Pech, Belize." Papers from the Institute of Archaeology 1: 1–5. London: University College London.

Awe, Jaime, and Paul F. Healy. 1994. "Flakes to Blades? Middle Formative Development of Obsidian Artifacts in the Upper Belize River Valley." *Latin American Antiquity* 5: 193–205.

Ball, Joseph W. 1993. "Pottery, Potters, Palaces, and Polities: Some Socioeconomic and Political Implications of Late Classic Maya Ceramic Industries." In *Lowland Maya Archaeology in the Eighth Century A.D.,* edited by Jeremy A. Sabloff and John S. Henderson, 243–272. Washington, DC: Dumbarton Oaks Research Library and Collections.

Ball, Joseph W., and Jennifer T. Taschek. 1991. "Late Classic Lowland Maya Political Organization and Central Place Analysis: New Insights from the Upper Belize Valley." *Ancient Mesoamerica* 2: 149–165.

Becker, Marshall J. 1973. "Archaeological Evidence for Occupational Specialization among the Classic Period Maya at Tikal, Guatemala." *American Antiquity* 38: 396–406.

Blake, Michael, B. Chisholm, John Clark, Barbara Voorhies, and Michael Love. 1992a. "Prehistoric Subsistence in the Soconusco Region." *Current Anthropology* 33: 83–94.

Blake, Michael, John Clark, B. Chisholm, and K. Mudar. 1992b. "Non-Agricultural Staples and Agricultural Supplements: Early Formative Subsistence in the Soconusco Region, Mexico." In *Transitions to Agriculture in Prehistory,* edited by A. B. Gebauer and T. Douglas Price, 133–152. Madison, WI: Prehistory Press.

Braswell, Geoffrey E., ed. 2003. *The Maya and Teotihuacan: Reinterpreting Early Classic Interaction.* Austin: University of Texas Press.

Braswell, Geoffrey E., John E. Clark, Kazuo Aoyama, Heather I. McKillop, and Michael D. Glascock. 2000. "Determining the Geological Provenance of Obsidian Artifacts from the Maya Region: A Test of the Efficacy of Visual Sourcing." *Latin American Antiquity* 11: 269–282.

Carr, H. Sorraya. 1986. "Preliminary Results of Analysis of Fauna." In *Archaeology at Cerros, Belize, Central America,* edited by Robin Robertson and David A. Freidel, 127–146. Dallas: Southern Methodist University Press.

Chase, Diane Z., and Arlen F. Chase. 1996. "Maya Multiples: Individuals, Entries, and Tombs in Structure A34 of Caracol." *Latin American Antiquity* 7: 61–79.

Christie, Jessica J., ed. 2003. *Maya Palaces and Elite Residences.* Austin: University of Texas Press.

Clark, John E. 1994. "The Development of Early Formative Ranked Societies in the Soconusco, Chiapas, Mexico." Ph.D. dissertation, Department of Anthropology, University of Michigan, Ann Arbor.

Clark, John E., and Richard Hansen. 2001. "The Architecture of Early Kingship: Comparative Perspectives on the Origin of the Maya Royal Court." In *Royal Courts of the Ancient Maya,* vol. 2, edited by Takeshi Inomata and Stephen Houston, 1–45. Boulder: Westview.

Clark, John E., and Stephen Houston. 1998. "Craft Specialization, Gender, and Personhood among the Post-Conquest Maya of Yucatan, Mexico." In *Craft and Social Identity,* edited by Cathy Costin and Rita Wright, 31–46. Archeological Papers 8. Washington, DC: American Anthropological Association.

Coe, Michael D. 1978. *Lords of the Underworld: Masterpieces of Classic Maya Ceramics.* Princeton, NJ: Art Museum, Princeton University, and Princeton University Press.

———. 1982. *Old Gods and Young Heroes: The Pearlman Collection of Maya Ceramics.* Jerusalem: Israel Museum.

Coe, Michael D., and Justin Kerr. 1998. *The Art of the Maya Scribe.* New York: Harry N. Abrams.

Coe, Michael D., and Mark Van Stone. 2001. *Reading the Maya Glyphs.* New York: Thames & Hudson.

Culbert, T. Patrick. 1974. *The Lost Civilization: The Story of the Classic Maya.* New York: Harper & Row.

———, ed. 1991. *Classic Maya Political History: Hieroglyphic and Archaeological Evidence.* New York: Cambridge University Press.

Davidson, William V. 1991. "Geographical Perspectives on Spanish-Pech (Paya) Indian Relationships, Northeast Honduras, Sixteenth Century." In *Columbian Consequences,* vol. 3, edited by David Hurst Thomas, 205–226. Washington, DC: Smithsonian Institution Press.

Demarest, Arthur. 1996. "The Maya State: Centralized or Segmentary? Closing Comment." *Current Anthropology* 37: 821–824.

Dockall, J. E., and Harry J. Shafer. 1993. "Testing the Producer-Consumer Model for Santa Rita Corozal, Belize." *Latin American Antiquity* 4: 158–179.

Dull, Robert A., John R. Southon, and Payson Sheets. 2001. "Volcanism, Ecology, and Culture: A Reassessment of the Volcán Ilopango TBJ Eruption in the Southern Maya Realm." *Latin American Antiquity* 12: 25–44.

Emery, Kitty, ed. 2004. *Maya Zooarchaeology.* Los Angeles: Costen Institute of Archaeology, University of California.

Estrada Belli, Francisco. 1999. *The Archaeology of Complex Societies in Southeastern Pacific Coastal Guatemala: A Regional GIS Approach.* Oxford: British Archaeology Reports, International Series 820.

Fash, William. 2001. *Scribes, Warriors, and Kings,* 2d ed. New York: Thames & Hudson.

Fedick, Scott, ed. 1996. *The Managed Mosaic.* Salt Lake City: University of Utah Press.

Feldman, Lawrence. 1974. "Shells from Afar: 'Panamic' Mollusca in Maya Sites." In *Mesoamerican Archaeology: New Approaches,* edited by Norman Hammond, 129–134. Austin: University of Texas Press.

Ferguson, William M., and Richard E. W. Adams. 2001. *Mesoamerica's Ancient Cities,* rev. ed. Albuquerque: University of New Mexico Press.

Foias, Antonia E., and Ronald L. Bishop. 1997. Changing Ceramic Production and Exchange in the Petexbatun Region, Guatemala: Reconsidering the Classic Maya Collapse. *Ancient Mesoamerica* 8: 275–291.

Fox, John W., and Garrett W. Cook. 1996. "Constructing Maya Communities: Ethnography for Archaeology." *Current Anthropology* 37 (5): 811–830.

Freidel, David A. 1979. "Culture Areas and Interaction Spheres: Contrasting Approaches to the Emergence of Civilization in the Maya Lowlands." *American Antiquity* 44: 36–54.

———. 1981. "The Political Economics of Residential Dispersion among the Lowland Maya." In *Lowland Maya Settlement Patterns,* edited by Wendy Ashmore, 371–382. Albuquerque: University of New Mexico Press.

———. 1992. "Children of the First Father's Skull: Terminal Classic Warfare in the Northern Maya Lowlands and the Transformation of Kingship and Elite Hierarchies." In *Mesoamerican Elites: An Archaeological Assessment,* edited by Diane Z. Chase and Arlen F. Chase, 99–117. Norman: University of Oklahoma Press.

Freidel, David A., and Vernon Scarborough. 1982. "Subsistence, Trade, and Development of the Coastal Maya." In *Maya Subsistence,* edited by Kent V. Flannery, 131–155. New York: Academic Press.

Freidel, David A., and Linda Schele. 1988. "Kingship in the Late Preclassic Maya Lowlands: The Instruments and Places of Ritual Power." *American Anthropologist* 90: 547–567.

Fry, Robert E. 1979. "The Economics of Pottery at Tikal, Guatemala: Models of Exchange for Serving Vessels." *American Antiquity* 44 (3): 494–512.

———. 1980. "Models of Exchange for Major Shape Classes of Lowland Maya Pottery." In *Models and Methods in Regional Exchange,* edited by Robert E. Fry, 3–18. Society for American Archaeology Papers 1. Washington, DC: Society for American Archaeology.

Garber, James F., ed. 2004. *The Ancient Maya of the Belize Valley.* Gainesville: University Press of Florida.

Garber, James F., M. Kathryn Brown, Jaime J. Awe, and Christopher J. Hartman. 2004. "Middle Formative Prehistory of the Central Belize Valley: An Examination of Architecture, Material Culture, and Sociopolitical Change at Blackman Eddy." In *The Ancient Maya of the Belize Valley,* edited by James F. Garber, 25–47. Gainesville: University Press of Florida.

Graham, Elizabeth. 1987. "Resource Diversity in Belize and Its Implications for Models of Lowland Trade." *American Antiquity* 52: 753–767.

———. 1991. "Archaeological Insights into Colonial Period Maya Life at Tipu, Belize." In *Columbian Consequences,* vol. 3, edited by David H. Thomas, 319–335. Washington, DC: Smithsonian Institution Press.

———. 1994. The Highlands of the Lowlands: Environment and Archaeology in the Stann Creek District, Belize, Central America. Monographs in World Archaeology 19. Madison, WI: Prehistory Press.

Graham, Elizabeth, Grant D. Jones, and Robert R. Kautz. 1985. "Archaeology and Ethnohistory on a Spanish Colonial Frontier: An Interim Report on the Macal-Tipu Project in Western Belize." In *The Lowland Maya Postclassic,* edited by Arlen F. Chase and Prudence M. Rice, 206–214. Austin: University of Texas Press.

Guderjan, Thomas H., and James F. Garber, eds. 1995. *Maya Maritime Trade, Settlement, and Populations on Ambergris Caye, Belize.* Lancaster, CA: Labyrinthos.

Haggett, Peter. 1965. *Locational Analysis in Human Geography.* London: Edward Arnold.

Hamblin, Nancy. 1984. *Animal Use by the Cozumel Maya.* Tucson: University of Arizona Press.

Hammond, Norman. 1972. "Obsidian Trade Routes in the Mayan Area." *Science* 178: 1092–1093.

———, ed. 1991. *Cuello.* New York: Cambridge University Press.

Harrison, Peter D. 1978. "Bajos Revisited: Visual Evidence for One System of Agriculture." In *Pre-Hispanic Maya Agriculture,* edited by Peter D. Harrison and B. L. Turner II, 247–254. Albuquerque: University of New Mexico Press.

Harrison, Peter D., and B. L. Turner, eds. 1978. *Ancient Maya Agriculture.* Austin: University of Texas Press.

Haviland, William A. 1967. "Stature at Tikal, Guatemala: Implications for Ancient Maya Demography and Social Organization." *American Antiquity* 32: 117–125.

Healy, Paul F., and Jaime J. Awe. 2001. "Middle Preclassic Jade Spoon from Belize." *Mexicon* 23: 61–64.

Healy, Paul F., John D. H. Lambert, J. T. Arnason, and Richard J. Hebda. 1983. "Caracol, Belize: Evidence of Ancient Maya Agricultural Terraces." *Journal of Field Archaeology* 10: 397–410.

Healy, Paul F., Heather I. McKillop, and Bernetta Walsh. 1984. "Analysis of Obsidian from Moho Cay, Belize: New Evidence on Classic Maya Trade Routes." *Science* 225: 414–417.

Hester, Thomas R., Harry B. Iceland, Dale B. Hudler, and Harry B. Shafer. 1996. "The Colha Preceramic Project: Preliminary Results from the 1993–1995 Field Seasons." *Mexicon* 18: 45–50.

Houston, Stephen D. 1993. *Hieroglyphs and History at Dos Pilas: Dynastic Politics of the Classic Maya.* Austin: University of Texas Press.

Hult, Weston, and Thomas R. Hester. 1995. "The Lithics of Ambergris Caye." In *Maya Maritime Trade, Settlement, and Population on Ambergris Caye, Belize,* edited by Thomas H. Guderjan and James F. Garber, 139–161. Lancaster, CA: Labyrinthos.

Iceland, Harry B. 1997. "The Preceramic Origins of the Maya: The Results of the Colha Preceramic Project in Northern Belize." Ph.D. dissertation, Department of Anthropology, University of Texas, Austin.

Inomata, Takeshi. 1997. "The Last Day of a Fortified Maya Center: Archaeological Investigations at Aguateca, Guatemala." *Ancient Mesoamerica* 8: 337–351.

———. 2001. "The Power and Ideology of Artistic Creation: Elite Craft Specialists in Classic Maya Society." *Current Anthropology* 42): 321–349.

Inomata, Takeshi, and Kazuo Aoyama. 1996. "Central-Place Analysis in the La Entrada Region, Honduras: Implications for Understanding the Classic Maya Political and Economic Systems." *Latin American Antiquity* 7: 291–312.

Jacobi, Keith. 2000. *Last Rites for the Tipu Maya: Genetic Structuring in a Colonial Cemetery.* Tuscaloosa: University of Alabama Press.

Jones, Grant D. 1989. *Maya Resistance to Spanish Rule: Time and History on a Colonial Frontier.* Albuquerque: University of New Mexico Press.

Jones, John. 1994. "Pollen Evidence for Early Settlement and Agriculture in Northern Belize." *Palynology* 18: 205–211.

Joyce, Rosemary A. 2000. *Gender and Power in Prehispanic Mesoamerica.* Austin: University of Texas Press.

Kowaleski, Jeff. 2003. "Evidence for the Functions and Meanings of Some Northern Maya Palaces." In *Maya Palaces and Elite Residences,* edited by Jessica Joyce Christie, 204–252. Austin: University of Texas Press.

Kurjack, Edward B. 2003. "Palace and Society in the Northern Maya Lowlands." In *Maya Palaces and Elite Residences,* edited by Jessica Joyce Christie, 274–290. Austin: University of Texas Press.

Lange, Frederick W. 1971. "Marine Resources: A Viable Subsistence Alternative for the Prehistoric Lowland Maya." *American Anthropologist* 73: 619–639.

Leventhal, Richard M. 1990. "Southern Belize: An Ancient Maya Region." In *Vision and Revision in Maya Studies,* edited by Flora S. Clancey and Peter D. Harrison, 125–141. Albuquerque: University of New Mexico Press.

Marcus, Joyce. 1976. *Emblem and State in the Classic Maya Lowlands.* Washington, DC: Dumbarton Oaks.

———. 1993. "Ancient Maya Political Organization." In *Lowland Maya Archaeology in the Eighth Century A.D.,* edited by Jeremy A. Sabloff and John S. Henderson, 111–183. Washington, DC: Dumbarton Oaks Research Library and Collections.

———. 1995. "Where is Lowland Maya Archaeology Headed?" *Journal of Archaeological Research* 3: 3–53.

Martin, Paul S. 1973. "The Discovery of America." *Science* 179: 969–974.

Masson, Marilyn, and David A. Freidel, eds. 2002. *Ancient Maya Political Economies.* New York: Altamira.

McAnany, Patricia A. 1989a. "Stone-Tool Production and Exchange in the Eastern Maya Lowlands: The Consumer Perspective from Pulltrouser Swamp." *American Antiquity* 54: 332–346.

———. 1989b. "Economic Foundations of Prehistoric Maya Society: Paradigms and Concepts." In *Prehistoric Maya Economies of Belize,* edited by Patricia A. McAnany and Barry Isaac, 347–372. Research in Economic Anthropology, Supplement 4. Greenwich, CT: JAI Press.

McAnany, Patricia A., and Barry Isaac, eds. 1989. *Prehistoric Maya Economies of Belize.* Research in Economic Anthropology Supplement 4. Greenwich, CT: JAI Press.

McKillop, Heather. 1980. "Moho Cay, Belize: Preliminary Investigations of Trade, Settlement, and Marine Resource Exploitation." Master's thesis, Department of Anthropology, Trent University, Peterborough, Ontario, Canada; Ann Arbor: University Micrfilms.

———. 1984. "Prehistoric Maya Reliance on Marine Resources: Analysis of a Midden from Moho Cay, Belize." *Journal of Field Archaeology* 11: 25–35.

———. 1985. "Prehistoric Exploitation of the Manatee in the Maya and Circum-Caribbean Areas." *World Archaeology* 16: 337–353.

———. 1987. "Wild Cane Cay: An Insular Classic Period to Postclassic Period Maya Trading Station." Ph.D. dissertation, Department of Anthropology, University of California, Santa Barbara; Ann Arbor: University Microfilms.

———. 1989. "Coastal Maya Trade: Obsidian Densities from Wild Cane Cay, Belize." In *Prehistoric Maya Economies of Belize,* edited by Patricia McAnany and Barry Isaac, 17–56. Research in Economic Anthropology, Supplement 4. Greenwich, CT: JAI Press.

———. 1994. "Ancient Maya Tree Cropping: A Viable Subsistence Adaptation for the Island Maya." *Ancient Mesoamerica* 5: 129–140.

———. 1995a. "Underwater Archaeology, Salt Production, and Coastal Maya Trade at Stingray Lagoon, Belize." *Latin American Antiquity* 6: 214–228.

———. 1995b. "The Role of Northern Ambergris Caye in Maya Obsidian Trade: Evidence from Visual Sourcing and Blade Technology." In *Maya Maritime Trade, Settlement, and Populations on Ambergris Caye, Belize,* edited by Thomas H. Guderjan and James F. Garber, 163–174. Lancaster, CA: Labyrinthos.

———. 1996a. "Prehistoric Maya Use of Native Palms." In *The Managed Mosaic: Ancient Maya Agriculture and Resource Use,* edited by Scott L. Fedick, 278–294. Salt Lake City: University of Utah Press.

———. 1996b. "Ancient Maya Trading Ports and the Integration of Long-Distance and Regional Economies: Wild Cane Cay in South-Coastal Belize." *Ancient Mesoamerica* 7: 49–62.

———. 2002. *Salt: White Gold of the Ancient Maya.* Gainesville: University Press of Florida.

———. 2003a. "Catastrophic and Other Environmental Factors in the Classic Maya Collapse." Paper presented at the annual meeting of the American Association of Geographers, New Orleans, March.

———. 2004. "The Ancient Maya Trading Port on Moho Cay." In *The Ancient Maya of the Belize Valley: Half a Century of Archaeological Research,* edited by James F. Garber. Gainesville: University Press of Florida.

———. 2005. *In Search of Maya Sea Traders.* College Station: University of Texas Press.

McKillop, Heather, and Paul F. Healy, eds. 1989. *Coastal Maya Trade.* Occasional Papers in Anthropology 8. Peterborough, Ontario: Trent University.

McKillop, Heather, and L. J. Jackson. 1988. "Ancient Maya Obsidian Sources and Trade Routes." In *Obsidian Dates Monograph 4,* edited by Clement Meighan and Janet Scalise, 130–141. Los Angeles: Institute of Archaeology, University of California.

McKillop, Heather, L. J. Jackson, Helen Michel, Fred Stross, and Frank Asaro. 1988. "Chemical Sources Analysis of Maya Obsidian Artifacts: New Perspectives from Wild Cane Cay, Belize." In *Archaeometry 88,* edited by R. M. Farquhar, R. G. V. Hancock, and Larry A. Pavlish, 239–244. Department of Physics, University of Toronto.

McKillop, Heather, and Terance Winemiller. 2004. "Ancient Maya Environment, Settlement, and Diet: Quantitative and GIS Analyses of Mollusca from Frenchman's Cay." In *Maya Zooarchaeology,* edited by Kitty Emery. Los Angeles: Costen Institute of Archaeology, University of California.

Miksicek, Charles H. 1991. "The Ecology and Economy of Cuello." In *Cuello: An Early Maya Community in Belize,* edited by Norman Hammond, 70–97. New York: Cambridge University Press.

Mitchum, Beverly A. 1991. "Lithic Artifacts from Cerros, Belize: Production, Consumption, and Trade." In *Maya Stone Tools: Selected Papers from the Second Maya Lithic Conference,* edited by Thomas R. Hester and Harry J. Shafer, 45–54. Madison, WI: Prehistory Press.

Moholy-Nagy, Hattula. 1990. "The Misidentification of Mesoamerican Lithic Workshops." *Latin American Antiquity* 1: 268–279.

———. 1997. "Middens, Construction Fill, and Offerings: Evidence for the Organization of Classic Period Craft Production at Tikal, Guatemala." *Journal of Field Archaeology* 24: 293–313.

———. 1999. "Mexican Obsidian at Tikal, Guatemala." *Latin American Antiquity* 10: 300–313.

Moholy-Nagy, Hattula, Frank Asaro, and Fred H. Stross. 1984. "Tikal Obsidian: Sources and Typology." *American Antiquity* 49: 104–117.

Moholy-Nagy, Hattula, and Fred Nelson. 1990. "New Data on Sources of Obsidian Artifacts from Tikal, Guatemala." *Ancient Mesoamerica* 1: 71–80.

Nelson, Fred W. 1985. "Summary of the Results of Analysis of Obsidian Artifacts from the Maya Lowlands." *Scanning Electron Microscopy* 2: 631–649.

Pendergast, David M. 1979. *Excavations at Altun Ha,* vol. 1. Toronto: Royal Ontario Museum.

———. 1981. "Lamanai, Belize: Summary of Excavation Results 1974–1980." *Journal of Field Archaeology* 8: 29–53.

———. 1982. "Ancient Maya Mercury." *Science* 217: 533–535.

Pohl, Mary D., ed. 1990. *Ancient Maya Wetland Agriculture: Excavations on Albion Island, Northern Belize.* Boulder, CO: Westview.

Rathje, Williams L. 1971. "The Origin and Development of Lowland Classic Maya Civilization." *American Antiquity* 36 (3): 275–285.

Reents Budet, Dorie. 1994. *Painting the Maya Universe.* Durham, NC: Duke University Press.

Reina, Ruben E., and Robert M. Hill III. 1978. *The Traditional Pottery of Guatemala.* Austin: University of Texas Press.

Reina, Ruben E., and John Monaghen. 1981. "The Ways of the Maya: Salt Production in Sacapulas, Guatemala." *Expedition* 23: 13–33.

Rice, Don S., and Prudence M. Rice. 1990. "Population Size and Population Change in the Central Peten Lakes Region, Guatemala." In *Precolumbian Population History in the Maya Lowlands,* edited by T. Patrick Culbert and Don S. Rice, 123–148. Albuquerque: University of New Mexico Press.

Rice, Prudence M. 1984. "Obsidian Procurement in the Central Peten Lakes Region, Guatemala." *Journal of Field Archaeology* 11: 181–194.

———. 1987a. "Economic Change in the Lowland Maya Late Classic Period." In *Specialization, Exchange, and Complex Societies,* edited by Elizabeth M. Brumfiel and Timothy K. Earle, 76–85. New York: Cambridge University Press.

———. 1987b. *Pottery Analysis: A Source Book.* Chicago: University of Chicago Press.

Robles C., Fernando, and Anthony P. Andrews. 1985. "A Review and Synthesis of Recent Postclassic Archaeology in Northern Yucatan." In *Late Lowland Maya Civilization,* edited by Jeremy A. Sabloff and E. Wyllys Andrews V, 53–98. Albuquerque: University of New Mexico Press.

Sabloff, Jeremy A., and William L. Rathje, eds. 1975. *A Study of Changing Pre-Columbian Commercial Systems: The 1972–73 Seasons at Cozumel, Mexico.* Monographs of the

Peabody Museum of Archaeology and Ethnology, vol. 3. Cambridge, MA: Harvard University.

Sanders, William T., and Barbara Price. 1968. *Mesoamerica: The Evolution of a Civilization.* New York: Random House.

Saturno, William. 2003. Proyecto San Bartolo. http://www.sanbartolo.org/index.htm.

Scarborough, Vernon L. 1991. *Archaeology at Cerros, Belize, Central America,* vol. 3: *The Settlement System in a Late Preclassic Maya Community.* Dallas: Southern Methodist University Press.

———. 1998. "Ecology and Ritual: Water Management and the Maya." *Latin American Antiquity* 9: 135–159.

Schele, Linda, and David A. Freidel. 1990. *A Forest of Kings: The Untold Story of the Ancient Maya.* New York: William Morrow.

Schele, Linda, and Peter Mathews. 1991. "Royal Visits and Other Intersite Relationships among the Classic Maya." In *Classic Maya Political History,* edited by T. Patrick Culbert, 226–252. New York: Cambridge University Press.

Schele, Linda, and Mary Miller. 1986. *The Blood of Kings: Dynasty and Ritual in Maya Art.* New York: George Braziller.

Shafer, Harry J., and Thomas R. Hester. 1983. "Ancient Maya Chert Workshops in Northern Belize, Central America." *American Antiquity* 48: 519–543.

———. 1986. "Maya Tool Craft Specialization and Production at Colha, Belize: A Reply to Mallory." *American Antiquity* 51: 158–166.

Sheets, Payson D., Kenneth Hirth, Fred Lange, Fred Stross, Frank Asaro, and Helen Michel. 1990. "Obsidian Sources and Elemental Analyses of Artifacts in Southern Mesoamerica and the Northern Intermediate Zone." *American Antiquity* 55: 144–158.

Shipley, Webster E., III, and Elizabeth Graham. 1989. "Petrographic Analysis and Preliminary Source Identification of Selected Stone Artifacts from the Maya Sites of Seibal and Uaxactun, Guatemala." *Journal of Archaeological Science* 14: 367–383.

Siemens, Alfred H. 1978. "Karst and the Pre-Hispanic Maya in the Southern Lowlands." In *Prehispanic Maya Agriculture,* edited by Peter D. Harrison and B. L. Turner II, 117–143. Albuquerque: University of New Mexico Press.

Sluyter, Andrew. 1993. "Long-Distance Staple Transport in Western Mesoamerica: Insights through Quantitative Modeling." *Ancient Mesoamerica* 4: 193–199.

Spence, Michael W. 1996. "Commodity or Gift: Teotihuacan Obsidian in the Maya Region." *Latin American Antiquity* 7: 21–39.

Stephens, John Lloyd. [1843] 1963. *Incidents of Travel in Yucatan.* 2 vols. New York: Dover.

———. [1841] 1969. *Incidents of Travel in Central America, Chiapas, and Yucatan.* New York: Dover.

Stross, F. H., H. R. Bowman, H. V. Michel, F. Asaro, and N. Hammond. 1978. "Mayan Obsidian: Source Correlations for Southern Belize Artifacts." *Archaeometry* 20: 83–93.

Tourtellot, Gair, and Jeremy A. Sabloff. 1972. "Exchange Systems among the Ancient Maya." *American Antiquity* 37: 126–135.

Turner, B. L., and Peter D. Harrison, eds. 1983. *Pulltrouser Swamp: Ancient Maya Habitat, Agriculture, and Settlement in Northern Belize.* Austin: University of Texas Press.

Turner, B. L., II and Charles H. Miksicek. 1984. "Economic Plant Species Associated with Prehistoric Agriculture in the Maya Lowlands." *Economic Botany* 38: 179–193.

Wauchope, Robert. 1938. *Modern Maya Houses.* Carnegie Institution of Washington Publication 502. Washington, DC: Carnegie Institution of Washington.

White, Christine D., ed. 1999. *Reconstructing Ancient Maya Diet.* Salt Lake City: University of Utah Press.

White, Christine D., Fred J. Longstaffe, and Kimberley R. Law. 2001. "Revisiting the Teotihuacan Connection at Altun Ha: Oxygen-Isotope Analysis of Tomb F-8/1." *Ancient Mesoamerica* 12: 65–72.

White, Christine D., Fred J. Longstaffe, Michael W. Spence, and Kimberley R. Law. 2000. "Testing the Nature of Teotihuacan Imperialism at Kaminaljuyu Using Phosphate Oxygen-Isotope Ratios." *Journal of Anthropological Research* 56: 535–558.

White, Christine D., David M. Pendergast, Fred J. Longstaffe, and Kimberley R. Law. 2001. "Social Complexity and Food Systems at Altun Ha, Belize: The Isotopic Evidence." *Latin American Antiquity* 12: 371–393.

Whittington, Stephen, and David Reed, eds. 1997. *Bones of the Maya.* Washington, DC: Smithsonian Institution Press.

Winemiller, Terance. 1997. "Limestone Resource Exploitation by the Ancient Maya at Chichen Itza, Yucatan, Mexico." Unpublished Master's thesis, Department of Geography and Anthropology, Louisiana State University, Baton Rouge.

Wing, Elizabeth S. 1978. "Use of Dogs for Food: An Adaptation to the Coastal Environment." In *Prehistoric Coastal Adaptations,* edited by Barbara L. Stark and Barbara Voohries, 29–41. New York: Academic Press.

Wright, Lori E. 1997. "Biological Perspectives on the Collapse of the Pasion Maya." *Ancient Mesoamerica* 8: 267–273.

Wright, Lori E., and Christine D. White. 1996. "Human Biology in the Classic Maya Collapse: Evidence from Paleopathology and Paleodiet." *Journal of World Prehistory* 10: 147–198.

CHAPTER 6

Social Organization
and Social Structure

SETTLEMENT PATTERNS

The way in which ancient Maya settlements were distributed across the landscape, the organization of buildings and spaces within communities, and the spatial organization within structures reflect on the social, economic, and ideological aspects of Maya society. The late Maya archaeologist Gordon R. Willey, Bowditch Professor of Central American Archaeology at Harvard University, is credited with the introduction of settlement pattern studies to the discipline of archaeology. Willey's research defined settlement patterns in the Viru Valley, Peru, in the late 1940s (Willey 1953). He subsequently directed a settlement pattern study in the upper Belize River Valley, initially focusing on residential house mounds at Barton Ramie and later focusing on other sites of various sizes along the Belize River, including Xunantunich, Floral Park, and Baking Pot (Willey et al. 1965). The Belize River Valley survey was a dramatic shift from the focus on large sites that was previously characteristic of Maya studies. The study was carried out from 1953 to 1956 and set the pace for subsequent regional settlement pattern projects in the Maya area. Settlement pattern studies are now an integral part of Maya fieldwork (Ashmore 1981; Culbert and Rice 1990; Garber 2004).

COMMUNITY PATTERNS

The basic settlement unit within an ancient Maya community was the plazuela (plaza) group. It is evident in the spatial organization throughout Maya settlements, from the monumental architecture in the center of the largest cities, to the modest households in the periphery of cities, and in towns, villages, hamlets, and even isolated homesteads. A residential plaza group contained houses, outbuildings, and exterior space utilized by related family groups, perhaps members of the same lineage or extended family. The plaza group also defined the spatial organization of public architecture consisting of temples, palaces (which may also have been administrative buildings), and ball courts. Central plazas at the larger cities contain stelae and altars with carvings of Maya kings and queens and hieroglyphic texts commemorating important dates and events, all for public viewing.

Sites mentioned in the text about social organization

Tikal central plaza (Courtesy H. McKillop)

The dispersed pattern of plaza groups within Maya communities has led some researchers, such as William T. Sanders, to interpret Maya society as less urban in character than its contemporary in highland Mexico, Teotihuacan (Sanders and Price 1968). In comparing maps of Tikal and the city of Teotihuacan, Sanders observed that Teotihuacan was built according to a grid system of streets in cardinal directions and was densely settled with buildings. By way of contrast, Tikal's map shows plazas dispersed across the landscape according to undulations in the landscape and the locations of aguadas (water reservoirs) and swamps. As a result, the density of settlement is much less at Tikal than at Teotihuacan.

Sanders concluded that the differences in urban population density reflected differences in the organization of the societies, with the Maya being socially and economically less complex than Teotihuacan (Sanders and Price 1968). He argued that the differences in community settlement patterns reflected the organization of Tikal as a chiefdom and Teotihuacan at a state level of organization. However, the spatial organization may simply reflect the featureless plain on which the city of Teotihuacan was built in contrast to the undulating landscape of the Maya capital. Although accepting that the Classic Maya had a dispersed community settlement pattern, Maya archaeologists have argued that the hierarchical distribution of settlements regionally across the landscape is a better indicator of the Maya's level of social and economic organization than the physical landscape and that this regional settlement pattern indicates that the Maya had a state level of organization, as will be discussed further below.

Estimations of the size of Maya communities and their boundaries are hindered by the tropical rainforest setting and have contributed to difficulty in estimating population size and density. Pioneering fieldwork (Pulesten 1983) at Tikal used four transects cut through the rainforest in cardinal directions to investigate the size of Tikal, extending the search for Maya settlement beyond the central area of the city. This method has also been utilized at other Maya cities, such as Pacbitun in western Belize, where Paul F. Healy (1990) of Trent University had students cut transects to discover the extent of suburban settlement. Another method was used by Vernon Scarborough (1991) at the Late Preclassic city of Cerros in northern Belize. Whereas transect surveys normally followed Puleston's (1983) method of walking a certain distance on either side of the trail, Scarborogh more intensively searched the entire area. An exhaustive settlement survey around the Late Classic city of La Milpa directed by Gair Tourtellot (Tourtellot, Clarke, and Hammond 1993; Tourtellot, Wolf, Estrada-Belli, et al. 2000) of Boston University has used transects as well, but also has predicted the location of outlying satellite communities around La Milpa from what Tourtellot calls the "Maya cosmogram." This is the ritualized, idealized view of the Maya world, divided into four quadrants, that is recorded in historical records such as the *Popol Vuh*. With the concept of La Milpa as a cosmogram of the quadripartite organization of the ancient Maya cosmos, Tourtellot and his colleagues predicted the location of an outlying community, and, using a GPS (global positioning system) unit, they walked to that location and discovered a satellite community perched on a hilltop with monumental architecture, in contrast to the more modest settlement remains in the surrounding area.

Arlen and Diane Chase of the University of Central Florida used the Maya road systems, called causeways (sacbes), evident at Caracol to investigate the size and nature of the city (Chase and Chase 2001). In a finding that would only have been possible with a long-term, multiyear field project, the Chases discovered that the causeways facilitated the centralized control by Caracol rulers of a large suburban region. The causeways were routes of communication and control by the central Caracol Maya to the suburban population, as well as routes for transporting goods produced in outlying areas to the downtown area. In an innovative model, the Chases describe Caracol as a modern "garden city," with at least the beginnings of a middle class living in the suburbs and intimately connected to the Caracal leadership in the city center.

Causeways were an important feature of Maya cities, although researchers such as Maya archaeologist Edward Kurjack and others (Kurjack and Garza 1981) have discovered more causeways in the northern Maya lowlands, where the vegetation cover is less dense, than in the southern Maya lowlands. However, even at smaller communities such as Cahal Pech in western Belize, Jaime Awe's (Aimers, Powis, and Awe 2000) team has investigated outlying plazuela groups linked to the site core by causeways. Although causeways have been known for decades as important avenues of political and economic control and communication between Maya cities, especially in the northern Maya lowlands, Maya archaeologists now realize their importance as a feature within Maya communities as well. The potential ritual value of roadways should also not be ignored.

Where causeways facilitate movement of people within and between communities, walls restrict access. The Late Postclassic Maya city of Mayapan is a walled community containing a much higher density of monumental and residential architecture than is seen in earlier cities, particularly in the southern Maya lowlands. Clearly, the defensive feature of the wall as well as the more open and uniform landscape contributed to the distinctiveness of the settlement. Karl Ruppert, Tatiana Proskouriakoff, and colleagues (Pollock et al. 1962) investigated Mayapan in the 1950s as part of their research at Chichen Itza, mapping the buildings within the city wall as well as carrying out excavations in the monumental architecture. The high density of settlement within the wall at Mayapan contrasts to other cities, but of course most predate this late Maya city. The relationship between walled cities and community patterning may become more of of a focus of study, as more walled cities are excavated, such as Chunchucmil.

Caves

Subterranean caves are a ubiquitous feature in the karstic topography of the Maya lowlands. Perhaps because of the rich symbolic imagery of the watery underworld, many of these caves were used for ancient Maya rituals. Early cave explorations by David Pendergast (1969, 1970, 1971, 1974) in the Maya Mountains of western Belize in the 1960s revealed human burials as well as an abundance of water storage vessels and other pottery. Ongoing study of caves in the Maya Mountains by Jaime Awe and colleagues reveals that although caves are often obscured in the landscape of rainforest vegetation, many, even the smallest and difficult to enter, were utilized in antiquity. Naj Tunich cave in the Peten of Guatemala contains human and other images painted on interior walls (Stone 1995). Human figures drawn with black paint are shown participating in penis bloodletting and other rituals, copulation, and contemplation. The paintings are accompanied by hieroglyphic text. Overlay of images suggests successive visits, perhaps pilgrimages, to caves. James Brady's (Brady et al. 1997) team found caves used by the Maya in the Petexbatun region of Guatemala. An underground cave system mirrored the east-west orientation of the site of Dos Pilas. One entrance to the cave was sealed by a tomb in an ancestor shrine in the royal family's residential plaza at the center of the city. Arthur Demarest and colleagues (2003) refer to the sacred geography of Dos Pilas, with the royal shrine as a sacred mountain linking the living world and the underworld, Xibalba, by a sacred tree of life, the grave shaft.

REGIONAL SETTLEMENT PATTERNS

At the height of Late Classic Maya civilization, the southern lowlands consisted of about eighty regional polities, each with a capital city and surrounding towns and villages that were linked to the capital economically, politically, and ideologically (Martin and Grube 2000). Although there is some discussion about the level of central political and economic organization of Maya polities (see chapter 5 of this book), there was a hierarchical organization that is visually evident in the distribution and size of Maya communities. The hierarchical organization reflected a centralization of political and economic power, although the degree of centralization is a topic of some debate among Maya archaeologists. The capital of each polity was the seat of royal power, as reflected in hieroglyphic records written on stelae about each Maya ruler's military and political accomplishments. The capital was normally the largest settlement in the region, again reflecting its political power.

In an innovative although controversial model, Joyce Marcus used the concept of Central Place Theory from geography to evaluate the distribution of Late Classic Maya polities in the southern Maya lowlands. According to Marcus (1976, 1993), the regular spacing of Maya cities was due to administrative factors that kept competing cities equally spaced from one another and distributed smaller towns and villages around the cities. Marcus backed her model by describing the distribution of "emblem glyphs" or city names on stelae. She assumed that captors mentioned on stelae the emblem glyphs of cities that they conquered and thereby controlled.

PAN-LOWLAND SETTLEMENT PATTERNS

In addition to the regional polities that, by the time of the Late Classic, were engaged in bitter conflicts with one another, archaeologists and Maya epigraphers also interpret higher-level organization. By the Late Classic, for example, Tikal was undoubtedly a "supercapital" in the southern Maya lowlands, as indicated by its size and the hieroglyphic record of Maya leaders on stelae. Although acknowledging the supreme power of Tikal, glyphic evidence from Stela A at Copan, erected by the ruler 18 Jog (erroneously noted in some places as 18 Rabbit) indicates that the Copan ruler regarded the southern Maya lowlands as having four superpowers, Tikal, Calakmul (or El Peru?), Copan, and Palenque, during the Late Classic. Marcus (1976) argued that this mirrored the mythical view of the Maya world as a quadripartite division. Decipherment of Mayan hieroglyphs, histories of Maya royal families recorded on carved stelae and painted pots, and offerings recovered from their graves provide details of changing political alliances, military defeats, and geopolitics.

MARRIAGE AND THE FAMILY

Hieroglyphic records on stelae at large Maya cities record marriages and family composition of the Maya royalty. In contrast, modern Maya families are used as the basis for understanding the nonroyal Classic Maya families. Emphasis on gender studies in archaeology has resulted in growing interest among Mayanists about the nature of marriage and the family among the ancient Maya (Ardren 2002). Rosemary Joyce (2000) interpreted male and female activities from pottery figurines, particularly those at the island site of Jaina, as well as those from Lubaantun and elsewhere in the Maya lowlands.

Royal Maya women obtained status and rank by marriage, were used by royalty to gain or solidify political power, and occasionally ruled (Martin and Grube 2000). Wives of rulers are shown on carved monuments and on painted pots, usually engaged in ritual, either with their husbands or occasionally on their own. Mothers of rulers are mentioned in texts on monuments reporting dynastic lines. The ruler normally married locally, and usually from among the royalty. The local origin of a ruler's wife, however, is often assumed, as she is not named by a separate emblem glyph recording her origin from another polity. From hieroglyphic texts, we know that the Maya, at least the rulers, were polygamous. The first wife had the highest status, as indicated by her participation in rituals with the ruler, as depicted in art. In one case—that of Shield Jaguar from Yaxchilan—his third wife, who was the mother of the heir, Bird Jaguar, was evidently not of royal blood.

Hieroglyphic records indicate that about 10 percent of royal marriages involved foreign women (women from other polities). Presumably, both royal houses hoped to gain by the intermarriage. Lesser sites may have hoped to gain prestige, trade benefits, and the support of a more powerful ally. Dominant sites may have wanted to extend their political domain or perhaps just extend their network of trading partners. Intermarriage fostered alliances between or within regional polities, enhanced a site's (or a ruler's) status if a woman was from a high-ranking polity, and sometimes facilitated control of a lesser site. For example, a ruler at Dos Pilas, who proclaimed himself the first ruler of the city, married women from El Chorro and Itzan, perhaps in an attempt to gain power and acceptance within the region. Certainly the status of Copan improved when a royal woman from Palenque was married to the successor of 18 Jog. It is unclear whether or not Lady Six Sky from Dos Pilas married the local ruler in Naranjo, but her arrival at the site presaged a time of great florescence, following the site's defeat (twice) by Calakmul, Naranjo's humiliation in recounting the defeat on a Hieroglyphic Stairway (a temple staircase carved with heiroglyphs), and a lapse of forty years in erecting carved stelae. The son of a royal woman from Dos Pilas who married into the Tamarindito lineage proclaimed his subservience to Dos Pilas, perhaps as a result of a timely marriage alliance by Dos Pilas.

Royal Maya Households

Hieroglyphic records on stelae indicate that the Classic Maya had patrilineal descent patterns, in which descent and inheritance, including rulership, was through the father. There are rare instances in which Maya queens were rulers, though. Marriage was regarded as an opportunity to initiate, maintain, or solidify political ties with other polities within the Maya lowlands, and occasionally beyond, as with Teotihuacan or its Maya highland outpost of Kaminaljuyu in the outskirts of modern Guatemala City. As such, foreign (from beyond the Maya lowlands) women sometimes married local Maya royalty.

Maya kings, queens, and their royal children evidently lived in the residential palaces in city centers and participated in public and private ceremonies in the adjacent temple buildings (Christie 2003). Royal rituals were performed for public viewing from the plaza at important events in the king's life, notably at accession to the throne, marriage, defeat of another polity, and death. The royal rituals involved bloodletting, trances, and communication with the supernatural forces that made kingship divine. Depictions of lancets of obsidian or stingray spines being used to pierce the body and draw blood, or of ropes being pulled through the tongue, are graphically shown on Maya stelae with accompanying hieroglyphic text. These depictions underscore the nature and importance of blood sacrifice among the Classic Maya.

The Common Maya Family

The image of the common Maya is based on comparisons with the Maya encountered by the Spaniards in the sixteenth century and with the relict Maya living in small villages throughout the Maya lowlands in modern times. These ethnographic and ethnohistoric analogies provide a picture of Maya farmers living in small communities, using slash and burn (swidden) agriculture at varying distances from the settlement and cultivating kitchen gardens around the house. Archaeologically, the mounded remains of houses—often built with stone foundations, but sometimes with only earthen floors—identify the Maya households. Diane Chase (1990) and K. Anne Pyburn (1990), among others, note that many of the more modest Maya houses have left no mounded remains and are invisible to Maya archaeologists equating mounds with families (see also Culbert and Rice 1990; Steiner 1994).

In a seminal study of modern Maya houses, Robert Wauchope (1934, 1938) noted that the excavated remains of ancient Maya houses resemble modern Maya houses, despite the major economic, social, and political changes that have affected the Maya since the Classic period. The village of Ceren, El Salvador, was preserved under volcanic tephra around A.D. 600 (Sheets 2002). Excavations of houses, fields, and plazas focused on activities that took place in Maya households and found that it was the use of space within and around buildings, rather than the house itself, that gives researchers information about Maya families. Focus on ancient Maya households, rather than on the houses themselves, may therefore better enable Maya archaeologists to understand the nature and composition of Maya families (Wilk and Ashmore 1988).

Although the transition from the Late Preclassic to the Classic period in the southern Maya lowlands witnessed a change from the role of kinship to kingship in the inheritance of power among Maya royalty, kinship continued to be the symbol of rank and importance among the common Maya (Freidel and Schele 1988). In an insightful study of kinship, Patricia McAnany (1995) of Boston University enunciated the importance of kinship to the common Maya, as reflected in the mounded remains of superimposed houses containing the buried remains of lineally related family members. The common Maya traced their importance through their lineal descent from a common ancestor. What better way to record lineage and importance than by burying the dead at home? Especially as public display of power and kingship on stone monuments was evidently reserved for Maya royalty.

Limestone Lintel 25 from Yaxchilan, showing serpent evoked in a vision by Lady Xook after bloodletting (The Art Archive/Museum of Mankind London/Eileen Tweedy)

SOCIAL STRATIFICATION

It is not surprising from the complexity of Classic Maya civilization that there would be a number of social levels in the society (Marcus 1993), and the range in size and decoration of residential buildings has long been an indicator of differing ranks in Maya society. However, it was not until the decipherment of the hieroglyphs that the extent of social stratification has emerged, at least for the upper echelons of Maya society. From hieroglyphic texts, we know that the highest rank in Maya society was that of ahau, or lord, which included both the ruler and a larger group of males and females, not all of whom were of equal rank. Paramount rulers, the kings and queens, of the oldest and largest cities began a tradition in the late fourth century A.D. that subsequently spread elsewhere, of referring to themselves as divine lord, k'uhal ahau. Emblem glyphs of Maya cities consist of the glyph ahau, the glyph for the word divine, as well as the polity name (Martin and Grube 2000, 17). The most powerful dynastic leaders called themselves kaloomte, denoting power over more than one polity. Some kings added the title ochk'in, meaning west, to denote they claimed legitimacy from Teotihuacan, when the influence of this rival highland state became evident in the Maya area, which was at the end of the fourth century A.D. By the Late Classic, some of the most powerful dynastic leaders were recording their political dominance over dynastic leaders by displaying accession glyphs at the subservient city: The accession glyph is followed by a glyph "ukab'jiiy, " translated as "he supervised it, " followed by the name of the more powerful king. For example, the accession to the throne of the ruler of Cancuen in A.D. 677 is recorded in hieroglyphs at the city showing his overlord, Yuknoon of Calakmul (Martin and Grube 2000, 20).

The next lower level, still considered nobility, was the cahal. Cahals were rulers of small sites, as well as nobles who assisted the ahau in battle and in various royal ceremonies. Both ahau and cahal were inherited statuses. In the few recorded instances in which a cahal female married an ahau male, their children had the rank of ahau.

The social order was maintained by a downward flow of honors, responsibilities, and titles and an upward flow of resources and goods. The upward flow of resources also helped to maintain the functioning and existence of the social hierarchy. The ruling dynasty in the polity capital was at the top of the social hierarchy. From Morley (1946) and Thompson's (1970) early characterizations of the social order of the Classic Maya consisting of priests and peasants, to the current views of elite and commoner, all agree that the Classic Maya society was stratified.

There were at least two classes of elites (ahau and cahal), then two classes of commoners (macehualob), and perhaps slaves. Although the hieroglyphs record the lives of a small number of the royal dynasties, the overwhelming majority of Maya lives are unrecorded. Richard E. W. Adams (1974, 294–295) estimates that 98 percent of the Classic Maya were commoners. Hammond (1982) describes slaves at the bottom of the social order, followed by the rural farmer who produced food to support the infrastructure of Maya society. In urban settings, the lowest class of society was the common unskilled laborer,

King Yax Pasah on Late Classic stela from Copan, Honduras (The Art Archive/ Archaeological Museum Copan Honduras/Dagli Orti)

who quarried and hauled stone; this class also included cleaners, porters, and servants. Skilled artisans included stone and wood carvers, stucco workers, painters, potters, scribes and sculptors not belonging to the elite, traders, and low-level bureaucrats carrying out orders of the ruling elite.

The ruling dynasty, other noble lineages, and many commoner lineages lived in the polity capital. At least some of the nobles and commoners were craft workers, worked as scribes, or pursued other nonfarming occupations.

Occupational specialization may have been class-specific, with intellectual activities (especially those requiring literacy) being the prerogative of the elite (royalty and nobility). Adams (1970) describes occupational specialization among the Maya, based on the level of skill (unskilled, semiskilled, and skilled) and the kind of activity (managerial, production for the elite, or production for the bulk of society). The ruling elite managed war, administration, astronomy, and the calendar. The upper levels of commoner society carried out skilled crafts. As with Teotihuacan, occupational specialization may have been tied to lineages. Certainly in some cases, as with chert tool production at Colha, craft specialization was carried out in households.

Adams (1970) defines four levels of occupational specialization. The top level (fourth tier) was exclusive to elites and included administrators, architectural planners, and religious and military leaders, as well as traders. The third tier of specialists included scribes, sculptors, costumiers, and armorers. The second tier included part-time semiskilled workers such as masons and chert workers, with unskilled labor forming the lowest level of occupational specialists. In contrast to Teotihuacan where residential craft workshops were common throughout the city, evidence for craft workers or other evidence for a middle class has been more ephemeral for the Classic Maya. However, community studies—such as at Caracol showing the variation in Maya settlement, at the Punta Ycacos Salt Works on the southern Belize coast, in household chert tool workshops at Colha, and those of pictorial evidence on Late Classic Maya pots for scribes, vessel painters, and other artisans—all point to the existence of a middle class.

Secondary (and sometimes tertiary, depending on the size of the polity) communities in the polity were ruled by lesser nobles, either ahau or cahalob. The central plazas of polity capitals and second-tier communities consisted of temples and palace or administrative buildings. Those in the second-tier sites were small-scale versions of those in the capital, although not replicas. Norman Hammond (1991) notes that the temples in the second-tier sites were foci of ancestor veneration for the ruling lineage of the community. The power of the second-tier ahau or cahal grew during the Terminal Classic breakdown of dynastic power in the polity capitals. At that time, some secondary lords in the smaller communities seized power and publicly announced their power by the erection of carved monuments showing their lineage (now royal?) and history, as at Xunantunich and Chichen Itza, or by the erection of impressive public buildings, as at Baking Pot and Cahal Pech (see Culbert 1991; Garber 2004).

Gordon Willey and Richard Leventhal (1979) identified four levels of socioeconomic complexity in sites in the Copan valley. The two uppermost levels, three and four, have inscriptions that demonstrate interaction between the ruler and members of the nobility or upper class. For example, a hieroglyphic text on a bench at a type-three site reports a scattering ritual (involving blood offerings on bark paper) by the Copan ruler Yax Pac to honor an unnamed noble. The Copan ruler actually names the higher-status noble in a type-four site. A noble who was a brother of Yax Pac evidently had even higher status, as he was named in several texts, including two altars at the site where he lived (destroyed by the modern Copan village) and one altar in the main group at Copan. He was also of sufficiently high status to use the Copan emblem glyph (Culbert 1991; Webster 2002).

POPULATION ESTIMATES

Without census data, cemeteries to give clues about community population, or other written information, population estimates for the ancient Maya vary considerably. Not only is the question of how many people lived in a particular community of general interest, but population size also tells researchers about various aspects of society. Generally, Maya archaeologists estimate ancient population by counting the number of low mounds interpreted as house mounds at a site or part of a site, excavating a sample of the mounds to determine their age, and multiplying the number of occupied mounds per time period by a numerical factor representing an estimate of the number of people in a household. For most Maya sites, chronologies are based on ceramics, so that demographic reconstructions include quite a broad time span: either a ceramic complex of 100 to 200 years' duration, or a time period of 200 to 300 years' duration. Clearly, not all mounds were utilized for the entire ceramic complex or time period. At Copan, obsidian hydration dating provided a more detailed, although controversial, chronology.

The most secure demographic reconstructions are for the latest time of occupation, particularly in the southern Maya lowlands at the height of Late Classic settlement when virtually all the mounds were used. Demographic estimates are more tenuous for earlier times. Some researchers use the presence of pottery sherds from particular time periods in the fill of house mounds as an indicator that the mound was used in those times. This method follows extensive surface surveys in arid regions of highland Mexico by William T. Sanders, and colleagues (Sanders, Parsons, and Santley 1979), among others, who used the frequencies of datable pottery sherds on the surface to reconstruct demographic changes over time. Some Maya archaeologists question the validity of using pottery sherds as demographic indicators, though, as they may have been moved from their original places of use.

Maya archaeologists usually adjust their population estimates to account for other factors that may have influenced the equation of mounds to people. The methodology of translating mounds to people has been carefully considered in terms of the various factors that influence the recovery of accurate demographic information for a particular time (A. Chase 1990; Pyburn 1990; Rice and Culbert 1990). Of course, some mounds had nondomestic uses. Clearly, not all houses were occupied at the same time. Some buildings are obscured by debris from adjacent structures. Some, perhaps many, houses leave no mounded remains and so are omitted from mound-to-people population estimates.

The most extensive and reliable data for structure density at southern lowland Maya cities are for the Late Classic period, during which figures vary from a high of 1,232 structures per square kilometers at Copan to a low of 58 for Nohmul (Rice and Culbert 1990, table 1.2). Most estimates are between 128 and 223 structures per square kilometers in the city center, and lower in the site periphery. In rural areas, the densities are between 30 and 60 structures per square kilometer. Estimates are much lower if nonhabitable swampland is omitted.

Dzibilchaltun, Central Plaza and sacbe (Courtesy Ed Kurjack)

Structure densities are higher for the northern Maya lowlands than they are for the southern Maya lowlands. For example, Ed Kurjack (1974) estimated a high density of 477 structures per square kilometers at Dzibilchaltun. Ringle and Andrews (1990) estimated 500 structures per square kilometer at Preclassic period Komchen. Estimates are 400 structures per square kilometers at Chunchucmil (Vlcek, de Gonzalez, and Kurjack 1978), and 220 structures per square kilometers at Sayil (Tourtellot 1990). For the Postclassic, Santa Rita had from 400 to 712 structures per square kilometers (D. Chase 1990).

Estimates of how many of the mounds were nonresidential vary from 5 to 30 percent and may vary over time and space in the Maya lowlands (Rice and Culbert 1990). William Haviland (1965) estimated that 16.5 percent of the small structures in his study at Tikal were nonresidential. For Copan, Webster and Freter (1990) estimated that 20 to 30 percent of small structures were nonresidential. Diane Chase (1990) made a significantly lower estimate of 6.6 percent nonresidential mounds for Late Postclassic Santa Rita Corozal in northern Belize.

There is no consensus among Maya archaeologists about estimating which house mounds were contemporaneous, whether they were used continuously throughout a time period, and if house platform use changed over time. Early demographic studies were based on the view that the Maya had a low population density because they were swidden farmers. Consequently, Uaxactun population estimates based on counting mounds and multiplying that number by family size were reduced by 75 percent, for example, to account for mounds not occupied at the same time. Sir J. Eric S. Thompson (1971) suggested that the Maya abandoned their houses after a family member died. However, extensive excavation of house mounds at Tikal indicated to William Haviland (1972) that houses were remodeled, extended, or otherwise renovated periodically, including at the death of a family member, but they were not abandoned. In some cases, as at Copan, there was periodic abandonment of house platforms, but the extent of this practice or of periodic or seasonal disuse of residences and differences over time are unknown and are subject to much discussion by Maya archaeologists. Bill Ringle and E. Wyllys Andrews IV (1990) found that 13 percent of Maya houses at Komchen in the Yucatan of Mexico were unoccupied during the Late Preclassic period. Whether or not this figure is transferable to the Classic period or earlier is, of course, a matter of debate.

Upward adjustments to account for unmapped structures vary from 10 percent at Tikal (Culbert et al. 1990), to 50 to 100 percent at Santa Rita Corozal (D. Chase 1990), to 37.4 percent in the Tayasal area of the Peten (D. Chase 1990), to 38 percent and 50 percent for small and large structures, respectively, at Copan (Webster and Freter 1990). The number of unmapped structures likely varied temporally within sites and across the Maya area, so that adjustments are best made for particular sites or regions, as noted by K. Anne Pyburn (1990) from her settlement survey at Nohmul in northern Belize.

Although early population estimates such as those made by the Ricketsons (Ricketson and Ricketson 1937) for Uaxactun were based on 5 people per mound, more recent researchers multiply the number of house mounds at a site by 5.6 people. This figure is an estimate based on an ethnographic survey by Robert Redfield and Villa Rojas (1962) of the average number of people in a nuclear family in the Maya village of Chan Kom in Yucatan. This figure was used for Mayapan, Tikal, and Seibal. Sanders (Sanders and Price 1968) suggested that a figure of 4 people per family based on sixteenth-century Mexican census data better reflects the ancient family size. Various other estimates include Haviland's (1965) estimate of 4.9 people based on ethnohistoric data from Cozumel Island, Dennis Puleston's (1983) estimate of 6.07 people based on census data on Maya in the Yucatan, and an estimate of 10 people per household composed of more than one nuclear family, at the time when the Spaniards arrived in the sixteenth century. Don and Prudence Rice (1990) suggest that their Postclassic house mounds in the Peten Lakes region housed up to 10 individuals as noted in the contact period data from the Itza capital. Although there is no consensus, most estimates currently range between 4.0 and 5.6 people per house (see Rice and Culbert 1990 for details and syntheses of demographic research).

Several other methods have been used to reconstruct ancient Maya demography. Individual rooms were used as the basis for calculating population numbers at Sayil and Copan. At Sayil, a city in the arid Puuc Hills region of the northern Maya lowlands, Gair Tourtellot and colleagues were able to map the stone architectural remains because of the lack of vegetation cover in the region (Sabloff and Tourtellot 1992). At Copan, David Webster and Corrine Freter were able to infer population estimates from extensive excavation of individual

Three-story building at Sayil in Puuc style (Courtesy T. Winemiller)

rooms at the site (Webster 2002). The plazuela group (patio group) was used for studying demographics at various sites including Quirigua by Wendy Ashmore (1990), Seibal by Gair Tourtellot (1990), and the Belize River by Anabel Ford (1990). Significantly different approaches were used by Patricia McAnany (1990), who based her population estimates of Sayil on the water storage capabilities of chultuns (underground storage pits dug into the limestone hardrock), and by Heather McKillop (1989), who used estimates of household obsidian blade use for estimating the population of Wild Cane Cay (see below).

The population of the Postclassic community on Wild Cane Cay, a trading port off the southern coast of Belize, was estimated by comparing the mound count method with an estimate derived from household stone tool use. Using the mount count method, the island's six mounds indicate an uncorrected population estimate of 33.6 people. Considering the 3.5-acre extent of the island with dense midden deposits throughout the island to a depth of 2.5 meters, this population estimate seemed too low. The alternative population estimate using stone tool use was based on a study in highland Mexico by archaeologist Robert Santley (1984), where cutting stone tools were made of locally available obsidian and an average household used twenty-one obsidian tools per year. As both obsidian and chert were traded to Wild Cane Cay in approximately equal quantities, an estimate of 10.5 obsidian blades per year per household was used. Extrapolating the density of obsidian in excavated Postclassic deposits to the 3.5-acre size of the island, an estimated 2,710,700 obsidian blades were used in the 300 years of the Postclassic period at Wild Cane Cay, or 9,036 blades per year. Based on 10.5 blades per year per household, the obsidian blade index indicates that there were 861 households on the island at any given time during the Postclassic. Clearly, then, the population of Wild Cane Cay was somewhere between 33.6 people and 861 households (McKillop 1989; McKillop 2005).

Exacerbating the difficulty in population estimates is the issue of determining the boundaries of settlements in the rainforest setting. Population estimates for peripheral and suburban parts of communities have been made from mound densities along transects, as at Tikal and Pacbitun, or between Tikal and Yaxha. Transect survey at Tikal has revealed that the population densities diminished dramatically outside the earthworks, which marked the boundary of the bajos. Still, the edges of most sites in the southern Maya lowlands covered in rainforest are more difficult to place. Uaxactun is an exception, where the mound density dropped precipitously about 2 kilometers from the site center. In the northern Maya lowlands, the lack of dense vegetation cover facilitates regional survey. At some sites, such as Sayil, the site boundary was marked by a virtual cessation of construction.

Estimating the population of cities, regional polities, and the lowlands in general throughout prehistory is central to evaluating subsistence strategies, whether or not the Classic Maya were an urban state, and economic and political organization: In terms of subsistence, only low populations could have been supported by slash and burn agriculture. This extended form of farming requires a lot of land, as fields must be allowed to lie fallow after several years of cultivation in order to replenish the nutrients in the soil. Large populations and particularly high population densities in Maya cities would have required more intensive cultivation practices in order to produce more food than could be supplied by slash and burn farming. The lowland demand for food—including carbohydrates, protein, and various vitamins and minerals, such as salt, depended on the size and density of the population.

The level of population density of lowland cities is a measure of how urban the Maya cities were, particularly in comparison with their highland counterpart, Teotihuacan, which was demonstrably urban. The size and population density of Maya cities is linked to the organization of ancient Maya society. What was the relationship between farmers who supplied food to the non-farming residents of cities? Did farmers live seasonally in cities?

Early views of Maya cities incorrectly viewed them as empty ritual centers (Morley 1946; Thompson 1970). Accumulated evidence from settlement pattern studies now indicates that Maya cities were not empty ceremonial centers but that they instead housed thousands or tens of thousands of residents (Harrison 1999). Although it was clear that slash and burn agriculture alone would not have satisfied the hunger of the urban Maya, many hypotheses have been advanced to explain how enough food was produced to meet the needs of the population. Archaeologists debate the kind and intensity of food production needed for the overall Maya population and for the population density of some cities. More food is needed for larger populations, especially if the population density is high. This has fostered many interpretations of intensification of agriculture and other food production techniques.

ANCIENT MAYA DEMOGRAPHY

Anthony Andrews (1983) calculated population estimates for the southern Maya lowlands in order to determine how much salt the Classic period population living in the area needed. Peter Harrison (1999) provides estimates of the population of Tikal. The size and density of ancient Maya populations is documented from the archaeological settlement remains of masonry and earthen residential platforms and from superstructures of varying size and elaboration arranged in plaza groups or in isolation. Much of the research from individual sites and regional surveys is summarized in two edited volumes, *Lowland Maya Settlement Patterns,* edited by Wendy Ashmore in 1981, and *Precolumbian Population History in the Maya Lowlands,* edited by T. Patrick Culbert and Don S. Rice in 1990. Demography includes discussion of the size and composition of populations over time in particular places, with these traits regarded as the products of birth, death, and migration.

Studies of ancient Maya demography have lagged in comparison to demography studies in highland Mexico, where the lack of ground cover and arid conditions have facilitated comprehensive surface collections of artifacts on which population estimates over time have been made (Sanders, Parsons, and Santley 1979). In contrast, the forest cover over the Maya lowlands has meant that comprehensive surface collections of artifacts were restricted to a few locations and that population estimates were based on surface evidence of architecture and on excavation, both of which cover only parts of sites. Don Rice and T. Patrick Culbert (1990) suggest that the erroneous view that the tropical rainforest could only support a low population density meant that, historically, there was general disinterest among Maya archaeologists in investigating population size and density.

Early studies of ancient Maya demography were carried out by archaeologists from the Carnegie Institution of Washington between 1930 and 1958 at Uaxactun, Chichen Itza, and Mayapan, as well as by ethnographers and other researchers studying modern and historic Maya in the Yucatan (Rice and Culbert 1990). At Uaxactun, the archaeologists Oliver and Edith Ricketson (1937) surveyed a large cross-shaped area of the site in order to investigate the ancient population, searching for and recording house mounds. The Uaxactun study also included the complete excavation of five houses, as part of a study of modern Maya houses by Robert Wauchope (1938). They found 78 mounds in 953,040 square meters of habitable land, translated as 82 structures per square kilometer. Using an estimate of 5 people per house and assuming that each mound was a residence, they suggested a population density of 170 people per square kilometer. If only 25 percent of the house mounds were occupied at a time, they estimated the population density of Uaxactun was 43 people per square kilometer. The Ricketsons estimated the population of the Uaxactun region at 50,000 people, assuming the site extended 16 kilometers from the center (about half the distance to nearby Tikal) and included 458 square kilometers of habitable land.

Although the Ricketsons rejected the idea that slash and burn agriculture supported the high population densities at the height of the Classic period, the dominant view of Maya archaeologists, certainly spearheaded by the late Sir Eric S. Thompson (1970), was that Maya cites were essentially empty ceremonial centers supported by a dispersed rural Maya population of slash and burn farmers. This view of low population density was supported by a popular view that the tropical rainforest was not capable of supporting a large population. In a compelling article entitled "Environmental Limitation on the Development of Culture," Betty Meggers (1954) became the lead proponent of this "environmental determinist" perspective. Ursula Cowgill (1962) calculated that the carrying capacity of swidden agriculture in the southern Maya lowlands was much greater than Maya archaeologists had considered, allowing 58 to 77 people per square kilometer, and that this population level (carrying capacity) had not been reached during the Classic period.

A focus on regional settlement pattern studies in the late 1950s under the impetus of Gordon Willey and colleagues such as William Bullard (Bullard 1960; Willey et al. 1965) indicated that the population of the southern Maya lowlands was overall much greater and also denser than had been considered previously (Rice and Culbert 1990). Bullard (1960) carried out an important reconnaissance of the Peten in 1958, following known trails and recording mounds. In one area that had been cleared for oil exploration, he recorded 89 structures, indicating a density of 414 structures per square kilometer. Bullard's population estimate of 222 people per square kilometers was downgraded from 888 people per square kilometer, following the Ricketsons' estimate that only 25 percent of house mounds were occupied at a time. Similar estimates of population density were made for Barton Ramie, with a population of 2,000 people estimated for 262 mounds.

The central 9 square kilometers of Tikal included an average of 235 mounds per square kilometer, or a higher figure of 275 mounds per square kilometers if uninhabitable swamps were excluded. The periphery of Tikal, including an additional 7 square kilometers, indicated a density of 145 mounds per square kilometer. William Haviland (1965) estimated a population of 11,000 people for the 16 square kilometers of the mapped area of Tikal. He concluded that agriculture was not possible within the city and, furthermore, that much of the Tikal population was not engaged in farming and would have relied on others for sustenance. Four transect surveys radiating in a cross shape from Tikal, as well as a transect survey from Tikal to Uaxactun, were undertaken to investigate the hinterland farming zone that supported the urban population of the city. Surprisingly, the urban density of Tikal was found to continue much farther than originally estimated from the city center, and the overall settlement density was found to be higher than anticipated for slash and burn farming. Haviland proposed a new central zone of Tikal that included 40,000 people in 63 square kilometers, with a peripheral zone of 66 square kilometers. The population density of 600 to 700 people in the central zone, and even the density of 160 people per square kilometers in the periphery, were much higher than previous estimates.

The mounting evidence from Tikal and other Maya sites has been that the ancient population density was much higher than previously thought, and that the traditional view of a low population supported by slash and burn agriculture was no longer tenable (Culbert and Rice 1990; Rice and Culbert 1990). The Tikal demographic estimates and their implications for lowland Maya population density and subsistence practices called into question the accepted views of low population and swidden agriculture and prompted continued field studies. Important studies of alternative food production systems and more-intensive agriculture resulted during the 1970s and 1980s, and these are summarized in *Maya Subsistence,* edited by Kent Flannery (1982), *Pre-Hispanic Maya Agriculture,* edited by Peter Harrison and B. L. Turner (1978), and many articles in journals and books (Fedick 1996; White 1999; Emery 2004).

POPULATION DATA FOR THE MAYA LOWLANDS

Population data available for a number of lowland Maya sites indicate that the cities were densely occupied and that their peripheries had densities high enough to preclude farming adjacent to houses (Rice and Culbert 1990). Don Rice and T. Patrick Culbert (1990) summarize population changes over time based on data from fifteen sites and areas. They present the data for each time period as a percentage of the total population for a site, and they also adjust the data on the assumption that house platforms were occupied for about 150 years and then abandoned. The latter estimate adjusts downward the data for time intervals greater than 150 years. Over time, the earliest occupation of the lowlands in the latter Early Preclassic and early Middle Preclassic shows very low population densities, with only a few sites occupied. Generally only 10 percent of the maximum population size is represented at the earliest occupation. The late Middle Preclassic shows most lowland sites occupied and population figures at about 20 percent of their maximum.

For the Late Preclassic, which is a long time period, the population figures are dramatically different, with important implications for Maya demography, depending on whether or not the population figures are adjusted according to Rice and Culbert's 150-year house platform occupation criterion. If one follows their adjustments, accepting that houses were occupied for an average of 150 years and then abandoned, the Late Preclassic population figures show a gradual increase from earlier times, with about one-third of the Late Classic figures. However, if one believes that Late Preclassic house platforms were occupied and renovated during the entire 300-year time span of the Late Preclassic, then the populations for quite a number of spatially scattered Late Preclassic communities are dramatically higher than earlier times and presage a significant decline in population during the Early Classic period. All Early Classic sites fall below 50 percent of their Late Classic population figures, and there is considerable variability in populations.

Most sites reached their population heights during the Late Classic. Although the Terminal Classic witnessed tremendous population decline at Tikal and the Peten Lakes, elsewhere, population stayed constant and in some cases increased. Seibal and Altar de Sacrificios reached their maximum population size during the Terminal Classic. Although the royal dynasty at Copan fell, the city continued to be occupied during the Terminal Classic. In Belize, many communities continued to be settled during the Terminal Classic and into the

Ball player and dwarf, relief, Late Classic Maya Period A.D., 600-900, Yaxchilan (Maya city), Chiapas, Mexico (The Art Archive/Dagli Orti)

Postclassic as well. After the collapse of Classic Maya polities in the central Maya lowlands, population figures for cities in this area were quite low. However, many sites in northern Belize, such as Lamanai and Santa Rita, continued and even expanded during the Postclassic. There also was a population expansion in the northern Maya lowlands during the Postclassic and a continuation of coastal settlement from southern Belize at Wild Cane Cay to Ambergris Caye, Cozumel, and Isla Cerritos.

REFERENCES

Adams, Richard E. W. 1970. "Suggested Classic Period Occupational Specialization in the Southern Maya Lowlands." In *Monographs and Papers in Maya Archaeology,* edited by William R. Bullard Jr., 487–502. Papers of the Peabody Museum of Archaeology and Ethnology, vol. 61. Cambridge, MA: Harvard University.

———. 1974. "A Trial Estimation of Classic Maya Palace Populations at Uaxactun, Guatemala." In *Mesoamerican Archaeology: New Approaches,* edited by Norman Hammond, 285–296. London: Gerald Duckworth.

Aimers, James L., Terry G. Powis, and Jaime J. Awe. 2000. "Preclassic Round Structures of the Upper Belize Valley." *Latin American Antiquity* 11: 71–86.

Andrews, Anthony P. 1983. *Maya Salt Production and Trade.* Tucson: University of Arizona Press.

Ardren, Traci, ed. 2002. *Ancient Maya Women.* Walnut Creek, CA: Altamira Press.

Ashmore, Wendy, ed. 1981. *Lowland Maya Settlement Patterns.* Albuquerque: University of New Mexico Press.

———. 1990. "Ode to a Dragline: Demographic Reconstructions at Classic Quirigua." In *Precolumbian Population History in the Maya Lowlands,* edited by T. Patrick Culbert and Don S. Rice, 63–82. Albuquerque: University of New Mexico Press.

Brady, James E., et al. 1997. "Glimpses of the Dark Side of the Petexbatun Project: The Petexbatun Regional Cave Study." *Ancient Mesoamerica* 8: 353–364.

Bullard, William R., Jr. 1960. "Maya Settlement Patterns in Northeastern Peten, Guatemala." *American Antiquity* 25: 355–372.

Chase, Arlen F. 1990. "Maya Archaeology and Population Estimates in the Tayasal-Paxcaman Zone, Peten, Guatemala." In *Precolumbian Population History in the Maya Lowlands,* edited by T. Patrick Culbert and Don S. Rice, 149–165. Albuquerque: University of New Mexico Press.

Chase, Arlen F., and Diane Z. Chase. 2001. "Ancient Maya Causeways and Site Organization at Caracol, Belize." *Ancient Mesoamerica* 12 (2): 273–281.

Chase, Diane Z. 1990. "The Invisible Maya: Population History and Archaeology at Santa Rita Corozal." In *Precolumbian Population History in the Maya Lowlands,* edited by T. Patrick Culbert and Don S. Rice, 199–213. Albuquerque: University of New Mexico Press.

Christie, Jessica J., ed. 2003. *Maya Palaces and Elite Residences.* Austin: University of Texas Press.

Cowgill, Ursula. 1962. "An Agricultural Study of the Southern Maya Lowlands." *American Anthropologist* 64: 273–286.

Culbert, T. Patrick, ed. 1991. *Classic Maya Political History: Hieroglyphic and Archaeological Evidence.* New York: Cambridge University Press.

Culbert, T. Patrick, Laura J. Kosakowsky, Robert E. Fry, and William A. Haviland. 1990. "The Population of Tikal, Guatemala." In *Precolumbian Population History in the Maya Lowlands,* edited by T. Patrick Culbert and Don S. Rice, 103–121. Albuquerque: University of New Mexico Press.

Culbert, T. Patrick, and Don S. Rice, eds. 1990. *Precolumbian Population History in the Maya Lowlands.* Albuquerque: University of New Mexico Press.

Demarest, Arthur, Kim Morgan, Claudia Wooley, and Hector Escobedo. 2003. "The Political Acquisition of Sacred Geography: The Murcielagos Complex at Dos Pilas." In *Maya Palaces and Elite Residences,* edited by Jessica J. Christie, 120–153. Austin: University of Texas Press.

Emery, Kitty, ed. 2004. *Maya Zooarchaeology.* Los Angeles: Costen Institute of Archaeology, University of California.

Fedick, Scott, ed. 1996. *The Managed Mosaic.* Salt Lake City: University of Utah Press.

Flannery, Kent V., ed. 1982. *Maya Subsistence.* New York: Academic Press.

Ford, Anabel. 1986. *Population Growth and Social Complexity: An Examination of Settlement and Environment in the Central Maya Lowlands.* Anthropological Research Paper 35. Tempe: Arizona State University.

———. 1990. "Maya Settlement in the Belize River Area: Variations in Residence Patterns of the Central Maya Lowlands." In *Precolumbian Population History in the Maya Lowlands,* edited by T. Patrick Culbert and Don S. Rice, 167–181. Albuquerque: University of New Mexico Press.

Freidel, David A., and Linda Schele. 1988. "Kingship in the Late Preclassic Maya Lowlands: The Instruments and Places of Ritual Power." *American Anthropologist* 90 (3): 547–567.

Garber, James F., ed. 2004. *The Ancient Maya of the Belize Valley*. Gainesville: University Press of Florida.

Hammond, Norman. 1982. *Ancient Maya Civilization*. New Brunswick: Rutgers University Press.

———. 1991. "Inside the Black Box: Defining Maya Polity." In *Classic Maya Political History*, edited by T. Patrick Culbert, 253–284. New York: Cambridge University Press.

Harrison, Peter D. 1999. *The Lords of Tikal*. New York: Thames & Hudson.

Harrison, Peter D., and B. L. Turner, eds. 1978. *Pre-Hispanic Maya Agriculture*. Albuquerque: University of New Mexico Press.

Haviland, William A. 1965. "Prehistoric Settlement at Tikal, Guatemala." *Expedition* 7 (3): 14–23.

———. 1972. "Estimates of Maya Population: Comments on Thompson's Comments." *American Antiquity* 37: 261–262.

Healy, Paul F. 1990. "Excavations at Pacbitun, Belize: Preliminary Report on the 1986 and 1987 Investigations." *Journal of Field Archaeology* 7: 247–262.

Joyce, Rosemary A. 2000. *Gender and Power in Prehispanic Mesoamerica*. Austin: University of Texas Press.

Kurjack, Edward. 1974. *Prehistoric Lowland Maya Community and Social Organization: A Case Study at Dzibilchaltun, Yucatan, Mexico*. Middle American Research Institute Publication 38. New Orleans: Tulane University.

Kurjack, Edward B., and Silvia Garza T. 1981. "Pre-Columbian Community Form and Distribution in the Northern Maya Area." In *Lowland Maya Settlement Patterns*, edited by Wendy Ashmore, 287–309. Albuquerque: University of New Mexico Press.

Marcus, Joyce. 1976. *Emblem and State in the Classic Maya Lowlands*. Washington, DC: Dumbarton Oaks.

———. 1993. "Ancient Maya Political Organization." In *Lowland Maya Archaeology in the Eighth Century A.D.*, edited by Jeremy A. Sabloff and John S. Henderson, 111–183. Washington, DC: Dumbarton Oaks Research Library and Collections.

Martin, Simon, and Nicholai Grube. 2000. *Chronicle of the Maya Kings and Queens: Deciphering the Dynasties of the Ancient Maya*. New York: Thames & Hudson.

McAnany, Patricia. 1990. "Water Storage in the Puuc Region of the Northern Maya Lowlands: A Key to Population Estimates and Architectural Variability." In *Precolumbian Population History in the Maya Lowlands*, edited by T. Patrick Culbert and Don S. Rice, 263–284. Albuquerque: University of New Mexico Press.

———. 1995. *Living with the Ancestors*. Austin: University of Texas Press.

McKillop, Heather. 1989. "Coastal Maya Trade: Obsidian Densities from Wild Cane Cay, Belize." In *Prehistoric Maya Economies of Belize*, edited by Patricia McAnany and Barry Isaac, 17–56. Research in Economic Anthropology, Supplement 4. Greenwich, CT: JAI Press.

———. 2005. *In Search of Maya Sea Traders*. College Station: University of Texas Press. In press.

Meggers, Betty. 1954. "Environmental Limitation on the Development of Culture." *American Anthropologist* 56: 801–824.

Morley, Sylvanus. 1946. *The Ancient Maya*. Palo Alto, CA: Stanford University Press.

Pendergast, David M. 1969. *The Prehistory of Actun Balam, British Honduras*. Occasional Paper 16, Art and Archaeology. Toronto: Royal Ontario Museum.

———. 1970. *A. H., anderson's Excavations at Rio Frio Cave E, British Honduras (Belize)*. Occasional Paper 20, Art and Archaeology. Toronto: Royal Ontario Museum.

———. 1971. *Excavations at Eduardo Quiroz Cave, British Honduras (Belize)*. Occasional Paper 21, Art and Archaeology. Toronto: Royal Ontario Museum.

————. 1974. *Excavations at Actun Polbilche, Belize.* Archaeology Monograph 1. Toronto: Royal Ontario Museum.

Pollock, Harry E. D., Ralph L. Roys, Tatiana Proskouriakoff, and A. Ledyard Smith. 1962. *Mayapan, Yucatan, Mexico.* Carnegie Institution of Washington Publication 619. Washington, DC: Carnegie Institution of Washington.

Puleston, Dennis. 1983. *The Settlement Survey of Tikal.* Tikal Report No. 13. Philadelphia: University Museum Publications, University of Pennsylvania.

Pyburn, K. Anne. 1990. "Settlement Patterns at Nohmul: Preliminary Results of Four Excavation Seasons." In *Precolumbian Population History in the Maya Lowlands,* edited by T. Patrick Culbert and Don S. Rice, 183–197. Albuquerque: University of New Mexico Press.

Redfield, Robert, and Alfonso Villa Rojas. 1962. *Chan Kom: A Maya Village.* Chicago: University of Chicago Press.

Rice, Don S., and T. Patrick Culbert. 1990. "Historical Contexts for Population Reconstruction in the Maya Lowlands." In *Precolumbian Population History in the Maya Lowlands,* edited by T. Patrick Culbert and Don S. Rice, 1–36. Albuquerque: University of New Mexico Press.

Rice, Don S., and Prudence M. Rice. 1990. "Population Size and Population Change in the Central Peten Lakes Region, Guatemala." In *Precolumbian Population History in the Maya Lowlands,* edited by T. Patrick Culbert and Don S. Rice, 123–148. Albuquerque: University of New Mexico Press.

Ricketson, Oliver G., Jr., and Edith B. Ricketson. 1937. *Uaxactun, Guatemala, Group E: 1926–1937.* Carnegie Institution of Washington Publication 477. Washington, DC: Carnegie Institution of Washington.

Ringle, William M., and E. Wyllys Andrews IV. 1990. "The Demography of Komchen, an Early Maya Town in Northern Yucatan." In *Precolumbian Population History in the Maya Lowlands,* edited by T. Patrick Culbert and Don S. Rice, 215–243. Albuquerque: University of New Mexico Press.

Sabloff, Jeremy, and Gair Tourtellot. 1992. "Beyond Temples and Palaces: Recent Settlement Pattern Research at the Ancient Maya City of Sayil (1983–1985)." In *New Theories on the Ancient Maya,* edited by Elin C. Danien and Robert J Sharer, 155 160. Philadelphia: University Museum, University of Pennsylvania.

Sanders, William T., Jeffrey Parsons, and Robert Santley. 1979. *The Basin of Mexico: Ecological Processes in the Evolution of a Civilization.* New York: Academic Press.

Sanders, William T., and Barbara Price. 1968. *Mesoamerica: The Evolution of a Civilization.* New York: Random House.

Santley, Robert S. 1984. "Obsidian Exchange, Economic Stratification, and the Evolution of Complex Society in the Basin of Mexico." In *Trade and Exchange in Early Mesoamerica,* edited by Kenneth G. Hirth, 43–86. Albuquerque: University of New Mexico Press.

Scarborough, Vernon L. 1991. *Archaeology at Cerros, Belize, Central America,* vol. 3: *The Settlement System in a Late Preclassic Maya Community.* Dallas: Southern Methodist University Press.

Sheets, Payson, ed. 2002. *Before the Volcano Erupted: The Ancient Ceren Village in Central America.* Austin: University of Texas Press.

Steiner, Edward P. 1994. "Prehistoric Maya Settlement along Joe Taylor Creek, Belize." Unpublished Master's thesis, Department of Geography and Anthropology, Louisiana State University, Baton Rouge.

Stone, Andrea J. 1995. *Images from the Underworld: Naj Tunich and the Tradition of Maya Cave Painting.* Austin: University of Texas Press.

Thompson, J. Eric S. 1970. *Maya History and Religion.* Norman: University of Oklahoma Press.

———. 1971. "Estimates of Maya Population: Deranging Factors." *American Antiquity* 36: 214–216.

Tourtellot, Gair. 1990. "Population Estimates for Preclassic and Classic Seibal." In *Precolumbian Population History in the Maya Lowlands,* edited by T. Patrick Culbert and Don S. Rice, 83–102. Albuquerque: University of New Mexico Press.

Tourtellot, Gair, Amanda Clark, and Norman Hammond. 1993. "Mapping La Milpa: A Maya City in Northwestern Belize." *Antiquity* 67: 96–108.

Tourtellot, Gair, M. Wolf, Francisco Estrada-Belli, et al. 2000. "Discovery of Two Predicted Ancient Maya Sites in Belize." *Antiquity* 74: 481–482.

Vlcek, David T., Sylvia Garza de Gonzalez, and Edward B. Kurjack. 1978. "Contemporary Farming and Ancient Maya Settlements: Some Disconcerting Evidence." In *PreHispanic Maya Agriculture,* edited by Peter D. Harrison and B. L. Turner II, 211–223. Albuquerque: University of New Mexico Press.

Wauchope, Robert. 1934. *House Mounds of Uaxactun, Guatemala.* Carnegie Institution of Washington Publication 436, Contributions to American Archaeology 7. Washington, DC: Carnegie Institution of Washington.

———. 1938. *Modern Maya Houses.* Carnegie Institution of Washington Publication 502. Washington, DC: Carnegie Institution of Washington.

Webster, David. 2002. *The Fall of the Ancient Maya.* New York: Thames & Hudson.

Webster, David, and AnnCorinne Freter. 1990. "The Demography of Late Classic Copan." In *Precolumbian Population History in the Maya Lowlands,* edited by T. Patrick Culbert and Don S. Rice, 37–61. Albuquerque: University of New Mexico Press.

Webster, David, AnnCorinne Freter, and Nancy Gonlin. 2000. *Copan: The Rise and Fall of an Ancient Maya Kingdom.* Fort Worth: Harcourt Brace.

White, Christine D., ed. 1999. *Reconstructing Ancient Maya Diet.* Salt Lake City: University of Utah Press.

Wilk, Richard R., and Wendy Ashmore, eds. 1988. *Household and Community in the Mesoamerican Past.* Albuquerque: University of New Mexico Press.

Willey, Gordon R. 1953. *Prehistoric Settlement Patterns in the Viru Valley, Peru.* Bureau of American Ethnology, Smithsonian Institution Bulletin No. 155. Washington, DC: U. S. Government Printing Office.

Willey, Gordon R., William R. Bullard, John B. Glass, and James C. Gifford. 1965. *Prehistoric Maya Settlement Patterns in the Belize Valley.* Papers of the Peabody Museum of Archaeology and Ethnology, vol. 54. Cambridge, MA: Harvard University.

Willey, Gordon R., and Richard Leventhal. 1979. "Prehistoric Settlement at Copan." In *Maya Archaeology and Ethnohistory,* edited by Norman Hammond, 75–102. Austin: University of Texas Press.

CHAPTER 7
Politics

By the height of Late Classic Maya civilization, the lowlands were organized into as many as eighty city-states (Martin and Grube 2000). Just how they were organized internally and the political relations among city-states, are subjects of some discussion among Mayanists. Moreover, an understanding of the political climate bears on other aspects of Classic Maya society, such as the economy. Were the city-states fairly autonomous political entities that operated independently, as in what is regarded the "segmentary model" of political organization (Demarest et al. 2003; Dunham, Jamison, and Leventhal 1989; Leventhal 1990)? Or was there more centralization, with the waxing and waning of regional superpowers (A. Chase and D. Chase 1996; Marcus 1993)? Researchers differ in their answers to this question, but both camps acknowledge that there were hierarchies of settlements within each city-state and under the overall authority of the Maya royalty at the capital. Supporters of the segmentary model see power as decentralized within the polity, whereas the centralists view the power and control of the Maya royalty as pervasive throughout its geographic realm. In the segmentary model, the emblem glyph for each city is regarded as evidence for the existence of an independent polity under the capital's suzerainty. By way of contrast, the centralists see the use of emblem glyphs on carved monuments as evidence of political maneuvering of Maya royalty in negotiating alliances and waging war in a world of pan-lowland power politics.

Decipherment of the hieroglyphic writing on stone monuments and painted pottery has enhanced historical detail about the geopolitical landscape of the Classic Maya, known previously only through traditional "dirt" archaeology (Reents-Budet 2001). Modern researchers' ability to read texts on stelae and other stone monuments transformed the Maya into a historical culture. Individuals and their life histories are now identified. It is specifically the history of Maya royalty and their personal and political life events that are recorded on monuments and that facilitate interpretations of historical events in the Maya lowlands during the Classic period. Together, fieldwork and epigraphy provide details of changing political alliances, military defeats and conquests, royal visits, and the political history of the Maya lowlands. Although the broad framework of politics affected the lives of the common Maya, there is no hieroglyphic record of their lives or of the economy. Norman Hammond (1991, 256) provides a cautionary note about interpreting too extensively from the hieroglyphic record: "A dozen royal marriages, a score of battles or royal visits, and the genealogies of a handful of dynasties do not give us a broad historical foundation upon which to build, in the absence of economic information or any documentation of Maya society below the uppermost elite."

Late Classic Palenque (Corel)

There is indeed a patchy record of hieroglyphic and archaeological research in the southern Maya lowlands. The best epigraphic and archaeological records exist for Tikal, Dos Pilas (Houston 1993), and other sites in the Petexbatun of Guatemala; Caracol in Belize; Copan in Honduras; and the nearby city of Quirigua, Guatemala. Martin and Grube (2000) synthesize the information on Classic Maya cities with royal dynastic records. Some cities, notably Piedras Negras, Yaxchilan (Tate 1992), and Palenque in the Usumacinta region, have excellent epigraphic records, which need to be fleshed out by archaeological field research, as is ongoing at Piedras Negras under the direction of Stephen Houston. For northern Belize, there is very little epigraphic information, but there is unparalleled data from field archaeology. In southern Belize, there are tantalizing clues to a rich epigraphic record at Uxbenka, Nim li punit, and Pusilha from fieldwork by Phil Wayenka, but most research has focused on sites without a dynastic record, notably the my own work on the coast and offshore islands and Hammond's research at Lubaantun.

POLITICAL STRUCTURE

Most Mayanists accept the view introduced by David Freidel and Linda Schele (1988; see also Schele and Freidel 1990) that the transition from the Preclassic to the Classic in the southern Maya lowlands marks a qualitative change from one social and political order to another, with the introduction of the concept

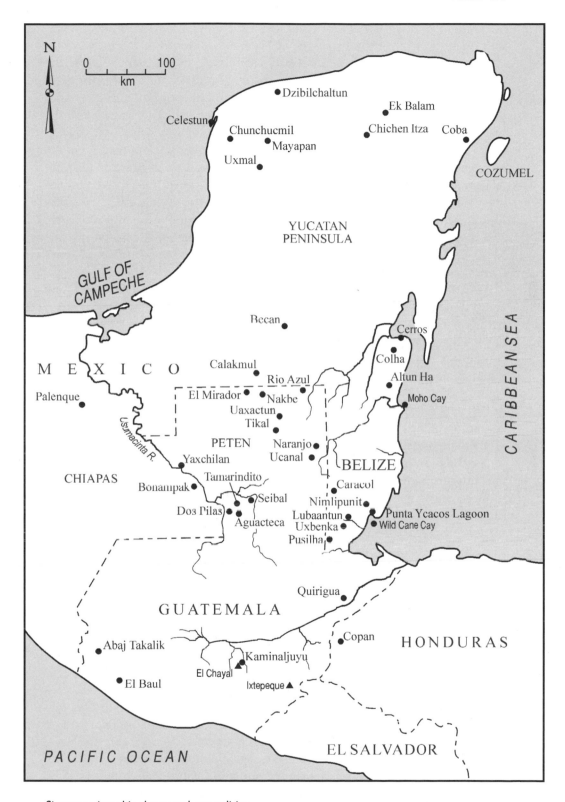

Sites mentioned in the text about politics

of kingship, although John Clark and Richard Hansen (2001) see kingship was introduced in the Middle Preclassic at Nakbe. Power and authority were focused on the king, articulated, publicly reinforced, and reinterpreted by the public display of carved stelae bearing his image and accounts of his (or occasionally a queen's) exploits. Rulers combined supreme political authority with a quasi-divine status. They were mediators between the supernatural and the real worlds. Through regular public and private ceremonies involving dance, blood sacrifice, trances, and enemas, the king engaged divine power. From the king's accession to the throne, to the ritual playing of the ball game, to his public burial in temple pyramids that became mortuary shrines for his veneration after his death, the king's life was a reinvention of the mythical history of the Maya, including the origin of the Maya world, particularly the origin of corn, and the journey and battles of the Hero Twins (as recounted in the historic Maya text, the *Popol Vuh*). With hereditary kingship, Maya royalty severed their lineage ties with the bulk of the Maya population.

It is not coincidental that the first carved stelae with dates in the Maya long count define the beginning of the Classic period. This marks the emergence of royal portraits on stone, with dates and historical texts, recording the first dynastic kingdoms. The origins of royal Maya kingship are evident earlier in the southern Maya highlands at Kaminaljuyu, El Baul, and Abaj Takalik, where dated stelae with portraits and historical records date to as early as A.D. 37. The emergence of kingship in the southern Maya lowlands dates to about A.D. 100 or earlier if one includes Middle Preclassic Nakbe. However, traditionally, the beginning of the Classic period is regarded as either A.D. 250 or A.D. 300, based on the date of A.D. 292 on Stela 29 from Tikal.

The Classic Maya had a concept of rulership that could be traced to an original founder. Kings were numbered from the founder by successor numbers (hel), so that a ruler had both a name, such as Animal Skull, and a successor number, such as the 22 hel of Tikal. Unfortunately for epigraphers' attempts to trace the Maya dynasties, few of the rulers record their successor numbers. Even though it is assumed that each ruler was a direct descendant of his predecessor, hieroglyphic texts record a few cases in which direct descent was not followed and many cases in which there is no textual evidence for a ruler's parentage. In the case of unrelated predecessors, the new ruler claimed authority and descent from the same dynastic "hel" line of rulers, despite a lack of lineal descent.

Royal succession was generally patrilineal, and primogeniture was the norm, resulting in the eldest male child of the king acceding to the throne. However, the fact there were exceptions to this ideal or norm of succession, and that in many cases a ruler's parentage is not given in texts, indicates that the reality of royal succession was quite different. The extent and elaboration of accession ceremonies may have been an attempt to help solidify the royal power of a ruler who may not have had a clear claim to the throne by virtue of lineal descent from the previous king (Martin and Grube 2000).

There are a number of exceptions to the pattern of patrilineal descent of kings from their fathers. In rare instances, queens ruled when the royal dynasty was without a male heir. Lady Zac Kuk ruled at Palenque until her son Pacal succeeded her when he reached age twelve. Lady Zac Kuk traced her royal descent through her father. Lady Six Sky, daughter of Ruler 1 from Dos Pilas, moved to Naranjo, where she was either de facto ruler or at least very influential during a time when the city prospered. She may have married into the Naranjo dynasty, but her husband is not mentioned in texts. Neither does the next Naranjo ruler, Smoking Squirrel, presumably Lady Six Sky's son, mention his father. At Yaxchilan, the ruler Bird Jaguar followed his father Shield Jaguar's reign, although only after eleven years for which rulership is in question (but presumably the ruler may have been Bird Jaguar's mother). She was not among his father's highly ranked wives; however, once Bird Jaguar succeeded to the throne, he went to great lengths to construct and record on monuments a regal past for his mother in which she participated in ceremonies appropriate for a highly ranked queen (Tate 1992). Sometimes the right to rule was gained through marriage, as in the case of Curl Nose of Tikal, who may have gained the throne by marrying the king's daughter. In other instances, a king has no apparent local dynastic ties. Animal Skull of Tikal names his parents in inscriptions, but they are evidently unrelated to the Tikal dynasty. The first named ruler of Dos Pilas, Ruler 1, came from Tikal. These and other examples indicate that the practice of patrilineal descent and primogeniture of Maya kings was not strictly followed.

Rituals and ceremonies, dictated by the Maya calendar and recorded on stelae, marked major transitions in the ruler's life. Hieroglyphic texts record that the heir engaged in various initiation rites (Martin and Grube 2000). There was a bloodletting ceremony at age five or six. As a young adult, the heir apparent began to build a reputation and demonstrate success in war by taking captives in wars against other city-states. Their names were often added to the heir's on the stela. The accession to kingship included the first of many ceremonies in the king's life. In the accession ceremony, the new ruler sat on a jaguar pelt, with a scarf bearing a depiction of the jester god—a symbol of royal authority around his forehead. He wore an elaborate headdress of jade and shell mosaic with quetzal feather plumage, and held a scepter carved in the image of the snake-footed god.

The prevalence of palaces—residential and administrative buildings for the Maya royalty—denotes an administrative structure beyond the king and points to a more complex political structure than in the preceding Preclassic period (Christie 2003; Inomata and Houston 2001; Marcus 1993). Some palaces, such as Tikal's central acropolis and northern acropolis (Harrison 1999), are extraordinarily large and complex multistructured edifices. Such administrative bureaucracy is characteristic of complex civilizations, arguably of a state; therefore, many researchers believe that the Maya society was a state. Painted pottery vessels depict the activities of Maya royalty and provide glimpses of court life and administration beyond the role of the ruler (Reents-Budet 1994; Reents-Budet 2001). Kings are depicted on thrones surrounded by wives and nobles. A court jester often is shown. Although some ceremonies took place in the small room at the top of temples, other ceremonies and administrative ac-

Jade mosaic death mask of King Pakal, Palenque, Mexico (The Art Archive/National Anthropological Museum Mexico/Dagli Orti)

tivities evidently were carried out elsewhere, notably in the palace and other structures included in the central plaza architecture of lowland cities. Feasting and dancing are often depicted, as they were important diplomatic events that built alliances. Some scenes show the king receiving slaves or tribute. Slaves are shown naked, with attendants holding them and presenting them to the ruler. Stelae depict a ruler standing on a slave. A procession of people with food and other tribute items in a scene from a painted pot demonstrates the power of the king, but also provides rare evidence of the Maya economy. There is ample evidence from archaeological work that trade was an important avenue by which goods and resources were obtained. Tribute payment fits well within the view of Classic Maya politics involving military imperialism, with conquered polities owing tribute to their new overlord. Of course, one might argue to the contrary that the depiction of tribute payment shows representatives of communities within a polity instead.

By Late Classic times, Marcus (1993) argues that the Maya were at a state level of organization consisting of a four-tiered hierarchy of settlements. The polity capital was the largest in size, containing the dynastic record on stone monuments focusing on the principal ahau, or royal dynastic ruler. The model of the single city polity creating a regional pattern of competing city-states is similar to Classical Greece, Sumer, and ancient Egypt. Next in the settlement hierarchy there were a number of smaller "minor ceremonial centers" that were smaller than the capital in general size and in the size and complexity of monumental architecture, and that generally lacked dynastic records on stone monuments. Next in the hierarchy were many small "minor centers" that were the seats of local elite rule and power, demarcated by small nonresidential buildings for local rule. Below this third tier in the hierarchy, there were many small hamlets and even isolated farmsteads that lacked elite or administrative architecture beyond the level of local lineage shrines.

There is hieroglyphic evidence for the existence of local governors, called cahalob, in smaller communities within a polity. Local governors of cahal rank are known from La Pasadita in the realm of Yaxchilan and Lacanha in the realm of Bonampak in the Usumacinta region. Local governors of ahau rank are known from Arroyo de Piedra in the realm of Dos Pilas.

Sanders (1977), Ford (1986), Hammond (1991), and others argue that the location of initial settlements in the lowlands and their continued growth into cities was correlated with the presence of critical resources, particularly arable land and water. In some cases smaller sites gained ascendancy because of their control of local resources, such as chert at Colha or salt in Punta Ycacos Lagoon, or control of trade, as at Wild Cane Cay.

THE PRECLASSIC ORIGINS OF MAYA KINGSHIP

The emergence of ruling dynasties in the Classic period can be traced to the erection of temples and stelae and the placement of elaborate elite burials that signify a growing complexity of political organization and regional and interregional communication and negotiation. Some southern lowland sites such as

El Mirador (Hansen 1984) and Nakbe (Hansen 1991) reached tremendous size and grandeur during the Preclassic. Others such as Cerros, Dzibilchaltun, Tikal, and Uaxactun shared a common ideology of rulership, manifested in elaborate painted stucco masks on temple façades, as well as in complex trade networks through which they acquired jade and other valuable resources. They publicly displayed these, then buried them; they also used these resources to begin negotiating powerful alliances with leaders in other emerging lowland polities. Freidel and Schele (1988; see also Schele and Freidel 1990) suggest that despite the undeniable Preclassic origins of political complexity, there was a dramatic shift at the beginning of the Classic period marked by the introduction of kingship. The concept of the king as an individual with divine and dynastically recorded rights of rulership differs from the theocratic rulership of earlier times. Although some Maya archaeologists, notably T. Patrick Culbert (1991), feel that there was more continuity than change from the Preclassic to the Classic, others, such as Freidel and Schele (1988), view a qualitative change at this transitional time. The definition of the Classic period as the time in which the Maya erected stelae with dates in the Maya long count lends support to Freidel and Schele's interpretation, as these dated stelae record the dynastic histories of the Maya kings.

POLITICS AND THE DEVELOPMENT OF KINGSHIP IN THE EARLY CLASSIC PERIOD

The Early Classic is an enigmatic time, as relatively little information is known either from the meager hieroglyphic record on stone monuments or from archaeological excavations. The beginning of the Early Classic is demarcated by the initiation of the cycle of carved monuments recording the dynastic histories of Maya rulers. The stelae depict an image of the individual, together with a hieroglyphic history of his or her life, provided with dates in the Maya long count. Until A.D. 435, all monuments are in the northeast Peten (Marcus 1993). Within 100 years, their presence across the Maya lowlands marks the emergence of Maya dynasties ruling regional polities. Even with the scant hieroglyphic and archaeological data for the Early Classic, there is evidence for the patterns of interpolity alliances and political takeover so common in the Late Classic. For example, Schele and Mathews (1991) point out that there were royal visits at Yaxchilan during the Early Classic. It was during the Early Classic that Tikal took over political control of Uaxactun (Sharer 2003a).

TEOTIHUACAN "INFLUENCE"

Perhaps the most debated and enigmatic political issue of the Early Classic in the Maya lowlands is the impact of Teotihuacan on the emergence and development of Classic Maya civilization (Braswell 2003; Sanders and Price 1968; Sharer 2003a; Sharer 2003b). There is ongoing discussion and debate about whether or not the influence of Teotihuacan catapulted the lowland Maya from chiefdom to state-level organization, a view energetically espoused by William Sanders (see Sanders and Price 1968). Others see the in situ development of the Maya as a state. There is no doubt about the evidence of Teotihuacan in the material remains of artifacts and architecture in the Maya area. The debate concerns the interpretation of this evidence either as representing trade, marriage, and other friendly alliances between the two great powers of Classic period Mesoamerica or as more direct political influence or military overthrow by Teotihuacan, with Kaminaljuyu directly or indirectly involved (if one accepts that the latter site was itself controlled for a time by Teotihuacan).

Both Teotihuacan-style architecture and pottery, as well as imported green obsidian and pottery, are found at a number of Maya sites between A.D. 400 and 700, demarcating a time in which Teotihuacan exerted significant influence throughout Mesoamerica (Braswell 2003). Green obsidian artifacts from Teotihuacan are found in burials, offerings, and other deposits at a number of lowland sites, notably at Altun Ha, Becan, and Tikal in the lowlands, as well as in the Maya highland city of Kaminaljuyu on the outskirts of present-day Guatemala City. Teotihuacan slab-foot, cylindrical pottery vessels were widely copied, both at major cities such as Kaminaljuyu, Tikal, Uaxactun, and Rio Azul, and at remote small communities such as the trading port of Moho Cay on the Belizean coast. There are even instances in which the distinctive Teotihuacan talud-tablero architectural style of alternating sloping and vertical facing stones is copied in the Maya area, notably at Tikal, Yaxha, Kaminaljuyu, and Copan.

Teotihuacan had its greatest influence at Kaminaljuyu, located in the outskirts of modern Guatemala City in the southern Maya highlands. William Sanders and others (Sanders and Michels 1977) have interpreted this enduring and pervasive influence as evidence of a military takeover by Teotihuacan, although not a few Maya archaeologists suggest that the contact was more likely trade. Long known from its precocious development in the Preclassic from excavations earlier in the twentieth century by Alfred V. Kidder and colleagues (1946), the buildings in the city center were renovated in Teotihuacan talud-tablero style around A.D. 400. The façades of buildings in this distinctive style consist of alternating inward sloping "talud" panels and vertical "tablero" (table) panels. However, the dimensions of the talud and tableros at Kaminaljuyu (as well as those at Tikal) are different from those at Teotihuacan, suggesting local copying by Maya people instead of construction overseen by Teotihuacanos (Valdes and Wright 2004). Elite burials at Kaminaljuyu have Teotihuacan tripod cylinder vessels, slender vessels called "floreros," and Thin Orange pottery made in central Mexico. Excavations under the direction of William T. Sanders and Joseph Michels (1977) in the 1970s through Pennsylvania State University suggested that Kaminaljuyu was conquered by Teotihuacan so that the central Mexican state could extend its control of resources and their distribution near Kaminaljuyu. This included the El Chayal obsidian outcrop that was the main source used by the lowland Classic Maya, as well as the rich cacao orchards somewhat farther away on the Pacific coast.

If Teotihuacan conquered Kaminaljuyu and replaced the city's leadership, were the new leaders native Teotihuacanos? The answer was equivocal with just Teotihuacan-style architecture, which could be local copies of trade goods. Chris White and colleagues' (2000) oxygen isotope study of human bone from

Kaminaljuyu burials indicates that two of the Kaminaljuyu individuals spent their youths at Teotihuacan, but that other individuals were from Kaminaljuyu. This innovative line of research is based on the absorption of different oxygen isotopes from drinking water into human bone and tissue at Teotihuacan and Kaminaljuyu. Oxygen isotope analysis of human bone from individuals buried in tombs with Teotihuacan-style goods indicate that the people lived their adult lives at Kaminaljuyu, an interpretation shared by Valdes and Wright (2004) who found no evidence to indicate Teotihuacan origins for individuals at Kaminaljuyu from another oxygen isotope study of Kaminaljuyu skeletal and dental remains. Whether or not one regards Kaminaljuyu has having been overtaken by Teotihuacan, most archaeologists regard Kaminaljuyu as the Maya highland outpost, even trading port, through which Teotihuacan traded goods, influence, and perhaps women, to the Maya lowlands.

There is considerable evidence for Teotihuacan influence at Tikal, but no consensus on how to interpret the evidence (Braswell 2003). The earliest glimmer of Teotihuacan influence at Tikal is associated with the takeover of Uaxactun by Smoking Frog of Tikal and the accession of Curl Nose to the throne at Tikal. Burials 10 and 48, probably of Curl Nose and his successor, Stormy Sky, include imported vessels made either at Teotihuacan or Kaminaljuyu. They include vessels with distinctive Teotihuacan painted decoration on stucco. Tikal Stela 31 consists of portraits of either Curl Nose or Stormy Sky wearing Teotihuacan military regalia, including the Teotihuacan god Tlaloc on shields, and spear throwers typical of Teotihuacan. Excavations by the University of Pennsylvania project revealed a temple with the distinctive Teotihuacan talud-tablero architecture just outside the central acropolis, and subsequent excavations by Guatemalan archaeologists under the direction of Juan Laporte as part of the Proyecto Nacional Tikal in what they called the Lost World Complex revealed a significant Early Classic architectural history in the central area of Tikal, including early evidence of talud-tablero architecture. At the Lost World Complex, the Teotihuacan architecture begins at the start of the Early Classic, and Teotihuacan iconography is added around A.D. 376. A ball court marker in Teotihuacan style and imagery has a date of A.D. 378. The marker names Smoking Frog three times.

From their research at the Lost World Complex, Laporte and Fialko (1995) see the local Tikal Maya royalty using their connections with Teotihuacan traders, perhaps including resident Teotihuacan merchants, to maneuver politically and perhaps to gain control and rulership. They think that the local Ma-Cuch lineage was able, through trading alliances with Teotihuacan, to outmaneuver two other lineages at Tikal and gain power. The Teotihuacan-style architecture, ceramic styles, and trade goods at Tikal may, on the other hand, reflect the presence of a trade emissary at the site or of trading and perhaps marriage alliances between two Early Classic superpowers (see Braswell 2003; Sharer 2003a; Sharer 2003b).

Teotihuacan influence elsewhere in the Maya lowlands is less pervasive, and there is some consensus among Maya archaeologists that it indicated trade and alliances rather than military or political takeover. At Yaxha, there is talud-tablero architecture and a stela with Tlaloc imagery indicative of Teotihuacan

Altar Q in front of Temple 16 at Copan (Courtesy B. Somers)

influence, as with Stela 31 from Tikal, but unfortunately little is known about the archaeology or epigraphy of Yaxha, so the interpretation of Teotihuacan impact at the site remains enigmatic at best. At Rio Azul, there is a small talud-tablero altar similar to one found in the Lost World Complex at Tikal, but no talud-tablero buildings. Rio Azul does, however, have a tremendous number of Teotihuacan-style cylindrical tripod vessels with distinctive Teotihuacan iconography, notably the "coffee bean" motif, but according to T. Patrick Culbert (see various articles in his 1991 edited volume), none of the Rio Azul burials has as much Teotihuacan iconography as Tikal's burials 10 and 48. Cylindrical tripod vessels also occur at Uaxactun but without the distinctive Teotihuacan imagery, suggesting that they may have been local copies.

Green obsidian eccentrics in an Early Classic burial from Altun Ha and an Altun Ha–style vessel in a Copan burial may reflect the extensive alliances undertaken by this city. Both of these finds may have been evidence of gift exchange among the Classic elite. Chris White and colleagues (2001a) suggest that the Teotihuacan goods in the Altun Ha burial were a one-time gift from Teotihuacan as a mark of appreciation. The results of oxygen isotope analysis of the Altun Ha tomb indicate that the adult male elite individual was local and not from Teotihuacan. Early Classic green obsidian found at Becan, associated with the defensive earthworks around the site, suggests some military intervention, but the dearth of other indications of Teotihuacan influence at Becan leaves conclusions about the Teotihuacan influence at Becan perplexing. The influence of Teotihuacan is evident in the founding of the Copan dynasty in A.D. 426, with the arrival of Yax Kuk Mo. This event is recorded on Altar Q, a stone monument at Copan (Martin and Grube 2000). Coincident with the arrival of Yax Kuk Mo, masonry buildings replaced earlier adobe construction, and the talud-tablero architectural style of Teotihuacan was dominant in Yax Kuk Mo's royal court buildings. Rather than directly from Teotihuacan, the new leader likely came from Tikal (Bell, Canuto, and Sharer 2004; Buikstra et al. 2004; Sharer 2003a; Sharer 2003b). Teotihuacan had previously exerted its political influence at Tikal with the arrival of a Siyaj Kak at the city in A.D. 378. Teotihuacan influence also is evident in the form of talud-tablero architecture, as well as pottery and obsidian trade goods, at Tikal. With the collapse of the Teotihuacan civilization about A.D. 600, its influence in the Maya area, both in the highlands at Kaminaljuyu and in the Maya lowlands, ceased. Having shaken off the "shackles" of the highland superpower, lowland Maya polities floresced after the fall of Teotihuacan. Maya royalty engaged their populace in extensive rebuilding projects and expansionistic military expeditions, and they nurtured the production of a spectacular record of decorative art in the form of sculpture, painted pottery, murals, stonework, and architecture.

LATE CLASSIC POLITICS AND WARFARE

The power of Tikal and the northeast Peten in the Early Classic halted temporarily during the "hiatus," a time between A.D. 534 and 593 when Tikal stopped erecting carved stelae. The Peten was in relative decline at this time. Caracol, located in present-day Belize just east of the Peten, dominated the lowland Maya political landscape, as reported by Diane and Arlen Chase of the University of Central Florida (Chase and Chase 1987a; Chase and Chase 1987b, Chase and Chase 1996; Chase and Chase 1994). An altar from Caracol reports two wars waged against Tikal in A.D. 556 and A.D. 562. Unfortunately, the text on the monument is eroded, so that although Diane and Arlen Chase (1994) interpret the fragmentary glyphs to record Tikal's defeat by Caracol, Martin and Grube (2000) think it was Calakmul rather than Caracol that defeated Tikal. In fact, although Caracol grew to prominence in the Late Classic, Calakmul dominated the political landscape, for a period of 130 years. With the defeat of Tikal, Caracol changed its allegiance from that city to its conqueror, Calakmul.

In addition to its successful military campaign against Tikal, Calakmul, with assistance from Caracol, embarked on an expansive military strategy. In A.D. 631, Naranjo was defeated by Calakmul, which had considerable impact on the history of Naranjo for forty years. A building campaign at Naranjo included a public record of the defeat of the city.

Both Tikal and Naranjo emerged from Calakmul's control during the Late Classic (beginning in Tepeu 2 times), Caracol fell into obscurity, and the northeast Peten in general experienced a boom in terms of population growth, construction activity, and artistic accomplishments. Apart from a slate stela dated to A.D. 702, Caracol erected no new monuments between A.D. 672 and A.D. 800. Tikal may have been involved in starting royal dynasties at Dos Pilas and Seibal and had continuing alliances with, or power over, these polities. The first ruler of Dos Pilas, Ruler 1, was inaugurated in A.D. 645 and evidently

Caana Structure at Caracol, Belize (Corbis/Macduff Everton)

came from Tikal (Demarest at al. 2003). The fact that Dos Pilas initially used, and continued to use, Tikal's emblem glyph indicates a strong political alliance between the two polities, perhaps even that Dos Pilas remained somewhat under the jurisdiction or political control of Tikal, despite its great distance. Dos Pilas went on to create a multicenter polity in the Pasion region (see Mathews and Willey in Culbert 1991), as well as engaging in military or political activities at Naranjo and Site Q (either El Peru or Calakmul) in the Peten. Dos Pilas commemorated the inauguration of Jaguar Paw-Jaguar at Site Q in A.D. 686, an event also recorded on a pottery vessel of unknown provenience reported by

Houston and Mathews (see Houston 1993), in which Jaguar Paw-Jaguar is seen kneeling before a Dos Pilas or Tikal ruler.

The emergence of Naranjo from under Calakmul's domination begins with intervention and continues with alliances with Dos Pilas and Tikal. Lady Six Sky was sent from Dos Pilas to restart the royal dynasty at Naranjo in A.D. 682. This event is recorded on a stela at Coba and is only 116 days after the inauguration of Ruler A at Tikal. The next ruler at Naranjo, Smoking Squirrel, was likely Lady Six Sky's son. He was born five years after her arrival at Naranjo, and he assumes the throne at age five. Smoking Squirrel subsequently reinforced his alliances with Tikal or Dos Pilas in mentioning two women with the Tikal emblem glyph, one of whom may have been his wife. Alliances between Dos Pilas and Tikal continued until the death of Ruler 2 at Dos Pilas, which is recorded on the carved bones in the tomb of Ruler A at Tikal.

As the cities rose again to prominence, both Tikal and Naranjo initiated expansionistic wars toward the west and south, respectively. Naranjo waged four wars between A.D. 693 and 695, ultimately capturing Ucanal, formerly in Caracol territory. The record of the capture of Ucanal includes mention of "he of Tikal/Dos Pilas," indicating some enduring contact between Tikal, Dos Pilas, and/or Naranjo. Ruler A led Tikal into war with Site Q in A.D. 695, capturing Jaguar Paw-Jaguar. His capture is recorded on the lintels of Temple 1 at Tikal. By A.D. 771 the time of military expansion and unification led by Tikal and Naranjo dissipated, and it was followed by a time of political fragmentation into many polities in the latter part of the Late Classic.

WARFARE

The Classic Maya were more warlike than considered by Thompson (1970), Morley (1946), and others in the 1940s and 1950s, but archaeologists do not agree on the role of warfare in the development and fall of Classic Maya society. Thompson viewed the ancient Maya as a pacific theocracy, based on interpretations at that time of empty ceremonial centers, low populations of contented rural farmers, and elite Maya engaged in cosmological and astronomical study. David Webster (1993; see also Webster 1976; Webster 2002), an archaeologist at Pennsylvania State University and a leading expert in Maya warfare, points out that the popular but erroneous view of the ancient Maya, particularly of the Classic period, was that they were unique among ancient civilizations and that they mysteriously rose and fell in the rainforest.

Warfare, capture, and sacrifice are commonly depicted in Maya art, especially art of the Late Classic, but these themes were largely ignored by Mayanists. Denial of the prevalence, even presence, of warfare in the Maya lowlands did not change until the dramatic breakthroughs in deciphering Mayan hieroglyphs that began with Heinrich Berlin's and Tatiana Proskouriakoff's (see Coe 1992; Houston, Mazariegos, and Stuart 2001; Proskouriakoff 1960) stunning discoveries that cities had emblem glyphs and that the glyphs were historical, not calendrical or astronomical records, respectively. Instead, the hieroglyphs recount the history of Maya dynasties, highlighting the battles won, captives taken and sacrificed, and cities conquered and subjugated.

The last quarter of the twentieth century witnessed a tremendous increase in the evidence of Classic Maya warfare, particularly from epigraphy and art, and increasingly from dirt archaeology. The hieroglyphs provide a military record of conquests by Maya rulers, even naming some captives. Battle scenes are depicted on the magnificent wall murals at Bonampak (Miller 1986), Chichen Itza, and elsewhere. Warfare, capture, and sacrifice are pervasive themes in stone carvings at Classic sites (Schele and Miller 1986). The pictorial scenes on painted pots from the Late Classic also are replete with themes of warfare (Reents-Budet 1994). Documentation of warfare archaeologically through discovery, excavation, and study of walls, weapons, and victims of war is necessarily a more lengthy process.

Elsewhere in Mesoamerica, warfare has been linked to the origins and development of civilization (Flannery and Marcus 2003). In ancient Oaxaca, intervillage raiding resulting from competition for access to water, good farmland, and other resources escalated as agricultural populations increased in size over time. Raiding escalated into the conquest of territory to obtain resources through tribute and the consolidation of power by military force. Since the conditions were similar in the Maya area, future researchers may find that raiding and warfare developed prior to the Classic period, as competition for scarce resources and population increased.

In addition to Webster's (1976) classic description of the defensive wall at Becan, defensive stone or earth walls have been reported from many sites in the southern and northern Maya lowlands. Although dating a defensive wall is often problematic, many evidently date to the Late Classic, although some date to the Early Classic or even the Late Preclassic. Southern lowland sites with defensive walls include Tikal, Calakmul, Becan (Webster 1976), El Mirador, Dos Pilas (Palka 1997), Aguateca (Inomata 1997), and Punta de Chimino (Demarest et al. 1997), among others. Dahlin (2000) describes a defensive wall around Chunchucmil in relation to walls around nine other sites in the northern Maya lowlands (see also Webster 1993; Webster 2002).

By Late Classic times, the Maya were engaged in frequent warfare, but was it related to the expansionistic, empire-building desires of Maya royalty, or was it to obtain captives for sacrifice, much like the Flowery Wars of the later Aztecs? Interpretations of the role and extent of Maya warfare are tied to Mayanists' views of the political structure of the lowlands during the Late Classic. Some Mayanists, like Culbert (1991) and the Chases (Chase and Chase 1996), regard warfare as expansionistic, resulting in the enlargement of political territories. In contrast, others (Martin and Grube 2000) regard warfare as more limited to the acquisition of captives for sacrifice and as a component of diplomacy—in fact, sometimes a tactic to maintain political dominance when diplomacy fails. Dahlin (2000) points to the destruction of walled cities to end their economic control over production and distribution. Joel Palka (1997), by way of contrast, suggests that the rulers may have abandoned walled cities such as Chunchucmil and Dos Pilas after they were attacked, but that the bulk of the city's residents may have continued to live in the city, except the abandoned downtown.

In the wider sphere of regional geopolitics, intermarriages sometimes oc-

Battle by Bonampak warriors against neighboring people; the halach uinic (lord, wearing jaguar skin) and his lieutenants stand on a platform as prisoners are tortured by having their fingernails pulled out. Reconstructed fresco from Bonampak, Maya culture (The Art Archive/National Anthropological Museum Mexico/Dagli Orti)

curred with polities at some distance, whereas warfare was usually initiated with polities closer geographically, usually neighbors. The greatest distance for interpolity marriage was between Palenque and Copan. For the other seven known instances of interpolity marriage, the average distance is 64 kilometers (with Palenque and Copan the distance is 109 kilometers). Hammond (1991) notes that for polities recorded in hieroglyphs as being engaged in warfare, each polity had an average territory of about 2,000 square kilometers, with the polity capital about 25 kilometers from each boundary, so that polity capitals were about 50 kilometers apart.

The patterns of royal visits and marriages are quite different from the patterns of warfare, a point well articulated by Hammond (1991) based on hieroglyphic data (Schele and Mathews 1991). In fact, patterns of visits and warfare are mutually exclusive. Rulers seem to have made shorter trips than did their royal representatives (lesser ahau). Rulers made short trips, as with the 45-kilometer trip downriver from Yaxchilan to Piedras Negras, or the 22-kilometer overland trek from Yaxchilan to Bonampak.

The possibility that Tikal conquered Rio Azul, some 100 kilometers to the northeast, also is under debate. Richard E. W. Adams (1999), who led the fieldwork at the site, believes that Tikal conquered Rio Azul and incorporated the site into the Tikal realm. Kneeling prisoners pictured on altars from Rio Azul are similar to those found by the Proyecto Nacional Tikal at the Lost World Complex. Adams also interprets the insignia of Ruler X from Rio Azul to indicate that he was related to Stormy Sky from Tikal. Other Maya archaeologists, notably Culbert (1991) and the participants of the School of American Research seminar on Maya politics, do not believe that Tikal's polity extended that far.

Mathews (in Schele and Mathews 1991) tabulates interpolity warfare and captures recorded in the hieroglyphs. Mathews reports about a dozen men of ahau status recorded as being captured in major battles. They include those portrayed on murals in a room in Bonampak. Two rulers were captured without their territories having been taken over. They were Kan-Xul of Palenque and 18 Rabbit of Copan, with their captors being 64 kilometers and 47 kilometers distant. On the other hand, when Ruler 3 of Dos Pilas, 24 kilometers away, captured Jaguar Paw-Jaguar of Seibal, Jaguar Paw-Jaguar's capital was subordinated to Dos Pilas. Hammond suggests that border skirmishes may have been quite common, with the purpose of obtaining captives for sacrifice and to enhance the captor's status, and that polity capitals were more interested in guarding the work force for construction efforts and food production closer to the city than in protecting the exact geographical boundaries of their polities.

The history of empire building in the Petexbatun region, as outlined by Arthur Demarest (1997), includes a series of military conflicts and alliances. Tamarindito was the main power in the Petexbatun before the rise of the Dos Pilas royal dynasty and after its downfall. From the late seventh to the mid-eighth century, the Petexbatun region was subsumed under the power of Dos Pilas. Initially, there were battles with Dos Pilas relatives at Tikal in order to claim that throne and subsume Tikal under the Dos Pilas polity, and later battles to conquer local neighbors.

The power of Dos Pilas and the Petexbatun in general expanded following a pattern of intensifying dynastic rivalries and interelite competition until A.D. 760, when Dos Pilas was invaded, destroyed, and abandoned. After the fall of Dos Pilas, the seat of regional dynastic power moved for a time to Aguateca until it, too, was sacked and abandoned. Generally, the Petexbatun region wallowed in endemic warfare until about A.D. 820 or 830, the beginning of the Terminal Classic period (marked by the introduction of Fine Orange pottery to the area). Demarest regards this incessant warfare as instrumental in the collapse of the region. The regional polity fragmented into warring centers, and continued to fragment, ultimately with villages themselves being fortified. This had a negative impact on the stability of the economic and demographic basis of the region, with disruption of production and trade; agriculture and the balance of subsistence in various environmental niches changing to strategically placed walled fields; emigration; and depopulation of the area. The Petexbatun collapsed into endemic siege and fortification warfare, from which it did not recover.

Military Organization

Wars were organized and led by the ahau, usually the king. The military of each city-state was evidently well organized with a trained and large corps, owing to the frequent success in taking high-ranking ahau and cahal captives and, in some cases, toppling the capital of another polity and taking its territory. Military strategy included the taking of captives, some high-ranking, for humiliation of their polity of origin and for sacrifice. The presentation of captives before the ahau is depicted on painted pottery vessels and stone monuments.

Military strategies varied from raids to obtain captives, to sacking and destroying the capital of a polity, as at Aguateca in the Petexbatun, to conquering and subjugating a polity, as Calakmul did with Tikal and Naranjo. Military tactics included attacking the central acropolis of capitals to capture the king and his entourage. Some cities took defensive measures to counter such attacks. At Aguateca, a city that became allied with Dos Pilas in the Petexbatun region, Takeshi Inomata (1997; Demarest et al. 1997, figure 7) mapped a series of three concentric defensive walls around the city, itself in a naturally defensive location with an escarpment forming the eastern side of the city center, deep gorges along the south and west, and sinkholes along the north. Most of the walls were constructed at the end of the Late Classic (Tepeu 2), when the bulk of the population lived in the city. Walls were built to protect the city center and were laid out in a preconceived concentric plan. The walls here did not cross over architecture as at Dos Pilas. The innermost circle protected the royal palace, which housed the ahau of the Petexbatun polity.

Aguateca became an important city allied with Dos Pilas around A.D. 700. After the defeat of the Dos Pilas Ruler 4 in A.D. 761, the royal dynastic seat evidently moved to Aguateca with the "Ruler of Aguateca." Demarest et al. (1997) believe that before the collapse of Dos Pilas, its royal dynasty may have periodically resided at Aguateca, with its better-planned and more-defensive wall system and its access to trade routes. After the fall of Dos Pilas, during the time

Calakmul temple with outset staircase, masks, and stelae in front (Courtesy T. Winemiller)

of increasing endemic warfare in the Petexbatun, Aguateca may have been more defensively situated to successfully hold the royal seat of power in the region. A nearby hilltop site, Quim Chi Hilan, included residences and agricultural terraces protected by defensive walls, contemporary with Aguateca and evidently defended to provide a secure food source for nearby Aguateca. Defensive walls also protected small villages and springs. Cerro de Cheyo was a true fort or garrison outpost for Aguateca located on a fortified hilltop, with few local residences.

By the late eighth century, defense was the first priority in settlement location, in contrast to earlier settlement choices in the Late Preclassic through the early part of the Late Classic (Tepeu 1) when settlements were located near arable land and water and along water transportation routes, especially along the edge of Lake Petexbatun. By the end of the eighth century, most hilltops were the locations of fortified villages or forts.

Inomata (1997) recounts how the epicenter of Aguateca was attacked and burned, with people fleeing and leaving their possessions behind. What he refers to as a deliberate attack and destruction by outsiders took place at some point after the last dated stela to the "Ruler of Aguateca" in A.D. 790 and before

A.D. 830, the beginning of the Terminal Classic. Demarest et al. (1997) suggest that the attackers may have laid logs across a narrow section of the gorge on the eastern side of Aguateca and quickly and effectively entered and ransacked the epicenter of the community (as depicted in *National Geographic* magazine, Demarest 1993). The attack and burning of buildings in the central area is clear from excavations in three buildings that had the shattered remains of artifacts on their floors, with reconstructible activity areas. There were thin layers of burnt daub on floors and evidence of burning on some of the walls, indicating that the buildings were burned when they were abandoned. In contrast, the buildings outside the epicenter were not burned, and their occupants had enough time to carry away household goods, as the floors were clean. It is of particular note that the invaders did not occupy Aguateca, but instead sacked the city and left it empty. The imperialist military strategy exhibited earlier by Caracol, Tikal, and Dos Pilas was not evident with the attack on Aguateca. The objective of these attackers was not to conquer or subjugate; the city was simply taken off the geopolitical map of power.

Defensive Walls

The Maya used defensive locations and walls to protect their cities. Defensive walls have been found at a number of southern lowland sites, notably Tikal, Becan, El Mirador, Seibal, and Becan, and a number of sites in the northern Yucatan. These walls are nowhere so common and pervasive as in the Petexbatun region, where even small communities, agricultural fields, and water sources were fortified in the Late Classic between A.D. 760 and 830 (Demarest 1997; Demarest et al. 1997).

Generally, the soils are thin in the region; defensive walls consisted of low rows of stones, 1.5–3.5 meters in height, into which posts were evidently placed. The stone bases vary in composition from crude piles of stones to carefully placed reused blocks (40–80 centimeters in length) stacked in horizontal courses. Vertical-facing slabs with stone fill are found at Aguateca and Quim Chi Hilan. Only in a few places, such as at Tamarindito where the soils are deep, were palisades constructed by placing posts directly in the ground, as evidenced by post molds and palisade impressions in burnt clay. Access through the fortified walls was restricted, often with the use of baffled gateways, which in some instances, as at Dos Pilas (Demarest et al. 1997, figure 5), led into a "killing alley," where the enemy was trapped in a long corridor for easy attack.

The quality and placement of the defensive features was a response to the increase in endemic warfare. At Dos Pilas, the defensive walls were crudely made and ran right over buildings, including the royal palace (Demarest et al. 1997, figure 1), whereas at Aguateca, the walls were better planned and did not cross over buildings (Demarest et al. 1997, figure 7). Whereas at Dos Pilas, elite architecture was raided for cut stone to build defensive walls, newly cut limestone blocks were used at Aguateca. After the defeat of Dos Pilas when Ruler 4 was driven from power in A.D. 761, a nearby hill was fortified with three concentric defensive walls enclosing a temple called El Duende (Demarest et al.

1997, figure 6). Demarest et al. (1997) note that similar defensive wall systems are found dating from later years in the Peten and Yucatan. The nature and dating of the defensive wall systems in the Petexbatun is known from extensive excavations. Better understanding of the defensive walls in the northern Yucatan awaits such fieldwork.

Seibal, a contemporary and a rival of Aguateca, was located in a defensible location above steep river bluffs and ravines, and the central group of buildings at the site has a low defensive wall around it similar to that at Aguateca. This wall also may have been further built up with wooden poles to form a palisade, as at Punta de Chimino.

At Punta de Chimino, located on a peninsula in Lake Petexbatun, a series of defensive moats and walls were constructed to protect the community and its fields and gardens and to cut off the island from the mainland. Demarest (1997) attributes the longevity of the site, from the Middle Preclassic into the Postclassic (unique in the region), to its participation in trade, along with its defensive position and its managed and defensible subsistence regime. The site evidently fell under the control of different powers as they waxed and waned, notably Tamarindito, Dos Pilas, Aguateca, and, after A.D. 830 during the Terminal Classic, perhaps as an outpost of Seibal and clearly associated with the florescence of Seibal and Altar de Sacrificios during the Terminal Classic.

The pattern of defense at ten communities in the northern Maya lowlands shows similarities with the Petexbatun. At Chunchucmil, Dahlin (2000) describes low walls built hastily from nearby buildings, causeways, and walled paths (albarradas) in a desperate attempt to defend the city. The walls were constructed over buildings and across roadways, and were not dismantled later. Apparently the city was sacked and was not repopulated. Whoever attacked Chunchucmil successfully ended its control over the nearby coastal salt works at Celestun and its management of the acquisition of exotic trade goods and distribution of goods and resources in northwestern Yucatan. Dahlin dates this event to the end of the Late Classic.

A similar pattern of hasty construction of defensive walls over existing buildings is reported at Dzonot Ake, Cuca, and Ake. At Dzonot Ake, a wall encloses the 6 ha of the main site area (Webster 1993). The wall may date to the Late Classic (Dahlin 2000) or the Late Postclassic (Webster 1993). At Cuca, buildings were cannibalized to construct the two walls that cross over existing buildings, suggesting to Dahlin that they were hastily made, perhaps by work gangs, in the face of threats of attack by outsiders during the Late Classic. David Webster (1993), on the other hand, contends that the walls were remodeled over time and that they were not built in response to an immediate threat.

Elsewhere in the northern Maya lowlands, defensive walls were more deliberately planned, as at Chacchob, Yaxuna, Xkanha, Ek Balam, Uxmal, and Mayapan (Dahlin 2000). Chacchob is a small site with three temples, several low stone platforms, two range or palace complexes, and residences. Walls 5–6 meters wide and 2.5 meters high were plastered and sloped on the exterior and on the interior. Benches 1–2 meters wide on the interior wall provided a platform upon which defenders could stand. There were three gates through the wall. Yaxuna is interesting because this large and important site south of Chichen Itza had defensive walls built during the Terminal Classic, likely in response to military threats from Chichen Itza (Dahlin 2000). The central acropolis at Yaxuna was protected by a low 1-meter-high wall, hastily constructed and varying in width from 0.6 to 3 meters in width. Entrances 1 to 2 meters wide and at least one switchback or bafflement controlled access. North of Yaxuna by 2 kilometers, the satellite community of Xkanha was transformed into a military garrison, protected by a massive wall that was actually constructed of two walls with faced stones set 4.5 meters apart, with loose boulders inside.

The defensive character of the wall system at Uxmal appears to have been created more to control pedestrian traffic than to defend the site from outsiders, even though it may have served a defensive purpose if the site were attacked. Walls joined buildings, but there were many gates and at least one baffled gate.

At the large city of Ek Balam, three concentric walls were well planned and built, with a fourth wall hastily constructed of rubble across the main plaza at the site (Dahlin 2000). A well-built inner wall enclosed the site center and was built of stone, faced with plaster, and was some 2 meters high and 3 meters wide (Bey, Hanson, and Ringle 1997). Where the walls cross causeways (sacbeob), the walls are baffled. The outer walls enclose large areas of Ek Balam, 9.55 and 11.9 ha respectively, and end at a large sinkhole (rejollada). Short walls between buildings further reinforce the defensive character of the city. Dahlin believes that the quick construction of the fourth wall, and the fact that it was not removed from the central plaza, indicate that Ek Balam did not recover from the attack, which he dates to the Late or Terminal Classic.

Weapons

Little attention has been directed to the weapons used in Maya warfare. The Classic Maya certainly had chert stone points suitable for hafting onto spears. Small dart points were introduced during the Postclassic, evidently from central Mexico. Caches of stone spear points were found along the defensive wall systems at Dos Pilas, as well as a cache of adult male skulls, decapitated while still fleshed, in a pit outside the exterior wall (Demarest et al. 1997, 234).

POLITICAL GEOGRAPHY

Mayanists disagree on the level of political integration and centralization of power during the Classic period and on the size of "typical" polities. Was Late Classic Maya society organized at a state level or a chiefdom level? Some view the lowlands as having been divided into many relatively autonomous polities whose royalty engaged in limited military ventures principally to obtain captives. Others see the development of alliances and larger political units based on military conquest. Part of the difficulty in defining polities is that their capitals are recorded in the hieroglyphic records, but the territorial boundaries of polities are not recorded. Even when there is a record of the successful capture of a ruler in warfare, the amount of territory added, if any, to the conqueror's polity is unstated. Conquerors may have preferred to secure tribute, rather than governing conquered polities, or to install a friendly ruler, perhaps a member of the conqueror's royal dynasty, instead of incorporating the polity.

Martin and Grube (2000) point to epigraphic evidence that relations among dynastic leaders were established by diplomacy (royal visits, gifting, feasting, and royal marriages) with powerful "over-kings" dominating the polities of less powerful kings in other polities. Martin and Grube view political expansion as an expansion of dynastic royal networks through alliances rather than as territorial expansion. Political subservience is noted on monuments that record royal accession to the throne by the word ukab'jiiy, meaning "he supervised it," referring to the role of the over-king in the coronation of the lesser king. Presumably if royal gifts were insufficient or the lesser king became too powerful, the over-king invaded the lesser king's city and captured high-ranking individuals as a show of supremacy.

As mentioned previously, Morley (1946) and Thompson (1970) dominated early views of Maya politics by their view that the Maya lowlands consisted of city-states that were vacant ceremonial centers supporting a low-density rural farming population practicing swidden agriculture. By the 1970s, a new view of Maya politics, including regional states, developed after the discovery of high population densities, both in urban and rural settings, as well as the discovery that a number of agricultural intensification techniques were practiced. Studies of site hierarchies based on labor investment, site size, and other factors argue for correlation of differences in site size with political structure, suggesting that political organization existed within the Maya lowlands at a higher level than the city-state (Hammond 1991). An insightful study by Joyce Marcus (1976, 1993) identifies emblem glyphs as the names of regional polities and points out that a subservient site mentioned a dominant site's emblem glyph. She then proposed a model of "large regional states . . . with primary, secondary, and tertiary centers forming an administrative-optimizing hierarchy " (Marcus 1993, 150, italics in original). Marcus notes that in A.D. 731, the ruler of Copan, 18 Jog, commissioned a monument that lists emblem glyphs for Copan, Tikal, Palenque, and another site that may be Calakmul (Marcus 1976; Marcus 1993). She insightfully points out that this represents 18 Jog's perception of the four superpowers of the Maya world at the time and that, interestingly, this also represents the quadripartite division of the Maya cosmos. In other studies, Richard F. W. Adams and Christopher Jones (1981) inferred five regional states based on counts of courtyards at Maya cities.

By the turn of the twenty-first century, with the decipherment of much of the historical records, many Mayanists (e.g., Hammond 1991) once again were considering the possibility that the lowlands were fragmented into small, politically autonomous units (Demarest 1996). Following this view, each small polity was identified by an emblem glyph, indicating that there were some eighty regional polities in the southern lowlands by the height of the Late Classic. Others, notably Joyce Marcus (1993), vehemently disagree with the correlation of emblem glyph to autonomous polity.

Hammond suggests that the average size of a Late Classic Maya polity was about 2,000 square kilometers. From this perspective, polity capitals were situated about 50 kilometers apart. In support of this size, Hammond marshals hieroglyphic data from Schele and Mathews (1991), who found that royal visits to subordinate cahalob were of distances less than 25 kilometers, whereas most royal visits to cahalob of equal or greater rank were of distances greater than 25 kilometers, presumably reflecting travel within and beyond the polity, respectively. Other Mayanists, notably Marcus (1993) and Arlen and Diane Chase (1996), argue that the military forays and political and marriage alliances between regional polities in the Late Classic indicate the conquest of territory and creation of larger political units. Even though Hammond appeals to the validity of Morley's (1946) model of a mosaic of small polities within the lowlands (based on the classical Greek model), he conceded that, from time to time, multipolities emerged as a result of military conquest (as with Tikal over Uaxactun in A.D. 378 and Dos Pilas over Seibal in A.D. 735) and marriage alliances (in the case of Dos Pilas and Tamarindito in A.D. 378). The Dos Pilas polity was about 3,500 square kilometers in size for about 40 years and about 1,800 square kilometers for about a century. Both Tikal and Caracol may have exceeded 2,500 square kilometers in size.

Although the size and extent of political unification of the southern lowlands during the Late Classic is unresolved, there are tantalizing clues that support contrasting interpretations. Views of a more unified Late Classic political landscape are based primarily on archaeological rather than epigraphic data, the latter of which is inconclusive on political unification. If one accepts a correlation of political structure and the differing sizes of sites with carved and dated monuments, then there is archaeological support for political unification beyond the regional polity. The model suggesting that the lowlands consisted of dozens of small polities is based on the assumption that the use of an emblem glyph was correlated with the distribution of independent and autonomous polities. This interpretation is supported by epigraphic data from the Usumacinta region, but not from the Pasion area. However, Culbert (1991, 142) points out several examples in which a subservient polity continues to use its own emblem glyph, such as Anonal, which expressed subservience to Seibal, and Bonampak, to Tonina. Tamarindito used local emblem glyphs after it was taken over by Dos Pilas in about A.D. 731. Secondary status within a larger polity did not necessarily result in the disuse of a polity's emblem glyph. Instead, some conquered polities use their emblem glyph as well as that of the conqueror: When Quirigua conquered Copan, Cauac Sky of Quirigua used both sites' names.

Although the issue is still debated, the high population density; intensification of subsistence techniques in order to feed the growing populations; increasingly greater displays of power and wealth in terms of larger monumental buildings and more finely made elite pots, costume, and other accoutrements all point to expansion of territory by warfare and military conquest of other polities in order to obtain their human and natural resources as well as marriage and economic alliances. Warfare, marriage alliances, and trading alliances led to the expansion of powerful lowland polities. This is clear evidence of the early existence of regional states (Marcus 1993).

With the disagreement over the extent of centralization and expansion of power between polities, it is not surprising that there is no consensus about the level of centralized organization and control, both politically and economically, within a polity. Based on the multiyear, multidisciplinary Petexbatun study (Demarest et al. 1997), the project director, Arthur Demarest of Vanderbilt University, describes a pattern of decentralized sites and agricultural systems loosely linked to local centers. With few exceptions, there was found to be little elite control in agriculture in the Petexbatun. Food production was well adapted to local environmental settings. Contrary to the findings of Chase and Chase (1996), who regard Classic Maya polities as centralized both politically and economically based on their research at Caracol, Demarest (1996) finds that the Petexbatun research supports a view that most Maya states were segmentary or at least poorly centralized and that they had only limited economic functions.

Marcus (1993) points out that not all functions were necessarily carried out within a polity capital, as with the production of elite chert objects called "eccentrics" at the small community of Colha, Belize. The idea that the Maya had a segmentary state organization finds support from a number of Maya archaeologists, notably Dunham, Jamison, and Leventhal (1989), Fox and Cook (1996), Hammond (1991), Ball and Taschek (1991), and Dunning and colleagues (Dunning, Beach, and Rue 1997). Certainly by the sixteenth-century arrival of the Spaniards to the Yucatan, the Maya settlements were coalesced into small polities. At that time, shared governance among leaders of settlements within a polity diminished the power of the Maya king. Kowalski (2003) sees the transition from divine royal kingship to shared governance by a council as taking place at Chichen Itza in the Terminal Classic, after the collapse of the Classic Maya civilization in the southern Maya lowlands. Even during the Late Classic period, there were council houses, called Popol Nas, at Copan and Palenque in the southern Maya lowlands, as well as at several settlements in the northern Maya lowlands, including Uxmal and Yaxuna. Even with the advances in Maya epigraphy and extensive fieldwork, the nature of Late Classic Maya politics—whether decentralized or centralized—remains unresolved. In and of itself, an understanding of Maya politics is important to defining the nature of the Maya state, but it also bears on interpretations of other aspects of Maya society and economy.

REFERENCES

Adams, Richard E. W. 1999. *Río Azul: An Ancient Maya City.* Norman: University of Oklahoma Press.

Adams, Richard E. W., and R. Christopher Jones. 1981. "Spatial Patterns and Regional Growth among Classic Maya Cities." *American Antiquity* 46: 301–322.

Ashmore, Wendy, ed. 1981. *Lowland Maya Settlement Patterns.* Albuquerque: University of New Mexico Press.

Ball, Joseph W., and Jennifer T. Taschek. 1991. "Late Classic Lowland Maya Political Organization and Central Place Analysis: New Insights from the Upper Belize Valley." *Ancient Mesoamerica* 2: 149–165.

Bell, Ellen E., Marcello A. Canuto, and Robert J. Sharer, eds. 2004. *Understanding Early Classic Copan.* Philadelphia: University of Pennsylvania Museum of Archaeology and Anthropology.

Bey, George J., III, Craig Hanson, and William M. Ringle. 1997. "Classic to Postclassic at Ek Balam, Yucatan: Architectural and Ceramic Evidence for Defining the Transition." *Latin American Antiquity* 1: 237–254.

Braswell, Geoffrey, ed. 2003. *The Maya and Teotihuacan: Reinterpreting Early Classic Interaction.* Austin: University of Texas Press.

Buikstra, Jane E., T. Douglas Price, Lori E. Wright, and James E. Burton. 2004. "Tombs from the Copan Acropolis: A Life-History Approach." In *Understanding Early Classic Copan,* edited by Ellen E. Bell, Marcello A. Canuto, and Robert J. Sharer, 191–212. Philadelphia: University of Pennsylvania Museum of Archaeology and Anthropology.

Chase, Arlen F., and Diane Z. Chase. 1987a. *Glimmers of a Forgotten Realm: Maya Archaeology at Caracol, Belize.* Orlando, FL: Orlando Museum of Art and Loch Haven.

———. 1987b. *Investigations at the Classic Maya City of Caracol, Belize: 1985–1987.* Monograph 3. San Francisco: Pre-Columbian Art Research Institute.

———. 1996. "More than Kin and King: Centralized Political Organization among the Late Classic Maya." *Current Anthropology* 37: 803–810.

Chase, Diane Z., and Arlen F. Chase, eds. 1994. *Studies in the Archaeology of Caracol, Belize.* Monograph 7. San Francisco: Pre-Columbian Art Research Institute.

Christie, Jessica J., ed. 2003. *Maya Palaces and Elite Residences.* Austin: University of Texas Press.

Clark, John E., and Richard Hansen. 2001."The Architecture of Early Kingship: Comparative Perspectives on the Origin of the Maya Royal Court." In *Royal Courts of the Ancient Maya,* vol. 2, edited by Takeshi Inomata and Stephen Houston, 1–45. Boulder: Westview.

Coe, Michael D. 1992. *Breaking the Maya Code.* New York: Thames & Hudson.

Culbert, T. Patrick, ed. 1991. *Classic Maya Political History.* New York: Cambridge University Press.

Dahlin, Bruce. 2000. "The Barricade and Abandonment of Chunchucmil: Implications for Northern Maya Warfare." *Latin American Antiquity* 11: 283–298.

Demarest, Arthur. 1993. "The Violent Saga of a Maya Kingdom." *National Geographic Magazine* 183 (2): 94–111.

———. 1996. "The Maya State: Centralized or Segmentary? Closing Comment." *Current Anthropology* 37: 821–824.

———. 1997. "The Vanderbilt Petexbatun Regional Archaeological Project 1989–1994: Overview, History, and Major Results of a Multidisciplinary Study of the Classic Maya Collapse." *Ancient Mesoamerica* 8: 209–227.

Demarest, Arthur, Kim Morgan, Claudia Wooley, and Hector Escobedo. 2003. "The Political Acquisition of Sacred Geography: The Murcielagos Complex at Dos Pilas." In *Maya Palaces and Elite Residences,* edited by Jessica J. Christie, 120–153. Austin: University of Texas Press.

Demarest, Arthur A., Matt O'Mansky, Claudia Wolley, Dirk Van Tuerenhout, Takeshi Inomata, Joel Palka, and Hector Escobedo. 1997. "Classic Maya Defensive Systems and Warfare in the Petexbatun Region: Archaeological Evidence and Interpretations." *Ancient Mesoamerica* 8: 229–253.

Dunham, Peter S., Thomas R. Jamison, and Richard M. Leventhal. 1989. "Secondary Development and Settlement Economies: The Classic Maya of Southern Belize." In *Prehistoric Maya Economies of Belize,* edited by Patricia McAnany and Barry Isaac, 255–292. Research in Economic Anthropology, Supplement 4. Greenwich, CT: JAI Press.

Dunning, Nicholas, Timothy Beach, and David Rue. 1997. "The Paleoecology and Ancient Settlement of the Petexbatun Region, Guatemala." *Ancient Mesoamerica* 8 (2): 255–266.

Flannery, Kent V., and Joyce Marcus. 2003. "The Origin of War: New ^{14}C Dates from Ancient Mexico." *Proceedings of the National Academy of Sciences* 100: 11801–11805.

Ford, Anabel. 1986. *Population Growth and Social Complexity: An Examination of Settlement and Environment in the Central Maya Lowlands.* Anthropological Research Paper 35. Tempe: Arizona State University.

Fox, John W., and Garrett W. Cook. 1996. "Constructing Maya Communities: Ethnography for Archaeology." *Current Anthropology* 37: 811–830.

Freidel, David A., and Linda Schele. 1988. "Kingship in the Late Preclassic Maya Lowlands: The Instruments and Places of Ritual Power." *American Anthropologist* 90: 547–567.

Hammond, Norman. 1991. "Inside the Black Box: Defining Maya Polity." In *Classic Maya Political History,* edited by T. Patrick Culbert, 253–284. New York: Cambridge University Press.

Hansen, Richard D. 1984. "Excavation on Structure 34 and the Tigre Area, El Mirador, Peten, Guatemala: A New Look at the Preclassic Lowland Maya." Master's thesis, Department of Anthropology, Brigham Young University, Provo, UT.

——— 1991. "The Maya Rediscovered: The Road to Nakbe." *Natural History* 91 (5): 8–14.

Harrison, Peter. 1999. *The Lords of Tikal.* New York: Thames & Hudson.

Houston, Stephen D. 1993. *Hieroglyphs and History at Dos Pilas: Dynastic Politics of the Classic Maya.* Austin: University of Texas Press.

Houston, Stephen, Oswaldo Chinchilla Mazariegos, and David Stuart, eds. 2001. *The Decipherment of Ancient Maya Writing.* Norman: University of Oklahoma Press.

Inomata, Takeshi. 1997. "The Last Day of a Fortified Maya Center: Archaeological Investigations at Aguateca, Guatemala." *Ancient Mesoamerica* 8: 337–351.

Inomata, Takeshi, and Stephen D. Houston, eds. 2001. *Royal Courts of the Ancient Maya.* Boulder, CO: Westview.

Kidder, Alfred V., Jessie D. Jennings, and Edwin M. Shook. 1946. *Excavations at Kaminaljuyu, Guatemala.* Carnegie Institution of Washington Publication 561. Washington, DC: Carnegie Institution of Washington.

Kowalski, Jeff. 2003. "Evidence for the Functions and Meanings of Some Northern Maya Palaces." In *Maya Palaces and Elite Residences,* edited by Jessica Joyce Christie, 204–252. Austin: University of Texas Press.

Laporte, Juan Pedro, and Vilma Fialko. 1995. "Un Reencuentro Con Mundo Perdido, Tikal, Guatemala." *Ancient Mesoamerica* 6: 41–94.

Leventhal, Richard M. 1990. "Southern Belize: An Ancient Maya Region." In *Vision and Revision in Maya Studies,* edited by Flora S. Clancey and Peter D. Harrison, 125–141. Albuquerque: University of New Mexico Press.

Marcus, Joyce. 1976. *Emblem and State in the Classic Maya Lowlands.* Washington, DC: Dumbarton Oaks.

———. 1993. "Ancient Maya Political Organization." In *Lowland Maya Civilization in the Eighth Century A.D.*, edited by Jeremy A. Sabloff and John S. Henderson, 111–183. Washington, DC: Dumbarton Oaks Research Library and Collection.

Martin, Simon, and Nikolai Grube. 2000. *Chronicle of the Maya Kings and Queens: Deciphering the Dynasties of the Ancient Maya.* New York: Thames & Hudson.

Miller, Mary. 1986. *The Murals of Bonampak.* Princeton, NJ: Princeton University Press.

Morley, Sylvanus G. 1946. *The Ancient Maya.* Palo Alto, CA: Stanford University Press.

Palka, Joel W. 1997. "Reconstructing Classic Maya Socioeconomic Differentiation at the Collapse of Dos Pilas, Peten, Guatemala." *Ancient Mesoamerica* 8: 293–306.

Proskouriakoff, Tatiana. 1960. "Historical Implications of a Pattern of Dates at Piedras Negras, Guatemala." *American Antiquity* 25: 454–475.

Reents-Budet, Dorie. 1994. *Painting the Maya Universe.* Durham, NC: Duke University Press.

———. 2001. "Classic Maya Concepts of the Royal Court: An Analysis of Renderings on Pictorial Ceramics." In *Royal Courts of the Ancient Maya,* vol. 1, edited by Takeshi Inomata and Stephen Houston, 195–233. Boulder: Westview.

Sanders, William T. 1977. "Environmental Heterogeneity and the Evolution of Lowland Maya Civilization." In *The Origins of Maya Civilization,* edited by Richard E. W. Adams, 287–297. Albuquerque: University of New Mexico Press.

Sanders, William T., and Joseph W. Michels, eds. 1977. *Teotihuacan and Kaminaljuyu: A Study in Prehistoric Culture Contact.* University Park: Pennsylvania State University Press.

Sanders, William T., and Barbara Price. 1968. *Mesoamerica: The Evolution of a Civilization.* New York: Random House.

Schele, Linda, and David A. Freidel. 1990. *A Forest of Kings: The Untold Story of the Ancient Maya.* New York: William Morrow.

Schele, Linda, and Peter Mathews. 1991. "Royal Visits and Other Intersite Relationships among the Classic Maya." In *Classic Maya Political History,* edited by T. Patrick Culbert, 226–252. New York: Cambridge University Press.

Schele, Linda, and Mary Miller. 1986. *The Blood of Kings: Dynasty and Ritual in Maya Art.* New York: George Braziller.

Sharer, Robert J. 2003a. "Tikal and the Copan Dynastic Founding." In *Tikal: Dynasties, Foreigners, and Affairs of State,* edited by Jeremy A. Sabloff, 319–353. Santa Fe, NM: School of American Research Press.

———. 2003b. "Founding Events and Teotihuacan Connections at Copan, Honduras." In *Teotihuacan and the Maya,* edited by Geoffrey Braswell, 143–165. Austin: University of Texas Press.

Tate, Carolyn E. 1992. *Yaxchilan: The Design of a Maya Ceremonial City.* Austin: University of Texas Press.

Thompson, J. Eric S. 1970. *Maya History and Religion.* Norman: University of Oklahoma Press.

Valdes, Juan Antonio, and Lori Wright. 2004. "The Early Classic and Its Antecedents at Kaminaljuyu: A Complex Society with Complex Problems." In *Understanding Early Classic Copan,* edited by Ellen E. Bell, Marcello A. Canuto, and Robert J. Sharer, 337–355. Philadelphia: University of Pennsylvania Museum of Archaeology and Anthropology.

Webster, David. 1976. *Defensive Earthworks at Becan, Campeche, Mexico.* Middle American Research Institute Publication 41. New Orleans: Tulane University.

———. 1993. "The Study of Maya Warfare: What It Tells Us about the Maya and What It Tells Us about Maya Archaeology." In *Lowland Maya Civilization in the Eighth Cen-*

tury A.D., edited by Jeremy A. Sabloff and John S. Henderson, 415–444. Washington, DC: Dumbarton Oaks.

———. 2002. *The Fall of the Ancient Maya.* New York: Thames & Hudson.

White, Christine D., Fred J. Longstaffe, and Kimberley R. Law. 2001a. "Revisiting the Teotihuacan Connection at Altun Ha: Oxygen-Isotope Analysis of Tomb F-8/1." *Ancient Mesoamerica* 12: 65–72.

White, Christine D., Fred J. Longstaffe, Michael W. Spence, and Kimberley R. Law. 2000. "Testing the Nature of Teotihuacan Imperialism at Kaminaljuyu Using Phosphate Oxygen-Isotope Ratios." *Journal of Anthropological Research* 56: 535–558.

White, Christine D., David M. Pendergast, Fred J. Longstaffe, and Kimberley R. Law. 2001b. "Social Complexity and Food Systems at Altun Ha, Belize: The Isotopic Evidence." *Latin American Antiquity* 12: 371–393.

CHAPTER 8

Religion and Ideology

As a literate civilization with a long tradition of naturalistic painting and carving, the Maya have left a wealth of information on their ancient religion and ideology. Ancient and historic texts detail myths, gods, and rituals. Ceremonies are reenacted pictorially on pottery vessels and on carved wood and stone. Archaeologists recover the material traces of ancient rituals such as burials, dedications, and termination rituals for buildings. And they find the religious paraphernalia used in bloodletting, the vision quest, and sacrifice—objects such as stingray spines, obsidian blades sharper than surgical steel, tobacco, and pots for hallucinogenic enemas.

Although the Classic Maya stelae primarily describe and date political events such as battles won or accession to the throne, rituals often accompanied these events and are described in writing. Classic period kings and queens also commemorated various events associated with the calendar and recorded them on carved monuments. Yaxchilan seems to be particularly prolific in pictorial scenes of bloodletting rituals. A series of stone carvings at the site depict the ritual bloodletting and vision quest of a royal woman associated with the accession to the throne of a king (Tate 1992, figures 6, 13, 14). Bloodletting equipment, including lancets, bark paper (for collecting the blood that was then burned on the paper to produce smoke), and cords (for pulling through the tongue, ear, or penis) are shown on lintels at Yaxchilan. Carolyn Tate (1992, 68, figure 28) suggests that the cloth bundles often shown held by royal women during accession ceremonies at Yaxchilan actually contain the bloodletting equipment.

The naturalistic art style of the Maya reaches its peak in the Late Classic with supernatural and actual personages depicted in a variety of scenes on painted pots and carved stone. In particular, a variety of mythical and court scenes are painted on the exteriors of fine vases and the interiors of open bowls and dishes (Reents-Budet 2001). Some vases show a sequence of events in panels, evidently telling a story. Some of the stories have counterparts in historic texts.

The primary historical texts relevant for interpreting ancient Maya religion and ideology include documents written by native Maya and those written by Spanish clerics during the early colonial period. The *Popol Vuh,* written by the Quiché Maya of highland Guatemala during the sixteenth century, is most informative, as it tells the Quiché creation story and also tells about the adventures of the Hero Twin gods (Tedlock 1985). Many scenes on Late Classic painted pots correspond to the *Popol Vuh,* especially the adventures of the Hero Twins, but some scenes also elaborate on myths not told in the *Popol Vuh* or other documents. Four Maya books are informative on astronomy, religion,

Sites mentioned in the text about religion and ideology

and ideology. They are the Dresden Codex, the Madrid Codex, the Paris Codex, and the Codex Grolier, the last being a fragmentary codex recently found in Chiapas, Mexico (Glass 1975).

The books of Chilam Balam, written by native Maya priests in several Yucatecan communities during early colonial days, also are variously informative on religion and ideology. The Chilam Balam books of Chumayel (Roys 1967), Tizimin (Edmonson 1982), and Mani (Craine and Reindorp 1979) each discuss the destruction of an early people, followed by a great flood and the successful creation of the Maya world. The flood also is discussed briefly in the Dresden Codex (Thompson 1972). Bishop Diego de Landa's *Relación de las Cosas de Yucatan* refers briefly to the flood. His detailed description of Maya culture includes discussion of mythology and cosmology (Tozzer 1941). One of the more important parts of the Chilam Balam accounts is the discussion of the creation of the world with four pillars holding up the four corners of the world and with a central world tree. Each pillar is associated with a color and a bird. Red is east, white is north, black is west, green is south, and yellow is the center where the world tree is located. Some researchers, however, interpret the four corners of the Maya world as making the solstitial rising and setting points of the sun, instead of cardinal directions (Tedlock 1985). In any case, the directions and colors have pervasive and clear counterparts in ancient Maya iconography and cosmology (Taube 1995). On his elaborately carved stone sarcophagus, King Pacal of Palenque descends into the underworld on the world tree to join the gods and ancestors, to be conjured back to earth through vision quests by the living. The sarcophagus also shows Pascal's ascent (Schele and Freidel 1990).

MAYA IDEOLOGY: THE *POPOL VUH*

Scenes on painted pots from the Late Classic, as well as motifs and images on other pottery, refer to the Maya creation story and the adventures of the Hero Twins told in the *Popol Vuh,* a sixteenth-century Quiché Maya text (Tedlock 1985). The text was written anonymously by Quiché Maya scribes, perhaps in an attempt to preserve their culture. The story describes the creation of the Earth, plants and animals, and humans. In addition, the *Popol Vuh* explains humans' place in the world in relation to the gods in the sky and the underworld, the links between astronomy and the calendar, and the place of astronomy in people's lives. Many of the events take place around the adventures of the Hero Twins and their father and uncle, both on Earth and in the underworld, in part involving the ball game. The *Popol Vuh* provides important analogues for interpreting the ball game, the identities of various gods, the importance of corn to the Maya, and the ancient Maya worldview.

The *Popol Vuh* begins with the story of creation, with the meeting of the god from the primordial sea (Plumed Serpent) and the god from the primordial sky (Heart of Sky) to discuss the emergence of the Earth from the sea and the creation of plants; the sun, moon, and stars; and people. The gods discuss the process of creation as "sowing" and the subsequent growth of plants, passage of the sun, moon, and stars, and birth and death of people as the process of

Pacal's sarcophagus lid, showing him descending into the underworld (Drawing by Kay A. Read)

"dawning." The first attempt to create humans fails, as the gods are disappointed that the animals they create cannot speak or offer prayers. Consequently, animals are destined to be providers of flesh to be consumed. After another unsuccessful attempt to make humans, this time from clay, which dissolves in water, the gods consult very old gods, Xpiyacoc, the divine matchmaker, and Xmucane, a divine midwife, who suggest that humans should be made from wood. These gods are known as day keepers because they understand the 260-day calendar of 13 day numbers and 20 day names and are able to divine information using the calendar. The attempt to make humans from wood fails, but results in the origin of monkeys.

The story is interrupted before the successful creation of humans from corn by the adventures of the Hero Twins, Hunahpu and Xbalanque. Their experiences, and those of their father and uncle, establish the relationships between humans and the celestial and underworld gods and the place of the calendar and the ball game in facilitating human existence. In fact, their adventures set the stage for the arrival of humans. Their adventures take place before the creation of the world and humans.

The first adventures are by the Hero Twins, Hunahpu and Xbalanque. These adventures are important symbolically because they define the quadripartite division of the Maya cosmos by assigning stars to each corner. They also establish a pattern of the celestial world as a metaphor for the Earth, with the two being linked through astronomy. In the first adventure, Hunahpu and Xbalanque encounter the monstrous Vucub Caquix, or Seven Macaw, who pretends to be the most powerful being, the sun and moon. They use their blowguns to shoot Vucub Caquix from a tree, and they remove his godly prowess by pulling out his teeth and removing metal disks from around his eyes. Metaphorically, the Hero Twins show their mastery of nature by killing Vucub Caquix. Seven Macaw becomes the Big Dipper, with his rise in the sky in mid-October marking the approach of the dry season and his setting in mid-July marking the approach of the hurricane season. He also marks north in the sky, as does the actual Big Dipper. This story has similaritites to the story of the attempt to create humans from wood. In that story, the "brothers" shoot Seven Macaw with a blowgun, which results in the flood.

Seven Macaw's son Zipacna, a crocodile monster claiming to be the god of mountains, destroys the gods of alcohol, known as the Four Hundred Boys, and they become the Pleiades, which rise late in the day and mark the proper time of day to plant crops. As they set in the western sky, the Pleiades mark the west. The brothers avenge the Four Hundred Boys' deaths by tempting Zipacna to wrestle (or have sex with?) a large crab at the base of a mountain, but the mountain collapses on top of Zipacna and he turns to stone. The twins lure Zipacna's younger brother, Earthquake, who pretends to be the destroyer of mountains, to eat a bird cooked in earth, resulting in Earthquake's burial in the east. These adventures place three of the cardinal directions within the Maya cosmos.

The next adventures establish the relationships between people and the gods of the underworld, Xibalba. The first story begins with the Hero Twins' father, Hun Hunahpu, and uncle, Vucub Hunahpu, born to the old gods Xpiyacoc and Xmucane. The lords of Xibalba become annoyed with the noise from

Hun Hunahpu and Vucub Hunahpu's ball playing. The brother's ball court is located on the eastern edge of the Earth near the great abyss. One Death and Seven Death, the primary lords of Xibalba, send owls to lure the twins to play ball in the ball court of Xibalba, located on the western edge of the underworld. It is a dangerous trip and the brothers fall asleep. They are sacrificed by the lords of Xibalba and buried in the ball court. This story ties the playing of the ball game with sacrifice. Hun Hunahpu's head is cut off and placed in a fruit tree, which bears calabash gourds for the first time. Xquic, the daughter of a lord of Xibalba, is miraculously impregnated when Hun Hunahpu spits in her hand after she looks at his head, which had deteriorated to a skull. Xquic's father orders her heart to be offered as a sacrifice, but his owl messengers instead escort Xquic to Earth and make a surrogate heart to sacrifice from sap of the croton bush. This story shows that the lords of Xibalba can be out-maneuvered and tricked.

Xmucane sees the journey of her sons to Xibalba and the arrival of Xquic as a metaphor for the movements of celestial beings as recorded in the calendar, and so she accepts Xquic's story that Hun Hunahpu is the father of her unborn children (the Hero Twins). In the calendrical metaphor, Venus rose as the morning star on a day called Hunahpu, analogous to her sons playing ball in their eastern court (celestial bodies rise in the east). Venus's reappearance on a day called Death is analogous to the death of her sons in Xibalba and to Hun Hunahpu's head being placed in the west in a tree. Venus is reborn on a day named Net, which corresponds to the impression of a net Xmucane found where Xquic was gathering corn. Xmucane interprets the net as a sign that Xquic's sons will be a reincarnation of Hun Hunahpu.

After they are born, Hunahpu and Xbalanque become tired of being taunted by their half-brothers, One Monkey (Hun Batz) and One Artisan (Hun Chouen), born earlier to Hun Hunahpu and a previous wife, Xbaquiyalo. Hun Batz and Hun Chouen had become proficient in a variety of arts and crafts, including music, writing, carving, and metallurgy. Eventually the Hero Twins become annoyed with being teased by their half-brothers and send them up a tree, where they become monkeys. They also become the planet Mars and the gods of arts and crafts. Mars is afterward visible on a day called One Monkey One Artisan. Hunahpu and Xbalanque return to their usual activities, planting corn and tending to their confields, as well as hunting.

Hunahpu and Xbalanque find ball game equipment in their father's house and start playing the ball game, to the annoyance of the gods of Xibalba, who summon them to Xibalba. Unlike their father and uncle, the twins survive various tests, with the help of a mosquito (who bites each of the gods of Xibalba, forcing them to identify themselves to the boys). They go on to play the ball game with the lords of Xibalba. They are quite successful and pass through a number of other tests set by the lords of Xibalba. Along the way, the twins deceive the lords of Xibalba into thinking the twins are dead when they jump into a soup. Miraculously the twins are reborn as catfish, change back to human form, and perform mock sacrifices in which the victim is allegedly resurrected. When a couple of the lords of Xibalba, One Death and Seven Death, offer themselves for a mock sacrifice, the twins trick the gods and carry out a real sacrifice.

Detail of Monkey from Lintel No. 48 from Yaxchilan (Archivo Iconografico, S.A./Corbis)

The twins spare the lives of the remaining gods of Xibalba, but tell them that
henceforth they will only be allowed to be offered sacrifices of animal blood
and croton sap and that they can only bother people on Earth who are weak or
have guilt. The twins are unsuccessful in their attempts at reviving their father,
Hunahpu, so they leave him buried in the ball court at Xibalba. In his memory,
the day called Hun Hunahpu is the day for remembering the dead, and the
words *ball court* and *graveyard* are synonymous. Xbalanque and Hunahpu become the sun and moon and are known thereafter as the Hero Twins.

The hero twins are commonly depicted on painted pictorial vessels of the
Late Classic period, but they are shown even earlier on Late Preclassic stelae.

The Hero Twins and Vucub Caquix are depicted on two Late Preclassic carved stelae at Izapa on the Pacific coast. The implication of the imagery on these stelae is that the mythical story of the Hero Twins as told in the *Popol Vuh* predates Classic Maya civilization. In Late Classic depictions, Vucub Caquix is a monstrous bird, possibly a vulture, with serpents on his wings and a long beak, instead of the macaw described in the *Popol Vuh*. On a Late Preclassic stela at Izapa, the Hero Twins knock Vucub Caquix from a tree, as in the *Popol Vuh*. The stela shows the Hero Twins running toward a tree with Vucub Caquix on top. The same stela shows the vanquished bird with a skeletal jaw and broken wing at the base of the tree. Another stela from Izapa shows Vucub Caquix, a man with one arm, and a severed arm spurting blood. This scene corresponds to the battle between the Hero Twins and Vucub Caquix in the *Popol Vuh*, when the bird temporarily gets Hunahpu's arm.

In the Classic period, the Hero Twins are common on painted pictorial pots and other media where Hunahpu is called Hun-Ahau and Xbalanque is called Yax-Balam. They are often depicted wearing red and white cloth headbands, signifying rulership. To further distinguish them from ordinary people, the Hero Twins have god markings on their faces and bodies. Hun-Ahau often has large black spots on his body and cheeks. His face is the glyph for the day name Ahau, which also means king. Yax-Balam has jaguar skin on his body, arms, and legs and around his mouth, denoting his affinity with the jaguar, itself associated with dynastic power. In addition to vanquishing Vucub Caquix, the imagery on Classic art shows the Hero Twins in a variety of other activities. The Hero Twins also are depicted in Classic art with the monkey scribes, their half-brothers. The theme of the Hero Twins playing ball in Xibalba is quite prominent. A Late Classic ball court marker at Copan, for example, shows Hun-Ahau playing ball against an underworld god.

The fate of Hun Hunahpu in Classic iconography differs from the story told in the *Popol Vuh*. In the *Popol Vuh*, the Hero Twins are unable to resurrect Hun Hunahpu, and leave him buried in the ball court of Xibalba. In Classic period iconography, Hun Hunahpu and the Hero Twins are directly tied to the creation story: In Classic images, Hun Hunahpu is resurrected from Xibalba by the Hero Twins and becomes the Maize God (Taube 1995, 66–67). One theme shows a scene of the Hero Twins with their father as he emerges from the carapace of a turtle. Metaphorically, this image refers to the emergence of the Maize God from Xibalba, as the turtle symbolized the Earth floating on the sea, which is the underworld. The rebirth of Hun Hunahpu as the Maize God symbolizes the renewal of life and the sowing of corn on Earth (Taube 1995, 67). Classic period iconography depicts the Hero Twins assisting Hun Hunahpu in his activities as the Maize God. This includes the theme of sowing and dawning, shown as planting and harvesting corn. Another theme features the Hero Twins standing in water with young, attractive women and holding the Maize God's accoutrements, including his sack of corn and distinctive jewelry. Tedlock (1985) interprets the presence of the young women as pertaining to the sometimes-licentious behavior of the Hero Twins.

At that point in the *Popol Vuh*, the story returns to the creation of humans, this time with the successful creation of humans from corn. (Remember that the Hero Twins were born to the old gods Xpiyacoc and Xmucane before the creation of humans). For the final and successful creation of humans, Xmucane makes flour from a mountain filled with yellow corn and white corn, and mixes it with water, following the advice of a fox, coyote, parrot, and crow. The corn mixture creates the first four men, Jaguar Quitze (Balam Kitza), Jaguar Night (Balam Aquals), Mahucutah (Naught), and Wind Jaguar (Iq'i Balam); A wife is created for each. The men are the first four leaders of the Quiché lineages. They are living in a predawn world in the east before the creation of the world.

The men go on a pilgrimage to find patron deities. Finding them, the men offer the deities blood (by piercing their bodies) in thanks and to request a safe return home. On the journey home, the men fast and hide the deities in the forest, in fear of the unknown, particularly the primordial sea and the great abyss. Still in the predawn world, the men travel cautiously, waiting on mountaintops for the sun to rise for the first time. When it does, the sun is so hot it turns the deities to stone. The men offer blood to the stone gods, who then speak as spirits to the men and assist them safely home. The story establishes the metaphorical link between blood sacrifice and the rising of the sun for the Maya. After the original four men die, their three sons (one father had no sons) follow their fathers' footsteps on a pilgrimage to the east. The sons arrive in a kingdom where the king gives them titles and also knowledge (the *Popol Vuh*).

One title is Keeper of the Mat, meaning head of state. The other title, Keeper of the Reception House Mat, means overseer of tribute collection. They evidently bring back the *Popol Vuh*—as it is referred to as "the light that came from across the sea" (Tedlock 1985, 55). The reference to the overseer of tribute collection provides a tantalizing clue about the organization of the Maya economy. A reference to a specific building associated with tribute collection suggests that this building was significant in the Maya economy. However, was the reference to tribute collection influenced by the Spaniards who exacted and recorded extensive tribute, or did it have much greater antiquity, perhaps from the Classic period? Unfortunately, the Classic Mayan hieroglyphs are silent on this issue.

The *Popol Vuh* continues with the regional settlement of the Quiché people and the rise to power of a shamanistic leader called Plumed Serpent, who is able to transform himself (or "reveal himself") into a snake, eagle, jaguar, or pool of blood and rise to the sky or descend into Xibalba, the underworld. A subsequent leader, Quicab, gains power by military prowess. These and other leaders further their powers by retreats in temples where they pray, fast, abstain from sex with their wives, offer blood sacrifice to the gods, and eat nothing but tree fruits, abstaining from meat and corn. The fasts last from 180 days, corresponding to half of a complete calendar year, to the full 260-day cycle, or even 340 days, corresponding to the departure of Venus as the morning star, its time in darkness, and its reemergence as the morning star. The story of the *Popol Vuh* was written and passed down for generations from antiquity to colonial days and although there is only one sure text in book form, the classic images and heirglyphs in the southern lowlands, as well as Late Preclassic stone and painted images, expand our knowledge of the Maya story of creation and world views.

COSMOLOGY

The Maya cosmos was a sky-Earth, with the actions of humans intertwined with celestial movement of the stars as recorded in the calendar. The balance and continuity of daily life among the Maya required ritual interactions with the gods. The world consisted of the heavens, populated with gods; the Earth, populated with humans; and the underworld (Xibalba), populated with underworld gods. The earth was quadripartite, with directions associated with different colors. There were thirteen layers of heaven and nine layers of the underworld. The nine layers of Xibalba were materially recreated in the stepped temple pyramids, which commonly had nine layers. Maya temples were sacred mountains, whose temple room doors provided access to the temple room, the mountain, and the underworld. Bloodletting rituals involved the vision quest by the royal dynastic king or queen to enlist vision serpents to bring the spirits of the dynastic ancestors and underworld gods to the temple to show the living ruler's power and affiliation. Cosmology figured prominently in the Maya's lives. In the creation story told in the *Popol Vuh*, the Earth emerged from the primordial sea, which was beside the great abyss—the unknown. The sea is a portal to the underworld, associated with darkness where the sun, moon, and stars disappear in the west and from which they emerge in the east. The sea was a source of ritual paraphernalia, such as stingray spines used in bloodletting and hallucinogens made from the *Bufo marinus* frog (McKillop 1996; McKillop 2002; McKillop 2004; McKillop 2005). Caves also are entrances to the underworld (Demarest et al. 2003).

THE BALL GAME

Playing ball engaged one in the maintenance of the cosmic order of the universe and the ritual regeneration of life (Day 2001, 67). The game was a game of chance, skill, and trickery reflecting life. The team effort engaged individuals in shared behavior and culture, introducing, reinforcing, and reinventing the game of life and peoples' place in the cosmic order. By Late Classic times, the ball game was ritually associated with the endemic warfare among citystates of the times. The success of military conquest was recreated in a public and ritual ball game, in which high-ranking war captives were defeated and sacrificed. Sometimes they were kept, tortured, and displayed for years before their sacrifice.

The origins of the Maya ball game date to about 1500 B.C. with the Olmec. The tradition of two teams playing with a rubber ball in a stone-lined court became a hallmark of Mesoamerica, spreading to the Caribbean and into North America. There was no European counterpart of this game or of the bouncing rubber ball. Both the game and the rubber ball quickly became popular when the Spaniards arrived in the sixteenth century and laid the foundations for modern football, soccer, basketball, volleyball, and other ball games (Day 2001, 65).

The *Popol Vuh* establishes the ritual importance of the Maya ball game as more than just sport. Two underlying and pervasive themes in the *Popol Vuh* are creating the world and establishing the relationships between humans and the gods—both the celestial gods and those of Xibalba, the underworld. The system of death and rebirth, mediated by offerings, is established when the Hero Twins, Hunahpu and Xbalanque, play the ball game with the gods of the underworld. Their death and resurrection, mediated by sacrifice, becomes a metaphor for death and rebirth on Earth, embedded in the cycles of planting corn; the trajectories of peoples' lives; the movements of the sun, moon, and stars as known from Maya astronomy; and the cycles of the Maya calendar. In the case of the Hero Twins, they become the ultimate offering, human sacrifice. More commonly, as told metaphorically in the *Popol Vuh*, the offering is self-mutilation to provide blood offerings, burning of copal or other incense, or sacrifice of animals or war captives. After the Hero Twins win their ball game with the lords of Xibalba by trickery, the twins set the relationship between the gods of Xibalba and humans. The twins decide that, unlike the celestial gods who are offered human blood sacrifice, the gods of Xibalba can only be offered animal sacrifices or incense, including croton sap.

Ball courts became ritually linked with death in perpetuity, as the Hero Twins are not able to resurrect their father, Hun Hunahpu, who was killed by the gods of Xibalba when he and Vucub Hunahpu were defeated in an earlier game, although not part of the story of the Hero Twins in the *Popol Vuh*, in their adventures as depicted on Classic period pottery. The subsequent resurrection of Hun Hunahpu as the Maize God symbolizes the planting of corn on Earth. Corn also requires annual decapitation (harvesting), like the decapitation that happened to Hun Hunahpu. Maya kings sought to be reborn as the Maize God, as shown on King Pacal's sarcophagus, where dead kings fall into Xibalba rise as maize gods. The Maize God also is often shown as a scribe, as on a painted vessel from a burial at Altar de Sacrificios. A ceramic plate was placed over the deceased, and a "kill hole" provided a conduit for the king's soul to be reborn as the youthful creator.

One lesson from the *Popol Vuh* is that playing the ball game is potentially life-threatening, as in the sacrifice of Hun Hunahpu, but that trickery may be the way to deceive your opponent, as with the successful defeat of the lords of Xibalba by the Hero Twins. The ball court became a place of transition, a liminal state between life and death. The ball court markers along the centerline of the playing field showed mythical scenes of the ball game, usually bordered by a quatrefoil that marked an opening or portal into another world (Miller 2001, figure 92). The players in the ball game pitted themselves against the gods, with the winners emerging symbolically as the Hero Twins from the *Popol Vuh*.

Ball courts, especially those of the major political cities of the Late Classic Maya, were public spaces used for a variety of elite ritual activities including the ball game. An alabaster bowl from Copan depicts King Yax Pac in war regalia in the ball court, wearing, among other things, a belt with the goggle eyes of Tlaloc, the Teotihuacan rain god who was symbolic of warfare among the Late Classic Maya (Whittington 2001, plate 251). The public space of royal Maya ball courts afforded a ritual location for the performance of other elite activities, including plays, musicals, or festivals. Pictorial depictions often show musicians playing at ball games. The depiction of masked players underscores the dramatic, ritual aspect of the ball game and the link with other forms of drama that may have unfolded on the court, as suggested by the painted murals at Bonampak, for example. Certainly ordinary people also played the ball game, using fields unmarked by the grandiose stone-lined courts of the royal Maya.

Most ball courts were I-shaped, with a long, narrow playing field flanked by vertical, sloping, or stepped walls that were plastered and brightly painted (Proskouriakoff 1963, 39). The end zones evidently held temporary scaffolding for seating. Day (2001, 65) estimates that the average size of the field measured 36.5 meters by 9 meters, although there was tremendous variation. Stone friezes on the walls, as at Chichen Itza, depicted ritual sacrifice. The largest ball court is the main one at Chichen Itza, measuring 185 meters long and 70 meters wide—longer than an American football field.

As warfare became endemic during the Late Classic in the Maya lowlands, human sacrifice became a more common outcome of the ball game, particularly at the royal courts of powerful cities. Late Classic Maya nobles were warriors and ball players. A step on a hieroglyphic staircase at Yaxchilan, for example, shows King Bird Jaguar defeating a war captive in the ball game (Miller 2001, figure 88), and there is a written reference to a war captive on an altar in Tikal (Miller 2001, 83). War captives played ball against the war victors, with the outcome being predetermined. Following the game, which was a ritual reenactment of the defeat of a city-state, the captives were commonly decapitated or their hearts were torn out for blood sacrifice. The walls of the principal ball court at Chichen Itza depict opposing teams, with the leader of the winning team holding the decapitated head of the opposing leader, who kneels with blood in the form of snakes spewing from his neck (Day 2001, figure 74). A stone carving of a skull rack (Tzompantli) at Chichen Itza attests to the practice of displaying war captives' heads for public viewing and for humiliation of the losers (Day 2001, figure 77). As depicted on a painted wall mural at Bonampak, captives were stripped of their elite clothing and were tortured and subjected to bloodletting and to various atrocities, including having their fingernails ripped off.

How the Ball Game Was Played

Depictions on pottery vessels and stone carvings show two players at a time. Each player often had a backup player directly behind him or her. The ball was thrown by hand into the court, and thenceforth the players hit it back and forth with hips, thighs, and upper arms (but not by kicking or throwing with one's hands) and through hoops set along the side walls of the court. Both men and women played the game. There are obviously no eye-witnesses to the Classic Maya ball game, but perhaps the sixteenth century Aztec ball game that the Spaniards witnessed may provide some comparisons. In the Aztec ball game, as reported by Bernard de Sahagun (Day 2001), points were lost by a player who let the ball bounce more than twice before returning it to the other team, who let the ball go outside the court, or who failed to pass the rather heavy ball (weighing 3 to 4 kilograms) through one of the stone hoops placed on each wall along the center line. In the Maya area there are similar hoops, some of which were quite high, as at Chichen Itza, where they were set 6 meters from the ground.

The Maya used a solid rubber ball made from the latex of the rubber tree (*Castilla elastica*), which was indigenous to Central America. The latex can be made into rubber by heating. This rubber was quite startling to the sixteenth-century Spaniards. Europeans of the time had no similar ball that could bounce for their sports. Although no rubber balls have been recovered from ancient Maya sites, three bowls from the sacred cenote at Chichen Itza contain a mixture of rubber, copal, jade, and shell that had been burned as an offering before the vessels were thrown into the cenote (Whittington 2001, plates 2–4). Somewhat deformed from centuries in the ground, an actual Olmec rubber ball from El Manatí, Veracruz, Mexico, was preserved because of its water-logged setting (Whittington 2001, plate 1). The balls evidently varied in size up to 30 centimeters (12 inches) in diameter and were solid.

The regalia of the ball players is preserved in stone replicas and shown in pictorial representations on pottery and carved stone monuments. Figurines of ball players are common among the Late Classic Jaina figurines and also among the Late Classic figurine whistles from southern Belize, such as from Village Farm. The players wore protective quilted cotton armor, perhaps filled with unspun cotton, wrapped around waist yokes probably made of wood, but certainly not the stone yokes found at some sites (Miller 2001, 81). Hachas, or carved heads, often trophy heads, were set into the yokes, as shown on a Late Classic pottery figurine ball player wearing a yoke with a bird hacha (Whittington 2001, plate 100). Brightly painted deer hides adorned with feathers were worn around the hips and provided some additional protection, as well as adding to the rich attire of the players. Players also wore knee pads (Miller 2001, figure 85) and had protective wrappings on their legs and lower arms. On certain occasions, the players wore elaborate headdresses representing Maya gods of war and sacrifice or deer and vulture headdresses, the latter commonly depicted on painted pottery vessels (Miller 2001, figure 87). Mary Miller (2001, 82) points out that both war and hunting were the activities of young men, both took place in the dry season, both could end in a ball game, and that the Hero Twins from the *Popol Vuh* were hunters and ball game players (the word *Hunahpu* means hunter and *Xbalanque* means jaguar deer, both references to the hunting activities of the Hero Twins). Some of the players were masked, as in the case of Yax Pac from Copan, underscoring the ritual play of the ball game. Each community had a playing field, although some were less elaborate, perhaps just a cleared space for sports and other community activities.

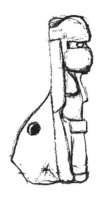 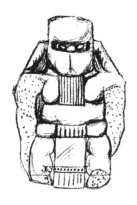

Pottery figurine whistle of a ball
player from Village Farm site, Belize
(Drawing by H. McKillop)

PANTHEON OF GODS, GODDESSES, AND OTHER SUPERNATURAL BEINGS

A host of gods, goddesses, and other supernatural beings mediated the world of the ancient Maya. Some of these gods are known historically from their appearance in the *Popol Vuh,* the codices, or the books of Chilam Balam. From his studies of the Dresden, Madrid, and Paris codices, a nineteenth-century German researcher named Paul Schellhas (1904) studied the gods in the Maya codices, assigned each Maya god a letter, and attempted to assign the Maya glyph name to each. With some revision, the letter assignments have persisted in use, although some Maya gods are now known by their depicted names as well. If for no other reason, using letters avoids the assumption of particular roles of the gods in the Postclassic period when the codices were writted or in earlier times as depicted in Maya pots and stone carvings, including stelae (Miller and Taube 1993, 146–148; also figure on p. 147 from Schellhas's work). Here, the god's name is used, unless there is no name, in which case the letter Schellhas assigned is used. Maya gods variously revealed themselves in different identities, depending on the situation, making it difficult to identify specific gods. Each celestial god was believed to have an underworld guise for passage through Xibalba (after the corresponding celestial body set below the horizon) before reappearing in the eastern sky to rise again. For example, the sun god Kinich Ahau may be Itzamna (the creator) as he travels in Xibalba. Some had counterparts as the other sex, as with Itzamna and Ix Chel in her form as an old fearsome goddess. The lack of distinction between spiritual powers of gods and animals meant that the physical manifestations of animals as gods was on a scale from anthropomorphic to zoomorphic. Spirit companions to the Classic elite called wayoob, who usually have an animal shape, are depicted on Classic period painted pots (Coe and Van Stone 2001, 121).

Several gods stand out as particularly powerful, notably Itzamna, Kinich Ahau, Pauahtun, K'awiil, Chac, God E (the Maize God), and God L (Coe and Van Stone 2001; Miller and Taube 1993; Taube 1995). Itzamna, or Lizard House, is the aged creator god, Schellas's god D, and is commonly depicted in Classic and Postclassic art. He is identifiable as an aged god with a Roman nose. Itzamna and his consort, Ix Chel, are the progenitors of all other gods and also the old couple, Xpiyacoc and Xmucane, in the *Popol Vuh.* Itzamna is credited with inventing writing. He is shown as a Maya scribe on pottery vessels and also is shown engaged in divination and other scribal and priestly activities (Coe and Kerr 1998). The Hero Twins' twin half-brothers, Huan Chuen and Hun Batz (but also known as One Monkey and One Artisan), also are godly scribes; they are depicted as a spider monkey and howler monkey, respectively (the Hero Twins were said to have tricked them and turned them into monkeys). They are identified as scribes by the depiction of a deer ear over their human ears and they hold an inkpot, pen, or codex. They are known as the patron gods of art, writing, and counting.

Another important god, Kinich Ahau, the sun god (also known as god G) transforms himself into a jaguar each night as he travels through Xibalba. He is otherwise closely associated with the jaguar. Kinich Ahau may actually be a variant of Itzamna. Perhaps the most famous Classic Maya depiction of Kinich Ahau is the large (4.4 kilograms) carved jade head from a tomb in a temple at Altun Ha, Belize (Pendergast 1979). The head of Kinich Ahau is also featured as stone or stucco masks on temple façades. In addition, the head of Kinich Ahau is a glyphic substitute for the number 4. The Classic period prominence of Kinich Ahau and his identification with Maya rulers (and Hun Hunahpu or Hun Ahau—translated as ruler) diminished in the Postclassic period.

Pauahtun, also known as god N, is an old quadripartite god who stands at the four corners of the universe and holds up the earth and the sky. He is shown wearing a turtle shell or conch shell on his back in the Classic period and in the codices. He also is identified by his cutout shell nose and crocodile jaw headdress (Whittington 2001, plate 113). When the Spaniards arrived in the sixteenth century, Pauahtun was known as the four bacabs (bearers of the world) who each held up a corner of the sky, according to Bishop de Landa (Tozzer 1941). God K (K'awiil) was associated with royal descent, fire, and lightning. He was shown as a scepter held by rulers, and also as a figure with an upturned snout; a celt, smoking tube, or torch on his forehead; and a serpent-shaped foot. Kulkulkan succeeded him in the Postclassic. Chac, the god of rain and lightning, is often shown with axes and snakes, which he uses to affect the weather.

Karl Taube (1995) identified the Maize God, god E, as Hun Hunahpu from the *Popol Vuh* or Hun Nah Yeh. He is depicted in the Classic period as the tonsured Maize God, representing Hun Hunahpu, the father of the Hero Twins from the *Popol Vuh*. He sometimes has his head flattened like a mature maize ear. Alternatively, he is shown as a foliated Maize God with a maize ear emerging from a human head. The resurrection of Hun Hunahpu symbolizes the planting and growth of a new maize crop. His death by decapitation is a metaphor for the harvesting of corn and for death. In the Late Postclassic, the Maize God may be represented as the diving god, a youthful figure descending headfirst from the sky, shown on murals at Tulum and also depicted at Mayapan and Moho Cay.

The merchant god and the god of war were one and the same, both known as God L (Whittington 2001, plate 112), but his Maya name is unknown. He is shown as an old man or as a black jaguar, often wearing a cape and a large wide-brimmed hat with owl features and sometimes an actual head of an owl on top. His bundle or backpack identifies him in his merchant role. Among the various painted Maya murals at Caxcatla, Tlaxcala, in central Mexico, one shows the merchant god with bundle including feathers and a variety of other trade goods. The merchant god burned incense to Xaman Ek, the North Star, for a safe voyage. The Classic period merchant god was eclipsed during the Postclassic by another merchant god, known as god M, who is identified by his pendulous lower lip, black face, and a long, pointed nose. At the time of the conquest of the Maya by the Spaniards, Ek Chuah was the god of merchants and cacao growers and was probably introduced from central Mexico; contacts between Maya merchants (called p'olom) and central Mexican merchants have great antiquity and clearly were important in dispersing information as well as goods.

Ix Chel, also known as Chak Chel, was clearly the most important goddess. Ix Chel, or Lady Rainbow, is the consort of the sun. However, as goddess of the moon and ruler of the night sky (and consort to Itzamna), she opposes the sun in her efforts to defeat the sun each day and make it descend into darkness (Miller and Taube 1993, 101). At the time of European contact, Ix Chel was the goddess of childbirth, pregnancy, and fertility. Ix Chel also is associated with weaving, fertility, and midwifery. There were shrines for her on Cozumel and Isla Mujeres off the eastern coast of the Yucatan to which people would make pilgrimages (Freidel 1975).

Ix Chel appears to be split into several individuals as represented in the codices. In the Dresden codex, Ix Chel is called Chac Chel (Schellhas's Goddess O), an old and fearsome goddess with jaguar claws and with snakes in her headdress. Sometimes she has a skull and crossbones on her skirt. Goddess I is a beautiful young goddess associated with love and fertility, not Ix Chel, who is old. Ix Ch'up, a youthful moon goddess depicted in the codices who has amorous adventures with various gods, may be a youthful variant of Ix Chel.

Several others figure prominently among the corps of celestial beings (Miller and Taube 1993; Taube 1995). The paddler gods transported people in canoes to the underworld. Their most famous depiction is on four incised bones accompanying the king in a temple burial at Tikal. The Old Jaguar Paddler God and the Old Stingray Paddler God guide the canoe through Xibalba, with the jaguar usually in the front. The Old Stingray Paddler God has a stingray peircing the septum of his nose and sometimes a helmet with a fish depicted on it. The Old Jaguar Paddler God has jaguar skin on his cheek, a jaguar ear, and sometimes wears a helmet with a jaguar head depicted on it. Jaguars are very common in ancient Maya iconography and mythology, perhaps because both the Maya and jaguars shared the rainforest. The jaguar is especially identified with the sun, both its daytime and nighttime form, with the latter being associated with Xibalba, where he sometimes rides a caiman across the nighttime sky. Other jaguar gods include the Water Lily Jaguar, a zoomorphic creature with a water lily on his forehead and often a collar of bulging eyeballs around his neck. Among many roles, the Water Lily Jaguar symbolized rulership and is shown as a throne (Miller and Taube 1993, 104). Scenes on Late Classic period painted pots show the royal throne draped in jaguar skins. God L often sits on a jaguar throne, in which case the head faces forward, the legs support the throne, and the tail forms the back of the chair. The jaguar was used to represent other gods, notably the Jaguar Baby God, and as a feature of supernatural powers for Xbalanque, one of the Hero Twins who wears a jaguar pelt.

The Water Lily Serpent symbolizes still water and is a substitute for the number 13 (Miller and Taube 1993, 184). The Water Lily Serpent has a snake body and a downturned bird head with a lily pad and flower headdress, often accompanied by a fish nibbling at the flower. Water lily imagery is common at Dzibilchaltun, Altun Ha, and Lamanai. The Water Lily Serpent is a common headdress for Classic Maya royalty, as in a figure on a stela at Machaquilá, for example (Miller and Taube 1993, 185). Vision serpents (which appear from the smoke created when blood offering is burned), particularly prominent on the carved stone monuments of Yaxchilán, were used as a vehicle for Maya royalty and others to attain supernatural powers in a vision quest to contact their dynastic ancestors and the gods.

Vuqub Caquix, defeated in the *Popol Vuh* as pretender to the sun and moon, is reincarnated in Classic times as a more benevolent avian creature, Itzam Yeh, sometimes depicted with Maya kings. Vuqub Caquix was an important icon during the Late Preclassic along the Pacific coast as well as in the southern Maya lowlands, depicted in a painted mural from San Bartolo, in the Peten district of Guatemala, for example, as well as on masks adorning the façades of temples.

The Jester God is common in Classic Maya iconography but has its origins in earlier Olmec times at La Venta. The Jester God has a head ornament dangling over his head and is often, but not exclusively, associated with Maya royalty, as with King Pacal's grave at Palenque. The zoomorphic version of the Jester God is the glyph for ahau, and association of the Jester God with a person and animal transforms its status to ahau. Kings most often were associated with the Jester God, held as a sceptor in his hand, on the king's headband, or worn on his chest as a pectoral (Schele and Freidel 1990, 411). God A, the skeletal god of death and also of violent sacrifice, such as decapitation, usually is denoted by a black band across his eyes. He appears in Early Classic Maya art and in the codices. God C is the personification of the concept of sacredness and not, according to Miller and Taube (1993, 146), the god of the north, as often assumed. There is some confusion about the various long-lipped deities, also sometimes referred to as long-nosed gods; these are a variety of Maya gods, including Chac, the Jester God, serpents, birds, or jaguars (Miller and Taube 1993, 107–108). Also somewhat enigmatic is the fat god, a potbellied figure found on Late Classic painted pottery vessels and figurines, often shown as a dancer. The ancient Maya also quite prominently depict dwarves and hunchbacks in scenes showing the royal Maya court on Classic painted pots. Dwarves and hunchbacks were evidently prominent members of the royal court. They are shown on painted vessels from the Naranjo-Holmul area and also are depicted at Lamanai. Dwarves were children of Chac and could bring rain, explaining at least part of their importance to the ancient Maya.

The Personified Perforator appears in Classic period images of bloodletting, depicted as a long-nosed head (which personifies inanimate objects), with an obsidian or chert blade, a stingray spine or thorn (for bloodletting), and three dots symbolizing bloodletting (Schele and Freidel 1990, 415).

Three symbols further define the relationships between the living and supernatural worlds: Wacah Chan (the world tree), the Cosmic Monster, and the Foliated Cross. Wacah Chan, meaning "raised-up tree, " holds up the sky at the center of the Maya universe. The Cosmic Monster holds up the sky at the edge of the universe. The Foliated Cross is a maize plant that represents the central axis of the earth. Wacah Chan is depicted as a cross with the Celestial Bird Deity (the Classic period version of Vucub Caquix) on top (Schele and Freidel 1990, 418). The Celestial Bird Deity has the head of a zoomorphic creature, a long tail, and wings with faces and is usually associated with the Foliated Cross, Wacah Chan, or the Cosmic Monster. Metaphorically, the Celestial Bird Deity represents the supremacy of the Classic Maya king (or queen), just as Vucub Caquix was vanquished by the Hero Twins in the *Popol Vuh* and on Late Preclassic stelae from Izapa. God C markings on Wacah Chan demarcate its sacred status. (God C, depicted as a monkey face, attaches sacred, holy, or divine status to anything to which it is attached.) Wacah Chan represents the divine king, as the king's Double-Headed Serpent bar is draped in the branches of the tree, which themselves end in snakes denoting blood or other offerings (Schele and Freidel 1990).

The Cosmic Monster, also called the Celestial Monster or the Bicephalic Monster, has two heads. One head is that of a crocodile with deer ears, denoting an affiliation with Venus. The other head hangs upside down. It is the Quadripartite Monster, identified by a skeletal jaw and the kin sign for sun. The heads represent the movement of Venus, the sun, and other plants across the sky, both in the day and at night. The body of the Cosmic Monster is either that of a crocodile or is depicted as a sky band, a horizontal band with glyphs of the planets and stars divided by vertical lines.

The Foliated Cross has water imagery, with the Waterbird (affiliated with water) on top and a Celestial Bird mask and the Waterlily Monster (personification of water) at the base of the cross. God C markings on the stalk of the plant denote sacred status.

RITUALS

Rituals, including blood sacrifice to the celestial gods and incense offerings to the underworld gods, were important to maintain the world of the living, to obtain the advice of the gods, and to ensure the movement of the sun, moon, and stars. Humans sought advice from the gods through vision quests aided by ritual fasting, bloodletting, or hallucinogens. Ordinary folk also cut themselves with sharp implements and offered their blood to the Maya gods, but the lives of ordinary Maya are not depicted in Maya stela, monuments, or heiroglyphs. While the kings and queens engaged in bloodletting and the vision quest in the small room at the top of the temples, the crowd gathered in

Two figures in scattering ritual at Nim li punit (Courtesy B. Somers)

the plaza below also let blood in an attempt to call the gods and ancestors in a vision quest (Schele and Freidel 1990). Most in demand for this purpose, evidently, were obsidian blades and stingray spines. Obsidian blades, with edges at least twice as sharp as surgical steel, and stingray spines, with their barbed edges, are commonly recovered in burials throughout the Maya area.

The majestic Ceiba tree was depicted in ancient Maya art as the tree of life and remains a dominant feature of the landscape (Courtesy H. McKillop)

Maya kings and queens called the vision serpent to bring forth from their blood offerings and fasting the dynastic ancestors and gods to reaffirm the divine right on kingship and to call the gods to seek advice, allowing the royal Maya access to supernatural powers and information to make superhuman decisions (Freidel, Schele, and Parker 1993; Schele and Freidel 1990). Royal rituals were public events, later recorded on public stone monuments. Royal bloodletting is a common theme on the carved stelae at Nim li punit, where blood drips from fingers onto bark paper held in a bowl to be burned in offering to the gods. Carved stones at Yaxchilan show smoke rising from the burning paper. Access to the upper world was ritually had via the tree of life, the great Ceiba tree. Rituals, including blood offerings, were made at astronomically significant dates, at the beginning of calendar cycles, at the dedication of a building, at the death of a person, and at many other important events. The end of a fifty-two-year cycle when the interlocking two calendars meshed on the same date was particularly worrisome and marked by blood sacrifice rituals that were recorded on stone monuments.

EVIDENCE

The quadripartite worldview of the Maya universe with the world tree at its center is pervasive in Maya art and architecture. Freidel, Schele, and Parker (1993) discuss the sacred space created by the quadripartite structure of architectural space. They suggest that the two axes formed by the intersection of the cardinal directions (the axis mundi or "tree of life") represent the sun's path and the Milky Way. Their replication in architectural spaces symbolically reenacted the creation of the Maya world.

Wendy Ashmore and Jeremy A. Sabloff (2002) suggest that the layout of Maya cities conformed to this mental template. They follow up on Clemency Coggins's (1980) observations that the layout of the twin-pyramid groups at Tikal in cardinal directions functions to map the east-west daily travel of the sun. The north and south buildings mark the time between the rise and setting of the sun—the heavens and the underworld, respectively (Ashmore and Sabloff 2002, 202–203). The rulers depicted on stelae on the north side of Tikal's main plaza are therefore "located" in Maya heaven at midday.

In a comparison of site plans, Ashmore and Sabloff (2002) find significant differences in the orientation of Preclassic and Classic cities. All followed the basic pattern of four-sided plazas formed by temples, palaces, or other structures. Cities such as El Mirador and Seibal, laid out during the Preclassic period, followed an east-west orientation, reflecting the cosmological and political importance of astronomy in the lives of the Preclassic Maya. By way of contrast, Classic cities, such as Tikal, Copan, Calakmul, and Quirigua, were established on a north-south axis, reflecting a major change to the power of dynastic succession. Xunantunich and Naranjo closely duplicated the site plan and orientation of the greater and earlier power of Calakmul, perhaps in order to emulate that city's dynastic authority.

Caches of broken pots found in ancient temples are interpreted as having been used during termination rituals, when the building was no longer used or before it was rebuilt (Mock 1998). It was the entrenched practice of the ancient Maya to rebuild on the same spot, be it a modest home or the tallest temple at Tikal. The frequency or periodicity at which buildings were renovated or rebuilt is unknown. In some cases, the renovation of a building, particularly a temple, coincided with the death of a king or queen. The dead royal body was placed in a tomb either dug into a temple or, more commonly, on the foundations or steps of the temple. Then the building received a "facelift," with a new foundation, façade, and temple room. However, buildings were not always rebuilt upon the death of the occupant. The practice of multiple burials, in which a royal tomb was reopened upon the death of another member of the royal court, as at Caracol (Chase and Chase 1996), Lubaantun (Hammond, Pretty, and Saul 1975), Caledonia (Healy, Awe, and Helmuth 1998), or Wild Cane Cay (McKillop 2005), underscores the reuse of tombs without new building construction. The common folk buried their dead relatives at home, either during the renovation of a building or in pits dug into the floors of existing homes (Lund and McKillop 2003; McKillop et al. 2004). In some cases, people were sacrificed to dedicate new construction, as at Wild Cane Cay, where a young woman was buried in prone (face-down) position, her hands and legs trussed and tied behind her back, on the floor of a building before coral rock was piled on top of her as the foundation for a new building (McKillop 2005). In this case, the burial was also an offering (see Becker 1992 for an insightful discussion of burials and caches).

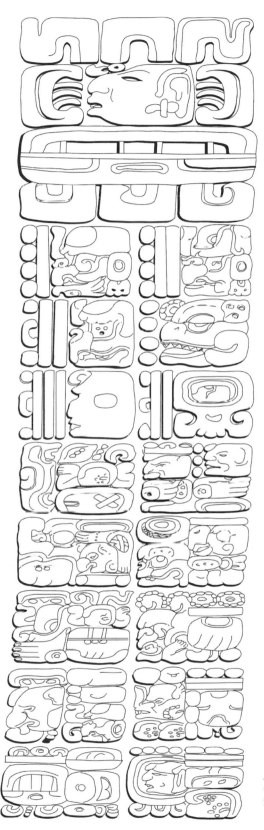

A Long Count date from Stela E, Quirigua, Guatemala (Drawing by Sandy Windelspecht)

Building renovation evidently required some form of ritual, either one associated with interment of a dead person or simply some other offering. Caches of complete or ritually smashed artifacts are frequently encountered by archaeologists along the centerline of a building or under staircases, associated with construction activities (Becker 1992). In addition to these consecration events, the ancient Maya smashed pots or other artifacts as part of termination rituals, as if to deconsecrate the space (Mock 1998). The ancient Maya traced their importance and rank in society through their lineages, physically present in the bodies of their ancestors in earlier homes built below their own. The royal Maya traced their authority through their dynastic roots, materially manifested by the bodies and sumptuous grave offerings of their dynastic forefathers and foremothers, and promulgated by public banner stones—the stelae in front of the temple-burial mounds. With buildings serving both as repositories for dead relatives and as spaces for living, they were both sacred and profane spaces, intimately intertwined in ancient Maya cosmology and the daily lives of individuals of both the royal Maya court and the common folk.

REFERENCES

Anders, F., ed. 1967. *Codex Tro-Cortesianus (Codex Madrid), Museo de América, Madrid.* Graz, Austria: Akademische Druck und Verlagsanstalt.

———. 1968. *Codex Peresianus (Codex Paris), Bibliothèque National, Paris, Madrid.* Graz, Austria: Akademische Druck und Verlagsanstalt.

Ashmore, Wendy, and Jeremy A. Sabloff. 2002. "Spatial Orders in Maya Civic Plans." *Latin American Antiquity* 13: 201–215.

Becker, Marshall J. 1992. "Burials as Caches; Caches as Burials: A New Interpretation of the Meaning of Ritual Deposits among the Classic Period Lowland Maya," In *New Theories on the Ancient Maya,* edited by Elin C. Danien and Robert J. Sharer, 185–196. University Museum Monograph 77, University Museum Symposium Series Volume 3. Philadelphia: University of Pennsylvania.

Chase, Diane Z., and Arlen F. Chase. 1996. "Maya Multiples: Individuals, Entries, and Tombs in Structure A34 of Caracol." *Latin American Antiquity* 7: 61–79.

Coe, Michael D., and Justin Kerr. 1998. *The Art of the Maya Scribe.* New York: Harry N. Abrams.

Coe, Michael D., and Mark Van Stone. 2001. *Reading the Maya Glyphs.* New York: Thames & Hudson.

Coggins, Clemency. 1980. "The Shape of Time: Some Political Implications of the Four-Part Figure." *American Antiquity* 45: 727–739.

Craine, E., and R. Reindorp. 1979. *The Codex Pérez and the Book of Chilam Balam of Maní.* Norman: University of Oklahoma Press.

Day, Jane. 2001. "Performing on the Court." In *The Sport of Life and Death: The Mesoamerican Ballgame,* edited by E. Michael Whittington, 64–77. New York: Thames & Hudson.

Demarest, Arthur, Kim Morgan, Claudia Wooley, and Hector Escobedo. 2003. "The Political Acquisition of Sacred Geography: The Murcielagos Complex at Dos Pilas." In *Maya Palaces and Elite Residences,* edited by Jessica J. Christie, 120–153. Austin: University of Texas Press.

Edmonson, M. 1982. *The Ancient Future of the Itza: Chilam Balam of Tizimin.* Austin: University of Texas Press.

Förstemann, Ernst W. 1906. *Commentary on the Maya Manuscript in the Royal Public Library of Dresden.* Papers of the Peabody Museum of Archaeology and Ethnology, vol. 4, no. 2. Cambridge, MA: Harvard University.

Freidel, David A. 1975. "The Ix Chel Shrine and Other Temples of Talking Idols." In *A Study of Changing Pre-Columbian Commerical Systems.* Monographs of the Peabody Museum of Archaeology and Ethnology, vol. 3, edited by Jeremy A. Sabloff and William L. Rathje, 107–113. Cambridge, MA: Harvard University.

Freidel, David A., Linda Schele, and Joy Parker. 1993. *Maya Cosmos: Three Thousand Years on the Shaman's Path.* New York: Morrow.

Glass, John B. 1975. "A Survey of Native Middle American Pictorial Manuscripts." *Handbook of Middle American Indians* 14: 3–81.

Hammond, Norman, Kate Pretty, and Frank P. Saul. 1975. "A Classic Maya Family Tomb." *World Archaeology* 7: 57–71.

Healy, Paul F., Jaime J. Awe, and Hermann Helmuth. 1998. "An Ancient Maya Multiple Burial at Caledonia, Cayo District, Belize." *Journal of Field Archaeology* 25: 261–274.

Lund, Erin, and Heather McKillop. 2003. Maya Burials from Moho Cay, Belize. Paper presented at the Southern Anthropological Association meeting, Baton Rouge, LA, February.

McKillop, Heather. 1996. "Ancient Maya Trading Ports and the Integration of Long-Distance and Regional Economies: Wild Cane Cay in South-Coastal Belize." *Ancient Mesoamerica* 7: 49–62.

———. 2002. *Salt: White Gold of the Ancient Maya.* Gainesville: University Press of Florida.

———. 2005. *In Search of Maya Sea Traders.* College Station: Texas A & M University Press.

McKillop, Heather, Aline Magnoni, Rachel Watson, Shannon Ascher, Bryan Tucker, and Terance Winemiller. 2004. "The Coral Foundations of Coastal Maya Architecture." In *Archaeological Investigations in the Eastern Maya Lowlands: Papers of the 2003 Belize Archaeology Symposium.* Edited by Jaime Awe, John Morris, and Sherilyne Jones, pp. 347 358. Research Reports in Belizean Archaeology Volume 1, Institute of Archaeology, National Institute of Culture and History (NICH), Belmopan, Belize.

Miller, Mary. 2001. "The Maya Ballgame: Rebirth in the Court of Life and Death." In *The Sport of Life and Death: The Mesoamerican Ballgame,* edited by F. Michael Whittington, 78–87. New York: Thames & Hudson.

Miller, Mary, and Karl Taube. 1993. *The Gods and Symbols of Ancient Mexico and the Maya.* New York: Thames & Hudson.

Mock, Shirley Boteler, ed. 1998. *The Sowing and the Dawning: Termination, Dedication, and Transformation in the Archaeological and Ethnographic Record of Mesoamerica.* Albuquerque: University of New Mexico Press.

Pendergast, David M. 1979. *Excavations at Altun Ha,* vol. 1. Toronto: Royal Ontario Museum.

Proskouriakoff, Tatiana. 1963. *An Album of Maya Architecture.* Norman: University of Oklahoma Press.

Reents-Budet, Dorie. 2001. "Classic Maya Concepts of the Royal Court: An Analysis of Renderings on Pictorial Ceramics." In *Royal Courts of the Ancient Maya,* vol. 1, edited by Takeshi Inomata and Stephen Houston, 195–233. Boulder, CO: Westview.

Roys, Ralph, trans. 1967. *Chilam Balam of Chumayel.* Norman: University of Oklahoma Press.

Schele, Linda, and David A. Freidel. 1990. *A Forest of Kings: The Untold Story of the Ancient Maya.* New York: Morrow.

Schellhas, Paul. 1904. *Representation of Deities of the Maya Manuscripts*. Papers of the Peabody Museum of Archaeology and Ethnology, vol. 4, no. 1. Cambridge, MA: Harvard University.

Tate, Carolyn E. 1992. *Yaxchilan: The Design of a Maya Ceremonial City*. Austin: University of Texas Press.

Taube, Karl. 1995. *Aztec and Maya Myths*. Austin: University of Texas Press.

Tedlock, Dennis, trans. 1985. *Popol Vuh: The Definitive Edition of the Mayan Book of the Dawn of Life and the Glories of Gods and Kings*. New York: Simon and Schuster.

Thompson, J. Eric S. 1972. *Dresden: A Commentary on the Dresden Codex*. American Philosophical Society Memoir 93. Philadelphia: American Philosophical Society.

———. 1975. *The Grolier Codex*. Contributions of the University of California Archaeological Research Facility 27: 1–9. Los Angeles: University of California.

Tozzer, Alfred M., trans. 1941. *Landa's Relación de las Cosas de Yucatan*. Papers of the Peabody Museum of Archaeology and Ethnology, vol. 18. Cambridge, MA: Harvard University.

Whittington, E. Michael, ed. 2001. *The Sport of Life and Death: The Mesoamerican Ballgame*. New York: Thames & Hudson.

CHAPTER 9

Material Culture

The lives and deaths of the ancient Maya are fleshed out by available material evidence that has been preserved to varying degrees over the millennia in the rainforest environment. Abandoned buildings, roads (sacbes), carved stone monuments, and decorated pottery vessels in tombs provide a direct link for reconstructing ancient activities. However, the most frequently recovered artifacts are broken and discarded remains of everyday life dumped in refuse heaps (middens) outside buildings, incorporated with the rock and earth of building platforms and foundations, or discarded elsewhere. Much attention is directed to these potsherds and broken stone tools, and to the fragmentary remains of bone, shell, metal, and wooden artifacts.

There are three distinct traditions of study in Maya archaeology. Art historians look at material culture as art, with an emphasis on painted pots and carved monuments (Coe 1978; Kerr 1989–1994; Reents-Budet 1994). Epigraphers such as the late Linda Schele, David Stuart, and Stephen Houston read and decipher hieroglyphic texts on carved monuments, painted pots, and the four remaining codices (books) that survived destruction by sixteenth-century Spanish priests. Epigraphers are thus able to interpret the dynastic histories of royal Maya and the ancient Maya's knowledge of religion, astronomy, and their calendars. "Dirt archaeologists," in contrast, excavate buildings and artifacts at ancient sites, looking at material culture as the artifacts of a people's way of life. The project director, often a field archaeologist supervising excavations and the interpretation of the architectural renovations, enlists experts to study artifacts of different material classes such as pottery, chert, obsidian, human bone, animal bone, plant remains, shells, and metal artifacts. With significant strides in decipherment of the hieroglyphs, epigraphers and dirt archaeologists occasionally collaborate in interpreting the Maya past, as with *A Forest of Kings* (Schele and Freidel 1990), *The Chronicle of Maya Kings and Queens* (Martin and Grube 2000), and *Classic Maya Political History* (Culbert 1991).

NATURAL RESOURCES

What materials were available to the ancient Maya for buildings and for making tools, containers, and objects of art? Throughout most of the Maya lowlands, stone buildings and their associated carved stelae, altars, and other monuments, as well as sacbes, were constructed of the limestone that forms the bedrock of the Yucatan peninsula. Limestone was quarried from pits of various sizes (Winemiller 1997) in and around Maya communities. Some of the quarries were subsequently used as aguadas (water reservoirs), wells, or other storage pits. Plaster was obtained by burning quarried limestone, a practice that continues in modern times in parts of the Maya lowlands. Abrams (1994) provides a detailed analysis of the construction efforts put into the buildings at Copan. In places where limestone was absent or scarce, other local stone was used in building construction. Sandstone was used to build stone platforms at Nim li punit and Lubaantun in southern Belize, as well as at Quirigua along the Motagua River in Guatemala. Sandstone also was used to make stelae at both Quirigua and Nim li punit, which, incidentally, were the tallest and second tallest stelae in the Maya area, respectively. Other local resources, such as slate, were used for monuments at some sites near the Maya Mountains of southern Belize, where slate occurs. Underscoring the use of local stone in building construction, at the offshore island communities of Wild Cane Cay and Frenchman's Cay in the Port Honduras of southern Belize, coral rock mined from the sea was used to build stone platforms that were faced with cut limestone and with sandstone ferried from the mainland (McKillop 2004; McKillop et al. 2004).

As with materials used in building construction, resources used in making tools, pottery, and other objects were affected by the local availability of various rocks, minerals, and other resources (Graham 1987). The distribution of artifacts made from nonlocal materials is important in reconstructing patterns of ancient Maya trade and communication. The origin of some materials, such as obsidian and granite, can be "fingerprinted" to particular locations, whereas the origin of many other materials, including chert, jade, seashells, and limestone, cannot be specifically identified.

The lowland Maya used both chert and obsidian as cutting instruments, but these resources have restricted distributions. Chert occurs in limestone deposits throughout much of the Maya lowlands, but high-quality chert occurs in large outcrops suitable for making stone tools in an area of northern Belize centered on the chert quarry and manufacturing community of Colha (Shafer and Hester 1983). Colha chert was widely traded within northern Belize and even beyond, where local chert, often of inferior quality, also was used (Mitchum 1991; McAnany 1989). By way of contrast, obsidian is a volcanic rock that does not occur in the Maya lowlands but was traded there in some quantity throughout Maya prehistory. Although most obsidian recovered from lowland Maya sites was from three outcrops in the southern Maya highlands of Guatemala, obsidian from many other outcrops from Mexico to Honduras was utilized in smaller quantities. Green obsidian from Pachuca, north of modern Mexico City, is one of the minor sources, easily identified by its "bottle-green" color. Its distribution to the Maya area may have been controlled by central Mexican states, notably Teotihuacan in the Classic period and Tula in the Early Postclassic. Reconstruction of the origins and distributions of chert and obsidian artifacts forms the basis of many models of Maya trade (Hammond 1972; Healy, McKillop, and Walsh 1984; McKillop et al. 1988; Nelson 1985).

Corn was an important dietary starch, as well as figuring in the Maya origin story recounted in the *Popol Vuh* and depicted on painted pots. Figurines and painted scenes on pottery vessels show corn being ground with hand-held

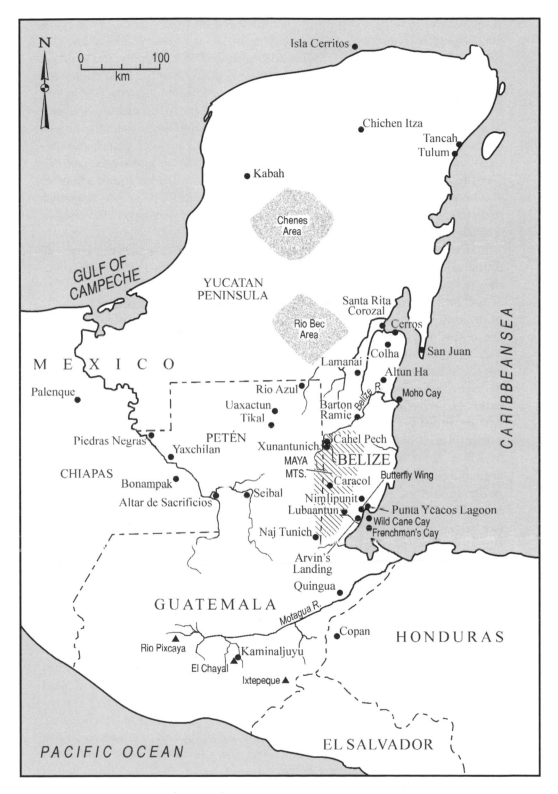

Sites mentioned in the text about architecture, artifacts, and natural resources

stone manos on large, flat grinding stones called metates. Manos and metates are commonly found at Maya sites and are made of a variety of local and imported stone (Anderson 1997; Sidrys and Andreson 1976; Shipley and Graham 1989). Although it might seem that limestone would make a poor choice for grinding corn due to the porosity and softness of limestone, it was commonly used in the northern Maya lowlands in particular, where other harder stones were not locally available (Anderson 1997). The Maya Mountains of southern Belize were identified by petrographic study as the source of granite metates from Uaxactun in the Peten district of Guatemala (Shipley and Graham 1989). Granite was used for metates at Wild Cane Cay and Frenchman's Cay in southern Belize as well. In some cases, basalt, a volcanic rock, was imported from the Maya highlands to sites in both southern and northern Belize (Sidrys and Andreson 1976).

Marine resources were widely used by the ancient Maya in ceremonies, as found in offerings and burials, and as food (McKillop 1996b; 2002). Most marine resources are only generally referred to "the sea," although some species of fish and shells have restricted distributions that allows for a more specific trade route to be documented, as with shells from the Pacific found at Altun Ha in northern Belize (Feldman 1974). Most other marine resources, including fish, stingray spines used in ritual bloodletting, shells, manatee bones, and coral generally document coastal-inland trade, and the assumption is that the nearest coast was probably the place of supply (Andrews 1969; Cobos 1989). Salt is an interesting resource, as it is a biological requirement for humans and was restricted to the Maya coasts, apart from a few inland salt springs and the salt produced by burning palm trees or from eating meat (McKillop 1996a; McKillop 2002). In an insightful and provocative model, Tony Andrews (1983) argued that salt was gathered in massive amounts from the salt flats along the north coast of the Yucatan peninsula and traded in bulk to the southern Maya lowlands. In contrast, McKillop (2002) suggests that salt was produced by boiling brine in pots over fires along the coast of Belize and was traded over shorter distances to the Maya interior. Furthermore, McKillop documents a 1-meter rise in sea level that submerged Maya salt works in Punta Ycacos Lagoon and left them "invisible" to modern archaeologists until her team discovered them in 1991 by underwater archaeology. This debate over long-distance import or local production of salt is unresolved.

Jade and other greenstones, including serpentine and albite, are found along the Motagua River in Guatemala, but the materials are too chemically variable to allow fingerprinting to specific locations (Hammond et al. 1977). Copper was traded to the Maya area in Postclassic times from Honduras and west Mexico. Gold was brought from lower Central America, generally in the Postclassic. Gold artifacts are reported from the Cenote of Sacrifice at Chichen Itza, Santa Rita Corozal in northern Belize, and Wild Cane Cay in southern Belize. Mercury, naturally occurring in Honduras, was recovered under a ball court marker at Lamanai (Pendergast 1982a).

Tohil Plumbate pottery was imported to the Maya lowlands from the Pacific coast of Chiapas, Mexico, and adjacent Guatemala during the Early Postclassic (Shepard 1948; Neff 1989). Other fancy pottery vessels were traded, either as royal gifts or as a part of more general trade, as with quantities of Tulum Red pottery (distinctive red-painted vessels with incised decoration and three cylindrical vessel supports) either copied or traded from Tulum on the east coast of the Yucatan to Colha in northern Belize and Wild Cane Cay in southern Belize. Slab-foot, cylindrical tripod pottery vessels in distinctive Teotihuacan style were widely traded and copied both at Kaminaljuyu in the Maya highlands and at Tikal, Moho Cay, and elsewhere in the Maya lowlands (see Braswell 2003). Fine Orange and Fine Grey pottery, chemically identified to the locations along the Gulf coast of Mexico, is a marker of the Terminal Classic period (A.D. 800–900) wherever it is found in the southern Maya lowlands.

Some researchers reconstruct an extensive trade in volcanic ash from the Maya highlands to the southern and northern Maya lowlands for use as a tempering agent in pottery vessels (Simmons and Brem 1979). However, the possibility of lowland availability of volcanic ash from volcanic eruptions that cast volcanic dust over the lowlands (as documented in modern times with the El Chichon volcanic eruption of 1982, for example) raises the questions of whether volcanic ash was obtained locally instead of by long-distance trade (Ford and Rose 1995). Considering the rather common use of volcanic ash as a tempering agent, including its use in utilitarian storage jars, a local source seems likely, although this issue remains unresolved.

A variety of materials were traded locally from the environs of a given community and over short distances within the Maya lowlands (Graham 1987) that are important in reconstructing the economy of the ancient Maya, although this shorter distance exchange may not be as dramatic as the long-distance import of obsidian, gold, copper, or exotic pottery. Clays and tempering agents were obtained either through direct procurement or through trade for use in everyday pottery manufacture.

Scenes on Late Classic painted pottery vessels indicate that perishable resources were traded or, in some cases, offered in tribute. Royal Maya are shown wearing jaguar skin robes with quetzal feather headdresses. A tribute offering of cacao on a painted mural at Bonampak shows the value of this lowland crop. By the time of European contact, chocolate was a currency in Mesoamerica. Barbara Voorhies (1982) lists perishable resources available in the Maya lowlands that may have been traded. Certainly, foodstuffs must have been required as tribute payments to Late Classic Maya polities to feed the people of the Maya court and to supply food to help support the warfare that became endemic. The bulk import of marine resources to feed the inland Maya (Lange 1971) seems unlikely given the limited amounts of fish bones and marine shells at inland sites, but certainly corn and other field and tree crops must have been collected for storage and redistribution over fairly short distances. Long-distance bulk trade in foodstuffs (Sluyter 1993) seems less likely (McKillop 1994).

ARCHITECTURE AND URBAN PLANNING

The basic settlement unit within an ancient Maya community is the plazuela (plaza) group, as mentioned previously. This unit is evident in the spatial organization throughout settlements, from the monumental architecture in the

Chichen Itza overview (Courtesy Ed Kurjack)

centers of the largest cities (Ferguson and Adams 2001) to the modest households in the periphery of cities and in towns, villages, hamlets, and even isolated homesteads. Many images of Maya sites, buildings, and artifacts can be viewed on websites (see, for example, Hixson 2001; McNelly 1997; Ruggles 2003). The dispersed array of plaza groups at Tikal and other Maya cities at first appears chaotic and unplanned. Maya cities lack the ordered streets in cardinal directions of modern cities or of Tikal's contemporary, the highland city of Teotihuacan in central Mexico. However, closer inspection reveals that plaza groups are situated in areas of high and dry land, and they avoid the swamps and low-lying areas typical of the rainforest setting of the Maya lowlands. Raised stone roads linked major plaza groups within the urban center at cities such as Tikal and Chichen Itza, provided access to suburban areas at Caracol and Chichen Itza, and formed a network for travel among lowland cities (Chase and Chase 2001; Cobos and Winemiller 2001; Harrison 1999).

A residential plaza group contains the mounded remains of houses, outbuildings, and exterior space utilized by related family groups, who may have been members of the same lineage or extended family. The plaza group also defines the spatial organization of public architecture consisting of temples, palaces (which may also have been administrative buildings), and ball courts (Inomata and Houston 2001). Central plazas at the larger cities contain stelae and altars with carvings of Maya kings and queens and hieroglyphic texts commemorating important dates and events for public viewing.

Public and residential architecture within a community is distinguished by location and by the size, height, construction materials, and grandeur of the buildings (see Proskouriakoff 1963 for reconstruction drawings of Maya buildings). Public architecture is centrally located within communities, with residential plaza groups extending in all directions around the site center. The density of residential plazuelas diminishes farther from the center, and the boundaries of a community are not always clear. Research programs to identify the extent of settlement and the site boundaries have been carried out at a number of Maya communities. At Tikal, Dennis Puleston and others cut trails through the rainforest in cardinal directions away from the city center, recording the location of house mounds on either side of the transects (Harrison 1999). A defensive earthen wall marked the boundary of the city, although settlement continued beyond the wall. In the 27-kilometer transect between Tikal and the neighboring city of Yaxha, Anabel Ford (1986) found that settlement was concentrated in well-drained uplands and was absent in swamps and other low-lying areas.

Elite residential architecture, including palaces used by the royal Maya, was more similar to public buildings than to residences used by the common Maya (Christie 2003). Public architecture in urban centers is characterized by large stone-faced substructures often supporting stone buildings, as at Tikal (Harrison 1999), although at some cities, such as Lubaantun (Hammond 1975) or Nim li punit (Leventhal 1990) in southern Belize, the superstructures were of perishable construction materials, probably pole and thatch. Public buildings

Puuc-style Nunnery at Uxmal (building on west side of quad of four that form the Nunnery) (Courtesy T. Winemiller)

also were often adorned with stone carvings as at Yaxchilan, Chichen Itza, and Uxmal, such as the House of the Governor (Ferguson and Adams 2001, 223). In the Chenes and Puuc region, the façades of public buildings were often quite ornate.

A typical house evidently resembled the traditional pole and thatch houses of the modern Maya, such as those studied by anthropologist Robert Wauchope (1938), who also studied ancient Maya houses at Uaxactun (Wauchope 1934). The houses were often built on a low earth mound that was sometimes faced with cut stone or river cobbles. The mapping and excavation of modest houses at Barton Ramie on the Belize River, directed by Gordon R. Willey (Willey et al. 1965) in the 1950s, set the tone for further community settlement pattern studies. The Barton Ramie researchers found a variety of earth- and stone-faced platforms for perishable pole and thatch houses. In many instances, new houses had been constructed on the same location as an old house, with the old house torn down and a new platform placed on top of the earlier one. All that remained in the archaeological record were the low platform mounds. A house platform at Arvin's Landing along Joe Taylor Creek in southern Belize was constructed using thousands of baseball-sized chert cobbles (McKillop 1995; Steiner 1994).

The widespread occurrence of "invisible" residential architecture presents quite a problem for Maya archaeologists searching for the houses of the common Maya, as well as for attempts to reconstruct the distribution of ancient houses, population densities, and site boundaries. Diane Chase (1990) estimated that a considerable percentage of the houses at Santa Rita Corozal left no mounded remains. K. Anne Pyburn (1990) found a similar situation elsewhere in northern Belize. Similarly, there was extensive evidence of ancient settlement on the coast and the offshore islands in the Port Honduras of southern Belize, but there were virtually no mounded remains of houses (McKillop 1996b; McKillop 1997). Furthermore, some sites had been submerged by rising seas and had no visible artifactual or mounded remains on the ground surface. Some sites are currently underwater, whereas others are deeply buried under mangrove peat among red mangroves that are themselves underwater (McKillop 2002). The fact that Maya archaeologists have found such extensive evidence of residential settlement in the form of mounds is perhaps a testimony to the high populations in ancient times. But it is unknown how many residences might have remained unnoticed because the houses were built directly on the ground surface or because of sea level rise or other environmental changes.

The Preclassic origins of public buildings in the Maya area were elaborated upon in the Late Preclassic and became entrenched and defined during the Classic period. Temples and palaces created large public spaces for gatherings such as markets, festivals, and the viewing of royal rituals and ceremonies in the temple rooms above. Stone temples were stuccoed and brightly painted in red, green, white, and blue during the Late Preclassic at Cerros and during the Classic period, as with the Rosalila temple at Copan. These painted temples had façades with masks of the sun god, as at Altun Ha, or with masks of Itzamna, as with the House of the Masks at Kabah in the northern Maya low-

Stone carving from Chichen Itza showing human skulls displayed on a skull rack, suggesting the practice of sacrifice and public display of actual skulls (Corel)

lands. Graphic depictions of war captives, including their torture, dismemberment, and sacrifice, were publicly displayed on Maya buildings. These images certainly acted as propaganda and intimidation tactics, or a reminder of the fate of disobedience. Images of war captives were carved on building façades in the northeast court of the Palace at Palenque (Miller 1999a, figure 26). A giant image of the death god holding a captive's head was displayed at Tonina (Miller 1999a, figure 31). Pictures of captives carved on stones that are three stories high formed the roof comb of the main building at Hochcob in the northern Maya lowlands (Miller 1999a, 43). The stone skull rack at Chichen Itza was also for public viewing.

Although the basic template of a Maya city is replicated over and over again, many cities are easily recognizable by their distinctive architecture. Public and residential buildings are dispersed in plaza groups according to the peculiarities of the local topography; however, local artists and craftspeople sponsored by the royal Maya followed regional practices that must have been fostered by apprenticeship and tradition. The height of the temples at Tikal rising above the rainforest canopy and the sheer size of the places in the main acropolis are overwhelming in their size and grandeur (Ferguson and Adams 2001, 88–91). Although the public architecture at the site was undoubtedly

Roof comb above room at top of Tikal's Temple 2 (Courtesy H. McKillop)

plastered and painted in bright colors in antiquity, the buildings were otherwise unadorned with stone carvings, apart from plaster masks flanking the stairs of early temples, as well as the roof combs and carved wooden lintels of the Late Classic temples. Stelae are rectangular, with low-relief images of royal personages and hieroglyphs.

By way of contrast, the buildings and stone sculpture at Copan are ornate. In addition to the Hieroglyphic Staircase, buildings are adorned with stone carvings or by decorative stonework, as with the Mat House. The stelae are more like sculptures, with Maya royalty shown in three dimensions. The stone carvings adorning buildings at Yaxchilan are easily recognized by their naturalistic renditions of human figures and their detailed portrayal of royal rituals. The colonnaded rooms and the tower at Palenque are distinctive, as is the naturalistic tradition of rendering human figures on stelae. The Rio Bec and Chenes sites in the northern Maya lowlands are easily recognized by their elaborate stone façades and roof combs. The high density of public and residential architecture within the walled city of Mayapan in the northern Maya lowlands reflects in part its Late Postclassic age as well as the defensive nature of the walled city (Pollock et al. 1962). The age and extent of influence or even invasion from the central Mexican Toltec state at Chichen Itza is unresolved. At least some of the public architecture is copied from the Early Postclassic Toltec city of Tula northwest of modern Mexico City. The round columns forming a colonnaded building and the stone reclining figure holding a plate for blood offering are among the architectural traits common to both Chichen and Tula.

Temples

Maya temples consisted of a substructure platform supporting a room or larger structure, sometimes with a decorative roof comb (Ferguson and Adams 2001, 91). Maya temples served Maya royalty in both life and death. During their lives, Maya royalty performed rituals and ceremonies in temples on public and private occasions. Temples also served as royal cemeteries tracing royal Maya dynasties and publicly proclaiming the ancestry and divine right of kingship of the next in line.

The substructure platform of Maya temples was made from earth or rubble. Throughout much of the Maya lowlands, the rubble was quarried limestone and the buildings were faced with cut limestone. In areas where sandstone formed the bedrock, it was used instead, as at Nim li punit and Lubaantun in southern Belize and at Quirigua along the Motagua River in Guatemala. The temple substructure platform often rose in nine layers, corresponding with the nine layers of the Maya underworld. An outset central staircase led from the plaza below to a room at the top. Both the steep slope of the substructure and the difficulty of walking up the staircase—which typically had treads so narrow that only part of the foot could rest on them, and a riser much higher than modern stairs—restricted easy access to the temple building and made this access precarious. Hieroglyphs recounting the dynastic history of Copan are carved into the stones that form a steep staircase for a Late Classic temple at that site (Fash 2001; Ferguson and Adams 2001, 104). Barbara Fash is engaged in recording these glyphs and assembling them in their correct chronological and historical order. On a more modest scale, hieroglyphs on a staircase at Aguateca record the defeat of a Tikal ruler. Stone and stucco masks flank the central outset staircases of temples at various Classic period cities, notably Tikal, Lamanai, and Altun Ha. The masks, like the entire stone temples, were plastered and painted, with only traces of plaster and paint today to hint at the multicolored splendor of the monumental architecture during its use by the Classic Maya. The Rosalila structure at Copan was perfectly preserved under a

Hieroglyphic Staircase at Copan (Courtesy B. Somers)

subsequent construction episode and includes red-, green-, and white-painted stucco masks.

The temple room at the top of Maya temples was small but was the center of important royal rituals that are depicted on stelae and on painted pots (Schele and Miller 1986; Reents-Budet 1994, 2001). Rituals helped to codify and reinforce the power, authority, and royal lineage rights of the royal Maya. Accession to power as well as other rights of passage were publicly commemorated with blood offerings using lancets made of obsidian, stingray spines, or ropes piercing tongues, ears, lips, and genitals. These bloodlettings helped to induce a state of trance in which the royal person attained supernatural powers by contact with the gods following age-old shamanistic practices. Blood offerings are depicted on carved monuments at Palenque, Yaxchilan, Nim li punit, and elsewhere, with droplets of blood falling onto bark paper in a brazier where they were burned, allowing smoke to rise, to conjure the vision serpent.

The top temple room was small because of the building construction technique known as the corbelled vault, which was used for constructing stone walls and roofs (Harrison 1999; Ferguson and Adams 2001). The Maya did not use the true arch in buildings, but instead used the corbelled vault; it resulted in narrow rooms that could be of considerable length, but not width. In making a corbelled vault roof, successive cut stone blocks were placed on opposite walls progressively closer to the centerline, with a capstone placed over the center. The corbelled vault roof required thick stone walls to transfer the weight of the roof and just a narrow distance between the supporting walls. The original corbelled vault rooms, complete with plastered walls and ceilings and wooden beam supports, still remain at two of Tikal's temples. Decorative roof combs added additional height to temples, which today tower above the rainforest at Tikal and other sites.

Palaces

Palaces flanking the sides of central plazas were for residential and administrative uses by the Classic Maya royalty and associated elite (Christie 2003; Harrison 1999; Inomata and Houston 2001). Palaces consisted of large stone-faced platforms, often with stone buildings on top, as at Tikal. In other cases, there would have been pole and thatch structures that have not been preserved, as at Nim li punit, Lubaantun, and Altun Ha, among others. The palaces at Tikal include multiroom buildings with corbelled vaults and interior chambers, some of which have stone benches, used for ceremonies and for sleeping. Tatiana Proskouriakoff (1963) provides some of the best reconstructions of Maya palaces, as well as other ancient Maya buildings.

Popol Na Council or "Mat" Houses

Perhaps a cross between a temple and a palace, Maya archaeologists have identified Popol Na council houses at Copan and a number of other cities where the Maya king or queen met with top advisors in the administration of the city and public affairs, including battles. A small stone building reached by a low staircase, the Mat House at Copan is identified as such by the cut stone decoration forming a mat, the symbol of power and authority, along the building's façade (Fash 2001). The role of the Maya court in governance is not well understood, but certainly there was a sizable retinue of advisors, servants, craftspeople, merchants, and others who were closely associated with the Maya kings, queens, and other nobility (Inomata and Houston 2001). Popol Nas have also been identified in the northern Maya lowlands during the Ter-

Ball court at Nim li punit, Belize (Courtesy B. Somers)

minal Classic and Postclassic periods at Chichen Itza (the Monjas building), Uxmal (House of the Governor) and elsehwere (Kowalski 2003).

Ball Courts

The ball game, an important feature of the Maya origin myth and likely commonly played in Maya communities, was a central part of life in Maya city states, as stone ball courts are found in the central areas of the cities (Whittington 2001). At Tikal, for example, there is a stone ball court behind a temple in the central plaza. The ball courts were formed by two buildings whose walls form a court between them, often with one or more circular ball court markers placed along the centerline of the playing field (Proskouriakoff 1963). The central ball court marker from Lubaantun (Hammond 1975; Whittington 2001) depicts men in elaborate ball game attire playing the ball game. The game was played with a large rubber ball about the size of a basketball, as indicated by an actual ball made of solid rubber preserved in waterlogged soil in Mexico (Whittington 2001).

Sacbes

Raised stone roads called causeways or sacbes linked various parts of a community and also provided means of communication and transportation among different communities. Sacbes linked different parts of city centers that were dispersed across the landscape on high ground, away from swamps and aguadas. The distribution of public architecture in downtown Tikal, for example, followed higher ground in the undulating landscape. Major architectural groups were linked by sacbes. Sacbes at Caracol extended from the site center to suburban and peripheral areas of the site and provided a means of linking disparate parts of Caracol economically (Chase and Chase 2001). The lack of public architecture along the sacbes in the suburbs suggested to the site's researchers, Diane and Arlen Chase, that the central urban elite of Caracol did not politically control the suburban Caracol Maya. Two episodes of road construction are evident at Chichen Itza, corresponding to the major building phases at the site (Cobos and Winemiller 2001). The sacbes linked major building groups within the urban center. The roads also provided access to peripheral groups.

MAYA POTTERY

Maya archaeologists have found that painted or incised decoration on pottery vessels is a sensitive temporal indicator, unlike vessel shape, which is more tied to the uses of a vessel. Most Mayanists use the type-variety system of Maya ceramic classification, in which pottery sherds are divided into groups (types) that have similar decoration and surface finish. Classifying sherds consists of dividing them into slip categories (unslipped, slipped, polychrome) and then grouping sherds together according to similarities in decoration (painting, incising, impressing, gouging, molding) and surface finish (glossy, waxy).

Commonly, massive quantities of pottery sherds from stratigraphic excavations in middens and from buildings are sorted into types. For example, Sabloff (1975) studied more than 200,000 sherds from Seibal, and Adams (1971) studied more than 800,000 sherds from Altar de Sacrificios. Less commonly, complete vessels from burials and caches, as at Tikal (Culbert 1993), form the foundation of the temporal sequence. Pottery types that occur together "stratigraphically" (at the same depths in excavations) are assumed to represent the pottery used at a particular time and are designated a "ceramic complex." Ceramic complexes from other sites are compared to see if they are contemporary. In this way, Maya archaeologists build a picture of the cultural history of a region and are able to place the various sites in chronological order. Even outside the immediate region of a site, some other Maya sites have quite similar pottery. The percentage of pottery types shared among sites is the basis for defining a "ceramic sphere." Archaeologists suggest that these similarities indicate cultural ties, even trade.

A number of Maya archaeologists have demonstrated that there is more to be learned about the ancient Maya from pottery than chronology alone using the type-variety system. Technological studies of the clay from which vessels were made (as well as the sand, shell, or other tempering material added to the clay) have provided information on the origins of pottery, allowing archaeologists to reconstruct trade patterns and other forms of distribution of pots, such as gift giving. Such technological "fingerprinting" also distinguishes trade pieces from local copies, which was evidently a common practice among the ancient Maya. Technological studies include petrography, in which minerals and other materials in the clay are observed and identified under a binocular microscope (Shepard 1976), as well as a variety of chemical techniques for identifying the components of the clay, including neutron activation analysis (NAA) and X-ray fluorescence (XRF). In an innovative study of Maya pottery, archaeologist Antonia Foias collaborated with chemist Ron Bishop (Foias and Bishop 1997) to carry out neutron activation analysis on a sample of pottery sorted by the type-variety system. They assumed that finished vessels were traded instead of clay or temper. Local manufacture was then interpreted from the highest frequency of a particular clay and temper. Foias and Bishop were able to reconstruct patterns of local production and trade of fine ware pottery in the Petexbatun region of Guatemala during the Late and Terminal Classic periods.

Despite the abundance of pottery at Maya sites, little is known about pottery workshops. Kilns for firing vessels have not been located. General areas of pottery production have been suggested from similarities between the clay and temper in pots with clay sources (Graham 1987). A number of studies have linked the standardization of pottery vessels with specialized workshop manufacture. For example, jars used to boil brine to produce salt in Punta Ycacos Lagoon along the southern coast of Belize were very standardized, suggesting mass production of the vessels (McKillop 2002). In addition, the low diversity of pottery types there (only four) was not the regular complement of types for a Maya community, suggesting a specialized, limited activity, in this case, salt production. This research follows innovative studies by Prudence Rice (1987a, 1987b), who examined standardization of pottery production as well as diversity (of types) and evenness (relative percentages of pots in each type) in ceramic complexes.

Most researchers, with some important exceptions, have largely overlooked the actual use of Maya pottery as containers used in ancient activities. Beyond classifying sherds into jars, vases, bowls, dishes, and plates, the type-variety system does not address vessel use. In the absence of contextual information on the use of Maya pots, researchers have information from their depiction in scenes on Late Classic painted vessels (Reents-Budet 1994), from analysis of food remains inside, and from studies of modern Maya pottery making and use (Reina and Hill 1978). Michael Coe (1978), Dorie Reents-Budet (2001), and Justin Kerr (1989–1994) focus on the iconography of Late Classic Maya pottery, especially the scenes of court life depicted on high-status vases. Some vessels identify their contents by hieroglyphs. Many vases show pots with food as part of royal feasts and other rituals, allowing researchers to link vessel shape and decoration with function. Scenes include depictions of tamales in red-painted bowls, unpainted jars for beverages, finely painted dishes for serving food, and pictorial painted vases for beverages. Reents-Budet (1994) discusses the importance of royal feasting and of gifting painted pottery vessels to create and maintain alliances and to help coalesce political power.

Actual chocolate was identified in a rare chemical analysis of residue inside a painted pot from Rio Azul (Hall et al. 1990). Lisa LeCount (1999) focused on the types of pottery containers recovered from various contexts at the Late Classic city of Xunantunich in western Belize. She was able to associate serving vessels, notably open bowls and dishes, with feasting ceremonies that she argued were used by the local rulers to engage others in alliances and to develop and maintain social and political power. In a test of the functional categorization of Maya pottery vessels into bowls, jars, vases, dishes, and plates, Brad Ensor and this author (Ensor and McKillop 2003) use vessel hardness and porosity to evaluate the suitability of pottery from Wild Cane Cay for a variety of uses based on vessel shape. The results of the porosity and hardness testing were compared with the function based on morphology to see how technologically well suited the vessels were for tasks suggested by their morphology and by ethnographic studies.

Changing Styles of Maya Pottery

The styles of Maya pottery changed over time, so that generally researchers can say that Preclassic pottery has a red slip, Classic Maya pottery is polychrome, and Postclassic pottery often has a red slip but also has modeled, carved, or incised decoration. Maya ceramicists have spent countless years sorting, refining, and describing pottery to provide quite detailed classifications that reflect fluctuations in time and place.

The earliest known pottery from the Pacific coast and from the southern Maya lowlands, dated at 1800 B.C. and 1000 B.C. respectively, is quite sophisticated in form and surface finish, so that Maya archaeologists often wonder about the earlier origins and development of Preclassic pottery. Widespread settlement of the Maya lowlands in the Late Preclassic is reflected in broad similarities in ceramic styles, such as Sierra Red. Late Preclassic pottery has a characteristic "waxy" surface finish (Kosakowsky 1987). The introduction of distinctive and innovative styles in the Protoclassic has invoked much controversy as to the origins and significance of the pottery, the Protoclassic period, and the origins of the people who made this style of pottery (Merwin and Vaillant 1932). Protoclassic pottery includes Usulutan, a type with wavy lines on the exterior of vessels. Four-legged open bowls with mammiform vessel supports are diagnostic of the Protoclassic, as is the use of polychrome painted decoration on the exterior of these tetrapod and other vessels (Gifford 1976). It is noteworthy that polychrome decoration, a hallmark of the subsequent Classic period, was not used prior to the Protoclassic.

What is the Protoclassic and what was its impact on the course and development of the Classic period in the Maya lowlands where it was so pervasive? Some tie the introduction of Protoclassic ceramics to the Ilopango volcanic eruption in El Salvador, where the same pottery was recovered. In this scenario, the Maya fled the devastation following the volcanic eruption and traveled to the Maya lowlands, bringing their innovative pottery. In this model, the Protoclassic is a time period between the Late Preclassic and the Early Classic. However, recent refinements of dating place the Ilopango volcanic eruption to the early fifth century A.D., which is during the Early Classic (Dull, Southon, and Sheets 2001). Alternatively, the Protoclassic could simply be a specialized suite of pottery or a "subcomplex" characteristic of burials, either dating to the Late Preclassic or the Early Classic. Most Maya archaeologists favor this latter scenario (Brady et al. 1998). Elizabeth Graham (1994) also noted that there was local experimentation with polychromes in the Late Preclassic within the southern lowlands, indicating that there was no need to suggest import of the polychrome tradition.

Polychrome painted pottery is a defining characteristic of the Classic period, but there was much variety in decoration and in vessel form over this 600-year time span. At any one time period, however, there were broad similarities, both at the level of pottery types, such as Belize Red, red-painted pots with volcanic ash temper—and modes, such as basal-flange—a characteristic of Early Classic pottery. The polychrome decoration was typically red and black paint on an orange or cream background. Variations include red, black, and orange on cream. Other colors, including brown and blue, were occasionally used. The painted or slipped pottery of the Classic period had a characteristic glossy surface finish, in sharp contrast to the waxy feel of Preclassic pottery. Maya ceramicists use the nomenclature from Uaxactun for temporal refinements within the Classic period, in addition to defining and naming pottery complexes at particular sites or regions. At Uaxactun, the Early Classic is divided into the Tzakol 1 and Tzakol 2 pottery complexes; the Late Classic consists of Tepeu 1, Tepeu 2, and Tepeu 3, with the last complex referred to as the Terminal Classic period (Smith 1955). Typical Tzakol 1 pottery included open bowls with polychrome decoration on the vessel exterior, a basal-flange around the lower part of the vessel exterior, and three oval vessel supports. A common Tzakol 2 pottery vessel was an open bowl with interior black lines below the rim and an animal or other figure painted in the interior.

By Tepeu 1 and Tepeu 2, the open bowls often had exterior ridges, with impressed or incised notches, and included both polychrome and red-slipped examples. Deep bowls and vases with elaborately painted pictorial scenes of rulers, ceremonies, rituals, and feasting were introduced in Tepeu 1 and are characteristic of Late Classic Maya pottery (Coe 1978; Kerr 1989–1994; Reents-Budet 1994). The finest "codex-style" vases had finely painted figures with hieroglyphic inscriptions recounting the activities. Some included the painter's signature. Ceramic figurines are common from the Late Classic, but perhaps none are as exquisite and informative of Maya culture as those from the island of Jaina off the west coast of the Yucatan. Naturalistically depicting Maya people engaged in a variety of mundane activities, many with the unusual Maya blue paint, these figures provide a rare glimpse of ancient lifeways. Lubaantun-style figurine whistles, though unpainted and not as finely made, also show figures engaged in a variety of activities, including ball game players. Red-slipped and black-slipped deep bowls, open bowls, and jars also were made in the Classic period, as was unslipped, undecorated pottery. These utilitarian vessels served the daily needs of the ancient Maya. Terminal Classic pottery shows some of the characteristics of the succeeding Postclassic, particularly the use of incision and gouging as decorative techniques on red-slipped or black-slipped vases and deep bowls.

The painted decoration of the Classic period changed to incised or grooved decoration on red-slipped or orange-slipped vessels during the Postclassic (Pendergast 1981; Smith 1971; Graham 1989). Open bowls with incised decorations on the vessel exterior have a variety of vessel support styles, including animal heads and human heads. Tohil Plumbate jars made on the Pacific coast of Chiapas and Guatemala were widely traded throughout the Maya area around A.D. 1000 (Neff 1989; Shepard 1948). These small jars often are in the form of an animal or bird. Fine Orange pottery made on the Gulf Coast near the Usumacinta also was widely traded in the Maya lowlands at about the same time. Short, cylindrical vessel supports on open bowls with double-line incisions are typical of Tulum on the east coast of the Yucatan (Sanders 1960) and were traded or perhaps copied farther south in Belize. Large incense burners with spikes and large, hollow figurines are part of the Postclassic Maya pottery assemblages.

The Maya continued their traditional pottery making after the arrival of the Spaniards in the sixteenth century, but archaeologists have found it difficult to differentiate between prehistoric pottery and early historic Maya pottery. Certainly where Spanish or, later, British ceramics occur, as at Lamanai, Tipu (Pendergast 1985), and the Port Honduras in southern Belize (McKillop 1995; McKillop 2005; McKillop and Roberts 2003), associated plain pottery can be attributed to the historic Maya. The ancient tradition of pottery making continues in highland Guatemala (Hill and Monaghen 1978). The Yucatan of Mexico has provided important analogues to the production process and the use of ancient Maya pottery vessels.

STONE TOOLS AND OTHER ARTIFACTS

From ritual bloodletting to cleaning fish and grinding corn, the study of stone tools has provided valuable insights into the daily lives of the common folk, as well as the rituals and ceremonies of the royal Maya. "Knappers" have duplicated the process of stone tool manufacture, providing clues to interpret the chipping debris at ancient sites and the production of finished stone artifacts. Site reports are replete with descriptions of the forms of stone tools that provide important comparative and chronological tools. Visual, petrographic, and chemical studies of the stone material itself has formed the basis of many models of ancient Maya trade, from the sources to the ancient Maya communities. Studies of the quantity of stone tools, the degree of conservation of the stone in the manufacture of artifacts, and the amount of debris in relation to finished artifacts have allowed archaeologists to reconstruct Maya production and trade locally and with more distant lands. Microscopic analysis of wear on the working edges of stone tools provides clues to their ancient use. Even blood residue has been identified on the edges of stone tools, providing an important link with depictions of ritual bloodletting on carved monuments and painted pots.

For purposes of study, Maya stone artifacts are divided into classes based on their manufacture, by chipping or by grinding, and then into the kind of material. Ground stone artifacts include manos and metates, jade and other greenstones, as well as artifacts in fewer numbers ground from other materials, such as coral and pumice. Chipped stone artifacts include chert and obsidian artifacts. Early studies of stone artifacts emphasized their description based on morphology. The study of the shape of Maya stone tools continues to be important for establishing site chronologies, as at least some forms change over time, and for making comparisons with other sites. Newer approaches include determination of the source locations of the stones, functional studies based on microscopic observation of the working edges of stone tools, and behavioral studies based on the production process. They add to the modern understanding of how the Maya used stone tools in everyday and ritual activities.

Ground Stone Artifacts: Manos, Metates, and Jade

A variety of materials obtained locally, from within the Maya lowlands, and from beyond were made into artifacts by grinding and polishing. They include the ubiquitous corn grinding tools in domestic contexts and exotic jade artifacts from offerings and burials. The corn grinding implements consist of the flat grinding surface of the metate and the hand-held cylindrical grinder, the mano. Common forms of metates include the oval "turtle back" metate, the rectangular tripod metate, and the rectangular metate with a deep trough created from extensive wear (Sidrys and Andreson 1976; Willey et al. 1965). Bryan Anderson (1997) provides a comprehensive description of manos and metates throughout the Maya area. Local limestone often was used to make manos and metates, particularly in the northern Maya lowlands where other hard stones suitable for making grinding stones were unavailable. Granite from the Maya Mountains of southern Belize often was used in the southern Maya lowlands, as identified by petrographic observation of thin sections of metates from Uaxactun in the Peten of Guatemala (Shipley and Graham 1989) and by macroscopic observation of artifacts from northern Belize (Sidrys and Andreson 1976), in southern Belize (McKillop 1987; McKillop 2004), and elsewhere in the southern Maya lowlands (Willey et al. 1965). Less commonly, basalt was imported from the volcanic Maya highlands, where it was made into tripod metates with manos at Lubaantun (Hammond 1975), Wild Cane Cay (McKillop 1987), and northern Belize (Sidrys and Andreson 1976).

Little has been said about manos and metates beyond descriptions of the sources of the stones from which they were made and their morphology. William Rathje (1971) advanced a provocative model of Maya trade in which he contended that the complex Maya civilization of the southern Maya lowlands developed as a consequence of the need to develop sophisticated organization to import basic materials that were locally unavailable. Basalt for making metates was one of the three materials he noted, along with obsidian and salt. Subsequent research has rejected his "local resource deficiency model." Even though basalt was imported in small quantities, the southern Maya lowlanders more commonly used local limestone and granite from the nearby Maya Mountains. Other researchers have identified local chert instead of obsidian, as well as southern lowland sources of salt. Still, Rathje's (1971) model has been important in provoking other researchers to provide alternative models of Maya trade.

Jade and other greenstones, including serpentine and albite, naturally occurring along the Motagua River in Guatemala, are assumed to be the sources of jade used by the ancient Maya (Hammond et al. 1977). Wherever it is found, jade is a status item, usually recovered in burials of important personages or in dedicatory offerings in public buildings. Although rare compared to pottery and other stone artifacts, jade has been recovered as undecorated beads at many sites; as small objects formed into heads, such as the human heads in a dedicatory building offering at Cerros (Freidel 1979); as larger and more elaborate hunchbacks and felines at Classic period Lamanai (Pendergast 1981); and as elaborate masks like the one covering Lord Pacal's face in his sarcophagus in a tomb at Palenque. Jade and other greenstones were frequently made into ceremonial axes that are recovered from burials at many sites. Modern studies attempting to replicate jade artifacts indicate that the material was ground using a variety of techniques, including standing a thin stick between one's hands and rolling it against the object to perforate or partially perforate the surface. The import of jade in the Late Preclassic was emphasized in support of a model of the precocious development of Cerros and other early cities, with masked temples and other artifactual and architectural elements that presaged subsequent Classic period civilization (Freidel 1979). Certainly, jade was utilized by the royal Maya of the Classic period dynasties to demonstrate their high rank and ability to import exotic material. They hired court artisans to fashion this material into a variety of highly crafted objects.

Chipped Stone Artifacts: Obsidian and Chert

Obsidian was highly desired for various cutting purposes, including ritual bloodletting as graphically depicted on carved stone monuments (Reents-Budet 1994). Modern experiments indicate that a freshly struck obsidian blade has edges that are at least twice as sharp as surgical steel. In fact, prior to the introduction of laser surgery, modern replicas of obsidian blades were made for surgical use on the suggestion of Maya archaeologist and obsidian expert Payson Sheets. The lowland Maya valued obsidian to make blades, but they did have other locally available stones suitable for making cutting implements, such as chert. These other stones were regularly used instead of or in addition to obsidian, especially for subsistence activities. Because of its ability to make a clean and directed incision, obsidian was evidently preferred for ritual bloodletting.

Small blades are the most common obsidian artifact found at Maya sites, with stemmed points (triangular-shaped blades with stems) and "eccentric" objects of various shapes found less frequently and in smaller numbers. Clues to the production and transport of obsidian derive from the occurrence of the cylindrical "cores" from which blades and other artifacts were made. Cores were made at the highland outcrop workshop, where large flakes have been found indicating the production of cores. A typical core measures some 10 centimeters in length and 4 centimeters in diameter with one flat end, which is the "striking platform" from which blades are flaked. Experiments indicate that a typical core can produce 125 to 200 blades, depending on the size of the blades (Sheets 1975). The cores were flattened at one end, and this end was often ground or scratched. Long, thin blades were struck from the roughened end, either by direct percussion with another rock or by indirect pressure using an antler tine pressed against the edge of the core and indirectly hitting the antler tine with a rock.

A freshly made blade has edges at least twice as sharp as surgical steel, but the blade is easily broken, as obsidian is a volcanic glass. A number of other artifacts were fashioned from obsidian. Bifacial points, which were chipped on each side or bifacially, are found in small numbers in burials and caches and are usually made from central Mexican obsidian (Moholy-Nagy 1999). A bifacial point from a Wild Cane Cay burial came from an unknown source (McKillop et al. 1988). Small obsidian "eccentrics" include artifacts chipped into half-moon shapes, as in a Wild Cane Cay Postclassic burial (McKillop 2005), human figures made from green Pachuca obsidian from a Classic burial at Altun Ha (Pendergast 1979), and other shapes (Moholy-Nagy 1999). The bifacial points and eccentrics may have been transported as finished objects, as were green obsidian blades, as chipping evidence for their on-site manufacture is lacking.

A small but growing trend in Maya obsidian studies includes behavioral studies of the artifacts based on the microscopic examination of the cutting edges. Chemical identification of blood residue on the edge of obsidian blades from El Ceren, El Salvador, is only generally identifiable as primate blood, so that it could either be human or monkey blood (including howler and spider monkeys, which are indigenous to Central America). Suzanne Lewenstein (1987) examined the edge wear on obsidian stone tools from Cerros and compared the microscopic scratches and polishes to the wear produced on modern tools used in a variety of activities. She was not able to identify particular tasks, but the generalized conclusions, such as scraping on a hard or soft material or cutting a soft material, provide important advances in discovering the uses of obsidian blades. Although their frequent depiction in ritual bloodletting on painted pots and carved monuments at Classic Maya sites points to their ritual use, obsidian blades also were well suited to cutting a variety of other materials. Their abundance at Wild Cane Cay, for example, calls for an additional interpretation besides ritual bloodletting, such as cleaning fish.

Obsidian has sometimes been called the preferred material for cutting purposes for the ancient Maya. However, chert is a local alternative widely found throughout the Maya lowlands, albeit with varying quality. The best information on chert production derives from a project at the chert quarry and manufacturing community of Colha in northern Belize directed by Harry Shafer and Tom Hester (1983). Particularly high-quality chert forms outcrops at the site where workshops for the production of chert tools date to the Late Preclassic, Classic, and Postclassic. The workshops are associated with Maya house mounds and so represent "household workshops," akin to cottage industries. The evidence for tool production is piles of flaking debris and artifacts broken in the process of production ("production errors"). These piles of flaking debris were the discards that accumulated or were moved from the production area, presumably in the immediate area. Other known workshops for producing household goods are the salt works in Punta Ycacos Lagoon, where brine or sea water was boiled in pots over fires to produce salt (McKillop 2002).

A variety of stone tools and other objects were made from chert (Hester and Shafer 1991). The same "core-blade" technology used to make obsidian blades formed the basis of chert tool production. Initially, a large blade (macroblade) was struck off a core, and this blade was either chipped into a final object or traded as a "blank" to be made into the desired final artifact at a later time, as at Moho Cay (McKillop 1980; McKillop 2004). The blades were chipped either on one side (unifacially) or on both sides (bifacially). Thin blades that had been carefully flaked bifacially were made into "laurel leaf" points at each end. Stemmed blades included bifacially worked stems with the blade worked on one side to produce unifacial stemmed points or on each side to produce bifacial stemmed points. Thicker blades were used to make axes, which were bifacially chipped around their circumference, and which are regarded as the basic agricultural tool used by the ancient Maya for clearing forests and working fields (Willey et al. 1965). An axe still hafted to a wooden handle, preserved in an inundated swamp in northern Belize (Shafer and Hester 1990) indicates how these "general utility tools" were used. Adzes were produced by removing a large flake at the distal end of a general utility tool, producing what Shafer and Hester (1983) termed an "orange peel adze."

As well as chert tools used for a variety of utilitarian and domestic uses, some chert objects had no possible or clear utilitarian use. As with obsidian, chert was chipped into eccentrics, but the chert eccentrics were both larger and often more elaborate than those made from obsidian. Large half-moon shapes, animal figures, and apparently nonrepresentational carvings figure in the inventory of "eccentrics" from Maya sites. Perhaps the most splendid eccentrics were discovered in a cache associated with the Rosalila building at Copan (Fash 2001). These elaborate carvings depict naturalistic renditions of Maya rulers, and their complex method of manufacture defies modern replication.

FOOD PLANTS

The triad of maize (corn), beans, and squash witnessed by the sixteenth-century Spaniards as forming the basis of the Maya diet of that time is often used as a model of the ancient Maya diet. This interpretation is reinforced by the frequent recovery of manos and metates at Maya sites, suggesting that corn was ground there (Anderson 1997; Willey et al. 1965). The recovery of plant food remains from ancient Maya sites, however, suggests that the interpretation of corn as the mainstay of the ancient diet may be erroneous. There was both regional variation in the plant foods that were consumed by the ancient Maya and a greater diversity in the types of foods than maize, beans, and squash. This finding is not surprising, as some 600 years had passed between the collapse of the Classic Maya civilization and the time the Spaniards encountered the Maya.

In addition to the variety of plant foods identified from ancient sites, a variety of ancient agricultural techniques have been discovered and excavated that were not observed at the time of first contact. For the typical Maya milpa field, a section of the forest was burned, cleared, and planted for several years until the soil was depleted of nutrients and overcome with weeds. At that point a new section of the forest was selected, resulting in an "extensive" form of agriculture that requires large tracts of forest to support a Maya community and results in the fissioning of population into new communities in order to remain close to milpas. Maya archaeologists have discovered that the Classic Maya, and perhaps their Preclassic predecessors, used more "intensive" forms of agriculture, including drained and raised fields, terraces, kitchen gardens, tree cropping, and forest management, in addition to the milpa so characteristic of modern Maya villages. A variety of food production techniques, including orchards and fields, were perserved by the volcanic eruption that covered the ancient community of Ceren, El Salvador (Sheets 2002).

MINERALS

A variety of minerals were available to the ancient Maya from the Maya Mountains of Belize and from the volcanic regions of Mesoamerica. The single instance of mercury is from under a ball court marker in a ball court at Lamanai in northern Belize (Pendergast 1982a). Mercury occurs naturally in Honduras, so the Lamanai mercury establishes trade connections. Hematite, an iron oxide, was used to make red pigment used in the Maya codices (Coe and Kerr 1998). Travertine, a dense banded calcium carbonate likely imported form Oaxaca, Mexico, to the Maya lowlands, was occasionally used to make bowls (Coe and Kerr 1998, figure 101). Pyrite was used as the reflective part of mirrors in the temple of the Sun God's tomb at Altun Ha (Pendergast 1982b), in burial 116 from Tikal's temple (Trik 1963), and in burials at Kaminaljuyu (Kidder, Jennings, and Shook 1946). Other minerals include jade and obsidian, discussed previously. Both were widely used by the ancient Maya.

MURAL PAINTING

Although few murals have survived on Maya buildings, inside rooms and caves, or in tombs, when complete or partial murals are discovered they provide a vivid reminder of the once-colorful appearance of Maya cities. The tradition of painting on dry stucco began in the Preclassic, reached its apogee in the Classic period, and was continued throughout the Postclassic. In addition to murals, Maya artists painted elaborate "mural" scenes on pottery vessels, as well as in books, four of which have survived. The Classic murals show historical scenes that have ritual significance in terms of Maya ideology, whereas the Terminal or Postclassic murals at Chichen Itza focus on religious themes and lack accompanying hieroglyphs.

The earliest Maya wall painting was accidentally discovered at the site of San Bartolo, Guatemala, by Harvard University archaeologist William Saturno (2003). The painting was exposed in a looter's trench at the site, and although much of the mural has been damaged or destroyed, a significant portion remains. The painting includes a scene with naturalistic human figures, including a man and a woman, perhaps participating in a corn ritual, as well as a depiction of Vucub Caquix. This exciting find puts the origin and development of mural painting back to the Late Preclassic period.

Early Classic mural paintings are known from Tikal, Uaxactun, and Rio Azul. Richard E. W. Adams (1999) uncovered walls painted in red and black on several Early Classic tombs at Rio Azul. In one of the Rio Azul painted tombs, the interred individual was placed at the center of the tomb, with painted glyphs on the walls denoting the cardinal directions of the Maya universe, as if the deceased was symbolically at the center of the Maya world. A burial at Tikal, dating to A.D. 445, contains stylized symbols in black paint. A mural in a palace at Uaxactun represents the only Early Classic palace painting known. The painting is on one wall of a room and depicts Maya royalty engaged in ritual bloodletting, with the ritual 260-day calendar dates below, perhaps correlating with ritual events depicted in the scene above. The scenes of court life include musicians, a warrior in Teotihuacan dress being received warmly by a Maya lord, and various other members of the Maya court, including women. The mural also shows the palace roof decorated with woven mat signs, which denote power and authority.

Late Classic mural paintings have been found from the western region of the southern Maya lowlands and the Puuc region in the northern Maya lowlands. Palace wall paintings in a structure at Bonampak are undoubtedly the most spectacular mural paintings in the Maya area, but there also are nearby murals at Yaxchilan and La Pasadita. Many Puuc sites have remnants of murals, with significant portions visible at Chacmultun and Mulchic, and painted doorway capstones usually depicting K'awiil or the Maize God (Miller 1999a, figure 159). In addition to the palace murals, the Late Classic Maya engaged in elaborate cave paintings, notably at Naj Tunich, as well as continuing the tradition of tomb wall painting, as at Caracol. Outside the Maya area in central Mexico, there are enigmatic Maya murals painted on a building at Caxcatla. Contemporary with the Bonampak murals, the Caxcatla paintings depict traders and warfare.

Bonampak Mural Paintings

The Bonampak murals show wonderful scenes of royal court life in red, blue, green, orange, and brown on the walls and ceilings of the three palace rooms that form one particular structure (Miller 1986; Hixson 2001). As indicated by a glyph on the wall of one room, the building was dedicated in A.D. 791. The murals show hundreds of figures depicted at one-third to one-half actual life size, so they present an imposing and powerful view. Traces of paint indicate that the exterior of the building also was painted. Following study by Mary Miller, the murals were conserved, making them visible for scholars and other visitors. A replica of the Bonampak murals forms part of an exhibit at the Florida Museum of Natural History at the University of Florida in Gainesville.

Hieroglyphs in one room name the Bonampak king, Yahaw Chan Muwan, as the owner of the building, and the murals depict the power and successful military campaigns he led along with the neighboring cities of Yaxchilan, 26 kilometers distant, and Lacanha. The murals depict hundred of members of the Bonampak royal court engaged in rituals and other dynastic activities not depicted elsewhere. They provide primary evidence for court life, social stratification, and warfare. The Bonampak murals include some of the finest Maya fig-

A mural painting from a Maya room at Late Classic Bonampak, Mexico (Art Directors/Ask Images)

ure painting, with delicate lines that capture naturalistic renditions of the human figure, including emotion, through body positions and facial expressions.

The throne room was probably the one designated by archaeologists as Room 2, as it is centrally located, is the largest of the three rooms in the building, and has the largest stone bench (throne). Upon entering this room, the viewer is met with a painting of a single, large battle scene. On the back wall, Yahaw Chan Muwan leads his army into battle against the advancing charge of warriors shown on the adjacent east wall. Yahaw Chan Muwan strikes the enemy, and captives are taken by groups of two or three warriors, as shown on the west wall. The battle is a series of scenes that progress around the room, beginning with the advance of warriors on the east wall and culminating with the capture of men on the west wall, with some individuals shown more than once, underscoring the interpretation of a sequence of events. Yahaw Chan Muwan, along with his wife (from Yaxchilan), warriors, and various royal women, receives the war captives in a scene on the north wall of the room (Miller 1999a, figure 153). A row of captives, wearing only loincloths, sit on the stairs with blood dripping from their fingers as if either the fingernails or the last finger joints were ripped off. A dead, sprawled captive lies draped on the stairs with cuts on his body. At his feet on the step below, there is a decapitated head with brains extruding. A naked captive pleads with the king above.

The scene continues in another room, with the killing and dismemberment of captives and with sacrifice, notably royal Maya men piercing their penises, accompanied by musicians. All of this is shown as occurring on the steps of a temple (Miller 1999a, figure 152). Smaller scenes on the ceiling show Maya women piercing their tongues on the throne, along with a child whose hand is held out for piercing (Miller 1999a, figure 154). Another scene depicts deformed musicians.

Another room shows several Maya lords paying tribute in the form of a bundle, identified by accompanying hieroglyphs as five portions of 8,000 cacao beans. The north wall over the doorway shows three lords preparing to dance wearing jaguar pelts, quetzal feathers, and boa constrictors. The dance is shown on the south wall. The skill of the Maya artists is underscored by the depiction of musicians in the panel below the dancers. By showing a drummer's hands blurred as if drumming and by changing positions of the maracas players' hands in subsequent frames, the artist visually captures the sense of sound and motion, respectively. Mary Miller (1999a, 174) points out that the Maya painters were precocious in showing frame-by-frame action, which was not shown in other Western art until the late nineteenth century with early photography.

In 1976, Maya murals were discovered at Caxcatla in central Mexico that stylistically are quite similar to the murals at Bonampak, but the presence of these murals well outside the Maya area is perplexing (for photos of the Caxcatla, see Ruggles 2003). A Maya scene is depicted along the sides of the central staircase of the red temple, featuring the Merchant God (god L) and several other Maya gods walking along a stream of water. The Merchant God is shown wearing his typical jaguar-skin clothing, with his backpack of trade goods (Miller 1999a, figure 155). Other murals at Caxcatla show scenes of battle and sacrifice, as at Bonampak. The battle is thought by some to be between central Mexican and Maya warriors, showing the defeat of the Maya (Miller 1999a, figure 156), but Ferguson and Adams (2001, 55) disagree. They contend that the battle is between two mercenary groups formerly associated with Teotihuacan. Another scene shows Maya lords in jaguar and bird clothing guarding a sacred mountain, known to the Maya by the word *witz* (Miller 1999a, figures 157 and 158).

Naj Tunich Cave Paintings

Some 100 paintings adorning the walls of Naj Tunich cave were painted over no more than 80 years ending at A.D. 771. Investigated by Andrea Stone (1995), these black line drawings of Maya figures and glyphs show many separate scenes, including the ball game and erotic images.

Chichen Itza Mural Painting

Paintings on all four walls of the inner room of the Temple of the Jaguars at Chichen Itza include the sun god and the Maize God on one wall (Miller 1999, figure 161) and scenes of warfare, where captives are killed on the battlefield instead of being taken alive for their sacrifice as in the Bonampak murals. The Chichen Itza murals are difficult to interpret historically, as they feature repeated representations of the Maize God and sun god instead of historical personages typical of the Bonampak murals.

Late Postclassic Murals

Wall paintings in buildings at Late Postclassic sites along the eastern coast of the Yucatan include murals at Tulum, Tancah, and other sites in Quintana Roo, Mexico, as well as at Santa Rita Corozal in northern Belize. Paintings in two structures at Tulum show the Maya cosmos from the sky to the sea, representing the heavens to the underworld, with various Maya gods approaching Maya lords in between. The scenes have a dark background, which emphasizes the figures.

SCULPTURE

The ancient Maya were masters of stone carvings, using them to adorn buildings, as separate monuments, and, of course, as stelae. The giant stuccoed and painted masks on the exteriors of temples underscore the decorative tradition of painting that characterized the Classic period. By the Postclassic, in Puuc and Chenes architecture, the decorative tradition of carving was shown in the elaborate roof combs, carved stones forming building façades, and tenon heads protruding from the façades. Chichen Itza shows giant serpents on buildings.

Although a few stelae are known from the Late Preclassic, it is the giant painted stucco masks that adorn the exteriors of temples from that period, usually on either side of the central outset staircase, that were a prominent feature of the emerging elite and the architectural display of their claim to power

Copan's Stela H (Courtesy B. Somers)

and authority. At Cerros, Uaxactun, Tikal, Lamanai, and elsewhere, these giant masks of the sun god aligned the Late Preclassic rulers with the gods.

Classic period sculpture focused on the divine authority of the Maya kings and queens; their battles won; enemies captured, tortured, and sacrificed; and the hierarchy of power and authority of the royal Maya shown in tribute payments and other presentations to them. Stelae record the histories of Maya kings and queens and identify their divine power and authority. It is the kings and queens who are displayed pictorially and naturalistically on stelae and other carved stone monuments instead of the gods displayed on Late Preclassic temples. With an image of the Maya king or queen on one side of the stela, hieroglyphs recount important personal and public events in his or her life. These include birth, marriage, and death, as well as cities conquered and annexed. Royal ancestry, including parentage, is usually detailed.

The stone carvings on buildings at Yaxchilan in particular include images of royal Maya engaged in rituals associated with accession to the throne and other important events. Shamanistic transformation into gods is induced by bloodletting. One image shows a kneeling royal woman pulling a thorn-covered rope through her tongue, with blood dripping onto paper and the smoke rising as a snake to conjure the vision serpent (Miller 1999b, figures 103 and 104).

Other stone carvings, such as those at Piedras Negras (Miller 1999, figure 97), focus on battles, the capture of enemies, the later sacrifice of captives at temples, and other signs of submission, humiliation, and royal power. Perhaps none is surpassed in grisly imagery than the carvings of decapitated human heads at Chichen Itza.

Regional stylistic differences in stone carving are evident when one compares sculptures from Copan, Tikal, and Palenque. The round sculptures of Copan, the detailed high-relief stone carvings on building façades at Palenque, and the dynastic records on stelae and altars at Tikal underscore separate regional traditions (Ferguson and Adams 2001, 92, 100, 106–108).

PAPER BOOKS

The Classic Maya were literate and wrote extensively. Researchers are taunted with the meager material evidence, including disintegrating fragments of Maya codices from Altun Ha and Copan. Vivid naturalistic images of scribes writing on paper are depicted on Late Classic Maya vases (Coe and Kerr 1998; Reents-Budet 2001). The books were written on paper made from the bark of the fig tree (*Ficus cotinifolia*). The text and images were mainly in black and red paint, with other colors used occasionally, including blue. The pages were fanfolded like an accordion to form books.

Four codices survived destruction by Spanish priests, notably the horrific book burning in 1562 in the town of Mani in the Yucatan, hosted by Diego de Landa. The Spanish Inquisitors, who regarded his actions as excessive, subsequently recalled him to Spain, but this is small recompense for the loss of information contained in the Maya books. De Landa's account of the Maya way of life, written to vindicate himself and show how terrible or heathen the Maya were (Tozzer 1941), remains a lasting and most important document of the contact period Maya and is widely cited by archaeologists.

The four codices contain religious, astronomical, and calendrical information and were written in the Postclassic period. Three of the codices were discovered in Europe during colonial times, and the last found in Chiapas, Mexico, in the mid-twentieth century. A variety of publications in print and on the Internet are available that include copies of the codices. Images of the Paris

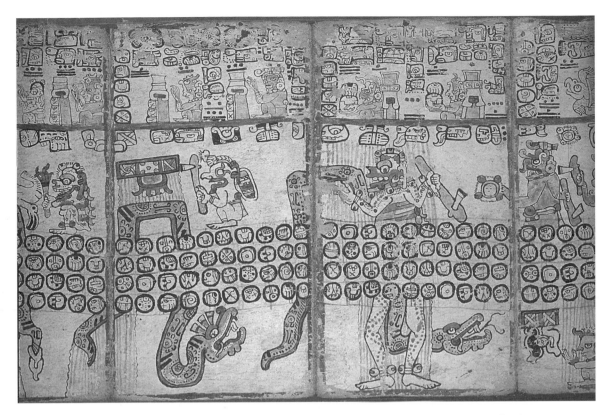

Detail of serpents and figures on the Madrid Codex, one of four known postclassic Maya books (Artephot/Corbis Sygma)

Codex are available in print (Anders 1968; Love 1994; Willard 1933) and on the Internet (Mann 2003). Images of the Dresden Codex are available in print (Förstemann 1906) and on the Internet (Burger 2001). The Madrid Codex is available in print (Anders 1967) and on the Internet (Vail 2002). The Grolier Codex was first published in print by Michael Coe (1973) as part of an exhibit of painted pottery vessels at the Grolier Club in New York City. The same images of the Grolier Codex are available on the Internet (Kerr 2003b). Images of the four codices are also available on the Internet at the Foundation for the Advancement of Mesoamerican Studies (FAMSI) website (Marhenke 2003). The FAMSI images include digital images of the Paris Codex from the original in the National Library in Paris, digital images of the Dresden Codex from Förstemann's (1906) publication, digital images of the Madrid Codex compiled from Brasseur de Bourbourg's (1869–1870) and de Rosny's (1883) publications, and digital images of the Grolier Codex by Justin Kerr (2003), which were also in Coe's (1973) publication.

METALWORK: GOLD AND COPPER

The virtual lack of gold among the sixteenth-century Maya was a great disappointment to the Spaniards, who financed their personal wealth, their voyages of exploration and conquest, and the European wars from Native American gold. Apart from an object of gold and copper alloy from Classic-period Altun Ha, metalwork was a Postclassic import to the Maya area. Small amounts of gold were imported to a few Maya communities from lower Central America during Postclassic times. Copper objects also were imported, but from closer sources in Honduras and western Mexico, and these have been recovered in greater frequency at Postclassic Maya communities. Edward Thompson dredged the finest examples of Maya gold and copper objects from the Cenote of Sacrifice at Chichen Itza in the early part of the twentieth century (Coggins and Shane 1984).

Gold was hammered into sheets that once covered wooden boxes or other objects, as traces of gold foil from a Wild Cane Cay burial suggest (McKillop 2004). In some cases, the gold sheet was impressed with a decoration, as at Chichen Itza. Copper bells and rings have been recovered from Chichen Itza and Wild Cane Cay. Their stylistic similarities suggest that they were obtained along the coastal Caribbean trade route via Wild Cane Cay.

WOODEN ARTIFACTS

Wood does not normally preserve in the tropical setting of Maya sites. A few wooden objects have been preserved in unusual settings, including dry caves of Belize and the waterlogged mud at the bottom of the Cenote of Sacrifice at Chichen Itza (Coggins 1992; Coggins and Shane 1984; Miller 1999b). Wooden lintels have been preserved in temple rooms at Tikal, including some that were elaborately carved. Most wooden objects, both in terms of variety and abundance, were recovered from the Cenote of Sacrifice at Chichen Itza. Items in the inventory include spears, arrow shafts, scepters, idols, buttons, batons, backs for mirrors, beads, spindle whorls, boxes, tubes, and disks. Jennifer Taschek (1981) describes twenty-one small wooden objects, including ear flares, rings, beads, and a spindle whorl, from the Cenote Xlacah at Dzibilchaltun.

A variety of wooden weapons have been recovered in caves and cenotes. David Pendergast (1974) recovered a sharpened wooden spear made from Sapodilla wood (*Achras zapote*) from Actun Polbiche, a dry cave in Belize. Sharpened wooden spears also were found in the Cenote of Sacrifice at Chichen Itza (Coggins and Ladd 1992, figures 8.26–8.29). Several wooden atlatls, spear throwers for launching spears, also were found in the Cenote (Coggins and Ladd 1992, figures 8.14–8.24). Thin shaft pieces from the same Cenote were interpreted as arrow or dart shaft fragments (Coggins and Ladd 1992, figure 8.30). A stone axe hafted at right angles to one end of a wooden handle made from custard apple wood (*Annona*) from a waterlogged field on Albion Island in northern Belize (Shafer and Hester 1990, figure 9.1) shows stone axes were actually used as axes, instead of being hand held. A chert biface hafted to a carved wooden handle in the shape of a snake was recovered from the Cenote of Sacrifice at Chichen Itza (Coggins and Ladd 1992, figure 8.37). The Chichen biface was inserted into a groove at one end of the handle, with the sharpened end point in the same direction, in contrast to the orientation of the Albion Island tool. Perhaps the Albion Island tool was an axe used in land clearing, whereas the Chichen Itza object was used as a spear.

Scepters, decorated sticks of ceremonial office carried in one hand by the dynastic kings of the Classic period, are depicted on carved stone monuments and on painted pottery vessels with scenes of royal court activities. Several wooden scepters were found in the Cenote of Sacrifice at Chichen Itza (Coggins and Ladd 1992, figures 8.40–8.45). One scepter in particular resembles Classic period scepters with a kneeling human figure carved at the top of the wand (Coggins and Ladd 1992, figure 8.45). Several other scepters each has a carved rendition of a diving figure (Coggins and Ladd 1992, figures 8.47–8.49), similar to the "diving gods" of unknown meaning depicted on Postclassic murals at Tulum and elsewhere, including a stone carving from Moho Cay, Belize.

A variety of other wooden objects have been found in caves and cenotes. David Pendergast (1974) recovered a rectangular wooden box with a fitted lid from Actun Polbiche cave in Belize. The Madrid Codex includes images of gods carving wooden idols similar to small wooden figures, less than 20 cm in height, from the Cenote of Sacrifice at Chichen Itza (Coggins and Ladd 1992, figures 8.49–8.64). The figures have traces of stucco, paint, and copal incense. Pine (*Pinus caribaea*) wood was used to make at least two of the figures. Ornately carved earplugs, including some with images of human figures, also were recovered from the Cenote of Sacrifice at Chichen Itza (Coggins and Ladd 1992, figures 8.1–8.13). Also recovered from the Cenote is a realistic carving of a human phallus with one of the testicles carved in the shape of a bird, perhaps a Maya pun on their word for testicle (he), also the word for egg (Coggins and Ladd 1992, figure 8.79). Coggins and Ladd (1992, 305) report pottery phalli used as vessel supports in Belize and Honduras, but some are just cylindrical supports used to hold pots over fires to boil brine or seawater to make salt (McKillop 2002, figures 3.10–3.18).

BONE AND SHELL ARTIFACTS

With an animal's fleshy parts often contributing to a Maya meal, the remaining bones or and shells were carved into tools and other objects for everyday use and rituals, often appearing in caches and burials and often far from their places of origin. A carved feline mandible from a burial at Lamanai has glyphs and Maya numbers (Pendergast 1981, figure 25). Even unaltered bone and shell were used in rituals or as offerings, with the stingray spine being the most notable example. With its jagged and sharp "teeth" along both sides of the spine, and with the teeth directed away from the tip of the spine, the living stingray embeds the spine into its target and is difficult to remove. So frequently depicted in Maya art on Late Classic painted pots, on carved monuments, and painted murals, stingray spines also were featured in Maya burials and offerings. At Moho Cay, a Late Classic burial included two stingray spines along with three obsidian blades, ritually equivalent sacrificial implements (McKillop 2004; McKillop 2005).

Other marine resources carved or used without modification included manatee rib bones, coral rock, and pumice, as well as a variety of seashells, notably *Spondylus americanus, Turbinella angulata, Strombus gigas, Melongena melongena,* and *Olivella* sp. shells (Andrews 1969; Cobos 1989; McKillop 1996b; McKillop 2004; McKillop 2005; McKillop and Winemiller 2004). The association of the sea with the Maya underworld did not go unnoticed in the selection of marine resources for rituals, offerings, and use as grave offerings. Certainly the value of any marine resource at a city distant from the sea would have been enhanced by its "exotic" origin. Manatee ribs, which are solid and quite large, were carved into figurines and boat models at Altun Ha (Pendergast 1979) and Moho Cay (McKillop 1984; McKillop 1985; McKillop 2004), as well as being deposited without modification in ritual deposits at inland sites, such as San Jose, Belize (Thompson 1939). *Spondylus* shells, perhaps owing to their bright red color (Pendergast and Graham 1998), were used in offerings and as grave goods without further modification, but they also were carved into bead necklaces as at Santa Rita Corozal. Maya musicians used the large *Turbinella* conch shells as trumpets (Moholy-Nagy and Ladd 1992, figure 5.35). At Wild Cane Cay, *Strombus* and *Melongena* conch shells were carved into shell disks, perhaps worn as ornaments; these were also found in burials at Wild Cane Cay (McKillop 2005) and elsewhere. The small *Olivella* shells were perforated and sometimes carved with happy faces (McKillop 1987) for use as clothing ornaments.

Marine resources were used in everyday life as well. At coastal communities in particular, the lip of large *Strombus* conch shells was modified into oval scraping tools, as at Moho Cay (McKillop 1984). Pumice is ubiquitous along the Caribbean littoral and the offshore cays. It was transported from the volcanic highlands of Guatemala, down the Motagua River to the sea, and carried in the sea by northerly coastal currents. Pieces of this pumice were modified by piercing a hole in the center for use as a float in fishing (McKillop 1984). Coral was the building block for stone houses at some coastal communities in the Port Honduras of southern Belize (McKillop 1996b; McKillop 2005; McKillop et al. 2004).

Human and mammal bones also were carved to make utilitarian implements and were used as decorative objects in offerings and graves. A feline mandible was elaborately incised for ritual use at Lamanai (Pendergast 1981, figure 25). A tapir scapula found at the Cenote of Sacrifice at Chichen Itza was carved with hieroglyphs (Coggins 1992, figure 5.43). Human long bones were carved into flutes in the Belize Valley (Willey et al. 1965) and at Moho Cay (McKillop 1980). Some of the most elaborate and informative scenes of Maya canoe transport are on the incised long bones from a temple burial at Tikal (Trik 1963). The carvings on the bones depict canoes similar in shape to the boat models from Altun Ha and Moho Cay, paddled by various supernatural creatures.

FOOD ANIMALS

The extinction of more than thirty-one genera of animals in Mesoamerica at the end of the last ice age left few animals available to the ancient Maya that were suitable for domestication. Still, a wide variety of animals were available to the ancient Maya (Schlesinger 2001). The ancient Maya relied on wild and sometimes tamed animals, fish, and birds for meat. The domestic dog, as well as being companion, guard, and hunter, was perhaps the most frequently consumed domestic animal among the ancient Maya. This is not surprising when one considers that only the Muscovy duck and the stingless bee filled the complement of domestic "animals."

The Spaniards noticed the importance of honey production and trade among the Maya in the sixteenth century and, one might assume, its importance in antiquity as a sweetener for chocolate and other beverages and foods. The importance of honey to the ancient Maya is underscored when one considers that salt was in high demand, both as a biological necessity for humans as well as an acquired taste. Salt and sugar represent two of the four taste sensations recognized by humans and, importantly, sugar (or honey) can reduce somewhat the need for salt (McKillop 2002).

Although chemical studies of human bone have identified the relative contributions of various meats and plants to the diet of individual Maya (Wright and White 1996), the study of animal bones from many Maya sites provides a pattern of community-wide access to specific animals (Emery 2004; Fedick 1996; White 1999). White-tailed deer and peccary (including both the collared peccary and the white-lipped peccary) are the most common animals whose remains are at inland Maya sites. Communities located on the coast, such as Cerros, included both land and sea animals in their diet. Not surprisingly, the Maya on offshore islands, such as Wild Cane Cay and Moho Cay, focused on sea fishes and other animals, such as manatee and sea turtle, that were available in the coastal waters (Hamblin 1984; McKillop 1984; McKillop 1985; McKillop 2004; McKillop 2005).

DEATH

The zeal with which Maya archaeologists search for burials and their associated pottery vessels and other grave offerings might erroneously lead one to wonder if they are no better than grave robbers or looters in search of beautiful objects. However, Maya burials hold particular significance for understanding ancient Maya culture. Because the Maya had no separate cemeteries, but instead buried their dead on or under the floors of houses and temples, depending on the status of the deceased and his or her family and lineage, burials are associated with Maya buildings. Families defined their social standing within ancient Maya society from their ancestry, so that "keeping the dead at home" was a material reminder of one's ancestors (McAnany 1995).

Because houses of the common Maya and temples of the elite were rebuilt over time on the same spots, the burials therein, and in particular the decorative pottery vessels deposited as grave offerings, can date the buildings. In addition, the recovery of complete pottery vessels is extremely informative of the shape and complete decoration of pottery so often recovered as fragmentary potsherds and used as the building blocks of chronologies for Maya sites. Because burials are one of the few "events" recovered by Maya archaeologists, they are important for recovering information about individuals (sometimes named by hieroglyphs as with Maya royalty), trade (due to the origin of the vessels or other grave goods), diet (when food items are offered as grave goods), and even environmental change (as with inundated burials at Moho Cay indicating sea level rise since the time of the interment) (McKillop 2004). Quite apart from the grave goods, archaeologists—or, more commonly, biological anthropologists—can estimate the age, sex, and health status of a deceased from his or her skeletal remains. This information can be correlated with the grave goods to build models of ancient Maya demography, status differences by age and gender, and health and dietary profiles of various socioeconomic sectors of ancient Maya society.

From burial in a simple pit to interment within a tomb with painted walls, the manner of Maya burial reflects social standing and cultural tradition. Maya kings and queens generally were buried with elaborate ceremony within temples in the centers of cities, their deaths proclaimed, along with a record of their personal lives and public achievements, on stelae placed in the main plaza in front of the temple that became their mausoleum.

King Pacal of Palenque, who died in A.D. 683, had one of the most elaborate Classic Maya burials (Schele and Freidel 1990). Pacal was buried in an enormous carved stone sarcophagus in a room deep inside the Temple of the Inscriptions at Palenque. The burial crypt is reached by a staircase that leads from the room at the top of the temple. The staircase winds three times as one descends to the burial crypt. The exterior of the temple has nine layers, perhaps reflecting the nine layers of the Maya underworld. The existence of King Pacal's tomb was only discovered after the late Alberto Ruiz, a prominent Mexican archaeologist, noticed finger holes in a stone that formed part of the floor of the temple room of the Temple of the Inscriptions.

After lifting the stone, and after devoting four field seasons to the removal of stones that filled the stairway, archaeologists discovered Pacal's burial crypt. From the initial discovery of the staircase in 1949, the burial chamber was opened on June 13, 1952. The lid of the sarcophagus depicts Pacal on his back in a crouched position falling into the open jaws of death, with a tree, representing the tree of life, emerging from his stomach and indicating his rebirth (Miller 1999, figure 86). Pacal is dressed as the Maize God and shown being reborn as a maize plant. Depictions of his ancestors on the sides of the sarcophagus show each with a different plant, including nance or craboo (*Byrsonima crassifolia*) and avocado (*Persea americana*). The Temple of the Inscriptions was constructed both as a temple with a room at the top for rituals and as a tomb to honor King Pacal, unlike other royal burials that were either excavated into existing temple substructures or placed on the exterior and overlain with a new temple construction, as with a temple burial Tikal, for example (Trik 1963).

Although without hieroglyphs to identify him personally, the Maya king buried in the Temple of the Sun God at Altun Ha also had an elaborate burial (Pendergast 1982b). His rectangular stone tomb, constructed of cut limestone, was outset on the central staircase midway up the temple substructure. Grave goods at the site include the largest carved jade object in the Maya world, 4.4-kilogram image of the head of Kinich Ahau, the sun god.

Fighting Conch, a modest stone temple forming the eastern side of the main plaza at the trading port of Wild Cane Cay, housed at least eighteen burials in a variety of graves (McKillop 2005). In one burial, an adult male sat on a bed of charcoal within a circular stone tomb. A pottery vessel had been smashed over his head. Neither his bones nor the stone tools buried in the ashes under the charcoal were burnt. In another burial, a sandstone block tomb housed a pedestal-base carved vase in the style of Fine Orange, with the bones of two adults extruding into the rock fill outside the tomb itself, where gold foil was scattered. A young adult woman was buried on her back on the floor of a building, her hands and feet tied behind her back, in the "bound-captive" position depicted so often on Late Classic painted pots. An heirloom painted pot was placed alongside her before coral rock entombed her with the construction of a new building foundation. Perhaps she was an offering or dedication for the new building.

At Moho Cay, an island site located in the mouth of the Belize River providing port facilities for coastal and river traders during the Late Classic period, burials were in simple pits associated with houses (McKillop 2004). Jade and obsidian grave goods connect the island community with sources of the raw material to the south, along the Motagua River and in the Maya highlands, respectively (Healy, McKillop, and Walsh 1984; McKillop 2004). Stingray spines, seashells, and a leg from a brine-boiling pot for salt making point to the ritual and utilitarian importance of the sea in the lives of the ancient Maya, who equated the sea with the underworld; a transportation route; and a source of salt, fish, and other foods (McKillop 1996b). One burial at Moho Cay provided clear evidence of environmental change since the Late Classic use of the island as a trading port. The burial, with its skeletal remains and associated grave offerings, was both offshore and well below modern sea level. Consistent with the inundated deposits on the island itself, the burial was clear evidence of sea level rise. An inundated burial also was excavated from the coral rock foundation of a Late Classic building at Frenchman's Cay, Belize (McKillop et al. 2004; McKillop 2005).

Most complete pottery vessels, stone tools, jade, and other objects recovered from Maya sites are from burials or other special "events" such as dedicatory offerings. The recovery of these complete objects, the associated skeletal remains, and the remains of any burial structure from the core of the burial event are a rare occasion for Maya archaeologists, when an event is associated with a specific person and set of artifacts. The contextual study of the burial, the separate classification of artifacts by material classes, and the correlations of skeletal, artifactual, and building constructions are the building blocks for understanding Maya history. In some cases, the interment is of a historical personage, a royal Maya, whose important life events are recorded nearby on a carved and dated stela. More often, the grave is of a common Maya man, woman, or child—or sometimes a family grave—but the identity of the individual or individuals interred centuries ago is unknown.

What is known about the ancient Maya from their skeletal remains? Age, sex, and health status are estimated from many observations and measurements. A constellation of traits of the skull and hipbones, in particular, are used to estimate the age and sex of the deceased. Height, as estimated from the length of various long bones, is a measure of dietary health. A reduction in stature during the Late Classic at Tikal was used to suggest the declining health of the masses, supporting a proposed model of civil unrest (Haviland 1967). However, Marie Danforth (1999) found much variability in stature within the lowlands and only a slight Late Classic decrease, notably at Tikal. Pinpoint holes in the eye orbits and on the skull indicate anemia. X-rays of long bones reveal horizontal "growth arrest" lines called Harris lines, and, together with other skeletal and dental markers of dietary or health stress, such as horizontal bars on the front teeth called dental hypoplasias, these build a picture of nutritional stress in infants or children.

The supposition that corn was the mainstay of the ancient Maya diet, like that of the modern and contact-period Maya observed by the sixteenth-century Spaniards, is supported by the frequent appearance of calculus on the teeth, often very extensive. Cavities often result from a diet rich in carbohydrates, such as corn. The incidence of cavities is quite high among the ancient Maya. Similarly, tooth wear, as results from a gritty diet of corn ground on stone metates, is common among the ancient Maya. Just as studies of ancient Maya agriculture indicate that there was considerable dietary diversity related to environmental diversity and regional differences in population densities, dental studies suggest that the diet was not concentrated on corn in all places. Certainly at Wild Cane Cay, trees with edible fruits and nuts formed a considerable portion of the diet, along with a wide variety of sea fishes (McKillop 1994; McKillop 1996a). Dental study of individuals interred in a Fighting Conch mound site indicates a diet low in grit and high in calculus-forming carbohydrates (Seidemann and McKillop 2004). Palm fruits, the most common of the tree crops from Wild Cane Cay, are rich in carbohydrates and may have contributed to the high calculus but low dental wear of the teeth. Dental wear was higher at Late Classic Moho Cay, suggesting stoneground corn, which included grit from the grinding process, was common in the diet (Lund and McKillop 2003).

A variety of chemical tests, notably carbon and nitrogen isotope analyses, provide general information on the deceased person's diet during his or her life. These and other chemical tests destroy the bone but provide dietary or other information about the interred person (White et al. 2001b). Carbon isotope analysis provides a measure of the presence and importance of corn in the diet, and nitrogen isotopes measure the relative contribution of meat from animals from the sea, the land, or freshwater rivers and lakes. Carbon and nitrogen isotope analyses carried out on individual Maya complement other lines of dietary reconstruction, notably the study of ancient plant and animal remains, usually recovered from garbage heaps used by many individuals. The manatee (*Trichechus manatus*) formed a significant portion of the meat diet at Moho Cay (McKillop 1984). Lynette Norr's carbon isotope analysis of human bone from burials indicate that the diet was overwhelmingly composed of seafood, although corn has the same carbon signature (McKillop 1980). Subsequent nitrogen isotope study by Norr (Wright and White 1996) indicate that seafood was a significant part of the Moho Cay diet. In a synthesis of chemical and other studies of Maya skeletons, Wright and White (1996; see also Wright 1997) found that the Late Classic Maya did not decline in health or stature (see also Danforth 1999). Furthermore, there was no decline in quality of diet, in contrast to models of the Classic Maya collapse correlating it with ecological collapse as would be indicated by declining nutrition.

Oxygen isotope analysis of human bone, along with oxygen isotope study of water, indicates the place where a dead person had lived during his or her youth. From such analyses, an individual buried at Altun Ha with grave offerings from Teotihuacan in central Mexico was found to be a Maya who grew up at Altun Ha, instead of being a foreign trader or diplomat (White et al. 2001b). Oxygen isotope analyses of individuals from the Maya highland city of Kaminaljuyu by Christine White and colleagues (2000) were identified as local Maya, except for one person who spent his youth at Teotihuacan. Another oxygen isotope study by Lori Wright (Valdes and Wright 2004) found no evidence of Kaminaljuyu people originating at or living at Teotihuacan. As with the Altun Ha study, the Kaminaljuyu isotope studies indicated that although the city may have been conquered by Teotihuacan so that city could control nearby obsidian and cacao, at least the royal dynasty remained in local hands (White et al. 2000). Oxygen isotope analysis of skeletal and dental remains of Kax Kuk Mo, Copan's founding ruler, indicate he may have come from the central Peten (Buikstra et al. 2004).

The ancient Maya practiced several body modification techniques, some painful, that evidently were status markers. The pointed heads of royal and other high-status Maya depicted on painted pots and carved monuments also are found in skeletal remains. The heads were shaped in infancy by pressing flat sufaces against the skull to elongate the skull with a sloped forehead. A cross-eyed appearance also was highly esteemed, as one can observe in pictorial depictions. Pictures, as well as earrings, indicate that the Maya pierced their ears, often with the ear "plug" being of considerable diameter. Some Maya endured considerable pain when their teeth were filed or when holes were drilled in their teeth to place jade or other inlays. Teeth were filed in a variety of styles, such as pointed teeth, as with an individual from Fighting Conch at Wild Cane Cay (McKillop 2005), or other patterns of side and corner notching.

Recent advances in DNA research have enhanced modern understanding of genetic relationships within and among ancient Maya communities (Whittington and Reed 1997). In addition to DNA studies indicating the manner of original settlement of the Maya area (Gonzalez-Oliver et al. 2001), DNA studies, along with oxygen isotope studies, hold promise for distinguishing local Maya from foreigners. Such chemical analyses complement observations of genetic relationships among individuals from their skeletal remains. Michael Spence (1987), for example, noted a number of dental traits that are inherited but have no apparent impact on one's health or lifestyle, including Caribelli's cusp, an extra cusp on a molar tooth. With all of the information available from Maya skeletal remains, it is perhaps surprising that until the 1980s few studies were carried out. Certainly the future is promising for Maya skeletal studies and their contribution to researchers' knowledge of ancient diet, health, and demography, and to addressing larger questions such as the Classic Maya collapse.

REFERENCES

Abrams, Elliot. 1994. *How the Maya Built Their World.* Austin: University of Texas Press.

Adams, Richard E. W. 1971. *The Ceramics of Altar de Sacrificios.* Papers of the Peabody Museum of Archaeology and Ethnology, vol. 63, no. 1. Cambridge, MA: Harvard University.

———. 1999. *Río Azul: An Ancient Maya City.* Norman: University of Oklahoma Press.

Anders, F., ed. 1967. *Codex Tro-Cortesianus (Codex Madrid) Museo de América, Madrid.* Graz, Austria: Akademische Druck und Verlagsanstalt.

———. 1968. *Codex Peresianus (Codex Paris) Bibliothèque National, Paris.* Graz, Austria: Akademische Druck und Verlagsanstalt.

Anderson, Bryan. 1997. "Ka'o'ob: The Metates of Chichen Izta within the Context of the Greater Maya Realm." Unpublished Master's thesis, Department of Geography and Anthropology, Louisiana State University, Baton Rouge.

Andrews, Anthony P. 1983. *Maya Salt Production and Trade.* Tucson: University of Arizona Press.

Andrews, E. Wyllys, IV. 1969. *The Archaeological Use and Distribution of Mollusca in the Maya Lowlands.* Middle American Research Institute, Publication 34. New Orleans: Tulane University.

Brady, James E., Joseph W. Ball, Ronald L. Bishop, Duncan C. Pring, Norman Hammond, and Rupert A. Housley. 1998. "The Lowland Maya 'Protoclassic:' A Reconsideration of its Nature and Significance." *Ancient Mesoamerica* 9 (1): 17–38.

Brasseur de Bourbourg, Etienne C. 1869–1870. *Manuscrit Troano.* Paris: Imprimerie Imperiale.

Braswell, Geoffrey E., ed. 2003. *The Maya and Teotihuacan: Reinterpreting Early Classic Interaction.* Austin: University of Texas Press.

Buikstra, Jane E., T. Douglas Price, Lori E. Wright, and James E. Burton. 2004. "Tombs from the Copan Acropolis: A Life-History Approach." In *Understanding Early Classic Copan,* edited by Ellen E. Bell, Marcello A. Canuto, and Robert J. Sharer, 191–212. Philadelphia: University of Pennsylvania Museum of Archaeology and Anthropology.

Burger, Thomas. 2001. *Die Maya-Handschrift Codex Dresdensis.* Available at http://www.tu-dresden.de/slub/proj/maya/maya/html.

Chase, Arlen F., and Diane Z. Chase. 2001. "Ancient Maya Causeways and Site Organization at Caracol, Belize." *Ancient Mesoamerica* 12: 273–281.

Chase, Diane Z. 1990. "The Invisible Maya: Population History and Archaeology at Santa Rita Corozal." In *Precolumbian Population History in the Maya Lowlands,* edited by T. Patrick Culbert and Don S. Rice, 199–213. Albuquerque: University of New Mexico Press.

Christie, Jessica J., ed. 2003. *Maya Palaces and Elite Residences.* Austin: University of Texas Press.

Cobos, Raphael. 1989. "Shelling In: Marine Mollusca at Chichen Itza," In *Coastal Maya Trade,* edited by Heather McKillop and Paul F. Healy, 49–58. Occasional Papers in Anthropology 8. Peterborough, Ontario: Trent University.

Cobos, Raphael, and Terance L. Winemiller. 2001. "The Late and Terminal Classic-Period Causeway Systems of Chichen Itza, Yucatan, Mexico." *Ancient Mesoamerica* 12 (2): 283–291.

Coe, Michael D. 1973. *The Maya Scribe and His World.* New York: Grolier Club.

———. 1978. *Lords of the Underworld: Masterpieces of Classic Maya Ceramics.* Princeton, NJ: Art Museum, Princeton University and Princeton University Press.

Coe, Michael D., and Justin Kerr. 1998. *The Art of the Maya Scribe.* New York: Harry N. Abrams.

Coggins, Clemency C., ed. 1992. *Artifacts from the Cenote of Sacrifice, Chichen Itza, Yucatan.* Memoirs of the Peabody Museum of Archaeology and Ethnology, vol. 10, no. 3. Cambridge, MA: Harvard University.

Coggins, Clemency C., and John M. Ladd. 1992. "Wooden Artifacts." In *Artifacts from the Cenote of Sacrifice, Chichen Itza, Yucatan,* edited by Clemency C. Coggins, 235–344. Memoirs of the Peabody Museum of Archaeology and Ethnology, vol. 10, no. 3. Cambridge, MA: Harvard University.

Coggins, Clemency, and Orrin C. Shane III, eds. 1984. *Cenote of Sacrifice: Maya Treasures from the Sacred Well at Chichen Itza.* Austin: University of Texas Press.

Culbert, T. Patrick. 1993. *The Ceramics of Tikal.* Philadelphia: University of Pennsylvania Museum.

———, ed. 1991. *Classic Maya Political History: Hieroglyphic and Archaeological Evidence.* New York: Cambridge University Press.

Danforth, Marie. 1999. "Coming up Short: Stature and Nutrition among the Ancient Maya of the Southern Lowlands." In *Reconstructing Ancient Maya Diet,* edited by Christine White, 103–117. Salt Lake City: University of Utah Press.

Dull, Robert A., John R. Southon, and Payson Sheets. 2001. "Volcanism, Ecology, and Culture: A Reassessment of the Volcán Ilopango TBJ Eruption in the Southern Maya Realm." *Latin American Antiquity* 12 (1): 25–44.

Emery, Kitty, ed. 2004. *Maya Zooarchaeology.* Los Angeles: Costen Institute of Archaeology, University of California.

Ensor, Bradley, and Heather McKillop. 2003. "Morphological and Technological Suitability of Maya Pottery from Wild Cane Cay, Belize." In *New Horizons for Ancient Maya Ceramics,* edited by Heather McKillop and Shirley Mock. Unpublished book manuscript.

Fash, William. 2001. *Scribes, Warriors, and Kings,* 2d ed. New York: Thames & Hudson.

Fedick, Scott, ed. 1996. *The Managed Mosaic.* Salt Lake City: University of Utah Press.

Feldman, Lawrence. 1974. "Shells from Afar: 'Panamic' Mollusca in Maya Sites." In *Mesoamerican Archaeology: New Approaches,* edited by Norman Hammond, 129–134. Austin: University of Texas Press.

Ferguson, William M., and Richard E. W. Adams. 2001. *Mesoamerica's Ancient Cities,* rev. ed. Albuquerque: University of New Mexico Press.

Foias, Antonia E., and Ronald L. Bishop. 1997. "Changing Ceramic Production and Exchange in the Petexbatun Region, Guatemala: Reconsidering the Classic Maya Collapse." *Ancient Mesoamerica* 8: 275–291.

Ford, Anabel. 1986. *Population Growth and Social Complexity: An Examination of Settlement and Environment in the Central Maya Lowlands.* Anthropological Research Paper 35. Tempe: Arizona State University.

Ford, Anabel, and W. I. Rose. 1995. "Volcanic Ash in Ancient Maya Ceramics of the Limestone Lowlands: Implications for Prehistoric Volcanic Activity in the Guatemalan Highlands." *Journal of Volcanology and Geothermal Research* 66: 149–162.

Förstemann, Ernst W. 1906. *Commentary on the Maya Manuscript in the Royal Public Library of Dresden.* Papers of the Peabody Museum, vol. 4, no. 2, 49–266. Cambridge, MA: Harvard University.

Freidel, David A. 1979. "Culture Areas and Interaction Spheres: Contrasting Approaches to the Emergence of Civilization in the Maya Lowlands." *American Antiquity* 44: 36–54.

Garber, James F., ed. 2004. *The Ancient Maya of the Belize Valley: Half a Century of Archaeological Research.* Gainesville: University Press of Florida.

Gifford, James C. 1976. *Prehistoric Pottery Analysis and the Ceramics of Barton Ramie in the Belize Valley.* Papers of the Peabody Museum of Archaeology and Ethnology, vol. 18. Cambridge, MA: Harvard University.

Gonzalez-Olivier, Angelica, Lourdes Marquez-Mofin, Jose C. Jiminez, and Alfonso Torre-Blanco. 2001. "Founding Amerindian Mitochondrial DNA Lineages in Ancient Maya from Xcaret, Quintana Roo." *American Journal of Physical Anthropology* 116: 230–235.

Graham, Elizabeth. 1987. "Resource Diversity in Belize and Its Implications for Models of Lowland Trade." *American Antiquity* 52 (4): 753–767.

———. 1989. "Brief Synthesis of Coastal Site Data from Colson Point, Placencia, and Marco Gonzalez, Belize." In *Coastal Maya Trade,* edited by Heather McKillop and Paul F. Healy, 135–154. Occasional Papers in Anthropology 8. Peterborough, Ontario: Trent University.

———. 1994. *The Highlands of the Lowlands: Environment and Archaeology in the Stann Creek District, Belize, Central America.* Monographs in World Archaeology 19. Madison, WI: Prehistory Press.

Hall, Grant D., Stanley M. Tarka Jr., W. Jeffrey Hurst, David Stuart, and Richard E. W. Adams. 1990. "Cacao Residues in Ancient Maya Vessels from Rio Azul, Guatemala." *American Antiquity* 55 (1): 138–143.

Hamblin, Nancy. 1984. *Animal Use by the Cozumel Maya.* Tucson: University of Arizona Press.

Hammond, Norman. 1972. "Obsidian Trade Routes in the Mayan Area." *Science* 178: 1092–1093.

———. 1975. *Lubaantun: A Classic Maya Realm.* Peabody Museum of Archaeology and Ethnology Monograph, vol. 2. Cambridge, MA: Harvard University.

Hammond, Norman, Arnold Aspinall, Stuart Feather, John Hazelden, Trevor Gazard, and Stuart Agrell. 1977. "Maya Jade: Source Location and Analysis." In *Exchange Systems in Prehistory,* edited by Timothy K. Earle and Jonathon E. Ericson, 35–67. New York: Academic Press.

Harrison, Peter D. 1999. *The Lords of Tikal.* New York: Thames & Hudson.

Haviland, William A. 1967. "Stature at Tikal, Guatemala: Implications for Ancient Maya Demography and Social Organization." *American Antiquity* 32: 117–125.

Healy, Paul F., Heather I. McKillop, and Bernetta Walsh. 1984. "Analysis of Obsidian from Moho Cay, Belize: New Evidence on Classic Maya Trade Routes." *Science* 225: 414–417.

Hester, Thomas R., and Harry J. Shafer, eds. 1991. *Maya Stone Tools.* Monographs in World Archaeology No. 1. Madison, WI: Prehistory Press.

Hill, Robert, and John Monaghen. 1978. *The Traditional Pottery of Guatemala.* Austin: University of Texas Press.

Hixson, David. 2001. *Mesoamerican Photo Archives.* Available at http://www.mesoamerican-archives.com (accessed February 27, 2004).

Inomata, Takeshi, and Stephen D. Houston, eds. 2001. *Royal Courts of the Ancient Maya.* Boulder, CO: Westview.

Kerr, Justin. 2003. *The Grolier Codex.* http://www.mayavase.com/grol/grolier.html

———, ed. 1989–1994. *The Maya Vase Book.* 4 vols. New York: Kerr Associates. http://www.famsi.org/research/kerr and http://www.mayavase.com.

Kidder, Alfred V., Jessie D. Jennings, and Edwin M. Shook. 1946. *Excavations at Kaminaljuyu, Guatemala.* Carnegie Institution of Washington Publication 561. Washington, DC: Carnegie Institution of Washington.

Kosakowsky, Laura J. 1987. *Preclassic Maya Pottery at Cuello, Belize.* Anthropological Papers of the University of Arizona 47. Tucson: University of Arizona Press.

Kowalski, Jeff. 2003. "Evidence for the Functions and Meanings of Some Northern Maya Palaces." In *Maya Palaces and Elite Residences,* edited by Jessica Joyce Christie, 204–252. Austin: University of Texas Press.

Lange, Frederick W. 1971. "Marine Resources: A Viable Subsistence Alternative for the Prehistoric Lowland Maya." *American Anthropologist* 73: 619–639.

LeCount, Lisa J. 1999. "Polychrome Pottery and Political Strategies in Late and Terminal Classic Lowland Maya Society." *Latin American Antiquity* 10 (3): 239–258.

Leventhal, Richard M. 1990. "Southern Belize: An Ancient Maya Region." In *Vision and Revision in Maya Studies,* edited by Flora S. Clancey and Peter D. Harrison, 125–141. Albuquerque: University of New Mexico Press.

Lewenstein, Suzanne. 1987. "Mesoamerican Obsidian Blades: An Experimental Approach to Function." *Journal of Field Archaeology* 8: 175–188.

Love, Bruce. 1994. *The Paris Codex: Handbook for a Priest.* Austin: University of Texas Press.

Lund, Erin, and Heather McKillop. 2003. Maya Burials from Moho Cay, Belize. Paper presented at the Southern Anthropological Association meeting, Baton Rouge, LA, February.

Mann, Tom. 2003. *The Paris Codex.* Available at http://digital.library.northwestern.edu/codex.

Marhenke, Randa. 2003. *The Ancient Maya Codices.* Available at http://www.famsi.org/mayawriting/codices/.

Marsden, Anne-Michelle, and Eric Leupold. 2001. *The Living Maya.* CD. Punta Gorda, Belize: Maya Viewkeeper.

Martin, Simon, and Nicholai Grube. 2000. *Chronicle of the Maya Kings and Queens: Deciphering the Dynasties of the Ancient Maya.* New York: Thames & Hudson.

McAnany, Patricia A. 1989. "Stone-Tool Production and Exchange in the Eastern Maya Lowlands: The Consumer Perspective from Pulltrouser Swamp." *American Antiquity* 54: 332–346.

———. 1995. *Living with the Ancestors.* Austin: University of Texas Press.

McKillop, Heather. 1980. "Moho Cay, Belize. Preliminary Investigations of Trade, Settlement, and Marine Resource Exploitation." Master's thesis, Department of Anthropology, Trent University, Peterborough; Ann Arbor, MI: University Microfilms.

———. 1984. "Prehistoric Maya Reliance on Marine Resources: Analysis of a Midden from Moho Cay, Belize." *Journal of Field Archaeology* 11: 25–35.

———. 1985. "Prehistoric Exploitation of the Manatee in the Maya and Circum-Caribbean Areas." *World Archaeology* 16: 337–353.

———. 1987. "Wild Cane Cay: An Insular Classic Period to Postclassic Period Maya Trading Station." Ph.D. dissertation, Department of Anthropology, University of California, Santa Barbara. Ann Arbor, MI: University Microfilms.

———. 1994. "Ancient Maya Tree Cropping: A Viable Subsistence Adaptation for the Island Maya." *Ancient Mesoamerica* 5: 129–140.

———. 1995. "The 1994 Field Season in South-Coastal Belize." *LSU Maya Archaeology News* 1, Department of Geography and Anthropology, Louisiana State University, Baton Rouge. http://www.ga.lsu.edu/ArchaeologyNews95.htm/.

———. 1996a. "Prehistoric Maya Use of Native Palms." In *The Managed Mosaic: Ancient Maya Agriculture and Resource Use,* edited by Scott L. Fedick, 278–294. Salt Lake City: University of Utah Press.

———. 1996b. "Ancient Maya Trading Ports and the Integration of Long-Distance and Regional Economies: Wild Cane Cay in South-Coastal Belize." *Ancient Mesoamerica* 7: 49–62.

———. 1997. *Excavations in Coral Architecture at Frenchman's Cay, 1997.* LSU Maya Archaeology New 2. Baton Rouge: Department of Geography and Anthropology, Louisiana State University. Available at http://www.ga.lsu.edu/Archaeology-News97.htm.

————. 2002. *Salt: White Gold of the Ancient Maya.* Gainesville: University Press of Florida.

————. 2003. "Catastrophic and Other Environmental Factors in the Classic Maya Collapse." Paper presented at the annual meeting of the American Association of Geographers, New Orleans, March.

————.2004 "The Ancient Maya Trading Port on Moho Cay." In *The Ancient Maya of the Belize Valley: Half a Century of Archaeological Research,* edited by James F. Garber, 257–272. Gainesville: University Press of Florida.

————. 2005. *In Search of Maya Sea Traders.* College Station: University of Texas Press, in press.

McKillop, Heather, L. J. Jackson, Helen Michel, Fred Stross, and Frank Asaro. 1988. "Chemical Sources Analysis of Maya Obsidian Artifacts: New Perspectives from Wild Cane Cay, Belize." In *Archaeometry 88,* edited by R. M. Farqhuar, R. G. V. Hancock, and Larry A. Pavlish, 239–244. Department of Physics, University of Toronto.

McKillop, Heather, Aline Magnoni, Rachel Watson, Shannon Ascher, Bryan Tucker, and Terance Winemiller. 2004. "The Coral Foundations of Coastal Maya Architecture." In *Archaeological Investigations in the Eastern Maya Lowlands: Papers of the 2003 Belize Archaeology Symposium,* edited by Jaime Awe, John Morris, and Sherilyne Jones, 347–358. Research Reports in Belizean Archaeology Volume 1, Institute of Archaeology, National Institute of Culture and History (NICH), Belmopan, Belize.

McKillop, Heather, and Erika Roberts. 2003. *Nineteenth-Century Settlement of the Port Honduras Coast, Southern Belize.* Unpublished manuscript, Department of Geography and Anthropology, Louisiana State University, Baton Rouge.

McKillop, Heather, and Terance Winemiller. 2004. "Ancient Maya Environment, Settlement, and Diet: Quantitative and GIS Analysis of Shell from Frenchman's Cay." In *Maya Zooarchaeology,* edited by Kitty Emery, 57–80. Los Angeles: Costen Institute of Archaeology, University of California.

McNelly, Nancy. 1997. *Rabbit in the Moon.* http://www.halfmoon.org/.

Merwin, Raymond E., and George C. Vaillant. 1932. *The Ruins of Holmul, Guatemala.* Memoirs of the Peabody Museum, vol. 3, no. 2. Cambridge, MA: Harvard University.

Miller, Mary. 1986. *The Murals of Bonampak.* Princeton, NJ: Princeton University Press.

————. 1999a. *Maya Art and Architecture.* New York: Thames & Hudson.

————. 1999b. "Mexican Obsidian at Tikal, Guatemala." *Latin American Antiquity* 10: 300–313.

Mitchum, Beverly A. 1991. "Lithic Artifacts from Cerros, Belize: Production, Consumption, and Trade." In *Maya Stone Tools: Selected Papers from the Second Maya Lithic Conference,* edited by Thomas R. Hester and Harry J. Shafer, 45–54. Madison, WI: Prehistory Press.

Moholy-Nagy, Hattula. 1990. "The Misidentification of Mesoamerican Lithic Workshops." *Latin American Antiquity* 1: 268–279.

————. 1999. "Mexican Obsidian at Tikal, Guatemala." *Latin American Antiquity* 10: 300–313.

Moholy-Nagy, Hattula, and John M. Ladd. 1992. "Objects of Stone, Shell, and Bone." In *Artifacts from the Cenote of Sacrifice, Chichen Itza, Yucatan,* edited by Clemency C. Coggins, 99–152. Memoirs of the Peabody Museum of Archaeology and Ethnology, vol. 10, no. 3. Cambridge, MA: Harvard University.

Neff, Hector. 1989. "The Effect of Interregional Distribution on Plumbate Pottery Production." In *Ancient Trade and Tribute: Economics of the Soconusco Region of Mesoamerica,* edited by Barbara Voorhies, 249–267. Salt Lake City: University of Utah Press.

Nelson, Fred W. 1985. "Summary of the Results of Analysis of Obsidian Artifacts from the Maya Lowlands." *Scanning Electron Microscopy* 2: 631–649.

Pendergast, David M. 1974. *Excavations at Actun Polbilche, Belize.* Archaeology Monograph 1. Toronto: Royal Ontario Museum.

———. 1982a. "Ancient Maya Mercury." *Science* 217: 533–535.

———. 1982b. *Excavations at Altun Ha,* vol. 2. Toronto: Royal Ontario Museum.

———. 1981. "Lamanai, Belize: Summary of Excavation Results 1974–1980." *Journal of Field Archaeology* 8: 29–53.

———. 1985. "Stability through Change: Lamanai, Belize, from the Ninth to the Seventeenth Century." In *Late Lowland Maya Civilization,* edited by Jeremy Sabloff and E. Wyllys Andrews V, 223–249. Albuquerque: University of New Mexico Press.

Pendergast, David M., and Elizabeth Graham. 1998. *What Do We Know About Lamanai?* http://www.rom.on.ca/digs/belize/what-we-know.html.

Pollock, Harry E. D., Ralph L. Roys, Tatiana Proskouriakoff, and A. Ledyard Smith. 1962. *Mayapan, Yucatan, Mexico.* Carnegie Institution of Washington Publication 619. Washington, DC: Carnegie Institution of Washington.

Proskouriakoff, Tatiana. 1963. *An Album of Maya Architecture.* Norman: University of Oklahoma Press.

Pyburn, K. Anne. 1990. "Settlement Patterns at Nohmul: Preliminary Results of Four Excavation Seasons." In *Precolumbian Population History in the Maya Lowlands,* edited by T. Patrick Culbert and Don S. Rice, 183–197. Albuquerque: University of New Mexico Press.

Rathje, Williams L. 1971. "The Origin and Development of Lowland Classic Maya Civilization." *American Antiquity* 36 (3): 275–285.

Reents-Budet, Dorie. 1994. *Painting the Maya Universe.* Durham, NC: Duke University Press.

———. 2001. "Classic Maya Concepts of the Royal Court: An Analysis of Renderings on Pictorial Ceramics." In *Royal Courts of the Ancient Maya,* vol. 1, edited by Takeshi Inomata and Stephen Houston, 195–233. Boulder, CO: Westview.

Reina, Ruben E., and Robert M. Hill III. 1978. *The Traditional Pottery of Guatemala.* Austin: University of Texas Press.

Rice, Prudence M. 1987a. "Economic Change in the Lowland Maya Late Classic Period." In *Specialization, Exchange, and Complex Societies,* edited by Elizabeth M. Brumfiel and Timothy K. Earle, 76–85. New York: Cambridge University Press.

———. 1987b. *Pottery Analysis: A Source Book.* Chicago: University of Chicago Press.

Rosny, Leon de. 1883. *Codex Coretsianus.* Paris: Librairies de la Societe d'Ethnographie.

Ruggles, Clive. 2003. *Images of Sites in Mesoamerica.* Available at http://www.le.ac.uk/archaeology/rug/image_collection/hier/am/r2.html.

Sabloff, Jeremy A. 1975. *Excavations at Seibal, Guatemala, Department of the Peten, Guatemala: The Ceramics.* Memoirs of the Peabody Museum of Archaeology and Ethnology, vol. 13, no. 2. Cambridge, MA: Harvard University.

Sanders, William T. 1960. *Prehistoric Ceramics and Settlement Patterns in Quintana Roo.* Contributions to American Anthropology and History 60, Carnegie Institution of Washington Publication 606. Washington, DC: Carnegie Institution of Washington.

Saturno, William. 2003. *Proyecto San Bartolo.* http://www.sanbartolo.org/index.htm.

Schele, Linda, and David A. Freidel. 1990. *A Forest of Kings: The Untold Story of the Ancient Maya.* New York: William Morrow.

Schele, Linda, and Mary Miller. 1986. *The Blood of Kings: Dynasty and Ritual in Maya Art.* New York: George Braziller.

Schlesinger, Victoria. 2001. *Animals and Plants of the Ancient Maya.* Austin: University of Texas Press.

Seidemann, Ryan, and Heather McKillop. 2004. "Dental Indicators of Diet and Health for the Postclassic Coastal Maya on Wild Cane Cay, Belize." Unpublished manuscript.

Shafer, Harry J., and Thomas R. Hester. 1983. "Ancient Maya Chert Workshops in Northern Belize, Central America." *American Antiquity* 48: 519–543.

———. 1990. "The Puleston Axe: A Late Preclassic Maya Hafted Tool from Northern Belize." In *Ancient Maya Wetland Agriculture,* edited by Mary Pohl, 279–294. Boulder, CO: Westview.

Sheets, Payson D. 1975. "Behavioral Analysis and the Structure of a Prehistoric Industry." *Current Anthropology* 16: 369–391.

———, ed. 2002. *Before the Volcano Erupted: The Ancient Ceren Village in Central America.* Austin: University of Texas Press.

Shepard, Anna O. 1948. *Plumbate: A Mesoamerican Trade Ware.* Carnegie Institute of Washington Publication 573. Washington, DC: Carnegie Institution of Washington.

———. 1976. *Ceramics for the Archaeologist.* Washington, DC: Carnegie Institution of Washington.

Shipley, Webster E., III, and Elizabeth Graham. 1989. "Petrographic Analysis and Preliminary Source Identification of Selected Stone Artifacts from the Maya Sites of Seibal and Uaxactun, Guatemala." *Journal of Archaeological Science* 14: 367–383.

Sidrys, Raymond V., and John Andreson. 1976. "Metate Import in Northern Belize." In *Maya Lithic Studies: Papers from the 1976 Belize Field Symposium,* edited by Thomas R. Hester and Norman Hammond, 151–176. Special Report 4. San Antonio: Center for Archaeological Research, University of Texas.

Simmons, Michael P., and Gerald F. Brem. 1979. "The Analysis and Distribution of Volcanic Ash-Tempered Pottery in the Lowland Maya Area." *American Antiquity* 44: 79–91.

Sluyter, Andrew. 1993. "Long-Distance Staple Transport in Western Mesoamerica: Insights through Quantitative Modeling." *Ancient Mesoamerica* 4: 193–199.

Smith, Robert E. 1955. *Ceramic Sequence at Uaxactun, Guatemala.* 2 vols. New Orleans: Middle American Research Institute, Tulane University.

———. 1971. *The Pottery of Mayapan.* 2 vols. Papers of the Peabody Museum of Archaeology and Ethnology, vol. 66. Cambridge, MA: Harvard University.

Spence, Michael W. 1987. "Report on the Burials of Wild Cane Cay, Belize." In *Wild Cane Cay: An Insular Classic Period to Postclassic Period Maya Trading Station,* by Heather McKillop, 282–295. University of California, Santa Barbara; University Microfilms, Ann Arbor.

Steiner, Edward P. 1994. "Prehistoric Maya Settlement along Joe Taylor Creek, Belize." Master's thesis, Department of Geography and Anthropology, Louisiana State University, Baton Rouge.

Stone, Andrea. 1995. *Images from the Underworld: Naj Tunich and the Tradition of Maya Cave Painting.* Austin: University of Texas Press.

Taschek, Jennifer. 1981. "The Non-Ceramic, Non-Chipped Stone Artifacts from Dzibilchaltun, Yucatan, Mexico." Ph.D. dissertation, Department of Anthropology, University of Wisconsin, Madison.

Thompson, J. Eric S. 1939. *Excavations at San Jose, British Honduras.* Carnegie Institution of Washington Publication 506, Washington, DC: Carnegie Institution of Washington.

Tozzer, Alfred M., trans. 1941. *Landa's Relación de las Cosas de Yucatan.* Papers of the Peabody Museum of Archaeology and Ethnology, vol. 18. Cambridge, MA: Harvard University.

Trik, Aubrey S. 1963. "The Splendid Tomb of Temple 1 at Tikal, Guatemala." *Expedition* 6: 2–18.

Vail, Gabrielle. 2002. *The Madrid Codex: A Maya Hieroglyphic Book, Version 1.0.* A website and database available online at http://madrid.doaks.org/codex/madcod.asp.

Valdes, Juan Antonio, and Lori Wright. 2004. "The Early Classic and Its Antecedents at Kaminaljuyu: A Complex Society with Complex Problems." In *Understanding Early Classic Copan,* edited by Ellen E. Bell, Marcello A. Canuto, and Robert J. Sharer, 337–355. Philadelphia: University of Pennsylvania Museum of Archaeology and Anthropology.

Voorhies, Barbara. 1982. "An Ecological Model of the Early Maya of the Central Lowlands." In *Maya Subsistence,* edited by Kent V. Flannery, 65–95. New York: Academic Press.

Wauchope, Robert. 1934. *House Mounds of Uaxactun, Guatemala.* Carnegie Institution of Washington Publication 436, Contributions to American Archaeology 7. Washington, DC: Carnegie Institution of Washington.

————. 1938. *Modern Maya Houses.* Carnegie Institution of Washington Publication 502. Washington, DC: Carnegie Institution of Washington.

White, Christine D., ed. 1999. *Reconstructing Ancient Maya Diet.* Salt Lake City: University of Utah Press.

White, Christine D., Fred J. Longstaffe, and Kimberley R. Law. 2001a. "Revisiting the Teotihuacan Connection at Altun Ha: Oxygen-Isotope Analysis of Tomb F-8/1." *Ancient Mesoamerica* 12 (1): 65–72.

White, Christine D., Fred J. Longstaffe, Michael W. Spence, and Kimberley R. Law. 2000. "Testing the Nature of Teotihuacan Imperialism at Kaminaljuyu Using Phosphate Oxygen-Isotope Ratios." *Journal of Anthropological Research* 56: 535–558.

White, Christine D., David M. Pendergast, Fred J. Longstaffe, and Kimberley R. Law. 2001b. "Social Complexity and Food Systems at Altun Ha, Belize: The Isotopic Evidence." *Latin American Antiquity* 12: 371–393.

Whittington, E. Michael, ed. 2001. *The Sport of Life and Death: The Mesoamerican Ballgame.* New York: Thames & Hudson.

Whittington, Stephen, and David Reed, eds. 1997. *Bones of the Maya.* Washtington, DC: Smithsonian Institution Press.

Willard, Theodore A. 1933. *The Codex Perez: An Ancient Mayan Hieroglyphic Book.* Glendale, CA: Arthur H. Clark.

Willey, Gordon R., ed. 1965. *Handbook of Middle American Indians,* vols. 2 and 3. Austin: University of Texas Press.

Willey, Gordon R., William R. Bullard, John B. Glass, and James C. Gifford. 1965. *Prehistoric Maya Settlement Patterns in the Belize Valley.* Papers of the Peabody Museum of Archaeology and Ethnology, vol. 54. Cambridge, MA: Harvard University.

Winemiller, Terance. 1997. "Limestone Resource Exploitation by the Ancient Maya at Chichen Itza, Yucatan, Mexico." Master's thesis, Department of Geography and Anthropology, Louisiana State University, Baton Rouge.

Wright, Lori E. 1997. "Biological Perspectives on the Collapse of the Pasion Maya." *Ancient Mesoamerica* 8: 267–273.

Wright, Lori E., and Christine D. White. 1996. "Human Biology in the Classic Maya Collapse: Evidence from Paleopathology and Paleodiet." *Journal of World Prehistory* 10: 147–198.

CHAPTER 10

Intellectual Accomplishments

The Classic Maya were a literate civilization with a complex hieroglyphic writing system, sophisticated knowledge of mathematics including the concept of zero, a complex calendar, and a deep understanding of astronomy. The counting system and calendar were deciphered during the nineteenth century. By the turn of the twenty-first century, much of the hieroglyphic writing system also had been deciphered. The ancient texts researchers have are on carved stone and painted pots, with only four paper books having been preserved from the time of European contact in the sixteenth century. The paper books that have survived pertain mainly to astronomy and ritual. As a result, until the mid-twentieth century, scholars mistakenly interpreted the Classic Maya writing and dates as being focused on astronomy.

The Classic Maya recorded historical and ritual events pertaining to Maya royalty, but with the collapse of the civilization around A.D. 900, there was no longer any need to publicly record dates and events, as the cities were abandoned and the Maya royalty disbanded. An abbreviated calendar was used by a few surviving members of the royalty at Chichen Itza and elsewhere during the Postclassic. Of course, much of the ancient Maya culture is excluded from the written records, but exciting opportunities do arise for assigning names, dates, and historical events to long-dead Maya kings and queens.

MATHEMATICS

The ancient Maya had symbols for writing virtually any whole number, including zero, but not fractions or negative numbers. Mathematically, the concept of zero is quite sophisticated and was rarely used in other ancient civilizations. In contrast to the modern Western system, which is based on multiples of ten and written left to right, their system was vigesimal, based on multiples of twenty. The position of a number in a column designated its value. Numbers were written vertically in a column, with each position increasing in value from bottom to top. The numbers 1 through 19 were in the lowest position. The next position was for multiples of 20, followed by multiples of 400 (20 × 20), and so on.

The Maya were able to create any number using just three symbols—a dot for 1, a horizontal bar for 5, and a stylized shell for 0. To write the number 19, for example, they wrote three horizontal bars with four dots arranged side by side above the uppermost bar. To write the number 20, the Maya placed the stylized shell symbol in the lowest place, designating zero, with a dot above it in the next position, denoting 20 × 1 (Coe and Van Stone 2001; Harris and Stearns 1997; Montgomery 2002a).

Maya numbers example (ABC-CLIO)

Researchers no longer believe that the ancient Maya were preoccupied with numbers and mathematics per se. Diego de Landa reported that during the sixteenth century, Maya merchants used mathematics for calculating the value of trade goods, particularly for establishing equivalences between cacao beans and other commodities (Tozzer 1941). The Dresden Codex, written during the Postclassic period, includes multiplication tables to figure out how the various Maya time cycles, with different lengths of months and years, correlated with each other, so that a calendar date could be read (Burger 2001; Förstemann 1906; Marhenke 2003; Thompson 1972).

CALENDARS

The Classic Maya used the Maya Long Count for dates on stelae and other carved monuments. The Maya Long Count differs from the Maya's regular counting system in that the third position of Maya counting (multiples of 400) was substituted with multiples of 365 to represent the 365-day year (of 18 months and 20 days, with 5 extra days). A date on a Classic period stela was read from top to bottom in five groups. The top numbers referred to the number of Baktuns (periods of 400 years or 20 × 20 × 365 days); the next group of numbers referred to the number of Katuns (periods of 20 years or 20 × 365 days); the third group referred to the number of Tuns (365-day periods or Maya years); the fourth group referred to the number of Uinals (the 20-day periods or

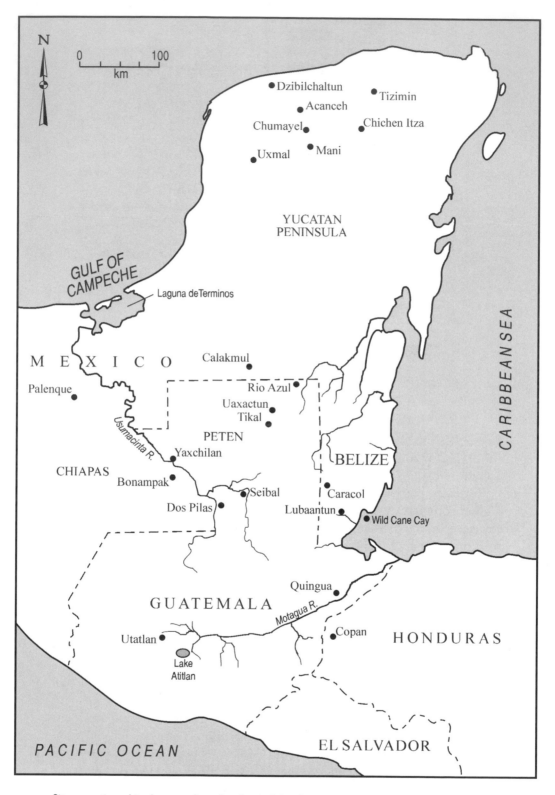

Sites mentioned in the text about intellectual developments

Maya months), and the bottom group of numbers referred to the Kins (number of days from 1–19). Adding the numbers provided the number of days, months, and years that had elapsed since the beginning of Maya time, September 8, 3114 B.C. The convention of modern researchers for writing the dates is to separate them by periods into the five sections, such as 8.9.3.4.15. The first number, that of the Baktun, designates its "cycle" as an eight-cycle date.

In addition to the Long Count, the Maya also used the Calendar Round, which was shared among many ancient cultures of Mesoamerica and long predated the Maya Long Count (Edmonson 1988). The Preclassic Maya used both the Calendar Round and the Long Count by 100 B.C. (Justeson 1989, 78–79). The Calendar Round was formed by the intersection of the sacred Tzolkin cycle of 260 days and the 365-day solar cycle (Coe and Van Stone 2001; Harris and Stearns 1997). It took fifty-two years for the same day on each cycle to co-occur (260 × 365 − 18,980 days).

The 260-day Tzolkin time cycle was the ritual count, as documented by Diego de Landa and the Postclassic Maya codices, as well as documents written in earlier times. The Tzolkin cycle was used to predict a person's destiny using his or her birth date and also to predict proper times to plant corn—an ancient "farmer's almanac." The 260-day count is still used by the Quiche Maya, who compare it with the 9-lunar-month human gestation period. In some areas, art historian and archaeoastronomer Susan Milbrath (1999, 2) points out that it also corresponds to the 9-month agricultural cycle. Maya scribes used the Tzolkin cycle to record the movements of the sun, the moon, Venus, and perhaps other celestial planets and stars as well (Love 1995; Mann 2003; Marhenke 2003; Milbrath 1999). In the Tzolkin cycle, the numbers 1–13 rotate with 20 named days (Matthews 2003a). The numbers and days can be viewed as two gears that intersect on a particular number and day, so that the same number and day repeat every 260 days. The first day of the Tzolkin cycle is 1 Imix, and the last day is 13 Ahau.

The 365-day Maya year or "Haab" cycle closely approximates the true solar year of 365.2422 days. It is often referred to as the "vague" year cycle because it includes 5 extra days at the end of its cycle of 18 named months, each with 20 numbered days (Matthews 2003a). A year in the solar vague year is one Haab. The 5 extra days, called "wayeb," were considered unlucky and were the time of preparation for extensive New Year ceremonies to ensure a successful renewal of the annual cycle. The 365-day cycle lists the day number followed by the name of the month, such as 1 Pop, 2 Pop, 3 Pop. Instead of writing 20 Pop for the last day of the month, the Maya substituted a sign foretelling the approach of the next month to accompany the number twenty. The 5 extra days were referred to as 1 Wayeb, 2 Wayeb, and so forth.

A Calendar Round date consisted of the Tzolkin date followed by the Haab date, such as 1 Kan 1 Pop. The next dates in the Calendar Round are 2 Chik'chan 2 Pop, 2 Kimi 3 Pop, and 4 Manik 4 Pop. The dates are best viewed as interlocking gears of different sizes, with each 260-day rotation bringing a new pattern of dates until the initial dates co-occur after fifty-two vague years. The Calendar Round is a time cycle that repeats the same date every fifty-two years, making it not useful for dating historical events beyond the fifty-two-year cycle. Moreover, the Calendar Round is not anchored in time, with a specific beginning date, but instead continues to cycle through the blocks of fifty-two years. In contrast, the Maya Long Count is fixed in time, with a beginning date of August 18, 3114 B.C. Using the Maya Long Count, any date, in the past or in the future, can be recorded. The Maya Long Count was useful to date the important events in the life of a Maya king or queen, as well as the dynastic history of past rulers. Recording the dynastic history of past ancestors was considered important to publicly proclaiming dynastic right to the throne. Altar Q from Copan, for example, depicts images of Yax Kuk Mo's dynastic ancestors as well as important dates in their lives.

The Calendar Round obviously did not provide enough time for recording historical events of the Classic period. In fact, some Classic period stelae refer to events before the creation of the Maya world. Dates on Classic Maya stelae were written in the Maya Long Count and expressed as the number of days, months, and years that had passed since the beginning of recorded time. The Maya developed and elaborated the Long Count used earlier by the Olmec. The earliest Long Count date is 31 B.C. on a stela from the Olmec site of Tres Zapotes, Veracruz, Mexico. Other early dates are written on the Mojarra stela with dates of A.D. 143 and 156.

Reading a Date on a Classic Maya Stela

A typical Classic period stela has an initial event dated in the Maya Long Count. This date is referred to as the Initial Series date. The Maya Long Count date begins with the Baktun and records the time elapsed since August 18, 3114 B.C. Other events described on the same stela are only given dates in the Calendar Round, not in the Maya Long Count. A Calendar Round date is not anchored in time. The Calendar Round date provides a day in its fifty-two-year cycle. The Classic rulers were interested in dating events that were longer than fifty-two years: Some rulers, such as King Pacal of Palenque, lived to over eighty years of age. Clearly, the lengthy dynastic records of kings and queens required more than fifty-two years. Calendar Round dates are tied to the Initial Series date on the stela by Distance Dates, the number of years, months, and days from the Initial Series date to each Calendar Round date. Distance Dates can count forward or backward in time from the Initial Series date. A hieroglyph denoting the forward or backward direction is affixed or suffixed to the Distance Date.

The end of dynastic rule by Maya kings and queens at the end of the Classic period meant the end to stelae with dated events about the dynastic heritage and royal achievements of kings and queens with dates in the Maya Long Count. The Classic Maya kings and queens were preoccupied with proclaiming their right to rule through their dynastic heritage, as well as publicly recording their military and other public activities in recorded time. In contrast, the Postclassic kings at Chichen Itza and elsewhere did not derive their authority through their dynastic predecessor, but instead proclaimed their divine right to rule through the sun god. Moreover, in contrast to the absolute authority of the Classic kings and queens, the power and authority of Postclassic kings was diffused by shared governance through a council of prominent city and regional leaders, as evidenced in the presence of Popol Na council houses in Postclassic Maya cities.

Postclassic kings did continue to broadcast their achievements in written records on stone monuments. However, the Postclassic Maya did not share their Classic predecessor's concern with lengthy historical records. The Postclassic Maya used the Maya Short Count, which is based on the 7,200-day rotation of Katuns. The problem with reading dates in the Short Count is that they lack the initial Baktun, so that, without other information, the date cannot be traced to the beginning of the Maya calendar: The Maya Short Count did not use Baktuns to tie a date to 3114 B.C. Nor was the Short Count anchored in time in any other way. With the regular 20-day rotation of the Uinal and 7,200-day rotation of the Katun, a Tzolkin date of Ahau marked the end of each Katun, with the accompanying number decreasing by two for each Katun in a cycle of 13 Katuns (about 256 years). Short Count dates float in time.

Time was cyclical for the ancient Maya. The cyclical nature of Maya time was writ large through the structure of the Classic Maya Long Count dates. The origin and end of calendrical time are consistent with the sequence of creation and destruction of the Maya world, as told by the Maya in colonial times in the *Popol Vuh* and as seen in Classic Maya iconography. From the beginning date of the Maya calendar on August 18, 3114 B.C., a complete cycle of 13 Baktuns will end on December 21, A.D. 2012, corresponding to the winter solstice or 13.0.0.0.0, which is 4 Ahau 3 Kankin. At that point, theoretically, the count will start at zero again. The Calendar Round defined a cycle of 52 years of 365 days each. The movements of the sun, moon, planets, and stars defined cycles recorded in astronomical tables in the four known surviving Maya codices. Astronomical data also are recorded in Classic Maya imagery on painted pots and on buildings. Many Late Classic rituals, even battles, coincided with important astronomical days as defined by the calendar, such as the Katun (twenty-year cycle) endings (Coggins 1980, 736–737). The agricultural cycle was linked to the various time cycles, to the celestial and underworld gods, and to creation itself through the reincarnation of Hun Hunahpu as the Maize God. By the time of the arrival of the Spaniards in the sixteenth century, the Maya were using a time cycle focusing on festivals that specified the rituals, ceremonies, pilgrimages, and fairs for each day of the solar year (Tozzer 1941, 151–167).

The four surviving ancient Maya codices, written in the Postclassic period, variously use the Maya Long Count, Short Count, and the Calendar Round. Some twenty-seven Long Count dates were used, albeit with quite a few errors, in the Dresden Codex to record events of astronomical significance (Burger 2001; Förstemann 1906; Marhenke 2003; Thompson 1972). The Dresden Codex may have been written around A.D. 1210. This is the most recent Long Count date in the codex and also the last known recorded Maya Long Count date (Milbrath 1999, 7). Calendar Round dates were accurately used to record the movements of the planet Venus in the Dresden Codex. The Long Count was not used in the Madrid Codex, which dates to between A.D. 1350 and 1450 (Anders 1967; Marhenke 2003; Vail 2002). The Maya Short Count was used in the Paris Codex, which likely dates to about A.D. 1450 (Love 1994; Love 1995; Mann 2003; Marhenke 2003; Willard 1933). The Chilam Balam books only date events to a given year and Katun.

ASTRONOMY

The ancient Maya's knowledge of astronomy permeated many parts of their culture (Aveni 1980; Milbrath 1999). They viewed their world as the center of the universe, with gods traveling to earth from the underworld and heavens. The Dresden, Paris, Madrid, and Grolier Codex provide details of Late Postclassic astronomical knowledge, but much has also been gleaned from Classic Maya visual images, the layout of buildings, and from the story of the *Popol Vuh*. The Maya recorded and predicted the daily, seasonal, and yearly trajectories of the sun, moon, planets, and stars in relation to the Earth, as well as solar and lunar solstices and equinoxes, the rising and setting of planets, and the likelihood of shooting stars and comets (Aveni 1980; Bricker and Bricker 1983; Milbrath 1999; Ortiz 1997). Astronomy was integrally linked to religion in that the Maya believed that the sun, moon, planets, and stars were gods who impacted, and in some cases controlled, human destiny (Milbrath 1999). Classic Maya kings and queens adopted the names of gods, thereby claiming divine status (Houston and Stuart 1996, 295). Maya royalty correlated important events in their lives with celestial movements of the sun, moon, and stars. Warfare, accession, and other ceremonies and activities were evidently associated with seasonality or astronomical events (Milbrath 1999, 64–65). "Maya rulers manipulated celestial imagery to make themselves central to the cosmos. Different rulers or lineages claimed descent from the Sun, the Moon, and Venus. . . . King Pacal was transformed into a god linked with Jupiter. . . . Other rulers were transformed into Venus after death. They traveled on the Milky Way, to reach their celestial abode. The Precolumbian Maya . . . believed their stars were gods, and their rulers derived power from their connection with the cosmos in life and in the afterlife" (Milbrath 1999, 11).

Sun and Moon

The ancient Maya observed the movements of the sun and moon—particularly the eclipses, but also the summer and winter equinoxes, the zenith position of the sun (when it was directly overhead, casting no shadow), as well as their paths across the sky as observed from Earth and in relation to the stars and planets. This interest in the movement of the sun and moon is evident in early colonial times from Diego de Landa's *Relación de las Cosas de Yucatan,* from the Postclassic codices, and from astronomical alignments of ancient buildings and from images on stones and pottery dating as early as the Classic period (Burger 2001; Förstemann 1906; Thompson 1972).

The Dresden Codex includes seven pages of eclipse tables. They record eclipses over 46 Tzolkin (260-day) years, including 405 lunations or 11,960 days. This allowed the Maya to coordinate eclipses with their sacred Tzolkin time cycle. The eclipse tables provide dates for when eclipses could occur, based on the knowledge that they can occur within 18 days on either side of the moon's path crossing the sun's path (Aveni 1980; Bricker and Bricker 1983; Bricker and Bricker 1986, 60; Milbrath 1999).

Venus

The ancient Maya predicted the heliacal rise and setting of planets—the point when they become visible after being obscured by the sun's glare or the point when they are once again hidden (Bricker and Bricker 1986, 60). In particular, the Maya made extensive calculations on Venus, perhaps because they associated it with warfare, as noted first by Maya epigrapher Floyd Lounsbury (1974). He found an association between war images and the appearance of Venus in the morning or evening sky, a point further investigated by Susan Milbrath (1999), John Justeson (1989), and Anthony Aveni (1980), among others. The Late Classic glyph for war included the Venus sign, sometimes along with the glyph for the city to be attacked. In fact, some battles evidently were timed to coincide with the celestial movements of this planet. Dos Pilas attacked Seibal when Venus was first visible as the evening star on December 3, A.D. 735. The captured Seibal ruler was sacrificed at a ritual ball game twelve years later, at the inferior conjunction of Venus. Floyd Lounsbury suggested that a battle scene depicted in Bonampak wall murals, dated to 6 August A.D. 792, occurred at the inferior conjunction of Venus and the zenith position of the sun. Although pessimists might view the relationships between Venus and earthly events as mere coincidences, Venus was apparently astronomically important, at least to the Postclassic Maya, who recorded its movements in the codices (Burger 2001; Förstemann 1906; Thompson 1972).

The Dresden Codex includes extensive discussion of Venus (Thompson 1972), and both the Dresden and Grolier (Coe 1973) codices provide tables correlating the trajectories of Venus and the sun around the Earth. Movements of the planet Venus between A.D. 1100 and 1250 are recorded in Calendar Round dates in the Venus pages of the Dresden Codex (Milbrath 1999). The ancient Maya recognized and recorded Venus when it appeared in the east as the morning star around dawn and in the west as the evening star around dusk. As the brightest planet in Earth's solar system, Venus is visible in the morning or evening sky for 263 days of each year.

Both the Dresden and Grolier codices contain an eight-year table following the cyclical rotations of Venus in relation to the sun's rotation. The Maya Venus year was 584 days, closely approximating the 583.92 actual days of the planet's year. Every five Venus years (5×584 or 2,920 days), Venus's rotation coincided with the solar rotation (8×365 days) around the Earth.

Stars

The stars—suns in other solar systems—also follow a regular movement in the sky, which makes them good seasonal markers in particular. The nighttime rising of the Pleiades coincided with the onset of the Maya rainy season, whereas the rise of Scorpio, also located in the Milky Way but on the opposite side of the sky, marked the onset of the Maya's dry season. Shooting stars (meteor showers) occur in particular constellations at certain times of the year, as do comets, so that their occurrence could also be used by the Maya to predict events (Milbrath 1999).

The Ancient Maya Zodiac

Westerners are familiar with the zodiac devised by ancient Egyptian and Baby-lonian astronomers, but Linda Schele, David Kelley, Susan Milbrath, and other Maya epigraphers believe that the ancient Maya had their own zodiac. The Maya evidently divided the night sky into groups of stars to form a zodiac, based on the positioning of constellations on the ecliptic—the apparent path of the sun, moon, and planets as they cross the Milky Way. The ancient Maya used a serpent (sometimes shown as a sky band) to denote the ecliptic. Diego de Landa noted that Venus, the Pleiades, and Gemini were the most frequently observed celestial bodies among the Maya (Tozzer 1941). Both the Paris and Dresden codices refer to the zodiac, and it is represented on sculptures at Chichen Itza, at Acanceh, and in Classic Maya iconography. A number of re-searchers have continued the early twentieth-century pioneering research on the Maya zodiac done by researchers such as Herbert Spinden (1916), notably Harvey and Victoria Bricker (1992), David Kelley (1976), Michael Love (1994), Susan Milbrath (1999), and Gregory Severin (1981). However, even the basic details about the number and positioning of the Maya constellations, the tim-ing of their zodiac, and their constellations' places in the night sky are the sub-ject of some disagreement.

Susan Milbrath (1999, 249–293) makes a compelling argument that the Maya zodiac consisted of thirteen groups of stars that cycled every twenty-eight days. Milbrath (1999) interprets the sky band in Maya iconography as the Milky Way, often shown as a serpent (see also Freidel and Schele 1993; Freidel, Schele, and Parker 1993). A scorpion, a peccary, and other animals suspended from a sky band on pages 23 and 24 in the Paris Codex represent constellations on the Milky Way or at its edge (Love 1994; Milbrath 1999, figure 7.2a; Willard 1933). A second group of animals dangling from a white band below are on the ecliptic but not near the Milky Way. The Venus pages in the Dresden Codex reinforce Milbrath's interpretation, as they show the sun, moon, and planets as gods on sky-band thrones crossing the Milky Way (Burger 2001; Förstemann 1906). Use of this zodiac in the Classic period is suggested from a number of monuments with dates corresponding to times when the sun, moon, and planets were aligned with the Milky Way (Milbrath 1999, 288). Milbrath found a correspon-dence between the ascension to heaven of Maya kings and the position of a planet on the Milky Way. Iconography featuring the Milky Way associated with living Maya kings and queens placed them at the center of the Maya universe.

Do the positions of the constellations in the Paris Codex represent the order of the constellations in the Maya zodiac (Love 1994; Milbrath 1999; Willard 1933)? There are differences in the order of the images of constellations in the various Postclassic codices and also where they are depicted on the façades of buildings, painted murals, and carved stone monuments from the Classic period. Since the order of the depicted images varies, researchers do not agree on what constellation each image represents. A variation of the zodiac in the

Paris Codex (Courtesy Northwestern University Library, Mann 2003)

Paris Codex is depicted on the façade of the Nunnery (Las Monjas) at Chichen Itza. Seven of these zodiac figures are represented in the Paris Codex, including a turtle, scorpion, peccary, snake, skeletal figure, and two birds, but they are not in the same order as in the Paris Codex (Bricker and Bricker 1992). Of the animals depicted on the north façade of the Palace of the Stuccoes at Acanceh, the bat, owl, and rattlesnake are also in the Paris Codex zodiac, but the frog, bat, feline, spider monkey, and howler monkey are not. The Madrid Codex shows rattlesnakes representing the Pleiades (Milbrath 1999, figure 7.3; Vail 2002). And the Pleiades may also be represented in serpent iconography, such as the rattlesnake's rattle, on stelae at Yaxchilan, Palenque, Tikal, and Bonampak (Milbrath 1999, 262–263). Several buildings at Chichen Itza are oriented to view the Pleiades, including one window at Caracol, from which the Pleiades could be seen as they set heliacally at dusk in late April near the end of the dry season (Aveni 1980, 266).

Both a scorpion and peccaries are depicted on a sky band on the Nunnery building at Chichen Itza (Milbrath 1999, 265, figure 7.2b). The scorpion may be represented as a segmented or skeletal snake with scorpion characteristics, as in Classic Maya images at Copan, Yaxchilan, Tikal, and Palenque. At Palenque, a skeletal snake on King Pacal's sarcophagus was a portal to the otherworld in the Milky Way (Milbrath 1999, plate 10; Freidel, Schele, and Parker 1993, 269–270). Peccaries depicted in celestial images on the ceiling of Room 2 at the Classic Maya site of Bonampak, on a sky band on the Nunnery building at Chichen Itza, and in the Paris Codex are viewed as representing either the constellation Leo (Bricker and Bricker 1992, 178; Milbrath 1999, 268) or Gemini (Freidel, Schele, and Parker 1993, 80–82).

Several Postclassic buildings at the Quiche site of Utatlan in the southern Maya highlands were oriented toward Orion as it sets (Freidel, Schele, and Parker 1993, 103). Orion's three stars were viewed as the three stones of creation in the *Popol Vuh*, the book of Chilam Balam of Chumayel, and in Classic period inscriptions at Palenque and Quirigua, where they are referred to as "three-stone place" (Freidel, Schele, and Parker 1993, 82–83). The three hearth-stones act as guides in the night sky and were created by Hun Hunahpu, the Maize God, who was taken by the paddler gods to the sky. This is depicted on a stela at Quirigua, which also shows the Maize God's creation of the world on the Milky Way with a central world tree, Wakah Chan.

King Pacal of Palenque's sarcophagus shows him ascending a tree, which Milbrath (1999, 273) interprets as the Southern Cross. Her interpretation shows Pacal entering the Milky Way at Scorpius and ascending the Southern Cross to reach Jupiter.

Pacal's son and successor, Chan Bahlum, is depicted with a giant maize plant and another cosmic tree in an image of his accession to the throne in the Temple of the Foliated Cross and an image marking him as heir designate in the Temple of the Cross, both at Palenque. Crosses, symbolizing the tree of life and ascent to the otherworld, and represented by the Ceiba tree according to the modern day Lacandon Maya of Chiapas, Mexico, were also important in Classic Maya iconography, particularly at Palenque.

What are the celestial signs of the Maya zodiac? Although researchers agree about the existence of a Maya zodiac, information from the codices, as well as from Classic and Postclassic iconography provide a fragmentary and sometimes contradictory picture of the Maya zodiac. Images in both the Paris Codex and on the façade of the Nunnery (Monjas) building at Chichen Itza show a turtle, scorpion, peccary, snake, skeletal figure, and two birds. The Paris Codex and a Postclassic façade of a building at Acanceh show a bat, an owl, and a rattlesnake. The Acanceh façade also shows a frog, feline, spider monkey, and a howler monkey. For the Classic period, peccaries are depicted at Bonampak, skeletal snakes at Palenque, the Southern and Northern crosses at Palenque, and a turtle in imagery at Quirigua. The details of the ancient Maya zodiac remain to be worked out. Some further evidence comes from the astronomical alignment of Maya buildings, as discussed below.

ASTRONOMY AND MAYA ARCHITECTURE

The ancient Maya oriented buildings according to the position of the sun on the horizon at the solstices and equinoxes, as well as the zenith passages (Aveni 1980; Milbrath 1999). Observations of celestial movements from the summits of buildings were especially useful to them, given the featureless landscape of the rainforest canopy across much of the Maya lowlands. Also, if rituals were timed to coincide with particular celestial events, this reinforced the power of the Maya royalty and their control over cosmic events (Milbrath 1999, 70).

A particular architectural grouping called E groups (named from the E group excavations at Uaxactun where they were first discovered), found at many lowland sites, notably Uaxactun, Tikal, Dzibilchaltun, and Chichen Itza, have clear astronomical importance as observatories. A Late Preclassic group of buildings at Uaxactun faces a platform with a line of three temples. From this group, the summer solstice sun rises behind the northern temple, the equinox sun rises behind the central temple, and the winter solstice sun rises behind the southern temple (Aveni 1980, 277–280). There is a similar E group in the Lost World Complex at Tikal, where a structure called the Great Pyramid faces three temples aligned with the rising sun at solstices and equinoxes (Milbrath 1999, 66).

Astronomical sightings were made from the doorways and windows of ancient Maya buildings, according to archaeoastronomer Anthony Aveni (1980) and others. Aveni and architect Horst Hartung (1991) have noticed, for example, that looking out the doorway of the House of the Governor at Uxmal in A.D. 750, the Maya would have seen Venus at its southerly extreme rising above a mound located 5.6 kilometers in the distance, suggesting there was an astronomical significance pertaining to Venus for the placement of the unexplored mound that remains unexplained to modern researchers. All buildings at Uxmal, except the House of the Governor, are oriented in the same direction, suggesting site planning and specific astronomical orientation for the House of the Governor. Aveni, Sharon Gibbs, and Hartung (1975) found that the Caracol building at Chichen Itza is aligned to the northerly travels of Venus at A.D. 1000, as is a diagonal sight line from a window in the tower. Another diagonal viewing sights Venus in its setting position at its maximum southerly declination.

LANGUAGE AND WRITING

Maya scribes continued writing books with hieroglyphs and dates even after the collapse of the Classic period dynasties and the cessation of the practice of commemorating their lives on stelae. The sixteenth-century Spanish missionaries burned many Maya books as part of their attempt to convert indigenous peoples to the Catholic religion. The most extensive of these book burnings was the auto-da-fé held by de Landa in 1562 at Mani, Yucatan. He also tortured many Maya who he believed were worshipping idols. Three surviving books were at some point during early colonial times taken to Europe, where they eventually were discovered in libraries in Madrid, Dresden, and Paris, respectively, and became known as the Madrid, Dresden, and Paris codices (Anders 1967; Anders 1968; Förstemann 1906; Love 1994; Thompson 1972; Willard 1933; Vail 2002). Part of a fourth book, the Grolier Codex, was found in a cave in Chiapas, where it was preserved due to the dry conditions (Coe 1973). The codex is housed in the Grolier Collection in the United States.

In addition to the many books lost in the book burnings, the Maya wrote a number of books replacing their hieroglyphs with the Spanish alphabet. As part of their attempts to convert the Maya, missionaries wrote prayers and other religious texts in Mayan languages, adapting the Spanish alphabet to incorporate the sounds of the Mayan languages. As part of the conversion effort, the missionaries also created dictionaries and grammars of Mayan languages. Among the most informative about Maya culture are the *Popol Vuh* (Tedlock 1985) and the Chilam Balam of the Yucatan (meaning "jaguar priests' books of the Yucatan").

Quiché Maya scribes wrote the *Popol Vuh*. These scribes were descendants of the royal lineages who had founded the Quiché kingdom in the Maya highlands after the Classic Maya collapse. Friar Francisco Ximénez found a copy of their text in Chichicastenango, where he was the parish priest, and he transcribed it and translated it into Spanish. Charles Etienne Brasseur de Bourbourg (1861) took the Ximénez text to Paris and published a copy, along with his French translation. Ximénez's copy is the only surviving transcription of the *Popol Vuh*, and it is now housed in the Newberry Library in Chicago (see Houston, Mazariegos, and Stuart 2001; Tedlock 1985).

Of twelve Chilam Balam books written in different towns in the Yucatan in Colonial times, the Chilam Balam of Chumayel (Roys 1967), Chilam Balam of Tizimin (Edmonson 1982), and the Chilam Balam of Mani are best known. They provide information on ceremonies coinciding with astronomical events and calendar dates during Colonial times.

Ancient and Modern Mayan Languages

What language did the Classic Maya speak and use for their hieroglyphs? Historical linguists, such as Lyle Campbell, John Justeson, and Terrence Kaufman tell us that now-extinct Chol Mayan was the language of the Classic period writing throughout the Maya area and that it was also the spoken language. Historical linguists have studied modern Mayan languages in order to reconstruct the ancestral "Proto-Mayan" language. Their classifications of modern Mayan languages also provide a family tree tracing the Mayan languages spoken in antiquity back in time to the Proto-Mayan language. There are thirty-one Mayan languages spoken today. Campbell (1984) notes that shared innovations and sound correspondences are critical in estimating which languages are more closely related to one another and therefore historically share a common parent language. Some Maya historical linguists use glottochronology—a system that measures the time of divergence of languages based on the number of key words that they share—to reconstruct the timing and sequence of divergence of Mayan languages over time (Kaufman 1976). Campbell (1984, 4) cautions that glottochronology is only valid when supported by independent radiocarbon, calendrical, and other archaeological evidence.

Using the controversial glottochronological method, Kaufman (1976) provides the most widely accepted classification of modern Mayan languages and their origins from ancestral Proto-Mayan. Huastec Mayan was probably the first language to split off in antiquity from ancestral Proto-Mayan. Modern Huastec Mayan is now spoken outside the Maya area to the north along the Gulf coast of Mexico. Huastec Maya is only distantly related culturally and linguistically to the ancient and modern Maya so is not used in understanding the culture of people in the Maya area. Proto-Mayan also was ancestral to Highland Mayan and Greater Lowland Mayan. Highland Maya includes several language groups used in antiquity in the southern Maya highlands, including Greater Kanjobalan, Mamean, and Quichean. The modern languages belonging to these groups are useful in understanding colonial documents from the highlands, such as the *Popol Vuh* (Tedlock), written in Quiche.

The Quiche Maya dominated a number of polities in the eastern and central Maya highlands during the Late Postclassic. The Quichean languages spoken by Maya people living in the eastern highland around Lake Atitlan include Quiche, Cakchiquel, Tzutuhil, Sacapultec, and Sipacapa. They only became distinct languages (from ancestral Quichean) around A.D. 1000. Other Quichean languages spoken in the eastern Maya highlands include Kekchi and Uspantec in the north and Pocom in the east.

Several languages of the Tzeltalan branch of Mayan were spoken in the western Maya highlands. Mam, Teco, Ixil, and Aguatecac of the Mamean language group diverged from ancestral Proto-Mayan around 1500 B.C. and remain closest linguistically to the ancestral language. In the Postclassic period, Mam was spoken by a large and powerful group of Mam people who had their capital at Zaculeu, now an archaeological site.

Greater Lowland Mayan includes Yucatecan and Cholan-Tzeltalan language groups. Greater Lowland Mayan has been further subdivided into Western Mayan (Tzeltalan) and Lowland Mayan (Yucatecan and Cholan). Now-extinct Cholan was the spoken and written language of the Classic Maya of the southern Maya lowlands (Campbell 1984; Kaufman 1976). Cholan includes two language groups: One includes Chol and Chontal. The other includes Cholti and Chorti. Floyd Lounsbury (1974) identified Chol in the Palenque hieroglyphs, which corroborates the use of Chol by the Classic Maya scribes in the western lowlands. The hieroglyphic writing used by the Chol Maya of the southern Maya lowlands spread to Yucatec and other Mayan languages, possibly including Tzeltalan (Campbell 1984). Historical linguists and epigraphers use modern descendants of the Chol language group to help decipher Classic Maya writing.

Although Classic-period Chol is an extinct language, other Cholan languages are still spoken today. Lacandon Mayan is still spoken by indigenous Maya people west of the Usumacinta River in Chiapas, Mexico. Chontal Maya was spoken farther north and around the Laguna de Terminos of the Gulf of Mexico. The people of the coastal plan from southern Belize to the area of Quirigua on the Motagua River of Guatemala, the north coast of Honduras, and inland to Copan were Chol speakers. Chorti was spoken farther inland. A variety of non-Mayan languages were spoken farther east in Honduras outside the Maya cultural area. Cholti, sometimes called Manche Chol, became extinct during colonial times.

Yucatecan includes modern Yucatec, Lacandon, Mopan, and Itza languages. Yucatec Maya emerged as a distinct language before 1000 B.C. This date is consistent with the earliest archaeological evidence of the Maya in the lowlands at about 1000 B.C. The Dresden, Madrid, and Paris codices were written during the Postclassic in the northern Maya lowlands in Yucatec Mayan. Therefore epigraphers and historical linguists use modern Yucatec as an aid in deciphering the codices, as well as other colonial documents written in Mayan in the northern Maya lowlands, such as the Chilam Balam books. A transition from the Chol language of the Classic period texts throughout the Maya lowlands is evident in the relatively few Postclassic texts on carved stone monuments in the northern Maya lowlands. The paucity of written texts, the use of the Maya Short Count instead of the Long Count, and the reduced need for historical records carved in stone meant that the prominence of Maya scribes and their central place in Maya royal courts was diminished during the Postclassic in the northern Maya lowlands compared to earlier times. Glyphs on stone monuments are not as well executed as in the Classic period. The surviving codices contain errors in writing dates. Campbell (1984, 7) notes that Yucatec Mayan borrowed many Cholan words in writing the codices. Also, many of the numbers and month names can be traced to Cholan. In contrast, Yucatecan words were not used in Cholan texts of the Classic period. Campbell further noted that the use of Cholan words in the Yucatecan Mayan codices further substantiates the view that Cholan was an older language and that it was the language of the Classic period, both for written and spoken Mayan. Matthews (2003a) includes spoken Maya hieroglyphs from Montgomery's (2002b) *Dictionary of Maya Hieroglyphics.*

The distribution of Mayan languages has changed considerably in antiquity and historic times with movement of Maya people within and beyond the ancient Maya area. With the fall of Chichen Itza and the rise to power of Mayapan, some of the Chichen Itza Maya established a new settlement at Tayasal in the Peten district of Guatemala during the Late Postclassic. Their Itza language became prominent in a sea of Chol Mayan speakers. In early colonial times, the

Spaniards and British drove indigenous Maya out of Belize. Beginning in the nineteenth century and continuing in the twenty-first century, Kekchi and Mopan Maya fled persecution in Guatemala, settling in southern Belize (McKillop 2005). Although Chol Mayan was the spoken and written language of southern Belize during the Classic period, modern Maya people in the area speak Kekchi and Mopan. Kekchi, a Highland Mayan language, is distantly related to Yucatec and Mopan Mayan, both Lowland Mayan languages. Yucatec Maya fled Mexico after the Caste War of the Yucatan in the 1840s, settling in northern Belize. Consequently, Maya people in northern Belize speak Yucatec Mayan.

Maya Hieroglyphs

The Classic Mayan writing system was used to record dynastic histories of Maya kings and queens for public display on stone monuments and other stone carvings, and on painted walls and wooden lintels (as at a temple in Tikal). Written text also was used for more private expression on painted pots and on carved bone and jade objects used during a person's life and then deposited as a grave offering. Writing also was used to record calendrical rituals and ceremonies. Although no paper books have been preserved from the Classic period, researchers know they existed. Disintegrating paper books have been recovered from Classic period sites, such as Altun Ha. The depiction of books on Classic stone carvings and on painted pots indicates that books were common in the Classic period. The books, like their four preserved Postclassic counterparts, had text and images painted on fig bark paper whose surface was coated with a white coating that was probably plaster or gesso, a calium sulphate (Coe and Kerr 1998, 144). The Dresden Codex shows fine calligraphy using a sharp quill pen. The other codices were written using a brush pen (Coe and Kerr 1998, 179–181). The pages were fan-folded with text and images on both sides.

Mayan hieroglyphs were (and are) easier to read than to write. As records of public information on stelae and other stone carvings in public places, hieroglyphic texts were intended to be understood by the masses—at least in a general sense. However, it was a select group of elite scribes who evidently wrote text on stone, painted it on pottery vessels and other objects, and wrote it in books. Scribes were part of the royal Maya court and at least sometimes part of a royal family (Coe and Kerr 1998; Inomata and Houston 2001; Inomata et al. 2002; Reents-Budet 2001). Some scribes signed their names on stone carvings or painted pots (Reents-Budet 1994). Mayan glyphs are quite variable, reflecting the flexibility that the scribes had to express themselves. The variations on glyphs make them more difficult to read, of course. The variability may reflect a decentralized nature of the Classic Maya political landscape in which polities were actively at war with one another. As a result of such a decentralization, scribes may have passed down their knowledge to apprentices without much direct contact with scribes from other polities.

A major breakthrough in deciphering ancient Mayan hieroglyphs was the realization that many of them represent sounds. The basic sound represented

Woman presenting offering to priest, relief on lintel 53, A.D. 766, Late Classic Maya, from Yaxchi-lan (Chiapas), Mexico (The Art Archive/National Anthropological Museum Mexico/Dagli Orti)

by a hieroglyph is a syllable consisting of a consonant-vowel combination. A hieroglyph often has two of these consonant-vowel combinations as the root or base of the glyph. Yuri Knorozov (1958) met with strong opposition when he suggested this phonetic origin of Maya glyphs in the mid-twentieth century. The prevailing view, spearheaded by the eminent Sir J. Eric S. Thompson (1971), was that the glyphs represented letters, following the alphabet recorded by Bishop de Landa (Tozzer 1941). However, David Kelley, Floyd Lounsbury, and other Mayan linguists supported the idea of a phonetic basis for the hieroglyphs. The acceptance of this view after a publication by Yuri

Knorozov (1958) enabled tremendous advances in deciphering the hiero-glyphs by Linda Schele, David Stuart, Stephen Houston, Barbara MacLeod, and John Justeson, among others. Much progress has been made in finding glyphic equivalences of consonant-vowel combinations (Campbell 1984; Houston et al. 2001; Justeson and Campbell 1984, Appendix A).

Mayan hieroglyphs, like other writing systems, followed a developmental sequence in which logograms (letters or signs) were initially used to represent words (Campbell 1984, 12–13). The introduction of rebus writing, in which an abstract concept such as "I" is represented by an eye symbol, for example, ex-panded the use of the written language. When the final consonant was dropped from a Maya logogram composed of a consonant-vowel-consonant combination, the direct link between meaning and sound was weakened, al-lowing more flexibility in the written language. Ultimately, the Maya began to use sounds (called syllabograms or phonetic complements; see below) that had no independent meaning to spell out words syllabically. By the Classic pe-riod in the southern lowlands, Maya scribes were using both logograms and phonetic complements to write hieroglyphic records on stone, wood, pottery, bark paper books, and other materials.

Some Maya glyphs represent words, but others are sounds that are used to-gether to form words. The glyphs for words (such as *king, tree,* and *water*) are called logograms. The syllable glyphs consist of a consonant-vowel-consonant cluster called a syllabogram. Syllabograms are phonetic sounds from a spoken language that have no meaning by themselves. Many words could be either written as a logogram or formed by several syllabograms. All logograms could be expressed by syllabograms. The Classic Maya created sentences by linking syllabograms or by combining them (as phonetic complements) with lo-gograms. According to Coe and Van Stone (2001), there are some 800 separate glyphs, of which perhaps 400 to 500 were commonly used in texts that still ex-ist today.

Mayan glyphic texts were read from top to bottom, left to right, by pairs of glyphs. To read a glyphic text on a Classic stela, for example, one begins at the top left corner, reads the first two glyphs, and then continues reading glyphs below them, by pairs. Once at the bottom, one returns to the top of the text and reads the next column of glyphs, again by pairs.

Classic Maya grammar was quite complex (Coe and Van Stone 2001; Juste-son and Campbell 1984; Schele 1982). Sentences were constructed by adding prefixes and suffixes to glyphs. Verbs came first in Classic Maya texts. The structure of a written Maya sentence usually conformed to the pattern verb-object-subject (VOS) or verb-subject (VS). Different verbs were used for the two types of sentences, with transitive verbs used with VOS sentences and in-transitive verbs used with VS sentences. Intransitive verbs could be made pas-sive by adding a suffix; the passive form was very common in Classic Maya writing (Coe and Van Stone 2001, 32). Most verbs in Classic Maya texts were in the present tense, although there was a past and future tense.

Classic Mayan was written in stone carvings in the third person singular (Coe and Van Stone 2001, 29–30). First person and plural constructions were rare. Second person was sometimes used on painted pottery vessels, but it was otherwise almost nonexistent. Plural was quite rare; the only example is *taak,* meaning people. Interestingly, there were no gender pronouns, which are so common in many Indo-European languages such as English, French, and Spanish. However, there were gender prefixes added to nouns to distinguish male (*aj*) or female (*ix*) occupations or activities. There were two types of pronouns used in Classic Maya texts, for transitive and intransitive sentences, respectively. They were used with nouns or verbs and also were used to denote possession. Some nouns were possessive and were distinguished by the presence of a possessive prefix. Possession was denoted by *u* or, if the glyph began with a vowel, by *y* or *w.* Adjectives preceded nouns.

In the late twentieth century, a standard orthography for writing Maya words, developed by Maya linguists and indigenous Maya people in Guatemala, became widely used (Coe and Van Stone 2001, 19; Freidel, Schele, and Parker 1993). The new orthography gives better phonetic representations of words than did the orthography imposed by the Spaniards in colonial times, by replacing words like *Uaxactun* with *Waxaktun,* and *Yukatek* with *Yucatec.* As mentioned at the beginning of this book, acceptance of the new orthography will standardize the various spellings used by researchers, missionaries, and others that have resulted in a confusing array of spellings of Maya words and place names. For example, Freidel, Schele, and Parker (1993, 16) point out that the word *lord* is variously written *ahaw, ahau, ajau, ajaw,* or *axaw.*

Epigraphers follow several conventions in transcribing and translating Mayan hieroglyphs (Coe and Van Stone 2001, 19). Direct transcriptions are written in bold type, with logograms capitalized and syllabograms in lowercase. Brackets are used to indicate that a sound is not pronounced. Mayan words are written in italics. Translations are in quotes.

History of Decipherment of Hieroglyphs

The tragic burning of Maya books in 1562 by Diego de Landa at Mani, Yucatan, certainly delayed the subsequent decipherment of Mayan hieroglyphs. Evidently priests had been burning Maya books before de Landa's infamous auto-da-fé (Houston, Chinchilla, and Stuart 2001). Eyewitness accounts by European explorers and chroniclers report that Maya books were quite common and often were taken to Europe by them. Houston, Chinchilla, and Stuart (2001) publish an excerpt from Peter Martyr's chronicles describing Maya hieroglyphs and books that he saw. Cline (1972–1975) provides a guide to early eyewitness accounts of Maya books in volumes 13 to 15 of the *Handbook of Middle American Indians.* Although there are only four known ancient Maya texts, there are undoubtedly more Maya manuscripts in archives or private collections that remain to be discovered.

It was not until the nineteenth century that a connection was made between the hieroglyphs carved in stone at ancient Maya sites and ancient texts that were being discovered in Europe, leading to a much attention directed at deciphering the glyphs. The director of the Royal Library of Dresden purchased the first text discovered in 1739. This text became known as the Dresden Codex (Burger 2001; Marhenke 2003; Förstemann 1906). The famous naturalist and traveler to the American tropics, Alexander von Humboldt (1810, plate 45), published five pages of the text. The public's attention was drawn to hiero-glyphs at ancient Maya sites with the publication of a drawing of a stone monument from Palenque in 1822. By this time, most of the Central American countries had gained their independence from Spain and there was great interest in traveling there and reading about the area (Stuart 1992, 5). An American antiquarian, James McCulloh (1829) recognized the link between the writing in the Dresden Codex and at Palenque. Another important step in decipherment was made by Constantine Rafinesque, who observed that the hieroglyphs were written in the same language as spoken by modern Maya people (G. Stuart 1992, 11). The publication of accurate illustrations of hieroglyphs accompanying the travel account of exploration of Maya ruins by John Lloyd Stephens (1963, 1969), made a large corpus of glyphs available for study by the educated and interested public.

In addition to the Dresden Codex, the discovery and study of various other indigenous books and records added to a growing understanding of ancient Maya writing and culture. Studies of chronicles written in Mayan during colonial times and collected by Yucatecan scholar Juan Pio Perez, including an important chronicle about the town of Mani, Yucatan, were published in John Lloyd Stephens 1841 and 1843 publications (Stephens 1963; Stephens 1969). Leon de Rosny (1887) found and published a fragment of what became known as the Paris Codex in a basket of old papers in a Parisian Library that had purchased the manuscript in 1832 (Marhenke 2003; Stuart 1992). Brasseur de Bourbourg (1869–1870) found and published part of another codex, which he acquired from Don Juan Troy Ortolanao, a professor of paleontology in Madrid. Leon de Rosny (1882) found and published the remaining part of the same codex, which had been purchased by the Museo Arqueologico de Madrid from a collector in 1875. The two parts of the codex became known as the Madrid Codex (Marhenke 2003; Vail 2002).

Brasseur de Bourbourg discovered several other important manuscripts, including the *Popol Vuh,* which he published in its original Quiche Mayan in addition to his own translation (Brasseur de Bourbourg 1861; Todlock 1985). He discovered an abbreviated copy of Diego de Landa's *Relación de Las Cosas de Yucatan* in the collections of the Royal Academy of History in Madrid (Brasseur de Bourbourg 1864). This text is the most important account of the indigenous Maya at the time of European contact, originally written in about 1566 (see translation by Tozzer 1941). Unfortunately, de Landa's original and longer text is lost. De Landa's text provides critical information for researchers interested in Mayan hieroglyphs (Stuart 1992, 21). The names of the Yucatec days and months were useful in figuring out the Maya calendar. However, de Landa confused scholars by providing a hieroglyphic alphabet, which obscured the phonetic basis of the written language. Although de Landa argued for a phonetic basis of Maya glyphs, in which glyph corresponds to a spoken sound, many scholars incorrectly argued that the glyphs were pictographic or ideographic, in which the glyph corresponded to its meaning, such as a picture of a hand indicating the word for hand. This debate continued until Yuri Knorozov's 1958 publication, where he conclusively demonstrated the phonetic basis of Mayan hieroglyphs.

Ernst Förstemann, librarian at the Royal Library of Dresden, made major breakthroughs in decipherment of Maya glyphs. After publishing a limited edition of the Dresden Codex in 1880 (see Förstemann 1906), Förstemann published his identifications of the multiplication charts and Venus cycle astronomical tables from the Dresden Codex, as well as reading Long Count dates, and other insights in deciphering the glyphs and numbers. A colleague of Förstemann, Paul Schellhas (1904), categorized the deities in the Dresden Codex, identifying glyphs associated with them. The ability of scholars to study the ancient glyphs was dramatically enhanced with the publication of Alfred Maudslay's drawings and photographs of inscriptions painstakingly recorded over the course of his travels over some thirteen years to Tikal, Copan, Palenque, Yaxchilan, Quirigua, Chichen Itza, and other ancient ruins (Maudslay 1902). Further important documentation of glyphic records at sites, many now too eroded to see, was made by Teobert Maler (1901, 1903, 1908a, 1908b, 1910, 1911), who drew and photographed carved monuments at many lowland Maya sites. Sylvanus Morley (1920) continued this tradition of careful documentation in *The Inscriptions of Copan,* and the multivolume *The Inscriptions of Peten* (Morley 1937–1938). Morley focused on interpretation of the dates on carved monuments, which helped archaeologists date sites. John Graham (1972) continued this careful documentation of inscriptions. In 1968 Graham began a monumental project, The Corpus of Maya Hieroglyphic Inscriptions, to accurately record all known hieroglyphs in codices, on pottery vessels, and at archaeological sites.

Meanwhile, other important strides were made by an American newspaperman, Joseph Goodman (1905). He provided the first correlation of the Maya calendar with the Christian calendar. Juan Martinez Hernandez (1926) later modified this correlation, as did J. Eric S. Thompson (1927, 1950). Thompson's version, known as the Goodman-Martinez-Thompson (GMT) correlation, is the generally accepted correlation used by researchers. The GMT correlation places the beginning of the Maya calendar at 3114 B.C. in the Christian calendar. Thompson (1950) dominated Maya archaeology in the mid-nineteenth century, and although he made many important decipherments of the glyphs, his opposition to their phonetic basis to Mayan hieroglyphs continued, even after the Russian scholar Yuri Knorosov (1958) demonstrated the phonetic basis of the writing. Thompson's views impeded the decipherment of the hieroglyphs.

The roots of decipherment of Mayan hieroglyphs can be attributed to insights by three scholars: Knorozov, Heinrich Berlin, and Tatiana Proskouriakoff. Heinrich Berlin (1958) identified "emblem glyphs" on stelae that he assumed named individuals or places, in stark contrast to the previous view that names identified priests, but certainly not dynastic rulers. Joyce Marcus (1976) later provided the first glyphic study of Classic Maya polities. Based on study of monuments from the site of Piedras Negras, Proskouriakoff (1960) recognized that the stelae at Classic Maya sites recorded historical information about Maya kings, along with dates for birth, marriage, accession to the throne, and other important events. Knorozov's correct identification of the phonetic basis of Mayan hieroglyphs was further examined and substantiated by epigrapher David Kelley (1976).

With these important strides, the pace of decipherment since 1960 escalated, and changed from a solitary pursuit to more collaborative endeavors, with regular meetings. The first Palenque round table meeting in 1973 resulted in the decipherment of the dynastic record of the site by Floyd Lounsbury, Peter Matthews, and Linda Schele (Matthews and Schele 1974). Michael Coe (1973) demonstrated the importance of glyphic texts on Classic Maya pottery vessels in *The Maya Scribe and His World,* a book accompanying an exhibition of Maya pots. Coe showed texts on ceramics contained important ritual and historical information, and often portrayed the same mythical stories told in the historic Quiche text, the *Popol Vuh.* The book also included publication of the newly discovered Grolier Codex (Kerr 2003b; Marhenke 2003). By the turn of the second millennium, much of Mayan hieroglyphs had been deciphered, thanks to the collaborative insights of many epigraphers who continue to work together at annual workshops, such as the "Texas Maya meetings" at the University of Texas, Austin (see also Coe 1992; Houston et al. 2001; Matthews 2003a; Matthews 2003b; Montgomery 2002a; Montgomery 2002b; G. Stuart 1992).

Hieroglyphs on Maya Pottery

A band of hieroglyphs (called the primary standard sequence or PSS) below the rim on Late Classic painted pottery vessels provided the name of the owner (who commissioned the vessel) or painter of the vessel and/or the vessel's intended contents, as well as other information such as the type of vessel or the manner of decoration (D. Stuart 2001). Many pots were used to hold cacao drinks, as with the Rio Azul vessel that contained traces of cacao and whose contents were identified by hieroglyphs on the pot (D. Stuart 1988). Occasionally there was a date preceding the text, which David Stuart suggests was the date the pot was made. Use of the PSS to denote ownership also appears on clothing and monuments and indicates that ownership of material possessions was an important dimension of royal Maya life. The same PSS is seen on other objects denoting ownership, such as a lintel from Yaxchilan (D. Stuart 2001, figure 47.7) that identifies the owner of the house as Lady Fist-Fish, or on clothing, as on a woman's skirt on one of the Bonampak murals (D. Stuart 2001, figure 47.8) or on a woman's clothing at Calakmul (D. Stuart 2001, 483–484).

Some Late Classic pots have hieroglyphs denoting the artist's signature (D. Stuart 2001). Gifting of vessels was a frequent aspect of Late Classic Maya royal alliances and politics, so that although hieroglyphs may name the commissioner or original owner of a vessel, it may have subsequently been given or traded elsewhere, used in local feasts, and ultimately deposited in a royal grave. Therefore, hieroglyphs provide little use in identifying the site from which the many unprovenienced painted pots derived (D. Stuart 2001).

SAMPLE MAYA TEXT WITH TRANSLATION

Lintel 24 from the Classic Maya city of Yaxchilan depicts Lady K'ab'al Xook, the main wife of Itzamnaaj B'alam II (the king), in a ritual bloodletting cere-

Lady Xook draws a rope through her tongue to let blood in a vision quest. Limestone Lintel from Yaxchilan, Chiapas (The Art Archive/Museum of Mankind London/Eileen Tweedy)

mony. The stone carving is from a set of three stone lintel carvings in Structure 23, known as the house of Lady Xook. The other lintels depict Lady Xook conjuring a vision serpent (after she has made the blood offering) and holding a jaguar helmet for the king for an unknown military event to follow—perhaps heading off to war. The rich iconography of Lintel 24 is complemented by the text, which further explains the depicted event. The king holds a torch above his principal wife, suggesting the ritual is at night. Lady Xook kneels in front of him, pulling a rope with thorns through her tongue. Blood drips onto the rope and onto bark paper in a basket that also holds a stingray spine, the implement she used to pierce her tongue before pulling the rope through it. Both figures are well dressed in regalia indicative of their royal status, with finely woven capes, his decorated with the cross-shaped "*tau*" sign of power and authority, hers edged with a sky band hinting at her knowledge of the Maya zodiac. The king is wearing a sun god pendant on a necklace and a shrunken head—probably from a sacrificed war victim—on his head.

The accompanying text provides a Calendar Round date for the event described in the hieroglyphs. The horizontal text above the king's head provides the date and identifies the king. Reading from left to right, the first glyph is the date 5 Kimi, identified by the horizontal bar (for five) above the head glyph for the month Kimi. The next glyph is in two parts. On the left, there is 15 Mak, identified by the three horizontal bars above the head glyph for Mak. The right part of the glyph is translated as "his semblance" or in Mayan "*u baab*" (Coe and Van Stone 2001, 138). The next three glyphs continue the text as follows: at the penance ("*ti ch'abil*"), with a fiery spear ("*ti k'ak'al jul*"), the penance of the 4 k'atun king ("*kan ajaw*"; Coe and Van Stone 2001, 138). The last glyphs on the right name the king, Itzamnaaj B'alaam.

The upper vertical text provides the name of the king's wife. Her title as "Lady Autocrat" ("Ix kaloomte"; Coe and Van Stone 2001, 138) is the lowest glyph. The lower vertical group of glyphs is the artist's signature, identified by Linda Schele and Mary Miller (1986, 186) as the "Cookie Cutter Master" from the depth that the background is recessed from the images of the figures. The existence of the artist's signature is a measure of the high status of the artist, both from the perspective of the artist and the king and queen. Carolyn Tate (1992, 44) suggests that more than one artist prepared the carving, since the size and shapes of the glyphs are different, and the hands are more finely executed than the rest of the image. Tate suggests that it was a workshop of several artists who drew and carved the image, and so the signature is a reflection of the workshop name instead of an individual.

REFERENCES

Anders, F., ed. 1967. *Codex Tro-Cortesianus (Codex Madrid)*. Museo de América, Madrid, Graz, Austria: Akademische Druck und Verlagsanstalt.

———. 1968. *Codex Peresianus (Codex Paris)*. Bibliothèque National, Paris, Graz, Austria: Akademische Druck und Verlagsanstalt.

Aveni, Anthony. 1980. *Skywatchers of Ancient Mexico*. Austin: University of Texas Press.

Aveni, Anthony F., Sharon L. Gibbs, and Horst Hartung. 1975. "The Caracol Tower at Chichen Itza: An Ancient Astronomical Observatory?" *Science* 188: 977–985.

Aveni, Anthony F., and Horst Hartung. 1991. "Archaeoastronomy and the Puuc Sites." In *Arqueoastronomia y Etnoastronomia en Mesoamerica*, edited by Johanna Broda, Stanislaw Iwaniszewski, and Lucrecia Maupome, 65–96. Mexico City: Universidad Nacional Autonoma de Mexico.

Berlin, Heinrich. 1958. "El glifo 'emblema' en las inscripciones Mayas." *Journal de la Société des Americanistes* 47: 111–119.

Brasseur de Bourbourg, Etienne C. 1861. *Popol Vuh: le livre sacre et les mythes de l'antiquite Americaine, avec les livres heroiques et historiques des Quiches.* Paris: Arthus Bertrand.

———. 1864. *Relacion des choses de Yucatan de Diego de Landa.* Paris: Arthus Bertrand.

———. 1869–1870. *Manuscrit Torano: Études sur le systeme graphique et al. langue des Mayas.* Paris: Imprimerie Imperale.

Bricker, Harvey, and Victoria Bricker. 1983. "Classic Maya Prediction of Solar Eclipses." *Current Anthropology* 24: 1–23.

———. 1992. "Zodiacal References in the Maya Codices." In *The Sky and Mayan Literature,* edited by Anthony F. Aveni, 148–183. Oxford University Press, New York.

Bricker, Victoria and Harvey Bricker. 1986. "The Mars Table in the Dresden Codex." In *Research and Reflections in Archaeology and History: Essays in Honor of Doris Stone,* edited by E. Wyllys Andrews V, 51–79. Middle American Research Institute Publication 47. New Orleans: Tulane University.

Burger, Thomas. 2001. *Die Maya-Handschrift Codex Dresdensis.* Available at http://www.tu-dresden.de/slub/proj/maya/maya.html.

Campbell, Lyle R. 1984. "The Implications of Mayan Historical Linguistics for Glyphic Research." In *Phoneticism in Mayan Hieroglyphic Writing,* edited by John Justeson and Lyle Campbell, 1–16. Institute for Mesoamerican Studies Publication 9. Albany: State University of New York.

Cline, H. F., ed. 1972–1975. *Handbook of Middle American Indians,* vols. 12–15. Austin: University of Texas Press.

Coe, Michael D. 1973. *The Maya Scribe and His World.* New York: Grolier Club.

———. 1992. *Breaking the Maya Code.* New York: Thames & Hudson.

Coe, Michael D., and Justin Kerr. 1998. *The Art of the Maya Scribe.* New York: Harry N. Abrams.

Coe, Michael D., and Mark Van Stone. 2001. *Reading the Maya Glyphs.* New York: Thames & Hudson.

Coggins, Clemency. 1980. "The Shape of Time: Some Political Implications of the Four-Part Figure." *American Antiquity* 45: 727–739.

Edmonson, Munro S. 1982. *The Ancient Future of the Itza: The Book of Chilam Balam of Tizimin.* Austin: University of Texas Press.

———. 1988. *The Book of the Year. Middle American Calendrical Systems.* Salt Lake City: University of Utah Press.

Fash, Barbara. 1992. "Late Classic Architectural Sculpture Themes in Copán." *Ancient Mesoamerica* 3: 89–104.

Förstemann, Ernst W. 1880. *Die Mayahandschrift der Koniglichen Offentlichen Bibliothek zu Dresden.* Leipzig, Deutschland: Verlag der A. Naumannschen Lichtruckerei.

———. 1906. *Commentary on the Maya Manuscript in the Royal Public Library of Dresden.* Papers of the Peabody Museum, vol. 4, no. 2, 49–266. Cambridge, MA: Harvard University.

Freidel, David A., Linda Schele, and Joy Parker. 1993. *Maya Cosmos: Three Thousand Years on the Shaman's Path.* New York: William Morrow.

Goodman, Jospeh T. 1905. "Maya Dates." *American Anthropologist* 7: 642–647.

Graham, Ian 1975. *Corpus of Maya Hieroglyphic Inscriptions,* vol. 2, part 1: *Naranjo.* Cambridge, MA: Peabody Museum of Archaeology and Ethnology, Harvard University.

Graham, John 1975. *The Hieroglyphic Inscriptions and Monumental Art of Altar de Sacrificios.* Papers of the Peabody Museum of Archaeology and Ethnology, vol. 64, no. 2. Cambridge, MA: Harvard University.

Harris, John F., and Stephen K. Stearns. 1997. *Understanding Maya Inscriptions.* 2d rev. ed. Philadelphia: University of Pennsylvania Museum of Archaeology and Anthropology.

Houston, Stephen, Oswaldo Chinchilla Mazariegos, and David Stuart, eds. 2001. *The Decipherment of Ancient Maya Writing.* Norman: University of Oklahoma Press.

Houston, Stephen, and David Stuart. 1996. "Of Gods, Glyphs, and Kings: Divinity and Rulership among the Classic Maya." *Antiquity* 70: 289–312.

Humboldt, Alexander von. 1910. *Vues des cordilleras, et monuments des peoples indigenes de l'Amerique.* Paris: F. Schoell.

Inomata, Takeshi, and Stephen D. Houston, eds. 2001. *Royal Courts of the Ancient Maya.* 2 vols. Boulder, CO: Westview.

Inomata, Takeshi, Daniela Triadan, Erick Ponciano, Estela Pinto, Richard E. Terry, and Markus Eberl. 2002. "Domestic and Political Lives of Classic Maya Elites: The Excavation of Rapidly Abandoned Structures at Aguateca, Guatemala." *Latin American Antiquity* 13: 305–330.

Justeson, John S. 1989 "The Ancient Maya Ethnoastronomy: An Overview of Hieroglyphic Sources." In *World Archaeoastronomy: Selected Papers from the Second Oxford International Conference on Archaeoastronomy,* edited by Anthony Aveni, 76–129. New York: Cambridge University Press.

Justeson, John S., and Lyle Campbell, eds. 1984. *Phoneticism in Mayan Hieroglyphic Writing.* Institute for Mesoamerican Studies Publication 9. Albany: State University of New York.

Kaufman, Terrence. 1976. "Archaeological and Linguistic Correlations in Mayaland and Associated Areas of Mesoamerica." *World Archaeology* 8: 101–118.

Kelley, David H. 1976. *Deciphering the Maya Script.* Austin: University of Texas Press.

Kerr, Justin. 2003a. *Maya Vase Data Base: An Archive of Rollout Photographs Created by Justin Kerr.* http://www.famsi.org/research/kerr/ or, http://www.mayavase.com

———. 2003b. *The Grolier Codex.* http://www.mayavase.com/grol/grolier.html.,

Knorozov, Yuri. 1958. "The Problem of the Study of the Maya Hieroglyphic Writing." *American Antiquity* 23: 284–291.

Lounsbury, Floyd G. 1974. "The Inscription of the Sarcophagus Lid at Palenque." In *Primera Mesa Redonda de Palenque,* part 2, edited by Merle Greene Robertson, 5–19. Pebble Beach, CA: Robert Louis Stevenson School.

Love, Bruce. 1994. *The Paris Codex: Handbook for a Priest.* Austin: University of Texas Press.

———. 1995. "A Dresden Codex Mars Table?" *Latin American Antiquity* 6: 350–361.

Maler, Teobert. 1901. *Researchers in the Central Portion of the Usumatsintla Valley: Report of Explorations for the Museum 1898–1900.* Memoirs of the Peabody Museum of Archaeology and Ethnology, vol. 2, no. 1. Cambridge, MA: Harvard University.

———. 1903. *Researches in the Central Portion of the Usumatsintla Valley: Report of Explorations for the Museum.* Memoirs of the Peabody Museum of Archaeology and Ethnology, vol. 2, no. 2. Cambridge, MA: Harvard University.

———. 1908a. *Explorations of the Upper Usumatsintla and Adjacent Region: Altar de Sacrificios; Seibal; Itsimte-Sacluk; Cancuen.* Memoirs of the Peabody Museum of Archaeology and Ethnology, vol. 4, no. 1. Cambridge, MA: Harvard University.

———. 1908b. *Explorations in the Department of Peten, Guatemala, and Adjacent Regions: Topoxte; Yaxha; Benque Viejo; Naranjo.* Memoirs of the Peabody Museum of Archaeology and Ethnology, vol. 4, no. 2. Cambridge, MA: Harvard University.

———. 1910. *Explorations in the Department of Peten, Guatemala, and adjacent Regions: Motul de San Jose; Peten-Itza.* Memoirs of the Peabody Museum of Archaeology and Ethnology, vol. 4, no. 3. Cambridge, MA: Harvard University.

————. 1911. *Explorations in the Department of Peten, Guatemala: Tikal.* Memoirs of the Peabody Museum of Archaeology and Ethnology, vol. 5, no. 1. Cambridge, MA: Harvard University.

Mann, Tom. 2003. *The Paris Codex.* Available at http://digital.library.northwestern.edu/codex.

Marcus, Joyce. 1976. *Emblem and State in the Classic Maya Lowlands.* Washington, DC: Dumbarton Oaks.

Marhenke, Randa. 2003. *The Ancient Maya Codices.* Available at http://www.famsi.org/mayawriting/codices/.

Martinez Hernandez, Juan. 1926. *Cronicas Mayas: Cronica de Yaxkukul.* Merida: Tipografia Yucateca.

Matthews, Peter. 2003a. *John Montgomery's Dictionary of Maya Hieroglyphs.* Available at http://www.famsi.org/mayawriting/dictionary/montgomery/index.html.

————. 2003b. *The Linda Schele Drawings.* Availble at http://www.famsi.org/research/schele/bypmathews.htm.

Matthews, Peter, and Linda Schele. 1974. "Lords of Palenque: The Glyphic Evidence." In *Primera Mesa Redonda de Palenque,* part 1, edited by Merle Greene Robertson, 63–75. Pebble Beach, CA: Robert Louis Stevenson School.

Maudslay, Alfred. 1902. *Archaeology.* 5 vols. London: R. H. Porter and Dulau.

McCulloh, James H. 1829. *Researches, Philosophical and Antiquarian, Concerning the Aboriginal History of America.* Baltimore: Fielding Lucas Jr.

McKillop, Heather. 2005 . *In Search of Maya Sea Traders.* College Station: Texas A & M University Press. In press.

Mesdia, Sharon. 2003. *The Tikal Digital Access Project.* Available at http://www.museum.upenn.edu/tdap/.

Milbrath, Susan. 1999. *Star Gods of the Maya: Astronomy in Art, Folklore, and Calendars.* Austin: University of Texas Press.

Montgomery, John. 2002a. *How to Read Maya Hieroglyphs.* New York: Hippocrene.

————. 2002b. *Dictionary of Maya Hieroglyphs.* New York: Hippocrene.

Morley, Sylvanus. 1920. *The Inscriptions of Copan.* Carnegie Institution of Washington Publication 219. Washington, DC: Carnegie Institution of Washington.

————. 1937–1938. *The Inscriptions of Peten.* 5 vols. Carnegie Institution of Washington Publication 437. Washington, DC: Carnegie Institution of Washington.

Proskouriakoff, Tatiana. 1960. "Historical Implications of a Pattern of Dates at Piedras Negras, Guatemala." *American Antiquity* 25: 454–475.

Reents-Budet, Dorie. 1994. *Painting the Maya Universe.* Durham, NC: Duke University Press.

————. 2001. "Classic Maya Concepts of the Royal Court: An Analysis of Renderings on Pictorial Ceramics." In *Royal Courts of the Ancient Maya,* vol. 1, edited by Takeshi Inomata and Stephen Houston, 195–233. Boulder, CO: Westview.

Rosny, Leon de. 1882. *Les documents écrits de l'antiquité Americaine.* Paris: Masionneuve et Cie.

————. 1887. *Codex Peresianus. Manuscrit hieratique des anciens Indiens de l'Amerique Centrale conserve a la Bibliotheque Nationale de Paris.* Paris: Bureau de la Société Americaine.

Roys, Ralph, trans. 1967. *Chilam Balam of Chumayel.* Norman: University of Oklahoma Press.

Schele, Linda. 1982. *Maya Glyphs: The Verbs.* Austin: University of Texas Press.

Schele, Linda, and Mary Miller. 1986. *The Blood of Kings: Dynasty and Ritual in Maya Art.* New York: George Braziller.

Schellhas Paul. 1904. *Representations of Deities of the Maya Manuscripts.* Papers of the Peabody Museum of Archaeology and Ethnology, vol. 4, no. 1, Cambridge, MA: Harvard University.

Spinden, Herbert. 1916. "The Question of the Zodiac in America." *American Anthropologist* 18: 53–80.

Stephens, John Lloyd. [1843] 1963. *Incidents of Travel in Yucatan.* 2 vols. New York: Dover.

———. [1841] 1969. *Incidents of Travel in Central America, Chiapas and Yucatan.* 2 vols. New York: Dover.

Stuart, David. 1988. "The Rio Azul Cacao Pot: Epigraphic Observations on the Function of a Maya Ceramic Vessel." *Antiquity* 62: 153–157.

———. 2001. "Hieroglyphs on Maya Vessels." In *The Decipherment of Ancient Maya Writing,* edited by Stephen Houston, Oswaldo Chinchilla Mazariegos, and David Stuart, 474–485. Norman: University of Oklahoma Press.

Stuart, George E. 1992. "Quest for Decipherment: A Historical and Biographical Survey of Maya Hieroglyphic Investigation." In *New Theories on the Ancient Maya,* edited by Elin C. Danien and Robert J. Sharer, 1–63. University Museum Monograph 77. Philadelphia: University Museum, University of Pennsylvania.

Tate, Carolyn E. 1992. *Yaxchilan: The Design of a Maya Ceremonial City.* Austin: University of Texas Press.

Tedlock, Dennis, trans. 1985. *Popol Vuh: The Definitive Edition of the Mayan Book of the Dawn of Life and the Glories of Gods and Kings.* New York: Simon and Schuster.

Thompson, J. Eric S. 1927. *A Correlation of the Mayan and European Calendars.* Field Museum of Natural History, Anthropological Series, vol. 17, no. 1. Chicago: Field Museum.

———. 1950. *Maya Hieroglyphic Writing: An Introduction.* Carnegie Institution of Washington Publication 589. Washington, DC: Carnegie Institution of Washington.

———. 1971. *Maya Hieroglyphic Writing.* 3d ed. Norman: University of Oklahoma Press.

———. 1972. *Dresden: A Commentary on the Dresden Codex.* American Philosophical Society Memoir 93. Philadelphia: American Philosophical Society.

Tozzer, Alfred M., trans. 1941. *Landa's Relacion de las Cosas de Yucatan.* Papers of the Peabody Museum of Archaeology and Ethnology, vol. 18. Cambridge, MA: Harvard University.

Vail, Gabrielle. 2002. *The Madrid Codex: A Maya Hieroglyphic Book, Version 1.0.* A website and database available at http://www.doaks.org/codex.

Weeks, John. 2003. *Bibliografia Mesoamericana.* Available at http://www.famsi.org/research/bibliography.htm.

Willard, Theodore A. 1933. *The Codex Perez: An Ancient Mayan Hieroglyphic Book.* Glendale, CA: Arthur H. Clark.

PART 3
Current Assessments

CHAPTER 11

Major Controversies and Future Directions in the Study of the Maya Civilization

I t should not be surprising that Maya archaeologists often strongly disagree about the course of Maya prehistory. Some information seems more ephemeral than other information. Classic Maya society is recreated from fragmentary remains from a sample of sites that are partially excavated. The hieroglyphic record structures modern knowledge of Classic politics, history, and warfare associated with the dynastic Maya. The carved and dated stelae of the Classic period provide a rich dynastic history of the Maya kings and queens and their public and ritual lives. However, they provide little information on the lives of the common folk or on the ancient economy. A historical focus on large sites and big temples has provided detailed information on Maya architecture, but less is known about the ancient diet, the lives of the common Maya, or trade. That kind of information can be obtained from excavating household garbage from the houses of the common Maya. Problem-oriented field projects aimed at collecting artifacts and other material evidence to help answer specific questions have advanced researchers' knowledge of the ancient Maya. Still, there are many controversies about the ancient Maya, several of which will be discussed in this chapter.

THE CLASSIC MAYA COLLAPSE

From the nineteenth-century explorations of ruined Maya cities in the jungle to modern times, the collapse of the Maya civilization has perplexed both scholars and the public. Archaeological research has identified the collapse of the Classic period civilization by A.D. 900, associated with abandonment of most cities in the southern lowlands. Stelae were no longer erected detailing the dynastic histories of Maya kings and queens with dates in the Maya Long Count. However, settlement either continued or expanded in the northern Maya lowlands as well as along the Caribbean coasts of Belize and Mexico. By the time of the arrival of the Spaniards in the sixteenth century, the Maya area was divided into many independent polities. Why did the Classic Maya civilization collapse?

Some Maya archaeologists argue that the Classic civilization did not collapse, but that it instead just changed and relocated. The city of Lamanai, located on the shores of the New River Lagoon in Belize, continued uninterrupted settle-

Numbers	Glyph	Time	Date
••• ▬		Baktun (20 Katuns)	8 x 400
•••• ▬		Katun (20 Tuns)	9 x 20
•••		Tun (20 Winals)	3 x 360
••••		Winal (20 Kins)	4 x 20
▬ ▬ ▬		Kin (1-19 Days)	15

Maya Long Count, showing the date 8.9.3.4.15 (Courtesy H. McKillop)

ment from the Classic through much of the Postclassic. Other communities in northern Belize, such as Colha and Santa Rita, also witnessed significant Postclassic use. Perhaps these Belizean sites continued to prosper with the rise of Chichen Itza and other communities in the northern Maya lowlands because of their role in coastal trade. The emerging Maya elite at Chichen Itza had a taste for exotic paraphernalia, some of which was nicely preserved in the famous Cenote of Sacrifice at the site. Gold foil from lower Central America, copper objects from west Mexico or Honduras, and turquoise from northern Mexico attest to the expensive tastes of the Chichen Itza Maya court. Wild Cane Cay certainly expanded and prospered from participation in the circum-Yucatan sea trade linking Chichen Itza to places farther south.

Still, the major cities in the southern Maya lowlands were abandoned, and this begs explanation. Did the Maya "overextend" the agricultural capacity of the rainforest, with their increasing need for more food to feed the growing population? Did this overuse of the land result in catastrophic health problems and population decline? Or was there a popular revolt of the common Maya, who were overtaxed and overworked by the Late Classic? Was it endemic warfare, as Arthur Demarest would have us believe, that led to the downfall of lowland polities, one by one, like a house of cards? Were there catastrophic climatic changes, such as drought, or other major perturbations, such as earthquakes, that led to the untimely demise of the cities in the southern lowlands? There are proponents of all of these—ecological overload, endemic warfare, and climatic catastrophes—to explain the collapse of the Classic Maya civilization.

Sites mentioned in the text about current issues and future directions

David Webster (2002) points out that it was systemic ecological disaster that led to the collapse of the Late Classic lowland polities. This ecological view of the Maya collapse was the consensus of Mayanists gathered at a conference on the Classic Maya collapse whose proceedings were subsequently published (Culbert 1973), and the view has remained popular. Maya archaeologists agree that population growth was tremendous during the Classic period and that, by the Late Classic, the cities had reached high densities and large sizes, prompting questions of how the urban Maya were fed. William Haviland (1967) found a diminution in stature at Tikal during the Late Classic, although more recent research by Mary Danforth (1999) indicates that there was no overall reduction in height in the southern lowlands.

The Late Classic also was the time of large construction programs across the southern lowlands, resulting in the limestone temples at Tikal that still protrude above the rainforest canopy, for example. The temples, palaces, and other elite public and private buildings were built with the skilled labor of various craft workers attached to the royal courts. But it was the common Maya from the surrounding hinterland who provided unskilled labor to build the urban landscape and produce increasingly larger quantities of food to feed the urban Maya. Did the increasing demands of labor and food (and perhaps other) taxation lead to civil unrest and revolt, as once proposed by the eminent J. Eric S. Thompson (1970)?

More recent views add overuse of the land and systemic disaster to the picture of increasing population and taxation. The idea that the ancient Maya may have cut down the rainforest and overused the farmland in a desperate attempt to feed the growing population of the Late Classic is compelling to the modern Western reader: The Maya example provides a sobering analogue to the potential ecological risks faced today. The modern Maya need some twenty acres of rainforest per family for their milpa system of slash and burn or swidden farming. In that system, most of the land lays fallow, naturally replenishing nutrients, while a small field is cultivated for two to four years until its nutrients are depleted and weeds become plentiful, overtaking the planted crops. If the fallow cycle were reduced, the land would eventually become useless for agriculture due to soil erosion and weed growth. Lowe (1985) has modeled this systemic collapse using a computer simulation. This view paints a dismal picture of the dietary prospects for the Late Classic Maya.

Arthur Demarest is among the leading proponents of the endemic warfare model of the downfall of the Classic Maya dynasties, the collapse of their royal courts, and the abandonment of their cities (Demarest 1997; Demarest et al. 1997; Inomata 1997). Based on his multiyear field Petexbatun project in the Peten district of Guatemala, Demarest was able to reconstruct the rise of a lowland polity and its demise by chronic warfare. According to Lori Wright (1997), a biological anthropologist and part of Demarest's team, there was no systemic ecological decline that precipitated the abandonment of lowland cities at the end of the Classic period. She found no decline in health, judging from her chemical analysis of human bone by oxygen and nitrogen isotopes. Instead, Demarest and his colleagues paint a horrific picture of endemic warfare, from

Palace at Tikal consisting of stone buildings on a raised platform (Courtesy H. McKillop)

the fortification and sacking of Dos Pilas, to the fortification of hilltop camps, and fields, to the transfer of Dos Pilas's royal court to Aguateca. The residents of Aguateca ravaged stone buildings in the town center to construct defensive walls. Walls ran over the foundations of old buildings and through the middle of plazas. This was a desperate group of Dos Pilas royalty eking out a threadbare existence, under siege or threat of siege. They apparently fled Aguateca when it was sacked, leaving their household and workshop goods behind. Had the quest for power by the Maya royalty led to the downfall of the Classic polities throughout the southern Maya lowlands, one polity at a time, until the area was abandoned—except for the Maya farmers, who eventually returned to their fields and villages?

Was there a major environmental change that precipitated or exacerbated the collapse? A number of scientists specializing in the reconstruction of ancient vegetation and climate have reported significant climatic changes around A.D. 900 coinciding with the Classic Maya collapse. Since the cultural anthropologist Julian Steward (1955) introduced the concept of "cultural ecology," archaeologists have accepted that the natural environment plays a role in cultural change. Maya archaeologists discounted Betty Meggers's (1954) provocative idea that the tropical rainforest environment of the southern Maya lowlands "limited" the development of the Maya. Still, no one would deny that the natural environment impacts on the course of culture, including that of the ancient Maya. Scientists engaged in research on the ancient civilizations in the Andes of South America have given the environment a causal role in cultural change.

For example, changes in the availability of water in the southern Andes created environmental thresholds that scientists argue limited cultural development (Binford et al. 1997). The most dramatic limitation was a reduction in water that forced a reduction in agricultural production and led to a dramatic loss of population and, ultimately, the collapse of the Tiwanaka civilization. Did climatic changes in the Maya area have similar catastrophic consequences for the Classic period civilization?

David Hodell and colleagues (Hodell, Curtis, and Brenner 1995) propose that a drought between A.D. 800 and 1000 precipitated the Classic Maya collapse. Richardson Gill (2000) has also popularized the idea that drought caused the collapse. They cite as evidence climatic changes evident from changes in sediments and oxygen isotopes in sediment cores from Lake Chichanacanab in the Yucatan, Mexico. Drought conditions at the time of the Classic period collapse also were found from analysis of a sediment core from Lake Punta Laguna, near Coba, Quintana Roo, Mexico (Curtis, Hodell, and Brenner 1996).

McKillop (2002, 2003) suggests that researchers should expect regional variability in the climatic changes and that the Classic Maya response also was variable. Based on her coastal research on the eastern margins of the southern Maya lowlands, she identified a significant rise in sea level at the end of the Classic period. The Classic Maya responded in various ways to this catastrophic environmental change. In some cases, such as Pelican Cay, communities were inundated and abandoned and now lie deeply buried in mangrove swamps. Further settlement was not possible at Pelican Cay. By way of contrast, the Maya at Wild Cane Cay took preventive measures to ward off the rising seas. They constructed stone foundations to elevate their houses. Elizabeth Graham (1989, 1997) has underscored the importance of the impact of human settlement and their centuries of garbage on changing the ancient Maya landscape. McKillop (2002) argues that the salt works in Punta Ycacos Lagoon could have been relocated to nearby higher ground, but that their abandonment was due to the abandonment of the nearby inland cities whose inhabitants were supplied with the Punta Ycacos salt. In this way, one should expect a complex interplay between cultural and environmental factors in the collapse. Moreover, the marked environmental differences from the north coast of the Yucatan to its base near Wild Cane Cay need to be included in models of the collapse based on climatic catastrophe. A significant diminution in rainfall in the north, where there is relatively little rainfall, might be more catastrophic than in the south, where there is significantly more rainfall.

Although advances have been made in understanding the Classic Maya collapse, the answers to the fall of this great civilization remain enigmatic. Instead of one catastrophic event, scholars now know from decipherment of the dynastic records on Late Classic stelae that cities fell one by one over the course of 150 years, so that it was a long collapse. There is now a better acceptance of the environmental and cultural variability within the Maya lowlands, which needs to be considered in any explanations of the collapse. The plethora of field projects in the Maya area since 1980 have underscored the fact that many settlements, particularly in northern Belize, along the coast, and in the northern Maya lowlands, actually floresced after the collapse of the lowland polities in the southern Maya lowlands.

CITY-STATE, EMPIRE, OR CHIEFDOM

Despite decades of fieldwork uncovering ancient cities and despite scholars' ability to read the dynastic histories of the royal Maya, there is no consensus on the nature of the Classic Maya civilization. Certainly the Classic Maya were a civilization, with a hierarchy of settlements with complex social, economic, and political systems, all criteria for a civilization. The royal Maya ruled by "divine kingship," had a standing army, and controlled a political economy that allowed them, by conquest, tribute, taxation, and trade, to support a substantial court of artisans, servants, and other royal and nonroyal personages in cities. Stephen Houston's view is quite popular that there were perhaps eighty independent city-states in the southern Maya lowlands at the height of the Late Classic period (Martin and Grube 2000). Arlen and Diane Chase (1996), among others, view the Late Classic Maya kings and queens as more centralized and "empire-building."

Was there a qualitative difference between the Classic Maya civilization and the large, empire-building central state based at Teotihuacan? William T. Sanders and Barbara Price (1968) wrote an influential treatise arguing that the Classic Maya was a chiefdom until Teotihuacan's influence catapulted the Maya into a state level of organization. What is the difference between a chiefdom and a state, and is there any evidence for Sanders and Price's claim? A state-level society is more complex, has a central bureaucracy backed by a military, and has a larger population with a higher population density than that of a chiefdom (Flannery and Marcus 2003). The chief in a chiefdom maintains power by virtue of popularity through public feasts and gifts to other powerful individuals. Most Maya archaeologists consider the Late Classic Maya to have been a state-level organization. The extensive evidence of royal armies and warfare supports the view of a Late Classic Maya state in the southern lowlands.

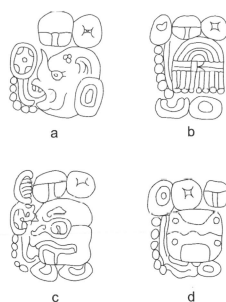

a   b

c   d

Examples of Maya emblem glyphs that represent major classic era polities: a) Copan; b) Tikal; c) Calakmul; d) Palenque. Each is actually a royal title that reads "divine ruler of (name of city)." (Drawing by Sandy Windelspecht)

Did Teotihuacan's contact with the Maya precipitate the Maya's rise to a state? Sanders and Price, among others, have argued that the pervasive evidence of Teotihuacan contact with the Maya included a takeover of Kaminaljuyu and usurpation of the Tikal throne by an interloper from Teotihuacan. Indeed, the Teotihuacan

Early Classic stela 31 from Tikal showing Nun Yax Ayin, father of Siyah Chan K'Awil on reverse side of stela (Courtesy H. McKillop)

"influence" is widespread in the Maya area (Braswell 2003). Some researchers contend that the hieroglyphic record of Tikal indicates a takeover by a member of the Teotihuacan dynasty (Miller 1999). Other evidence, including oxygen isotope studies, indicate that dead Maya interred with Teotihuacan grave offerings at Altun Ha and Kaminaljuyu "drank the local water" instead of being from Teotihuacan (White, Longstaffe, and Law 2001a; White, Longstaffe, and Law 2001b). Hieroglyphic evidence from Tikal points to the "arrival of strangers," likely a conquest by Smoking Frog from Teotihuacan in A.D. 378, coinciding with the death of Tikal ruler Great Jaguar Paw and the installation of Curl Nose (Martin and Grube 2000; Sharer 2003a; Sharer 2003b; Braswell 2003).

During the reign of Curl Nose and continuing with his son Stormy Sky, Tikal embarked on a successful campaign of geopolitical domination, involving both military battles and royal marriage alliances. The plan extended to other emerging lowland powers, including a political takeover at Copan and the establishment of the ruling dynasty at Copan's subsidiary city, Quirigua, in A.D. 426 or 427 (Sharer 2003a; Sharer 2003b). The military takeover of Copan by K'uk' Mo' in the same year led to his installation as king. Sharer, who directed research at both Quirigua and Copan, believes that Tikal's motivation was to control the jade sources along the Motagua via Quirigua and to use Copan as a gateway for trade with lower Central America, in addition to territorial aggrandizement. In both the Tikal and Copan takeovers, there is a clear Teotihuacan connection, which will be better resolved by oxygen isotope analysis of skeletal remains of the royalty and other studies. Exciting fieldwork at the site of Chac in the northern Maya lowlands indicates Teotihuacan architecture and other influence at that site, based on research by Michael Smyth re-

Nun Yax Ayin wears Teotihuacan style military regalia, A.D. 445 from Tikal, Guatemala (The Art Archive/Archaeological Museum Tikal Guatemala/Dagli Orti)

ported in *National Geographic* magazine (Stuart 2002). Whether the Teotihuacan connection was a military takeover or was symptomatic of prevailing international communication among Classic royalty throughout Mesoamerica will remain, undoubtedly, an area of heated discussion among Maya archaeologists. Further interpretation of heiroglyphs, oxygen isotope studies, and excavation of sites with Teotihuacan-style buildings and trade goods will help clarify the role of Teotihuacan in the development of the Maya state.

FEEDING THE MASSES

The high population of the southern Maya lowlands is no longer contested by scholars, but there remain many unanswered questions about how the masses were fed and what agricultural systems were in use. Although the modern Maya's use of milpa slash and burn (swidden) agriculture surely has great antiquity, this system could not have supported the high populations of the Late Classic (Harrison and Turner 1978; Turner and Harrison 1983). The terracing of hillslopes brought more land into cultivation and actually may have intensified its use by water management (Healy et al. 1983). The environmental diversity within the Maya lowlands meant that tree cropping, kitchen gardens, agroforestry (managing economically useful trees in the rainforst), and other systems of cultivation and plant management were practiced (McKillop 1994; McKillop 1996).

The age and extent of drained or raised-field agriculture remains unresolved. Excavations at Pulltrouser Swamp, Cerros, and Albion Island in northern Belize document water management and cultivation of low-lying land, even swamps. The Bajo de Morocoy in Quintana Roo also was cultivated. Turner and Harrison (1983) think Pulltrouser Swamp was drained and managed as a result of Late Classic population increases. But some researchers think drained field agriculture actually preceded the dramatic population increases of the Late Classic period. David Freidel (Freidel and Scarborough 1982) reports that the canal system and drained fields at Cerros were a successful attempt by the precocious Late Preclassic Maya elite at the community to harness control of local agricultural workers. In a similar interpretation, Mary Pohl (1990) interprets the drained fields at Albion Island as a way for the Preclassic Maya elite to garner power by management and control of the farming system.

The case for widespread use of drained field agriculture throughout the Maya lowlands presented by Richard E. W. Adams and colleagues (Adams, Brown, and Culbert 1981) from radar imagery needs to be checked from the ground. For example, the canal between Tikal and Yaxha shown in the images is actually a trail made by Anabel Ford's survey team. The greatest need for food was not in the periphery of the Maya area at places such as Pulltrouser Swamp where there are few large sites in the vicinity, but near Tikal in the Peten area of Guatemala where the largest cities with dynastic rulers lived. The Bajo de Santa Fe at Tikal has been investigated for drained field agriculture, but there are no conclusive results.

ILLEGAL TRADE IN MAYA ANTIQUITIES

Should Maya archaeologists study artifacts from private collections or museums, which often were looted from Maya sites? Certainly these artifacts are without context, so that their potential for interpretation of ancient Maya culture is limited. It has been contended that by studying artifacts in collections, Maya archaeologists legitimize and encourage further looting, destruction of

Maya sites, and collecting of antiquities. Although this ethical debate among Maya archaeologists is unresolved, laws governing the import and export of Maya artifacts limit their legal trade and collection. Countries signatory to the UNESCO (United Nations Educational, Scientific, and Cultural Organization) Convention of 1970 agreed to respect each other's cultural patrimony. Ensuing federal legislation in each country made it illegal to import and export antiquities, including Maya artifacts. Unfortunately, the United States, Japan, and West Germany, countries where much collecting of antiquities occurs, did not initially sign the UNESCO convention. The United States signed the UNESCO Convention in 1982 and passed related federal legislation, after which it became illegal to import artifacts, including Maya artifacts from Mexico, Guatemala, Honduras, El Salvador, and Belize, into the United States without a permit from the country of origin. Those countries prohibit the export of Maya artifacts without a permit from the government.

The art history tradition in Maya archaeology includes study of a considerable corpus of highly crafted painted pots and sculpture of unknown origin, obtained from private collections or museums. Some of the items undoubtedly were looted from Maya sites and acquired through the antiquities trade before legislation made these activities illegal. Art historians, antiquities collectors, and the public often appreciate Maya artifacts for their artistic value alone. The painted pots, murals, carved jade ornaments, and stone monuments with hieroglyphic inscriptions of the Late Classic period in particular are finely crafted. Many have scenes of Maya royalty and court life, including feasting, tribute payment, ritual bloodletting, torture, sacrifice, delivery of captives, and the ball game, that provide significant insights into the way of life of Maya royalty and other members of the royal court. They include attendants, wealthy merchants, artisans, women, musicians, and shaman-priests. Some scenes of Maya ritual and political events on Late Classic painted vases have no counterparts from excavated contexts (Coe 1978; Coe 1982; Kerr 1989–1994; Reents-Budet 1994). Some Maya archaeologists argue that without examination of such artifacts, even if they are of questionable legal status, modern knowledge of the ancient Maya would be greatly diminished.

However, other archaeologists contend that it is only with knowledge of the context of artifacts that their full value for interpreting ancient Maya culture can be recognized. They argue that without context, a Maya vessel is just another pretty pot and should not be studied, as study exonerates looting and collecting of artifacts. Context includes the location of the artifact and its association with other remains. The location in which an artifact is found situates the artifact temporally, and its association with other artifacts in a burial, fire pit, house floor, or building dedication provides clues to ancient activities—the building blocks that dirt archaeologists use to reconstruct ancient culture. Maya archaeologists study the decoration and form of artifacts as well as the context from which the artifacts were recovered in order to reconstruct ancient activities. Although no Maya archaeologist condones the looting of archaeological sites, whether or not artifacts from unprovenienced locations should be studied remains a controversial issue.

Pottery vase with fat merchant in obeissance to ruler from Tikal, Guatemala (The Art Archive/ Francesco Venturi)

Widespread interest in ecotourism, which brings together a concern with local involvement in tourism with preserving the natural and cultural heritage, may hold part of the key to reducing looting of Maya sites. Or, tourism may bring more foreign tourists interested in Maya antiquities closer to artifacts. Some indigenous Maya people, many still living a way of life little changed for hundreds of years, are becoming interested in preserving their past and participating in ecotourism. It is more often people of other ethnic backgrounds in the Maya-area countries, though, who have become active in developing tourism and have made important strides in protecting and promoting the cultural and natural heritage, including Maya ruins. The Toldeo Institute for Development and the Environment (TIDE) in Belize is one example of ecotourism integrating Maya people. Will tourism, ecotourism, and increased interest by indigenous Maya people in preserving their ancient past and acquiring rights to some of the land help preserve ancient Maya sites and their antiquities? Tourism underwrites much of the economy of the modern Mexican and Central American countries, which are home to ancient ruins and living Maya descendants. Who and what will benefit from tourism?

FUTURE DIRECTIONS IN MAYA ARCHAEOLOGY

Emphasis has been on the big cities, large architecture, great names, fancy goods, and exotic resources in Maya history, including the "earliest," "largest," and most "unique." Future research will focus on variability within Maya society by more regional settlement surveys, ceramic studies that go beyond the type-variety system, a search for a middle class or artisan class, a consideration of gender and age, and a better understanding of craft production and distribution within the lowlands that will extend researchers' understanding of ancient Maya people.

REFERENCES

Adams, Richard E. W., Walter E. Brown, Jr., and T. Patrick Culbert. 1981. "Radar Mapping, Archaeology, and Ancient Maya Land Use." *Science* 213: 1457–1463.

A Kekchi boy holds a slingshot carved like a quetzal in a cloud forest village near Coban, Guatemala (Corbis/Natalie Fobes)

Binford, Michael W., Alan L. Kolata, Mark Brenner, John W. Janusek, Matthew T. Seddon, Mark Abbott, and Jason H. Curtis. 1997. "Climate Variation and the Rise and Fall of an Andean Civilization." *Quaternary Research* 47: 235–248.

Braswell, Geoffrey E., ed. 2003. *The Maya and Teotihuacan. Reinterpreting Early Classic Interaction.* Austin: University of Texas Press.

Chase, Arlen F., and Diane Z. Chase. 1996. "More Than Kin and King: Centralized Political Organization among the Late Classic Maya." *Current Anthropology* 37 (5): 803–810.

Coe, Michael D. 1978. *Lords of the Underworld: Masterpieces of Classic Maya Ceramics.* Princeton, NJ: Art Museum, Princeton University, and Princeton University Press.

———. 1982. *Old Gods and Young Heroes: The Pearlman Collection of Maya Ceramics.* Jerusalem: Israel Museum.

Culbert, T. Patrick, ed. 1973. *The Classic Maya Collapse.* Albuquerque: University of New Mexico Press.

Curtis, Jason H., David A. Hodell, and Mark Brenner. 1996. "Climate Variability on the Yucatan Peninsula (Mexico) during the Past 3,500 Years, and Its Implications for Maya Cultural Evolution." *Quaternary Research* 46: 37–47.

Danforth, Marie. 1999. "Coming up Short: Stature and Nutrition among the Ancient Maya of the Southern Lowlands." In *Reconstructing the Ancient Maya Diet,* edited by Christine White, 103–117. Salt Lake City: University of Utah Press.

Demarest, Arthur. 1997. "The Vanderbilt Petexbatun Regional Archaeological Project

1989–1994: Overview, History, and Major Results of a Multidisciplinary Study of the Classic Maya Collapse." *Ancient Mesoamerica* 8: 209–227.

Demarest, Arthur A., Matt O'Mansky, Claudia Wolley, Dirk Van Tuerenhout, Takeshi Inomata, Joel Palka, and Hector Escobedo. 1997. "Classic Maya Defensive Systems and Warfare in the Petexbatun Region: Archaeological Evidence and Interpretations." *Ancient Mesoamerica* 8: 229–253.

Flannery, Kent V., and Joyce Marcus. 2003. "The Origin of War: New 14C Dates from Ancient Mexico." *Proceedings of the National Academy of Sciences* 100: 11801–11805.

Freidel, David A., and Vernon Scarborough. 1982. "Subsistence, Trade, and Development of the Coastal Maya." In *Maya Subsistence,* edited by Kent V. Flannery, 131–155. New York: Academic Press.

Gill, Richardson. 2000. *The Great Maya Droughts.* Albuquerque: University of New Mexico Press.

Graham, Elizabeth. 1989. "Brief Synthesis of Coastal Site Data from Colson Point, Placencia, and Marco Gonzalez, Belize." In *Coastal Maya Trade,* edited by Heather McKillop and Paul F. Healy, 135–154. Occasional Papers in Anthropology 8. Peterborough, Ontario: Trent University.

———. 1997. "Metaphor and Metaphorism: Some Thoughts on Environmental Metahistory." In *Advances in Historical Ecology,* edited by William Balee, 119–137. New York: Columbia University Press.

Harrison, Peter D., and B. L. Turner, eds. 1978. *Pre-Hispanic Maya Agriculture.* Albuquerque: University of New Mexico Press.

Haviland, William A. 1967. "Stature at Tikal, Guatemala: Implications for Ancient Maya Demography and Social Organization." *American Antiquity* 32: 117–125.

Healy, Paul F., John D. H. Lambert, J. T. Arnason, and Richard J. Hebda. 1983. "Caracol, Belize: Evidence of Ancient Maya Agricultural Terraces." *Journal of Field Archaeology* 10: 397–410.

Hodell, David A., Jason H. Curtis, and Mark Brenner. 1995. "Possible Role of Climate in the Collapse of Classic Maya Civilization." *Nature* 375: 391–394.

Inomata, Takeshi. 1997. "The Last Day of a Fortified Maya Center: Archaeological Investigations at Aguateca, Guatemala." *Ancient Mesoamerica* 8: 337–351.

Kerr, Justin, ed. 1989–1994. *The Maya Vase Book.* 4 vols. New York: Kerr.

Lowe, John W. G. 1985. *The Dynamics of Apocalypse: A Systems Simulation of the Classic Maya Collapse.* Albuquerque: University of New Mexico Press.

Martin, Simon, and Nicholai Grube. 2000. *Chronicle of the Maya Kings and Queens: Deciphering the Dynasties of the Ancient Maya.* New York: Thames & Hudson.

McKillop, Heather. 1994. "Ancient Maya Tree Cropping: A Viable Subsistence Adaptation for the Island Maya." *Ancient Mesoamerica* 5: 129–140.

———. 1996. "Prehistoric Maya Use of Native Palms." In *The Managed Mosaic: Ancient Maya Agriculture and Resource Use,* edited by Scott L. Fedick, 278–294. Salt Lake City: University of Utah Press.

———. 2002. *Salt: White Gold of the Ancient Maya.* Gainesville: University Press of Florida.

———. 2003. "Catastrophic and Other Environmental Factors in the Classic Maya Collapse." Paper presented at the annual meeting of the American Association of Geographers, New Orleans, March.

Meggers, Betty. 1954. "Environmental Limitation on the Development of Culture." *American Anthropologist* 56: 801–824.

Miller, Mary. 1999. *Maya Art and Architecture.* New York: Thames & Hudson.

Pohl, Mary D., ed. 1990. *Ancient Maya Wetland Agriculture: Excavations on Albion Island, Northern Belize.* Boulder, CO: Westview.

Reents-Budet, Dorie. 1994. *Painting the Maya Universe.* Durham, NC: Duke University Press.

Sanders, William T., and Barbara Price. 1968. *Mesoamerica: The Evolution of a Civilization.* New York: Random House.

Sharer, Robert J. 2003a. "Tikal and the Copan Dynastic Founding." In *Tikal: Dynasties, Foreigners, and Affairs of State,* edited by Jeremy A. Sabloff, 319–353. Santa Fe, NM: School of American Research Press.

———. 2003b. "Founding Events and Teotihuacan Connections at Copan, Honduras." In *Teotihuacan and the Maya,* edited by Geoffrey Braswell, 143–165. Austin: University of Texas Press.

Steward, Julian. 1955. *Theory of Culture Change.* Chicago: Aldine.

Stuart, George. 2002. "Yucatan's Mysterious Hill Cities." *National Geographic* 201 (4): 54–69.

Thompson, J. Eric S. 1970. *Maya History and Religion.* Norman: University of Oklahoma Press.

Turner, B. L., and Peter D. Harrison, eds. 1983. *Pulltrouser Swamp: Ancient Maya Habitat, Agriculture, and Settlement in Northern Belize.* Austin: University of Texas Press.

Webster, David. 2002. *The Fall of the Ancient Maya.* New York: Thames & Hudson.

White, Christine D., Fred J. Longstaffe, and Kimberley R. Law. 2001a. "Revisiting the Teotihuacan Connection at Altun Ha: Oxygen-Isotope Analysis of Tomb F-8/1." *Ancient Mesoamerica* 12 (1): 65–72.

Wright, Lori E. 1997. "Biological Perspectives on the Collapse of the Pasion Maya." *Ancient Mesoamerica* 8: 267–273.

Glossary

AGUATECA: CLASSIC-period walled city in PETEXBATUN, Guatemala, investigated by Takeshi Inomata, where evidence of elite CRAFT PRODUCTION was found. The city was abandoned suddenly due to WARFARE.

AHAU: The highest rank in Maya society was that of ahau, lord; this included both the ruler and a larger group of males and females, not all of whom were of equal rank. Ahau was an inherited status.

ALTAR DE SACRIFICIOS: CLASSIC Maya city along the Pasion River, Guatemala, excavated under direction of GORDON R. WILLEY, with major ceramic study by Richard E. W. Adams.

ALTUN HA: MINOR CENTER north of Belize City investigated by David Pendergast and famous for a 4.4-kilogram carved JADE head of the Maya sun god from a TEMPLE tomb. The JADE head is stored in Belize Bank in Belize City.

ARCHAIC: Time period of development of agriculture, hunting of small animals, and gathering wild plants before the introduction of pottery and farming villages in the Maya area. It is best known at COLHA and by Belize surveys by Richard MacNeish, and it predates 1000 B.C. in the MAYA LOWLANDS.

ASTRONOMY: The DRESDEN CODEX provides details of Late POSTCLASSIC astronomical knowledge, but much has also been gleaned from CLASSIC Maya visual images, the layout of buildings, and analogies with the POPOL VUH. The Maya recorded and predicted the daily, seasonal, and yearly trajectories of the sun, moon, planets, and stars in relation to the Earth, as well as solar and lunar solstices and equinoxes, the rising and setting of planets, and the likelihood of comets.

BAKING POT: MINOR CENTER along the Belize River, investigated by Oliver and Mary Ricketson of CARNEGIE INSTITUTION, Gordon Willey's Belize Valley survey in 1950s, and more recently by Belize archaeologists Jaime Awe and Allan Moore.

BAKTUN: The largest unit of time in the Maya counting system, referring to a period of 400 years.

BALL COURT: Usually at the center of cities, a rectangular playing field with sloped or vertical walls and sometimes circular ball court markers along the centerline. Here, according to depictions on painted pots and stone carvings and recounted in the POPOL VUH, two or more players used a RUBBER BALL in a game that may have been for life or death, sometimes played with war captives.

BALL GAME: A Maya game of chance, skill, and trickery reflecting life. Playing ball engaged one in the maintenance of the cosmic order of the universe and the ritual regeneration of life. War captives were brought to play ball, but also the central location of BALL COURTS at Maya cities places them as central to the political lives of the Maya court in many additional ways.

BARRA PHASE: Earliest pottery in Maya area, on Pacific littoral about 1800 B.C.

BARTON RAMIE: A small community consisting mainly of house mounds, which was the focus of Gordon Willey's pioneering settlement pattern study along the Belize River during the 1950s.

BECAN: The defensive wall at Becan suggests early WARFARE, involving the central Mexican state of Teotihuacan, since GREEN OBSIDIAN was associated with the defensive wall and Teotihuacan controlled the green obsidian quarry.

BERLIN, HEINRICH: Made critical discovery that EMBLEM GLYPHS are names of Maya cities, which, along with discoveries by PROSKOURIAKOFF and KNOROZOV, were instrumental in the decipherment of Mayan HIEROGLYPHS.

BLOODLETTING: Blood offerings made by the Maya to their GODS. OBSIDIAN blades, stingray spines, and knotted ropes are shown in scenes on carved monuments and painted pictorial pots being used to pierce the tongue, lips, genitals, or other body parts to make blood offerings to the GODS, such as on a stone sculpture from Yaxchilan. The cloth bundles often shown held by royal women during accession ceremonies at Yaxchilan may have contained the BLOODLETTING equipment.

BOATS: Canoes depicted on carved bones from a BURIAL in a TEMPLE at TIKAL, in carved manatee rib bones from ALTUN HA and MOHO CAY, from pottery replicas from ORLANDO'S JEWFISH in southern Belize, and on painted murals from CHICHEN ITZA were powered by canoe paddlers, with no evidence of the use of sails.

BONAMPAK: Painted murals on interior walls of buildings depict scenes of WARFARE, capture, and torture by the Late CLASSIC Maya of this city in the southern MAYA LOWLANDS, as studied by Mary Miller.

BURIALS: Interment of the common Maya was normally under house floors or in the construction fill of a new building, whereas the royal Maya were buried in their TEMPLES. Both types of burials were associated with grave offerings.

CAHAL: After the AHAU, the next lower social level, still considered nobility. Cahals were rulers of small sites, as well as nobles who assisted the AHAU in battle and in various royal ceremonies. Both AHAU and cahal were inherited statuses.

CAHAL PECH: MINOR CENTER in the outskirts of the modern town of San Ignacio, Belize, important for Middle Preclassic development. The site was investigated by Jaime Awe, and the reconstruction of Late CLASSIC architecture was done by Joseph Ball and Jennifer Taschek.

CALENDAR: Using the GMT (Goodman-Martinez-Thompson) correlation to the Christian CALENDAR, the Maya CALENDAR originated in 3114 B.C. and was used to provide dates using a base 20, with numbers written from the top in multiples of 400 years, multiples of 20 years, and multiples of 20 days (months), using a sophisticated MATHEMATICAL SYSTEM and the numbers 1 through 19 indicating the date.

CALENDAR ROUND: The 365-day vague year and the 260-day TZOLKIN CALEN-DARS combined to form the Maya Calendar Round. It took 52 (vague) years for the same day on each calendar to co-occur (260 × 365 = 18,980 days). A Calendar Round date consists of the Tzolkin date followed by the vague year date, such as 1 Kán 1 Pop.

CANCUEN: Southern Maya lowland city at juncture of highland-lowland trade route, investigated by Arthur Demarest.

CARACOL: Maya city in western Belize, excavated by Diane and Arlen Chase, with sacbes linking a large suburban area to central city.

CARNEGIE INSTITUTION: Focus of major research at UAXACTUN in the southern MAYA LOWLANDS, CHICHEN ITZA and MAYAPAN in the northern MAYA LOWLANDS, and KAMINALJUYU in the southern Maya highlands until its closure in 1958. Notable archaeologists were Alfred V. Kidder, Oliver and Mary Ricketson, A. LEDYARD SMITH, ROBERT E. SMITH, Harry Pollock, Jesse Jennings, Ed Shook, and TATIANA PROSKOURIAKOFF.

CAVES: Common in the limestone topography of the MAYA LOWLANDS, and commonly used by the ancient Maya for rituals. This was perhaps due to the rich symbolic imagery in Maya mythology of the watery underworld. Caves have been studied in western Belize by Jaime Awe (following earlier studies by David M. Pendergast), in the PETEXBATUN by James Brady, and in Naj Tunich by Andrea Stone. Caves in the Maya area contained painted images, pottery vessels, and sometimes BURIALS.

CEREN: CLASSIC Maya community buried by the Loma Calerda volcanic eruption and later discovered and excavated by Payson Sheets, with outstanding preservation of houses and volcanic casts of plants and furrows in fields. Now a World Heritage site (listed with the United Nations), Ceren is protected by the government of El Salvador and open to the public for tourism.

CERROS: Late Preclassic community on the shores of Corozal Bay in northern Belize (opened as a tourist site by Belize government), famous for painted masks on TEMPLES and other monumental buildings and for iconography that archaeologist David Freidel demonstrated to show precocious development leading to CLASSIC civilization.

CHAC: Maya rain god and name of northern Maya lowland site near SAYIL, investigated by Michael Smyth, with TEOTIHUACAN-style architecture indicating some form of trade or contact with central Mexico. Chac, the god of rain and lightning, is often shown with axes and snakes, which he used to affect the weather.

CHAU HIIX: MINOR CENTER between ALTUN HA and LAMANAI in northern Belize, investigated by K. Anne Pyburn.

CHERT: A hard stone naturally occurring in the limestone platform of the MAYA LOWLANDS and used widely for chipping stone tools.

CHICHEN ITZA: A city in the northern MAYA LOWLANDS that grew to prominence after the collapse of the Late CLASSIC cities in the southern lowlands. Research here by the CARNEGIE INSTITUTION of Washington focused on restoration; the age of the city and the explanation for the Toltec-style architecture remain under discussion.

CHILAM BALAM: Books written by native Maya in several Yucatecan communities during early colonial days, variously informative on religion and ideology. Chilam Balam was a native priest who evidently foretold the arrival of the Spaniards. The Chilam Balam of Chumayel, Tizimin, and Mani are the most famous, having been translated into English.

CHOLAN: The spoken and written language of the CLASSIC Maya of the southern lowlands. Cholan includes two groups: the Chol and Chontal group and the Cholti and Chorti group. Chorti may have dominated the southern MAYA LOWLANDS before A.D. 1000. The coastal plain from southern Belize to the area of Quirigua on the MOTAGUA RIVER of Guatemala, the north coast of Honduras, and inland to COPAN was populated by Chol speakers.

CHUNCHUCMIL: Northern Maya lowland city investigated by Bruce Dahlin, without monumental architecture. It arguably was a trading depot controlling coastal SALT from nearby SALT flats.

CITY-STATES: By the Late CLASSIC, the lowlands were divided into city-states, each with a capital city and smaller towns, villages, and agricultural lands. The degree to which they were independent or centralized under one or more larger polities is controversial, but it likely changed over time and space with WARFARE and alliances.

CLASSIC MAYA COLLAPSE: Many explanations have been proposed to explain the abandonment of Late CLASSIC cities in the southern MAYA LOWLANDS, depopulation of much of the area, and the collapse of the CLASSIC royal dynasties. Proposed explanations include WARFARE, ecological disaster, climatic change (drought), disease, overpopulation, and popular revolt.

CLASSIC PERIOD: The time roughly between A.D. 300 and 900, when Maya royalty erected STELAE at lowland cities with dates in the MAYA LONG COUNT corresponding to the time of royal dynasties.

CLIMATE CHANGE: Sediment cores in lagoons provide pollen and soil evidence for a changing landscape, including drier weather. These changes coincided with major political upheavals in the MAYA LOWLANDS, including the CLASSIC MAYA COLLAPSE, HIATUS, and abandonment of CHICHEN ITZA, all of which have been proposed as either explanatory or coincidental.

COBA: City in the northern MAYA LOWLANDS, investigated by William Folan. It did not collapse but continued into POSTCLASSIC, perhaps due to the proximity of water.

CODEX (PLURAL = CODICES): Maya book made using bark from fig trees that was prepared with a gesso and then painted with HIEROGLYPHS and images. Only four codices are known to have survived—Madrid, Dresden, Paris, and Grolier—and they focus on astronomical matters and date to after the CLASSIC period.

CODICES: See CODEX.

COLHA: A site located beside an outcrop of high-quality CHERT in northern Belize, where vast quantities of CHERT stone tools were produced by household WORKSHOPS and distributed within northern Belize and beyond from the Late Preclassic to Early POSTCLASSIC, according to the site's excavators, Tom Hester and Harry Shafer.

COPAN: A city in modern Honduras that grew to prominence in the CLASSIC period and is known in particular for its hieroglyphic staircase and artistic style of sculpting STELAE in the round. From the time of John Stephens's nineteenth-century accounts, the site has received intensive investigation by archaeologists from Harvard, Tulane, Penn State, the University of Pennsylvania, and the country of Honduras.

COPPER: Bells, rings, and other items made from copper alloy traded from Honduras or west Mexico were found at a variety of lowland Maya sites dating from the POSTCLASSIC period, notably from the Cenote of Sacrifice at CHICHEN ITZA.

COSMOLOGY: The Maya cosmos was a sky-Earth with the actions of humans intertwined with celestial movement of the stars as recorded in the CALENDAR. The balance and continuity of daily life among the Maya required ritual interactions with the GODS. The world consisted of the heavens, containing GODS, the Earth, containing humans; and the underworld, containing underworld GODS. The living world was quadripartite, with directions associated with different colors. There were thirteen layers of heaven and nine layers of the underworld.

COUNTING SYSTEM: Numbers were written using a dot to represent the value 1, a horizontal bar for 5, and a stylized shell for 0. The counting system was based on multiples of 20 and the Maya had the concept of 0, which was quite sophisticated and was rarely used in other ancient civilizations.

COZUMEL: A POSTCLASSIC island trading locale off the eastern coast of the Yucatan, also the location of a pilgrimage shrine, investigated by Jeremy Sabloff and William Rathje.

CRAFT PRODUCTION: CHERT tools manufactured in household WORKSHOPS at COLHA; SALT produced in independent WORKSHOPS at STINGRAY LAGOON, DAVID WESTBY, ORLANDO'S JEWFISH, and other underwater sites in Paynes Creek National Park; and elite pots and hooks at AGUATECA indicate variability in production from household to specialized, with elite control of production also variable.

CREATION STORY: As told in the *POPOL VUH* and depicted in scenes on CLASSIC painted pots, the Maya world was created from a meeting of the GODS from the primordial sea (Plumed Serpent) and the primordial sky (Heart of Sky) to discuss the emergence of the Earth from the sea and the creation of plants, the sun, the moon, and stars, and people. The first people were created from corn, with an earlier attempt from wood having ended up creating monkeys.

CUELLO: Northern Belize site where the earliest Maya pottery, farming, and architecture were first identified by Norman Hammond, dating to 1000 B.C.

CURL NOSE: A ruler whose accession to the throne at TIKAL marks the beginning of TEOTIHUACAN influence at the city. Two BURIALS thought to be those of Curl Nose and his successor, Stormy Sky, include imported vessels, made at either TEOTIHUACAN or KAMINALJUYU. They include vessels with distinctive TEOTIHUACAN painted decoration on stucco. A TIKAL STELA bears portraits of either Curl Nose or Stormy Sky wearing TEOTIHUACAN military regalia, including the TEOTIHUACAN god Tlaloc on shields, and spear throwers typical of TEOTIHUACAN.

DAVID WESTBY SITE: A Late CLASSIC SALT works in Punta Ycacos Lagoon, Paynes Creek National Park, Belize, excavated by Heather McKillop.

DEFENSIVE WALLS: Defensive walls have been found at a number of southern lowland sites, notably TIKAL, EL MIRADOR, SEIBAL, and BECAN, and at a number of sites in the northern Yucatan. They are nowhere so common and pervasive as in the PETEXBATUN region, where even small communities, agricultural fields, and water sources were fortified during the Late CLASSIC period.

DE LANDA, BISHOP: Franciscan priest who was appointed the first Bishop of the Yucatan but was recalled to Spain for overzealous conversion of the Maya, including an auto-da-fé at Mani in the northern Yucatan in which Maya CODICES were gathered and burned. In his defense while in jail in Spain, de Landa wrote *Relación de las Cosas de Yucatan,* which, ironically, is regarded as a major documentary source of the contact period Maya.

DEMOGRAPHY: Ancient population estimates are usually based on counting the number of house mounds and multiplying by a factor representing an estimate of an average family, often 5.6 people. Although this method neglects to include houses for which there are no mounded remains, the lack of cemeteries or written death records makes any other method of population estimating difficult.

DISTANCE DATES: Often used to record dates of CLASSIC Maya events on STELAE. A Distance Date refers to the time since the initial LONG COUNT date on the STELA.

DOS PILAS: City in the PETEXBATUN region of the southern MAYA LOWLANDS, investigated by Arthur Demarest, where endemic WARFARE and alliances with other CITY-STATES were a feature of Late CLASSIC.

DRESDEN CODEX: One of four surviving Maya books, or codices, with hieroglyphic text and images painted on prepared bark paper and fan-folded. The Dresden Codex was found in the Dresden Library in Germany by Ernst Förstemann, who translated it and brought it to the attention of scholars.

DZIBILCHALTUN: City in the northern MAYA LOWLANDS that enjoyed prominence from the Late Preclassic through the CLASSIC period.

ECOTOURISM: A form of tourism that brings together a concern for local involvement in tourism with preserving an area's natural and cultural heritage. Ecotourism may hold part of the key to reducing the looting of Maya sites by increasing local interest in preserving sites for tourism and increasing tourists' interest in preserving sites.

E GROUP: Groups of buildings found at many lowland sites, notably UAXACTUN, TIKAL, DZIBILCHALTUN, and CHICHEN ITZA that have clear astronomical importance as observatories. A Late Preclassic building at UAXACTUN, for example, faces a platform with a line of three TEMPLES. From the building, the summer solstice sun rises behind the northern TEMPLE, the equinox sun rises behind the central TEMPLE, and the winter solstice sun rises behind the southern TEMPLE.

EK BALAM: Northern MAYA LOWLAND city with occupation from the Preclassic period onward, investigated by George Bey and Bill Ringle.

EL CHAYAL: Outcrop of high-quality OBSIDIAN near modern Guatemala City, widely used by the CLASSIC Maya for making blades and other objects.

EL MIRADOR: Large southern LOWLAND MAYA city that grew to prominence in the Late Preclassic and was then abandoned, investigated by Ray Matheny and Bruce Dahlin and, subsequently, by Richard Hansen.

EL PILAR: City that straddles the border between western Belize and Guatemala, reconstructed as an archaeological and ecological binational park by Anabel Ford and open to the public.

EMBLEM GLYPH: The hieroglyphic name of a CLASSIC city; more than eighty such glyphs have been identified. Written on STELAE, they often recorded the defeat of a city and are now used by archaeologists to reconstruct the political history of the CLASSIC period.

E-VII-SUB: A TEMPLE at UAXACTUN with four staircases and monumental masks, regarded as a prototype of Late Preclassic architecture. Excavated by Oliver Ricketson of the CARNEGIE INSTITUTION of Washington project.

FRENCHMAN'S CAY: Late CLASSIC Maya trading port with the remains of three coral rock building platforms, in the Port Honduras Marine Reserve, investigated by Heather McKillop.

GOD A: The skeletal god of death, God A also was the god of violent sacrifice such as decapitation and was usually denoted by a black band across his eyes. He appears in Early CLASSIC Maya art and in the CODICES.

GOD K: God of royal descent (K'awiil), fire, and lightning. He was shown as a scepter held by rulers and also as a figure with an upturned snout; a celt, smoking tube, or torch on his forehead; and a serpent foot. Kulkulkan succeeded him in the POSTCLASSIC.

GOD L: CLASSIC period MERCHANT GOD.

GOD M: The CLASSIC period MERCHANT GOD was eclipsed during the POSTCLASSIC by this MERCHANT GOD, who is identified by his pendulous lower lip, black face, and long, pointed nose.

GODS: A host of gods, goddesses, and other supernatural beings mediated the world of the ancient Maya. Some of these gods are known historically from their appearance in the *POPOL VUH*, the codices, or the books of CHILAM BALAM and were prehistorically depicted on painted pots, carved monuments, clay figurines, and other artwork.

GREEN OBSIDIAN: Stone used by the Maya for blades and other objects. The only known source of green obsidian is Pachuca, north of modern Mexico City, which was controlled by TEOTIHUACAN during the CLASSIC period and was part of the POLITICAL ECONOMY of the CLASSIC Maya. This indicates some level of communication, direct or indirect, between TEOTIHUACAN and the Maya. Green obsidian found at POSTCLASSIC Maya sites indicates trade with later highland people.

HAAB CALENDAR: A 365-day CALENDAR that closely approximates the true solar year of 356.2422 days. It is often referred to as the "vague" year CALENDAR, because it includes five days called "wayeb" at the end of each cycle of eighteen named months, each with twenty numbered days.

HALLUCINOGENS: Used by dynastic leaders in pursuit of VISION QUESTS. Nobles sought altered mental states by using hallucinogenic enemas, by smoking tobacco, by fasting, and by BLOODLETTING. Figures painted on CAVE walls at Naj Tunich are depicted as if they were in an altered state of consciousness. Hallucinogens included extract from the *Bufo marinus* frog, mushrooms, and perhaps poison from stingray spines and other marine fauna used by the CLASSIC Maya.

HERO TWINS: A pair of twins discussed in the historic text the POPOL VUH and depicted graphically on CLASSIC Maya painted pots and scenes on carved stone. The adventures of the Hero Twins, Hunahpu and Xbalanque, establish the relationships between humans and the celestial and underworld GODS and the place of the CALENDAR and the BALL GAME in facilitating human existence. In one adventure, they assign a star to each of the four corners of the world, establishing the quadripartite "worldview," or COSMOLOGY, of the Maya. The Hero Twins battle VUCUB CAQUIX and play the original BALL GAME with the lords of the underworld (XIBALBA), thus establishing the relations between the underworld and the living world.

HIATUS: A time between A.D. 534 and 593, when the power of TIKAL and the northeast PETEN in the Early CLASSIC halted temporarily. TIKAL stopped erecting carved STELAE during this period, coinciding with the dominance of other lowland Maya cities.

HIEROGLYPHS: Maya writing. Maya glyphs are phonetic in that they are based on spoken language, Chol being the language at the time of the CLASSIC period in the southern MAYA LOWLANDS. The basic component of a glyph is a sound consisting of a consonant-vowel-consonant combination. Some Maya glyphs represent words, but others are sounds that are used together to form words. The hieroglyphs were used to record historical information about the lives of the dynastic Maya during the CLASSIC period and continued to be used in writing in the POSTCLASSIC, with some focus on ASTRONOMY, the CALENDAR, and rituals.

HOLMUL: Prototype site in the southern MAYA LOWLANDS where George Vaillant and Robert Merwin reported distinctive PROTOCLASSIC pottery vessels, sparking debate about their local or intrusive origin, subsequently investigated by Francisco Estrada-Belli.

HUN HUNAHPU: Father of the HERO TWINS, also known as the MAIZE GOD.

ILOPANGO: Volcanic eruption in the fifth century that caused regional devastation in the Zapotitan Valley in El Salvador, making the area uninhabitable for about 200 years. Ceren, itself later destroyed by the Loma Caldera volcanic eruption radiocarbon dated to between A.D. 610 and 671, was one of the first communities to occupy the valley after the Ilopango eruption.

INGENTA: An electronic journal retrieval service available at university libraries and by subscription for downloading articles from the Internet.

INTENSIVE AGRICULTURE: Modification of the landscape by terracing or by draining wetlands in order to increase production, often related to increased population of the Late CLASSIC MAYA LOWLANDS, as at PULLTROUSER SWAMP, Belize, or the MAYA MOUNTAINS of western Belize.

"INVISIBLE ARCHITECTURE": Refers to houses built directly on the ground without stone platforms or any other type of foundation. Many such houses leave no mounded remains and are invisible to modern archaeologists, which may cause researchers to dramatically underestimate population estimates that are based on house mound counts.

ISLA CERRITOS: An Early POSTCLASSIC trading port located off the north coast of Yucatan for the inland city of CHICHEN ITZA. Excavated by Anthony P. Andrews, the site has a harbor and abundant central Mexican OBSIDIAN.

ISOTOPE ANALYSIS: A chemical test done on human bone and teeth that provides dietary and other information about individual Maya. Carbon isotopes (C^{13}/C^{12}) distinguish between corn and other plant foods consumed, as the foods have different photosynthetic pathways (different ways that plants absorb sunlight). Nitrogen isotopes (N^{18}/N^{16}) distinguish between marine and terrestrial or riverine animals eaten. Oxygen isotope analysis (O^{18}/O^{16}) identifies the source location of water consumed, thereby identifying an individual's area of origin.

ITXTEPEQUE: A source of high-quality OBSIDIAN in the Maya highlands east of modern Guatemala City. It was a common source of OBSIDIAN in the Late CLASSIC, and it dominated POSTCLASSIC OBSIDIAN production in the MAYA LOWLANDS for blade making.

ITZAMNA: The paramount male god, also known as "Lizard House." He is the aged creator god, God D, and is commonly depicted in CLASSIC and POSTCLASSIC art. He is identifiable as an aged god with a Roman nose. Itzamna and his consort, IX CHE, are the progenitors of all other GODS and also are the old couple in the *POPOL VUH*. Itzamna is credited with inventing writing. He is shown as a Maya scribe on pottery vessels and also is shown engaged in divination and other scribal and priestly activities.

IX CHEL: Also known as Lady Rainbow. She is clearly the most important goddess and is consort of the sun. However, as goddess of the moon and ruler of the night sky, she opposes the sun in her efforts to defeat the sun each day and make it descend into darkness. At the time of European contact, Ix Chel was the goddess of childbirth, pregnancy, and fertility. Ix Chel also was associated with weaving, fertility, and midwifery. There were shrines dedicated to her on COZUMEL and Isla Mujeres off the eastern coast of the Yucatan to which people made pilgrimages.

IZAPA: A Preclassic site on the Pacific coastal plain of Chiapas that has art styles and iconography midway between OLMEC and later Maya, and has depictions of VUCUB CAQUIX and the long-lipped god.

JADE: Greenstones, including jade, serpentine, and albite, have been identified from outcrops along the MOTAGUA RIVER drainage in Guatemala and were elaborately carved at lowland Maya sites into elite pendants, later recovered from burials and caches.

JAGUAR: A very common animal in ancient Maya iconography and mythology, perhaps because both the Maya and jaguars shared the rainforest. The jaguar was especially identified with the sun in both its daytime and nighttime form, the latter associated with XIBALBA, where he sometimes rode a caiman across the nighttime sky. Other jaguar gods included the Water Lily Jaguar, a zoomorphic creature with a WATER LILY on his forehead and often a collar of bulging eyeballs around his neck. Among his many roles, the Water Lily Jaguar acted as a throne and walked in underworld processions. As a powerful rainforest animal, the jaguar is common in shamanistic or ritual transformations in Mesoamerica.

JESTER GOD: A god common in CLASSIC Maya iconography but having its origins in earlier OLMEC times at La Venta. The Jester God had a head ornament dangling over his head and was often, but not exclusively, associated with Maya royalty, as with King Pacal's grave at Palenque.

JSTOR: An electronic journal retrieval service ("journal storage") at http://www.jstor.org for downloading the text of articles from the Internet, available at many libraries or by subscription.

KAMINALJUYU: A site located on the outskirts of modern Guatemala City, investigated by Alfred V. Kidder, Jesse Jennings, and Ed Shook in the 1940s and by William T. Sanders and Joseph Michels of Penn State in the 1970s. Kaminaljuyu was an important Late Preclassic and CLASSIC city, with TEOTIHUACAN-style architecture and pottery vessels, suggesting military takeover, trade, or alliances with central Mexico between A.D. 400 and 700.

KATUN: A unit of time in counting and the CALENDAR, representing a period of twenty years.

KILLER BEE: A Late CLASSIC SALT works excavated by Heather McKillop in Paynes Creek National Park.

KIN: A Maya day.

KINGSHIP: During the CLASSIC period, power and authority were focused on the king, articulated and publicly reinforced and reinterpreted by the public display of carved STELAE bearing his image and accounts of his (or occasionally a queen's) exploits. Rulers combined supreme political authority with a quasi-divine status. They were mediators between the supernatural and the real worlds. Through regular public and private ceremonies involving dance, blood sacrifice, trances, and enemas, the king engaged divine power.

KINICH AHAU: The Maya sun god, also known as God G. He transformed himself into a JAGUAR each night as he traveled through XIBALBA (the underworld). He was otherwise closely associated with the JAGUAR. Kinich Ahau may actually have been a variant of ITZAMNA. Perhaps the most famous CLASSIC Maya depiction of Kinich Ahau is the large (4.4 kilogram) carved JADE head taken from a tomb in a TEMPLE at ALTUN HA, Belize. The head of Kinich Ahau also was featured on stone or stucco masks on TEMPLE façades. In addition, the head of Kinich Ahau was a glyphic substitute for the number 4.

KINSHIP: The ancient Maya identified their place in society from their kinship, identified by the ancestral home with ancestors buried under earlier houses at the same location. This tracing of kinship laid the foundations for the CLASSIC period concept of KINGSHIP, in which a ruler governed by divine power and authority through dynastic ties.

KNOROZOV, YURI: Correctly determined that Mayan HIEROGLYPHS were phonetic rather than pictographs, which was critical in decipherment of the glyphs.

LADYVILLE: A location near Belize City's International Airport, site of surface recovery of the first PALEOINDIAN fluted point by Thomas Kelley of the COLHA Project.

LA ESPERANZA: An OBSIDIAN outcrop near the modern community by that name in western Honduras. La Esperanza was a minor source of OBSIDIAN used at Quirigua and WILD CANE CAY, but its OBSIDIAN was more commonly used by people in lower Central America, outside the Maya area.

LAMANAI: City on Northern Lagoon dating from the Middle Preclassic through the POSTCLASSIC, without suffering the CLASSIC period collapse. This city had a Franciscan mission and nineteenth-century sugar mill and was excavated by David Pendergast and Elizabeth Graham.

LA MILPA: CLASSIC Maya city in northwestern Belize, investigated by SIR J. ERIC S. THOMPSON and subsequently by Norman Hammond, with a site layout reflecting the quadripartite cosmogram of the Maya universe, according to project surveyor Gair Tourtellot.

LONG COUNT: A CALENDAR system that defined a period of about 5,200 years based on 13 BAKTUN cycles (multiples of 400 years), reflecting the CREATION of the world as described in CLASSIC images and the *POPOL VUH.*

LUBAANTUN: City in southern Belize investigated in the 1920s by the British Museum and subsequently in 1970 by Norman Hammond, known for its sandstone buildings and lack of STELAE, dating to the Late CLASSIC. Famous for the alleged discovery by Anna Mitchell-Hedges of a human-shaped crystal skull, now in Kitchener, Canada, which was more likely obtained from a European antique store and planted at the site.

MACEHUALOB: The lowest social status among the Maya. Below the AHAU and CAHAL, these were the commoners in Maya society.

MAIZE GOD: Also known as God E. He is HUN HUNAHPU from the *POPOL VUH* or Hun Nah Yeh. He was depicted in the CLASSIC period as the tonsured Maize God, representing HUN HUNAHPU, the father of the HERO TWINS from the *POPOL VUH.* He sometimes was shown with his head flattened like a mature maize ear. Alternatively, he was shown as the foliated Maize God, with a maize ear emerging from a human head. The resurrection of HUN HUNAHPU symbolized the planting and growth of a new maize crop. His death by decapitation was a metaphor for the harvesting of corn and for death. In the Late POSTCLASSIC, the Maize God was sometimes represented as the diving god, shown on murals at Tulum and also depicted at MAYAPAN and MOHO CAY.

MAJOR CENTERS: The capitals of lowland polities, showing the hieroglyphic records on carved stone monuments (STELAE) of the ruling Maya dynasty of the particular CITY-STATE.

MAMON POTTERY: Middle Preclassic pottery (700–300 B.C.) found at many sites in the southern MAYA LOWLANDS.

MANO: A cylindrical stone held in two hands and used to grind corn on the surface of a METATE, or stone grinding implement.

MARCO GONZALEZ: Trading site in the southern part of Ambergris Cay, Belize, that played an important role in SEA TRADE and coastal-inland trade, as investigated by Elizabeth Graham and David Pendergast.

MARRIAGE ALLIANCES: Royal Maya engaged in marriage alliances to cement interpolity relations. In the wider sphere of regional geopolitics, intermarriages sometimes occurred with politics at some distance, whereas WARFARE was usually initiated with polities closer geographically, usually neighbors. The greatest distance for interpolity marriage was between Palenque and CO-

PAN, which are 109 kilometers apart. For the other seven known instances of interpolity marriage, the average distance is 64 kilometers.

MATHEMATICS: Using a dot to indicate 1, a bar for 5, and a stylized shell for 0, the Maya could write any number, and they used their mathematics to record historical and astronomical events.

MAYA LONG COUNT: CALENDAR system used in the CLASSIC PERIOD, based on bars and dots, that provides dates for events with the year zero corresponding to 3114 B.C.

MAYA LOWLANDS: A flat, tropical rainforest area on the limestone platform of the Yucatan peninsula of Mexico, Guatemala, and Belize. The lowlands are environmentally diverse and include the MAYA MOUNTAINS and Puuc Hills. The CLASSIC Maya civilization developed in the southern Maya lowlands of Belize and the PETEN district of Guatemala, whereas the northern Maya lowlands of Mexico's Yucatan peninsula were the focus of POSTCLASSIC florescence.

MAYA MOUNTAINS: Three granite batholiths that rise to over 1,000 meters in southern Belize, providing GRANITE, quartz, and other minerals, as well as the origins of many rivers, notably the Belize River, Deep River, and Rio Grande.

MAYAPAN: A walled city in the northern lowlands that dominated the Late POSTCLASSIC in the northern MAYA LOWLANDS, investigated by the CARNEGIE INSTITUTION of Washington in the 1930s and 1940s and later by Marilyn Masson.

MERCHANT GOD: The god of XIBALBA, known as God L. As lord of the underworld, God L transformed himself into a JAGUAR each night as he traveled through XIBALBA. He was shown as an old man or as a black JAGUAR, often wearing a cape and a large wide-brimmed hat with owl feathers and sometimes an actual head of an owl. His bundle or backpack identified him in his merchant role.

MERCURY: A cache of mercury was recovered from under a BALL COURT marker at LAMANAI. The mineral was available in Honduras during ancient Maya times.

METATE: A rectangular stone grinding surface, often with three supports, used by the ancient Maya to grind corn and ubiquitous at ancient Maya sites. Metates were made of GRANITE, limestone, or imported volcanic basalt, with a hand-held cylindrical MANO used to grind on the surface.

MIDDEN: Garbage heaps, commonly associated with households and containing broken pottery and other broken artifacts disposed of along with food remains. Middens were often moved and used as fill in construction; they are now also used by archaeologists to reconstruct the changes in pottery styles that form the backbone of the system for dating sites.

MILITARY STRATEGIES: Reasons for WARFARE varied from raids to obtain captives, to sacking and destroying the capital of a polity (as at AGUATECA in the PETEXBATUN), to conquering and subjugating a polity (as Calakmul did with TIKAL and Naranjo. Military tactics included attacking the central acropolis of capitals to capture the AHAU and his entourage. Some cities took defensive measures to counter such attacks, such as building DEFENSIVE WALLS.

MILPA/SLASH AND BURN/SWIDDEN AGRICULTURE: A form of agriculture in which a section of the forest is burned and then the land is planted by dropping seeds into holes made with a stick as the farmer walks. The fields are used for two to eight years and then abandoned to regenerate, as nutrients are eventually lost and weeds take over. This extensive form of farming, used by the modern Maya, uses more land than intensive farming methods such as raised or drained fields and terracing, which the ancient Maya also used.

MINOR CENTER: Small cities, not the political capitals of a CLASSIC Maya CITY-STATE, often having significant monumental architecture and carved monuments with hieroglyphic records of ties with a royal dynasty.

MITOCHONDRIAL DNA: DNA extracted from ancient bones and modern Maya people, and used to reconstruct population movement and settlement in the Maya area.

MOHO CAY: A CLASSIC Maya trading port located in the mouth of the Belize River. The city tied coastal canoe trade with riverine trade, providing the Maya at inland cities with resources from the sea and from farther away along coastal Caribbean transportation routes.

MOTAGUA RIVER: An important avenue of trade and transportation between the southern Maya highlands around KAMINALJUYU, the EL CHAYAL OBSIDIAN outcrop, and the Caribbean coast of modern Guatemala for canoe trade to the MAYA LOWLANDS. Also the location of major known sources of JADE and other greenstones desired by the Maya for highly crafted status objects.

MOTUL DE SAN JOSE: A southern Maya lowland city investigated by Antonia Foias.

NAKBE: A prominent Middle Preclassic city investigated in the southern MAYA LOWLANDS by Richard Hansen.

NIM LI PUNIT: A site discovered by oil workers and subsequently investigated by Jaime Awe, Norman Hammond, and Richard Leventhal. This MINOR CENTER in the foothills of southern Belize has some twenty-five carved monuments, in contrast to their absence at nearby LUBAANTUN.

NOHMUL: A MINOR CENTER in northern Belize investigated by Norman Hammond. The site has two areas of monumental architecture connected by a SACBE.

OBSIDIAN: Volcanic glass occurring in the volcanic areas of highland Mesoamerica and widely traded throughout Maya prehistory to make sharp-edged blades, used for ritual BLOODLETTING (as seen depicted on Maya painted pottery and stone carvings) and other more mundane uses. Chemical identification of trace elements of OBSIDIAN can link artifacts to their outcrops, making OBSIDIAN the basis for many studies of ancient Maya trade.

OCCUPATIONAL SPECIALIZATION: The CLASSIC Maya had skilled workers for constructing buildings, quarrying stone for buildings and monuments, producing the most finely made painted pots and stone tools, and for writing records on paper, STELAE, architecture, and pottery and other objects.

OLMEC: The earliest civilization in Mesoamerica, with capitals at San Lorenzo (1200–900 B.C.) and La Venta (900–400 B.C.) on the Gulf of Mexico coast, predating the Maya and influencing its development (number system, CALENDAR, and precious development) throughout the Pacific coast and particularly around IZAPA.

ORLANDO'S JEWFISH: Underwater site in Punta Ycacos Lagoon, Paynes Creek National Park, in southern Belize, submerged by sea level rise, where brine was boiled in pots to produce SALT in specialized WORKSHOPS, excavated by Heather McKillop.

PACBITUN: A city in western Belize investigated by Paul F. Healy, known for musical instruments from elite graves and for a long prehistoric record.

PADDLER GODS: Gods that transported people in canoes to the underworld. Their most famous depiction is on incised bones accompanying the king in a TEMPLE BURIAL in TIKAL. The Maize Paddler God and the JAGUAR Paddler God guided the canoe through XIBALBA, with the JAGUAR usually in the front and the Stingray Paddler God in the center.

PALEOINDIANS: The earliest post-PLEISTOCENE occupants of the Maya area, not identifiable ethnically as Maya, known by isolated recoveries of distinctive OB-SIDIAN or CHERT fluted projectile points, as at LADYVILLE, Belize.

PAUAHTUN: The old quadripartite god, also known as God N, who supported the four corners of the sky. He was shown wearing a turtle carapace or conch shell on his back during the CLASSIC period and in the CODICES. He also is identified by his cutout shell nose and crocodile jaw headdress. By the contact period, Pauahtun was known as the four bacabs, who each held up a corner of the sky.

PETEN: Modern political district in Guatemala located in the southern MAYA LOWLANDS, dominated by tropical rainforest and the central area where the CLASSIC civilization developed, including TIKAL.

PETEXBATUN: A region between the Pasion and Usumacinta Rivers in the southern MAYA LOWLANDS investigated by Arthur Demarest and colleagues Takeshi Inomata, Juan Valdes, Hector Escobedo, Joel Palka, Antonia Foias, Nicholas Dunning, Lori Wright, and James Brady. Endemic WARFARE, CRAFT PRO-DUCTION, and political and military alliances were forged here during the Late CLASSIC, including such cities as DOS PILAS, Tamarindito, Punta de Chimino, and AGUATECA.

PIEDRAS NEGRAS: A city on the Usumacinta River in Guatemala, investigated by University of Pennsylvania researchers and subsequently by Stephen Houston. The city had drains for water management.

PLAZUELA GROUP: The basic unit of Maya settlement, in which several buildings are arranged around a square plaza. The system was used both for Maya households and for TEMPLES and palaces in city centers.

PLEISTOCENE: The most recent ice age, ending about 9500 B.C., after which there is artifactual evidence in the form of isolated OBSIDIAN and CHERT projectile points of the first human use of the Maya area by people termed PALEOINDIANS.

POLITICAL ECONOMY: Control of the production and distribution of some goods, particularly high-status pottery vessels and exotic goods of high value, by Maya royalty at urban cities. Contrast with SUBSISTENCE ECONOMY.

POLYCHROME POTTERY: A feature of the CLASSIC period in which vessels were painted using multiple colors, usually red and black on an orange or cream base, with brown and blue less common. This style was in contrast to the predominantly red pots of the Preclassic and the incised decoration of the POST-CLASSIC.

POPOL VUH: A historic text from highland Guatemala that recounts the Maya story of CREATION, in particular the exploits of the HERO TWINS. It is depicted pictorially in scenes on CLASSIC painted pottery vessels and carved stone monuments, and so has great antiquity and use for interpreting the ancient Maya worldview.

POSTCLASSIC PERIOD: The time after the collapse of the southern MAYA LOW-LAND CITY-STATES (A.D. 900–1500) until the arrival of the Spaniards, when cities in the northern MAYA LOWLANDS such as CHICHEN ITZA and, later, MAYAPAN rose to prominence.

PRESTIGE ECONOMY: Often referred to as the POLITICAL ECONOMY or ritual economy, this included the production, distribution, and use of goods and resources for the royal Maya and other elites.

PRIMARY STANDARD SEQUENCE (PSS): A band of HIEROGLYPHS below the vessel rim of Late CLASSIC vases with HIEROGLYPHS indicating the date and other essential information about the activity depicted.

PROSKOURIAKOFF, TATIANA: Trained as an architect, she worked for the CARNEGIE INSTITUTION of Washington and then the Peabody Museum at Harvard, making a major breakthrough in the decipherment of Mayan HIEROGLYPHS by discovering that they recorded historical information about Maya royalty.

PROTOCLASSIC: A period of distinctive POLYCHROME POTTERY including dishes with four mammiform supports. The style is regarded variously as intrusive from El Salvador following a volcanic eruption or as a local development, either part of the Late Preclassic or Early CLASSIC.

PULLTROUSER SWAMP: Drained or RAISED FIELDS and associated settlements in northern Belize investigated by Peter D. Harrison and Billie Lee Turner, who suggested that they were built to intensify agricultural production resulting from a Late CLASSIC population increase.

PUSILHA: Major Late CLASSIC site investigated by the British Museum in the 1920s, with carved monuments removed to Britain, and subsequently investigated by Geoff Braswell. The site also has a bridge over the Moho River and has distinctive Late CLASSIC "unit-stamped" pottery.

RAISED (OR DRAINED) FIELDS: Swamps that are drained by digging canals and piling the muck on top of the resulting raised beds, which are continuously cultivated. Such fields produce multiple crops per year and make more-intensive use of the land than SLASH AND BURN agriculture, thereby supporting more people. This draining of swamps may have been done as a response to Late CLASSIC population increases at PULLTROUSER SWAMP, Albion Island, or along the Candelaria River, or as a Late Preclassic tactic of aggrandizing elites, as at Albion Island. Some swamps may also be naturally canalized. Regular rectilinear patterns called gilgae develop in swamps during the dry season when the swamps become dessicated and the ground cracks.

RELACIÓN DE LAS COSAS DE YUCATAN: A treatise that BISHOP DE LANDA wrote while in prison in Spain, written in defense of his treatment of the Maya of the Yucatan. The book was later to become the most detailed account of the sixteenth-century Yucatecan Maya. Tragically, DE LANDA had burnt most of the existing Maya books, which was part of the reason he was recalled to Spain and imprisoned.

RUBBER BALL: A solid rubber ball used in the ritual BALL GAMES of the Maya. It was made from the sap of the Sapodilla tree.

SACBE: A raised roadway, also called a causeway, made of limestone rubble and surfaced with plaster. It connected parts of a single community, as at TIKAL, CHICHEN ITZA, and CARACOL, or ran between communities, as the road departing COBA.

SALT: A very important commodity among the Maya. WORKSHOPS excavated in Punta Ycacos Lagoon in Paynes Creek National Park by Heather McKillop supplied salt for the Late CLASSIC inland Maya in nearby cities, but the temporal and geographical importance of salt produced by this method of boiling brine in pots over fires is unknown. This method also contrasts with the extraction and use of salt gathered from the salt flats along the north coast of the Yucatan, proposed by Anthony Andrews as supplying the CLASSIC Maya of the southern MAYA LOWLANDS.

SAN BARTOLO: Site of a discovery of rare painted wall murals in the southern MAYA LOWLANDS by William Saturno, dating to Late PRECLASSIC period.

SAN MARTIN JILOTEPEQUE: A source of high-quality OBSIDIAN west of modern Guatemala City that was commonly used by the Preclassic lowland Maya, but used less in other times. Also known as Rio Pixcaya.

SANTA RITA: Coastal community, now mainly buried under the modern Belize city of Corozal, well known for now-destroyed Late POSTCLASSIC painted murals. One building here is maintained by the Belize government as a tourist site.

SAYIL: A TERMINAL CLASSIC city in the northern MAYA LOWLANDS investigated by Jeremy Sabloff and Gair Tourtellot. The site has little ground cover, allowing surface collection of artifacts to interpret ancient activities.

SEA TRADE: Trade and travel of varying distances along the Yucatan coast that facilitated trade and settlement of the coast and offshore islands (cays).

SEGMENTARY MODEL: A model in which power is seen as having been decentralized within a CITY-STATE and in which the MAYA LOWLANDS are seen as having consisted of some eighty rather independent CITY-STATES during the CLASSIC period. The segmentary model contrasts with the centralist model, in which the lowlands are viewed as having been more centrally organized.

SEIBAL: A lowland Maya city along the Pasion River, which was the focus of major excavations under GORDON R. WILLEY. Jeremy Sabloff's ceramic study here set standards for recording using the TYPE-VARIETY SYSTEM of ceramic classification.

SETTLEMENT PATTERNS: Pioneered by Maya archaeologist GORDON R. WILLEY. Settlement pattern studies include examination of the way in which ancient Maya settlements were distributed across the landscape, the organization of buildings and spaces within communities, and the spatial organization within structures; this information reflects the social, economic, and ideological aspects of Maya society.

SHORT COUNT DATES: TERMINAL CLASSIC and POSTCLASSIC dates that were written without the BAKTUN number, so that, without other information, the date cannot be traced to the beginning of the Maya CALENDAR.

SKY BAND: A representation of the Milky Way, depicted by a rectangular band divided into sections with images of animals interpreted as representing ancient Maya constellations. Depicted in the Dresden and Paris CODICES and on the face of buildings at CHICHEN ITZA and Acanceh. The Milky Way is also sometimes shown with a Cosmic Monster and sometimes as a double-headed snake.

SLAVES: May or may not have been used by the Maya. Whether or not slaves were a regular part of CLASSIC Maya society, it is known that war captives were temporarily enslaved before eventual sacrifice, torture, and/or being forced to participate in a terminal BALL GAME.

SMITH, A. LEDYARD: A CARNEGIE INSTITUTION of Washington archaeologist who directed major architectural excavations at UAXACTUN and later for Harvard University at SEIBAL and ALTAR DE SACRIFICIOS. He set the standards for excavation of Maya architecture.

SMITH, ROBERT E.: A CARNEGIE INSTITUTION of Washington archaeologist best known for his seminal ceramic study of UAXACTUN, which formed the foundation for all subsequent Maya pottery studies. The UAXACTUN ceramic complex terms are now standard terminology, including Late Preclassic "Chicanel," Early CLASSIC "Tzakol," and Late CLASSIC "Tepeu."

STELA (PLURAL = STELAE): Stone slabs placed vertically in the ground in front of TEMPLES in the central plazas of cities and carved with images of Maya royalty, HIEROGLYPHS, and—during the CLASSIC period—dates in the Maya LONG COUNT.

STINGRAY LAGOON: A Late CLASSIC SALT works excavated by Heather McKillop in Punta Ycacos Lagoon in Paynes Creek National Park. The site is also used to demonstrate sea level rise, as it is now 110 centimeters below sea level.

SUBSISTENCE ECONOMY: The production of food and resources basic to daily life by individual households and within Maya communities. This model is in contrast to the POLITICAL ECONOMY controlled by the urban royalty.

SWASEY: The earliest pottery known from the MAYA LOWLANDS, first identified by Norman Hammond at CUELLO and subsequently found at other northern Belize sites and beyond, consisting of well-made vessels and dating to about 1000 B.C.

TALUD-TABLERO: A distinctive style of façades on buildings, consisting of alternating inward-sloping "talud" panels with vertical "tablero" panels. This style was characteristic of TEOTIHUACAN architecture and was a marker of the influence of that highland state, as at KAMINALJUYU, TIKAL, and CHAC.

TEMPLE: A stone rubble-filled platform supporting a small upper room of stone or of pole and thatch, used for ceremonies. The platform was reconstructed over time and contained BURIALS of important personages, with Maya royalty buried in the largest temples in lowland cities.

TEOTIHUACAN: A competing and coeval state in central Mexico, with a city of the same name north of modern Mexico City. Teotihuacan dominated highland Mexico between A.D. 100 and 700, making military and MARRIAGE ALLIANCES with the CLASSIC Maya, possibly including the cities of KAMINALJUYU, COPAN, and TIKAL. The relationship between Teotihuacan and the Maya is hotly debated among Maya archaeologists and epigraphers, however.

TERMINAL CLASSIC: Time of endemic WARFARE, political unrest, and economic unrest in the southern MAYA LOWLANDS (A.D. 800–900), when CITY-STATES fell and were abandoned. This period, however, witnessed the rise to prominence of cities such as CHICHEN ITZA in the northern MAYA LOWLANDS and coastal communities, especially trading ports.

TERMINATION RITUALS: Rituals performed when a building was no longer to be used or before it was rebuilt. Caches of broken pots or other offerings found in ancient TEMPLES are interpreted as termination rituals.

TERRACED HILLSLOPES: A series of horizontal ridges made in a hillslope. In the MAYA MOUNTAINS of Belize, the Rio Bec region in Mexico had slopes that were terraced to prevent soil erosion, make farming possible, and arguably to allow fertilization and more-intensive use of the land than MILPA farming, perhaps as a response to Late CLASSIC population increases.

THOMPSON, SIR J. ERIC S : A leading Maya archaeologist from Britain who excavated at LUBAANTUN, San Jose, MAYAPAN, and elsewhere, coined the term "PLAZUELA GROUP," and made many important strides in hieroglyphic research.

TIKAL: A Maya city that became one of the major powers during the CLASSIC period in the southern lowlands. It was the focus of a major research project by the University of Pennsylvania and then the Guatemalan government, in which several of the major TEMPLES as well as outlying structures have been investigated.

TIPU: A Maya community in western Belize where Fransiscan missionaries established a mission. Excavations have been made there of a church with more than 500 Maya buried in Christian fashion and with a Spanish-style community layout.

TREE CROPPING (ORCHARDS): Remains of fruits of trees with edible fruits such as chocolate, native palms, mammee apple, and nance indicate deliberate planting and tending of trees around ancient houses to supplement the Maya diet, especially on small Caribbean islands with limited arable land.

TRIBUTE: May have been demanded of those conquered by the Maya. Tribute payment fits well within the view of CLASSIC Maya politics involving military imperialism, with conquered polities owing tribute to their new overlords. Although HIEROGLYPHS record historical and political rather than economic events, scenes on painted pots show offerings, including tribute payments.

TUN: A unit of time in Maya counting and the CALENDAR, corresponding to one year.

TURQUOISE: A trade good for the Maya. Late POSTCLASSIC trade tied the Maya area into a broader Mesoamerican interaction sphere, with turquoise being among the trade goods recovered from SANTA RITA Corozal, Belize, and elsewhere.

TYPE-VARIETY SYSTEM: A system of classifying pottery sherds widely used by Mayanists to establish a site's chronology based on changes in decoration and surface finish.

TZOLKIN CALENDAR: A 260-day Maya ritual CALENDAR, as documented by Diego de Landa and the POSTCLASSIC Maya CODICES, as well as in earlier times. The Tzolkin CALENDAR was used to predict a person's destiny from his or her birth date and also to predict proper times to plant corn—an ancient "farmer's almanac."

UAXACTUN: A site near TIKAL that was extensively excavated in the 1920s and 1930s by Oliver Ricketson, A. LEDYARD SMITH, and others of the now-defunct CARNEGIE INSTITUTION of Washington. This site is most famous for E-VII-SUB, a Late Preclassic TEMPLE decorated with masks. ROBERT E. SMITH'S ceramic report on this site is the foundation for all subsequent studies of Maya pottery.

UINAL: A period of twenty days comprising a Maya month.

UNESCO CONVENTION OF 1970: An international agreement by most world countries to respect each other's cultural patrimony. Ensuing federal legislation in each country made it illegal to import or export antiquities, including Maya artifacts.

VENUS: A very important celestial body to the Maya. The Maya made extensive calculations on Venus, perhaps because they associated it with WARFARE. The appearance of Venus in the morning or evening sky was often associated with war imagery in CLASSIC-period art, and there are tables about Venus in the DRESDEN and Grolier CODICES.

VISION QUEST: A mental trance state sought by Maya rulers and other elite. Dynastic leaders are depicted in scenes such as those in carved stone at Yaxchilan, engaged in vision quests: Blood offerings dripped onto bark paper are ignited, and the leader is transformed in the ensuing smoke to communicate with the GODS and seek their power and insights to lead the people. Vision quests were aided by smoking tobacco, fasting, using HALLUCINOGENS from mushrooms or the *Bufo marinus* frog, and from blood loss through ritual BLOODLETTING.

VUCUB CAQUIX: A anthropomorphic vulture found in the *POPOL VUH*, first depicted at IZAPA and common in CLASSIC Maya iconography.

WARFARE: Practiced extensively among the Maya. Historical records of defeat on Maya STELAE, DEFENSIVE WALLS, and pictorial depictions of battles such as the murals of BONAMPAK indicate that warfare was endemic by the Late CLASSIC and may have precipitated the Maya collapse. Warfare continued in the POSTCLASSIC, as evidenced by fortifications at many cities in the northern MAYA LOWLANDS.

WATER LILY: A common motif in Maya imagery. The Water Lily Serpent symbolized still water and was a substitute for the number 13; it was shown with a snake body and a downturned bird head wearing a lily pad and flower headdress, often accompanied by a fish nibbling at the flower. Water lily imagery is common at DZIBILCHALTUN, ALTUN HA, and LAMANAI. The Water Lily Serpent was a common headdress for CLASSIC Maya royalty.

WEAPONS: Scenes on CLASSIC Maya painted pots and stone carvings show royal Maya with spears and war captives, but little attention has been directed to research on the weapons used in WARFARE. The CLASSIC Maya had CHERT stone points suitable for hafting onto spears. Small dart points were introduced during the POSTCLASSIC, evidently from central Mexico. Caches of stone spear points were found along the DEFENSIVE WALL systems at DOS PILAS along with a cache of adult male skulls, decapitated while still fleshed, in a pit outside the exterior wall.

WILD CANE CAY: A coastal Maya trading port in the Port Honduras Marine Reserve of southern Belize, excavated by Heather McKillop, that was important in the Late CLASSIC and grew to prominence during the POSTCLASSIC canoe trade.

WILLEY, GORDON R.: Bowditch Professor of Archaeology at Harvard University, who directed major projects at BARTON RAMIE, the Belize River, SEIBAL, ALTAR DE SACRIFICIOS, and COPAN. He was a leading and influential figure in Maya archaeology in the latter part of the twentieth century.

WORKSHOP: A location where goods were produced for use elsewhere, for purposes beyond the needs of regular household production. Some examples were CHERT tools produced in household workshops at COLHA, SALT produced in independent workshops in Punta Ycacos Lagoon in Paynes Creek National Park, and elite paraphernalia produced in royal households at AGUATECA.

WORLD TREE: Symbolized by the Ceiba tree, or axis mundi. The quadripartite worldview of the Maya universe with the world tree at its center is pervasive in Maya art and architecture.

XIBALBA: The Maya underworld, equated with the primordial sea. It was the locus of a battle in form of the BALL GAME, fought by the HERO TWINS, as told in the *POPOL VUH.*

XUNANTUNICH: A MINOR CENTER in western Belize occupied late in the Late CLASSIC and abandoned at the end of the CLASSIC period, investigated and restored by Wendy Ashmore and Richard Leventhal and currently open to the public.

YAXUNA: A northern lowland Maya city investigated by David Freidel.

ZODIAC: The Maya version, including VENUS, the Pleiades, and Gemini, among others, may have consisted of thirteen groups of stars that cycled every twenty-eight days. Both the Paris and DRESDEN CODICES refer to the zodiac, and it is represented on sculptures at CHICHEN ITZA and Acanceh, as well as in CLASSIC Maya iconography.

Chronology

9500 B.C.	Palaeoindian period marked by stone fluted spear points at Ladyville, Belize, and Los Tapiales and Huehuetenango, Guatemala, reflecting a hunting and gathering way of life, perhaps hunting now-extinct ice age large animals such as giant horse, mammoth, and armadillo
7000–2000 B.C.	Archaic period, recognized by stemmed stone points and constricted unifaces for hunting and butchering deer, rabbits, and other small animals at Colha and Pulltrouser Swamp in northern Belize
3114 B.C.	Beginning date of calendar used by Classic Maya
c. 2500 B.C.	Corn pollen at Cobweb Swamp, Belize, indicates clearing of forest and planting of corn by people in the southern Maya lowlands
2000 B.C.–A.D. 300	Preclassic period
2000–1000 B.C.	Early Preclassic period
1800–1500 B.C.	Barra complex, earliest known Maya pottery on the Pacific coast of Guatemala, with sites associated with permanent villages
1700–1500 B.C.	Locona complex on Pacific coast of Guatemala, with sites associated with ranked society
1500–1400 B.C.	Ocos complex, with cord-marked pottery at Salinas La Blanca site, on the Pacific coast of Guatemala
1200 B.C.	rise of Olmec civilization on the Gulf coast of Mexico, with first Olmec capital city, San Lorenzo, having monumental public architecture and widely influencing art styles, including what becomes the Maya area
1000–300 B.C.	Middle Preclassic period in the Maya area
1000–700 B.C.	Early part of Middle Preclassic
1000 B.C.	earliest pottery (called Swasey) in the Maya lowlands first reported by Norman Hammond at Cuello in northern Belize, but later also recognized at Santa Rita, Colha, Cahal Pech, and other sites in Belize and marks the beginning of the Middle Preclassic period in the Maya lowlands, the first agriculture and permanent village life, as well as the earliest evidence the people who were ethnically Maya
1000 B.C.	Middle Preclassic (called Xe) pottery at Seibal and Altar de

	Sacrificios in Peten district of Guatemala contemporary with Swasey
900 B.C.	Demise of first Olmec capital, San Lorenzo, and rise of second capital, La Venta, which imported quantities of jade for carving objects that were widely copied in style and sometimes traded throughout Mesoamerica, including the Maya area
700 B.C.	Rise of social complexity in Maya lowlands during latter part of the Middle Preclassic (700–300 B.C.) indicated by temples as at Nakbe, Guatemala
700 B.C.	(until 300 B.C.) Expansion of Maya people throughout lowlands indicated by presence of red-painted pottery of Mamom complex
600 B.C.	Earliest known hieroglyph at non-Maya site of San Jose, Mogote, Oaxaca
300 B.C.–A.D. 300	Late Preclassic period
300 B.C.	Beginning of Late Preclassic period (300 B.C.–A.D. 300) rise of social complexity in the Maya area
c. 300 B.C.	Earliest known painted murals at San Bartolo, Guatemala, with depictions of Vucub Caquix
200 B.C.	Miraflores Complex of Late Preclassic at Kaminaljuyu shows increasing social complexity, with elaborate temples and fancy grave offerings
c. 150 B.C.	Large stucco and painted masks on façades of temples at Cerros (Belize); Nakbe, Uaxactun, and Tikal (Guatemala); and Dzibilchaltun (northern Maya lowlands)
A.D. 36	Herrera stela from El Baul is earliest Maya stela
A.D. 143	(and A.D. 156) Long Count dates on carving at La Mojarra, a non-Maya site in Mexico, shows early precursor of Maya writing
A.D. 162	Long Count date on statue in Tuxtla Mountains of Mexico, shows pre-Maya origins of writing
c. 75 B.C.	(to A.D. 400) Distinctive pottery, including mammiform four-legged pots, polychrome painting, and Usulutan style pottery of coastal Guatemala common in southern Maya lowlands and characteristic of development of lowland pottery and not, as previously thought, an invasion of people fleeing a volcanic eruption in El Salvador
A.D. 300–900	Classic Period
A.D. 292	Stela 29 at Tikal provides first Maya Long Count date on Maya stela, marking the beginning of the Classic Period (rounded to A.D. 300–900) and time of dynastic rule of Maya polities in the southern Maya lowlands when stelae were erected with dates in the Maya Long Count
A.D. 378	arrival of Siyaj K'ak' at Tikal, associated with introduction of Teotihuacan styles of art, clothing, and architecture at the city

A.D. 411	Siyaj Chan K'awill II ascends to throne at Tikal
A.D. 426	Yax Kuk Mo, founder of Copan dynasty, arrives at Copan from west (likely Tikal), introducing Teotihuacan styles of pottery, clothing, and architecture to Copan
A.D. 426	Quirigua's first dynastic ruler, Tok Casper, inaugurated under supervision of Copan's Yax Kuk Mo, demonstating inclusion of Quirigua within Copan hegemony
A.D. 431	inauguration of K'uk' B'alam I as first ruler of Palenque, at time of Siyaj Chan K'awiil II's rule at Tikal, suggesting inception of Palenque dynasty may be related to arrival of Teotihuacanos in the Peten
A.D. 435	Accession of Palenque's second ruler, Casper
A.D. 437	(or somewhat earlier) Death and burial of Yax Kuk Mo in Hunal (Temple 16) at Copan, accompanied by Teotihuacan-style pots
c. A.D. 450	Construction of elaborately stuccoed and painted Margarita temple at Copan as a memorial shrine to Yax Kuk Mo
A.D. 487	Accession to throne of Palenque's third ruler, B'utz'aj Kak Chiik
A.D. 501	B'utz'aj Kak Chiik's brother, Ah kal Mo' Naab' I, becomes Palenque's fourth ruler
c. A.D. 504	Reign of Balam Nehn, seventh in the dynastic line of kings at Copan and responsible for major expansion of the Copan acropolis buildings
A.D. 529	Accession to Palenque throne of K'an Joy Chitam I after a four-year hiatus apparently without a ruler at the city
A.D. 551	Accession of Ruler 9 at Copan, recorded on a stone on the Hieroglyphic Staircase
A.D. 553	Inauguration of Tzik Balam at Copan, the ruler responsible for building the splendidly stuccoed and painted (in red, green, and yellow) Rosalila Temple, dedicated to the founder, Yax Kuk Mo (with chert objects elaborately chipped in the forms of gods and humans in a building termination offering)
A.D.553	Tikal's twenty-first ruler, Wak Chan K'awill, sponsors inauguration of Caracol ruler Yajaw Te' K'inich II
A.D. 562	Wak Chan K'awill defeated in battle, likely by Calakmul, and Tikal's power dissipated, initiating the Classic Maya "hiatus," when no dated carved stelae are erected at Tikal
A.D. 565	Inauguration of Palenque ruler Ahkal Mo' Naab' (grandson of earlier ruler of same name)
A.D. 572	Inauguration of Palenque ruler Kan B'alam I
A.D. 578	Accession to throne of Butz' Chan, Copan's eleventh ruler
A.D. 583	Lady Yohl Ik'nal, either sister or daughter of Kan B'alam I, inaugurated as Palenque's first queen
c. A.D. 595	Accession to the throne of the first great Tonina king, K'inich Hix Chapat
c. A.D. 599	Defeat and sacking of Palenque, likely by Calakmul, recorded in hieroglyphic stairway at Palenque
A.D. 600–900	(Late Classic Period)

c. A.D. 600	Ceren site, El Salvador, buried by volcanic eruption
A.D. 604	Death of Queen Yohl Ik'nal and accession to Palenque throne of her son, Aj Ne' Ohl Mat
A.D. 611	Palenque defeated and sacked by Calakmul, under leadership of Calakmul King Scroll Serpent
A.D. 615	After short rule by Lady Sak K'uk' (granddaughter of Aj Ne' Ohl Mat) or possibly another ruler, her son, K'inich Janaab' Pakal ascends to Palenque throne
c. A.D. 626	Pakal marries Lady Tz'akb'u Ajaw, from another city, Toktan
Late 500s	(or early 600s) Much of Quirigua flooded and covered by river silt from hurricane or volcanic eruption, resulting in reorientation of construction at the city
A.D. 628	Accession to throne of K'ak' Na K'awill (Smoke Imix) at Copan, who had many stelae erected and also the beautiful Chorcha temple, now under the Hieroglyphic Stairway, with an elaborate tomb containing pottery effigies of the Copan dynastic rulers
A.D. 640	Death of Lady Sak K'uk'
A.D. 659	Tikal ruler Nuun Ujol Chaak is driven from Tikal by Calakmul and visits King Pacal at Palenque
A.D. 668	Inauguration of Tonina Ruler 2
A.D. 672	Nuun Ujol Chaak of Tikal ousts a rival from Dos Pilas
A.D. 677	Nuun Ujol Chaak defeated by Calakmul
A.D. 679	Nuun Ujol Chaak defeated by Dos Pilas and Calakmul
A.D. 683	King Pakal of Palenque dies and is buried in the Temple of the Inscriptions, a building completed by his son and successor, K'inich Kam B'alam II.
A.D. 684	K'inich Kam B'alam II ascends to Palenque throne
A.D. 687	Tonina raided by Palenque, perhaps including capture of Tonina Ruler 2
A.D. 688	Third Tonina ruler, K'inich B'aaknal Chaak, inaugurated and begins campaign of battles against Palenque and other nearby cities
c. A.D. 692	Ballcourt 1 at Tonina depicts six named prisoners from nearby cities reported as subservient to Palenque that likely refers to "star wars" campaign undertaken by K'inich Baaknal Chaak c. A.D. 692
A.D. 692	Kam B'alam II dedicates the Temples of the Cross, Sun, and Foliated Cross at Palenque, a glorious display of Palenque's dynastic history and spiritual place in the Maya world
A.D. 692	End of Classic Maya "hiatus" at Tikal
A.D. 695	Nuun Ujol Chaak's son, Jasaw Chan K'awiil I, defeats Calakmul and returns Tikal to its former power (as pictorially depicted on a doorway lintel at Tikal's Temple 1)
A.D. 695	Waxaklajuun Ub'aah K'awiil, Copan's thirteenth ruler, ascends to the throne
A.D. 702	K'an Joy Chitam II, second of K'inich Janaab' Pakal's sons, ascends to Palenque throne
A.D. 710	Waxaklajuun Ub'aah K'awiil oversees construction of Esmeralda temple, Copan's first hieroglyphic stairway, over the Chorcha

A.D. 711	K'an Joy Chitam II of Palenque captured by K'inich B'aaknal Chaak, ruler of nearby Tonina, as recorded on a stone carving at Tonina
A.D. 715	Stone carving describes Bonampak King Etz'nab Jawbone as a vassal lord of B'aaknal Chaak of Tonina
c. A.D. 717	Tonina Ruler 4 ascends to throne and among his accomplishments is the capture of Aj Chiik Naab, a person from Calakmul, depicted as a bound captive on a stone carving
A.D. 721	Inauguration of Akhal Mo'Naab' III at Palenque, ten years after capture of his predecessor (who is likely his brother)
A.D. 723	Ascension of K'inich Ich'aak Chapat to throne of Tonina
A.D. 724	Quirigua's ruler K'ak' Tiliw Chan Yoaat inaugurated under the supervision of Copan's ruler, Waxaklajuun Ub'aah K'awiil
A.D. 730	K'inich Ich'aak Chaapat of Tonina conducts ritual re-entry of the royal tomb of his predecessor, B'aaknal Chaak
A.D. 731	Stela A depicting Copan, Tikal, Calakmul, and Palenque as the four centers of the Maya world, erected by Copan's ruler, Waxaklajuun Ub'aah K'awiil
A.D. 738	Waxaklajuun Ub'aah K'awiil captured by Quirigua's King K'ak' Tiliw Chan Yoaat and beheaded, resulting in florescence at Quirigua and its domination of Motagua River trade
A.D. 738	K'ak' Joplaj Chan K'awiil inaugurated at Copan, thirty-nine days after death of his predecessor, and reigns during a time of weakness of Copan, while Quirigua rises to prominence
A.D. 742	Ahkal Mo'Naab' III's successor (likely his son), Upakal K'inich of Palenque, installs a secondary lord to an important office (the only known date for his reign)
c. A.D. 742	Lady Chak Nik Ye' Xook sent from Palenque to Copan, where she later becomes the mother of Yax Pasaj Chan Yoaat, Copan's sixteenth ruler
A.D. 743	Jasaw's son, Yik'in Chan K'awiil, defeats El Peru
A.D. 749	Death of K'ak Joplaj Chan K'awiil and succession of his son, K'ak' Yipyaj Chan K'awiil, who led a revitalization of Copan, including rebuilding and expansion of the Hieroglyphic Stairway and its underlying temple
A.D. 756	Last great king of Tonina, Ruler 8, born, although the date he ascended to the throne is unknown
A.D. 762	After absence of known dated monuments at Tonina since A.D. 739, Stela 47 reports the death or burial of Tonina king K'inich Tuun Chapat
A.D. 763	Copan's sixteenth ruler, Yax Pasaj Chan Yoaat (whose mother was Lady Xook from Palenque), ascends to throne
A.D. 764	K'uk B'alam II (a son of Ahkal Mo'Naab' III) ascends to Palenque throne
A.D. 775	Monument 69 at Tonina records the death of Tonina king Wak Chan K'ak' and his burial in A.D. 776
A.D. 776	Dedication of Copan's Altar Q, depicting the sixteen kings of Co-

pan with their name glyphs (an associated offering includes the skeletal remains of sixteen jaguars)

A.D. 783   Commission of Tablet of the 96 Glyphs, arguably the finest Classic Maya calligraphy, commemorating K'uk' B'alam's first Katun (twenty-year) anniversary of rulership at Palenque

A.D. 785   Death of Quirigua's ruler K'ak' Tiliw, after a long reign during which he commissioned the construction of many public buildings and monuments at the city

A.D. 785   Inauguration of Sky Mul at Quirigua

A.D. 789   Tonina Ruler 8 undertakes battle with Pomoy (linked with Calakmul at the time) and captures Ucha'an Aj Chih, described in Tonina Monument 20 as the vassal of B'olon K'awiil, possibly the ruler of Calakmul

A.D. 799   Palenque's last known ruler, Wak Kimi Janaab' Pakal ascends to throne, and with this last date at the city, it is abandoned shortly thereafter

C. A.D. 800   Inauguration of Quirigua's sixteenth and last king, Jade Sky

A.D. 810   Last dated monument at Quirigua, after which city is deserted

A.D. 822   Inauguration of Copan's seventeenth and last ruler, Ukit Took', noted on Altar L, never completed or erected, mirroring the downfall of the city

A.D. 837   Stela fragment at Tonina mentions Ruler 9, Uh Chapat

A.D. 869   Last dynastic reference to a Tikal king, Jasaw Chan K'awiil II, at Tikal, after which site is virtually abandoned

A.D. 889   Last stela with Maya Long Count date erected at Caracol

A.D. 904   Monument 158 at Tonina erected by Tonina Ruler 10

A.D. 909   Monument 101 at Tonina is last stela with Maya Long Count date erected in southern Maya lowlands, January 15, 909

A.D. 750   (to A.D. 900) Terminal Classic period demise of cities in the southern Maya lowlands and rise to prominence of northern Maya lowland cities of Chichen Itza, Yaxuna, Sayil, Uxmal, and others

A.D. 900   (to A.D. 1250) Early Postclassic Period, with dominance of Chichen Itza

A.D. 1250   Fall of Chichen Itza and Late Postclassic rise to power of Mayapan, political fragmentation throughout the northern Maya lowlands, and apparent increase in sea trade around the Yucatan and beyond

A.D. 1519   arrival of Hernan Cortes on Gulf of Mexico and beginning of Spanish conquest of indigenous people in Mesoamerica

1525   Hernan Cortes travels up the Usumacinta River to the Peten, where he meets Ajaw Kan Ek, Itza ruler of Nojpeten (Tayasal), and continues travels to Gracias a Dios Falls on Sarstoon River

1528   Fransisco de Montejo and Alonso Davila travel by sea along the east coast of the Yucatan and battle with the Maya at Chetumal

1531   Davila establishes Villa Real at Chetumal but is driven away by the Maya within a year

1543   (or early 1544) Melchor and Alonso Pacheco set out from Merida to conquer the Maya, establishing Salamanca de Bacalar near Corozal and chocolate haciendas at Tipu and elsewhere in what is now Belize

1543   Dominican friars found a church at Ocosingo, near ancient city of Tonina

1500s   Fransiscan missionaries establish churches at Tipu and Lamanai in northern Belize, as well as throughout the Yucatan peninsula of Mexico, and elsewhere in Mexico and Central America

1547   Maya rebel against Spanish incursions in Belize and the Yucatan

1558   Rebellion of native Maya near Tonina lead to their forced resettlement at Ocosingo

1562   Diego de Landa supervises burning of indigenous Maya books at Mani, Yucatan, and is recalled to Spain by the Spanish Inquisition

c. 1566   Diego de Landa writes his account of the Maya, *Relación de Las Cosas de Yucatan,* after having been recalled to Spain by the Spanish Inquisition for having been too harsh with the Maya

c. 1616   Fray Juan de Orbita, a Fransiscan missionary, travels to NojPeten and brings 150 Itzas to Merida

1616   Orbita travels with Fray Bartolome de Fuensalida to Tipu and Nojpeten

1624   Maya revolt at Spanish town of Sakalum

1697   Spanish defeat of Itza Maya at Nojpeten, the last unconquered Maya kingdom

1739   Dresden Codex is purchased from private collection in Vienna for the Royal Library in Dresden

1810   Alexander Von Humbolt publishes five pages of the Dresden Codex

1822   First publication of Maya hieroglyphs carved in stone, part of a tablet from the Temple of the Cross at Palenque

1829   James McCulloch of Baltimore notes that the hieroglyphs in the Dresden Codex and from Palenque are in the same language

1841   John Lloyd Stephens's publication of *Incidents of Travel in Central America, Chiapas, and the Yucatan* stirs widespread interest in the ancient Maya ruins by people in Europe and North America

1842   Manuscript of what later became known as the Paris Codex purchased by a Parisian library

1861   Etienne Brasseur de Bourbourg copies and translates the *Popol Vuh,* a sixteenth-century Quiche Maya text

1864   Etienne Brasseur de Bourbourg finds de Landa's manuscript *Relación de las Cosas de Yucatan* in the collections of the Royal Academy of History in Madrid and publishes the manuscript

1869   Etienne Brasseur de Bourbourg finds part of the Madrid Codex in a private collection in Spain and calls it the Codex Troano

1875   Missing portion of Madrid Codex found

1877   Maler visits Palenque, beginning a long career of photographing, exploring, and recording Maya sites

1881   Alfred Maudslay begins important research, photographing and recording Maya ruins (1881–1894)

1887   Leon de Rosny publishes twenty-two-page fragment of the Paris Codex

1896   George Gordon's publication of first Harvard Maya project at Copan

1905   American newspaperman, Joseph Goodman, publishes first correlation of the Maya calendar with the Christian calendar.

1906   Ernst Förstemann deciphers much of the Maya calendar and counting system portrayed in the Dresden Codex

1913   Publication of Herbert Spinden's *A History of Maya Art,* which remains an important reference for understanding ancient Maya art styles and motifs

1924   CIW (Carnegie Institution of Washington) begins research at Uaxactun under direction of Oliver Ricketson (with fieldwork continuing until 1938)

1925   Middle American Research Institute (MARI) established at Tulane University under direction of William Gates, assisted by Frans Blom

1926   Juan Martinez Hernandez modifies Goodman's calendar correlation

1926   J. Eric S. Thompson begins his career in Maya archaeology at Chichen Itza

1926   Frans Blom appointed acting director and later head of MARI (1926–1941)

1926   British Museum expedition to southern British Honduras (Belize) with work at Wild Cane Cay and Lubaantun

1927   J. Eric S. Thompson modifies Goodman's and Hernandez's Maya calendar correlation and publishes the GMT (Goodman-Martinez-Thompson) correlation, which became the most widely accepted Maya calendar correlation

1927   Thompson joins second British Museum expedition to British Honduras, under direction of Thomas Joyce, working at Lubaantun and Pusilha

1927   Anna Mitchell-Hedges discovers a crystal skull at Lubaantun, Belize, but the circumstances of the discovery on her sixteenth birthday and accompanied by her father, Frederick Mitchell-Hedges, and the medical officer of health for then British Honduras (Belize), and the fact there are no other "Maya" crystal skulls, indicate to archaeologists that it was likely placed at Lubaantun for her discovery

1929   University of Pennsylvania begins research at Piedras Negras under direction of J. Alden Mason

1929   Thompson's fieldwork at Tzimin Kax in the Maya Mountains of Belize lays the foundation for his definition of the plazuela group (plaza group) as the basic architectural unit of ancient Maya household and community planning

1932   Holmul ceramic report published by Robert Merwin and George Vaillant describing distinctive Protoclassic pottery

1936   Thompson joins the CIW and continues his fieldwork at San Jose, Belize

1938   Thompson carries out fieldwork at Xunantunich, then called Benque Viejo

1940   Clyde Klukhohn publishes scathing criticism of Maya archaeology as merely descriptive and not interpretive or explanatory in "The Conceptual Structure in Middle American Studies"

1940   CIW closes Chichen Itza project

1946   Publication of CIW's research at Kaminaljuyu by Alfred V. Kidder, Jesse Jennings, and Ed Shook

1950   Gordon R. Willey appointed first Charles P. Bowditch Professor of Central American and Mexican Archaeology and Ethnology at Harvard University

1950   Publication of A. Ledyard Smith's excavations at Uaxactun, documenting large-scale architectural style of excavation that set a standard for Maya excavations

1953   Gordon R. Willey initiates settlement pattern study along Belize River (1953–1956)

1955   Publication of Robert E. Smith's ceramic study of Uaxactun

1958   End of Carnegie Institution of Washington research on the ancient Maya with closing of Division of Historical Research of the institution (after projects at Uaxactun, Chichen Itza, Mayapan, and Kaminaljuyu), with remaining Maya archaeologists, Proskouriakoff, Shook, and Pollock, moving next door to Harvard's Peabody Museum

1955   University of Pennsylvania project begins at Tikal under direction of Edwin Shook (1955–1961), Robert Dyson (1962), and William Coe (1963–1969), becoming the largest archaeological project in the Americas

1958   Heinrich Berlin publishes study of Maya emblem glyphs as names of Classic Maya cities

1958   Yuri Knorozov publishes study that Maya hieroglyphs are phonetic, leading to decipherment of ancient texts based on study of the glyphs as sounds instead of picture writing

1958   Gordon R. Willey initiates project at Altar de Sacrificios, Guatemala (1958–1963)

1960   Tatiana Proskouriakoff publishes study of hieroglyphs of Piedras Negras site, indicating that glyphs on Maya stelae provide historical information about ancient kings and queens

1960   Publication of William Bullard's regional survey in the Peten

1962   Publication of CIW's research at Mayapan by Harry Pollock and colleagues

1964   Gordon R. Willey initiates project at Seibal (1964–1968)

1964   David M. Pendergast initiates project at Altun Ha, Belize, under auspices of the Royal Ontario Museum, Toronto (1964–1970)

1969   Government of Guatemala initiates research at Tikal under direction of Juan Pedro Laporte, focusing on the Lost World Complex

1970   Norman Hammond excavates at Lubaantun

1972   Cozumel Archaeological Project directed by Jeremy Sabloff and William Rathje

1974   David Pendergast begins fieldwork at Lamanai, Belize

1974   Field work at Cerros, Belize, initiated under direction of David Freidel, found to be primarily Late Preclassic in age

1974   Hammond begins excavations at Cuello, defining the earliest Maya settlement in the southern Maya lowlands at 1000 B.C.

1975   Elizabeth Graham begins regional settlement survey of Stann Creek District, Belize

1978   Payson Sheets begins excavations at Ceren, a well-preserved Classic Maya community buried by a volcanic eruption about A.D. 600

1979   Survey and excavation of terraced fields in Maya Mountains of Belize by Paul Healy

1979   Excavations of raised fields by Peter Harrison and B. L. Turner at Pull-trouser Swamp, Belize

1979   Excavations at Santa Rita Corozal by Diane Chase

1979   Excavations at the trading port of Moho Cay, Belize, by Heather Mc-Killop

1979   Thomas Hester directs excavations at Colha, Belize, a major stone tool manufacturing community

1982   Richard "Scotty" MacNeish explores coast and rivers of Belize for pre-ceramic sites

1982   Thomas Kelly (1993) discovers Paleoindian spear point at Ladyville, Belize

1982   Excavations initiated at Wild Cane Cay by Heather McKillop

1982   Major excavations at Nohmul, Belize, by Hammond

1983   Fieldwork initiated at Sayil, Yucatan, Mexico, by Jeremy Sabloff and Gair Tourtellot

1984   Fieldwork initiated at Ek Balam by George Bey and Bill Ringle

1985   Caracol project initiated by Arlen and Diane Chase

1986   Freidel begins research at Yaxuna, Yucatan, Mexico

1989   Petexbatun project, including work at Aguateca, Dos Pilas, begins un-der direction of Arthur Demarest

1990   Xunantunich fieldwork begun by Richard Leventhal and Wendy Ashmore

1993   T. Patrick Culbert publishes study of Tikal ceramics from University of Pennsylvania project

1992   Excavations begun at La Milpa by Hammond

1992   Programme for Belize archaeological research project (under direction of Fred Valdez) begins in northwestern Belize

1997   (to 2000) Piedras Negras fieldwork initiated under direction of Stephen Houston

1997   Death of Linda Schele, epigrapher and scholar at University of Texas, Austin, who also founded the Maya Hieroglyphic Workshop at the University of Texas in 1977, an event that continues annually

1999   Peter Harrison publishes study of architecture of central acropolis at Tikal from University of Pennsylvania project

2002   Death of Gordon R. Willey, retired Bowditch Professor of Central

American and Mexican Archaeology and Ethnology at Harvard University

2003   Belize government creates Institute of Archaeology, part of the National Institute of Culture and History (NICH), and holds the first Belize Archaeology Symposium

Resources for Further Study

Abrams, Elliot. 1987. "Economic Specialization and Construction Personnel in Classic Period Copan, Honduras." *American Antiquity* 52 (3): 485–499.

Craft specialization at Copan and, by inference, elsewhere among the Late Classic Maya was by part-time craft specialists and was low in intensity.

Abrams, Elliot. 1994. *How the Maya Built Their World.* Austin: University of Texas Press.

Based on his Ph.D. research at Copan, Abrams examines the energetics involved in construction at Copan, with important implications for other Maya communities.

Adams, Richard E. W. 1970. "Suggested Classic Period Occupational Specialization in the Southern Maya Lowlands." In *Monographs and Papers in Maya Archaeology,* edited by William R. Bullard Jr., 487–502. Papers of the Peabody Museum of Archaeology and Ethnology, vol. 61. Cambridge, MA: Harvard University.

A Classic study of Maya craft specialization drawing on available sources. It provides a starting point for most studies of specialization in the Maya area.

Adams, Richard E. W. 1971. *The Ceramics of Altar de Sacrificios.* Papers of the Peabody Museum of Archaeology and Ethnology, vol. 63, no. 1. Cambridge, MA: Harvard University.

Adams published what was perhaps the first full report of a type-variety classification of Maya pottery, and it forms a standard reference for Maya ceramicists.

Adams, Richard E. W. 1974. "A Trial Estimation of Classic Maya Palace Populations at Uaxactun, Guatemala." In *Mesoamerican Archaeology: New Approaches,* edited by Norman Hammond, 285–296. London: Gerald Duckworth.

In this paper, Adams estimates that 98 percent of the Classic Maya were commoners.

Adams, Richard E. W. 1999. *Río Azul: An Ancient Maya City.* Norman: University of Oklahoma Press.

This monograph reports on excavations at Rio Azul directed by Adams.

Adams, Richard E. W., Walter E. Brown Jr., and T. Patrick Culbert. 1981. "Radar Mapping, Archaeology, and Ancient Maya Land Use." *Science* 213: 1457–1463.

From side-looking radar imagery of the Maya lowlands, the authors traced lines they interpreted as canals for intensive agriculture, an idea that remains controversial. In some areas these lines have been inspected on the ground.

Adams, Richard E. W., and R. Christopher Jones. 1981. "Spatial Patterns and Regional Growth among Classic Maya Cities." *American Antiquity* 46: 301–322.

The authors present a model of site hierarchies ranked according to the number of courtyards and other factors.

Aimers, James L., Terry G. Powis, and Jaime J. Awe. 2000. "Preclassic Round Structures of the Upper Belize Valley." *Latin American Antiquity* 11: 71–86.

Four late Middle Preclassic round structures dated to between 650 and 300 B.C. were excavated at Cahal Pech. They were used as performance platforms as part of burial or ancestor shrines. See also Clark and Hansen (2001) for the precocious developments at Nakbe at the same time, and Garber et al. (2004) for a general discussion of the time in the Upper Belize valley. Hammond (1991a) provides evidence for settlement in the early part of the Middle Preclassic at Cuello.

Alexander, Rani. 1998. "Community Organization in the Parroquia de Yaxcaba, Yucatan, Mexico, 1750–1847: Implications for Household Adaptation within a Changing Colonial Economy." *Ancient Mesoamerica* 9: 39–54.

Alexander examines changes in the Maya household and economy, using archaeological and historical evidence. She traces a population increase after initial decimation by sixteenth-century European diseases to the time of the Caste War of the Yucatan, finding that being cut off from the means of production and extension of credit are major factors in the dynamics of rural-urban economy.

Ambrosino, Michael, prod. [1981] 1993. *Maya: Lords of the Jungle.* VHS video, PBS Home Video, Los Angeles: The Pacific Arts Corporation.

The video provides an informative discussion of population increase and methods of intensifying agricultural production during the Late Classic, with interviews of Maya archaeologists and video coverage of a wide variety of Maya sites.

Amlin, Patricia. 1989. *Popol Vuh: The Creation Myth of the Maya.* VHS Video. Extension Center for Media and Independent Learning, University of California, Berkeley; also available through http://www.ucmedia.berkeley.edu.

An animated video of the story of the *Popol Vuh,* a Quiche text describing the creation of the world and origin of the Maya people, as well as the adventures of the Hero Twins and the place of people in the world in relation to the gods (see also Tedlock 1985).

Anders, F., ed. 1967. *Codex Tro-Cortesianus (Codex Madrid).* Museo de América, Madrid, Graz, Austria: Akademische Druck und Verlagsanstalt.

This is a translation of the indigenous Maya text, with annotations.

Anders, F., ed. 1968. *Codex Peresianus (Codex Paris),* Bibliothèque National, Paris, Graz, Austria: Akademische Druck und Verlagsanstalt.

This is a translation of the indigenous Maya text, with annotations.

Anderson, Bryan. 1997. "Ka'o'ob: The Metates of Chichen Izta within the Context of the Greater Maya Realm." Unpublished Master's thesis, Department of Geography and Anthropology, Louisiana State University, Baton Rouge.

A comprehensive study of metates made by the ancient Maya, with particular reference to those recovered or observed from Anderson's fieldwork at Chichen Itza. Anderson includes linguistic, biological, and cultural information of interest in the use of these corn grinding implements.

Andrews, Anthony P. 1983. *Maya Salt Production and Trade.* Tucson: University of Arizona Press.

This book is an extensive archival and archaeological survey of historic and prehistoric salt making in the Maya area, making this a standard reference for Maya salt studies. The apparent lack of salt in the southern Maya lowlands led Andrews to suggest that salt was imported from the north coast of the Yucatan where there are vast salt flats, an idea that has been questioned by the discovery and excavation of salt works along the Belize coast by McKillop (2002a) and others.

Andrews, Anthony P. 1991. "The Rural Chapels and Churches of Early Colonial Yucatan and Belize: An Archaeological Perspective." In *Columbian Consequences,* vol. 3, edited by David Hurst Thomas, 355–374. Washington, DC: Smithsonian Institution Press.

Andrews describes the various types of churches that were built in the Yucatan by Franciscan missionaries.

Andrews, Anthony P., Frank Asaro, Helen V. Michel, Fred H. Stross, and Pura Cervera Rivero. 1989. "The Obsidian Trade at Isla Cerritos, Yucatan, Mexico." *Journal of Field Archaeology* 16: 355–363.

A significant part of the obsidian found at Isla Cerritos was from a variety of Mexican sources, tying the island site to central Mexican trade connections.

Andrews, E. Wyllys, IV. 1969. *The Archaeological Use and Distribution of Mollusca in the Maya Lowlands.* Middle American Research Institute, Publication 34. New Orleans: Tulane University.

A standard reference for the identification of marine shells from Maya sites, this source also presents information from archaeological sites on ancient Maya use of seashells.

Andrews, E. Wyllys, IV, and E. Wyllys Andrews V. 1980. *Excavations at Dzibilchaltun, Yucatan, Mexico.* Middle American Research Institute Publication 48. New Orleans: Tulane University.

Tulane University excavations at this ancient Maya city in the northern Maya lowlands are described.

Andrews, E. Wyllys, V., and Norman Hammond. 1990. "Redefinition of the Swasey Phase at Cuello, Belize." *American Antiquity* 54: 570–584.

This article discusses the fact that the earliest age of Cuello pottery in the Swasey Phase was adjusted to 1000 B.C. instead of the previous age of 2000 B.C. Therefore, the earliest Maya use of the lowlands is 1000 B.C.

Andrews, E. Wyllys, IV, Michael P. Simmons, Elizabeth S. Wing, and E. Wyllys Andrews V. 1975. "Excavations of an Early Shell Midden on Isla Cancun, Quintana Roo, Mexico." *Middle American Research Institute, Publication* 31: 147–197. New Orleans: Tulane University.

A variety of maritime resources were identified from this Late Preclassic community.

Ardren, Traci, ed. 2002. *Ancient Maya Women.* New York: Altamira Press.

With its emphasis on women, this book marks an important departure from the typical literature on the Maya.

Ashmore, Wendy. 1990. "Ode to a Dragline: Demographic Reconstructions at Classic Quirigua." In *Precolumbian Population History in the Maya Lowlands,* edited by T. Patrick Culbert and Don S. Rice, 63–82. Albuquerque: University of New Mexico Press.

Ashmore presents an overview of population at Quirigua.

Ashmore, Wendy, and Jeremy A. Sabloff. 2002. "Spatial Orders in Maya Civic Plans." *Latin American Antiquity* 13: 201–215.

The layout of Maya cities conformed to the ancient Maya mental template of a quadripartite worldview of the Maya universe with the world tree at its center. The authors include maps of many sites with their discussion.

Ashmore, Wendy, ed. 1981. *Lowland Maya Settlement Patterns.* Albuquerque: University of New Mexico Press.

Summaries of Maya settlement throughout the Maya area by leading Mayanists are presented in this edited volume, the result of a School of American Research seminar.

Aveni, Anthony. 1980. *Skywatchers of Ancient Mexico.* Austin: University of Texas Press.

Aveni is one of the leading archaeoastronomers and has carried out important research on Maya archaeoastronomy, some of which is provided in this general text.

Aveni, Anthony F., Sharon L. Gibbs, and Horst Hartung. 1975. "The Caracol Tower at Chichen Itza: An Ancient Astronomical Observatory?" *Science* 188: 977–985.

They note that the alignment of windows from the Caracol building coincides with the movements of the planet Venus across the sky, also discussed by Milbrath (1999) and others.

Aveni, Anthony F., and Horst Hartung. 1991. "Archaeoastronomy and the Puuc Sites." In *Arqueoastronomia y Etnoastronomia en Mesoamerica,* edited by Johanna Broda, Stanislaw Iwaniszewski, and Lucrecia Maupome, 65–96. Universidad Nacional Autonoma de Mexico, Mexico City.

They examine astronomical alignments of doorways, windows, and buildings at sites in the northern Maya lowlands, especially noting alignments with the movement of the planet Venus across the sky.

Awe, Jaime, Cassandra Bill, Mark Campbell, and David Cheetham. 1990. "Early Middle Formative Occupation in the Central Maya Lowlands: Recent Evidence from Cahal Pech, Belize." *Papers from the Institute of Archaeology* 1: 1–5. University College London, London, England; also available online at http://www.ucl.ac.uk/archaeology/pia/.

Early pottery contemporary with Swasey ceramics from Cuello (Kosakowsky 1987) were recovered from Cahal Pech in this project, directed by Jaime Awe.

Awe, Jaime, and Paul F. Healy. 1994. "Flakes to Blades? Middle Formative Development of Obsidian Artifacts in the Upper Belize River Valley." *Latin American Antiquity* 5: 193–205.

With obsidian from radiocarbon-dated contexts at Cahal Pech, the authors provide the first documented sequence of flakes used in the early part of the Middle Preclassic, followed by the introduction of the core-blade technology in the latter part of the Middle Preclassic.

Ball, Joseph W. 1993. "Pottery, Potters, Palaces, and Polities: Some Socioeconomic and Political Implications of Late Classic Maya Ceramic Industries." In *Lowland Maya Ar-*

chaeology in the Eighth Century A.D., edited by Jeremy A. Sabloff and John S. Henderson, 243–272. Washington, DC: Dumbarton Oaks Research Library and Collections.

Based on his fieldwork at Cahal Pech, Buenavista, and other sites in the upper Belize Valley, Ball suggests that pottery production of most utilitarian vessels was decentralized in the periphery of cities, as suggested by Robert Fry and others, but that there were specialized "palace" workshops for some of the finest painted pottery, as at Buenavista.

Ball, Joseph W., and Jennifer T. Taschek. 1991. "Late Classic Lowland Maya Political Organization and Central Place Analysis: New Insights from the Upper Belize Valley." *Ancient Mesoamerica* 2: 149–165.

Based on their research at Buenavista and Cahal Pech and on comparisons with other sites in the area, the authors suggest that a decentralized "segmentary" state model better reflects the organization of Late Classic Maya society than does a more centralized political model.

Becker, Marshall J. 1973. "Archaeological Evidence for Occupational Specialization among the Classic Period Maya at Tikal, Guatemala." *American Antiquity* 38: 396–406.

This is a Classic-period reference for occupational specialization that has prompted much research.

Becker, Marshall J. 1992. "Burials as Caches; Caches as Burials: A New Interpretation of the Meaning of Ritual Deposits among the Classic Period Lowland Maya," In *New Theories on the Ancient Maya,* edited by Elin C. Danien and Robert J. Sharer, 185–196. University Museum Monograph 77, University Museum Symposium Series, vol. 3. Philadelphia: University of Pennsylvania.

Becker discusses the overlap between burials and caches, both of which are associated with houses and other structures. Both may be dedicatory offerings with artifacts associated with building renovation, burials typically have articulated human skeletal remains, whereas caches may have skeletal remains.

Berlin, Heinrich. 1958. "El Glifo 'emblema' en La Inscripciones Mayas." *Journal de la Societe des Americanistes* 47: 111–119.

Berlin identified "emblem glyphs" on stelae that he assumed named individuals or places, in stark contrast to the previous view that names identified priests, certainly not dynastic rulers. His discovery of emblem glyphs that provided names for Classic Maya cities was a major breakthrough in decipherment of the hieroglyphs and understanding of the historical nature of the glyphs. Along with discoveries by Proskouriakoff (1960) and Knorozov (1958), Berlin's research set the stage for the decipherment of Maya hieroglyphs.

Bey, George J., III, Tara M. Bond, William M. Ringle, Craig A. Hanson, Charles W. Houck, and Carlos Peraza Lope. 1998. "The Ceramic Chronology of Ek Balam, Yucatan, Mexico." *Ancient Mesoamerica* 9: 101–120.

The basic time sequence for the site is established using the type-variety system of ceramic classification, previously used by Adams (1971), Gifford (1976), Sabloff (1975), and others.

Bey, George J., III, Craig Hanson, and William M. Ringle. 1997. "Classic to Postclassic at Ek Balam, Yucatan: Architectural and Ceramic Evidence for Defining the Transition." *Latin American Antiquity* 1: 237–254.

The authors report a C-shaped structure with Cepech complex ceramics, which they say characterizes the Terminal Classic period in the northern lowlands.

Binford, Michael W., Alan L. Kolata, Mark Brenner, John W. Janusek, Matthew T. Seddon, Mark Abbott, and Jason H. Curtis. 1997. "Climate Variation and the Rise and Fall of an Andean Civilization." *Quaternary Research* 47: 235–248.

Changes in the availability of water in the southern Andes created environmental thresholds that scientists argue limited cultural development of the Tiwanaka civilization in the southern highlands of Peru and Bolivia.

Black, Stephen L. 1990. "The Carnegie Uaxactun Project and the Development of Maya Archaeology." *Ancient Mesoamerica* 1: 257–276.

Black provides an insightful historical study of the research carried out at Uaxactun, Chichen Itza, and other Maya sites by the Carnegie Institution of Washington and of the relationship between Carnegie and Harvard in the development of Maya archaeology.

Blake, Michael, B. Chisholm, John Clark, Barbara Voorhies, and Michael Love. 1992. "Prehistoric Subsistence in the Soconusco Region." *Current Anthropology* 33: 83–94.

Early adaptation on the coast of Chiapas, Mexico, is described here.

Blake, Michael, John Clark, B. Chisholm, and K. Mudar. 1992. "Non-Agricultural Staples and Agricultural Supplements: Early Formative Subsistence in the Soconusco Region, Mexico." In *Transitions to Agriculture in Prehistory*, edited by A. B. Gebauer and T. Douglas Price, 133–152. Madison, WI: Prehistory Press.

Coastal resources provided for sedentary lifestyle on the coast of Chiapas, Mexico, even without agricultural products.

Blom, Frans, and Oliver La Farge. 1926–1927. *Tribes and Temples.* New Orleans.

During his early days at Tulane's Middle American Research Institute, Frans Blom, accompanied by his assistant and a former fellow Harvard student, Oliver La Farge, traveled through Central America recording sites and their experiences and observations of the natural and cultural environment.

Brady, James E., et al. 1997. "Glimpses of the Dark Side of the Petexbatun Project: The Petexbatun Regional Cave Study." *Ancient Mesoamerica* 8: 353–364.

Results of the cave survey are presented in this report.

Brady, James E., Joseph W. Ball, Ronald L. Bishop, Duncan C. Pring, Norman Hammond, and Rupert A. Housley. 1998. "The Lowland Maya 'Protoclassic': A Reconsideration of its Nature and Significance." *Ancient Mesoamerica* 9 (1): 17–38.

The authors reevaluate Protoclassic pottery and find that some can be assigned to an early facet in the Late Preclassic and that some fits into a later facet in the Early Classic.

Brasseur de Bourbourg, Etienne C. 1857–1859. *Histoire de nations civilisees du Mexique and de l'Amerique Centrale.* Paris.

An early explorer and epigrapher, Bourbourg is perhaps most remembered for his discovery of the *Popol Vuh* document, which is also translated here.

Brasseur de Bourbourg, Etienne C. 1861. *Popol Vuh: le livre sacre et les mythes de l'antiquite Americaine, avec les livres heroiques et historiques des Quiches.* Paris: Arthus Bertrand.

Includes a Quiche text as well as de Bourbourg's translation.

Brasseur de Bourbourg, Etienne C. 1864. *Relacion des choses de Yucatan de Diego de Landa.* Paris: Arthus Bertrand.

Written in about 1566 by Diego de Landa and published after its discovery by Brasseur de Bourbourg, Landa's account is the single most important text about the contact period Maya. Tozzer's annotated (1941) translation is the standard reference for researchers.

Brasseur de Bourbourg, Etienne C. 1869–1870. *Manuscrit Torano: Etudes sur le systeme graphique et la. langue des Mayas.* Paris: Imprimerie Imperale.

First publication of the Troano part of the Madrid Codex.

Braswell, Geoffrey E., ed. 2003. *The Maya and Teotihuacan: Reinterpreting Early Classic Interaction.* Austin: University of Texas Press.

Researchers continue the debate over the impact of Teotihuacan on the Maya.

Braswell, Geoffrey E., John E. Clark, Kazuo Aoyama, Heather I. McKillop, and Michael D. Glascock. 2000. "Determining the Geological Provenance of Obsidian Artifacts from the Maya Region: A Test of the Efficacy of Visual Sourcing." *Latin American Antiquity* 11: 269–282.

Leading Maya obsidian researchers carry out a blind test of visual sourcing of obsidian and find a high degree of accuracy when compared to chemical analysis of the obsidian.

Bricker, Harvey, and Victoria Bricker. 1983. "Classic Maya Prediction of Solar Eclipses." *Current Anthropology* 24: 1–23.

This important text about Maya archaeoastronomy is available on the Internet through Jstor ("Journal Storage"), an electronic service that provides the text of articles on the Internet, for free at many universitites, or otherwise for a fee at http:// www.jstor.org.

Bricker, Harvey, and Victoria Bricker. 1992. "Zodiacal References in the Maya Codices." In *The Sky and Mayan Literature,* edited by Anthony F. Aveni, 148–183. Oxford University Press, New York.

This book discusses the idea that some of the constellations in the Paris Codex (an indigenous Maya book) are located at opposites sides of the night sky and follow 168-day intervals of 6 months, suggesting they were used to record half a year.

Bricker, Victoria, and Harvey Bricker. 1986. "The Mars Table in the Dresden Codex." In *Research and Reflections in Archaeology and History: Essays in Honor of Doris Stone,* edited by E. Wyllys Andrews V, 51–79. Middle American Research Institute, Publication 47. New Orleans: Tulane University.

An illustration of the Mars Table, a page from the Dresden Codex apparently depicting the movements of the planet Mars in the sky is provided, along with discussion of its astronomical significance and the authors' detailed analysis indicating that the table refers to Mars.

Brunhouse, Robert L. 1975. *Pursuit of the Ancient Maya.* Albuquerque: University of New Mexico Press.

Brunhouse presents a discussion of some of the important early figures in Maya archaeology that shaped it as a discipline.

Bullard, William R., Jr. 1960. "Maya Settlement Patterns in Northeastern Peten, Guatemala." *American Antiquity* 25: 355–372.

A pioneering survey along trails cut by chicleros (people tapping trees for chicle, used to make chewing gum) in the Peten indicated that there were abundant settlements of various sizes in the intervening areas between large Maya cities.

Burger, Thomas. 2001. *Die Maya-Handschrift Codex Dresdensis.* Dresden: Sachsische Landdesbibliothek-Staats-un Universitatsbibliothek; http://www.tu-dresden.de/slub/proj/maya/maya/html.

Images of the Dresden Codex housed in the Dresden Library, with additional commentary, in German. For an English digital version, see Marhenke (2003).

Campbell, Lyle R. 1984. "The Implications of Mayan Historical Linguistics for Glyphic Research." In *Phoneticism in Mayan Hieroglyphic Writing,* edited by John Justeson and Lyle Campbell, 1–16. Institute for Mesoamerican Studies, Publication 9. Albany: State University of New York.

This book discusses Maya hieroglyphic writing, which was based on the spoken language called Chol Maya of the southern lowlands during the Classic period and which spread to Yucatec and other Mayan languages. The book points out that surviving codices were written in the northern Yucatan, and Yucatec Maya is appropriate for deciphering them.

Cancian, Frank. 1965. *Economics and Prestige in a Maya Community: The Religious Cargo System in Zinacantan.* Palo Alto, CA: Stanford University Press.

As part of the Harvard project at Zinacantan, Chiapas, Mexico, Cancian provides a detailed study of the cargo system in use there, in which surplus wealth among the villagers is exchanged for a prestigious position. Use of the cargo system is widespread and provides a useful analogue for earlier times as well.

Carr, H. Sorraya. 1986. "Preliminary Results of Analysis of Fauna." In *Archaeology at Cerros, Belize, Central America,* edited by Robin Robertson and David A. Freidel, 127–146. Dallas: Southern Methodist University Press.

This article is an important inventory and quantification of animal remains from Cerros, more readily available than her dissertation of the same date.

Chamberlain, Robert S. 1948. *The Conquest and Colonization of Yucatan, 1517–1550.* Washington, DC: Carnegie Institution of Washington.

Historical accounts of various explorers and of the early European settlement of the Yucatan make this a standard reference.

Charnay, Desire. 1887. *Ancient Cities of the New World.* New York: Harper and Brothers.

This is an account by French photographer and explorer Desire Charnay of travels to the Yucatan in the nineteenth century. Charnay was likely first person to photograph Maya sites.

Chase, Arlen F. 1985. "Time Depth or Vacuum: The 11.3.0.0.0 Correlation and the Lowland Maya Postclassic." In *Late Lowland Maya Civilization,* edited by Jeremy A. Sabloff and E. Wyllys Andrews V, 99–140. Albuquerque: University of New Mexico Press.

Chase discusses how minor changes in the correlation of the Maya and Christian calendars affect our chronologies of Maya prehistory.

Chase, Arlen F. 1990. "Maya Archaeology and Population Estimates in the Tayasal-Paxcaman Zone, Peten, Guatemala." In *Precolumbian Population History in the Maya Lowlands,* edited by T. Patrick Culbert and Don S. Rice, 149–165. Albuquerque: University of New Mexico Press.

Based on a survey in 1971 and 1977, continuous settlement was found on high ground between the northern and southern arms of Lake Peten, dating from the Late Preclassic through the Terminal Classic, without a decline in population during the Early Classic. The chronology was based on stylistic changes of artifacts from burials and caches placed in buildings rather than potsherds from construction fill. Pitfalls of the latter method are discussed.

Chase, Arlen F., and Diane Z. Chase. 1987a. *Glimmers of a Forgotten Realm: Maya Archaeology at Caracol, Belize.* Orlando, FL: Orlando Museum of Art and Loch Haven.

This is a catalog from an exhibit of Caracol artifacts from the Chases' research.

Chase, Arlen F., and Diane Z. Chase. 1987b. *Investigations at the Classic Maya City of Caracol, Belize: 1985–1987.* Monograph 3. San Francisco: Pre-Columbian Art Research Institute

This is a monograph of the Chases' research.

Chase, Arlen F., and Diane Z. Chase. 1996. "More Than Kin and King: Centralized Political Organization among the Late Classic Maya." *Current Anthropology* 37: 803–810.

Based on their long-term field research at the Classic Maya city of Caracol, Belize, the Chases present a convincing argument for a model of centralized political organization of Late Classic Maya society.

Chase, Arlen F., and Diane Z. Chase. 2001. "Ancient Maya Causeways and Site Organization at Caracol, Belize." *Ancient Mesoamerica* 12: 273–281.

This is a discussion of a complex system of causeways that radiated from the center of Caracol to the suburban areas of the city during the Late Classic period.

Chase, Arlen F., and Prudence M. Rice, eds. 1985. *The Lowland Maya Postclassic.* Austin: University of Texas Press.

Important discussions of the Postclassic by various Mayanists are presented in this edited volume.

Chase, Diane Z. 1990. "The Invisible Maya: Population History and Archaeology at Santa Rita Corozal." In *Precolumbian Population History in the Maya Lowlands,* edited by T. Patrick Culbert and Don S. Rice, 199–213. Albuquerque: University of New Mexico Press.

Much of the domestic architecture of Postclassic Santa Rita was low lines of stones that left no visible remains on the ground surface. Chase discusses the factors Maya archaeologists use to adjust population estimates and adds adjustments for invisible buildings (structures that leave no artifacts or mounds on the ground surface and can only be discovered by excavation).

Chase, Diane Z., and Arlen F. Chase. 1986. *Offerings to the Gods: Maya Archaeology at Santa Rita Corozal.* University of Central Florida, Orlando.

This is a catalog of artifacts from the Chases' excavations at Santa Rita Corozal, Belize.

Chase, Diane Z., and Arlen F. Chase. 1988. *A Postclassic Perspective: Excavations at the Maya Site of Santa Rita Corozal, Belize.* Monograph 4. San Francisco: Pre-Columbian Art Research Institute.

This is a monograph on the Chases' research at Santa Rita Corozal, Belize.

Chase, Diane Z., and Arlen F. Chase. 1996. "Maya Multiples: Individuals, Entries, and Tombs in Structure A34 of Caracol." *Latin American Antiquity* 7: 61–79.

Clear evidence for multiple burials in the same tomb is presented, underscoring Hammond, Petty, and Saul's 1975 discussion that graves were reused.

Chase, Diane Z., and Arlen F. Chase, eds. 1994. *Studies in the Archaeology of Caracol, Belize.* Monograph 7. San Francisco: Pre-Columbian Art Research Institute.

This monograph includes research at Caracol done since the first monograph in 1987.

Cheek, Charles. 1997. "Setting an English Table: Black Carib Archaeology on the Caribbean Coast of Honduras." In *Approaches to the Historical Archaeology of Mexico, Central, and South America,* edited by Jan Gasco, Greg C. Smith, and Patricia Fournier-Garcia, 101–109. Los Angeles: Costen Institute of Archaeology, University of California.

Cheek's study is one of the few by archaeologists of the historical period in Central America. There are other important studies in this volume as well.

Christie, Jessica J., ed. 2003. *Maya Palaces and Elite Residences.* Austin: University of Texas Press.

Evidence from Classic and Postclassic cities in the southern and northern Maya lowlands, including Tikal, Copan, Dos Pilas, Aguateca, Yaxuna, Blue Creek, Chichen Itza, and Uxmal, indicate that a wide range of activities took place in palaces, which varied in size, number, and shape of rooms, and in degree of elaboration.

Clancy, Flora S., Clemency C. Coggins, T. Patrick Culbert, Charles Gallenkamp, Peter D. Harrison, and Jeremy A. Sabloff. 1985. *Maya: Treasures of an Ancient Civilization.* New York: Harry N. Abrams.

This catalog, from a major exhibition of Maya pottery and other artifacts, is well illustrated, with accompanying text.

Clancy, Flora, and Peter D. Harrison, eds. 1990. *Vision and Revision in Maya Studies.* Albuquerque: University of New Mexico Press.

This volume includes an eclectic yet important assortment of papers by leading Mayanists, from Postclassic trading ports by Anthony Andrews, to early pottery by E. Wyllys Andrews V, and Classic cities in southern Belize by Richard Leventhal.

Clark, John E. 1994. "The Development of Early Formative Ranked Societies in the Soconusco, Chiapas, Mexico." Ph.D. dissertation, Department of Anthropology, University of Michigan, Ann Arbor.

Excavations and analysis of obsidian and pottery from coastal Chiapas indicate precocious development in the area (see also Blake, Chisholm, Clark, Voorhies, and Love 1992 and Blake, Clark, Chisholm, and Mudar 1992).

Clark, John E., and Richard Hansen. 2001. "The Architecture of Early Kingship: Comparative Perspectives on the Origin of the Maya Royal Court." In *Royal Courts of the Ancient Maya*, vol. 2, edited by Takeshi Inomata and Stephen Houston, 1–45. Boulder, CO: Westview.

Large temples and other monumental architecture dated to the latter part of the Middle Preclassic at Nakbe, in the Peten district of Guatemala, indicate a precious development for the southern lowland Maya, contemporaneous with the Olmec at La Venta. This finding suggests that the Olmec and Maya may have developed complexity in tandem, rather than the Olmec preceding the rise to complexity in the Maya lowlands.

Clark, John E., and Stephen Houston. 1998. "Craft Specialization, Gender, and Personhood among the Post-Conquest Maya of Yucatan, Mexico," In *Craft and Social Identity*, edited by Cathy Costin and Rita Wright, 31–46. Archeological Papers 8. Washington, DC: American Anthropological Association.

By looking at documentary sources, the authors of this book discuss craft production.

Cline, H. F., ed. 1972–1975. "Guide to Ethnohistoric Sources." In *Handbook of Middle American Indians*, vols. 12–15. Austin: University of Texas Press.

Provides sources of important colonial documents for Mesoamerica, including texts about and by the Maya.

Cobos, Raphael. 1989. "Shelling In: Marine Mollusca at Chichen Itza," In *Coastal Maya Trade*, edited by Heather McKillop and Paul F. Healy, 49–58. Occasional Papers in Anthropology 8. Peterborough, Ontario: Trent University.

Cobos identifies marine shells from Chichen Itza and attributes their origin to their habitats on the nearest coasts.

Cobos, Raphael, and Terance L. Winemiller. 2001. "The Late and Terminal Classic-Period Causeway Systems of Chichen Itza, Yucatan, Mexico." *Ancient Mesoamerica* 12: 283–291.

The authors' mapping project extends the known causeways based on earlier research by others. There are two periods of construction and use of the causeways, which connect different parts of the city.

Coe, Michael D. 1973. *The Maya Scribe and His World.* New York: Grolier Club.

This is the catalog of an exhibition of Classic Maya pottery vessels at the Grolier Club, and it also includes the first publication of the eleven known pages of the Grolier Codex, the last of four known Maya codices.

Coe, Michael D. 1978. *Lords of the Underworld: Masterpieces of Classic Maya Ceramics.* Princeton, NJ: Art Museum, Princeton University, and Princeton University Press.

This catalogue of painted Maya pottery vessels provides important iconographic data for understanding Maya elite society.

Coe, Michael D. 1982. *Old Gods and Young Heroes: The Pearlman Collection of Maya Ceramics.* Jerusalem: Israel Museum.

Coe's catalog and text includes painted pottery vessels of use for interpreting Maya elite society.

Coe, Michael D. 1990. "Next Door to Olympus: Reminiscences of a Harvard Student." *Ancient Mesoamerica* 1: 253–255.

Important historical notes are provided here about the early beginnings of Harvard and the Carnegie Institution of Washington in the foundation of Maya field archaeology.

Coe, Michael D. 1992. *Breaking the Maya Code.* New York: Thames & Hudson.

Coe presents an engaging account of the history of decipherment of Mayan hieroglyphs.

Coe, Michael D., and Kent V. Flannery. 1967. *Early Cultures and Human Ecology in South Coastal Guatemala.* Washington, DC: Smithsonian Institution Press.

This is a classic report of early sedentary coastal settlers on the Pacific coast, including reports of excavations by the authors.

Coe, Michael D., and Justin Kerr. 1998. *The Art of the Maya Scribe.* New York: Harry N. Abrams.

Wonderful illustrations from painted pottery vessels, many produced from the famous "rollouts" photographed by Justin Kerr, provide a pictorial document of the role of scribes and writing in elite Maya society, with extensive text accompanying the pictures.

Coe, Michael D., and Mark Van Stone. 2001. *Reading the Maya Glyphs.* New York: Thames & Hudson.

This is a primer on understanding Maya glyphs that is introductory yet detailed.

Coggins, Clemency. 1980. "The Shape of Time: Some Political Implications of the Four-Part Figure." *American Antiquity* 45: 727–739.

This article points out that the twin-pyramid group at Tikal in cardinal directions functions to map the east-west daily travel of the sun.

Coggins, Clemency C., and John M. Ladd. 1992. "Wooden Artifacts." In *Artifacts from the Cenote of Sacrifice, Chichen Itza, Yucatan,* edited by Clemency C. Coggins, 235–344. Memoirs of the Peabody Museum of Archaeology and Ethnology, vol. 10, no. 3. Cambridge, MA: Harvard University.

Descriptions and illustrations of wooden objects dredged in the early 20th century by Edward Thompson (see Willard 1926) from the Cenote of Sacrifice. Also see Coggins 1992 and Coggins and Shane 1984 for other artifacts recovered from the Cenote.

Coggins, Clemency C., ed. 1992. *Artifacts from the Cenote of Sacrifice, Chichen Itza, Yucatan.* Memoirs of the Peabody Museum of Archaeology and Ethnology, vol. 10, no. 3. Cambridge, MA: Harvard University.

This monograph includes Edward Thompson's description of the Cenote, Coggins's description of Thompson's and others' recoveries, as well as descriptions of non-metal artifacts. These include textiles, basketry, stone, bone, shell, chipped stone, pottery, wood, copal, rubber, and ceramics, among others.

Coggins, Clemency, and Orrin C. Shane III, eds. 1984. *Cenote of Sacrifice: Maya Treasures from the Sacred Well at Chichen Itza.* Austin: University of Texas Press.

Prepared as a catalog to accompany an exhibit at the Science Museum of Minnesota from artifacts from Harvard's Peabody Museum, this volume includes color photos and text of the finest pottery, gold, copper, bone, shell, and other artifacts from the Cenote and other locations at Chichen Itza.

Cowgill, Ursula. 1962. "An Agricultural Study of the Southern Maya Lowlands." *American Anthropologist* 64: 273–286.

Her calculations indicate that the carrying capacity of slash and burn agriculture in the southern Maya lowlands was much greater than Maya archaeologists had previously considered, allowing 58–77 people per km^2, and that this population level (carrying capacity) had not been reached during the Classic period.

Craine, E., and R. Reindorp. 1979. *The Codex Pérez and the Book of Chilam Balam of Maní.* Norman: University of Oklahoma Press.

This is an authoritative annotated translation of the codex. Books written by native Maya in several Yucatecan communities during early colonial days called Chilam Balam are variously informative on religion and ideology. Chilam Balam was a native priest who evidently foretold the arrival of the Spaniards and the books are named after him.

Culbert, T. Patrick. 1974. *The Lost Civilization: The Story of the Classic Maya.* New York: Harper and Row.

A short introductory survey of the Classic Maya that summarizes the politics, economy, subsistence, and other aspects of the culture.

Culbert, T. Patrick. 1993. *The Ceramics of Tikal.* Philadelphia: University of Pennsylvania Museum.

This is the landmark study of the pottery from the University of Pennsylvania Tikal project, using the type-variety system of ceramic classification and based on complete vessels.

Culbert, T. Patrick, Laura J. Kosakowsky, Robert E. Fry, and William A. Haviland. 1990. "The Population of Tikal, Guatemala." In *Precolumbian Population History in the Maya Lowlands,* edited by T. Patrick Culbert and Don S. Rice, 103–121. Albuquerque: University of New Mexico Press.

In this, the first publication on the Tikal project to use data from all sources of survey and excavation in the 20 km^2 area of the 1956 to 1970 University of Pennsylvania project at the site, the authors calculate a population estimate of about 62,000 residents of Tikal (see also Harrison 1999). A detailed discussion of methodology and difficulty of estimating population is included.

Culbert, T. Patrick, ed. 1973. *The Classic Maya Collapse.* Albuquerque: University of New Mexico Press.

Based on a School for American Research seminar, this book provides a variety of explanations for the Classic period collapse of cities in the southern Maya lowlands. A consensus is reached that multiple factors, principal among which are ecological disaster and population increase, were important reasons for the collapse.

Culbert, T. Patrick, ed. 1991. *Classic Maya Political History: Hieroglyphic and Archaeological Evidence.* New York: Cambridge University Press.

>   In this School of American Research seminar book, the authors coalesce archaeological and epigraphic information to provide insightful discussions of areas oftentimes reported separately. Papers are included from across the Maya area on the Classic and Postclassic periods.

Culbert, T. Patrick, and Don S. Rice, eds. 1990. *Precolumbian Population History in the Maya Lowlands.* Albuquerque: University of New Mexico Press.

>   The editors provide a thorough summary of demography in the Maya area, followed by chapters by Mayanists describing populations. Of particular interest is the way Mayanists reconstruct population figures from mounds or other evidence and the missing population figures for houses without mounded remains.

Curtis, Jason H., David A. Hodell, and Mark Brenner. 1996. "Climate Variability on the Yucatan Peninsula (Mexico) during the Past 3,500 years, and Its Implications for Maya Cultural Evolution." *Quaternary Research* 46: 37–47.

>   This article discusses drought conditions at the time of the Classic period collapse, found from analysis of a sediment core from Lake Punta Laguna, near Coba, Quintana Roo, Mexico.

Dahlin, Bruce. 2000. "The Barricade and Abandonment of Chunchucmil: Implications for Northern Maya Warfare." *Latin American Antiquity* 11: 283–298.

>   Dahlin describes the defensive wall at Chunchucmil and provides comparative data for sites in the northern Maya lowlands.

Danforth, Marie. 1999. "Coming up Short: Stature and Nutrition among the Ancient Maya of the Southern Lowlands." In *Reconstructing Ancient Maya Diet,* edited by Christine White, 103–117. Salt Lake City: University of Utah Press.

>   This is a compilation of published data on ancient Maya height based on skeletal remains. It indicates much regional variability and only a slight decrease in male height in the Late Classic, in contrast to Tikal data studied by Haviland in 1967 that showed decline in stature attributed to the Classic Maya collapse.

Davidson, William V. 1991. "Geographical Perspectives on Spanish-Pech (Paya) Indian Relationships, Northeast Honduras, Sixteenth Century." In *Columbian Consequences,* vol. 3, edited by David Hurst Thomas, 205–226. Washington, DC: Smithsonian Institution Press.

>   From archival and historical linguistic evidence, Davidson finds that the trading canoe Columbus encountered off the north coast of Honduras was not a Maya vessel but that of another local native group.

Day, Jane. 2001. "Performing on the Court." In *The Sport of Life and Death: The Mesoamerican Ballgame,* edited by E. Michael Whittington, 64–77. New York: Thames & Hudson.

>   Day discusses the origin of the ball game, the Amerindian origin of the "rubber ball," the ritual importance of the ball game, and its association with warfare among the Maya.

Demarest, Arthur. 1993. "The Violent Saga of a Maya Kingdom." *National Geographic Magazine* 183 (2): 94–111.

>   This article's color illustrations show military defeat in the Petexbatun.

Demarest, Arthur. 1996. "The Maya State: Centralized or Segmentary? Closing Comment." *Current Anthropology* 37: 821–824.

Based on his research in the Petexbatun, and on comparisons with other Maya research, Demarest finds that a decentralized model fits Late Classic Maya organization.

Demarest, Arthur. 1997. "The Vanderbilt Petexbatun Regional Archaeological Project 1989–1994: Overview, History, and Major Results of a Multidisciplinary Study of the Classic Maya Collapse." *Ancient Mesoamerica* 8: 209–227.

The director of the project summarizes the fieldwork and findings here. The research was designed to investigate warfare, and the author found warfare to have been endemic and causal in the Classic collapse.

Demarest, Arthur A. 2001. "Climatic Change and the Classic Maya Collapse: The Return of Catastrophism." *Latin American Antiquity* 12 (1): 105–123.

In this review of Richardson Gill's (2000) book, *The Great Maya Droughts,* Demarest cautions that his model indicates a return to environmental determinism.

Demarest, Arthur, Kim Morgan, Claudia Wooley, and Hector Escobedo. 2003. "The Political Acquisition of Sacred Geography: The Murcielagos Complex at Dos Pilas." In *Maya Palaces and Elite Residences,* edited by Jessica J. Christie, 120–153. Austin: University of Texas Press.

Excavations in the Murcielagos complex at Dos Pilas revealed a shrine in the royal plaza linked by a tomb to an underground cave system that followed the east-to-west site plan and created a sacred cosmogram of the underworld (the cave system) and the living world (the settlement). See also Brady et al. 1997 for a discussion of the caves in the area and Demarest et al. 1997 for a discussion of Dos Pilas in the Petexbatun region.

Demarest, Arthur A., Matt O'Mansky, Claudia Wolley, Dirk Van Tuerenhout, Takeshi Inomata, Joel Palka, and Hector Escobedo. 1997. "Classic Maya Defensive Systems and Warfare in the Petexbatun Region: Archaeological Evidence and Interpretations." *Ancient Mesoamerica* 8: 229–253.

This article presents a summary of evidence of warfare in the Petexbatun.

Desmond, Lawrence, and Phyllis Messenger. 1988. *A Dream of Maya: Augustus and Alice Le Plongeon in Nineteenth-Century Yucatan.* Albuquerque: University of New Mexico Press.

The authors describe the travels by Augustus and Alice Le Plongeon in the Yucatan.

Dockall, J. E., and Harry J. Shafer. 1993. "Testing the Producer-Consumer Model for Santa Rita Corozal, Belize." *Latin American Antiquity* 4: 158–179.

This article discusses high-quality chert tools that were traded to Santa Rita from Colha.

Dull, Robert A., John R. Southon, and Payson Sheets. 2001. "Volcanism, Ecology, and Culture: A Reassessment of the Volcán Ilopango TBJ Eruption in the Southern Maya Realm." *Latin American Antiquity* 12 (1): 25–44.

In this article, the dating of the eruption is set at A.D. 410, which, according to some researchers seems late for the Protoclassic intrusion into Belize and Guatemala.

Dunham, Peter S., Thomas R. Jamison, and Richard M. Leventhal. 1989. "Secondary Development and Settlement Economies: The Classic Maya of Southern Belize." In *Pre-*

historic Maya Economies of Belize, edited by Patricia McAnany and Barry Isaac, 255–292. Research in Economic Anthropology, Supplement 4. Greenwich, CT: JAI Press.

An argument for segmentary state development among the Classic Maya is made using data from field work in southern Belize.

Dunning, Nicholas, Timothy Beach, and David Rue. 1997. "The Paleoecology and Ancient Settlement of the Petexbatun Region, Guatemala." *Ancient Mesoamerica* 8: 255–266.

Preclassic farmers practiced rainfall farming, clearing parts of the forest and subjecting it to erosion. After a diminution in population in the Early Classic period, population increased in the Late Classic, but farmers increasingly placed their fields in defensive locations, some walled and on uplands or ridges, coinciding with the increasingly endemic warfare in the region.

Edmonson, Munro S. 1982. *The Ancient Future of the Itza: The Book of Chilam Balam of Tizimin.* Austin: University of Texas Press.

This is the authoritative annotated translation of this text. Books written by native Maya in several Yucatecan communities during early colonial days called Chilam Balam are variously informative on religion and ideology. Chilam Balam was a native priest who evidently foretold the arrival of the Spaniards and the books are named after him.

Edmonson, Munro S. 1988. *The Book of the Year: Middle American Calendrical Systems.* Salt Lake City: University of Utah Press.

He places the Maya and other Mesoamerican calendars in a pan-Mesoamerican perspective, from the Olmec to Colonial times.

Emery, Kitty, ed. 2004. *Maya Zooarchaeology.* Los Angeles: Costen Institute of Archaeology, University of California.

In this book, a variety of studies on vertebrate and invertebrate animal remains are reported by the leading experts in Maya zooarchaeology.

Ensor, Bradley, and Heather McKillop. 2003. "Morphological and Technological Suitability of Maya Pottery from Wild Cane Cay, Belize." In *New Horizons for Ancient Maya Ceramics,* edited by Heather McKillop and Shirley Mock. Unpublished book manuscript.

This is a report on a study in which sherds from pottery vessels of various shapes from Wild Cane Cay were tested for hardness and porosity. Comparisons were made between the suitability of the material for various tasks.

Estrada-Belli, Francisco. 1999. *The Archaeology of Complex Societies in Southeastern Pacific Coastal Guatemala: A Regional GIS Approach.* Oxford, UK: British Archaeology Reports, International Series 820.

Regional survey and excavation was incorporated into a geographic information system (GIS), along with satellite imagery and aerial photos, to reconstruct the changing settlement patterns in relation to the landscape. This report was one of the first to use GIS for the Maya area.

Fagan, Brian. 1987. *The Great Journey: The Peopling of Ancient America.* New York: Thames & Hudson.

Fagan summarizes, in a readable fashion, the various theories and evidence for the peopling of the Americas. Although not dealing specifically with the Maya area, the text places the Paleoindian occupation of Central America in a broader context.

Fash, Barbara. 1992. "Late Classic Architectural Sculpture Themes in Copán." *Ancient Mesoamerica* 3: 89–104.

Fash's study of mosaic sculpture façade pieces from buildings at Copan showed a shift from religious and political images to images of warfare over time.

Fash, William. 2001. *Scribes, Warriors, and Kings,* 2d ed. New York: Thames & Hudson.

Fash presents a very readable discussion of the dynastic history of Copan, its monumental architecture, its hieroglyphs, and other information based on the author's research through Harvard's Copan project and drawing on research by others at the site and the surrounding hinterland.

Fedick, Scott, ed. 1996. *The Managed Mosaic.* Salt Lake City: University of Utah Press.

This book includes articles on Maya agriculture, tree cropping, and other forms of subsistence and is an important reference on ancient Maya diet and use of the land.

Feldman, Lawrence. 1974. "Shells from Afar: 'Panamic' Mollusca in Maya Sites." In *Mesoamerican Archaeology: New Approaches,* edited by Norman Hammond, 129–134. Austin: University of Texas Press.

In this paper, shells from the Pacific coast are identified from various lowland Maya sites.

Ferguson, William M., and Richard E. W. Adams. 2001. *Mesoamerica's Ancient Cities,* rev. ed. Albuquerque: University of New Mexico Press.

Color photos, black-and-white illustrations, and text provide a visual tour of Tikal, Quirigua, Copan, Altun Ha, Caracol, Palenque, Yaxchilan, Rio Bec, Becan, Xpuhil, Chicanna, Uxmal, Kahah, Sayil, Labna, Dzibilchaltun, Chichen Itza, Mayapan, Coba, Tulum, and other Maya sites.

Flannery, Kent V., and Joyce Marcus. 2003. "The Origin of War: New 14C Dates from Ancient Mexico." *Proceedings of the National Academy of Sciences* 100: 11801–11805.

They discuss the origins of complex society in Mesoamerica based on the appearance of raiding and warfare associated with the power of chiefs, with examples from their research in Oaxaca, Mexico. They also report the earliest known hieroglyph on a stone monument from San Jose Mogote, sealed under deposits radiocarbon-dated to about 600 B.C.

Flannery, Kent V., ed. 1982. *Maya Subsistence: Studies in Memory of Dennis E. Puleston.* New York: Academic Press.

Various agricultural and other systems are described here for the ancient Maya diet.

Foias, Antonia E., and Ronald L. Bishop. 1997. "Changing Ceramic Production and Exchange in the Petexbatun Region, Guatemala: Reconsidering the Classic Maya Collapse." *Ancient Mesoamerica* 8: 275–291.

This article discusses production and distribution of pottery in the Petexbatun region, which indicates that changes in the economy followed the political turmoil and warfare of the late eighth century.

Ford, Anabel. 1986. *Population Growth and Social Complexity: An Examination of Settlement and Environment in the Central Maya Lowlands.* Anthropological Research Paper 35. Tempe: Arizona State University.

> This study is based on a transect between Tikal and Yaxha, examining the settlement distribution by survey and excavation. In addition to the results, the study represents an important methodological contribution to the field.

Ford, Anabel. 1990. "Maya Settlement in the Belize River Area: Variations in Residence Patterns of the Central Maya Lowlands." In *Precolumbian Population History in the Maya Lowlands,* edited by T. Patrick Culbert and Don S. Rice, 167–181. Albuquerque: University of New Mexico Press.

> Three transects from the Belize River were surveyed, each passing through a known inland site on the north side of the river, with settlement distribution discussed in relation to distance from the river, access to well-drained uplands for farming, and the known sites. In contrast to Willey et al.'s (1965) finding that settlement was concentrated along the Belize River, Ford found that settlements were located inland wherever there was arable land.

Ford, Anabel, and W. I. Rose. 1995. "Volcanic Ash in Ancient Maya Ceramics of the Limestone Lowlands: Implications for Prehistoric Volcanic Activity in the Guatemalan Highlands." *Journal of Volcanology and Geothermal Research* 66: 149–162.

> Instead of the massive import of volcanic ash to mix with local clays as a tempering agent for pottery vessels, the authors suggest there were local sources of volcanic ash within the Maya lowlands.

Förstemann, Ernst W. 1880. *Die Mayahandschrift der Koniglichen Offentlichen Bibliothek zu Dresden.* Leipzig, Deutschland: Verlag der A. Naumannschen Lichtruckerei.

> Limited-edition publication of the Dresden Codex, discovered in the Dresden library in Germany; see Förstemann 1906 for an English edition more widely available and Burger 2001 and Marhenke 2003 for digital images.

Förstemann, Ernst W. 1906. *Commentary on the Maya Manuscript in the Royal Public Library of Dresden.* Papers of the Peabody Museum, vol. 4, no. 2, 49–266. Cambridge, MA: Harvard University.

> This author found and published the Dresden Codex, one of four surviving indigenous Maya texts.

Fox, John W., and Garrett W. Cook. 1996. "Constructing Maya Communities: Ethnography for Archaeology." *Current Anthropology* 37: 811–830.

> The authors provide evidence in support of centralized control of Classic Maya society.

Freidel, David A. 1975. "The Ix Chel Shrine and Other Temples of Talking Idols." In *A Study of Changing Pre-Columbian Commerical Systems.* Monographs of the Peabody Museum of Archaeology and Ethnology, vol. 3, edited by Jeremy A. Sabloff and William L. Rathje, 107–113. Cambridge, MA: Harvard University.

> In this article, Freidel describes a shrine to Ix Chel, the goddess of childbirth, pregnancy, and fertility. There were shrines on Cozumel and Isla Mujeres off the eastern coast of the Yucatan to which people would make pilgrimages.

Freidel, David A. 1979. "Culture Areas and Interaction Spheres: Contrasting Approaches to the Emergence of Civilization in the Maya Lowlands." *American Antiquity* 44: 36–54.

Based on his work at Cerros, Freidel explains the rise of cultural complexity due to elite communication and exchange of elite paraphernalia such as jade carvings, and he discusses architectural symbolism expressed in masks on temples.

Freidel, David A. 1981. "The Political Economics of Residential Dispersion among the Lowland Maya." In *Lowland Maya Settlement Patterns,* edited by Wendy Ashmore, 371–382. Albuquerque: University of New Mexico Press.

Freidel contrasts the decentralized organization of Mayapan with the centralized organization of earlier Chichen Itza, where elite residence and administration was centrally focused on three plaza groups around the Castillo.

Freidel, David A. 1992. "Children of the First Father's Skull: Terminal Classic Warfare in the Northern Maya Lowlands and the Transformation of Kingship and Elite Hierarchies." In *Mesoamerican Elites: An Archaeological Assessment,* edited by Diane Z. Chase and Arlen F. Chase, 99–117. Norman: University of Oklahoma Press.

This is a discussion of how Classic Maya kings fought wars to capture victims for sacrifice. This enhanced their title to the throne, prompting escalating warfare by competing city-states. By way of contrast, more expansionary warfare was promulgated by the competing Postclassic powers of Coba and Chichen Itza in the northern lowlands.

Freidel, David A., and Vernon Scarborough. 1982. "Subsistence, Trade, and Development of the Coastal Maya." In *Maya Subsistence,* edited by Kent V. Flannery, 131–155. New York: Academic Press.

The canal surrounding the ceremonial precinct and the system of raised fields is described, with more details provided in Scarborough's (1991) book.

Freidel, David A., and Linda Schele. 1988. "Kingship in the Late Preclassic Maya Lowlands: The Instruments and Places of Ritual Power." *American Anthropologist* 90 (3): 547–567.

The authors present a detailed description of the iconography and ritual of power as publicly displayed with symbols in Late Preclassic Cerros. These symbols laid the foundations for Classic Maya kingship rituals carved in stone monuments with hieroglyphs and pictures of kings and queens.

Freidel, David A., Linda Schele, and Joy Parker. 1993. *Maya Cosmos: Three Thousand Years on the Shaman's Path.* New York: Morrow.

This highly readable account of the importance of shamanism, iconography, and cosmology in ancient Maya culture draws on epigraphic, artistic, and archaeological data.

Freter, AnnCorinne. 1992. "Chronological Research at Copan: Methods and Implications." *Ancient Mesoamerica* 3: 117–133.

This article details major use of obsidian hydration dating for establishing a chronology for sites in a 135-square-kilometer area around Copan. Some 2,150 obsidian hydration dates, correlated with other dating methods, were used to assign ages to sites and structures in Penn State PAC II (Progecto Arqueologia Copan, phase 2) research directed by David Webster.

Fry, Robert E. 1979. "The Economics of Pottery at Tikal, Guatemala: Models of Exchange for Serving Vessels." *American Antiquity* 44: 494–512.

This is an important model of the production of everyday serving vessels in the city periphery and of their distribution to the city folk.

Fry, Robert E. 1980. "Models of Exchange for Major Shape Classes of Lowland Maya Pottery." In *Models and Methods in Regional Exchange,* edited by Robert E. Fry, 3–18. Society for American Archaeology Papers 1. Washington, DC: Society for American Archaeology.

This and other studies in this edited volume support production of utilitarian pottery vessels in the periphery of sites such as Palenque and Tikal.

Gann, Thomas H. F. 1925. *Mystery Cities: Exploration and Adventure in Lubaantun.* London: Duckworth.

This book is an account of the archaeological research carried out at Lubaantun and elsewhere while Gann was medical officer of health to what was then the colony of British Honduras.

Garber, James F. 1989. *Archaeology at Cerros, Belize, Central America,* vol. 2: *The Artifacts.* Dallas: Southern Methodist University Press.

In this revision of his Ph.D. dissertation, Garber provides descriptions of the artifacts recovered from David Freidel's (1979) Cerros project.

Garber, James F., ed. 2004. *The Ancient Maya of the Belize Valley.* Gainesville: University Press of Florida.

Studies by researchers carrying out fieldwork since the 1970s in the Belize Valley provide summaries of excavation and survey carried out and synthesize the regional cultural history. Although some of the sites have been published before in other venues, this is an important volume because it provides the first regional presentation and synthesis of data.

Garber, James F., Jaime J. Awe, M. Kathryn Brown, and Christopher J. Hartman. 2004. "Middle Formative Prehistory of the Central Belize Valley: An Examination of Architecture, Material Culture, and Sociopolitical Change at Blackman Eddy." In *The Ancient Maya of the Belize Valley,* edited by James F. Garber, 25–47. Gainesville: University Press of Florida.

Information is summarized from Garber's project at Blackman Eddy and from Awe's project (see also Awe et al. 1990) about the earliest occupation of the Belize Valley, which shows surprising cultural complexity in contrast to the simple farming groups in northern Belize at Cuello (Hammond 1991a), for example.

Gifford, James C. 1976. *Prehistoric Pottery Analysis and the Ceramics of Barton Ramie in the Belize Valley.* Papers of the Peabody Museum of Archaeology and Ethnology, vol. 18. Cambridge, MA: Harvard University.

This is a standard reference for ceramic studies and the first Maya pottery study to use the type-variety system of classification. It includes discussion on the system as well as reporting on the pottery.

Gill, Richardson. 2000. *The Great Maya Droughts.* Albuquerque: University of New Mexico Press.

A compelling and detailed argument for a sustained drought that precipitated the Classic Maya collapse is presented here.

Glass, John B. 1975. "A Survey of Native Middle American Pictorial Manuscripts." *Handbook of Middle American Indians* 14: 3–81.

The article includes a discussion of Maya codices.

Gonzalez-Oliver, Angelica, Lourdes Marquez-Morfin, Jose C. Jimenez, and Alfonso Torre-Blanco. 2001. "Founding Amerindian Mitochondrial DNA Lineages in Ancient Maya from Xcaret, Quintana Roo." *American Journal of Physical Anthropology* 116: 230–235.

This article discusses mitochondrial DNA studies of modern Yucatecan Maya and ancient human skeletal remains from Xcaret on the east coast of the Yucatan, which indicate that the high frequency of lineage group A corresponds to similar results from elsewhere in Mesoamerica and North America.

Goodman, Joseph T. 1905. "Maya Dates." *American Anthropologist* 7: 642–647.

Goodman provides the first correlation of the Maya calendar with the Christian calendar, a correlation subsequently updated, with the generally accepted version referred to as the Goodman-Martinez-Thompson (GMT) correlation, as published by Thompson (1927).

Gordon, George Byron. 1896. *Prehistoric Ruins of Copan, Honduras.* Memoirs of the Peabody Museum of Archaeology and Ethnology, vol. 1, no. 1. Cambridge, MA: Harvard University.

This source reports on the first major expedition sponsored by Harvard, which was carried out at Copan under the direction of Marshall Saville, John Owens, and George Gordon.

Gordon, George Byron. 1902. *The Hieroglyphic Stairway: Ruins of Copan.* Memoirs of the Peabody Museum, vol. 1, no. 6. Cambridge, MA: Harvard University.

The first Harvard Maya project at Copan included study of the hieroglyphic stairway, more recently reassembled and studied through another Harvard project by Barbara and Bill Fash (Fash 2001).

Graham, Elizabeth. 1987. "Resource Diversity in Belize and Its Implications for Models of Lowland Trade." *American Antiquity* 52: 753–767.

Graham here identifies many resources used by the ancient Maya that were available within the Maya lowlands of Belize, especially in the Maya Mountains, suggesting that trade within the lowlands was overlooked in contrast to long-distance trade.

Graham, Elizabeth. 1989. "Brief Synthesis of Coastal Site Data from Colson Point, Placencia, and Marco Gonzalez, Belize." In *Coastal Maya Trade,* edited by Heather McKillop and Paul F. Healy, 135–154. Occasional Papers in Anthropology 8. Peterborough, Ontario: Trent University.

Graham describes excavations at several coastal Belize sites, along with a schematic reconstruction of sea level rise in relation to the site at Marco Gonzalez.

Graham, Elizabeth A. 1991. "Archaeological Insights into Colonial Period Maya Life at

Tipu, Belize." In *Columbian Consequences,* vol. 3, edited by David H. Thomas, 319–335. Washington, DC: Smithsonian Institution Press.

> Graham's research at Tipu, a Franciscan mission site in western Belize, is discussed.

Graham, Elizabeth. 1994. *The Highlands of the Lowlands: Environment and Archaeology in the Stann Creek District, Belize, Central America.* Monographs in World Archaeology 19. Madison, WI: Prehistory Press.

> This book is a revision of Graham's Ph.D. dissertation, in which she discusses the many resources from the Maya Mountains, a highland area within the lowlands, used by the lowland Maya in Belize. Graham reports the survey and excavation of sites, as well as detailed reports of the artifacts and other remains, making this book the standard reference for the archaeology of the region.

Graham, Elizabeth. 1997. "Metaphor and Metaphorism: Some Thoughts on Environmental Metahistory." In *Advances in Historical Ecology,* edited by William Balee, 119–137. New York: Columbia University Press.

> Graham discusses the impact of human agency on the ancient Maya landscape, suggesting that these "anthropogenic" forces were important in creating and modifying cultural events.

Graham, Elizabeth, Grant D. Jones, and Robert R. Kautz. 1985. "Archaeology and Ethnohistory on a Spanish Colonial Frontier: An Interim Report on the Macal-Tipu Project in Western Belize." In *The Lowland Maya Postclassic,* edited by Arlen F. Chase and Prudence M. Rice, 206–214. Austin: University of Texas Press.

> The church at Tipu was discovered and its exterior walls excavated during the 1981 field season by Kautz and Jones. Subsequently, Graham continued excavations at this Franciscan mission site.

Graham, Elizabeth, David M. Pendergast, and Grant D. Jones. 1989. "On the Fringes of Conquest: Maya-Spanish Contact in Colonial Belize." *Science* 246: 1254–1259.

> The authors provide a discussion of the archaeological and archival research on the Spanish missions established at Tipu in western Belize and Lamanai in northern Belize.

Graham, Ian. 1975. *Corpus of Maya Hieroglyphic Inscriptions,* vol. 2, part 1: *Naranjo.* Cambridge, MA: Peabody Museum of Archaeology and Ethnology, Harvard University.

> This first volume of drawings of hieroglyphic texts from the Maya area provides a valuable resource for study of Maya hieroglyphs.

Graham, Ian. 2002. *Alfred Maudslay and the Maya.* Norman: University of Oklahoma Press.

> This very readable book is the first detailed biography of one of the early Maya scholars and fieldworkers, written by epigrapher Ian Graham.

Graham, John. 1975. *The Hieroglyphic Inscriptions and Monumental Art of Altar de Sacrificios.* Papers of the Peabody Museum of Archaeology and Ethnology, vol. 64, no. 2. Cambridge, MA: Harvard University.

> Graham continued the careful documentation of inscriptions begun by Maler (1901, 1903, 1908a, 1908b, 1910, 1911) and Maudslay (1961). In 1968, Graham began this monumental project, the Corpus of Maya Hieroglyphic Inscriptions, to accurately

record all known hieroglyphs in codices, on pottery vessels, and at archaeological sites.

Grove, David. 1997. "Olmec Archaeology: A Half Century of Research and Its Accomplishments." *Journal of World Prehistory* 11: 51–101.

Having devoted much of his career to the Olmec at Chalcatzingo, Guerrero, Mexico, Grove provides an insider's overview of this important early Mesoamerican civilization.

Guderjan, Thomas H., and James F. Garber, eds. 1995. *Maya Maritime Trade, Settlement, and Populations on Ambergris Caye, Belize.* Lancaster, CA: Labyrinthos.

This book includes reports of excavations at San Juan, Ek Luum, and Chac Balam on northern Ambergris Cay, as well as reports by specialists on chert, obsidian, human bone, pottery, and other materials.

Guderjan, Thomas H., James F. Garber, and Hermann A. Smith. 1989. "Maritime Trade on Ambergris Cay, Belize." In *Coastal Maya Trade,* edited by Heather McKillop and Paul F. Healy, 123–133. Occasional Papers in Anthropology 8. Peterborough, Ontario: Trent University.

This paper reports preliminary research on northern Ambergris Cay, Belize.

Haggett, Peter. 1965. *Locational Analysis in Human Geography.* London: Edward Arnold.

A classic reference for geographers, archaeologists, and other researchers interested in the spatial distribution of settlements over the landscape. The book includes discussion of Central Place Theory and various models and methods in spatial analysis. The concepts have been incorporated into computer-based spatial analyses using geographic information systems.

Hall, Grant D., Stanley M. Tarka Jr., W. Jeffrey Hurst, David Stuart, and Richard E. W. Adams. 1990. "Cacao Residues in Ancient Maya Vessels from Rio Azul, Guatemala." *American Antiquity* 55 (1): 138–143.

This article discusses chemical analysis of residues that were identified as cacao, or chocolate—known from pictorial depictions on painted pots to have been an elite beverage of the ancient Maya.

Hamblin, Nancy. 1984. *Animal Use by the Cozumel Maya.* Tucson: University of Arizona Press.

Hamblin presents a detailed identification and analysis of maritime resources exploited by the Maya, indicating a focus on seafood.

Hammond, Norman. 1972. "Obsidian Trade Routes in the Mayan Area." *Science* 178: 1092–1093.

Hammond's widely cited model posits trade of El Chayal obsidian by overland routes and Ixtepeque along the coast during the Classic period. The model has sparked much debate and research.

Hammond, Norman. 1975. *Lubaantun: A Classic Maya Realm.* Peabody Museum of Archaeology and Ethnology Monograph, vol. 2. Cambridge, MA: Harvard University.

Hammond describes his excavations at the Late Classic city of Lubaantun in southern Belize as well as a survey in the coastal and inland surrounding region he calls the realm of Lubaantun. He includes important early unpublished reports and specialist reports in the monograph.

Hammond, Norman. 1982. *Ancient Maya Civilization.* New Brunswick: Rutgers University Press.

This book is an overview of Maya prehistory that provides important theoretical directions as well as the culture's history.

Hammond, Norman. 1983. "Lords of the Jungle: A Prosopography of Maya Archaeology." In *Civilization in the Ancient Americas,* edited by Richard M. Leventhal and Alan L. Kolata, 3–32. Albuquerque: University of New Mexico Press.

Historical background is provided here about the development of Maya archaeology. This is an article in a book honoring Gordon R. Willey, written by his former students and associates.

Hammond, Norman. 1991b. "Inside the Black Box: Defining Maya Polity." In *Classic Maya Political History,* edited by T. Patrick Culbert, 253–284. New York: Cambridge University Press.

In this writing, Hammond presents an overview of Maya politics.

Hammond, Norman, Arnold Aspinall, Stuart Feather, John Hazelden, Trevor Gazard, and Stuart Agrell. 1977. "Maya Jade: Source Location and Analysis." In *Exchange Systems in Prehistory,* edited by Timothy K. Earle and Jonathon E. Ericson, 35–67. New York: Academic Press.

Chemical analysis of jade and other greenstone artifacts from Maya sites shows more chemical variability than for obsidian, making assignment to a specific location impossible. However, the Motagua River drainage is investigated as the only known source of jade, serpentine, and other greenstones in Mesoamerica and the apparent source of Maya jade.

Hammond, Norman, Amanda Clark, M. Horton, M. Hodges, Logan McNatt, Laura Kosakowsky, and K. Anne Pyburn. 1985. "Excavation and Survey at Nohmul, Belize, 1983." *Journal of Field Archaeology* 12: 177–200.

Hammond's multiyear excavation and survey project at Nohmul in northern Belize investigated the city with two main plaza groups connected by a sacbe.

Hammond, Norman, Kate Pretty, and Frank P. Saul. 1975. "A Classic Maya Family Tomb." *World Archaeology* 7: 57–71.

Hammond discusses his excavations at Lubaantun, which revealed burials of multiple individuals.

Hammond, Norman, Gair Tourtellot, Sara Donaghey, and Amanda Clark. 1998. "No Slow Dusk: Maya Urban Development and Decline in La Milpa, Belize." *Antiquity* 72: 831–837.

Excavations at La Milpa directed by Hammond revealed a major city dated primarily to the Classic period.

Hammond, Norman, ed. 1991a. *Cuello.* New York: Cambridge University Press.

In this edited volume, Cuello's project director draws together reports by various specialists, as well as the reports of the excavations that define the earliest known

Maya occupation in the southern lowlands (the Swasey Phase), first defined at Cuello by Hammond.

Hansen, Richard D. 1984. "Excavation on Structure 34 and the Tigre Area, El Mirador, Peten, Guatemala: A New Look at the Preclassic Lowland Maya." Master's thesis, Department of Anthropology, Provo, UT: Brigham Young University.

El Mirador developed as a large urban city during the Late Preclassic and then diminished in importance before the rise of the Classic period civilization.

Hansen, Richard D. 1991. "The Maya Rediscovered: The Road to Nakbe." *Natural History* 91 (5): 8–14.

Hansen's excavations at Nakbe, Guatemala, revealed that the Middle Preclassic Maya had monumental architecture, showing complexity in the culture much earlier in time than previously believed.

Hanson, Craig A. 1995. "The Hispanic Horizon in Yucatan: A Model of Franciscan Missionization." *Ancient Mesoamerica* 6: 15–28.

Hanson provides an overview of the Franciscan mission program in the Yucatan, the increasing complexity of the churches with time, and an example of his excavation of the Ek Balam church, as well as comparative data of interest to missions elsewhere in the New World.

Harris, John F., and Stephen K. Stearns. 1997. *Understanding Maya Inscriptions,* 2d rev. ed. Philadelphia: University of Pennsylvania Museum of Archaeology and Anthropology.

A text and workbook to learn Maya hieroglyphs, counting, and the calendar, appropriate for both the beginner and the more advanced epigrapher.

Harrison, Peter D. 1978. "Bajos Revisited: Visual Evidence for One System of Agriculture." In *Pre-Hispanic Maya Agriculture,* edited by Peter D. Harrison and B. L. Turner II, 247–254. Albuquerque: University of New Mexico Press.

Harrison provides a description of his research on agricultural use of bajos in Quintana Roo, Mexico.

Harrison, Peter D. 1999. *The Lords of Tikal.* New York. Thames & Hudson.

A readable text on Tikal by one of the University of Pennsylvania project archaeologists, focusing on Harrison's dissertation fieldwork on the central acropolis at Tikal. Harrison draws on the tremendous Tikal data to provide a comprehensive account of the history of this major Maya city.

Harrison, Peter D., and B. L. Turner, eds. 1978. *Pre-Hispanic Maya Agriculture.* Albuquerque: University of New Mexico Press.

A variety of agricultural techniques used by the ancient Maya included raised or drained fields and terracing of hillslopes, which were more intensive uses of the land in contrast to the modern Maya's use of more extensive swidden farming, in which fields are rotated in use and fallow. The articles in this book by Maya archaeologists reporting on various field projects find that intensive agriculture produced more food, which is in line with the high population estimates for the Classic Maya.

Haviland, William A. 1965. "Prehistoric Settlement at Tikal, Guatemala." *Expedition* 7 (3): 14–23.

Ethnohistoric data from Cozumel Island indicating an average family size of 4.9 people are used to reconstruct population size based on low mounds representing family residences. Various population estimates for Tikal include those by Haviland 1972, Culbert and Rice 1990, and Harrison 1999, all of whom worked on the University of Pennsylvania Tikal project.

Haviland, William A. 1967. "Stature at Tikal, Guatemala: Implications for Ancient Maya Demography and Social Organization." *American Antiquity* 32: 117–125.

Measurements of skeletal remains from burials at Tikal indicate a diminution in stature at the end of the Classic period and further indicate that the elite were taller, and hence better fed, than the common folk. These ideas have found little support in a more recent, larger sample by Danforth (1999).

Haviland, William A. 1972. "Estimates of Maya Population: Comments on Thompson's Comments." *American Antiquity* 37: 261–262.

Based on excavations at Tikal (see Culbert and Rice 1990), Haviland is critical of Thompson's 1971a view that houses were abandoned after a family member died. Haviland instead suggests instead that they were periodically remodeled, extended, or otherwise renovated, including at the death of a family member, but not abandoned.

Healy, Paul F., and Jaime J. Awe. 2001. "Middle Preclassic Jade Spoon from Belize." *Mexicon* 23: 61–64.

A jade object in the shape of a spoon was reported from the site of Uxbenka in southern Belize. The object is attributed to trade from the Olmec, who traded jade objects throughout much of Mesoamerica, particularly during the time of the Olmec capital of La Venta, 800–400 B.C.

Healy, Paul F., Jaime J. Awe, and Hermann Helmuth. 1998. "An Ancient Maya Multiple Burial at Caledonia, Cayo District, Belize." *Journal of Field Archaeology* 25: 261–274.

The authors report an interment of multiple individuals, similar to those at several other Maya sites, notably Lubaantun and Caracol.

Healy, Paul F., John D. H. Lambert, J. T. Arnason, and Richard J. Hebda. 1983. "Caracol, Belize: Evidence of Ancient Maya Agricultural Terraces." *Journal of Field Archaeology* 10: 397–410.

The authors discuss their finding that excavations of terraced hillslopes in the Maya Mountains of western Belize date primarily to the Late Classic, when populations were increasing.

Healy, Paul F., Heather I. McKillop, and Bernetta Walsh. 1984. "Analysis of Obsidian from Moho Cay, Belize: New Evidence on Classic Maya Trade Routes." *Science* 225: 414–417.

This article presents a discussion about obsidian from Late Classic burials, middens, and other contexts at Moho Cay which was chemically sourced by the Lawrence Berkeley Lab. The dominance of El Chayal obsidian at this Caribbean site contrasts with the expectation of Hammond's (1972) model.

Hester, Thomas R., Harry B. Iceland, Dale B. Hudler, and Harry B. Shafer. 1996. "The Colha Preceramic Project: Preliminary Results from the 1993–1995 Field Seasons." *Mexicon* 18: 45–50.

Summary report of excavations at Colha that revealed Archaic period layers strati-graphically below the Middle Preclassic Maya ceramic-bearing deposits previously excavated at the site (see Shafer and Hester 1983). The Archaic layers included the temporally distinctive constricted unifaces, also found later elsewhere in northern Belize (see Pohl et al. 1996).

Hester, Thomas R., and Harry J. Shafer, eds. 1991. *Maya Stone Tools*. Monographs in World Archaeology No. 1. Madison, WI: Prehistory Press.

An important compendium of articles on stone tools from various Maya sites, this volume provides a good starting point for researchers.

Hill, Robert, and John Monaghen. 1978. *The Traditional Pottery of Guatemala*. Austin: University of Texas Press.

Text and extensive photographs of modern pottery making in villages in highland Guatemala provide valuable information for understanding ancient production.

Hixson, David. 2001. *Mesoamerican Photo Archives*. New Orleans: Department of Anthropology, Tulane University; http://www.mesoamerican-archives.com.

Digital photos of ancient Maya sites including Ek Balam, Bonampak, Calakmul, and Loltun Cave.

Hodell, David A., Jason H. Curtis, and Mark Brenner. 1995. "Possible Role of Climate in the Collapse of Classic Maya Civilization." *Nature* 375: 391–394.

Based on analysis of soil cores, the authors suggest that there was a significant drought at the end of the Classic period.

Houston, Stephen D. 1993. *Hieroglyphs and History at Dos Pilas: Dynastic Politics of the Classic Maya*. Austin: University of Texas Press.

In this revision of his Ph.D. dissertation, Houston documents the political history of Dos Pilas in the Petexbatun region, providing important epigraphic information.

Houston, Stephen D., and David Stuart. 1996. "Of Gods, Glyphs, and Kings. Divinity and Rulership among the Classic Maya." *Antiquity* 70: 289–310.

The authors find that Classic Maya kings and queens adopted names of gods, thereby claiming divine status.

Houston, Stephen, Oswaldo Chinchilla Mazariegos, and David Stuart, eds. 2001. *The Decipherment of Ancient Maya Writing*. Norman: University of Oklahoma Press.

Key published articles, unpublished manuscripts, and portions of books pertaining to decipherment of Maya hieroglyphs are drawn together, with important commentary by the editors. This book provides a nice complement to historical accounts of decipherment by Coe (1992) and Stuart (1992), as well as studies by Coe and Van Stone (2001) and Montgomery (2002a and 2002b) on reading the glyphs.

Hult, Weston and Thomas R. Hester. 1995. "The Lithics of Ambergris Caye." In *Maya Maritime Trade, Settlement, and Population on Ambergris Caye, Belize*, edited by Thomas H. Guderjan and James F. Garber, 139–161. Culver City, CA: Labyrinthos.

The authors present a discussion of chert stone tools from Colha that were traded offshore to sites on northern Ambergris Cay.

Iceland, Harry B. 1997. "The Preceramic Origins of the Maya: The Results of the Colha Preceramic Project in Northern Belize." Ph.D. dissertation, Department of Anthropology, Austin: University of Texas.

> Detailed report and analysis of excavations at Colha that revealed Archaic period layers stratigraphically below the Middle Preclassic Maya ceramic-bearing deposits previously excavated at the site (see Hester et al. 1996; Shafer and Hester 1983). The Archaic layers included the temporally distinctive constricted unifaces, also found elsewhere in northern Belize (see Kelly 1993; Pohl et al. 1996).

Inomata, Takeshi. 1997. "The Last Day of a Fortified Maya Center: Archaeological Investigations at Aguateca, Guatemala." *Ancient Mesoamerica* 8: 337–351.

> This is a graphic description with illustrations of the city sacked by unknown intruders in the Petexbatun, leaving the remains of the houses and other buildings in place for the archaeologists to interpret evidence of warfare, elite craft production, and other activities.

Inomata, Takeshi. 2001. "The Power and Ideology of Artistic Creation: Elite Craft Specialists in Classic Maya Society." *Current Anthropology* 42: 321–349.

> The article discusses the classic city of Aguateca, which was abandoned rapidly with the tools of artisans and scribes trades left on the floors of elite residences, providing important evidence for elite craft specialization.

Inomata, Takeshi, and Kazuo Aoyama. 1996. "Central-Place Analysis in the La Entrada Region, Honduras: Implications for Understanding the Classic Maya Political and Economic Systems." *Latin American Antiquity* 7: 291–312.

> Settlements were located in order to allow the major cities to extract tribute and labor tax from Maya in the smaller communities, following the administrative principle in Central Place Theory.

Inomata, Takeshi, and Stephen D. Houston, eds. 2001. *Royal Courts of the Ancient Maya.* 2 vols. Boulder, CO: Westview.

> Volume 1 includes general and theoretical articles about the people, buildings, and spaces of the most elite Maya—the royalty and their court attendants, artisans, and others—which has previously been overlooked as a focus within Maya studies. Volume 2 provides case studies.

Inomata, Takeshi, Daniela Triadan, Erick Ponciano, Estela Pinto, Richard E. Terry, and Markus Eberl. 2002. "Domestic and Political Lives of Classic Maya Elites: The Excavation of Rapidly Abandoned Structures at Aguateca, Guatemala." *Latin American Antiquity* 13: 305–330.

> This article provides a discussion of Aguateca. The city was attacked and the people fled, leaving their possessions in situ for archaeologists to find hundreds of years later, including evidence of elite craft specialization in elite households.

Jacobi, Keith. 2000. *Last Rites for the Tipu Maya: Genetic Structuring in a Colonial Cemetery.* Tuscaloosa: University of Alabama Press.

> Jacobi provides an important overview of the history and archaeology of this Franciscan mission site, as well as a study of the inherited dental traits of almost 600 Maya buried in and around the church. He finds no evidence of Spanish biological

impact, in contrast to the cultural changes found by Elizabeth Graham's archaeological work (Graham, Pendergast, and Jones 1989).

Jones, Grant D. 1989. *Maya Resistance to Spanish Rule: Time and History on a Colonial Frontier.* Albuquerque: University of New Mexico Press.

With reference mainly to the Yucatec Maya of northern Belize, Jones finds that the indigenous Maya encountered by the Spaniards, and subsequently by the British, resisted the intruders' efforts to settle and use the land. This finding contrasts with earlier views that the Maya simply fled the area when the Europeans arrived.

Jones, John. 1994. "Pollen Evidence for Early Settlement and Agriculture in Northern Belize." *Palynology* 18: 205–211.

The author relates that coring of Cobweb Swamp near Colha indicated that the swamp edge had been cleared by 2500 B.C. and that corn was being grown in the area.

Joyce, Rosemary A. 2000. *Gender and Power in Prehispanic Mesoamerica.* Austin: University of Texas Press.

Joyce's focus on gender among the ancient Maya (as well as other Mesoamerican cultures) draws attention to this overlooked area of research. She brings epigraphic, artifactual, and other evidence to bear on her studies of both elite and common people.

Justeson, John S. 1989. "The Ancient Maya Ethnoastronomy: An Overview of Hieroglyphic Sources." In *World Archaeoastronomy: Selected Papers from the Second Oxford International Conference on Archaeoastronomy,* edited by Anthony Aveni, 76–129. New York: Cambridge University Press.

This paper discusses calendars, which were in use by the Preclassic Maya by 100 B.C.

Justeson, John S., and Lyle Campbell, eds. 1984. *Phoneticism in Mayan Hieroglyphic Writing.* Institute for Mesoamerican Studies, Publication 9. Albany: State University of New York.

Historical linguists Justeson and Campbell find that Mayan was spoken by 2000 B.C. Various authors in this edited volume discuss advances in Mayan hieroglyphs, in part derived from the knowledge that the writing was based on phonetics (sounds) rather than picture writing.

Kaufman, Terrence. 1976. "Archaeological and Linguistic Correlations in Mayaland and Associated Areas of Mesoamerica." *World Archaeology* 8: 101–118.

Using glottochronology, Kaufman traces the divergences of various Mayan languages and provides a classification of Mayan languages.

Kelley, David H. 1976. *Deciphering the Maya Script.* Austin: University of Texas Press.

An important study of Maya hieroglyphs that supported Knorozov's phonetic basis for the glyphs.

Kelly, Thomas C. 1993. "Preceramic Projectile-Point Typology in Belize." *Ancient Mesoamerica* 4: 205–227.

Kelly provides a description with illustrations of Archaic stone tools, as well as the Paleoindian point found at Ladyville, all as part of the Colha regional survey. The study is the first systematic analysis of Archaic points in Belize and is a starting point for further research. Kelly examines Richard MacNeish's sites and artifacts and includes them in this study.

Kerr, Justin. 2003a. *Maya Vase Data Base: An Archive of Rollout Photographs Created by Justin Kerr.* http://www.famsi.org/research/kerr/.

Digital photos of more than 1,400 Maya vases in a searchable database, with accompanying text and articles about Maya vase painting and a listing of many Maya vase rollouts published in print form. The images can also be viewed at http://www.mayavase.com.

Kerr, Justin. 2003b. *The Grolier Codex.* http://www.mayavase.com/grol/grolier.html or http://www.famsi.org/mayawriting/codices/pdf/grolier_kerr.pdf.

Rollout images providing a 360° view of the entire exterior of a Maya vase in two-dimensional space are shown on these Internet sites. The same images accompany Coe's 1973 paper on the Grolier Codex.

Kerr, Justin, ed. 1989–1994. *The Maya Vase Book.* 4 vols. New York: Kerr.

These books are illustrated with Kerr's "rollout" photographs of Maya vases. See http://www.famsi.org for the color photos on the Internet.

Kidder, Alfred V., Jessie D. Jennings, and Edwin M. Shook. 1946. *Excavations at Kaminaljuyu, Guatemala.* Carnegie Institution of Washington Publication 561. Washington, DC: Carnegie Institution of Washington.

This report of major architectural excavations at the Maya highland city by Carnegie Institute of Washington archaeologists includes description of buildings, burials, and artifacts, remaining a significant reference for Maya archaeology.

Kluckhohn, Clyde. 1940. "The Conceptual Structure in Middle American Studies." In *The Maya and Their Neighbors,* edited by Clarence L. Hay, Ralph L. Linton, Samuel K. Lothrop, Harry L. Shapiro, and George C. Vaillant, 41–51. D. New York: Appleton-Century.

This scathing attack on the descriptive nature of Maya archaeology is often cited. However, it had little impact on the course of the Maya fieldwork of the Carnegie Institution of Washington archaeologists and others of the time, who established detailed architectural and ceramic data invaluable to future generations.

Knorozov, Yuri V. 1958. "The Problem of the Study of Maya Hieroglyphic Writing," translated by Sophie Coe. *American Antiquity* 23: 284–291.

This landmark study by a Russian epigrapher, who contended that Mayan hieroglyphs were phonetic rather than picture words, precipitated the exponential decipherment of the glyphs.

Kosakowsky, Laura J. 1987. *Preclassic Maya Pottery at Cuello, Belize.* Anthropological Papers of the University of Arizona 47. Tucson: University of Arizona Press.

This report on Cuello pottery, defining the earliest known Swasey Phase ceramics from Norman Hammond's (1991) project, is based on Kosakowsky's Ph.D. dissertation.

Kowaleski, Jeff. 2003. "Evidence for the Functions and Meanings of Some Northern Maya Palaces." In *Maya Palaces and Elite Residences,* edited by Jessica Joyce Christie, 204–252. Austin: University of Texas Press.

Examination of the layout and iconography of elite structures at Uxmal, Chichen Itza, Sayil, and other northern Maya lowland settlements indicates that some were council houses, called Popol Nas. Their common occurrence indicates a shift from the dynastic authority of the Classic kings and queens to a shared governance by Postclassic kings and other leaders within a community and its hinterland.

Kurjack, Edward B. 1974. *Prehistoric Lowland Maya Community and Social Organization: A Case Study at Dzibilchaltun, Yucatan, Mexico.* Middle American Research Institute Publication 38. New Orleans: Tulane University.

In this writing, Kurjack discusses the settlement research he carried out at this site.

Kurjack, Edward B. 2003. "Palace and Society in the Northern Maya Lowlands." In *Maya Palaces and Elite Residences,* edited by Jessica Joyce Christie, 274–290. Austin: University of Texas Press.

Kurjack finds that palaces were simply residences writ large for the elite, in contrast to the views of many other researchers who found multiple uses for palaces.

Kurjack, Edward B., and Silvia T. Garza 1981. "Pre-Columbian Community Form and Distribution in the Northern Maya Area." In *Lowland Maya Settlement Patterns,* edited by Wendy Ashmore, 287–309. Albuquerque: University of New Mexico Press.

The authors describe house types, residential property walls, and sacbes within communities in the northern Maya lowlands, as well as intersite sacbes, noting the integrative and controlling functioning of these roads.

Kutscher, Gerdt, ed. 1971. *Teobert Maler: Bauten der Maya.* Berlin.

This study, written in German, is an important biography of the early Maya explorer and archaeologist.

Lambert, John D. H., and Thor Arnason. 1978. "Distribution of Vegetation on Maya Ruins and Its Relationship to Ancient Land-Use at Lamanai, Belize." *Turrialba* 28 (1): 33–41.

In this article, the presence of ramón trees at Maya sites is found to be due to an ecological adaptation to the lime-rich soil of the limestone buildings and not to ancient dietary reliance on ramón nuts.

Lange, Frederick W. 1971. "Marine Resources: A Viable Subsistence Alternative for the Prehistoric Lowland Maya." *American Anthropologist* 73: 619–639.

Lange's idea of seafood being traded inland during the Late Classic population boom prompted other researchers to also investigate the Maya's production and trade of seafood.

Laporte, Juan Pedro, and Vilma Fialko. 1995. "Un Reencuentro Con Mundo Perdido, Tikal, Guatemala." *Ancient Mesoamerica* 6: 41–94.

Description of excavations in the Lost World Complex at Tikal by the Guatemalan government after the University of Pennsylvania project ended. These excavations resulted in the discovery of significant Early Classic construction, among other findings reported in the article.

LeCount, Lisa J. 1999. "Polychrome Pottery and Political Strategies in Late and Terminal Classic Lowland Maya Society." *Latin American Antiquity* 10: 239–258.

LeCount studied pottery as containers from various contexts at the Late Classic city of Xunantunich, Belize, providing important information on vessel use.

Leventhal, Richard M. 1990. "Southern Belize: An Ancient Maya Region." In *Vision and Revision in Maya Studies,* edited by Flora S. Clancey and Peter D. Harrison, 125–141. Albuquerque: University of New Mexico Press.

Based on his fieldwork in southern Belize, Leventhal describes the organization of inland Maya cities, including Nim li punit, Pusilha, and Uxbenka.

Lewenstein, Suzanne. 1987. "Mesoamerican Obsidian Blades: An Experimental Approach to Function." *Journal of Field Archaeology* 8: 175–188.

The edge wear on obsidian artifacts from Cerros was compared with edges of modern tools made from obsidian for the study and used in a variety of tasks, in order to reconstruct ancient tool use.

Lincoln, Charles. 1985. "The Chronology of Chichen Itza: A Review of the Literature." In *Late Lowland Maya Civilization,* edited by Jeremy A. Sabloff and E. Wyllys Andrews V, 141–196. Albuquerque: University of New Mexico Press.

Pottery from Lincoln's fieldwork at the site is used to evaluate existing chronologies.

Lounsbury, Floyd G. 1974. "The Inscription of the Sarcophagus Lid at Palenque." In *Primera Mesa Redonda de Palenque,* part 2, edited by Merle Greene Robertson, 5–19. Pebble Beach, CA: Robert Louis Stevenson School.

Lounsbury here identifies Chol as the language of Maya glyphs at Palenque.

Love, Bruce. 1994. *The Paris Codex: Handbook for a Priest.* Austin: University of Texas Press.

This is an annotated translation and discussion of the Paris Codex, one of the four surviving ancient Maya books.

Love, Bruce. 1995. "A Dresden Codex Mars Table?" *Latin American Antiquity* 6: 350–361.

Love discusses how Maya scribes used the Tzolkin calendar to record the movements of the sun, the moon, and Venus, and perhaps other planets and stars as well.

Lowe, John W. G. 1985. *The Dynamics of Apocalypse: A Systems Simulation of the Classic Maya Collapse.* Albuquerque: University of New Mexico Press.

Multiple factors are brought together in this analysis of the Classic Maya collapse.

Lund, Erin, and Heather McKillop. 2003. Maya Burials from Moho Cay, Belize. Paper presented at the Southern Anthropological Association meeting, Baton Rouge, LA, February.

This paper provides a description of skeletal remains from Late Classic burials at Moho Cay, a Classic trading port in the mouth of the Belize River. The findings indicate good skeletal and dental health, attributed to the availability of seafood.

Maler, Teobert. 1901a. *Researches in the Central Portion of the Usumatsintla Valley: Report of Explorations for the Museum 1898–1900.* Memoirs of the Peabody Museum of Archaeology and Ethnology, vol. 2, no. 1. Cambridge, MA: Harvard University.

Important documentation of glyphic records at sites, many now too eroded to see, was made by Teobert Maler (see also Maler 1903; Maler 1908a; Maler 1908b; Maler 1910; Maler 1911), who drew and photographed carved monuments at many lowland Maya sites.

Maler, Teobert. 1903. *Researches in the Central Portion of the Usumatsintla Valley: Report of Explorations for the Museum.* Memoirs of the Peabody Museum of Archaeology and Ethnology, vol. 2, no. 2. Cambridge, MA: Harvard University.

See comments under Maler 1901.

Maler, Teobert. 1908a. *Explorations of the Upper Usumatsintla and Adjacent Region: Altar de Sacrificios, Seibal, Itsimte-Sacluk, Cancuen.* Memoirs of the Peabody Museum of Archaeology and Ethnology, vol. 4, no. 1. Cambridge, MA: Harvard University.

Maler reports here on early fieldwork that he carried out at sites later studied by Willey and Demarest.

Maler, Teobert. 1908b. *Explorations in the Department of Peten, Guatemala, and Adjacent Regions: Topoxte, Yaxha, Benque Viejo, Naranjo.* Memoirs of the Peabody Museum of Archaeology and Ethnology, vol. 4, no. 2. Cambridge, MA: Harvard University.

See comments under Maler 1901

Maler, Teobert. 1910. *Explorations in the Department of Peten, Guatemala, and Adjacent Regions: Motul de San Jose, Peten-Itza.* Memoirs of the Peabody Museum of Archaeology and Ethnology, vol. 4, no. 3. Cambridge, MA: Harvard University.

See comments under Maler 1901.

Maler, Teobert. 1911. *Explorations in the Department of Peten, Guatemala: Tikal.* Memoirs of the Peabody Museum of Archaeology and Ethnology, vol. 5, no. 1. Cambridge, MA: Harvard University.

See comments under Maler 1901.

Mann, Tom. 2003. *The Paris Codex.* Evanston, IL: Northwestern University Library; http://digital.library.northwestern.edu/codex.

Reproduction of Willard's (1933) images of the Paris Codex, along with informative text. For digital images of the Paris Codex from the National Library of Paris copy, see Marhenke 2003.

Marcus, Joyce. 1976. *Emblem and State in the Classic Maya Lowlands.* Washington, DC: Dumbarton Oaks.

This is a report on emblem glyphs that identify the name of a Classic period city and are used to build a model of the political and economic landscape of the lowland Classic Maya.

Marcus, Joyce. 1993. "Ancient Maya Political Organization." In *Lowland Maya Archaeology in the Eighth Century A.D.,* edited by Jeremy A. Sabloff and John S. Henderson, 111–183. Washington, DC: Dumbarton Oaks Research Library and Collections.

A convincing argument is made here for centralized control of Late Maya society. By the Late Classic period there were regional political powers at Copan, Tikal, Calakmul, and Palenque. Marcus presents a dynamic model of political organization, including both centralized and less centralized political organization over time.

Marcus, Joyce. 1995. "Where is Lowland Maya Archaeology Headed?" *Journal of Archaeological Research* 3: 3–53.

This article is an important treatise on the status of Maya archaeology.

Marhenke, Randa. 2003. *The Ancient Maya Codices.* Foundation for the Advancement of

Mesoamerican Studies, Inc. (FAMSI). Available at http://www.famsi.org/mayawriting/codices/.

> Digital images of the four known ancient Maya codices are provided for downloading and viewing as pdf files. Marhenke also provides informative commentary on each of the codices. Förstemann's 1906 (originally from 1880) images are used for the Dresden Codex; Brasseur de Bourbourg's (1869–1870) and de Rosny's (1882) sections of the Madrid Codex are used for the images of the Madrid Codex. The originals in the National Library in Paris are used for the images in the Paris Codex; Justin Kerr's (2003b) images from Coe's (1973) publication are reproduced for the images of the Grolier Codex. For other digital images of the codices, see Mann (2003) for the Paris Codex, Burger (2001) for the Dresden Codex, Vail (2002) for the Madrid Codex, and Kerr (2003b) for the Grolier Codex.

Martin, Paul S. 1973. "The Discovery of America." *Science* 179: 969–974.

> An innovative and widely accepted model for the rapid peopling of the Americas in about 1,000 years from an initial arrival at 9500 B.C. from the Bering Strait land bridge. The model is based on high population increase of people who were the first to follow the large Pleistocene animals into the Americas at the end of the last ice age, about 9500 B.C.

Martin, Simon, and Nicholai Grube. 2000. *Chronicle of the Maya Kings and Queens: Deciphering the Dynasties of the Ancient Maya.* New York: Thames & Hudson.

> Martin and Grube describe the dynastic histories and the known rulers of eleven Classic Maya cities, namely Tikal, Dos Pilas, Naranjo, Caracol, Calakmul, Yaxchilan, Piedras Negras, Palenque, Tonina, Copan, and Quirigua.

Martinez Hernandez, Juan. 1926. *Cronicas Mayas: Cronica de Yaxkukul.* Tipografia Yucateca, Merida, Mexico.

> Martinez Hernandez modified Goodman's (1905) correlation of the Maya and Christian calendars, subsequently modified again by J. Eric S. Thompson (1927), the result of which is the most commonly accepted correlation, known as the Goodman-Martinez-Thompson (GMT) correlation.

Masson, Marilyn and David Freidel, eds. 2002. *Ancient Maya Political Economies.* New York: Altamira.

> This book includes a series of articles discussing the economy of the ancient Maya, concentrating on the aspects controlled by the urban elite—the *political economy.*

Matthews, Peter. 2003a. *John Montgomery's Dictionary of Maya Hieroglyphs.* http://www.famsi.org/mayawriting/dictionary/montgomery/index.html.

> A digital version of Montgomery (2002b), updated and expanded, including sounds by a native Maya speaker to accompany the glyphs, a dictionary searchable in Maya or English, and other text by Mathews and from Montgomery (2002b).

Matthews, Peter. 2003b. *The Linda Schele Drawings.* http://www.famsi.org/research/schele/bypmathews.htm.

> Digital drawings in a searchable database of monuments and other images made by this epigrapher and art historian.

Matthews, Peter, and Linda Schele. 1974. "Lords of Palenque: The Glyphic Evidence."

In *Primera Mesa Redonda de Palenque,* part 1, edited by Merle Greene Robertson, 63–75. Pebble Beach, CA: Robert Louis Stevenson School.

> The first Palenque round table meeting in 1973 resulted in the decipherment of the dynastic record of the site by Floyd Lounsbury, Peter Matthews, and Linda Schele.

Maudslay, Alfred. 1902. *Archaeology.* 5 vols. London: R. H. Porter and Dulau.

> The ability of scholars to study the ancient glyphs was dramatically enhanced with the publication of Alfred Maudslay's drawings and photographs of inscriptions, painstakingly recorded over the course of his travels over some thirteen years to Tikal, Copan, Palenque, Yaxchilan, Quirigua, Chichen Itza, and other ancient Maya ruins.

McAnany, Patricia A. 1989a. "Stone-Tool Production and Exchange in the Eastern Maya Lowlands: The Consumer Perspective from Pulltrouser Swamp." *American Antiquity* 54: 332–346.

> Based on her Ph.D. dissertation research, McAnany finds in this article that chert stone tools produced at Colha workshops were traded to Pulltrouser Swamp, as were locally produced stone tools.

McAnany, Patricia A. 1989b. "Economic Foundations of Prehistoric Maya Society: Paradigms and Concepts." In *Prehistoric Maya Economies of Belize,* edited by Patricia A. McAnany and Barry Isaac, 347–372. Research in Economic Anthropology, Supplement 4. Greenwich, CT: JAI Press.

> McAnany provides an important overview of the ancient Maya economy in this summary of an edited volume.

McAnany, Patricia. 1990. "Water Storage in the Puuc Region of the Northern Maya Lowlands: A Key to Population Estimates and Architectural Variability." In *Precolumbian Population History in the Maya Lowlands,* edited by T. Patrick Culbert and Don S. Rice, 263–284. Albuquerque: University of New Mexico Press.

> The distribution of chultuns used for water storage and structural remains is examined at Sayil in the Puuc region, where McAnany notes that there is no surface water and the ground water is too deep for wells. The Terminal Classic surge in settlement at Sayil is attributed to the collapse of the southern lowland civilization and a climatic shift to wetter conditions.

McAnany, Patricia A. 1995. *Living with the Ancestors.* Austin: University of Texas Press.

> Based on her research at Kaxob in northern Belize, McAnany presents comparative data and archaeological support for the importance of kinship among the Maya in burying deceased relatives under floors of houses.

McAnany, Patricia A., and Barry Isaac, eds. 1989. *Prehistoric Maya Economies of Belize.* Research in Economic Anthropology, Supplement 4. Greenwich, CT: JAI Press.

> This volume includes studies of the production and distribution of chert and obsidian tools and pottery vessels, as well as the exploitation of plant and animal foods by the ancient Maya. It is therefore an important resource on the ancient Maya economy.

McCulloh, James H. 1829. *Researches, Philosophical and Antiquarian, Concerning the Aboriginal History of America.* Baltimore: Fielding Lucas Jr.

> McCulloh recognized the link between the writing in the Dresden Codex and at Palenque as being the same language.

McKillop, Heather. 1980. "Moho Cay, Belize: Preliminary Investigations of Trade, Settlement, and Marine Resource Exploitation." Master's thesis, Department of Anthropology, Trent University, Peterborough; University Microfilms, Ann Arbor, MI.

> This is a discussion of excavations that were carried out at this island site, located at the mouth of the Belize River, before it was destroyed by commercial development in 1980. The site yielded evidence of trade of obsidian and chert, as well as hunting of manatee during the Late Classic period.

McKillop, Heather. 1984. "Prehistoric Maya Reliance on Marine Resources: Analysis of a Midden from Moho Cay, Belize." *Journal of Field Archaeology* 11: 25–35.

> A midden composed of quantities of manatee as well as shell, dating to the Late Classic, is discussed here.

McKillop, Heather. 1985. "Prehistoric Exploitation of the Manatee in the Maya and Circum-Caribbean Areas." *World Archaeology* 16: 337–353.

> Based on a midden with abundant manatee bones at Moho Cay, the author investigates the use of manatees elsewhere in the Maya area and historically and prehistorically in Central America and the Caribbean.

McKillop, Heather. 1987. "Wild Cane Cay: An Insular Classic Period to Postclassic Period Maya Trading Station." Unpublished Ph.D. dissertation, Department of Anthropology, University of California, Santa Barbara; University Microfilms, Ann Arbor.

> Based on excavations in midden deposits and complete surface collection of obsidian in 10-by-10-meter areas, McKillop presents a model of the island as a trading port. Obsidian is chemically sourced, quantified, and other measurements are taken.

McKillop, Heather. 1989. "Coastal Maya Trade: Obsidian Densities from Wild Cane Cay, Belize." In *Prehistoric Maya Economies of Belize,* edited by Patricia McAnany and Barry Isaac, 17–56. Research in Economic Anthropology, Supplement 4. Greenwich, CT: JAI Press.

> McKillop points out here that the density of obsidian on the ground surface and from excavations supports the interpretation of Wild Cane Cay as a coastal trading port. The shortage of blades in relation to cores indicates that blades were produced at this location for distribution in the surrounding region.

McKillop, Heather. 1994. "Ancient Maya Tree Cropping: A Viable Subsistence Adaptation for the Island Maya." *Ancient Mesoamerica* 5: 129–140.

> This article outlines how the Classic and Postclassic Maya on Wild Cane Cay, Belize, focused on a variety of trees for their plant foods, including three species of native palms and other fruit trees, instead of the vegetables of the mainland Maya. Corn was recovered from this site as well.

McKillop, Heather. 1995a. "Underwater Archaeology, Salt Production, and Coastal Maya Trade at Stingray Lagoon, Belize." *Latin American Antiquity* 6: 214–228.

> This article discusses Stingray Lagoon, which was a Late Classic salt workshop located in Punta Ycacos Lagoon on the southern coast of Belize. Salt was made there by boiling brine in pots over fires; it was a nondomestic setting away from any settlements or control of elite urban Maya. The site is now submerged from sea level rise.

McKillop, Heather. 1995b. "The Role of Northern Ambergris Caye in Maya Obsidian

Trade: Evidence from Visual Sourcing and Blade Technology." In *Maya Maritime Trade, Settlement, and Populations on Ambergris Caye, Belize,* edited by Thomas H. Guderjan and James F. Garber, 163–174. Lancaster, CA: Maya Research Program and Labyrinthos.

McKillop uses visual identification to source obsidian in a blind test, which shows a high degree of accuracy. She also uses technological characteristics of blade production to help assign ages, such as the more common use of grinding core platforms and lack of core overhang removal in the Postclassic and compared to the Classic period.

McKillop, Heather. 1995c. "The 1994 Field Season in South-Coastal Belize." *LSU Maya Archaeology News* 1, Department of Geography and Anthropology, Louisiana State University, Baton Rouge. http://www.ga.lsu.edu/ArchaeologyNews95.htm.

Excavations at Frenchman's Cay, David Westby, Orlando's Jewfish, and Arvin's Landing, as well as a survey in the Port Honduras coastal area of southern Belize, are discussed.

McKillop, Heather. 1996a. "Prehistoric Maya Use of Native Palms." In *The Managed Mosaic: Ancient Maya Agriculture and Resource Use,* edited by Scott L. Fedick, 278–294. Salt Lake City: University of Utah Press.

This is a discussion of cohune, coyol, and poknoboy palms, which were used by the Late Classic Maya at Wild Cane Cay, Frenchman's Cay, Pelican Cay, and Tiger Mound in the Port Honduras of southern Belize. With the arrival of Europeans, the native palm fruits were replaced by more productive coconuts in popular use among the newcomers.

McKillop, Heather. 1996b. "Ancient Maya Trading Ports and the Integration of Long-Distance and Regional Economies: Wild Cane Cay in South-Coastal Belize." *Ancient Mesoamerica* 7: 49–62.

This article describes the Classic to Postclassic trading port on Wild Cane Cay as well as its role in the Port Honduras coastal region.

McKillop, Heather. 1997. "Excavations in Coral Architecture at Frenchman's Cay, 1997." *LSU Maya Archaeology News* 2. Baton Rouge: Department of Geography and Anthropology, Louisiana State University. http://www.ga.lsu.edu/ArchaeologyNews97.htm.

Summary of excavations in three mounds that contained coral rock foundations for structures, as well as a limestone façade around one mound, named Great White Lucine.

McKillop, Heather. 1998. *Archaeological Survey of Wild Cane Caye, Port Honduras, Toledo, Belize: Archaeological Impact Assessment.* Report on file, Institutue of Archaeology, National Institutue of Culture and History, Belmopan, Belize, Central America.

The Belize government requested this archaeological impact assessment of Wild Cane Cay, and this represents perhaps the first such study in Belize.

McKillop, Heather. 2002a. *Salt: White Gold of the Ancient Maya.* Gainesville: University Press of Florida.

The monograph includes reporting of the discovery and excavations of four salt workshops in Punta Ycacos Lagoon, with the type-variety analysis of pottery as well as tests of standardization suggesting mass-production. Evidence of sea level rise is gathered from sites in the coastal region, including three of the salt works that were submerged by rising seas.

McKillop, Heather. 2002b. "Central America." *Encyclopedia of Historical Archaeology,* edited by Charles Orser, 355–358. London: Routledge.

> A summary is provided here of archaeological research on contact, colonial, and later archaeological work, including discussion of work by archaeologists at Tipu, Lamanai, and other Maya sites.

McKillop, Heather. 2003. "Catastrophic and Other Environmental Factors in the Classic Maya Collapse." Paper presented at the annual meeting of the American Association of Geographers, New Orleans, March.

> Based on the different responses to rising sea level at Late Classic Maya communities in southern Belize, McKillop suggests that researchers should not expect to see evidence of a uniform collapse of Late Classic lowland Maya society if there was a major climatic change, such as a drought.

McKillop, Heather. 2004. "The Ancient Maya Trading Port on Moho Cay." In *The Ancient Maya of the Belize Valley: Half a Century of Archaeological Research,* edited by James F. Garber, 257–272. Gainesville: University Press of Florida.

> The author reports her excavations on the island, including the many burials, and ties the island into the upper Belize Valley sites by trade. Situated at the mouth of the Belize River, the Moho Cay Maya traded coastal resources as well as obsidian and other items from along the coast.

McKillop, Heather. 2005. *In Search of Maya Sea Traders.* College Station: University of Texas Press. In press.

> This book includes descriptions of the excavations and finds from Wild Cane Cay, Frenchman's Cay, and other sites in the Port Honduras coastal region of southern Belize, set within a narrative style.

McKillop, Heather, and Paul F. Healy, eds. 1989. *Coastal Maya Trade.* Occasional Papers in Anthropology 8. Peterborough, Ontario: Trent University.

> This book includes reports by most of the researchers carrying out fieldwork along the Caribbean coast of the Maya area, including Matthew Boxt at Sarteneja, Thomas Guderjan, Herman Smith, and James Garber on Ambergris Cay; Elizabeth Graham at Marco Gonzalez on Ambergris Cay; Diane and Arlen Chase at Santa Rita; J. Jefferson MacKinnon at Placencia; and the editors' own coastal research.

McKillop, Heather, and L. J. Jackson. 1988. "Ancient Maya Obsidian Sources and Trade Routes." In *Obsidian Dates IV,* edited by Clement Meighan and Janet Scalise, 130–141. Los Angeles: Institute of Archaeology, University of California.

> Changing patterns of obsidian source use for lowland Maya sites are indicated from published reports of chemical sourcing. However, sites with samples of less than ten items per time period show less diversity of sources and tend to emphasize the dominant source, compared to samples of greater than ten items.

McKillop, Heather, L. J. Jackson, Helen Michel, Fred Stross, and Frank Asaro. 1988. "Chemical Sources Analysis of Maya Obsidian Artifacts: New Perspectives from Wild Cane Cay, Belize." In *Archaeometry 88,* edited by R. M. Farqhuar, R. G. V. Hancock, and Larry A. Pavlish, 239–244. Toronto: Department of Physics, University of Toronto.

> This original report of chemical analysis by XRF (nondestructive X-ray florescence)

and NAA (neutron activation analysis) of obsidian from Classic and Postclassic excavations yielded obsidian from six known sources and one unknown source, Source Z.

McKillop, Heather, Aline Magnoni, Rachel Watson, Shannon Ascher, Bryan Tucker, and Terance Winemiller. 2004. "The Coral Foundations of Coastal Maya Architecture." In *Archaeological Investigations in the Eastern Maya Lowlands: Papers of the 2003 Belize Archaeology Symposium,* edited by Jaime Awe, John Morris, and Sherilyne Jones, 347–358. Research Reports in Belizean Archaeology, vol. 1. Institute of Archaeology, National Institute of Culture and History, Belmopan, Belize.

This paper discusses excavations of stone foundations on Frenchman's Cay dated to the Late Classic, which were platforms for perishable structures of pole and thatch that were periodically renovated. The architectural style, along with the practice of burying the deceased in structures, follows the tradition at mainland Maya sites, but the use of coral as a building material differs.

McKillop, Heather, and Erika Roberts. 2003. *Nineteenth-Century Settlement of the Port Honduras Coast, Southern Belize.* Unpublished manuscript.

This paper summarizes historic ceramics from Wild Cane Cay, Muschamp Creek, and Pineapple Grove sites in the Port Honduras and relates them to documentary evidence of historic non-Maya settlement.

McKillop, Heather, and Terance Winemiller. 2004. "Ancient Maya Environment, Settlement, and Diet: Quantitative and GIS Analysis of Shell from Frenchman's Cay." In *Maya Zooarchaeology,* edited by Kitty Emery, 57–80. Los Angeles: Costen Institute of Archaeology, University of California.

Shells recovered from transect excavations at Frenchman's Cay are identified, quantified, and displayed for this paper, using the geographic information system software Intergraph MGE.

McKillop, Heather, Terance Winemiller, and Farrell Jones. 2000. *A GIS Analysis of Obsidian from the Surface at Wild Cane Cay.* Paper presented at the annual meeting of the Society for American Archaeology, Philadelphia, March.

This paper discusses obsidian that was collected in 10-by-10-meter grids and analyzed using Intergraph Geomedia GIS, a geographic information system software allowing the display of information from a database on a computerized map to search for information about the Maya's production and distribution of obsidian.

McNelly, Nancy. 1997. *Rabbit in the Moon.* Boston: School of Medicine, Boston University. http://www.halfmoon.org.

Photos of Maya sites including Bonampak and Uxmal, as well as other useful information on the ancient Maya, including the calendar, hieroglyphs, and virtual buildings.

Meggers, Betty. 1954. "Environmental Limitation on the Development of Culture." *American Anthropologist* 56: 801–824.

An environmental determinist view of culture is presented here in which the limits of ancient Maya culture were predetermined by the tropical rainforest setting. This outlook is gaining popularity with models of Maya drought suggested by Gill 2000 and others.

Merwin, Raymond E., and George C. Vaillant. 1932. *The Ruins of Holmul, Guatemala.* Memoirs of the Peabody Museum of Archaeology and Ethnology, vol. 3, no. 2. Cambridge, MA: Harvard University.

The first stratigraphic ceramic sequence developed in the Maya area, the Uaxactun ceramic sequence, became the standard used by Maya archaeologists because it was available to researchers before its 1955 publication by R. E. Smith. The Holmul ceramics discussed here established a distinctive group of pottery known as the Protoclassic, still enigmatic in the twenty-first century.

Mesdia, Sharon. 2003. *The Tikal Digital Access Project.* http://www.museum.upenn.edu/tdap/.

An ambitious and ongoing digital project of the University of Pennsylvania Museum to make records from the University of Pennsylvania Tikal project available, including primary documents such as field notes; other documents such as theses, dissertations, and other publications; as well as images from slides, photos, and film. For part of the digital project data, see also http://www.famsi.org/research/tikal/index.html for a searchable online database of photos from the Tikal project.

Miksicek, Charles H. 1991. "The Ecology and Economy of Cuello." In *Cuello: An Early Maya Community in Belize,* edited by Norman Hammond, 70–97. New York: Cambridge University Press.

Miksicek describes the plant food and other botanical remains recovered from Cuello.

Milbrath, Susan. 1999. *Star Gods of the Maya: Astronomy in Art, Folklore, and Calendars.* Austin: University of Texas Press.

This book presents an overview of modern and ancient Maya astronomy, links ancient astronomical images and calendar cycles to show how the seasonal round is represented in art, explores the astronomical characteristics of ancient Maya gods and the astronomical regalia of Maya royalty, and provides a detailed appendix of Classic Maya dates associated with astronomical events.

Miller, Mary. 1986. *The Murals of Bonampak.* Princeton, NJ: Princeton University Press.

This monograph illustrates and describes the Late Classic painted murals on the walls and ceilings of rooms at Bonampak, showing scenes of Maya royalty engaged in a variety of activities. Interpretation of the murals' significance are also offered.

Miller, Mary. 1999. *Maya Art and Architecture.* New York: Thames & Hudson.

Art historian Mary Miller provides a detailed overview here of the artistic traditions of the ancient Maya on buildings, painted pots, murals, sculpture, wood, stelae, and other media. The book is well illustrated.

Miller, Mary. 2001. "The Maya Ballgame: Rebirth in the Court of Life and Death." In *The Sport of Life and Death: The Mesoamerican Ballgame,* edited by E. Michael Whittington, 78–87. New York: Thames & Hudson.

Miller discusses the artistic renditions associated with the ball game, including ball court markers and their ritual significance among the Classic Maya, as well as the linkages between warfare and the ball game.

Miller, Mary, and Karl Taube. 1993. *The Gods and Symbols of Ancient Mexico and the Maya.* New York: Thames & Hudson.

The authors discuss ancient Maya gods from the *Popol Vuh* and their depictions on pottery vessels, stone carvings, and other media.

Mitchell-Hedges, Frederick. 1931. *Land of Wonder and Fear.* New York: Century Co.

This book is mainly a travelogue account of Mitchell-Hedges's traveling adventures in Belize and elsewhere in the Caribbean, but the account also includes rare notes about his archaeological work in Wild Cane Cay.

Mitchum, Beverly A. 1991. "Lithic Artifacts from Cerros, Belize: Production, Consumption, and Trade." In *Maya Stone Tools: Selected Papers from the Second Maya Lithic Conference,* edited by Thomas R. Hester and Harry J. Shafer, 45–54. Madison, WI: Prehistory Press.

Based on her Ph.D. research, Mitchum studies stone tools in this writing, including chert traded from Colha.

Mock, Shirley Boteler, ed. 1998. *The Sowing and the Dawning: Termination, Dedication, and Transformation in the Archaeological and Ethnographic Record of Mesoamerica.* Albuquerque: University of New Mexico Press.

Articles by archaeologists and ethnographers describe the ritual cycles of death and rebirth associated with offerings placed during building construction and abandonment.

Moholy-Nagy, Hattula. 1990. "The Misidentification of Mesoamerican Lithic Workshops." *Latin American Antiquity* 1: 268–279.

This paper contends that instead of identifying workshops on the basis of abundance of finished stone tools, archaeologists should look for evidence of microdebitage (microscopic flakes that wouldn't have been cleaned in a workshop) embedded in floors. Finished goods would have been distributed elsewhere, the author maintains.

Moholy-Nagy, Hattula. 1997. "Middens, Construction Fill, and Offerings: Evidence for the Organization of Classic Period Craft Production at Tikal, Guatemala." *Journal of Field Archaeology* 24: 293–313.

In this article, Moholy-Nagy is critical of definitions of workshops, many of which were actually trash dumps. The work areas, she contends, were kept clean.

Moholy-Nagy, Hattula. 1999. "Mexican Obsidian at Tikal, Guatemala." *Latin American Antiquity* 10: 300–313.

Here, Moholy-Nagy reports on the green and gray obsidian from the University of Pennsylvania Tikal project and notes that chemical analysis of source locations is critical to estimating the source of gray obsidian from central Mexico.

Moholy-Nagy, Hattula, Frank Asaro, and Fred H. Stross. 1984. "Tikal Obsidian: Sources and Typology." *American Antiquity* 49: 104–117.

This is one of several studies of chemical identification of Tikal obsidian.

Moholy-Nagy, Hattula, and John M. Ladd. 1992. "Objects of Stone, Shell, and Bone." In *Artifacts from the Cenote of Sacrifice, Chichen Itza, Yucatan,* edited by Clemency C. Coggins, 99–152. Memoirs of the Peabody Museum of Archaeology and Ethnology, vol. 10, no. 3. Cambridge, MA: Harvard University.

The authors describe and illustrate artifacts dredged in the early twentieth century by Edward Thompson (Willard 1926) from the cenote.

Moholy-Nagy, Hattula, and Fred Nelson. 1990. "New Data on Sources of Obsidian Artifacts from Tikal, Guatemala." *Ancient Mesoamerica* 1: 71–80.

The authors compared visual and chemical sourcing of eighty-five obsidian items from Tikal and found the visual technique unreliable.

Montgomery, John. 2002a. *How to Read Maya Hieroglyphs.* New York: Hippocrene.

A basic introductory text for beginners, which explains the Maya calendar, counting, and hieroglyphic writing.

Montgomery, John. 2002b. *Dictionary of Maya Hieroglyphs.* New York: Hippocrene.

A companion volume to Montgomery 2002a, this dictionary includes some 1,100 Mayan glyphs, with discussion. The dictionary, with sounds and additional text added, is also available in a digital version (Matthews 2003a).

Morley, Sylvanus G. 1920. *The Inscriptions of Copan.* Carnegie Institution of Washington Publication 219. Washington, DC: Carnegie Institution of Washington.

Morley traveled and recorded monuments in the Maya area, producing detailed reports, including this early record of monuments at Copan.

Morley, Sylvanus G. 1937–1938. *The Inscriptions of the Peten.* 5 vols. Carnegie Institution of Washington Publication 437. Washington, DC: Carnegie Institution of Washington.

These volumes are valuable records of stelae in the Peten.

Morley, Sylvanus G. 1946. *The Ancient Maya.* Palo Alto, CA: Stanford University Press.

Although not the first general text on the ancient Maya, Morley's book was widely utilized and continues to be revised, with a more recent edition by Robert Sharer (1994). Historically, the book remains a valuable source of views on ancient Maya settlement, demography, religion, and hieroglyphs of the mid-twentieth century.

Neff, Hector. 1989. "The Effect of Interregional Distribution on Plumbate Pottery Production." In *Ancient Trade and Tribute: Economics of the Soconusco Region of Mesoamerica,* edited by Barbara Voorhies, 249–267. Salt Lake City: University of Utah Press.

Neff describes three kinds of Plumbate pottery, including Guayabal and San Juan, which are early and of limited distribution, and Tohil Plumbate, which was widely traded throughout Mesoamerica in the Early Postclassic. Tohil included new shapes and decorations for an export market.

Neivens, Mary, and David Libbey. 1976. "An Obsidian Workshop at El Pozito, Northern Belize." In *Maya Lithic Studies: Papers from the 1976 Belize Field Symposium,* edited by Thomas R. Hester and Norman Hammond, 137–149. Special Report No. 4. San Antonio: Center for Archaeological Research, University of Texas.

This report remains perhaps the only description of the important Maya site excavated by Mary Neivens.

Nelson, Fred W. 1985. "Summary of the Results of Analysis of Obsidian Artifacts from the Maya Lowlands." *Scanning Electron Microscopy* 2: 631–649.

Nelson summarizes the results of his and other obsidian source data to present a model of obsidian source use over time, from San Martin in the Preclassic, to El Chayal in the Classic, to Ixtepeque in the Postclassic, with some important variations.

Olsen, Stanley J. 1982. *An Osteology of Some Maya Mammals.* Papers of the Peabody Museum of Archaeology and Ethnology, vol. 73. Cambridge, MA: Harvard University.

These line drawings and descriptions of bones of mammals available in the Maya area provide a good starting point for identification of ancient bones at Maya sites.

Palka, Joel W. 1997. "Reconstructing Classic Maya Socioeconomic Differentiation at the Collapse of Dos Pilas, Peten, Guatemala." *Ancient Mesoamerica* 8: 293–306.

This is a description of the author's research in the Petexbatun.

Pendergast, David M. 1969. *The Prehistory of Actun Balam, British Honduras.* Occasional Paper 16, Art and Archaeology. Toronto: Royal Ontario Museum.

Describes excavations and recovered artifacts from the cave (meaning "cave of the jaguar or priest"), south of Caracol in the Maya Mountains of Belize. Late and Terminal Classic pottery vessels include some with stamped decoration and a polychrome vase showing Maya hunting a deer.

Pendergast, David M. 1970. *A. H. Anderson's Excavations at Rio Frio Cave E, British Honduras (Belize).* Occasional Paper 20, Art and Archaeology. Toronto: Royal Ontario Museum.

Describes A. H. Anderson's 1959 work in the cave, located in the Maya Mountains of western Belize, and Pendergast's study of the pottery. Recovered material included Late Classic polychrome pots, water jars, and stalagmites probably used in ritual.

Pendergast, David M. 1971. *Excavations at Eduardo Quiroz Cave, British Honduras (Belize).* Occasional Paper 21, Art and Archaeology. Toronto: Royal Ontario Museum.

Pendergast reports on his first cave excavation in Belize in 1963 near Caracol. The cave consists of several chambers, with burials, caches (offerings), and lots of pottery, with more than 90 percent of the vessels consisting of water jars, some with stamped decoration typical of the Late Classic in southern Belize (Hammond 1975; McKillop 2002a) and the Pasion area of Guatemala (Adams 1971).

Pendergast, David M. 1974. *Excavations at Actun Polbilche, Belize.* Archaeology Monograph 1. Toronto: Royal Ontario Museum.

A report on his 1971 work at the cave of the wood, located on the south side of the Sibun River. A wooden spear made from sapodilla wood and a wooden box with a fitted lid were recovered, along with many potsherds from water jars.

Pendergast, David M. 1979. *Excavations at Altun Ha,* vol. 1. Toronto: Royal Ontario Museum.

In one of three volumes describing the excavations between 1964 and 1970 at this northern Belize site, Pendergast provides detailed descriptions and illustrations of the artifacts in their context of the excavation descriptions and maps, making this a monograph that can be used for primary research by others. Volume 1 includes Plaza A.

Pendergast, David M. 1981. "Lamanai, Belize: Summary of Excavation Results 1974–1980." *Journal of Field Archaeology* 8: 29–53.

With no monograph on the extensive fieldwork at Lamanai, this article provides a useful description of the excavations, structures, and artifacts. The site was occupied from the Middle Preclassic through colonial and historic times, which is rare among Maya sites.

Pendergast, David M. 1982a. "Ancient Maya Mercury." *Science* 217: 533–535.

This article describes the only incidence of mercury recovered from a Maya site. The mineral was under a ball court marker.

Pendergast, David M. 1982b. *Excavations at Altun Ha,* vol. 2. Toronto: Royal Ontario Museum.

The buildings and artifacts from Pendergast's excavations in Plaza B are described, including Temple B4, which has the tomb with the 4.4 kg carved jade head.

Pendergast, David M. 1985. "Stability through Change: Lamanai, Belize, from the Ninth to the Seventeenth Century." In *Late Lowland Maya Civilization,* edited by Jeremy Sabloff and E. Wyllys Andrews V, 223–249. Albuquerque: University of New Mexico Press.

Pendergast discusses the Postclassic, colonial, and historic occupation at Lamanai. The site was not abandoned at the end of the Classic period, unlike many other cities in the southern lowlands.

Pendergast, David M., and Elizabeth Graham. 1998. *What Do We Know about Lamanai?* http://www.rom.on.ca/digs/belize/what-we-know.html.

A cultural historical overview of the research at Lamanai, with photos and descriptions of the architecture and artifacts recovered from the site from the Preclassic through historic times, that augments Pendergast's (1981) overview on the site.

Pohl, Mary D., ed. 1990. *Ancient Maya Wetland Agriculture: Excavations on Albion Island, Northern Belize.* Boulder, CO: Westview.

Pohl draws together all the work by Dennis Puleston and Alfred Siemens on the archaeological work on Albion Island, providing artifactual, botanical, and other evidence of raised-field agriculture by the Preclassic Maya in northern Belize.

Pohl, Mary D., Kevin O. Pope, John G. Jones, John S. Jacob, Dolores R. Piperno, Susan D. deFrance, David L. Lentz, John A. Gifford, Marie E. Danforth, and J. Kathryn Josserand. 1996. "Early Agriculture in the Maya Lowlands." *Latin American Antiquity* 7: 355–372.

The authors present archaeological, palynological, and other evidence indicating that corn was introduced to northern Belize by 3400 B.C., that fields were being drained with ditches by 1000 B.C. due to rising sea levels, and that by the Classic period the wetland fields were flooded and mostly abandoned.

Pollock, Harry E. D., Ralph L. Roys, Tatiana Proskouriakoff, and A. Ledyard Smith. 1962. *Mayapan, Yucatan, Mexico.* Carnegie Institution of Washington Publication 619. Washington, DC: Carnegie Institution of Washington.

This study is a report of mapping and excavations in the monumental architecture at a Late Postclassic city in the northern Maya lowlands, undertaken by Carnegie Institution of Washington archaeologists. The study remains a standard reference.

Powis, Terry G., Fred Valdez Jr., Thomas R. Hester, W. Jeffrey Hurst, and Stanley M. Tarka Jr. 2002. "Spouted Vessels and Cacao Use among the Preclassic Maya." *Latin American Antiquity* 13 (1): 85–106.

This analysis of residue from inside these vessels indicates that they contained chocolate.

Proskouriakoff, Tatiana. 1960. "Historical Implications of a Pattern of Dates at Piedras Negras, Guatemala." *American Antiquity* 25: 454–475.

Based on study of monuments from the site of Piedras Negras, Proskouriakoff recognized that the stelae at Classic Maya sites recorded historical information about Maya kings, along with dates for birth, marriage, accession to the throne, and other important events. With this important article, Maya archaeologists accepted that the Classic Maya stelae recorded historical information.

Proskouriakoff, Tatiana. 1963. *An Album of Maya Architecture.* Norman: University of Oklahoma Press.

Proskouriakoff provides pencil sketch reconstructions of Maya buildings from a variety of sites.

Puleston, Dennis. 1982. "The Role of Ramón in Maya Subsistence." In *Maya Subsistence,* edited by Kent V. Flannery, 353–366. New York: Academic Press.

Puleston points out here that the high population of Tikal during the Classic period was supported by ramón nuts, from trees that Puleston has observed to be abundant and to be prolific in their supply of nuts.

Puleston, Dennis. 1983. *The Settlement Survey of Tikal.* Tikal Report No. 13, University Museum Publications. Philadelphia: University of Pennsylvania.

In his transect survey beyond the central area of Tikal, Puleston made population estimates based on 6.07 people per household from census data in the Yucatan and 10 people per household where there was more than one nuclear family. Tikal population estimates are provided by Culbert and Rice 1990 and Harrison 1999.

Pyburn, K. Anne. 1990. "Settlement Patterns at Nohmul: Preliminary Results of Four Excavation Seasons." In *Precolumbian Population History in the Maya Lowlands,* edited by T. Patrick Culbert and Don S. Rice, 183–197. Albuquerque: University of New Mexico Press.

Among other findings, Pyburn notes that the lack of mounded remains of some houses underrepresents population estimates. She used posthole testing to discover these remains.

Randall, John E. 1983. *Caribbean Reef Fishes.* Neptune City, NJ: T. F. H.

This reference identification book has informative text and color photos of fish.

Rathje, Williams L. 1971. "The Origin and Development of Lowland Classic Maya Civilization." *American Antiquity* 36: 275–285.

Rathje's model of resource deficiency leading to complex organization in order to import basic daily resources of salt, basalt, and obsidian has prompted much research on Maya trade and social complexity.

Redfield, Robert and Alfonso Villa Rojas. 1962. *Chan Kom: A Maya Village.* Chicago: University of Chicago Press.

A classic ethnography of a modern Maya village in the Yucatan first published in 1934, this study remains an important reference and analogy for interpreting ancient Maya culture.

Reents-Budet, Dorie. 1994. *Painting the Maya Universe.* Durham, NC: Duke University Press.

In this richly illustrated book produced to accompany an art exhibit, Reents-Budet discusses the meaning of the iconography on Classic Maya painted pottery vessels, many from unknown source locations. She makes a convincing argument that they enhance our knowledge of the ancient Maya with information not available elsewhere.

Reents-Budet, Dorie. 2001. "Classic Maya Concepts of the Royal Court: An Analysis of Renderings on Pictorial Ceramics." In *Royal Courts of the Ancient Maya,* vol. 1, edited by Takeshi Inomata and Stephen Houston, 195–233. Boulder, CO: Westview.

Shows images of royal court life on painted vessels, including views of the steps of palaces, the interiors of palace rooms, and curtains and doorway fixtures, which inform on many of the perishable aspects of ancient Maya stone buildings at Classic cities (see Harrison 1999). Justin Kerr's (2003a) rollouts of Late Classic vases provide images of the entire exterior surfaces of the vessels.

Reina, Ruben E., and Robert M. Hill III. 1978. *The Traditional Pottery of Guatemala.* Austin: University of Texas Press.

This is a classic study of modern potters from the highlands of Guatemala.

Reina, Ruben E., and John Monaghen. 1981. "The Ways of the Maya: Salt Production in Sacapulas, Guatemala." *Expedition* 23: 13–33.

This article discusses salt, which was produced by boiling brine in pots over fires in this modern community, located near natural salt springs.

Rice, Don S., and T. Patrick Culbert. 1990. "Historical Contexts for Population Reconstruction in the Maya Lowlands." In *Precolumbian Population History in the Maya Lowlands,* edited by T. Patrick Culbert and Don S. Rice, 1–36. Albuquerque: University of New Mexico Press.

The authors provide a detailed summation of demography in the Maya area.

Rice, Don S., and Prudence M. Rice. 1990. "Population Size and Population Change in the Central Peten Lakes Region, Guatemala." In *Precolumbian Population History in the Maya Lowlands,* edited by T. Patrick Culbert and Don S. Rice, 123–148. Albuquerque: University of New Mexico Press.

Summary of long-term fieldwork traces settlement and population from the Middle Preclassic through the Early Postclassic periods.

Rice, Prudence. 1984. "Obsidian Procurement in the Central Peten Lakes Region, Guatemala." *Journal of Field Archaeology* 11: 181–194.

Rice discusses the obsidian source data analysis carried out at the Lawrence Berkeley Lab, as well as modeling obsidian distribution in the central Peten Lakes area.

Rice, Prudence M. 1987a. "Economic Change in the Lowland Maya Late Classic Period." In *Specialization, Exchange, and Complex Societies,* edited by Elizabeth M. Brumfiel and Timothy K. Earle, 76–85. New York: Cambridge University Press.

This examination of Late Classic utilitarian pottery and obsidian distribution indicates that pottery production was decentralized and outside the cities, whereas obsidian distribution was more centralized, albeit changing to a decentralized distribution by the Late Classic. Production was likely part-time work.

Rice, Prudence M. 1987b. *Pottery Analysis: A Source Book.* Chicago: University of Chicago Press.

Rice's text provides detailed methods for the analysis of prehistoric ceramics, including those of the Maya, for which she is an expert.

Ricketson, Oliver G., Jr., and Edith B. Ricketson. 1937. *Uaxactun, Guatemala, Group E, 1926–1937*. Carnegie Institution of Washington Publication 477. Washington, DC: Carnegie Institution of Washington.

This monograph is an important record of the Carnegie excavations, which established the foundations for the style of excavations, the ceramic chronology, and the intellectual lineage of Maya archaeology.

Ringle, William M., and E. Wyllys Andrews IV. 1990. "The Demography of Komchen, an Early Maya Town in Northern Yucatan." In *Precolumbian Population History in the Maya Lowlands,* edited by T. Patrick Culbert and Don S. Rice, 215–243. Albuquerque: University of New Mexico Press.

The authors note that an estimate of 500 structures per km^2 for Preclassic Komchen indicates a high human population.

Robertson, Robin A., and David A. Freidel, eds. 1986. *Archaeology at Cerros, Belize, Central America,* vol. 1: *An Interim Report.* Dallas: Southern Methodist University Press.

This book includes summary articles by Jim Garber on the artifacts, by H. Sorraya Carr on fauna, by Cathy Crane on plants, and on excavations from Freidel's project at Cerros. Some of the papers, such as Garber's, have been supplanted by monographs (see Garber 1989).

Robles, Fernando, and Anthony P. Andrews. 1985. "A Review and Synthesis of Recent Postclassic Archaeology in Northern Yucatan." In *Late Lowland Maya Civilization,* edited by Jeremy A. Sabloff and E. Wyllys Andrews V, 53–98. Albuquerque: University of New Mexico Press.

Discussion of their recent research in the northern Maya lowlands.

Rosny, Leon de. 1887. *Codex Peresianus: Manuscrit hieratique des anciens Indiens de l'Amerique Centrale conserve a la Bibliotheque Nationale de Paris.* Paris: Bureau de la Societe Americaine.

The author found and published a fragment of what became known as the Paris Codex; it was found, in a basket of old papers in a Paris library that had purchased the manuscript in 1832. See also Marhenke (2003) for a digital copy, combining the two parts of the Madrid Codex.

Roys, Ralph, trans. 1967. *Chilam Balam of Chumayel.* Norman: University of Oklahoma Press.

This is an authoritative annotated translation of this native text. Books written by native Maya in several Yucatecan communities during early colonial days called Chilam Balam are variously informative on religion and ideology. Chilam Balam was a native priest who evidently foretold the arrival of the Spaniards and the books are named after him.

Ruggles, Clive. 2003. *Images of Sites in Mesoamerica.* Leicester, UK: University of Leicester; http://www.le.ac.uk/archaeology/rug/image_collection/hier/am/r2.html.

Photos of Maya sites, including Chichen Itza, Dzibilchaltun, and Uxmal.

Sabloff, Jeremy A. 1975. *Excavations at Seibal, Guatemala, Department of the Peten,*

Guatemala: The Ceramics. Memoirs of the Peabody Museum of Archaeology and Ethnology, vol. 13, no. 2. Cambridge, MA: Harvard University.

> Sabloff's type-variety classification of the pottery from Seibal is an important reference for ceramicists. His use of principal identifying modes to describe the main traits of a pottery type has been widely used by Maya ceramicists.

Sabloff, Jeremy, and Gair Tourtellot. 1992. "Beyond Temples and Palaces: Recent Settlement Pattern Research at the Ancient Maya City of Sayil (1983–1985)." In *New Theories on the Ancient Maya,* edited by Elin C. Danien and Robert J. Sharer, 155–160. Philadelphia: University Museum, University of Pennsylvania.

> Extensive mapping and surface collection and excavation at this northern Maya city provides new information on the Terminal Classic in the Puuc Hills, including the possibility of a marketplace.

Sabloff, Jeremy A., ed. 2003. *Tikal: Dynasties, Foreigners, and Affairs of State*. Santa Fe, NM: School of American Research Press.

> This is a status report by some of the original University of Pennsylvania Tikal project archaeologists that summarizes more detailed published and unpublished reports on the site. The book includes papers by T. Patrick Culbert, Hattula Moholy-Nagy, William Haviland, Robert Fry, Peter Harrison, Christopher Jones, H. Stanley Loten, and Marshall Becker, as well as a dynastic summary by Simon Martin, a study on Tikal's relationship with Copan by Robert Sharer, and a summary of the Guatemalan government research by Juan Pedro Laporte.

Sabloff, Jeremy A., and E. Wyllys Andrews V, eds. 1986. *Late Lowland Maya Civilization: Classic to Postclassic*. Albuquerque: University of New Mexico Press.

> This collection of papers by leading Maya scholars investigating the Postclassic in the northern lowlands, as well as the continuity of some southern lowland cities (Lamanai), provides a rich discussion for the timing of the ceramic complexes, Cehpech and Sotuta, the age of Chichen Itza, and political and economic relationships after the Classic Maya collapse.

Sabloff, Jeremy A., and John S. Henderson, eds. 1993. *Lowland Maya Civilization in the Eighth Century A.D.* Washington, DC: Dumbarton Oaks Research Library and Collection.

> This volume is based on a Dumbarton Oaks symposium and includes insightful articles on the politics and economy of Late Classic Maya civilization before the collapse.

Sabloff, Jeremy A., and William L. Rathje, eds. 1975. *A Study of Changing Pre-Columbian Commercial Systems: The 1972–73 Seasons at Cozumel, Mexico*. Monographs of the Peabody Museum of Archaeology and Ethnology, vol. 3. Cambridge, MA: Harvard University.

> In this book, the directors of the Cozumel project present a model of a port of trade. The report includes studies by Richard Leventhal, David Freidel, David Gregory, David Phillips, Judith O'Connor, and Paula Sabloff, as well as a report on the geography of the island by William Davidson.

Sanders, William T. 1960. *Prehistoric Ceramics and Settlement Patterns in Quintana Roo*. Contributions to American Anthropology and History 60, Carnegie Institution of Washington Publication 606. Washington, DC: Carnegie Institution of Washington.

Sanders's excavations at Tulum include the main reference illustrations for Tulum Red pottery, which was so widely copied and/or traded in the Postclassic.

Sanders, William T. 1977. "Environmental Heterogeneity and the Evolution of Lowland Maya Civilization." In *The Origins of Maya Civilization*, edited by Richard E. W. Adams, 287–297. Albuquerque: University of New Mexico Press.

Contrary to previous views of a uniform physical landscape in the Maya lowlands, Sanders presents maps and information to indicate diversity within the lowlands, suggesting preferential use of certain areas.

Sanders, William T., Jeffrey Parsons, and Robert Santley. 1979. *The Basin of Mexico: Ecological Processes in the Evolution of a Civilization*. New York: Academic Press.

Provides an overview of settlement pattern studies from complete pedestrian survey and surface collection in the basin of Mexico near Mexico City.

Sanders, William T., and Barbara Price. 1968. *Mesoamerica: The Evolution of a Civilization*. New York: Random House.

The authors make a compelling and quite controversial argument that Teotihuacan was an ancient state, whereas the Maya society was a chiefdom that became more complex with contact with Teotihuacanos. They argue that Teotihuacan conquered the Maya highland city of Kaminaljuyu in order to control the El Chayal obsidian source as well as cacao on the Pacific coast. This is a classic text, which has both supporters and opponents.

Sanders, William T., and Joseph W. Michels, eds. 1977. *Teotihuacan and Kaminaljuyu: A Study in Prehistoric Culture Contact*. University Park: Pennsylvania State University Press.

Having carried out research in the Teotihuacan Valley, Sanders initiated work at Kaminaljuyu and the surrounding valley, suggesting that there was a military takeover of Kaminaljuyu by Teotihuacan between A.D. 400–700. This theory is based, in part, on Teotihuacan-style architecture in the city center.

Santley, Robert S. 1984. "Obsidian Exchange, Economic Stratification, and the Evolution of Complex Society in the Basin of Mexico." In *Trade and Exchange in Early Mesoamerica*, edited by Kenneth G. Hirth, 43–86. Albuquerque: University of New Mexico Press.

Describes obsidian tool production and distribution at Teotihuacan, in the region with itinerant obsidian blade traders and farther away with long-distance trade, over time.

Saturno, William. 2003. Proyecto San Bartolo. http://www.sanbartolo.org.

This Internet site provides images of Vucub Caquix and other painted murals on walls at this lowland Maya site, accidentally discovered during survey by Saturno in 2001. The site also includes descriptions of the fieldwork, the conservation efforts, and many color images of the site and murals. The text can be accessed in English or Spanish.

Scarborough, Vernon L. 1991. *Archaeology at Cerros, Belize, Central America*, vol. 3: *The Settlement System in a Late Preclassic Maya Community*. Dallas: Southern Methodist University Press.

In this revision of his Ph.D. dissertation, Scarborough describes the methods and results of his survey and excavations at Cerros, outside the ceremonial precinct, including the agricultural fields.

Scarborough, Vernon L. 1998. "Ecology and Ritual: Water Management and the Maya." *Latin American Antiquity* 9: 135–159.

The complex interplay between settlement and access to water for drinking and agriculture is examined in relation to his research at La Milpa and elsewhere in northwestern Belize.

Schele, Linda. 1982. *Maya Glyphs: The Verbs.* Austin: University of Texas Press.

A monograph by one of the leading epigraphers, this book provides important strides in decipherment of Maya glyphs.

Schele, Linda, and David A. Freidel. 1990. *A Forest of Kings: The Untold Story of the Ancient Maya.* New York: William Morrow.

The authors combine archaeological and epigraphic data on the ancient Maya, prefacing their chapters with stories about Maya kings and queens. These stories are based on facts but are a creative and stunning departure from Maya archaeology.

Schele, Linda, and Peter Matthews. 1991. "Royal Visits and Other Intersite Relationships among the Classic Maya." In *Classic Maya Political History,* edited by T. Patrick Culbert, 226–252. New York: Cambridge University Press.

These two eminent Maya epigraphers trace the marriage and other alliances between Classic Maya cities in their royal leaders' pursuits of political power.

Schele, Linda, and Mary Miller. 1986. *The Blood of Kings: Dynasty and Ritual in Maya Art.* New York: George Braziller.

The illustrations and text for this book, produced to accompany an art exhibit, provide important information about Classic Maya elite society, in particular the rituals of bloodletting, graphically depicted in Maya art.

Schellhas, Paul. 1904. *Representations of Deities of the Maya Manuscripts.* Papers of the Peabody Museum of Archaeology and Ethnology, vol. 4, no. 1. Cambridge, MA: Harvard University.

This English publication follows its first publication in German in 1886. Schellhas categorized the deities in the Dresden Codex, identifying glyphs associated with them, providing the basis for further study.

Schlesinger, Victoria. 2001. *Animals and Plants of the Ancient Maya.* Austin: University of Texas Press.

Line drawings and text provide a good introduction for both the layperson and the academic to the plants and animals available in the Maya area in ancient and modern times.

Schmidt, Peter, Mercedes de la Garza, and Enrique Nalda, eds. 1998. *Maya.* Venice: Bompiani.

This book is the catalog to an exhibit in Venice, Italy, and is well illustrated with accompanying text.

Seidemann, Ryan and Heather McKillop. 2004. "Dental Indicators of Diet and Health for the Postclassic Coastal Maya on Wild Cane Cay, Belize." Unpublished manuscript.

Examination of calculus (plaque), cavities, and abscesses, to assess the diet and health of people buried in Fighting Conch mound.

Shafer, Harry J., and Thomas R. Hester. 1983. "Ancient Maya Chert Workshops in Northern Belize, Central America." *American Antiquity* 48: 519–543.

Based on their excavations at Colha, the authors describe household workshops where stone tools were made in massive quantities from the Late Preclassic through Early Postclassic, using high-quality chert from outcrops at the site.

Shafer, Harry J., and Thomas R. Hester. 1986. "Maya Tool Craft Specialization and Production at Colha, Belize: A Reply to Mallory." *American Antiquity* 51: 158–166.

The authors present data in support of mass-production of chert stone tools for trade.

Shafer, Harry J., and Thomas R. Hester. 1990. "The Puleston Axe: A Late Preclassic Maya Hafted Tool from Northern Belize." In *Ancient Maya Wetland Agriculture,* edited by Mary Pohl, 279–294. Boulder, CO: Westview.

This paper discusses a chert axe that was recovered still hafted on a handle in water-logged soil on Albion Island, providing the only artifactual evidence of the way in which axes were used. The axe was interpreted as a land-clearing implement.

Sharer, Robert J. 1978. "Summary of Architecture and Construction Activity." In *The Prehistory of Chalchuapa, El Salvador,* vol. 1, edited by Robert J. Sharer, 121–132. Philadelphia: University of Pennsylvania Press.

The project director describes the excavations at this important Preclassic Maya community.

Sharer, Robert J. 1994. *The Ancient Maya.* 5th ed. Stanford: Stanford University Press.

Sharer's revision of Morley's 1946 publication is a profusely illustrated and up-to-date discussion of the ancient Maya.

Sharer, Robert J. 2003a. "Tikal and the Copan Dynastic Founding." In *Tikal. Dynasties, Foreigners, and Affairs of State,* edited by Jeremy A. Sabloff, 319–353. Santa Fe, NM: School of American Research Press.

Sharer discusses the role of Teotihuacan in the founding of Tikal and the takeover of Copan and Quirigua by Tikal in the Early Classic. Hieroglyphic evidence from Tikal points to the "arrival of strangers," likely a conquest by Smoking Frog from Teotihuacan in A.D. 378, coinciding with the death of Tikal ruler Great Jaguar Paw and the installation of Curl Snout.

Sharer, Robert J. 2003b. "Founding Events and Teotihuacan Connections at Copan, Honduras." In *Teotihuacan and the Maya,* edited by Geoffrey Braswell, 143–165. Austin: University of Texas Press.

Sharer discusses Tikal's military expansion, its political takeover at Copan, and the establishment of the ruling dynasty at Copan's subsidiary city, Quirigua, in A.D. 426 or 427, along with other evidence for Teotihuacan presence at Copan.

Sheets, Payson D. 1975. "Behavioral Analysis and the Structure of a Prehistoric Industry." *Current Anthropology* 16: 369–391.

In contrast to earlier emphasis on the form of finished stone tools, Sheets describes the stages of manufacture of obsidian blades from stone cores.

Sheets, Payson D., Kenneth Hirth, Fred Lange, Fred Stross, Frank Asaro, and Helen Michel. 1990. "Obsidian Sources and Elemental Analyses of Artifacts in Southern Mesoamerica and the Northern Intermediate Zone." *American Antiquity* 55: 144–158.

La Esperanza obsidian figures in these authors' data, as at Wild Cane Cay; it is rare elsewhere in the Maya area.

Sheets, Payson D., ed. 2002. *Before the Volcano Erupted: The Ancient Ceren Village in Central America.* Austin: University of Texas Press.

Detailed information and illustrations are presented on the excavations of this Classic Maya community, which has preserved, Pompeii-style, the casts of plants in fields and of collapsed houses, providing an important view of Classic Maya life of the common folk.

Shepard, Anna O. 1948. *Plumbate: A Mesoamerican Trade Ware.* Carnegie Institute of Washington Publication 573. Washington, DC: Carnegie Institution of Washington.

Shepard provides an inventory and discussion of this distinctive pottery made on the Pacific coast of Chiapas, Mexico, and neighboring Guatemala and widely traded throughout Mesoamerica in the Early Postclassic between A.D. 900 and 1200. The book remains the classic reference on the pottery.

Shepard, Anna O. 1976. *Ceramics for the Archaeologist.* Washington, DC: Carnegie Institution of Washington.

Shepard was an early practitioner of technological studies of Maya pottery including petrography, in which minerals and other materials in the clay are observed and identified under a binocular microscope. This report is a classic text for Maya ceramicists.

Shipley, Webster E., III, and Elizabeth Graham. 1989. "Petrographic Analysis and Preliminary Source Identification of Selected Stone Artifacts from the Maya Sites of Seibal and Uaxactun, Guatemala." *Journal of Archaeological Science* 14: 367–383.

Granite from the batholiths of the Maya Mountains is compared to grinding stones from Uaxactun and Seibal to identify the sources of the material and hence the exchange networks.

Sidrys, Raymond V. 1983. *Archaeological Excavations in Northern Belize, Central America.* Monograph XVII. Los Angeles: Institute of Archaeology, University of California.

This study reports on Raymond Sidrys's survey and excavations in northern Belize and on the artifacts and other remains discovered. The report provides a basis for many researchers subsequently working in the area.

Sidrys, Raymond V., and John Andreson. 1976. "Metate Import in Northern Belize." In *Maya Lithic Studies: Papers from the 1976 Belize Field Symposium,* edited by Thomas R. Hester and Norman Hammond, 151–176. Special Report 4. San Antonio: Center for Archaeological Research, University of Texas.

This important study of metates from Sidrys's 1974 survey in northern Belize assigns them to three sources based on visual inspection: locally available limestone, metamorphic and igneous intrusives (granite, porphyry, gneiss, quartzite, slate, and schist) from the Maya Mountains, and extrusive volcanics (basalt, vesicular lava, pumicious or andesitic tuff) from the volcanic regions of the southern Maya highlands.

Siemens, Alfred H. 1978. "Karst and the Pre-Hispanic Maya in the Southern Lowlands." In *Prehispanic Maya Agriculture*, edited by Peter D. Harrison and B. L. Turner II, 117–143. Albuquerque: University of New Mexico Press.

A discussion of the limestone karst topography of the Yucatan indicates that access to water for agriculture was a problem for the ancient Maya, which may have been relieved by use of bajos (swamps). Aerial photos of raised fields in the Candelaria region of Campeche, Mexico, and at Albion Island and Pulltrouser Swamp in northern Belize are discussed, as is the possibility that the bajo near Tikal was used for agriculture.

Simmons, Michael P., and Gerald F. Brem. 1979. "The Analysis and Distribution of Volcanic Ash-Tempered Pottery in the Lowland Maya Area." *American Antiquity* 44: 79–91.

The authors suggest that volcanic ash was imported over long distances from the southern Maya highlands to use as a tempering agent in pottery produced in the Maya lowlands, using extensive coastal Caribbean canoe trade.

Sluyter, Andrew. 1993. "Long-Distance Staple Transport in Western Mesoamerica: Insights through Quantitative Modeling." *Ancient Mesoamerica* 4: 193–199.

In an insightful model, Sluyter suggests that food may have been traded long distances in the Maya area, an idea that has prompted some debate.

Smith, A. Ledyard. 1950. *Uaxactun, Guatemala: Excavations of 1931–1937.* Carnegie Institution of Washington Publication 588. Washington, DC: Carnegie Institution of Washington.

Smith's extensive exactions set the standard for much of the architectural excavations of subsequent sites in the Maya area, combining trenching to search for structures followed by horizontal exposure of the structure.

Smith, A. Ledyard. 1972. *Excavations at Altar de Sacrificios: Architecture, Settlement, Burials, and Caches.* Papers of the Peabody Museum of Archaeology and Ethnology, vol. 62, no. 2. Cambridge, MA: Harvard University.

This is a description of major architecture and excavations by Smith.

Smith, A. Ledyard. 1982. *Major Architecture and Caches: Excavations at Seibal, Department of Peten, Guatemala.* Papers of the Peabody Museum of Archaeology and Ethnology, vol. 15, no. 1. Cambridge, MA: Harvard University.

This is a description of major architecture and excavations by Smith.

Smith, Robert E. 1955. *Ceramic Sequence at Uaxactun, Guatemala.* 2 vols. New Orleans: Middle American Research Institute, Tulane University.

In this research, Smith excavated test pits adjacent to structures and coordinated architectural and stratigraphic ceramic profiles. The Uaxactun ceramic sequence is the standard reference for Maya ceramicists. The time periods and their subdivisions are well known and are used in other pottery reports.

Smith, Robert E. 1971. *The Pottery of Mayapan.* 2 vols. Papers of the Peabody Museum of Archaeology and Ethnology, vol. 66. Cambridge, MA: Harvard University.

Smith's study of the pottery from Mayapan is a benchmark for studying Postclassic Maya pottery. It predates introduction of the type-variety system of ceramic classification.

Spence, Michael W. 1987. "Report on the Burials of Wild Cane Cay, Belize." In *Wild Cane Cay: An Insular Classic Period to Postclassic Period Maya Trading Station,* by Heather McKillop, 282–295. University of California, Santa Barbara, University Microfilms, Ann Arbor.

This paper includes skeletal and dental analyses of burials from midden excavations in 1982.

Spence, Michael W. 1996. "Commodity or Gift: Teotihuacan Obsidian in the Maya Region." *Latin American Antiquity* 7: 21–39.

Spence examines the distribution of green obsidian in the Maya lowlands during the Classic period and finds that there was relatively little obsidian traded, except in a couple of elite burials at Kaminaljuyu. Green obsidian did not drive economic relations between Teotihuacan and the Maya area, but rather reflected gifts cementing political relationships. Blades, eccentrics (blades further chipped into other shpaes including some that depict animals or human heads and other that are nonrepresentive), points, and other artifacts were traded.

Spinden, Herbert J. 1913. *A Study of Maya Art.* Memoirs of the Peabody Museum of Archaeology and Ethnology, vol. 6. Cambridge, MA: Harvard University.

This revision of Spinden's Harvard Ph.D. dissertation remains a standard resource for Maya studies of art.

Spinden, Herbert. 1916. "The Question of the Zodiac in America." *American Anthropologist* 18: 53–80.

Includes a discussion of the ancient Maya zodiac, further discussed by Milbrath (1999) and others.

Steiner, Edward P. 1994. "Prehistoric Maya Settlement along Joe Taylor Creek, Belize." Unpublished Master's thesis, Department of Geography and Anthropology, Louisiana State University, Baton Rouge.

Steiner contends here that the lack of mounded remains, apart from a single mound, lend support to the underrepresentation of population estimates based on mound counts.

Stephens, John Lloyd. [1841] 1969. *Incidents of Travel in Central America, Chiapas, and Yucatan* New York: Dover.

Accompanied by the accurate and detailed drawings of Maya sites temples and stone carvings of Frederick Catherwood, Stephens's accounts of their travels to Copan and other Maya ruins provided historical detail and sparked widespread interest among the public in North America and Europe for the ancient Maya.

Stephens, John Lloyd. [1843] 1963. *Incidents of Travel in Yucatan.* 2 vols. New York: Dover.

The companion to Stephens's first account of travels in Central America, this book also was well received by a public interested in accounts of travel to Maya cities in the jungle.

Steward, Julian. 1955. *Theory of Culture Change.* Chicago: Aldine.

In this book, Steward introduced the concept of cultural ecology to anthropology and stressed the role of the environment in cultural change.

Stone, Andrea. 1995. *Images from the Underworld: Naj Tunich and the Tradition of Maya Cave Painting.* Austin: University of Texas Press.

Fieldwork and analysis of cave paintings from this site in the lowlands of Guatemala are presented in this monograph.

Stross, F. H., H. R. Bowman, H. V. Michel, F. Asaro, and N. Hammond. 1978. "Mayan Obsidian: Source Correlations for Southern Belize Artifacts." *Archaeometry* 20: 83–93.

The authors report on chemical source identification of obsidian from Lubaantun and coastal sites in southern Belize, including Wild Cane Cay, Frenchman's Cay, and Moho Cay.

Stuart, David. 1988. "The Rio Azul Cacao Pot: Epigraphic Observations on the Function of a Maya Ceramic Vessel." *Antiquity* 62: 153–157.

For this paper, Stuart analyzed the hieroglyphs on a vessel identified by residue analysis to have contained chocolate.

Stuart, David. 2001. "Hieroglyphs on Maya Vessels." In *The Decipherment of Ancient Maya Writing,* edited by Stephen Houston, Oswaldo Chinchilla Mazariegos, and David Stuart, 474–485. Norman: University of Oklahoma Press.

Stuart discusses current knowledge of Maya hieroglyphs on pottery vessels, usually below the rim on the exterior of the vessel in what is termed the "Primary Standard Sequence," providing information on the owner or maker of the vessel and the type of vessel, with some identifying as containers of chocolate.

Stuart, George. 2002. "Yucatan's Mysterious Hill Cities." *National Geographic* 201 (4): 54–69.

This article's photos and discussion of Michael Smyth's fieldwork at Chac in the northern Maya lowlands include still-unexplained Teotihuacan influences at the city.

Stuart, George E. 1992. "Quest for Decipherment: A Historical and Biographical Survey of Maya Hieroglyphic Investigation." In *New Theories on the Ancient Maya,* edited by Elin C. Danien and Robert J. Sharer, 1–65. University of Pennsylvania Museum, Philadelphia: University of Pennsylvania.

This is an important companion to other historical accounts, notably Houston et al. 2001 and Coe and Van Stone 2001.

Taschek, Jennifer. 1981. "The Non-Ceramic, Non-Chipped Stone Artifacts from Dzibilchaltun, Yucatan, Mexico." Ph.D. dissertation, Department of Anthropology, University of Wisconsin, Madison.

Description of artifacts is useful in comparison with other Maya sites and for inform-ing on the ancient culture at this important northern Maya lowland city.

Tate, Carolyn E. 1992. *Yaxchilan: The Design of a Maya Ceremonial City.* Austin: University of Texas Press.

Tate provides a study of the site layout, architecture, and art as expressed in the stone sculpture at the site.

Taube, Karl. 1993. *Aztec and Maya Myths.* Austin: University of Texas Press.

Taube presents an overview of Maya myths, which is a good introduction. He pro-vides sources for further reading.

Tedlock, Dennis, trans. 1985. *Popol Vuh: The Definitive Edition of the Mayan Book of the Dawn of Life and the Glories of Gods and Kings.* New York: Simon and Schuster.

This colonial text from the highland Quiche Maya, translated and extensively anno-tated into English, describes the Maya creation of the world and the adventures of the Hero Twins. The stories have important analogues among the ancient Maya, be-ing widely depicted in Preclassic through Postclassic painted pots and carved stone.

Thompson, J. Eric S. 1927. *A Correlation of the Mayan and European Calendars.* Field Mu-seum of Natural History, Anthropological Series, vol. 17, no. 1. Chicago: Field Museum.

Thompson modified the earlier correlations of the Maya and Christian calendars provided by Martinez Hernandez (1926) and Goodman (1905). The result is the most commonly accepted correlation, known as the Goodman-Martinez-Thompson (GMT) correlation.

Thompson, J. Eric S. 1939. *Excavations at San Jose, British Honduras.* Carnegie Institution of Washington Publication 506. Washington, DC: Carnegie Institution of Washington.

This is a detailed description of the excavations and artifacts from a medium-sized Maya city in northern Belize by one of the leading Maya archaeologists of the twenti-eth century.

Thompson, J. Eric S. 1950. *Maya Hieroglyphic Writing: An Introduction.* Carnegie Institution of Washington Publication 589. Washington, DC: Carnegie Institution of Washington.

Although he provides much in the way of important translations, Thompson dis-misses the phonetic basis for Maya hieroglyphs.

Thompson, J. Eric S. 1970. *Maya History and Religion.* Norman: University of Oklahoma Press.

In this landmark study by one of the preeminent Maya scholars of the twentieth cen-tury, Thompson draws together many of his ideas on Maya prehistory.

Thompson, J. Eric S. 1971a. "Estimates of Maya Population: Deranging Factors." *American Antiquity* 36: 214–216.

Thompson suggests that Maya houses were abandoned upon the death of a family member and so is critical of Haviland's 1965 population estimates for Tikal. Al-though Thompson's view is not shared by other Maya archaeologists, the periodicity of abandonment of Maya houses remains unresolved. See Haviland (1972) for a reply and Culbert and Rice (1990) and Harrison (1999) for estimates of Tikal's population.

Thompson, J. Eric S. 1971b. *Maya Hieroglyphic Writing.* 3d ed. Norman: University of Oklahoma Press.

Thompson's monumental study in which he assigns a T (for Thompson) number to each glyph, along with a translation. The decipherment is somewhat out of date, but epigraphers still use his T numbers.

Thompson, J. Eric S. 1972. *Dresden: A Commentary on the Dresden Codex.* American Philosophical Society Memoir 93. Philadelphia: American Philosophical Society.

English translation of the Dresden Codex, an ancient Maya book from the Yucatan now housed in Dresden, that provides text and images of astronomy, mathematics, and the Maya calendar. See also Burger (2001) and Marhenke (2003) for digital images of the Dresden Codex.

Thompson, J. Eric S. 1975. "The Grolier Codex." *Contributions of the University of California Archaeological Research Facility* 27: 1–9.

The most recently discovered of four remaining indigenous Maya texts is described in this article.

Tourtellot, Gair. 1990. "Population Estimates for Preclassic and Classic Seibal." In *Precolumbian Population History in the Maya Lowlands,* edited by T. Patrick Culbert and Don S. Rice, 83–102. Albuquerque: University of New Mexico Press.

The plazuela (plaza) group is used for estimating population figures.

Tourtellot, Gair, Amanda Clark, and Norman Hammond. 1993. "Mapping La Milpa: A Maya City in Northwestern Belize." *Antiquity* 67: 96–108.

Results of Tourtellot's settlement survey around La Milpa are presented.

Tourtellot, Gair, Gloria Everson, and Norman Hammond. 2003. "Suburban Organization: Minor Centers at La Milpa, Belize." In *Perspectives on Ancient Maya Rural Complexity,* edited by Gyles Iannone and Samuel V. Connell, 95–107. Monograph 49. Los Angeles: Cotsen Institute of Archaeology, University of California.

Based on extensive mapping at the major center of La Milpa and in the hinterland beyond the site, the authors propose that the entire settlement pattern, including minor centers around La Milpa, is a replication of the ancient Maya cosmogram. They find two concentric rings of minor centers around La Milpa.

Tourtellot, Gair, and Jeremy A. Sabloff. 1972. "Exchange Systems among the Ancient Maya." *American Antiquity* 37: 126–135.

A widely cited article in which the authors make the distinction between elite and subsistence trade goods in terms of their origins from distant and local areas, respectively.

Tozzer, Alfred M., trans. 1941. *Landa's "Relación de las Cosas de Yucatan.* Papers of the Peabody Museum of Archaeology and Ethnology, vol. 18. Cambridge, MA: Harvard University.

The definitive translation, with important commentary, of the account of the first Catholic bishop of the Yucatan about the Maya at the time of Spanish contact. This book remains a critical source of information on the Maya.

Trik, Aubrey S. 1963. "The Splendid Tomb of Temple 1 at Tikal, Guatemala." *Expedition* 6: 2–18.

Grave goods described in this article include long bones incised with pictures of mythical figures in canoes, providing one of the few depictions of Maya boats.

Turner, B. L., and Peter D. Harrison, eds. 1983. *Pulltrouser Swamp: Ancient Maya Habitat, Agriculture, and Settlement in Northern Belize.* Austin: University of Texas Press.

As the directors of the Pulltrouser Swamp project, geographer Turner and archaeologist Harrison bring together the researchers who worked on various aspects of the fieldwork and analysis, providing a report on Late Classic intensive agriculture in raised or drained agricultural fields.

Turner, B. L., II, and Charles H. Miksicek. 1984. "Economic Plant Species Associated with Prehistoric Agriculture in the Maya Lowlands." *Economic Botany* 38: 179–193.

The authors provide a summary of plant foods used by the ancient Maya, summarizing data from a variety of sources.

Vail, Gabrielle. 2002. *The Madrid Codex: A Maya Hieroglyphic Book,* Version 1.0. http://madrid.doaks.org/codex/madcod.asp .

A website and database presentation with analysis of the Madrid Codex, one of the four known ancient Maya books. This publication is only available online.

Valdes, Juan Antonio. 1986. "Uaxactun: Recientes Investigaciones." *Mexicon* 7 (6): 125–128.

This is a summary in Spanish of the research by Guatemalan archaeologists at Uaxactun.

Valdes, Juan Antonio, and Jonathan Kaplan. 2000. "Ground-Penetrating Radar at the Maya Site of Kaminaljuyu, Guatemala." *Journal of Field Archaeology* 27: 329–342.

In this study, remote sensing was used to locate ancient buildings at the site that were previously obscured by urban sprawl from modern Guatemala City.

Vlcek, David T., Sylvia Garza de Gonzalez, and Edward B. Kurjack. 1978. "Contemporary Farming and Ancient Maya Settlements: Some Disconcerting Evidence." In *Pre-Hispanic Maya Agriculture,* edited by Peter D. Harrison and B. L. Turner II, 211–223. Albuquerque: University of New Mexico Press.

Early research at the northern Maya lowland settlement of Chunchucmil indicates 400 structures per km^2 with a poor agricultural base. Dahlin (2000) directed a subsequent survey and excavation project at the site.

Vogt, Evon Z. 1970. *The Zinacantecos of Mexico: A Modern Maya Way of Life.* New York: Holt, Rinehart, and Winston.

In this classic study of the village of Zinacantan initiated by Harvard University in 1959, Vogt provides an important ethnography that also is valuable for analogies with the ancient Maya.

Von Humboldt, Alexander. 1910. *Vues des cordilleras, et monuments des peoples indigenes de l'Amerique.* Paris: F. Schoell.

As part of von Humboldt's monumental natural history, he includes five pages from the Dresden Codex, in plate 45.

Voorhies, Barbara. 1976. *The Chantuto People: An Archaic Period Society of the Chiapas Littoral, Mexico.* Papers of the New World Archaeological Foundation 41. Provo, UT: Brigham Young University.

The author describes shell midden excavation that yielded evidence of seasonal use of the coast by Archaic people, who subsisted on shellfish, shrimp, and other maritime resources.

Voorhies, Barbara. 1982. "An Ecological Model of the Early Maya of the Central Lowlands." In *Maya Subsistence,* edited by Kent V. Flannery, 65–95. New York: Academic Press.

Discussion and itemization of the many natural forest products accessible in the rainforest that would have been available for exchange of highland resources.

Wauchope, Robert. 1934. *House Mounds of Uaxactun, Guatemala.* Carnegie Institution of Washington Publication 436, Contributions to American Archaeology 7. Washington, DC: Carnegie Institution of Washington.

Wauchope chose to study the ordinary houses of the Maya instead of the elite, and this monograph remains an important description of Uaxactun house mounds.

Wauchope, Robert. 1938. *Modern Maya Houses.* Carnegie Institution of Washington Publication 502. Washington, DC: Carnegie Institution of Washington.

This is a classic text, often cited, on the common Maya homes, based on the author's work as a Carnegie researcher.

Weber, Christie, director and producer. 1993. *Lost Kingdoms of the Maya.* VHS video. Washington, DC: National Geographic Society.

The video presents interviews with archaeologists at several Classic Maya sites and shows important new discoveries that illuminate the Classic Maya civilization. The video highlights Bill Fash, David Stuart, and Linda Schele at Copan; Diane and Arlen Chase at Caracol; and Arthur Demarest at Dos Pilas.

Webster, David. 1976. *Defensive Earthworks at Becan, Campeche, Mexico.* Middle American Research Institute Publication 41. New Orleans: Tulane University.

This is an account of early earthworks found at Becan.

Webster, David. 1993. "The Study of Maya Warfare: What It Tells Us about the Maya and What It Tells Us about Maya Archaeology." In *Lowland Maya Civilization in the Eighth Century A.D.,* edited by Jeremy A. Sabloff and John S. Henderson, 415–444. Washington, DC: Dumbarton Oaks.

This is a summary of Webster's views on Maya warfare. Webster recognized the existence of warfare among the ancient Maya long before it became more popularly investigated.

Webster, David. 2002. *The Fall of the Ancient Maya.* New York: Thames & Hudson.

This book provides a compelling account of the Classic Maya and the collapse, with discussions of various factors. Webster builds a convincing argument for ecological disaster, with warfare as part of the scenario. As well as the overall picture of the collapse, Webster discusses the collapse at Copan and its hinterland, based on the Penn State project that he directed.

Webster, David, and AnnCorinne Freter. 1990. "The Demography of Late Classic Copan." In *Precolumbian Population History in the Maya Lowlands,* edited by T. Patrick Culbert and Don S. Rice, 37–61. Albuquerque: University of New Mexico Press.

With reference to earlier research at Copan by others, the authors use their settlement data for a preliminary reconstruction of the population at Copan's maximum size from A.D. 700 to 850. Using estimates of both 4 and 5 persons per household, they that find Copan was quite small at its maximum size in comparison to other contemporary cities such as Tikal (see Culbert and Rice 1990; Harrison 1999), with estimates of less than 25,000 people.

Webster, David, AnnCorinne Freter, and Nancy Gonlin. 2000. *Copan: The Rise and Fall of an Ancient Maya Kingdom.* Fort Worth, TX: Harcourt Brace.

An ecological perspective on the regional settlement and the growth of the city of Copan.

Weeks, John. 2003. Bibliografia Mesoamericana. http://www.famsi.org/research/bibliography.htm.

A searchable digital database of published references on Maya and other Mesoamerican archaeology and culture, begun by Ignacio Bernal and continued by John Weeks through the Foundation for the Advancement of Mesoamerican Studies (FAMSI) Web page.

West, Robert C., and John P. Augelli. 1989. *Middle America: Its Land and Peoples,* 3d ed. Englewood Cliffs, NJ: Prentice Hall.

General reference for the physical and cultural geography of Mexico, Central America, and the Caribbean islands.

West, Robert C., ed. 1964. *Natural Environment and Early Cultures: Handbook of Middle American Indians,* vol. 1. Austin: University of Texas Press.

This is the first volume of an important series on the ancient cultures of Middle America. This volume summarizes the physical landscape.

White, Christine D., Fred J. Longstaffe, and Kimberley R. Law. 2001a. "Revisiting the Teotihuacan Connection at Altun Ha: Oxygen-Isotope Analysis of Tomb F-8/1." *Ancient Mesoamerica* 12: 65–72.

This article concludes that Teotihuacan contact with Altun Ha did not leave any lasting impact on the community, apart from some trade goods.

White, Christine D., David M. Pendergast, Fred J. Longstaffe, and Kimberley R. Law. 2001b. "Social Complexity and Food Systems at Altun Ha, Belize: The Isotopic Evidence." *Latin American Antiquity* 12: 371–393.

Isotopic data from Altun Ha are provided in this article, to estimate individuals ' place of origin.

White, Christine D., Fred J. Longstaffe, Michael W. Spence, and Kimberley R. Law. 2000. "Testing the Nature of Teotihuacan Imperialism at Kaminaljuyu Using Phosphate Oxygen-Isotope Ratios." *Journal of Anthropological Research* 56: 535–558.

This innovative technique tested isotopes in human remains to estimate the place of origin of individuals buried in central Kaminaljuyu. Oxygen isotope is laid down in teeth and bones as a measure of the source of water consumed by the individual during life.

White, Christine D., ed. 1999. *Reconstructing Ancient Maya Diet.* Salt Lake City: University of Utah Press.

This comprehensive discussion of diet, based on articles on plant foods, faunal remains, and chemical studies of human bone, provides a plethora of data on the diverse and abundant resources exploited by the ancient Maya.

Whittington, E. Michael, ed. 2001. *The Sport of Life and Death: The Mesoamerican Ballgame.* New York: Thames & Hudson.

Written to accompany an exhibit of the same name, this book includes informative chapters by various specialists, as well as color illustrations of the objects on display in the exhibit.

Whittington, Stephen, and David Reed, eds. 1997. *Bones of the Maya.* Washington, DC: Smithsonian Institution Press.

This volume draws together reports of the descriptive statistics of Maya skeletal and dental remains, as well as chemical studies of human bone, which provide a basis for researchers and students interested in Maya skeletal studies.

Wilk, Richard R. 1991. *Household Ecology: Economic Change and Domestic Life among the Kekchi Maya in Belize.* Tucson: University of Arizona Press.

Based on his Ph.D. dissertation fieldwork among the Kekchi in southern Belize, Wilk provides an in-depth study of the modern farming community and a valuable analogue for the ancient Maya.

Wilk, Richard R., and Wendy Ashmore, eds. 1988. *Household and Community in the Mesoamerican Past.* Albuquerque: University of New Mexico Press.

Articles compare modern and ancient Maya households and focus on the common Maya rather than the elite, with examples from Copan, Seibal, Tikal, Quirigua, Komchen, Cerros, and the Peten.

Willard, Theodore A. 1926. *The City of the Sacred Well.* New York: Century.

This is a popular account of Thompson's dredging of the Cenote at Chichen Itza.

Willard, Theodore A. 1933. *The Codex Perez: An Ancient Mayan Hieroglyphic Book.* Glendale, CA: Arthur H. Clark.

This publication of the Paris Codex is the basis for Mann's 2003 digital images.

Willey, Gordon R. 1973. *The Altar de Sacrificios Excavations: General Summary and Conclusions.* Papers of the Peabody Museum of Archaeology and Ethnology, vol. 64, no. 3. Cambridge, MA: Harvard University.

Willey directed the excavations at this Preclassic to Classic Maya city on the Pasion River of the Peten and here summarizes the excavations.

Willey, Gordon R. 1990. *Excavations at Seibal: General Summary and Conclusions.* Memoirs of the Peabody Museum of Archaeology and Ethnology, vol. 14, no. 4. Cambridge, MA: Harvard University.

Willey directed the excavations at this Preclassic to Classic Maya city on the Pasion River of the Peten and here summarizes the excavations.

Willey, Gordon R., William R. Bullard, John B. Glass, and James C. Gifford. 1965. *Prehistoric Maya Settlement Patterns in the Belize Valley.* Papers of the Peabody Museum of Archaeology and Ethnology, vol. 54. Cambridge, MA: Harvard University.

An important contribution to Maya archaeology and in particular to settlement pattern studies, this fieldwork was based on a settlement survey instead of excavation of a major city. The project laid the foundations for subsequent survey projects in the Maya area.

Willey, Gordon R., and Richard Leventhal. 1979. "Prehistoric Settlement at Copan." In *Maya Archaeology and Ethnohistory,* edited by Norman Hammond, 75–102. Austin: University of Texas Press.

Preliminary report on the Harvard University fieldwork at Copan and in the Copan Valley, describing four levels of socioeconomic complexity related to size and grandeur of architecture. The four levels are widely used in discussions of regional settlement patterns in the Maya area.

Willey, Gordon R., and Jeremy A. Sabloff. 1980. *A History of American Archaeology,* 2d ed. New York: Thames & Hudson.

The authors include a detailed history of archaeological exploration and fieldwork in the Maya area, set within a theoretical framework of the history of archaeology in the Americas through the 1970s.

Willey, Gordon R., ed. 1965. *Handbook of Middle American Indians,* vols. 2 and 3. Austin: University of Texas Press.

These articles by leading Maya archaeologists of the time are a standard reference, although many have been supplanted by subsequent field studies.

Winemiller, Terance. 1997. "Limestone Resource Exploitation by the Ancient Maya at Chichen Itza, Yucatan, Mexico." Unpublished Master's thesis, Department of Geography and Anthropology, Louisiana State University, Baton Rouge.

This is an account of surveys and excavation of chultuns within Chichen Itza that provide evidence for the source of limestone used to construct buildings at the city.

Wing, Elizabeth S. 1978. "Use of Dogs for Food: An Adaptation to the Coastal Environment." In *Prehistoric Coastal Adaptations,* edited by Barbara L. Stark and Barbara Voorhies, 29–41. New York: Academic Press.

A case is made for dogs as food in the coastal areas of Mesoamerica in antiquity, a view that has not been stressed by subsequent researchers but that remains a viable perspective.

Wright, A. Charles S., D. H. Romney, R. H. Arbuckle, and V. E. Vial. 1959. *Land Use in British Honduras: Report of the British Land Use Survey Team.* Colonial Research Publication 24. London: Colonial Office.

This report is the standard reference for the geology, vegetation, and land use in Belize based on fieldwork in the 1950s. Long out of print, the book still has important maps on geology, vegetation, and land use that are valuable for archaeological research.

Wright, Lori E. 1997. "Biological Perspectives on the Collapse of the Pasion Maya." *Ancient Mesoamerica* 8: 267–273.

In an analysis of the health of ancient Maya based on Petexbatun skeletal remains, Wright found no decline in health. She performed chemical analysis of human bone by oxygen and nitrogen isotopes.

Wright, Lori E., and Christine D. White. 1996. "Human Biology in the Classic Maya Collapse: Evidence from Paleopathology and Paleodiet." *Journal of World Prehistory* 10: 147–198.

> This article provides a summary of skeletal, dental, and chemical studies of human remains from the Maya area.

INTERNET REFERENCES

Antiquity: http://antiquity.ac.uk/Listing/listingindex.html. The journal *Antiquity* has an index of articles by subject and author, as well as the tables of contents of recent journal issues. It is available on line via Jstor ("Journal Storage"), an electronic service that provides the text of articles on the Internet, for free at many universitites, or otherwise for a fee.

Archaeology magazine: http://www.archaeology.org. *Archaeology* has an index of articles by author, with abstracts from 1991 to the present, as well as an archive of articles from 1996 to 2001, available at http://www.archaeology.org/index/msubject.html.

Ball game: http://www.ballgame.org/main.asp. The Mesoamerican ball game website is a sophisticated companion to the exhibit of the same name.

Belize sites: http://www.ambergriscaye.com/pages/mayan/mayasites.html. Information on many Maya sites in Belize is available through a Cubola Publications Web page made in Belize. http://www.archaeology.about.com/blbelize.htm provides links to Maya archaeology websites in Belize.

Bonampak: http://www.yale.edu/bonampak/. This is the Yale University digital documentation project, with images of murals from Bonampak and methods used to restore the murals.

Bonampak: http://www.halfmoon.org/bonampak.html. These pictures of murals on interior walls of rooms, with 1 to 3 in Structure 1 at Bonampak, provide the observer with a sense of being in the rooms and viewing the murals in person.

Bonampak: http://studentweb.tulane.edu/~dhixson/bonampak/bonampak.html, or access by the permanent Web page http://www.mesoamerican-archives.com.

Calendar, hieroglyphs, mathematics: http://www.michielb.nl/maya/astro.html. The Maya astronomy page provides very useful information on Maya mathematics, the calendars, hieroglyphic writing, and astronomy.

Caracol: http://www.caracol.org. This site, by Arlen and Diane Chase, has information about their project at Caracol. The site includes background on Caracol, field season summaries, photos, and information on publications. The site also has journals from the archaeologists and their children, plus fun Maya games for kids to play.

Ceren: http://www.ceren.colorado.edu. Payson Sheets's excavations at El Ceren, an ancient Maya community buried by a volcanic eruption in El Salvador, are highlighted in his Web page, which provides stunning graphics. This is a companion to the monograph *Before the Volcano Erupted* (Sheets 2002). Or see the CD on the Cerens Site, "An Interactive Guide to Ancient Cerén: Before the Volcano Erupted" (by Jen S. Lewin, Mark A. Ehrhardt, Mark D. Gross, and Payson Sheets).

Chiquibul Cave: http://www.nationalgeographic.com/chiquibul/intro.html. *National Geographic* covers Jaime Awe's cave research in Belize. Jaime Awe's Western Belize Cave Project at http://www.indiana.edu/~belize/ includes video tours and other information.

Colha: http://www.utexas.edu/cola/llilas/centers/publications/papers/

latinamerica/9503.html. This project, directed by Harry Shafer and Tom Hester, yielded evidence of household workshops for mass production of chert tools from local outcrops, as well as earlier Archaic settlement located stratigraphically below the Maya occupation.

Colonial sites: http://www.colonial-mexico.com. This is a valuable website for researchers and travelers interested in Spanish colonial sites in the Yucatan. Published by Richard Perry, the website has selected Yucatecan monasteries, churches, and other Spanish colonial monuments, with a focus on the art and architecture. The site also has links to related websites.

Copan: http://www.peabody.harvard.edu/profiles/fash.html. Bill and Barbara Fash present some of their research findings at Copan, Honduras in their Web page.

Copan: http://www.museum.upenn.edu/new/research/exp_rese_disc/Americas/copan.shtml. The Early Copan Acropolis Program, directed by Robert Sharer of the University of Pennsylvania Museum from 1989 to 2000, has a detailed text summary of the research on this website.

Copan: http://www.peabody.harvard.edu/Copan/text.html/. On this website, David Stuart of Harvard's Peabody Museum provides an outstanding introduction to the "hieroglyphs and history at Copan."

Copan: http://www.nationalgeographic.com/copan/index-m.html. *National Geographic* photos and text about Copan are included on this Web page.

Copan: http://maya-archaeology.org/vrhtml2/copanLRvrP.html. Rosalila temple reconstruction inside Copan Museum is shown on Nicholas Hellmuth's Web page, which also includes other photos of the site.

Copan: http://maya-archaeology.org/museums/copan/copangate2.html. This is another Nicholas Hellmuth Web page on Copan, including views of the site and of the museum.

Dresden Codex: http://www.tu-dresden.de/slub/proj/maya/maya.html (Burger 2003). This Web page has beautiful color illustrations of the Dresden Codex that can be enlarged. The page also has commentary in German. See also Marhenke (2003) for a digital copy of the Dresden, Paris, Madrid, and Grolier codices as pdf files.

Dumbarton Oaks: http://www.doaks.org/Pre-columbian.html. Pre-Columbian Studies at Dumbarton Oaks has useful online material and information for Maya archaeology, including an online tour of their Maya gallery. Maya pots, including rollouts, are shown on their "slide sets" listing. The Dumbarton Oaks website also lists conferences and other activities on Maya archaeology, as well as an important online library catalog of Maya books and articles in their collections. The site includes Gabrielle Vail's (2002) study of the Madrid Codex, which includes a digital version of the images.

Earthwatch: http://www.earthwatch.org. Earthwatch sponsors archaeological research in the Maya area by donations to Earthwatch and participation by the donors in the fieldwork.

El Pilar: http://marc.ucsb.edu/elpilar//. Anabel Ford's website on El Pilar provides sophisticated computer illustrations, informative illustrations, and text on her successful efforts to create a binational park at El Pilar, which straddles the border between Belize and Guatemala.

Foundation for Mesoamerican Research Inc. (FAMSI): http://www.famsi.org. FAMSI is the main source for Justin Kerr's (2003) "rollouts" of Maya vases and other pottery. The website also includes research reports from FAMSI grants. Their online "research facility" is an important source of primary information for students and researchers, who can search by word or phrase through the combined Kerr portfolio, John Montgomery Maya glyph dictionary (Matthews 2003a), and Linda Schele archives (Matthews 2003b). Randa Marhenke (2003) compiled digital versions of the Dresden, Paris, Madrid, and Grolier codices, available as downloadable pdfs. Other information is being added to the site.

Hieroglyphs: http://iath.virginia.edu/med/. The Mayan Epigraphic Database Project provides a stellar Glyph Catalog for the serious researcher, as well as other information for researchers and novice Maya hieroglyph aficionados. The Maya astronomy page at http://www.michielb.nl/maya provides very useful information on Maya mathematics, the calendars, hieroglyphic writing, and astronomy. John Montgomery's (Matthews 2003a) Maya dictionary includes words spoken by a native Maya speaker.

Ingenta: http://www.Ingenta.com. This Internet document delivery service provides articles by fax from thousands of journals for a fee. Articles can be accessed free of charge at some universities by faculty and registered graduate students. Ingenta also is useful for searching references on the Maya by journal or topic.

Isla Cilvituk: http://www.nmsu.edu/~anthro/islacilvituk/ICmast.html. Rani Alexander's excavations at Isla Cilvituk, an island off the west coast of the Yucatan, Mexico, are well documented in her website.

Journal of Field Archaeology (JFA): http://www.bu.edu/jfa/Indices/MesoAm.html/. JFA publishes reports of fieldwork and analysis, with a Web page providing an alphabetical listing of articles on the Maya by author under the category "Mesoamerica."

JStorr: Jstor (Journal Storage) provides electronic access to the full text of articles from *Latin American Antiquity, American Antiquity, World Archaeology, Current Anthropology,* and *Annual Review of Anthropology,* although not the most recent issues. Importantly, both Jstor and Ingenta can be used without charge as online search engines by topic or by the table of contents of journals. Jstor is available free of charge to faculty and registered students at many universities, as well as to members of the Society for American Archaeology.

K'axob and Sibun River: http://www.bu.edu/tricia/. Patricia McAnany's fieldwork at the Maya community of K'axob near Pulltrouser Swamp in northern Belize and Xibun, along the Sibun River in central Belize, is presented in her Web page.

Laguna de On: http://www.albany.edu/anthro/fac/masson.htm. Marilyn Masson's website is about northern Belize and Mayapan.

Lamanai, Altun Ha, Marco Gonzalez: http://www.rom.on.ca/digs/belize. Research at Lamanai, Altun Ha, and Marco Gonzalez in northern Belize by David Pendergast and Elizabeth Graham is detailed here. Much of the site highlights Lamanai, with a section on the history of excavations and a wonderful summary of the research.

La Milpa: http://www.bu.edu/lamilpa. Sophisticated GIS maps by Francisco Estrada-Belli, as well as informative reports, are on the La Milpa website, including a Tourtellot et al. 2003 article from Monograph 49 of the Cotsen Institute of Archaeology, UCLA, "Suburban Organization: Minor Centers at La Milpa, Belize."

Madrid Codex: http://madrid.doaks.org/codex/madcod.asp. This site has information and black-and-white illustrations from the Madrid Codex at Dumbarton Oaks, Washington, prepared by Maya epigrapher Grabrielle Vail, in 2002. The Madrid Codex: A Maya Hieroglyphic Book, Version 1.0. Vail includes an online database on the site.

Mathematics: http://www.michielb.nl/maya. The Maya astronomy page provides very useful information on Maya mathematics, the calendars, hieroglyphic writing, and astronomy.

Maya Research Program: http://www.mayaresearchprogram.org. The Maya Research Program provides opportunities for volunteers to participate in fieldwork at Maya sites at Blue Creek, Belize (directed by Jon Lohse; executive director Thomas H. Guderjan).

Mexican government: http://www.inah.gob.mx. In Mexico, the Instituto Nacional de Antropologia e Historia (INAH) is in charge of Maya archaeology, and you can find information about them on their website.

Mexican sites: http://www.mesoamerican-archives.com. This Web page has photos of Bonampak, Caxcatla, Calakmul, Ek Balam, and Loltun Caves by archaeologist David R. Hixson.

Mexicon: http://www.mexicon.de. *Mexicon* is a periodical that is a good source of recent research. It also lists recent journal articles and books that focus on Mesoamerica, including the Maya. Their Web page has an index of articles by author, including some articles with abstracts.

Middle American Research Institute (MARI): http //www.tulane.edu/~mari/ collections. MARI at Tulane University provides a listing of their collections, as well as their publication series (http://www.tulane.edu/~mari/pubmenu.html). The annual Tulane Maya Weekend began in 2002 and is an annual event through the Stone Center at Tulane (see http://stonecenter.tulane.edu).

Naj Tunich Cave: http://www.famsi.org/reports/96061/index.html. This is a report on the FAMSI Web page by James Brady and Gene Ware on their use of ultraviolet and infrared photography to enhance the views of paintings in Naj Tunich cave, Guatemala. Importantly, they noted the presence of overpainting and retouching of painting, and the fact that several pigments were used on the cave walls. The site http://www.archaeology.org/9707/etc/maya.html has an article by Angela Shuster in *Archaeology* magazine from 1997 discussing the modern and ancient use of Maya caves, including Naj Tunich.

National Geographic Society: http://www.nationalgeographic.com. *National Geographic* provides information on the ancient Maya. The companion website to the National Geographic Society video *Lost Kingdoms of the Maya* (Weber 1993) includes detailed information on the ancient Maya under the pages entitled Tour Copan with David Stuart, Incidents of Travel, Map of Maya World (which has a clickable map with information on fifteen Maya sites), and Reading Maya Hieroglyphs. These segments are available in video format or as a transcript online at http://www.pbs.org/wgbh/nova/maya.

Palenque: http://www.mesoweb.com/pari. This site has Merle Green Robertson's rubbings of Palenque stelae and other carved monuments; they are available on CD through the Pre-Columbian Art Research Institute (PARI) through the above website.

Paris Codex: http://digital.library.northwestern.edu/codex/codex.html (Mann 2003). This Northwestern University Library site has clear black and white illustrations of the Paris Codex that can be enlarged. Digital images of the Paris Codex, as well as the Madrid, Dresden, and Grolier codices, are available as downloadable pdf files on the FAMSI website (Marhenke 2003).

Pre-Columbian Art Research Institute (PARI): http://www.mesoweb.com/pari. PARI focuses on Palenque and publishes a newsletter with articles on Palenque and other Maya sites.

San Bartolo: http://www.sanbartolo.org. William Saturno's (2003) website of his excavation and restoration at San Bartolo, Guatemala, focuses on the painted murals.

School for American Research (SAR): http://www.sarweb.org. SAR, in Santa Fe, New
Mexico, periodically hosts seminars on Maya archaeology and publishes
proceedings through the University of New Mexico Press or its own press.

Tikal: http://www.tikalpark.com. Juan Antonio Valdes reviewed this Tikal website,
which includes the site map, general information about the ruins, history of
research, flora, and fauna, and photographs. See also Misdea (2003) for the
University of Pennsylvania's Tikal Digital Access Project.

University of California Research Expeditions (UREP): http://www.extension.
ucdavis.edu/urep. UREP sponsors archaeological projects to the Maya area for
university credit.

University Museum, University of Pennsylvania: http://www.museum.upenn.edu/
TDAP. The Tikal Digital Access Project is an ongoing project to bring information
about Tikal to the Internet. The project is organized by Sharon Aponte Misdea
(2003).

Wild Cane Cay, Frenchman's Cay, Paynes Creek National Park, and Port Honduras
Marine Reserve: http://www.ga.lsu.edu/Maya_Night.htm. The LSU Maya
Archaeology website includes descriptions, photos, and newsletters about my own
fieldwork at Wild Cane Cay, Frenchman's

Cay, Punta Ycacos Lagoon, and other sites in the Port Honduras, southern Belize.

Index

ABOUT THE AUTHOR

HEATHER McKILLOP is William G. Haag Professor of Archaeology at Louisiana State University. She received her Honors B.S. and M.A. in anthropology from Trent University in Canada and her Ph.D. in anthropology from the University of California at Santa Barbara. Her books include *Salt: White Gold of the Ancient Maya; In Search of Maya Sea Traders* (2005); and *Coastal Maya Trade* (with coeditor P. Healy, 1989). She has carried out Maya fieldwork on the coast of Belize since 1979 and has published many articles on the research. She is a Sigma Xi National Distinguished Lecturer (2003–2005).